Frommer's®

Alaska 2010

CHARLES WOHLFORTH

P9-DXT-672

Wiley Publishing, Inc.

Published by:
WILEY PUBLISHING, INC.
111 River St.
Hoboken, NJ 07030-5774

ISBN 978-0-470-49773-9

Editor: Anuja Madar
Production Editor: Heather Wilcox
Cartographer: Andrew Dolan
Photo Editors: Alden Gewirtz, Cherie Cincilla
Cover Photo Research: Richard Fox
Design and layout by Vertigo Design
Graphics and prepress by Wiley Indianapolis Composition Services

Front cover photo: Iceberg Portage Lake Chugach Mtns Portage Southcentral Alaska winter portrait © Randy Brandon/Alaska Stock LLC/Alamy Images
Back cover photos, left to right: Wildflowers in Alaska © Will Johnson/iStockphoto; Close-up view of a totem pole © Brandon Laufenberg/iStockphoto; Ketchikan: Creek Street Shops © America/Alamy Images; Grizzly bear rubbing its back on a log © Suzann Julien/iStockphoto

For information on our other products and services or to obtain technical support, please contact our Customer Care Department within the U.S. at 800/762-2974, outside the U.S. at 317/572-3993 or fax 317/572-4002.

Wiley also publishes its books in a variety of electronic formats. Some content that appears in print may not be available in electronic formats.

Manufactured in the United States of America

5 4 3 2

CONTENTS

8 THE KENAI PENINSULA & PRINCE WILLIAM SOUND 355

9 THE DENALI NATIONAL PARK REGION 451

LIST OF MAPS

ABOUT THE AUTHOR

Charles Wohlforth is a lifelong Alaskan who has been a writer and journalist since 1986. Wohlforth lives in Anchorage with his wife, Barbara, sons Robin and Joseph, and daughters Julia and Rebecca. Due this spring from St. Martin's Press is his book *The Fate of Nature,* which explores the history, ecology, and anthropology of Prince William Sound. His previous book, winner of the *Los Angeles Times* book prize, is *The Whale and the Supercomputer: On the Northern Front of Climate Change* (North Point Press, $14). Wohlforth can be reached through his website, www.wohlforth.net.

ACKNOWLEDGMENTS

This is my 13th edition of *Frommer's Alaska* and, as always, it is the product of teamwork. From the very start I received enormous help from friends, colleagues, and my family. The size and diversity of Alaska would otherwise make the project impossible. I want to acknowledge them all, but I need to give special note to the remarkable professionals who assisted with this 2010 edition. Karen Datko is my right hand, contributing creative and journalistic talents that greatly enhance the book. Researchers and writers around the state contributed as well, bringing new life to the book and giving it the insider information that I couldn't have produced alone, even as a life-long Alaskan. They include: Charlotte Glover, Eric Troyer, Kris Capps, Matt Hawthorne, Carolyn Edelman, and Martha Robinson. —Charles Wohlforth

FROMMER'S STAR RATINGS, ICONS & ABBREVIATIONS

Every hotel, restaurant, and attraction listing in this guide has been ranked for quality, value, service, amenities, and special features using a **star-rating system.** In country, state, and regional guides, we also rate towns and regions to help you narrow down your choices and budget your time accordingly. Hotels and restaurants are rated on a scale of zero (recommended) to three stars (exceptional). Attractions, shopping, nightlife, towns, and regions are rated according to the following scale: zero stars (recommended), one star (highly recommended), two stars (very highly recommended), and three stars (must-see).

In addition to the star-rating system, we also use **seven feature icons** that point you to the great deals, in-the-know advice, and unique experiences that separate travelers from tourists. Throughout the book, look for:

special finds—those places only insiders know about

fun facts—details that make travelers more informed and their trips more fun

kids—best bets for kids and advice for the whole family

special moments—those experiences that memories are made of

overrated—places or experiences not worth your time or money

insider tips—great ways to save time and money

great values—where to get the best deals

The following abbreviations are used for credit cards:

AE	American Express	DISC Discover	V Visa
DC	Diners Club	MC MasterCard	

HOW TO CONTACT US

In researching this book, we discovered many wonderful places—hotels, restaurants, shops, and more. We're sure you'll find others. Please tell us about them, so we can share the information with your fellow travelers in upcoming editions. If you were disappointed with a recommendation, we'd love to know that, too. Please write to:

Frommer's Alaska 2010
Wiley Publishing, Inc. • 111 River St. • Hoboken, NJ 07030-5774

AN ADDITIONAL NOTE

Please be advised that travel information is subject to change at any time—and this is especially true of prices. We therefore suggest that you write or call ahead for confirmation when making your travel plans. The authors, editors, and publisher cannot be held responsible for the experiences of readers while traveling. Your safety is important to us, however, so we encourage you to stay alert and be aware of your surroundings. Keep a close eye on cameras, purses, and wallets, all favorite targets of thieves and pickpockets.

TRAVEL RESOURCES AT FROMMERS.COM

Frommer's travel resources don't end with this guide. **Frommers.com** has travel information on more than 4,000 destinations. We update features regularly, giving you access to the most current trip-planning information and the best airfare, lodging, and car rental bargains. You can also book listen to podcasts, connect with other Frommers.com members through our active reader forums, share your travel photos, read blogs from guidebook editors and fellow travelers, and much more.

THE
BEST OF
ALASKA

As a child, when my family traveled outside Alaska for vacations, I often met other children who asked, "Wow, you live in Alaska? What's it like?" I never did well with that question. To me, the place I was visiting was far simpler and easier to describe than the one I was from. The Lower 48 seemed a fairly homogeneous land of freeways and fast food, a well-mapped network of established places. Alaska, on the other hand, wasn't even completely explored. Natural forces of vast scale and subtlety were still shaping the land in their own way, inscribing a different story on each of an infinite number of unexpected places. Each region, whether populated or not, was unique far beyond my ability to explain. Alaska was so large and new, so unconquered and exquisitely real, as to defy summation.

In contrast to many places you might choose to visit, it's Alaska's unformed newness that makes it so interesting and fun. Despite the best efforts of tour planners, the most memorable parts of a visit are unpredictable and often unexpected: a humpback whale leaping clear of the water, the face of a glacier releasing huge ice chunks, a bear feasting on salmon in a river, a huge salmon chomping onto your line. You can look at totem poles and see Alaska Native

PREVIOUS PAGE: **Chief Johnson totem pole in Ketchikan;** ABOVE: **A bear catches salmon.**

cultural demonstrations, and you can also get to know indigenous people who still live by traditional ways. And sometimes grand, quiet moments come, and those are the ones that endure most deeply.

As the writer of this guidebook, I aim to help you get to places where you may encounter what's new, real, and unexpected. Opening yourself to those experiences is your job, but it's an effort that's likely to pay off. Although I have lived here all my life, I often envy the stories visitors tell me about the Alaskan places they have gone to and what happened there. No one owns Alaska, and most of us are newcomers here. In all this immensity, a visitor fresh off the boat is just as likely as a lifelong resident to see or do something amazing.

THE BEST VIEWS

- **A First Sight of Alaska:** Flying north from Seattle, you're in clouds, so you concentrate on a book. When you look up, the light from the window has changed. Down below, the clouds are gone, and under the wing, where you're used to seeing roads, cities, and farms on most flights, you see instead only high, snowy mountain peaks, without the slightest mark of human presence, stretching as far as the horizon. Welcome to Alaska.

- **Punchbowl Cove (Misty Fjords National Monument):** A sheer granite cliff rises smooth and implacable 3,150 feet straight up from the water. A pair of bald eagles wheels and soars across its face, providing the only sense of scale. They look the size of gnats. See p. 164.

- **From the Chugach Mountains over Anchorage, at Sunset:** The city sparkles below, on the edge of an orange-reflecting Cook Inlet, far below the mountainside where you stand. Beyond the pink and purple silhouettes

Punchbowl Cove.

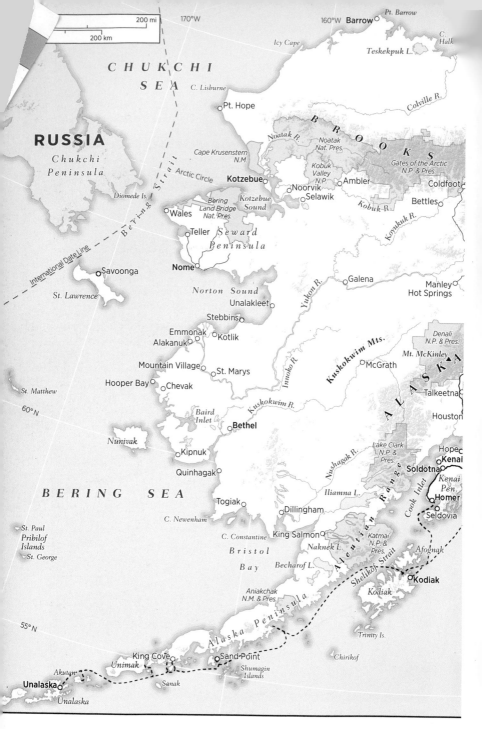

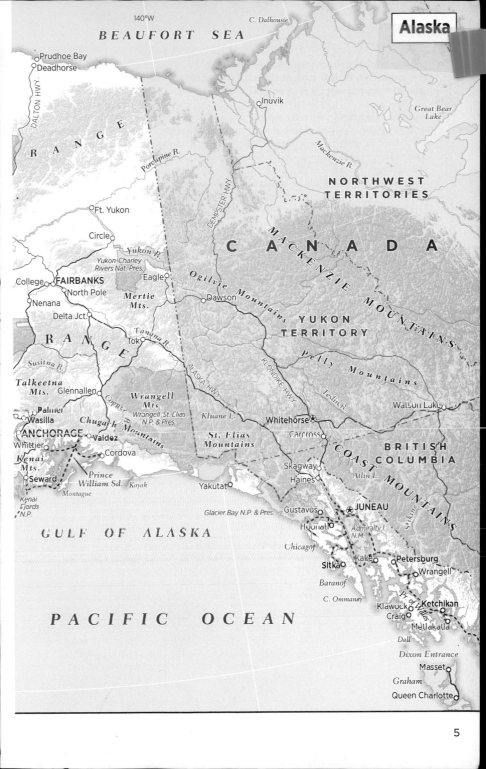

140°W

C. Dalhousie

BEAUFORT SEA

Prudhoe Bay
Deadhorse

DALTON HWY.

Inuvik

*Great Bear
Lake*

R A N G E

Porcupine R.

DEMPSTER HWY.

Mackenzie R.

NORTHWEST
TERRITORIES

Ft. Yukon

Circle

Yukon R.

C A N A D A

*Yukon-Charley
Rivers Nat. Pres.*

College FAIRBANKS
North Pole

Eagle

Ogilvie

Mountains

M A C K E N Z I E

Nenana

*Mertie
Mts.*

Dawson

YUKON
TERRITORY

M O U N T A I N S

Delta Jct.

R A N G E

Tanana R.

Tok

ALASKA HWY.

Pelly *Mountains*

Susitna R.

*Talkeetna
Mts.* Glennallen

Copper R.

*Wrangell
Mts.*

KLONDIKE HWY.

Teslin R.

Watson Lake

*Wrangell St. Elias
N.P. & Pres.*

Kluane L.

Whitehorse

Palmer
Wasilla

Chugach

Mountains

*St. Elias
Mountains*

Carcross

ANCHORAGE Valdez

Whittier

Cordova

Skagway

C O A S T

BRITISH
COLUMBIA

*Kenai
Mts.*

*Prince
William Sd.* *Kayak*

Haines

Atlin L.

M O U N T A I N S

Seward

Montague

Yakutat

*Kenai
Fjords
N.P.*

Glacier Bay N.P. & Pres. Gustavus

Stikine R.

JUNEAU

GULF OF ALASKA

Hoonah

*Admiralty I.
N.M.*

Chicagof

Kake

Petersburg

Sitka

Wrangell

Baranof

C. Ommaney

Klawock

P. of Wales

Ketchikan

Craig

Metlakatla

PACIFIC OCEAN

Dall

Dixon Entrance

Masset

Graham

Queen Charlotte

of mountains on the other side of the inlet, the sun is spraying warm, dying light into puffs of clouds. And yet it's midnight. See "Getting Outside" in chapter 7.

o **Mount McKinley from the Air (Denali National Park):** A bush pilot guides your plane up from the flatlands of Talkeetna into a realm of eternal white, where a profusion of insanely rugged peaks rises in higher relief than any other spot on Earth. After circling a 3-mile-high wall and slipping through a mile-deep canyon, you land on a glacier, get out of the plane, and for the first time realize the overwhelming scale of it all. See "Attractions & Activities Outside the Park" and "Talkeetna: Back Door to Denali" in chapter 9.

o **The Northern Lights (Alaska's Interior):** Blue,

The Northern Lights at the Talkeetna Mountains.

purple, green, and red lines spin from the center of the sky, draping long tendrils of slow-moving light. Bright, flashing, sky-covering waves wash across the dome of stars like ripples driven by a gust of wind on a pond. Looking around, you see that your companions' faces are rosy in a silver, snowy night, all gazing straight up with their mouths open. See p. 510.

THE BEST ALASKA CRUISES

Cruises provide comfortable, leisurely access to the Inside Passage and the Gulf of Alaska. Here are some of the best bets. See chapter 5 for details.

o **Best Up-Close Alaska Experience:** Lindblad Expeditions is an expert at soft adventure cruising, and its Alaska cruises are no exception. The *National Geographic Sea Bird* and *National Geographic Sea Lion* each carry only 62 passengers and offer routes where the focus is clearly on wildlife viewing and exploring the wilderness, with the National Geographic Society providing the expedition leaders, whose affiliation has lifted the Lindblad ships out of the realm of the ordinary in Alaska. National Geographic has been a part of the Lindblad experience since 2005, and the ships were recently renamed to reflect that affiliation.

- **Most Comfortable Small Ships:** Look to Cruise West's *Spirit of Endeavour* and *Spirit of Yorktown* in terms of relaxed comfort. The ships (both formerly with Clipper Cruise Line) offer more space to spread out than do smaller ships. And the yachts of American Safari Cruises are clearly in the high-end luxury category, although the educational aspects lag somewhat behind those of Lindblad—as do those of all other cruise lines in the market.

- **Most Luxurious Big Ships:** If you want a more casual kind of luxury, Radisson Seven Seas' *Seven Seas Navigator* offers just that. Meanwhile, Silversea Cruises' *Silver Shadow* offers pure luxury with an Italian edge, although it's arguably just a tad more formal (without being stuffy) than the *Navigator*. Among the mainstream cruise ships, Celebrity's *Infinity* and *Millennium* are the big winners, offering cutting-edge modern ships with great service, dining, and design. Also impressive are Princess's newest and biggest vessels in Alaska, the *Sapphire Princess* and *Diamond Princess*.

- **Best Cruise Tours:** Holland America Line and Princess are the leaders in linking cruises with land tours into the Interior, either before or after your cruise. They own their own hotels, deluxe motorcoaches, and railcars, and after many years in the business, they both really know what they're doing. Princess concentrates more on the Denali/Fairbanks and Kenai Peninsula routes, while Holland America has many itineraries that get you to the

The Music Library aboard Celebrity's ship.

Childs Glacier calving.

Yukon Territory, beginning in Fairbanks and ending with a 3-day cruise from Skagway to Vancouver, B.C. Royal Caribbean (which owns Royal Caribbean and Celebrity Cruises) has also made strides as the number three Alaska player, operating its own trains and motorcoaches, although it has yet to make a serious dent in the Yukon.

THE BEST GLACIERS

More of Alaska—more than 100 times more—is covered by glacier ice than is settled by human beings.

- o **Grand Pacific Glacier (Glacier Bay National Park):** Two vast glaciers of deep blue meet at the top of an utterly barren fjord. Three intimidating walls of ice surround boats that pull close to the glaciers. See "Glacier Bay National Park" in chapter 6.

- o **Childs Glacier (Cordova):** Out the Copper River Highway from Cordova, this is a participatory glacier-viewing experience. The glacier is cut by the Copper River, which is ¼ mile broad; standing on the opposite shore (unless you're up in the viewing tower), you have to be ready to run like hell when the creaking, popping ice gives way and a huge berg falls into the river, potentially swamping the picnic area. Even when the glacier isn't calving, you can feel the ice groaning in your gut. See "Cordova: Hidden Treasure" in chapter 8.

Exit Glacier.

1

- **Exit Glacier (Seward):** You can park near the glacier and walk the rest of the way on a gravel path. It towers above like a huge blue sculpture, the spires of broken ice close enough to breathe a freezer-door chill down on watchers. See "Exit Glacier" under "Kenai Fjords National Park," in chapter 8.

- **Western Prince William Sound:** On a boat from Whittier, you can see a couple dozen glaciers in a day. Some of these are the amazing tidewater glaciers that dump huge, office building–size spires of ice into the ocean, each setting off a terrific splash and outward-radiating sea wave. See "Whittier: Dock on the Sound" in chapter 8.

THE MOST BEAUTIFUL DRIVES & TRAIN RIDES

You'll find a description of each road in "Alaska's Highways a la Carte" on p. 502. Here are some highlights:

- **White Pass and Yukon Route Railway (Skagway to Summit):** The narrow-gauge excursion train climbs a steep grade that was chiseled into the granite mountains by stampeders to the Klondike gold rush. The train is a sort of mechanical mountain goat, balancing on trestles and steep rock walls high above deep gorges. See p. 277.

Aerial view of the Alaska Railroad.

o **Seward Highway/Alaska Railroad (Anchorage to Seward):** Just south of Anchorage, the highway and rail line have been chipped into the side of the Chugach Mountains over the surging gray water of Turnagain Arm. Above, Dall sheep and mountain goats pick their way along the cliffs, within easy sight. Below, white beluga whales chase salmon through the turbid water. Farther south, the route splits and climbs through the mountain passes of the Kenai Peninsula. See "Out from Anchorage: Turnagain Arm & Portage Glacier" in chapter 7 and "The Seward Highway: A Road Guide" in chapter 8 for information on the highway, and p. 378 for information on this Alaska Railroad route.

o **Denali Highway:** Leading east-west through the Alaska Range, the highway crosses terrain that could be another Denali National Park, full of wildlife and with views so huge and grand they seem impossible. See p. 456.

o **Richardson Highway:** Just out of Valdez heading north, the Richardson Highway rises quickly from sea level to more than 2,600 feet, switching back and forth on the side of a mountain. With each turn, the drop down the impassable slope becomes more amazing. North of Glennallen, the highway rises again, bursting through the tree line between a series of mountains and tracing the edges of long alpine lakes, before descending, parallel with the silver skein of the Alaska pipeline, to Delta Junction. See "The Richardson Highway & Copper Center," in chapter 10.

o **The Roads Around Nome:** You can't drive to Nome, but 250 miles of gravel roads radiate from the Arctic community into tundra that's populated mainly by musk oxen, bears, reindeer, birds, and other wildlife. See p. 592.

o **The Dalton Highway:** When you're ready for an expedition—a real wilderness trip by road—the Dalton Highway leads from Fairbanks across northern Alaska to the Arctic Ocean, a mind-blowing drive through 500 miles of spectacular virgin country. See "The Dalton Highway" in chapter 10.

The Dalton Highway.

THE BEST FISHING

The quality of salmon fishing in Alaska isn't so much a function of place as of time. See p. 82 for information on how to find the fish when you arrive.

Trophy salmon at the Kenai River.

○ **Bristol Bay:** This is the world's richest salmon fishery; lodges on the remote rivers of the region are an angler's paradise. See p. 82.

○ **Copper River Delta, Cordova:** The Copper itself is silty with glacial runoff, but feeder streams and rivers are rich with trout, Dolly Varden, and salmon, with few other anglers in evidence. See p. 365.

○ **The Kenai River:** The biggest king salmon—up to 98 pounds—come from the swift Kenai River. Big fish are so common in the second run of kings that there's a special, higher standard for what makes a trophy. Silvers and reds add to a mad, summer-long fishing frenzy. See p. 401.

○ **Homer:** Alaska's largest charter-fishing fleet goes for halibut ranging into the hundreds of pounds. See p. 422.

○ **Unalaska:** Beyond the road system, Unalaska has the biggest halibut. See p. 587.

Giant halibut in Homer.

o **Kodiak Island:** The bears are so big here because they live on an island that's crammed with spawning salmon in the summer. Kodiak has the best roadside salmon fishing in Alaska, and the remote fishing, at lodges or fly-in stream banks, is legendary. See p. 570.

THE BEST BEAR VIEWING

There are many places to see bears in Alaska, but if your goal is to make *sure* you see a bear—and potentially lots of bears—these are the best places:

o **Anan Wildlife Observatory:** When the fish are running, you can see many dozens of black bears feeding in a salmon stream from close at hand. Access is easiest from Wrangell. See p. 181.

o **Pack Creek (Admiralty Island):** The brown bears of the island, which is more thickly populated with them than anywhere else on Earth, have learned to ignore the daily visitors who stand at viewing areas along Pack Creek. Access is by air from Juneau. See p. 240.

o **Mendenhall Glacier (Juneau):** Bear viewing is supposed to be an expensive boutique activity—NOT! Here, at one of Alaska's busiest and most accessible tourist attractions, a group of about 10 black bears decided within the last 5 years that they really like being around large groups of people. Anyone who can walk to the edge of a parking lot can watch them feeding on spawning salmon and rearing their young. See p. 232.

o **Katmai National Park:** During the July and September salmon runs, dozens of giant brown bears congregate around Brooks Camp, where, from wooden platforms a few yards away, you can watch the full range of their

A large Kodiak brown bear.

Black bear cub at the Anan Wildlife Observatory.

behaviors. Flight services from Kodiak also bring guests at any time of the summer to see bears dig clams on the park's eastern seashore. See "Katmai National Park" and "Kodiak: Wild Island" in chapter 11.

o **Kodiak Island:** The island's incredible salmon runs nourish the world's largest bears, Kodiak brown bears; pilots know where to find them from week to week, landing floatplanes as near as possible. See p. 575.

o **Denali National Park:** The park offers the best and least expensive wildlife-viewing safari in the state. Passengers on the buses that drive the park road as far as mile 63 usually see at least some grizzlies. See chapter 9.

THE BEST MARINE MAMMAL VIEWING

You've got a good chance of seeing marine mammals almost anywhere you go boating in Alaska, but in some places it's almost guaranteed.

o **Frederick Sound (Petersburg):** A humpback jumped right into the boat with whale-watchers here in 1995. The whales show up reliably for feeding each summer. Small boats from Petersburg have no trouble finding them and watching in intimate circumstances. See p. 194.

o **Juneau:** A mom-and-pop whale-watching operation here claims 100% success in finding whales on every tour for 5 years running. You can count on seeing humpback whales, and often killer whales and spectacular Dalls porpoises. And the competition of many operators provides numerous choices and low prices. See p. 238

o **Icy Strait (Gustavus) and Bartlett Cove (Glacier Bay National Park):** Humpback whales show up, and often orcas are present off Point Adolphus, in Icy Strait, just a few miles from little Gustavus, a town of luxurious country inns. They can also be seen in Bartlett Cove within Glacier Bay National Park. See "Glacier Bay National Park" and "Gustavus: Country Inns & Quiet" in chapter 6.

o **Sitka Sound:** Lots of otters and humpback whales show up in the waters near Sitka. In fall, when the town holds its Whale Fest, you can spot them from a city park built for the purpose. See "Sitka: Rich Prize of Russian Conquest" in chapter 6.

o **Kenai Fjords National Park (near Seward):** You don't have to go all the way into the park—you're pretty well assured of sea otters and sea lions

ABOVE: **A pod of killer whales in Frederick Sound;** LEFT: **A sea otter in the Kenai Peninsula.**

in Resurrection Bay, near Seward, and humpbacks and killer whales are often seen in the summer, too. See "Kenai Fjords National Park" in chapter 8.

o **Prince William Sound:** Otters, seals, and sea lions are easy—you'll see them on many trips out of Valdez, Whittier, or Cordova—but you also have a chance of spotting both humpback and killer whales in the Sound. See chapter 8.

THE BEST ENCOUNTERS WITH NATIVE CULTURE

o **Ketchikan Totem Poles:** This Tlingit homeland has three unique places to see totem poles: historic poles indoors at the Totem Heritage Center, faithful reproductions outdoors in a natural setting at Totem Bight State Park, and brand-new poles as they are created in a workshop at the Saxman Native Village Totem Pole Park. See p. 157.

o **Sitka:** The Tlingits remain strong where they met Russian invaders in fierce battles 2 centuries ago. The totem poles and ancient Native art you can see here are second to none, and the setting makes them only more impressive. And the living tribe presents its own culture in a grand clan house. See "Sitka: Rich Prize of Russian Conquest," in chapter 6.

A woman explores the clan house at Totem Bight State Park.

○ **Alaska Native Heritage Center (Anchorage):** All of Alaska's Native groups joined together to build this grand living museum and gathering place, where dance and music performances, storytelling, art and craft demonstrations, and simple meetings of people happen every day. See p. 323.

○ **Iñupiat Heritage Center (Barrow):** A living museum, this is a place to meet and enjoy performances by the Native people who built it, and to see extraordinary artifacts they have made and recovered from digs in frozen ground. See p. 603.

THE BEST MUSEUMS & HISTORIC SITES

○ **Sitka National Historical Park:** The historic park, its buildings, and other structures in Sitka keep alive an alternate stream in history: one in which a Russian czar ruled Alaska and this little town was one of the most important on the west coast of North America. See p. 203.

○ **The Alaska State Museum (Juneau):** This richly endowed museum doesn't just show off its wealth of objects—it also uses them to teach about the state. A visit will put Alaska's Native cultures and pioneer history in context. See p. 221.

- **Anchorage Museum at Rasmuson Center:** Alaska's largest museum has the room and expertise to tell the story of Native and white history in Alaska, and to showcase contemporary Alaskan art and culture. A huge expansion project will be completed in the spring of 2010, returning to Alaska a large cultural collection from the Smithsonian Institution, and adding natural history to the museum's repertoire. See p. 321.

- **The Pratt Museum (Homer):** The Pratt explains natural history (especially the life of the ocean) in a clear and intimate way you'll find nowhere else in Alaska. See p. 416.

- **UA Museum of the North (Fairbanks):** The spectacular university museum includes a swooping new gallery to present Alaska's art and an extraordinary natural history collection, presented with the help of some of the world's top scientists on Alaskan subjects. A sound installation here has been recognized as one of the most important works of modern music of current times. See p. 512.

"The Great Alaska Outhouse Experience" at the UA Museum of the North.

THE BEST WINTER DESTINATIONS

- **Anchorage:** Anyone can enjoy the Fur Rendezvous and Iditarod sled-dog races, which keep a winter-carnival atmosphere going through much of February and March, but winter sports enthusiasts get the most out of winter here. The city has some of the best Nordic skiing in the country, close access to challenging downhill skiing, dog mushing, and groomed lake skating. See chapter 7.

- **Alyeska Resort (Girdwood):** Alaska's premier downhill skiing area has lots of snow over a long season, fantastic views, few lift lines, and the luxurious Hotel Alyeska. See "Out from Anchorage: Girdwood & Mount Alyeska," in chapter 7, and "The Best Hotels," below.

- **Chena Hot Springs Resort:** A 90-minute ride from Fairbanks, and you're out in the country, where the northern lights are clear on a starry winter afternoon and night. The resort has lots of activities to get you out into the snowy countryside, or you can just relax in the hot mineral springs. See p. 535.

- **Homer:** In March, you can fish for king salmon in the morning and cross-country ski over a high ridge with limitless ocean views in the afternoon. In the evening, check out Alaska's best art galleries and eat in its best restaurants. See "Homer & Kachemak Bay: Cosmic Hamlet by the Sea," in chapter 8.

- **Barrow:** Go to the shore of the frozen Arctic Ocean, and you have a chance to experience the most extreme winter conditions in the world. It's dark for 65 days except for the aurora blasting across the sky. There's not much to do, but you could run into a polar bear in the street. See "Barrow: Way North" in chapter 11.

TOP: **Snowboarder at Alyeska Resort;** ABOVE: **Cross-country skiing in Anchorage.**

THE STRANGEST COMMUNITY EVENTS

o **Cordova Ice Worm Festival (Cordova):** The truth is, ice worms do exist. Really. This winter carnival celebrates them in February. The highlight is the traditional annual march of the ice worm (a costume with dozens of feet sticking out) down the main street. See p. 443.

o **Midnight Sun Baseball Game (Fairbanks):** For more than 100 years they have played a baseball game without lights that doesn't begin until 10:30pm on the longest day of the year. See p. 508.

o **Bering Sea Ice Golf Classic (Nome):** The greens are AstroTurf, as the sea ice won't support a decent lawn in mid-March. Hook a drive and you could end up spending hours wandering among the pressure ridges, but you must play the ball as it lies. See p. 595.

o **Piuraagiaqta (Barrow):** This spring festival, in April, has included lots of strange contests, such as the tea-making race—contestants start with solid sea ice—and the white men versus Eskimo women tug-of-war contest, which the white men have yet to win after many years of trying. Or the community may have come up with some other silly contest this year. See p. 603.

o **Mountain Mother Contest (Talkeetna):** In this event in the July Moose Dropping Festival, mothers compete in a test of Bush skills, including splitting wood, carrying water, and diapering a baby. See p. 493.

o **Wild Cow Milking Contest (Kodiak):** The Labor Day Kodiak State Fair and Rodeo includes an event in which pairs of amateur cowboys and cowgirls pulled from the audience chase down and milk small cows unleashed in a ring. See p. 573.

THE BEST HOTELS

o **Cape Fox Lodge** (Ketchikan; **☎800/325-4000**): Clinging to cliffs above the downtown, amid the tops of huge spruce trees, the hotel feels like a peaceful treehouse. The elegance and proportions of the understated building perfectly enhance the setting, all framed in rich cedar. The Alaska Native owners complete the experience by filling the hotel with masterpieces of their culture's art. See p. 167.

o **Hotel Captain Cook** (Anchorage; **☎800/843-1950**): This is the grand old hotel of downtown Anchorage, with a heavy nautical theme, teak paneling, several terrific restaurants, and every possible amenity. It remains the state's standard of service and luxury. See p. 295.

o **Hotel Alyeska** (Girdwood; **☎800/880-3880**): The first sight of this ski resort hotel—designed in a château style and standing in an undeveloped mountain valley—will make you catch your breath. Wait until you get inside and see the starscape and polar bear diorama in the lobby atrium, or the saltwater swimming pool, with its high-beamed ceiling and windows,

Cape Fox Lodge.

The deck at the Land's End Resort.

looking out on the mountain. A tram carries skiers and diners to the mountaintop, and you can also ski from the back door. See p. 349.

o **Land's End Resort** (Homer; ☏800/478-0400): It's the location: right on the end of Homer Spit, 5 miles out in the middle of Kachemak Bay, where you can fish for salmon from the beach right in front of your room, or watch otters drifting by. The hotel itself is excellent, too, with a tremendous variety of rooms, some extraordinarily luxurious, and a complete spa. See p. 425.

o **Westmark Fairbanks Hotel & Conference Center** (Fairbanks; ☏800/544-0970): A tower rises over the flat river city of Fairbanks, a stylish and charming new wing of the city's oldest modern hotel. The owners, the Holland America Line, demolished much of the original building, leaping decades from the past to just a little into the future. See p. 524.

THE BEST WEBSITES

Many useful websites are listed throughout the book; some of the best are under "Visitor Information" near the beginning of each town section. Here's an idiosyncratic sampling of some fun or informative links.

o **www.trollart.com**: Ketchikan artist Ray Troll has created a website that carries you deep into his mind, which is full of odd and resonant humor about the evolution of fish, man, and our common relations. His vibrantly colored art makes it an aesthetic journey.

o **www.adfg.state.ak.us**: The Alaska Department of Fish & Game posts valuable information for anyone interested in fishing, hunting, wildlife watching, or just learning about creatures. Everyone from children to wildlife biologists will find something at their level. Try **www.wildlife.alaska.gov** for information about where to go and how to see Alaska's wild animals.

o **www.gi.alaska.edu**: The Geophysical Institute at the University of Alaska Fairbanks maintains a fascinating and cool site filled with real-time earth science information about Alaska, such as aurora predictions, volcano watches, earthquake and tsunami updates, rocketry, and space science.

o **www.adn.com**: The newspaper behind this site, the *Anchorage Daily News*, has shrunk to almost nothing, but the site itself has been recognized widely since the rise of former Governor Sarah Palin to national prominence. It's the place to look for the latest on her career, the rest of the crazy Alaska political scene, and a good deal of handy travel and outdoor information as well, including blogs by writers who know as much about their subjects as anyone around.

o **Some of Alaska's Liveliest Current Blogs: The Mudflats** (www.themud flats.net), a sassy political and community voice; **Alaska Dispatch** (www. alaskadispatch.com), a journalist-edited news and opinion channel on life in Alaska; and **Julia O'Malley,** a forum for one of the state's best homegrown writers, who pens a newspaper column and a blog about her life and views (http://community.adn.com/adn/blog).

o **Favorite Small-Town Sites:** Small-town Alaska newspapers, and people in communities too small to have a newspaper, communicate through the Internet; visitors to these sites can vicariously experience the pleasures and pitfalls of remote living, which can be touching and hilarious. The best I've found are Seldovia's **www.seldovia.com**, Nome's **www.nomenugget. com**, and Kotzebue's **www.cityofkotzebue.com.**

o **www.wohlforth.net**: A bit of self-promotion here, but readers can get something out of it. I've posted a long list of FAQ based on real reader questions, and supply links to many of the establishments listed in this book and some of my other writings on Alaska and other subjects. Other travelers have run into the same puzzles you have, and you'll find my advice here.

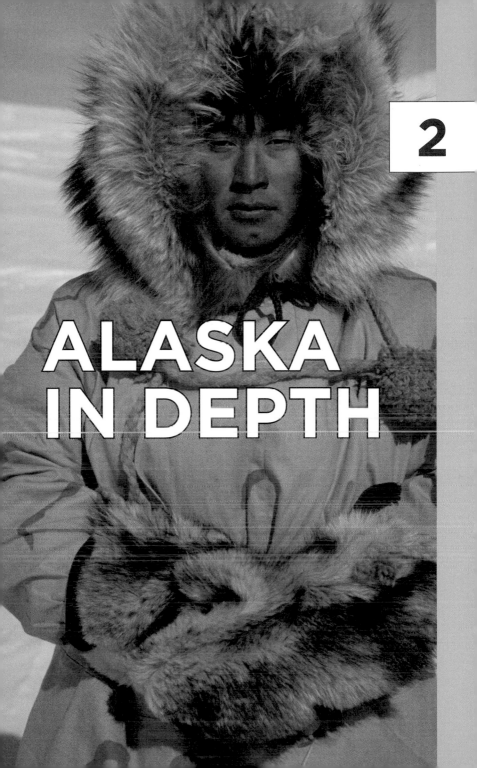

2

ALASKA IN DEPTH

An old photo album opens, emitting a scent of dust and dried glue. Inside, pale images speak wanly of shrunken mountains and glaciers, a huge blue sky, water, trees, and a moose standing way off in the background. No family photographer can resist trying to capture Alaska's vastness in the little box of a camera, and none, it seems, has ever managed it. Then, turning the page, there it is—not in another picture of the landscape, but reflected in a small face at the bottom of the frame: my own face, as a child. For anyone who hasn't experienced that moment, the expression is merely enigmatic—slightly dazed, happy, but abstracted. But if you've been to Alaska, that photograph captures something familiar: It's an image of discovery. When I began researching this book, I got to see it once again, on my own young son's face. And I knew that he, like me, had discovered something important.

So what, exactly, am I talking about? Like anything worth experiencing, it's not simple to explain.

Tour guides try to get it across with statistics. Not much hope of that, although some of the numbers do give you a general idea of scale. Once you've driven across the continental United States and know how big that is, seeing a map of Alaska placed on top of the area you crossed, just about spanning it, provides some notion of size. Alaska has 627,000 residents. If you placed them an equal distance apart, each would be almost a mile from any other. Of course, that couldn't happen. No one has ever been to some parts of Alaska.

But none of that expresses what really matters. It's not just a matter of how big Alaska is or how few people it contains. It's not an intellectual conception at all. None of that crosses your mind when you see a chunk of ice the size of a building fall from a glacier and send up a huge splash and a wave surging outward, or when you feel a wave lift your sea kayak from the fall of a breaching humpback whale. A realization of what Alaska means can come even in the car, at the end of a long day driving an Interior Alaska highway, as you climb into yet another mountain range, the sun still hanging high in what should be night, storm systems arranged across the landscape before you, when you realize that you haven't seen anyone else in an hour.

What's the soul alchemy of such a moment? I suppose it's different for each person, but for me it has something to do with realizing my actual size in the world, how I fit in, what it means to be just another medium-size mammal,

PREVIOUS PAGE: **Iñupiat Eskimo man.**

no longer armed with the illusions supplied by civilization. On returning to the city from the wilderness, there's a reentry process, like walking from a vivid movie to the mundane, gray street outside—it's the movie that seems more real. For a while, it's hard to take human institutions seriously after you've been deep into Alaska.

Anyone with the courage to come to Alaska—and the time to let the place sink in—can make the same discovery. You don't have to be an outdoors enthusiast or a young person. You only have to be open to wonder and able to slow down long enough to experience it. Then, in a quiet moment when you least expect it, things may suddenly seem very clear and all that you left behind oddly irrelevant.

How you find your way back to where you started is your affair.

ALASKA TODAY: WHAT IT MEANS TO BE ALASKAN

In the fall of 2008, when our governor became world famous as the Republican Party's candidate for vice president, Alaskans felt a strong mix of contradictory emotions. Coming from an exotic, often-misunderstand place with a small population means feeling proud and excited whenever one of our own gets the attention of the wider world—for example, the local media follow every step in the career of Alaskan athletes who make it into professional sports, although the closest major league teams are in Seattle. During her brief time in office, Governor Sarah Palin had built huge popularity as a post-partisan, new-generation leader, addressing some of Alaska's long-standing problems with vigor and fearlessness. But once she took the national stage, she came across very differently. And then

A Native of Beaver, Alaska, and his dog.

came the embarrassments: her misstatements and apparent shallowness, her tabloid-ready family life, and the "pit bull with lipstick" persona that made her an increasingly divisive figure. Around the time Palin appeared in a *Saturday Night Live* rap routine with comedian Amy Poehler gunning down a dancing stuffed moose, I realized that the world's impressions about Alaska might never be the same, and not for the better. And then came her sudden resignation.

I'll address the politics of the moment in the next section, "Alaska's Political Earthquake." But the Palin phenomenon extends well beyond politics to how we—and everyone else—defines what it means to be an Alaskan. It's probably obvious that the caricature isn't accurate—there's obviously more to Alaska's people than a trailer trash stereotype—but the subtler and more interesting truth is that aspects of Palin's image do reflect the Alaska character. Whatever that is.

Few questions can spark as lively a conversation or elicit as many diverse views as, "What makes a real Alaskan?" Despite being born in Idaho, Palin is certainly one species of real Alaska. But there are many others, as well. After half a century as a state, Alaska continues to define itself. We've all got our own idea of how to live here, and we're each charging ahead regardless of what anyone else says—and sometimes that seems to be all we have in common.

Alaska's population changes so rapidly, it's still a point of pride to say you were born here. The non-Native population arrived just over a century ago, with the Klondike Gold Rush of 1898, and even that's only a symbolic bookmark—oil and military development dating back less than 50 years brought the majority of the state's growth. There hasn't been enough time to develop a culture or a shared outlook on the world. Alaska is too young to have an accent or a cuisine. But the place itself is so overwhelming that people have molded to it in some distinctive ways that they hold in common. "Alaskan" is far more than a name.

So here I offer my own exploration of what it means to be an Alaskan, without reference to Sarah Palin's snow machines, Naughty Monkey red pumps, or

Flowers set against the Mendenhall Glacier.

Aurora Borealis.

sexy librarian glasses—but with the anticipation that you may see a shadow of her profile in this, more real picture of Alaskan lifestyles.

Living the Seasons

A small town in Alaska in March. Each time it snows, you have to throw shovels of it higher over your head to dig out. The air in the house is stale, and the view out the window is black, white, and gray. Everyone's going nuts with winter. It's time for a good political ruckus. No one can predict exactly what will set it off—it could just be an ill-considered letter to the editor in the local newspaper, or it could be something juicier, such as a controversial development proposal. At some point, when the cabin fever gets bad enough, it almost doesn't matter what sparks the inferno. Alaskans can generate outrage about almost anything, with a ritual of charges and countercharges, conspiracy theories, and impassioned public testimony.

It's particularly amusing when some outsider is involved, thinking he's at the town council meeting in a normal political process to get some project approved, only to wind up on the receiving end of a public hearing from hell. I'll never forget a sorry businessman who was trying to lease some land from the town of Homer. He endured hours of angry public testimony one night. He was sweating, the only person in the packed city hall meeting room wearing a tie, surrounded by flannel shirts, blue jeans, and angry faces. Finally, he stood up from his chair and, in a plaintive tone of frustration near tears, declared, "You're not very professional as a community!" For once, no one could disagree.

He gave up. He didn't know that if he had only waited a couple of months, the opposition would dry up when the salmon started running. Then most of the city council meetings are canceled, and the rest are brief and sparsely attended. If anything really important comes up, the council is smart enough to postpone it till fall. In the summer, Alaskans have more important things to attend to than government.

The sun shines deep into the night, so you can catch fish and tourists, not sit inside. It's the season when the money is made. The streets are full of new people, like a bird colony refreshed by migrants. Everyone stays awake late pounding nails, playing softball, and fly-casting for reds. Office workers in Anchorage depart straight from work for a 3-hour drive down to the Kenai Peninsula, fish through the night, catch a quick nap in the car in the wee hours, and make it to work on time the next morning, with fish stories to share. Sleep is expendable— you don't seem to need it that much when the sky is light all night.

In the Native villages of the Bush, everyone has gone to fish camp. Families load everything in an aluminum riverboat and leave town, headed upriver. On the banks and beaches, they set up wall tents and spruce-log fish-drying racks, maybe a basketball hoop and campfire, too. Extended families work as a unit. Men gather in the salmon, and the women gut them with a few lightning strokes of a knife and hang them to dry on the racks. Children run around in a countryside paradise, watched by whichever adults are handiest.

Suddenly, August comes. For the first time in months, you can see the stars. It comes as a shock the first time you have to use your car headlights. The mood gets even more frantic. There's never enough time in the summer to do everything that needs to get done. Construction crews can count the days now until snow and cold will shut them down. Anything that's not done now won't be done until next May. Labor Day approaches as fast as 5pm on a busy business day.

As September turns to October, the last tourists are gone and T-shirt shops are closed for the season. The commercial fishing boats are tied up back in the harbor, and the fishermen prepare for vacation. Cannery workers are already back at college. For the first time in months, people can slow down long enough to look at each other and remember where they left off in the spring. It's time to catch up on sleep and make big decisions. The hills of birch turn bright yellow, the tundra goes brick red, and the sky turns gray—there's the smell of wood smoke in the air—and then, one day, it starts to snow.

It's not the velvet darkness of midwinter that gets you. December is bearable, even if the sun rises after the kids get to school, barely cruises along the horizon, and sinks before they start for home. Nowhere is Christmas more real than in Alaska, where carolers sing with cheeks tingling from the cold. January isn't so hard. You're still excited about the skiing. The phone rings in the middle of the night—it's a friend telling you to put on your boots and go outside to see the northern lights. February is a bit harder to take, but most towns have a winter carnival to divert your attention from the cold.

March is when bizarre things start to happen. People are just holding on for the end of winter, and you never know what will set them off. That's when you hunker down and lay low, watch what you say, and bite your tongue when your spouse lets out a comment you'd like to jump on like a coho hitting fresh bait. Hold on—just until the icicles start to melt, the mud shows around the snow banks, and the cycle starts fresh.

The First People

Theories differ about how North America was originally populated. The textbook lesson says the first people walked across a land bridge from Asia over the dry Bering Sea around 15,000 years ago, when glacial ice sequestered enough of the earth's water to lower the sea level. The bridge, up to 1,000 miles wide, included the entire west coast of Alaska at its largest size and lasted longest in the area between Nome and Kotzebue.

But new archaeology and geology throw doubt on that theory, suggesting a migration story that's much more complex. People who know the Arctic know the land bridge simply wasn't necessary for migration: In the winter, you can sometimes walk on ice between Siberia and Alaska even today, and the seafaring skills of Alaska's Aleuts and Eskimos would have enabled them to travel back and forth to Asia at any time. Siberian and Alaskan Natives share language, stories, and kin. Perhaps the connection across the north was continuous and followed many routes after northern people learned to sew skin boats and clothing about 15,000 years ago. Certainly, the idea that they walked seems increasingly questionable. Geologists now believe the route south was largely impassable during the last glacial period; if migrants did use it, they must have used boats to connect coastal pockets that remained free of glacial ice.

However and whenever the first people arrived, they quickly spread through the Americas, creating cultures of incredible complexity and diversity. Most scientists believe migrants through Alaska were the ancestors of all the indigenous peoples of the hemisphere, from the Inca to the Algonquin. Those who stayed in Alaska became the Eskimos, who include the Iñupiat of the Arctic, the Yup'ik of the Southwest, and the Alutiiq of the Gulf of Alaska coastline. They also became Indians: the Athabascan of the Interior and the Tlingits, Haida, and Tsimshians of Southeast Alaska and British Columbia.

The Native groups of Alaska have a lot in common culturally, but before the white invasion, they had well-defined boundaries and didn't mix much. They didn't farm, and the only animal they domesticated was the dog—dog teams and boats were the primary means of transportation and commerce. But they generally were not nomadic, and no one in Alaska lived in ice igloos (farther east, in Canada, igloos were used as winter dwellings on the ice pack). On the treeless Arctic coast, houses were built of sod atop supports of whalebone and driftwood; where wood was plentiful, in the rainforests, large and intricately carved houses sheltered entire villages. Typically, a family-connected tribal group would have a winter village and a summer fish camp for gathering and laying up food. Elders guided the community in important decisions. A gifted shaman led the people in religious matters, relating to the spirits of ancestors, animals, trees, and even the ice that populated their world. Stories passed on through generations explained the universe.

Those oral traditions kept Native cultures alive. Twenty distinct Native languages were spoken. A few elders still speak only their Native language today, and only one language, Eyak, is essentially extinct. The languages break into four major families: Eskimo-Aleut, Athabascan–Eyak–Tlingit, Haida, and Tsimshian (the last two are primarily Canadian). The Eskimo-Aleut language group includes languages spoken by coastal people from the Arctic Ocean to the Gulf of Alaska, including Iñupiaq in the Arctic, Yup'ik in the Yukon–Kuskokwim and Bristol Bay region; Aleut in the Aleutian Islands; and Alutiiq on the Alaska Peninsula, Kodiak, and Prince William Sound. There are 12 Athabascan and Eyak languages in Alaska, and more Outside, including Apache and Navajo. In Southeast Alaska, Tlingit was spoken across most of the Panhandle. Haida was spoken on southern Prince of Wales Island and southward into what's now British Columbia, where Tsimshian also was spoken.

Anchorage.

The first arrival of whites was often violent and destructive, spanning a 100-year period that started in the 1740s with the coming of the Russian fur traders, who enslaved the Aleuts, and continued to the 1840s, when New England whalers first met the Iñupiat of the Arctic. There were pitched battles, but disease, resource depletion, and nonviolent destruction of oral traditions were more influential. Protestant missionaries, backed by government assimilation policy, drove the old stories and even Native languages underground. Lela Kiana Oman, who published traditional Iñupiaq stories to preserve them, told me of her memories of her father secretly telling the ancient tales at night to his children. She was forbidden to speak Iñupiaq in school and did not see her first traditional Native dance until age 18.

For the Aleut, whose cultural traditions were almost completely wiped out, the process of renewal involves archaeology, repatriation of stolen objects, and a certain amount of invention. On the other hand, some villages remain with unbroken traditions, especially deep in the country of the Yukon–Kuskokwim Delta, where Yup'ik is still the dominant language and most of the food comes from traditional subsistence hunting and gathering, altered only by the use of modern materials and guns.

Today's young adults have grown up in a Native cultural renaissance. It's not a moment too soon. Television, the Internet, and the lure of teen rebellion—common all over the world—compete with healthier traditional activities. Schools in many areas now require Native language classes, or even teach using language-immersion techniques. Alaska Natives also are fighting destruction fueled by alcohol and other substance-abuse problems. Rates of suicide, accidents, and domestic violence are high in the Bush. Statistically, nearly every Alaska Native in prison is there because of alcohol. A sobriety movement attacks the problem one person at a time. One of its goals is to use traditional Native culture to fill a void of rural despair where alcohol flows in. Politically, a "local option" law provides communities the choice of partial or total alcohol prohibition; it has been successfully used in many towns but remains controversial in others.

There are social and political tensions between Natives and whites on many levels and over many issues. The Alaskan city and Alaskan village have less in common than do most different nations. Although village Natives come to the city to shop, get health care, or attend meetings, urban Alaskans have no reason to go to the villages, and most never have made the trip.

The most contentious rural-urban issue concerns allocation of fish and game. Some urban outdoorsmen feel they should have the same rights to hunt and fish that the Natives do, and the state Supreme Court has interpreted Alaska's constitution to say they're correct. But rural Natives have federal law on their side, which overrules the state. A decade of political stalemate over the issue divided Alaskans until, in 2000, the feds finally stepped in and took over fish and game management in the majority of Alaska to protect Native subsistence. Many Natives were glad to see it happen, as humiliating as the move was for independent-minded Alaskans. Natives feel subsistence hunting and fishing are an integral part of their cultural heritage, far more important than sport, and should take priority. Darker conflicts exist, too, and it's impossible to discount the charges of racism that Native Alaskans raise in issues as diverse as school funding and public safety.

Alaska Natives have essentially become a minority in their own land. In 1880, Alaska contained 33,000 Natives and 430 whites. By 1900, with the gold rush, the numbers were roughly equal. Since then, non-Natives have generally outnumbered Natives in ever greater numbers. Today there are about 98,000 Alaska Natives—27,000 of whom live in the cities of Anchorage and Fairbanks—out of a total state population of 627,000 people of all races. Consequently, Alaska Natives must learn to walk in two worlds. The North Slope's Iñupiat, who hunt the bowhead whale from open boats as their forefathers did, must also know how

Main Street in Hyder.

to negotiate for their take in international diplomatic meetings. And they have to use the levers of government to protect the whale's environment from potential damage by the oil industry.

Non-Natives traveling to the Bush also walk in two worlds, but they may not even know it. In a Native village, a newly met friend will ask you in for a cup of coffee; it can be rude not to accept. Too much eye contact in conversation also can be rude—that's how Native elders look at younger people who owe them respect. If a Native person looks down, speaks slowly, and seems to mumble, that's not disrespect, but the reverse. Fast-talking non-Natives have to make a conscious effort to slow down and leave pauses in conversation because Natives usually don't jump in or interrupt—they listen, consider, and then respond. Of course, most Native people won't take offense at your bad manners. They're used to spanning cultures. When I was in a village a few years ago, I looked in confusion at a clock that didn't seem right. "That's Indian time," my Athabascan companion said. Then, pointing to a clock that was working, he said, "White man time is over there."

Urban visitors who miss cultural nuances rarely overlook the apparent poverty of many villages. Out on a remote landscape of windswept tundra, swampy in summer and frozen in winter, they may secretly wonder why Natives endure the hardships of rural Alaskan life when even the most remote villager can see on television how easy it is in Southern California. Save your pity. As Yup'ik social observer Harold Napoleon once said, "We're poor, all right, but we've got more than most people. Our most important asset is our land and our culture, and we want to protect it, come hell or high water."

The Culture of Boom & Bust

Alaska's history books are full of the stories of economic booms, the people who came, what kind of wealth they were after, and how they populated and developed the land. In a new land, you can make history just by showing up. But every wave is followed by a trough, the bust that comes after the boom, when those who came just for the money go back where they came from.

The first to leave were the Russians sent by the czar and the Russian-American Company. On October 18, 1867, their flag came down over Castle Hill in Sitka in a solemn ceremony, got stuck, and had to be untangled by a soldier sent up the pole. The territory was virtually empty of Russians before the check was even signed, as Congress didn't much like the idea of the purchase and took a while to pay. The gold-rush stampeders were the next to leave, abandoning the territory by 1914. The population of Nome went from 12,500 to 852 when gold rush excitement wore off. An economic crash also followed the end of World War II and, to some extent, the Cold War. The close of the oil industry's wildest years in the 1970s and '80s saw out-migration and a prolonged depression.

But each time the boom went bust, enough new arrivals stayed that Alaska ended up with more people than before. Over the long term, the population grew dramatically. And each migration brought young, vigorous people, ambitious to build Alaska's society as well as their own wealth. Most new Alaskans prior to 1980 were white, but that's changed, and strong minority communities have grown in many towns, especially Anchorage, where more than 90 languages are spoken in the schools.

Alaska's people are a mix of America's mix, made up of odds and ends from all over the United States and the world, without cohesive social commonalities. But great outfits can be made even from mismatched clothes, and variety itself has shaped the way Alaskans relate to one another. The lack of shared culture helped establish values for tolerance and equality, hospitality, and independence. Alaska is a classless society with a strong ethic for treating all with the same warm and respectful informality.

Everyone arrives with a clean slate and a chance to reinvent himself or herself. On occasion, that ability to start from scratch has created embarrassing discoveries when the past does become relevant. A series of political scandals erupted when reporters checked the resumes of well-known politicians, only to find out they had concocted their previous lives out of thin air. One leading legislative candidate's husband found out about his wife's real background from such a news story.

Frontier values also come with a darker side, including an acceptance of violence as part of the belief in personal independence. In the late 1980s in Homer, a gunfight over a horse left a man lying dead on a dirt road. In the newspaper the next week, the editorial called for people not to settle their differences with guns. A couple of letters to the editor shot back on the theme, "Don't you tell *us* how to settle our differences." Guns are necessary tools in Alaska. They're also a religion. I have friends who exchanged handguns instead of rings when they got married.

The tradition of tolerance made Alaska a destination for oddballs, religious cults, hippies, and people who just can't make it in the mainstream. Perhaps the most interesting of the religious groups that formed its own community is the Old Believers, who built villages of brightly painted houses around Kachemak Bay, near Homer. Their resistance to convention dates from Peter the Great's reforms to Russian Orthodoxy in the 18th century, which they reject. In Alaska they've found a place where they can live without interference—in fact, they've thrived as fishermen and boat builders. You'll likely see them around town in their 18th-century Russian peasant dress.

Today the era of boom and bust may be ending. The last 2 decades have seen Alaska's economy settle into a new pattern of stability, and, with it, society also has grown more permanent and conventional. An unbroken run of 20 years of slow but steady growth began in 1989, ending only with the worldwide economic downturn in 2009—more evidence that Alaska had become a connected part of the rest of the country. The 1990s had seen the arrival of national shopping chains and the disappearance of many unique independent businesses in the larger towns. The fishing industry entered a long-term decline as overseas salmon farming competed with Alaska's wild-caught output. More people worked for smaller, steadier paychecks; fewer were betting on seasonal wealth or one-time bonanzas from uniquely Alaskan pursuits. And, perhaps most important, no boom came along to flare up—and burn out—the state's economic fire.

Alaska grew older, more permanent, less colorful, and not as greedy for the next big boom at all costs. With our 50th anniversary as a state, we seemed to have come of age. But history never ends, and as the page turned for Alaska, the next chapter held even bigger surprises than the last one. Sarah Palin was the biggest shock of all, and the best evidence that, for all the changes, Alaska remains a place like no other. Whatever finally happens in her political career—a topic I'll take up below—her confidence, independence, and self-creation were about as Alaskan as it gets.

ALASKA'S POLITICAL EARTHQUAKE

For a century, Alaska politics were remarkably simple. The economy ran on cycles of boom and bust. To get elected, politicians promised more boom, less bust. To deliver, they fought the federal government, long seen as the overlord of Alaska's lands, and they got as close to industry as they could. It was impossible to be too pro-development or too anti-government.

But a tectonic shift in Alaska politics began about 10 years ago, capped in 2008 by the explosive rise of Gov. Sarah Palin as Sen. John McCain's running mate for the White House. She seemed to burst out of nowhere as McCain's selection just before the Republican Party's national convention that summer, and then stole the show with her confident, sassy acceptance speech. But that historic moment, which became an international cultural event, did have a background. Palin's success had bloomed from the ruins of an Alaskan political earthquake. Her role challenging Alaska's cracking establishment enabled the former small-town mayor to become governor despite serious questions about her qualifications and aptitude to run the state, and she used that position to make some rapid accomplishments, and from that perch she jumped even higher to a nomination for vice president.

The stresses that ruptured Alaska's political ruling elite had built up in the long, cozy, and ultimately corrupt relationship of state leaders with the oil industry. The old guard kept resource developers happy while beating up on Washington—and milking the federal treasury for Alaskan goodies. But times and Alaska's population changed. Rather than being migrants, more residents were people who had been raised here and planned to stay. Their values often included more than a greedy drive for another development boom.

John McCain and Sarah Palin.

The sheer inertia of power had kept the same group in office for decades. Gov. Frank Murkowski was elected in 2002, giving up a seat in the U.S. Senate he had held since 1980. Palin, a former beauty queen, high school basketball star, and Republican mayor, ran for lieutenant governor that year, and made ripples with her charisma and energy, but lost in the primary while still largely unknown. (I met Palin when she won her first race for Wasilla mayor in 1996. The town had complained about how I had described it in this book. She didn't impress me at the time, and Wasilla hasn't gotten any prettier since then.) Murkowski appointed Palin to a 6-year term on the Alaska Oil and Gas Conservation Commission, a well-paid sinecure used in the past for putting politicians out to pasture. He also appointed Randy Ruedrich, an influential political fundraiser and chairman of the Alaska Republican Party. Democrats complained that a party fundraiser shouldn't be regulating the oil industry from which he was soliciting funds, but the Republican-dominated legislature confirmed Ruedrich anyway. Palin took her seat without controversy, and that appeared to be a happy ending for her political career.

Another Murkowski appointment got much more attention at the time. As governor, he had the power to pick a new senator to fill out his unfinished term in Washington. As if passing on a family legacy, he appointed his daughter, Lisa. Alaska's other U.S. Senator, Ted Stevens, also a Republican, had held his office since 1968. His son, Ben, seemed to follow the path of hereditary power as well when he was appointed to complete a term in the State Senate, faced no opponent for reelection, and became Senate president, despite an imperious attitude that bothered voters. Some political observers said the Stevens and Murkowski families were simply too powerful to challenge.

But the habits of power finally wore thin. Although Gov. Murkowski's daughter proved an able legislator and was reelected 2 years after being appointed to office, her father never escaped the impression of arrogance and self-dealing created by the appointment. More scandals—and some tough decisions he made—contributed to the problem. An attorney general resigned under ethical accusations, and problems erupted at the oil and gas commission. Ruedrich used his office there to continue his party fundraising, and his co-commissioner, Palin, blew the whistle on him. Murkowski at first protected Ruedrich, even under threat that Palin would resign. Finally both resigned. The issue made Palin's name and won her respect from rank-and-file members of both parties.

Gov. Murkowski's biggest initiative in office was to encourage construction of a natural gas pipeline from Alaska's North Slope to the American Midwest, unsuccessfully, as it turned out. To win the support of the large producers that control the gas, he struck a deal to permanently set their taxes on oil and gas output at a rate they liked. The proposal would raise the taxes Alaska had been charging, but locked them in much lower than critics and consultants said was justified. The legislature at first balked, but finally went along. We now know its decision happened, at least in part, because Alaska's most influential oil industry executive, Bill Allen, won support for Murkowski's plan in a Juneau hotel room where he gave legislators cash and promises of jobs and other benefits. Allen, owner of Veco, an oil-field construction company that long had represented the industry's interests in Juneau, was caught on video by the FBI paying off legislators, and then directed their votes from a legislative gallery. Allen also paid illegally for a poll supporting Murkowski's reelection bid at the request of the Governor's powerful chief of staff. When Allen agreed secretly to cooperate with the FBI, Alaska's political earthquake hit full force.

In 2006, Palin took on Murkowski in the Republican primary for governor and routed him at the polls, next beating a pro-oil Democrat and two-time governor to win the general election. By that time, the FBI investigation was in the open. Palin's fresh face, her status as a reformer, and her direct challenge to the old guard struck a cord with disgusted and disappointed voters. She performed poorly in debates, showing the same lack of command of the issues that came up in the presidential campaign, but in the environment of voter anger against political corruption, her lack of experience counted in her favor rather than against her.

Meanwhile, the corruption scandals widened. The FBI investigated both Stevens senators, father and son, whom Allen implicated in trial testimony. Federal prosecutors put various legislators, lobbyists, and others in jail. Alaska's sole member of the House of Representatives for almost 30 years, Don Young, came under scrutiny for directing federal highway spending to wealthy campaign contributors, and the U.S. House and Senate both voted to refer his case to the Department of Justice for investigation. As the revelations mounted, Palin joined with legislative Democrats to push through a strong new ethics law. When the corruption of the oil tax came out in court, she sponsored a legislative redo of that issue at higher tax rates, which Democrats further sweetened for the state, leading to an enormous increase in revenues from an industry that recently had controlled all the levers of power. As oil prices spiked, the Governor was able to use some of the windfall of new oil tax money to send a check for $3,269 to every person living in the state, adult or child. Her popularity peaked at near unanimous levels.

There matters stood in August of 2008, when John McCain made his sudden decision to choose Palin as his running mate. On one hand, the scenario seemed like something out of a movie, a Cinderella story in which an unexceptional small-town politician's exceptional integrity suddenly was recognized and rewarded with national acclaim. But that story line ultimately didn't hold together. First, the qualities that had made Palin popular in Alaska didn't translate to her national role. Here she had pragmatically worked with Democrats to get her program through the legislature, avoiding divisive social issues; but as a vice-presidential candidate, her fiercely partisan role and Christian conservative rhetoric were unappealing outside her own party. Also, in Alaska she took on discrete, practical issues with the help of strong staff: oil taxes, a gas pipeline, and an ethics bill. When thrust onto the national stage, she didn't have her own background to speak convincingly on a broad range of complex issues. And then her own ethics and family problems emerged. As the national media descended on Wasilla like a vacuum cleaner, the Governor's reputation for integrity began to evaporate.

It was an unforgettable political season. After 40 years in office, Sen. Ted Stevens was indicted for failing to report thousands of dollars in gifts from Bill Allen, and asked for a lightning-fast trial in hopes of being acquitted before the election. Instead, he was convicted the week before Election Day and then defeated by Democratic challenger Mark Begich, a member of Palin's generation. (Rep. Don Young, remaining under a cloud but not charged with a crime, won reelection that year.) After losing in the presidential election, Palin went back to a restive legislature, her high approval ratings deflated and her relationships with Democrats soured. She accomplished little and seemed more interested in future national ambitions. That summer, she suddenly resigned from office, without giving a credible reason, but with plans to write a book and to maintain her high-media profile. Stevens left the Senate, but fought on in court and saw his conviction overturned due to misconduct by prosecutors, who had failed to turn over to defense attorneys some evidence favorable to his case. The judge ordered a special prosecutor to investigate the prosecutors. U.S. Attorney General Eric Holder additionally took the remarkable step of asking for already jailed legislators to be released pending the reviews.

As this is written, the story of the political earthquake goes on, still messy and with more rubble than rebuilding in evidence. The investigations continue, but with the investigators in disarray due to the Stevens case, and the new generation dealing with its own problems, the future is less clear than ever. The events of the last few years partially cleansed Alaska politics and cleared the ground for new debates on different terms than those that have dominated for the last half century. It's been interesting, to say the least, and now that anything seems possible, it's well worth waiting to see what happens next.

NATURAL HISTORY: ROUGH DRAFTS & ERASURES

Understanding some of the natural history behind Alaska's landscapes and wildlife will give context and meaning to your visit. I've arranged this section by the natural features and issues you will encounter; the section above explains their geographic relation.

Kayaking along the Inside Passage.

Portage Glacier.

Glaciers

In 1986, Hubbard Glacier, north of Yakutat, suddenly decided to surge forward, cutting off Russell Fjord from the rest of the Pacific Ocean. A group of warm-hearted but ill-advised wildlife lovers set out to save the marine mammals that had been trapped behind the glacier. Catching a dolphin from an inflatable boat isn't that easy—they didn't accomplish much, but they provided a lot of entertainment for the locals. Then the water burst through the dam of ice and the lake became a fjord again, releasing the animals anyway. In 2002 it happened again (no rescue this time). Ships were warned away as the 70-square-mile lake, having risen 61 feet above sea level, quickly drained through a 300-foot-wide channel with a whoosh. Geologists say it could happen again any time.

Bering Glacier, the largest in North America (about 30×145 miles in area), can't decide which way to go. Surging and retreating on a 20-year cycle, it reversed course in 1995 after bulldozing a wetland migratory bird stopover, and speedily contracted back up toward the mountains. Yanert Glacier surged 100 yards a day in 2000 after moving 100 yards a year since 1942. The next year, Tokositna Glacier started galloping after 50 years of quiet. In 1937, surging Black Rapids Glacier almost ate the Richardson Highway. In Prince William Sound, Meares Glacier plowed through old-growth forest. On a larger scale, all the land of Glacier Bay—mountains, forests, sea floor—is rising 1½ inches a year as it rebounds from the weight of melted glaciers that 100 years ago were a mile thick and 65 miles longer.

Yet these new and erased lands are just small corrections around the margins compared to all the Earth has done in setting down, wiping out, and rewriting the natural history of Alaska. In the last ice age, 15,000 years ago, much of what is Alaska today was a huge glacier. Looking up at the granite mountains of Southeast Alaska, especially in the Lynn Canal, you can see a sort of high-water mark near their towering peaks—the highest point to which the glaciers came in the ice age.

Some 7-year-old children worry about the bogeyman or being caught in a house fire. When I was that age, living with my family in Juneau, I was worried about glacier ice. I had learned how Gastineau Channel was formed, I had seen Mendenhall Glacier, and I had heard how it was really a river of ice, advancing and retreating. I came to fear that while I slept another ice age would come and grind away the city of Juneau.

It's possible that a glacier *could* get Juneau—the city fronts on the huge Juneau Ice Field—but there would be at least a few centuries' warning before it hit. Glaciers are essentially just snow that doesn't get a chance to melt. The snow accumulates at higher elevations until it gets deep enough to compress into ice and starts oozing down the mountainside. When the ice reaches the ocean, or before, the melt and calving of icebergs at the leading edge reaches equilibrium with the snow that's still being added at the top. The glacier stops advancing, becoming a true river of ice, moving a snowflake from the top of the mountain to the bottom in a few hundred years. When conditions change—more snow or colder long-term weather, for example—the glacier gets bigger; that's called advancing, and the opposite is retreating. Sometimes something strange will happen under the glacier and it will surge. Bering Glacier started to float on a cushion of water, and Yanert Glacier slid on a cushion of mud. But most of the time, the advance or retreat is measured in inches or feet a year.

It took some time to figure out how glaciers work. The living glaciers of Alaska, like living fossils from the last ice age, helped show the way. In the 1830s, scientists in Switzerland found huge rocks (now called glacial erratics) that appeared to have moved miles from where they had once been a part of similar bedrock. Scientists theorized that ancient glaciers shaping the Alps must have moved the rocks. John Muir, the famous writer and naturalist, maintained in the 1870s that the granite mountains of Yosemite National Park had been rounded and polished by the passing of glaciers that melted long ago (he was only partly right). He traveled to Alaska to prove it. Here, glaciers were still carving the land— they had never finished melting at the end of the last glacial period—and Muir could see shapes like those at Yosemite in the act of being created. Glacier Bay, which

Kenai Fjords National Park.

An Athabascan boy bringing in his catch.

Two Native children sit beneath a polar bear skin.

Muir "discovered" when guided there by his Alaska Native friends, was a glacial work in progress, as it still is today.

When you visit, you can see for yourself how the heavy blue ice and white snow are streaked with black rock and dust that were obviously gouged from mountains and left at the faces and along the flanks of the glaciers in debris piles called moraines. At Exit Glacier, in Kenai Fjords National Park, you can stand on a moraine that wraps the leading edge of the glacier like a scarf and feel the cold streaming off spires of clicking ice—like standing in front of a freezer with the door open. Find another hill like that, no matter where it is, and you can be pretty sure a glacier once came that way. Likewise, you can see today's glaciers scooping out valleys in the mountains.

Today Alaska's 100,000 glaciers cover about 5% of its landmass, mostly on the southern coast. There are no glaciers in the Arctic—the climate is too dry to produce enough snow. The northernmost large glaciers are in the Alaska Range, such as those carving great chasms in the side of Mount McKinley. At that height, the mountain creates its own weather, wringing moisture out of the atmosphere and feeding its glaciers. The Kahiltna Glacier flows 45 miles from the mountain, descending 15,000 feet over its course. The Ruth Glacier has dug a canyon twice as deep as the Grand Canyon, half filled with mile-deep ice. Similarly, fjords and valleys all over Alaska were formed by the glaciers of 50 ice ages that covered North America in the last 2.5 million years.

Earthquakes & Mountains

Despite my early glacier phobia, I never had a similar fear of earthquakes. Living in Anchorage, I'd been through enough of them that, as early as I can remember, I generally didn't bother to get out of bed when they hit. Alaska has an average of 13 earthquakes a day, or 11% of all the earthquakes in the world, including 3 of the 10 largest ever recorded. On November 3, 2002, Alaska felt the world's largest earthquake of the year and one of the largest ever in the United States. My car rocked as I drove in Anchorage. Waves slopped across the bayous of Louisiana, and geysers at Yellowstone changed their size and period of eruptions. No one died and few people were injured because the quake occurred in such a sparsely populated area, the region between Anchorage and Fairbanks in the Alaska Range east of Mount McKinley. A 140-mile-long crack appeared right across that region, running over mountains and through glaciers. The land on each side moved laterally as much as 22 feet and vertically up to 6 feet. The Glenn Highway section known as the Tok Cut-off, between Glennallen and Tok, broke into many deep cracks. A tractor-trailer fell into one of them. Where the Interior highways crossed the big fault-line crack, lanes no longer lined up, and the road got a new jog where it used to be straight.

It's all part of living in a place that isn't quite done yet. Any part of Alaska could have an earthquake, but the Pacific Rim from Southcentral Alaska to the Aleutians is the shakiest. This is where Alaska is still under construction. The very rocks that make up the state are something of an ad hoc conglomeration, still in the process of being assembled. The floor of the Pacific Ocean is moving north, and as it moves, it carries islands and mountains with it. When they hit the Alaska plate, these pieces of land, called terranes, dock like ships arriving, but slowly—an island moving an inch a year takes a long time to travel thousands of miles. Geologists studying rocks near Mount McKinley found a terrane that used to be tropical islands. In Kenai Fjords National Park, fossils have turned up that are otherwise found only in Afghanistan and China. The slowly moving crust of the earth brought them here on a terrane that makes up a large part of the south coast of Alaska.

The earth's crust is paper thin compared to the globe's forces, and, like paper, it folds where two edges meet. Alaska's coast oscillates, bending up and down. At Kenai Fjords National Park, you can see steep little rock islands flocked

St. Augustine volcano.

with birds: They are old mountaintops, shrinking down into the earth. At Denali National Park, it is bowing upward. The monolith of McKinley is a brand-new dent growing higher.

Here's how it works: Near the center of the Pacific, underwater volcanoes and cracks that constantly ooze molten new rock are adding to the tectonic plate that forms the ocean floor. As it grows from the middle, the existing sea floor spreads at a rate of perhaps an inch a year. At the other side of the Pacific plate, where it bumps up against Alaska, there's not enough room for more crust, so it's forced, bending and cracking, downward into the planet's great, molten, re-cycling mill of magma. Landmasses that are along for the ride smash into the continent that's already there. When one hits—the so-called Yakutat block is still in the process of docking—a mountain range gets shoved up. Earthquakes and volcanoes are byproducts.

Living in such an unsettled land is a matter of more than abstract interest. The Mount Spurr volcano, which erupted most recently in 1992, turned day to night in Anchorage, dropping a blanket of ash all over the region. A Boeing 747 full of passengers flew into the plume and lost power in all its engines, falling in darkness for several minutes before pilots were able to restart the clogged jets. After that incident, the airport was closed until aviation authorities could find a way to keep volcanic plumes and planes apart. Early in 2009 the Anchorage air-port repeatedly closed due to eruptions of Redoubt Volcano, stranding thousands of passengers for days here and in Seattle and other cities that are jumping-off points for Alaska. Such events underline the remoteness of Alaska—you can't just take a bus. (Your only defense is travel insurance, covered in chapter 3. Find up-to-date volcano monitoring information at the Alaska Volcano Observatory website, www.avo.alaska.edu.) More than 80 volcanoes have been active in Alaska in the last 200 years.

Sitka.

Drunken forest of spruce trees.

Earthquakes between 7 and 8 on the Richter scale—larger than the 1994 Los Angeles quake—occur once a year on average, and huge quakes over 8 averaged every 13 years over the last century. The worst of the quakes, on March 27, 1964, was the strongest ever to hit North America. It ranked 9.2 on the Richter scale, twisting an entire region of the state so land to the west sank 12 feet while on the east it rose more than 30 feet. More land moved laterally than in any other recorded earthquake as well. The earthquake destroyed much of Anchorage and several smaller towns, and killed about 131 people, mostly in sea waves created by underwater landslides. In Valdez, the waterfront was swept clean of people.

But even that huge earthquake wasn't an unusual occurrence, at least in the Earth's terms. Geologists believe the same Alaska coast sank 6 feet in an earthquake in the year 1090.

Permafrost & Sea Ice

The northern Interior and Arctic parts of the state are less susceptible to earthquakes and, since they receive little precipitation, they don't have glaciers, either. But there's still a sense of living on a land that's not permanent, since most of northern Alaska is solid only by virtue of being frozen. When it thaws, it turns to mush. The phenomenon is caused by permafrost, a layer of earth a little below the surface that never thaws—or at least, you'd better hope it doesn't. Buildings erected on permafrost without some mechanism for dispersing their own heat—pilings, a gravel pad, or even refrigerator coils—can thaw the ground below and sink into a self-made quicksand. With the climate warming, sections of the trans-Alaska pipeline are leaning, and many miles of highway in Interior Alaska are being rebuilt each year because the ground they traverse has turned to mush due to increased average temperatures (more on this below).

The Arctic and much of the Interior is a swampy desert. Annual precipitation measured in Barrow is the same as in Las Vegas. Most of the time, the tundra is frozen in white; snow blows around, but not much falls. It melts in the summer, but the water can't sink into the ground, which remains frozen. Liquid water on top of the permafrost layer creates huge, shallow ponds. Alaska is a land of 10 million lakes, with 3 million larger than 20 acres. Birds arrive to feed and paddle around those circles and polygons of deep green and sky blue.

Permafrost makes the land do other strange things. On a steep slope, the thawed earth on top of the ice can begin to slowly slide downhill like a blanket sliding off the side of a bed, setting the trees at crazy angles. These groves of black spruce—the only conifer that grows in this kind of ground—are called drunken forests, and you can see them in Denali National Park and elsewhere in the Interior. Permafrost also can create weird tundra, with shaky tussocks the size of basketballs that sit a foot or two apart on a wet, muddy flat. From a distance it looks smooth, but walking on real basketballs might be easier. In other places, freezing and thawing processes create ponds with straight sides and sharp corners, polygons that appear manmade.

The permafrost also preserves many things. Although few and far between, tractor tracks remain clearly delineated for decades after they're made, appearing as narrow, parallel ponds reaching from one horizon to the other. The meat of prehistoric mastodons, still intact, has been unearthed from the frozen ground. On the Arctic Coast, the sea eroded ground near Barrow that contained ancient ancestors of the Eskimos who still inhabit the same neighborhood. In 1982, a family was found that apparently had been crushed by sea ice up to 500 years ago. Two of the bodies were well preserved, sitting in the home they had occupied and wearing the clothes they had worn the day of the disaster, perhaps around the time Columbus was sailing to America.

Sea ice is the frozen ocean that extends from northern Alaska to the other side of the world. For a few months of summer, it pulls away from the shore. Then, in October, icebergs floating toward land are cemented together by new ice forming along the beach. But even when the ice covers the whole ocean, it still moves under the immense pressure of wind and current. The clash creates towering pressure ridges—piles of broken ice that look like small mountain ranges and are about as difficult to cross.

The National Weather Service keeps track of the ice pack and issues maps and predictions you can find on the Internet (www.arh.noaa.gov). Eskimo hunters traveling on the ice by snowmobile need this information, as do crabbers who tempt disaster by fishing the south-moving ice edge in the fall, and shippers looking for the right moment in the summer to venture north with barges of fuel and other supplies for the coast of the Arctic Ocean. Sometimes there is barely time in the summer to get there and back before the ice closes in again in the fall.

Rainforest

By comparison, southern coastal Alaska is warm and biologically rich. Temperate rainforest ranges up the coast from Southeast Alaska north into Prince William Sound and westward to Kodiak Island, with bears, deer, moose, wolves, and even big cats living among the massive western hemlock, Sitka spruce, and cedar. This old-growth forest, too wet to burn in forest fires, is the last vestige of the virgin, primeval woods that seemed so limitless to the first white settlers who arrived on the east coast of the continent in the 17th century. The trees grow on and on, sometimes rising more than 200 feet high, with diameters up to 10 feet, and falling only after hundreds or even thousands of years. When they fall, the trees rot on the damp moss of the forest floor and return to soil to feed more trees, which grow in rows upon their nursery trunks.

Here, at least, Alaska *does* seem permanent. That sense helps explain why logging the rainforest is so controversial. Just one of these trees contains thousands of dollars' worth of wood. Vast Southeast lands owned by Alaska Native corporations were stripped of their old trees for the money they brought to their owners. But the great majority of this rainforest land belongs to the federal government, and a combination of environmental campaigns and economics put a stop to large-scale logging on that land while most of it remained virgin. When the Southeast Alaska logging economy died in the 1990s, the towns there suffered heavy economic blows. Tourism is taking the place of logging (with its own environmental and cultural impacts), but deep antipathy remains against logging opponents.

The rivers of the great coastal forests bring home runs of big salmon, clogging in spawning season like a busy sidewalk at rush hour. The fish spawn only once, returning by a precisely tuned sense of smell to the streams where they were hatched from 2 to 5 years before. When the fertilized eggs have been left in the stream gravel, the fish conveniently die on the beach, making a smorgasbord for bears and other forest animals. The huge Kodiak brown bear, sometimes topping 1,000 pounds, owes everything to the millions of salmon that return to the island each summer. By comparison, the grizzly bears of the Interior—the same species as browns, but living on grass, berries, and an occasional ground squirrel—are mere midgets, their weight counted in the hundreds of pounds. Forest-dwelling black bears grow to only a few hundred pounds.

Boreal Forest

Rainforest covers only a small fraction of Alaska. In fact, only a third of Alaska is forested at all, and most of this is the boreal forest that covers the central part of the state, behind the rain shadow of coastal mountains that intercept moist clouds off the oceans. Ranging from the Kenai Peninsula, south of Anchorage,

Boreal conifer forest.

Giant spruce trees.

to the Brooks Range, where the Arctic begins, this is a taiga—a moist, subarctic forest of smaller, slower-growing, hardier trees that leave plenty of open sky between their branches. In well-drained areas, on hillsides and southern land less susceptible to permafrost, the boreal forest is a lovely, broadly spaced combination of straight, proud white spruce and pale, spectral paper birch. Along the rivers, cottonwoods grow, with deep-grained bark and branches that spread in an oaklike matrix—if they could speak, it would be as wise old men.

Forest fires tear through Alaska's boreal forest each summer. In the newly warmed climate, million-acre years have become common, and in 2004, a record 6.5 million acres burned—an area the size of Massachusetts. It's impossible to fight that much fire. Alaska has always allowed fire to take its course unless structures or certain resources are at risk. In most cases, forest managers do no more than note the occurrence on a map. Unlike the rainforest, there's little commercially valuable timber in these thin stands, and, anyway, trying to halt the process of nature's self-immolation would be like trying to hold back a river with your hands. The boreal forest regenerates through fire—it was made to burn. The wildlife that lives in and eats it needs new growth from the burns as well as the shelter of older trees. When the forest is healthiest and most productive, the dark green of the spruce is broken by streaks and patches of light-green brush in an ever-changing succession.

This is the land of the moose. They're as big as large horses, with a long, bulbous nose and huge eyes that seem to know, somehow, just how ugly they are. Their flanks look like a worn-out shag carpet draped over a sawhorse. But moose are survivors. They thrive on land that no one else wants. In the summer, they wade out into the swampy tundra ponds to eat green muck. In the winter, they like nothing better than an old burn, where summer lightning has peeled back the forest and allowed a tangle of willows to grow—a moose's all-time favorite food. Eaten by wolves, hunted and run over by man, stranded in the snows of a hard winter, the moose always come back.

In the summer, moose disperse and are not easily seen in thick vegetation. In the winter, they gather where walking is easy, along roads and in lowlands where people also like to live. Encounters happen often in the city, until, as a resident, you begin to take the moose for granted, or see them as a pest that eats decorative plantings and blocks bike trails. Then, skiing on a Nordic trail one day, you round a corner and come face to face with an animal that stands 2 feet over you. You can smell the beast's foul scent and see his stress, the ears pulled back on the head and the whites of the eyes showing, and you know that this wild creature, fighting to live until summer, could easily kill you.

Light & Darkness

There's no escaping the stress of winter in Alaska—not for moose or people—nor any shield from the exhilaration of the summer. In summer, it never really gets dark at night. In Fairbanks in June, the sun sets in the north around midnight, but it doesn't go down far enough for real darkness to settle, instead rising again 2 hours later. It's always light enough to keep hiking or fishing, and, in clear weather, it's always light enough to read. You may not see the stars from early May until sometime in August (the climate chart in chapter 3 gives seasonal daylight for various towns). Visitors have trouble getting used to it: Falling asleep in broad daylight can be hard. Alaskans deal with it by staying up late and being active outdoors.

In the winter, on the other hand, you forget what the sun looks like. Kids go to school in the dark and come home in the dark. The sun rises in the middle of the morning and sets after lunch. At high noon in December, the sun hangs just above the southern horizon with a weak, orange light, a constant sunset. Animals and people go into hibernation.

As you go north, the change in the length of the days gets bigger. In Ketchikan, the longest day of the year, on the June 21 summer solstice, is about 17 hours, 20 minutes; in Fairbanks, 22 hours; and in Barrow, the longest day is more than 2 months. In contrast, in Seattle, the longest day is 16 hours, 15 minutes; and in Los Angeles, 14 hours, 30 minutes. On the equator, days are always the same length, 12 hours. At the North Pole and South Pole, the sun is up half the year and down the other half.

The best way to understand this is to model it with a ball and a lamp. The earth spins on its axis, the North and South poles, once a day. When the axis is upright, one spin of the ball puts light on each point of the ball equally—that's the spring and fall equinox, March 21 and September 21, when the day is 12 hours long everywhere. In the summer, the North Pole leans toward the light and the Northern Hemisphere gets more light than darkness, so during the course of one rotation, each northern spot is lighted more than half the time. In winter, the Southern Hemisphere gets its turn, and more than half the Northern Hemisphere is in shadow, meaning shorter days. As you go farther north in winter, the shadow gets larger, and the day in any one spot shorter. But no matter how the axis leans, the equator is always half light and half dark, like the entire globe as a whole.

In the North, on a long summer evening, you can almost feel the planet leaning toward the sun. The world lies under a bright, endless dome. In the winter, darkness falls as deep as space, and you can almost feel the Earth's warmth wafting away into the universe as the freeze sinks ever deeper in the land. Now the rainforest rivers and permafrost lakes are hard ice, the salmon are away at sea, and the bears are asleep. The moose and other wintering animals burn their summer fat, a finite store of provisions that may or may not last. Up in the mountains, the glaciers grow.

The Warming Climate

In the past 2 decades, winters have warmed and shortened and summers have gotten hotter. Individual years are sometimes closer to the long-term norm, but the trend is for warming. Years of bizarrely warm weather have become common, and records have been broken so often they are hardly noted. In Anchorage, where I live, that has meant ski seasons ruined by rainy weather, massive insect kills of trees, and extraordinary forest-fire danger, among many other changes. My friends and I, who grew up in Anchorage, never heard thunder until our teens; now it's commonplace, even early in the summer. Starting in the summer of 2004, the ocean warmed so much we were able to swim in it in places, for the first time in any of our lives. Alaska didn't even smell like Alaska that summer. Something about how the sun heated the ground and the plants created an odor I remember from travels in the Lower 48, not here.

In Arctic Alaska, the changes are much more pronounced: Sea ice is thinning and withdrawing from shore to ever-increasing records. In 2007, the Northwest Passage over America was ice-free from one end to the other, completely navigable for the first time. The loss of ice has led to catastrophic erosion washing away bluffs and villages. Permafrost has softened and given way. With winters warming and shortening, ecosystems are disrupted, plant and animal life stressed by the new conditions. A team of 300 scientists from all the Arctic nations, including the United States, completed a 4-year *Arctic Climate Impact Assessment* in 2004 and 2005. The report documents the changes and says they were largely driven by human carbon dioxide emissions. Since then, changes have accelerated alarmingly, with the prospect of an ice-free summertime Arctic within the foreseeable future. That likelihood led U.S. government scientists to conclude polar bears could go extinct; indeed, without sea ice, it is difficult to imagine how they could survive.

Carbon dioxide warms the Earth by trapping the heat of the sun in the atmosphere, a phenomenon understood since the late 1800s. Climate records reconstructed from ancient ice show the amount of carbon dioxide in the atmosphere has closely matched average temperature and climate conditions for half a million years. Due to human burning of fossil fuels, the carbon dioxide level in the atmosphere now is higher than at any time in that period. And now Arctic temperatures are rising at a rate that appears unprecedented.

Does this mean adjusting your plans as a visitor? Yes and no. Tourists in recent years have enjoyed sunny weather but have also suffered through forest-fire smoke and rainy skiing. But how the changes will play out in any particular year cannot be predicted, just as you cannot set your vacation dates based on a TV weather forecast. On the other hand, we may all need to adjust our plans. The amount of carbon dioxide each of us is responsible for emitting relates directly to the nonrenewable energy we use. You can help save Alaska by carpooling or turning off an extra light.

I've written a book on this subject, *The Whale and the Supercomputer: On the Northern Front of Climate Change* (Farrar, Straus and Giroux, $14), which tells the story of how Alaska's Iñupiat and scientists are experiencing and learning about the changing climate. You can read more about it on my website at www. wohlforth.net.

HISTORY: SCENES ON AN OVERSIZE STAGE

The history of Alaska is largely the tale of what *didn't* happen. What counts for visitors is not what people accomplished or the few monuments they built, but how little they managed to change this magnificent place. Immense wilderness remains. Conservationists can take some credit. The great formative battle of the national conservation movement—now largely forgotten—centered on protection of Alaska lands, as did the largest conservation law ever passed. Indeed, a century of politics focused mostly on this conflict between development and environment. But the sheer size and ruggedness of Alaska played as much a part in insulating it from change as its human protectors. Alaska simply overwhelmed efforts to tame it. Yes, history is here, but in this setting it's as visible as a flashlight on a bright, sunny morning. If Alaska's story is one of man versus nature, nature won—at least so far.

St. Nikolas Russian Orthodox Church in Sitka.

Russian America

Vitus Bering's story is almost too sad to tell. Sent by Peter the Great to explore east of his Empire in 1724, he labored for 17 years over two expeditions—including the effort of sledging back and forth clear across Russia and building ships in on the eastern edge of the Kamchatka Peninsula. Imagine transporting enough iron to build a ship and equip it with anchors across thousands of miles of primitive wilderness. In 1741, he finally located the American mainland and his ship's naturalist, Georg Steller, landed for part of a day to explore. But terrible weather, disease on board, and impending winter drove the expedition toward home with little more to show for its suffering.

The Russian sailors wandered in a nightmare. They were trapped among Alaska's coastal islands and reefs without charts or a clear course, men dying daily, cloudy and foggy skies and constant storms defeating efforts to find their position by the sun or stars, and even the compass stopped working. "We had to sail in an unknown ocean, not described by anyone, like blind

THE IDITAROD

The Iditarod Trail Sled Dog Race, a 1,000-mile run from Anchorage to Nome that takes place over 2 weeks in mid-March, is the biggest event of Alaska's year, not only in terms of sports, but also culturally and as a unifying event. The race is big news—TV anchors speculate on the mushers' strategies at the top of the evening news and break away live to cover the top finishers, regardless of the time of day or night. Schoolchildren plot the progress of their favorite teams on maps and over the Internet. Increasingly, the world is joining in. Visitors, especially Europeans, fill hotels in Anchorage and Nome for the Iditarod. Voices speaking French and German waft through the restaurants. Flight services drop spectators at remote checkpoints along the trail to see the mushers come through. It's a wonderful time of year to visit, with light skies, excellent late-season skiing, and winter festivals enlivening many towns. Nome goes crazy when the mushers hit. Even if the first team crosses the finish line at 3am in –30°F (–34°C) weather, a huge crowd turns out to congratulate the winner. And crowds keep turning out for the also-rans, too.

Given all this, it's difficult for me to report objectively on the activities of animal rights opponents to the race, currently led by People for the Ethical Treatment of Animals (PETA). While PETA opposes all human use of animals, some mainstream animal welfare advocates also criticize the race. They charge that dogs can suffer and die on the trail and, while not racing, are inhumanely tethered in dog lots. Organized boycotts against race sponsors have peeled off some national companies, but the campaign doesn't seem to be affecting the race, which grows every year. Iditarod supporters—the universal view in Alaska—claim the critics exaggerate and distort their charges. Iditarod mushers insist that the dogs, which are worth thousands of dollars, receive veterinary care superior to the doctoring that most people get. Sick dogs have been evacuated from the trail by helicopter. Mushers who abuse dogs are kicked out of the sport.

But framing the debate by focusing on the sport's marquee event probably skews the facts in the mushers' favor. Harmful practices do occur in the lower ranks of mushing. For example, uncontrolled breeding by amateurs or careless professionals produces too many pups that end up being killed. Sadly, that problem isn't unique to mushing—it happens to pets in cities all over the U.S. It's also true that sled dogs can be tethered excessively or otherwise abused. Successful mushers—including Iditarod competitors—must give their dogs thorough exercise, as only that way can the animals perform as athletes, but there's no law limiting how many dogs an irresponsible musher or pet owner can acquire or how often they must be run.

Our society is inhumane to animals in many ways. The question for visitors to consider is if the Iditarod is a fit symbol of that inhumanity, or the opposite.

men, not knowing if we were sailing too fast or too slow and unable to determine our location," an officer wrote. "I do not know if there is anything more joyless or a more desperate condition."

The ship finally came upon an island that the men thought might be part of Kamchatka. The ship would soon be inoperable because too many sailors were ill or dead to sail it. They landed there, then lost the ship upon the beach. Bering died. The survivors scratched out an existence over the winter by eating marine mammals. The next summer they built a new ship out of parts from the old one and sailed on.

When they arrived back in a Russian port, they were rich men. The sea otters they had eaten to survive yielded 700 pelts that were worth enormous sums in China. Seeing this, Russian fur hunters launched back into ferocious Alaskan waters in search of these same islands of furs. They had little more idea of where they were going than did Bering, but they were powered by the hope of catching otters and making their fortune.

The courage and brutality of these men are similarly astonishing. Their courage was shown by sailing on some of the world's roughest waters, without charts, in river boats held together with leather thongs. Their brutality was shown by the eagerness with which they slaughtered Alaska Natives along with sea mammals. As time passed, Russian invaders backed by investors spread these effective tactics, wiping out both coastal people and sea otters as they voyaged east and south along Alaska's coast, and eventually reaching all the way to California and Hawaii.

But Russian America never became a true colony. The Russians at most had fewer than 1,000 people in Alaska. They treated it more as a military outpost in hostile territory than as a place to live. When the Tsar sold his interest in Alaska to the United States in 1867, the new U.S. Army garrison at the capital of Sitka lived in fear of surrounding Tlingit people who had never been truly conquered.

The Russians' legacy exists mainly in the Russian Orthodox religious faith they left behind in coastal Native communities and in the destruction of marine mammal populations, which took until the 1970s to rebound completely (except for the amazing Steller sea cow, which the Russians drove to extinction). Onion-domed churches and Russian names remain in some communities, and Sitka, Kodiak, Unalaska, and Kenai still have Russian buildings, original or reconstructed, that visitors can see.

Klondike Gold Rush

The United States paid Russia $7.2 million for Alaska, a price of about 2¢ an acre. Even at that, many Americans considered the deal a bad one, and cartoonists and others in the press made fun of the worthless land Secretary of State William Seward had bought. Congress didn't bother to so much as give Alaskans a government or basic rights. Those few prospectors and trappers who wandered its wilderness lived without law. When several settled together, they would form ad hoc committees to record their mining claims and to judge crimes, for which the only available punishments were banishment or summary execution.

A significant non-Native population arrived all at once. In 1897, steamers landed in Seattle and Portland carrying prospectors from beyond the rim of civilization with trunks and gunnysacks full of gold. Americans were suffering a deep economic depression caused in part because of a lack of gold—it backed the currency, and its scarcity had made money too valuable, driving down prices and rendering debts impossible to repay. The perceived opportunity of free wealth in the North created a worldwide rush to the Klondike River, a tributary of the Yukon River in the Yukon Territory just east of Alaska.

The first of the stampeders, among them writer Jack London, arrived in the fall of 1897 and built tent camps on Lynn Canal, at the northern end of the Inside Passage. Their plan was to climb over the coastal mountains, through the Chilkoot or White pass, build boats to sail over a series of lakes, and float down the Yukon, through deadly rapids, to the new town of Dawson City, a trek of more than 400 miles. Some 100,000 people set off for the odyssey from as far away as Australia, most coming in the summer of 1898. About 40,000 made it to Dawson, enduring hardship and disappointment that are hard to comprehend, as many knew nothing about surviving in the outdoors, and hardly any understood the arduous, technical process of finding and mining gold.

This was the last gasp of the Wild West, rich in stories of flamboyant con men, fleeting fortunes, and Main Street gun fights. And it was the first breath of a new Alaskan culture of optimism, individualism, and greed. The gold-rush migration didn't stop at Dawson City. Towns sprang up across Alaska with news of gold finds—both real and fraudulent—that kept the rush in constant motion. Everyone benefited from enthusiasm that led to new investment, and that eagerness led to the fantasy that Alaska was a land of easy money in fish, fur, oil, timber, coal, and copper as well as gold.

For the next 100 years, Alaska's boosters focused on bringing that fantasy to reality.

Conservation Movement

Teddy Roosevelt became president as the wave of gold-rush development washed over Alaska, and it collided with his conservation movement like a surge of water hitting a breakwater. Roosevelt's Boone and Crocket Club of elite big-game hunters ushered through laws to protect Alaskan wildlife, and his Forest Service chief, Gifford Pinchot, drew boundaries on the Alaska map to defend its rainforests. The Tongass and Chugach national forests took in an area the size of Pennsylvania, encompassing all of Southeast Alaska, Prince William Sound, the Kenai Peninsula, and even the land where Anchorage now stands.

Alaskans met Roosevelt's conservation decisions with fury, especially an order freezing coal lands, particularly the Bering River Coal Field, on the edge of Chugach National Forest, which a syndicate of the J. P. Morgan and Guggenheim fortunes hoped to use to develop the huge Kennecott copper mine in the mountains up the Copper River. As Roosevelt turned over the presidency to his hand-picked successor, William Howard Taft, the mining advocates saw their opportunity. Taft's Secretary of the Interior, formerly a lawyer for the owners of the coal claims, approved a release to allow mining to begin.

Pinchot, still heading the Forest Service, believed Taft was betraying Roosevelt's conservation plans and blew the whistle on the coal deal. A national scandal erupted, complete with a media frenzy and Congressional hearings. For a time, the whole nation knew the geography of the Bering River Coal Fields, as daily installments in the drama made headlines. In the end, Taft paid the biggest price when his attempt to cover up the scandal was exposed. Roosevelt broke with him and ran for president in 1912 on a third-party ticket, splitting the Republicans so Democrat Woodrow Wilson won the presidency. The loss of progressive votes from Roosevelt to Wilson set the future shape of our national political system, with Democrats as the more liberal and environmentally oriented party and the Republicans favoring business and development.

In Alaska, the controversy set the pattern for conservation battles to follow for decades more. Alaskans came to think of the federal government as a distant landlord that stifled development and mismanaged resources. As the gold-rush period died out with World War I, the territory fell into economic stagnation. With federal spending in World War II, however, the modern era began, Alaska becoming connected for the first time by road to the balance of the nation. Cold War spending further nourished the economy. Ironically, federal spending became Alaska's economic base, and the government remains one of the state's largest employers, despite the tradition of viewing Washington as the enemy of Alaska's development.

Statehood & Native Lands

The fight for Alaska's statehood was a fight for control of land and fishing resources. Except for a few homesteads and tiny towns, all of Alaska remained federally owned. The Statehood Act would transfer 103 million acres to the new state, about a third of its total landmass, to be selected over a 25-year period. Statehood leaders dreamed of using these lands to produce the resource boom dreamed about since the gold rush.

The founding of the State of Alaska in 1959 brought huge celebrations in Alaska cities, but worry in some Native communities. Alaska Natives had never abandoned traditional lifestyles of hunting, fishing, and gathering. Their claims to their land mostly had not been resolved, but as long as Alaska lacked property lines, it hadn't mattered much. The wording of the Statehood Act nodded to their land rights, but gave no real assurance they would receive title. The threat of losing their land to the State of Alaska forever forced Native groups to organize and become militant in the 1960s.

Westward expansion in the rest of the United States had robbed American Indians of land. In Alaska, invasion instead took health and culture. Salmon canneries destroyed fish runs and starved villages. Russian fur traders and Yankee whalers depleted marine mammals Natives used for food and clothing. Newcomers introduced alcohol abuse and disease epidemics that wiped out entire villages. Christian missionaries and teachers suppressed Native languages and culture and imposed social practices and ways of life inappropriate to the Alaskan environment. Natives faced official discrimination in their own land, denied economic opportunity and subject to racial segregation.

Alaska's leaders of the 1960s had little interest in a land settlement for the Natives, but new national awareness of American Indian rights had an impact in Washington, D.C. As Alaska Natives filed claims covering almost the entire state, the federal government froze release of land to the state, or to almost anyone else. Then, at the end of the decade, America's largest oil field was discovered at Prudhoe Bay, in northern Alaska, on land owned by the State of Alaska. Boosters saw that under the Native land freeze, construction of a pipeline to remove the oil could be indefinitely delayed. With the support of the oil industry, Alaska politicians lined up in support of a generous settlement of Native land claims to get things moving.

Prodevelopment Alaskans had feared that land transferred to the Natives would be used for traditional Native priorities—hunting and gathering—not for economic projects such as mining, timber cutting, or oil drilling. But the form of the Native claims settlement addressed that concern. Land was transferred into for-profit corporations owned by Native shareholders—corporations that would be forced to earn a profit, and therefore would be motivated to develop their lands.

When the Alaska Native Land Claims Settlement Act passed in 1971, it was the largest indigenous land settlement yet in history, returning 44 million acres of land. And it initiated a new way of Native people relating to their land—not as tribes or tenants of reservations, but as corporate stockholders. Three decades later, some of these corporations had become the largest and most successful in Alaska.

Big Oil & Big Money

The economic boom that arrived with construction of the trans-Alaska pipeline, completed in 1977, and the subsequent flow of high-priced oil, dwarfed any boom that came before or since. People flooded in looking for lucrative jobs, and they found them. Just as in the gold rush, prostitution and street crime flourished—plus organized crime, air pollution, and traffic congestion. Growth came fast and chaotically. The population changed, too, with a new mix of residents from the oil states who brought a new, socially conservative vein to civic life.

As taxes and royalties from the new oil wealth flooded into the state treasury, Alaska for a time found itself rivaling the richest Arab countries in its per capita petroleum income. All individual taxes were cancelled, grandiose projects were constructed, and programs were created to subsidize many aspects of middle-class life. For example, my wife and I were able to pay for most of our college educations with loans that were 50% forgiven just for coming back to Alaska to live, the mortgage on our first house had a state-backed low interest rate, and the milk in the grocery store came from a state-owned creamery that processed the output of state-sponsored dairy farms.

The most famous and unique form of new spending arrived in checks sent to every man, woman, and child in Alaska. Gov. Jay Hammond created the Alaska Permanent Fund to save some of the new wealth in an investment account, with half the annual earnings to be distributed equally to all Alaskans. Hammond called himself a Bush rat—he lived on remote Lake Clark and flew his own plane—and he was a true conservationist, one of those many Alaskans disturbed by the excesses of the oil boom who wanted to save the good things about Alaska's past. A major purpose of the Permanent Fund was to deny the legislature access to excess funds. Another was to create the dividend, which Hammond believed would transfer the public's own money to their own use. When oil production and prices ebbed in the 1980s and '90s, he favored imposing taxes while continuing to pay the dividend so government would have to earn its keep. The dividend never was cut. Varying with the fund's investments, it has sometimes exceeded $2,000 per person.

Change came to Alaska, but not to the great majority of its lands. The oil rush helped that happen, too. The grand compromise that brought about the Alaska Native Claims Settlement Act and pipeline authorization in Congress in the early 1970s included a deal for the environmentalists as well: It required study of a large part of the federal government's remaining Alaska lands for new national parks, refuges, preserves, and other land-conservation units. At the end of the decade, as President Jimmy Carter left office, Congress made good, over the infuriated objections of development-minded Alaskans. The Alaska National Interest Lands Conservation Act set aside an area the size of California to be preserved, including areas such as Kenai Fjords National Park that today are the most popular attractions for visitors.

Boom times ended in the mid-1980s with a drop in oil prices and political mismanagement of the economy that plunged Alaska into a devastating depression—the inevitable bust after the boom. Spending from the 1989 Exxon Valdez oil spill put the economy back on its feet, and since then growth has been slow and steady, without another boom to disrupt it. As the gold rush recedes from historical awareness, Alaskans may be starting to appreciate their land as it is.

I've written a new book covering Alaska's conservation history, *The Fate of Nature,* which is due to be published in 2010 by Thomas Dunne/St. Martin's Press.

BOOKS, FILM & TV

Alaska remains a popular setting upon which writers and directors can project their fantasies, and more is coming out now in popular culture than ever. Oddly, despite the many new movies and television programs about Alaska, few are produced in Alaska. Here are some notable examples of fiction and nonfiction books, film, and TV of potential interest to visitors.

Books

Jack London.

The Call of the Wild, by Jack London (1903): Classic tale of the Klondike gold rush from the point of view of a dog sent to pull a sled. London published it just 5 years after giving up on the gold rush himself after suffering scurvy in a Yukon cabin (Aladdin, $5).

Coming into the Country, by John McPhee (1976): A gifted nonfiction writer captures the spirit of Alaska during the years of transition that marked the end of the frontier. McPhee's vivid portraits of backcountry personalities portray the motivations of the sort of odd people you may yet encounter (Farrar, Straus and Giroux, $17).

The Fate of Nature, by Charles Wohlforth (2010): Due out this year, my new book traces the relationship of Alaska's people to the land and waters of the Gulf of Alaska to find the hopes and motivations for saving this magnificent place. It's history, science, and biography in a single story (Thomas Dunne/St. Martin's Press).

Ordinary Wolves, by Seth Kantner (2004): This harrowing autobiographical novel is the most compelling and realistic account ever written of life in the Alaska Bush, in all its beauty and hardship. Kantner grew up in a sod hut before his rough introduction to the urban world (Milkweed Editions, $15).

The Yiddish Policemen's Union, by Michael Chabon (2007): A novel of complete imagination sets a noir crime story in a large colony of Jews that, in an alternate version of history, resembles Israel placed in Southeast Alaska (Harper Perennial, $16).

Film

Mystery, Alaska (1999): A pond hockey team from small-town Alaska gets to play the New York Rangers. Some found the film heartwarming, but more were disappointed by the clichés and lack of substance. Weekend pond hockey is a real tradition in some of Alaska's rural communities.

Northern Exposure.

Insomnia (2002): A gritty police thriller set in a small town in Alaska during the summer when the sun never sets. Al Pacino gives a brilliant performance as an ethically stained detective who can't get to sleep.

Grizzly Man (2005): Probably the best movie yet made about Alaska, Werner Herzog's documentary explores humanity's relation to nature using film shot by a misguided animal lover who ultimately was eaten by the bears he befriended.

Into the Wild (2007): Director Sean Penn's dramatization of the true story of a young wanderer who died in the Alaska wilderness, the movie is packed with spectacular scenery and was filmed on location.

The Simpsons Movie (2007): The summer blockbuster cut uncomfortably close to home with its portrayal of greedy Alaskans eager to destroy the environment. Homer seemed so darned at home here, a place where "you can never be too fat or too drunk."

Television

Northern Exposure (1990–95): The comedy series about a spoiled New York doctor forced to practice medicine in an eccentric Alaskan town remains the most perceptive screen portrayal of such places. It sometimes shows in reruns and is available on DVD.

Deadliest Catch: Crab Fishing in Alaska (2005–present): This surprise hit records the real-life hazards and conflicts of hard-driving fishermen as they battle the notoriously bad weather of the Bering Sea (Discovery Channel).

ALASKA CUISINE: FRESH FISH SPECIAL

Alaska probably will never be a food destination, but you will find some excellent restaurants and many opportunities to dine on fresh Alaska seafood, primarily salmon and halibut. The true taste of Alaska summer is fresh fish cooked over a driftwood fire, and you won't do any better in the fanciest restaurant. The key to cooking Pacific salmon—or to ordering it in a restaurant—is to avoid preparation that spoils the rich flavor. With halibut, it's important to choose the right cut and preparation to enjoy flaky, delicate fish.

Salmon

FREEZE AS LITTLE AS POSSIBLE It's a sad fact that salmon loses some of its richness and gets more "fishy" as soon as it's frozen. Eat as much as you can fresh because it'll never be better. Ask if the salmon is fresh (never frozen) when you order it in a restaurant. If you have a lot of salmon, don't overlook smoking, the traditional Native way of preserving fish for the winter. See p. 423 for information on getting your salmon frozen and smoked.

CHOOSING THE BEST FISH The best restaurants advertise where their salmon comes from on the menu. In early summer, Copper River kings and reds are the richest in flavor; later in the summer, Yukon River salmon are best. The oil in the salmon gives it the rich, meaty flavor; the fish from the Copper and Yukon are high in oil content because the rivers are long and the fish need a lot of stored energy to swim upstream to spawn. King, red, and silver salmon are the only species you should find in a restaurant. Avoid farm-reared salmon, which is mushy and flavorless compared with wild Alaska salmon and doesn't come from here. (Fish farming is outlawed in Alaska.)

KEEP IT SIMPLE When salmon is fresh, it's best with light seasoning, perhaps just a little lemon, dill weed, and pepper and salt, or basted with soy sauce; or without anything on it at all, grilled over alder coals. Some restaurants prepare it blackened or with a reduction sauce. Their success depends on the skill of the chef, as they run the risk that the nuances of the fish's flavor will be hidden.

DON'T OVERCOOK IT Salmon should be cooked just until the moment the meat changes color and becomes flaky through to the bone, or slightly before. A minute

Restaurants incorporate Alaska's fresh fish in such dishes as this mustard- and potato-crusted filet with beets.

more, and the meat becomes "fishier" and loses its texture, taking on a dry, uniform feel rather than its exquisite delicacy. That's why those huge barbecue salmon bakes often are not as good as they should be—it's too hard to cook hundreds of pieces of fish just right and serve them all hot. Japanese chefs and some trendy restaurants serve salmon raw or cured, which is delicious if the fish is good. Fried salmon is a poor choice, due to both the too-strong flavor and the surfeit of fat.

FILETS, NOT STEAKS Salmon is cut two ways in Alaska: lengthwise filets or crosswise steaks. The filet is cut with the grain of the flesh, keeping the oil and moisture in the fish. Do not remove the skin before cooking—it holds in the oils and will fall off easily when the fish is done. If you have a large group, consider cooking the salmon bone-in (sometimes called a roast), stuffing seasonings in the body cavity. When it's done, the skin easily peels off and, after eating the first side, you can effortlessly lift out the skeleton.

Halibut

SEASONS & PROCESSING The halibut fishery continues through most of the year, so fresh fish is usually available, if you are willing to pay the prices. Halibut are large, so if you have a successful sportfishing charter, you will end up with more than you can eat fresh. If properly processed—and it is well worth using a professional with the right equipment—frozen halibut will last most of the winter in the freezer and will taste almost as good as fresh.

CHOOSING THE FISH If you are buying halibut or deciding which fish to keep while angling, consider this: The younger, smaller fish are better eating. Huge halibut make good pictures, but their flesh breaks into relatively tough chunks rather than thin, tender flakes of the under-20-pounders known as "chicken halibut." Keep the cheeks, which are prized as the best meat of the entire fish.

PREPARATION Some cooks believe low-fat halibut meat needs help with big globs of mayonnaise or cheese, and produce something that tastes like a grilled cheese sandwich. There are a lot of good ways to prepare halibut, both simple and more sophisticated, that compliment its healthy, lean flavor. Halibut is wonderful fried with light batter; grilled with lemon or soy; baked in foil with olive oil, basil, and garlic; or even baked encrusted with macadamia nuts or in parchment, as you find it at some gourmet restaurants. Fresh fish needs little help; if it has been frozen a while, some added fat in the form of oil or butter is a good idea.

DON'T OVERCOOK IT Because a halibut filet can be so thick, it's easy to mess up the cooking time. Overcooking quickly dries the fish. In the oven I use high heat and check frequently. Thinner pieces can be layered so they don't get done before the bigger chunks. It's even harder when grilling because halibut falls apart if you handle it much when cooking. Put bigger filets on first. As soon as the flakes separate, the fish is done.

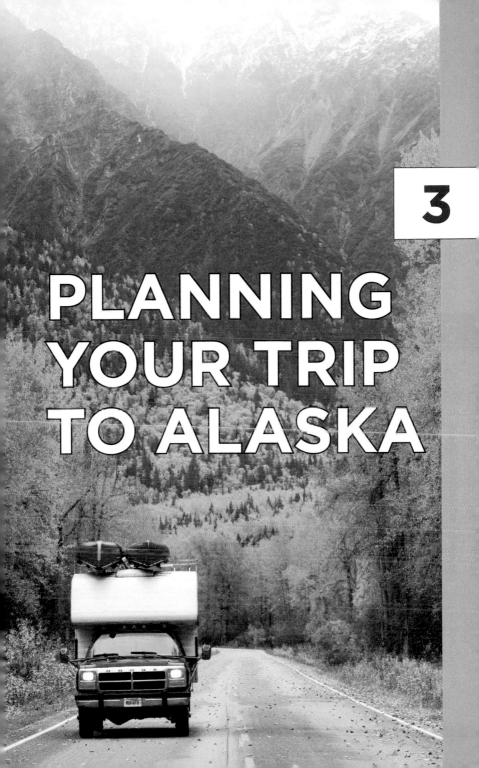

3

PLANNING YOUR TRIP TO ALASKA

Planning a trip to Alaska can be a bit more complicated than getting ready to travel in the rest of the United States. Aside from the vast distances and range of climatic conditions, the best places book up quickly for the high summer season. This chapter provides general orientation information, advice on when to go and how much it will cost, and then covers how to plan a trip to Alaska, including passport and visa information for international visitors, modes of travel, insurance, safety, and issues to watch out for. I will also point you to the best outdoor activities and places and the businesses to get you there. I've included primers on fishing and shopping for Alaska Native art as well.

WHEN TO GO

One of the questions I am asked most frequently is, "What's the best time to visit _____?" Alaska's vastness means the seasons change at different times in different parts of the state. Sports and cultural activities also happen at different times in different places.

Climate & Seasons

The weather in Alaska can be extreme and unpredictable. The state is the first to get whatever Arctic Siberia or the void of the North Pacific have to throw at North America. The extremes of recorded temperatures are a high of 100°F (38°C) and low of −80°F (−62°C). At any time of year, your vacation could be enlivened by weeks of unbroken sunny weather or weighed down by weeks of unbroken rain. All you can do is play the averages, hope for the best, and, if you do get bad weather, get out and have fun anyway—that's what Alaskans do. A statistical summary of weather probabilities in various Alaska places is found below in "Alaska's Climate, by Months & Regions." I've summarized the best visitor season in each destination in "Alaska by the Numbers," p. 74.

JUNE, JULY & AUGUST Summer in Alaska is a miraculous time, when the sun refuses to set, the salmon run upriver, and people are energized by limitless daylight. The sun dips below the horizon in Anchorage for only about 4 hours on June 21, the longest day of the year, and the sky is light all night. The state fills with people coming to visit and to work in the seasonal fishing, timber, and construction industries. Weather gets warmer, although how warm depends on where you go (see the chart below). June is the driest of the summer months, July the warmest, and August generally the rainiest month of the brief summer, but warmer than June. In most respects, June

PREVIOUS PAGE: **Driving along the Haines Highway.**

is the best summer month to make a visit, but it does have some drawbacks to consider: In the Arctic, snow can linger until mid-June; in Southcentral Alaska, trails at high elevations or in the shade may be too muddy or snowy; and not all activities or facilities at Denali National Park open until late June. It's also the worst time for mosquitoes.

Summer also is the season of high prices. Most operators in the visitor industry have only these 90 days to make their year's income, and they charge whatever the market will bear. July is the absolute peak of the tourist season, when you must book well ahead and when crowds are most prevalent. (Of course, crowding depends on where you are. With a population density of roughly one person per square mile, Alaska is never *really* crowded.) Before June 15 and after August 15, the flow of visitors relaxes, providing occasional bargains and more elbow room. Real off-season prices show up before Memorial Day and after Labor Day. But the length and intensity of the visitor season varies widely in different areas: In cruise-ship ports, it's busy from chilly early May into stormy October.

MAY & SEPTEMBER More and more visitors are coming to Alaska during these "shoulder months" to take advantage of the lower prices, reduced crowds, and special beauty.

May is the drier of the 2 months and can be as warm as summer if you're lucky, but as you travel farther north and earlier in the month, your chances of finding cold, mud, and even snow increase. In Alaska, there is no spring—the melt of snow and resultant seas of mud are called **breakup.** Flowers show up with the start of summer. Many outdoor activities aren't possible during breakup, which can extend well into May. Except in cruise-ship towns, most tourist-oriented activities and facilities are still closed before May 15, and a few don't open until Memorial Day or June 1. Where visitor facilities are open, they often have significantly lower prices. Also, the first visitors of the year usually receive an especially warm welcome. The very earliest salmon runs start in May, but for a fishing-oriented trip it's better to come later in the summer. Cruise ships begin calling May 1, and the towns they visit swing into action when they arrive.

Sometime between late August and mid-September, weather patterns change, bringing clouds, frequent rainstorms, and cooling weather, and signaling the trees and tundra to turn bright, vivid colors. For a week or two (what week it is depends on your latitude), the bright yellow birches of the boreal forest and the rich red of the heathery tundra make September the loveliest time of year. But the rain and the nip in the air, similar to late October or November in New England, mean you'll likely have to bundle up; and September is among the wettest months of the year. Most tourist-oriented businesses stay open, with lower prices, until September 15, except in the Arctic. After September 15, it's potluck. Some areas close up tight, but the silver salmon fishing is still active on the Kenai Peninsula, and the season there continues until the end of the month. A lucky visitor can come in September and hit a month of crisp, sunny, perfect weather, and have the state relatively to him- or herself. Or, it can be cold and rainy all month. Cruise ships continue to ply the Inside Passage well into October, while the sky dumps torrential rains: Ketchikan averages 22 inches and 24 rainy days in October.

OCTOBER, NOVEMBER, APRIL I always love Alaska, but I love it least during these transition months between winter and summer. From Southcentral Alaska northward, snow and ice arrive sometime in October; in Southeast Alaska, these are the month of cold, unending rain. Winter starts in November, but you can't count on being able to do winter sports, and darkness is prevalent as the year's shortest day approaches. April is a month of waiting, as winter sports come to an end and summer activities are blocked by melt and mud (although spring skiing can still be great in high-snow years). In-town activities are down in these months, too; with few visitors, many facilities are closed.

DECEMBER THROUGH MARCH Winter is the whole point of Alaska. For sightseeing, the scenery is at its best (although there are far fewer wildlife-viewing opportunities). This is the time to see the aurora borealis. Communities get busy with activities such as sled-dog and snowmobile races; theater, music, and other performing arts; ice-carving competitions and winter carnivals; and all the rest of the real local culture that takes a break in the summer,

Alaska's Climate, by Months & Regions

	JAN	FEB	MAR	APR	MAY
ANCHORAGE: **SOUTHCENTRAL ALASKA**					
AVERAGE HIGH**	21/-6	26/-3	33/1	44/7	55/13
AVERAGE LOW**	8/-13	11/-12	17/-8	29/-2	39/4
HOURS OF LIGHT*	6:53	9:41	12:22	15:20	18:00
SUNNY DAYS†	12	10	13	12	11
RAINY OR SNOWY DAYS	8	8	8	6	7
PRECIPITATION‡	0.8	0.8	0.6	0.6	0.7
BARROW: ARCTIC ALASKA					
AVERAGE HIGH**	8/-13	12/-24	-8/-22	6/-14	25/-4
AVERAGE LOW**	20/-29	-24/-31	-21/-29	-8/-22	15/-9
HOURS OF LIGHT*	0:00	8:05	12:33	17:43	24:00
SUNNY DAYS†	7	18	21	18	8
RAINY OR SNOWY DAYS	4	4	4	4	4
PRECIPITATION‡	0.2	0.2	0.1	0.2	0.2
COLD BAY: **ALEUTIAN ARCHIPELAGO**					
AVERAGE HIGH**	33/1	32/0	35/2	38/3	45/7
AVERAGE LOW**	24/-4	23/-5	25/-4	29/-2	35/2
HOURS OF LIGHT*	8:05	10:10	12:17	14:36	16:32
SUNNY DAYS†	8	6	8	4	3
RAINY OR SNOWY DAYS	19	17	18	16	17
PRECIPITATION‡	**2.8**	2.5	2.3	2.0	2.5

*Hours of light is sunrise to sunset on the 21st day of each month.
**All temperatures are given in degrees Fahrenheit first, with degrees Celsius after the slash.

when most visitors come. If you enjoy winter and its outdoor activities, an Alaska visit is paradise, with superb downhill, cross-country, and backcountry skiing; snowshoeing; snowmobiling; dog mushing; ice-skating—anything that can be done on snow and ice.

By far the best time to come is late winter, February and March, when the sun is up longer and winter activities hit their peak. Anchorage's Fur Rendezvous is in late February; the Iditarod Sled Dog Race is in early March. Visiting in late March could mean thin snow at lower elevations for cross-country skiing, but downhill skiing and skiing at backcountry locations keep going strong. At Alyeska Resort, south of Anchorage, skiing goes into April (they used to ski until Memorial Day, but not enough people came). In Homer, you can cross-country ski and go salmon fishing on the same day in March.

If you come in winter, you sacrifice some popular Alaska experiences. Some tourism-oriented towns such as Skagway close down almost completely. In places on the ocean, most activities and attractions are closed for

JUNE	JULY	AUG	SEPT	OCT	NOV	DEC
62/17	65/18	63/17	55/13	40/4	28/-2	22/-6
47/8	51/11	49/9	41/5	28/-2	16/-9	10/-12
19:22	18:00	15:15	12:19	9:29	6:46	5:27
10	9	9	9	10	10	10
8	11	13	14	12	10	11
1.0	1.9	2.7	2.6	1.9	1.1	1.1
39/4	46/8	43/6	34/1	20/-7	5/-15	-6/-21
30/-1	34/1	34/1	27/-3	10/-12	-6/-21	-17/-27
24:00	24:00	17:34	12:30	7:46	0:00	0:00
9	11	5	4	6	8	4
5	9	11	11	11	6	5
0.3	0.9	1.0	0.6	0.5	0.2	0.2
50/10	55/13	56/13	52/11	44/7	39/4	35/2
41/5	46/8	47/8	43/6	35/2	30/-1	27/-3
17:25	16:33	14:34	12:17	10:04	8.01	7:08
3	3	2	4	6	6	7
16	17	20	21	23	22	21
2.3	2.4	3.7	4.3	4.2	4.2	3.3

†Sunny days include the average observed clear and partly cloudy days per month.
‡Precipitation is the average water equivalent of rain or snow. [CONTINUED ON NEXT PAGE]

the season, but services remain open for business travelers. Inland, where winter sports are better, there is more to do. Hotel prices are often less than half of what you'd pay in the high season. Quite luxurious rooms can go for the cost of a budget motel.

What to Wear

Unless you're coming for business meetings, you'll find little use for a tie or any formal attire anywhere in Alaska, but you do need to prepare for broad swings in weather.

SUMMER You're not going to the North Pole, and you don't need a down parka or winter boots weighing down your luggage. But you do need to be ready for a variety of weather, from sunny, 80°F (27°C) days to windy, rainy 50°F

Alaska's Climate, by Months & Regions [CONTINUED FROM PREVIOUS PAGE]

	JAN	FEB	MAR	APR	MAY
FAIRBANKS: INTERIOR ALASKA					
AVERAGE HIGH**	-2/-18	8/-13	24/-4	42/6	60/16
AVERAGE LOW**	-19/-28	-15/-26	-2/-19	20/-7	38/3
HOURS OF LIGHT*	5:46	9:14	12:22	15:54	19:22
SUNNY DAYS†	15	14	17	14	16
RAINY OR SNOWY DAYS	8	7	6	5	7
PRECIPITATION‡	0.6	0.4	0.4	0.2	0.6
JUNEAU: SOUTHEAST ALASKA					
AVERAGE HIGH**	29/-2	34/1	39/4	48/9	55/13
AVERAGE LOW**	18/-8	23/-5	27/-3	32/0	39/4
HOURS OF LIGHT*	7:31	9:55	12:18	14:55	17:11
SUNNY DAYS†	8	7	7	8	8
RAINY OR SNOWY DAYS	18	17	18	17	17
PRECIPITATION‡	4.3	3.9	3.5	2.9	3.5
VALDEZ: PRINCE WILLIAM SOUND					
AVERAGE HIGH**	27/-3	30/-1	37/3	45/7	53/12
AVERAGE LOW**	18/-8	19/-7	24/-4	31/-1	39/4
HOURS OF LIGHT*	6:54	9:41	12:22	15:19	17:58
SUNNY DAYS†	9	9	11	11	9
RAINY OR SNOWY DAYS	17	14	16	14	17
PRECIPITATION‡	5.7	5.5	4.7	3.2	3.2

*Hours of light is sunrise to sunset on the 21st day of each month.
**All temperatures are given in degrees Fahrenheit first, with degrees Celsius after the slash.

(10°C) outings on the water. The way Alaskans prepare for such a range is with layers. The content of the layers depends on what you'll be doing, but everyone should bring at least this: warm-weather clothes, heavy long-sleeved shirts and pants, a wool sweater or fleece equivalent, a jacket, and a waterproof raincoat and rain pants. Gloves and wool hats are a good idea, too, especially for boating trips. If you'll be camping, add synthetic thermal long underwear and wool socks, and make sure your jacket is thick synthetic fleece. Combining these items, you'll be ready for any summer conditions. For hiking, bring sturdy shoes or cross trainers.

WINTER You can be warm and comfortable no matter how cold it is. Once you know how to dress, winter is not a time of suffering, and the world of snow opens up to you. First, what not to wear: People don't wear heavy Arctic

JUNE	JULY	AUG	SEPT	OCT	NOV	DEC
71/22	73/23	66/19	55/13	32/0	11/-12	1/-17
52/11	52/11	47/8	36/2	17/-8	-5/-21	-16/-27
21:48	19:26	15:52	12:24	9:04	5:39	3:43
13	12	10	10	9	12	12
11	12	12	10	11	11	9
1.4	1.8	1.8	1.1	0.8	0.7	0.8
62/17	64/18	63/17	56/13	47/8	37/3	32/0
45/7	48/9	48/9	43/6	37/3	28/-2	23/-5
18:17	17:13	14:54	12:20	9:49	7:27	6:22
8	8	9	6	4	6	5
15	17	17	20	24	20	21
3.1	4.2	5.3	7.2	7.8	5.4	5.1
60/16	63/17	61/16	54/12	43/6	33/1	29/-2
45/7	48/9	46/8	41/5	33/1	23/-5	19/-7
19:20	17:57	15:14	12:20	9:30	6:48	5:29
8	8	10	8	8	10	7
15	17	17	20	20	16	18
2.8	3.6	6.5	9.3	7.9	5.7	7.6

†Sunny days include the average observed clear and partly cloudy days per month.
‡Precipitation is the average water equivalent of rain or snow.

Only-in-Alaska Events

By the end of the winter, sports in Alaska can get extreme. The **Arctic Man Ski & Sno-Go Classic** (**☎907/456-2626;** www.arcticman. com) sounds insane just in the description: A skier goes straight down a steep 1,700-foot slope, then grabs a rope to be pulled up the next slope by a snow machine going as fast as 88 mph, then skis down the next, 1,200-foot slope; best total time for 5½ miles: 4 minutes, 1 second. Thousands of spectators build a hard-partying city of RVs, snow machines, and a big tent for beer and rock-and-roll in the remote, treeless hills of the Alaska Range near Summit Lake, 10 miles north of Paxson at mile 197.5 on the Richardson Highway. For a few days, it's the fourth largest community in Alaska. Parking is $100. The event will be held from April 8 to 11, 2010 (race day the 10th).

Another kind of insanity occurs in the **Tesoro Iron Dog Snowmobile Race** (**☎907/563-4414;** www.iron dog.org), which begins February 21, 2010. Teams of two racers leave from Wasilla, near Anchorage, take the Iditarod Trail to Nome, then turn around and ride to Fairbanks, in the middle of the state. Racers cover a distance of about 2,000 miles of rugged, roadless wilderness at speeds often well in excess of high-way-driving speed. In 2007, the winning duo included former Governor Sarah Palin's husband Todd, then better known as the "First Dude." He covered the distance in just more than 38 hours. The race is by far the longest and toughest in the world.

Muscle-powered sports also have big late winter events, including the 50km **Tour of Anchorage** Nordic ski race (www.tourof anchorage.com), which winds its way from one side of the city to the other on the first Sunday in March. With as many as 2,000 racers, it has become a major community happening and draws elite skiers, kids, and grandmothers. It is the second largest race in the U.S. I ski it every year. Other towns around Alaska have started their own ski marathons during the following weeks, including Homer, Talkeetna, and Fairbanks. For a calendar of events and other Alaska cross-country skiing information, contact the **Nordic Ski Association of Anchorage** (**☎907/276-7609;** www. anchoragenordicski.com).

And don't forget the various human-powered wilderness races that cross Alaska, winter and summer. In 2008, the Iditarod Invitational included a 350-mile division, from Knik to McGrath, and a 1,100-mile distance to Nome, with racers on skis, snowshoes, bikes, or on foot, in temperatures colder than −25°F (−31°C), some pushing bikes through deep snow. Twenty-eight of 45 starters made it to McGrath; one racer scratched after she was found wandering near the trail, blinded by frostbite. Sometimes these races have only a few competitors, and perhaps only one or two finishers. No one does it for glory, but somehow it makes sense where big, wild land is the dominant theme and trail sports are the primary form of recreation.

gear in town, even in the Arctic. To make the dash from car to heated building, all you need is an overcoat, sweater, hat, gloves, and wool socks. For outdoor pursuits, what to wear depends on how active you will be. The key to warmth and safety during vigorous outdoor activities is to wear layers of breathable clothing that will stay warm when wet, such as wool or synthetics. With the following layers, you can be ready for temperatures well below zero (at which point you won't want to ski or skate anyway): synthetic thermal long underwear, synthetic fleece pants and coat, wool sweater, wind-resistant pants and jacket, wool socks and hat, warm boots with liners or covers, and lined mittens. Remove layers for warmer temperatures. For more sedentary outdoor activities, such as watching the aurora or riding a snowmobile or dogsled, you need warmer clothing. Likewise, drives on rural highways in winter require warm clothing in case of breakdowns. On guided trips or at cold-weather resorts, they'll tell you what to bring or provide or rent it to you. A full cold-weather outfit includes synthetic thermal long underwear, the stoutest Sorel-style or Air Force bunny boots, insulated snow pants, a heavy down or fur parka with a hood, thick, insulated mittens (not gloves), a wool hat, a face-insulating mask, and ski goggles or quality sunglasses. You don't want any skin showing while riding a snowmobile or standing in a strong wind in below-zero (Fahrenheit) temperatures. Such a get-up costs more than $500. You can buy what you need in Anchorage at **Army Navy Store,** 320 W. 4th Ave. (☎888/836-3535 or 907/279-2401; www.army-navy-store.com); or in Fairbanks at **Big Ray's Store,** 507 2nd Ave. (☎800/478-3458 Alaska only or 907/452-3458; www.bigrays.com).

Alaska Calendar of Events

Here are some of the biggest community events of the year in Alaska's cities and towns. Event plans can change, so don't set up your vacation around any of these dates without checking for current details. I haven't listed fishing derbies, which go on in almost every coastal town in the summer and are listed in the sections on each town.

FEBRUARY

The Yukon Quest International Sled Dog Race (☎907/452-7954; www.yukonquest.com). Mushers say this rugged 1,000-mile race is even tougher than the Iditarod. It runs between Fairbanks and Whitehorse, Yukon Territory, trading the direction each year. Starts February 6, 2010, in Fairbanks.

The Anchorage Fur Rendezvous Winter Festival (☎907/274-1177; www.furrondy.net). The citywide winter celebration includes community events, fireworks, craft fairs, dogsled rides, and other fun. The main event has always been

the **World Champion Sled Dog Race,** a 3-day sprint event of about 25 miles per heat. The Rondy's end coincides with the start of the Iditarod (see directly below). February 26 through March 7, 2010.

MARCH

The Iditarod Trail Sled Dog Race (☎907/376-5155; www.iditarod.com). The world's most famous sled-dog race starts with fanfare from **Anchorage;** then the teams are loaded into trucks for the **Iditarod Restart,** north of the city, the real beginning of the race, where the historic gold-rush trail becomes continuous for the dogs' 1,000-mile run to

Nome. The start and the finish in Nome are the biggest sporting and cultural events of Alaska's year, drawing world media attention and turning Nome into a huge party for a few days (they even play golf out on the sea ice). Along the way, visitors can stay in remote lodges and fly bush planes to see the check points (with plenty of advance planning and a big budget). Animal-rights groups oppose the race on the grounds that it's cruel to dogs. For more on the issue, see p. 48. In 2010 the race starts March 6.

The Nenana Ice Classic (☎907/832-5446; www.nenanaakiceclassic.com), Nenana. This is a betting pool on the date of spring breakup that has happened every year for the last 9 decades. The kick-off is Tripod Days, when a "four-legged tripod" that will mark the ice going out on the Tanana River is erected during the first weekend in March, with a celebration of dance performances, dog mushing, and other activities. The ticket buyer who guesses the minute the tripod will move, usually about 2 months later, wins the jackpot, typically more than $300,000.

The World Ice Art Championships (☎907/451-8250; www.icealaska.com), Fairbanks. Carvers from all over the world sculpt immense chunks of clear ice cut from a Fairbanks pond. Among ice carvers, Fairbanks's ice is famous for its clarity and the great size of the chunks. Some spectacular ice sculptures stand as tall as a two-story building. In 2010, professional carving will be February 23 to 25 (single block) and February 28 to March 5 (multiblock), with the best viewing of completed sculptures March 5 to 15.

APRIL

The Alaska Folk Festival (☎907/463-3316; www.alaskafolkfestival.org), Juneau. This is a communitywide celebration, drawing musicians, whether on the bill or not, from all over the state. April 5 to 11, 2010.

MAY

The Kachemak Shorebird Festival (☎907/235-7740; www.homeralaska.org), Homer. The festival includes guided bird-watching hikes and boat excursions, natural-history workshops, art shows, performances, and other events. Early May.

The Last Frontier Theater Conference (☎907/834-1614; www.pwscc.edu/conference), Valdez. The conference brings playwrights and directors from all over the nation to the community for a week of seminars and performances. May 16 to May 23, 2010.

Little Norway Festival (☎907/772-3646; www.petersburg.org), Petersburg. This festival celebrates the May 17, 1814, declaration of the independence of Norway from Sweden. The town has several days of community events. The festival takes place on the third full weekend in May.

Kodiak Crab Festival (☎907/486-5557), Kodiak. This Memorial Day weekend event is the town's biggest of the year, including fun events, the solemn blessing of the fleet, and a memorial service for lost fishermen and other mariners.

JUNE

Celebration, Juneau. Sponsored by the Sealaska Heritage Institute (☎907/463-4844; www.sealaskaheritage.org), this every-other-year event is among Alaska's largest cultural gatherings. Alaska Natives come from every corner of the state to share dance and art, sell crafts, meet, and, well, celebrate. Book well ahead if you will be in Juneau at this time, as rooms will be in short supply. June 3 to 5, 2010.

The Sitka Summer Music Festival (☎907/747-6774; www.sitkamusicfestival.org), Sitka. Since 1972, this chamber-music series has drawn musicians from all over the world for most of June.

Performances take place Tuesdays and Fridays, with other events all week, over 3 weeks in June.

Midnight Sun Baseball Game, Fairbanks. A century-old summer-solstice tradition: a game without artificial lights beginning at 10:30pm. The local semipro baseball team, the Alaska Goldpanners (☎907/451-0095; www.goldpanners.com), has hosted since 1960. June 21.

Midnight Sun Festival, Nome. Over the summer solstice, Nome gets more than 22 hours of direct sunlight, ample reason for a parade, softball tournament, raft race, and polar bear swim. Call ☎907/443-5535 for information. Weekend closest to June 21.

JULY

Independence Day. Most of the small towns in Alaska make a big deal of the Fourth of July. Seward always has a huge celebration, exploding with visitors, primarily from Anchorage. Besides the parade and many small-town festivities, the main attraction is the **Mount Marathon Race,** which goes from the middle of town straight up rocky Mount Marathon to its 3,022-foot peak and down again. **Seldovia, Ketchikan, Skagway,** and **Juneau** also have exceptional Fourth of July events. See the individual town sections for more information.

The Southeast Alaska State Fair (☎907/766-2476; www.seakfair org), Haines. Held for 4 days in late July, this is a regional small-town get-together and music festival, with livestock, cooking, a logging show, a parade, and other entertainment.

AUGUST

The Alaska State Fair (☎907/745-4827; www.alaskastatefair.org), Palmer. The region's biggest event of the year is a typical state fair, except for the huge vegetables. The good soil and long Valley days produce cabbages the size of beanbag chairs. Try to imagine a 19-pound carrot. Held the 12 days before Labor Day.

OCTOBER

Alaska Day Festival (☎907/747-8806), Sitka. Alaska Day, commemorating the Alaska purchase on October 18, 1867, is a big deal in this former Russian and U.S. territorial capital city.

NOVEMBER

Sitka WhaleFest (☎907/747-7964; www.sitkawhalefest.org), Sitka. Over a weekend in early November, during the fall and early winter period when humpback whales congregate in Sitka Sound, experts from around the world present a 3-day symposium, and there are whale-watching tours, concerts, an art show, a run, and community events.

The Alaska Bald Eagle Festival (☎907/766-3094; www.baldeaglefestival. org), Haines. Seminars and special events mark an annual congregation of 3,000 eagles near Haines. Mid-November.

The Carrs/Safeway Great Alaska Shootout basketball tournament (☎907/786-1250; www.goseawolves. com), Anchorage. The University of Alaska Anchorage hosts top-ranked college teams at the Sullivan Arena over Thanksgiving weekend.

DECEMBER

Anchorage International Film Festival (www.anchoragefilmfestival.org). As many as a dozen screenings a day feature films from every corner of the world, including the obscure, the bizarre, and the profound. Two weeks in mid-December.

MONEY & COSTS

Alaska is an expensive destination any way you slice it. The recent economic downturn brought big discounts, but then it also cut how much money we all have to spend. It's too difficult to predict how the economic changes will shake out during the 2010 visitor season; on the whole, in 2009 operators seemed to be offering discounts without lowering their regular rates. I'll use those regular rates here in predicting how much you will pay, but keep in mind that when tourism drops drastically it is easy to negotiate breaks.

With the exception of rural highway motels, standard motel rooms are rarely less than $140 in the high season. (I've rated them this way: inexpensive, under $135; moderate, $135–$174; expensive $175–$250; very expensive, more than $250.) Airfare from Seattle to Anchorage fluctuates wildly with competition among the airlines and fuel prices, with a round-trip with 14-day advance

native art: FINDING THE REAL THING

In a gift shop in Southeast Alaska, I watched as a woman, who said she was an artist's assistant, sanding a Tlingit-style carving. When I asked who made the carving, the artist said, "It's my work." At the time, that seemed like an odd way of putting it. Only later did I learn from one of the artist's former assistants that his "work" involved ordering the carvings from Southeast Asia and shipping them to Alaska, where he hired locals to pretend to be working on them in the shop.

Journalists have repeatedly documented shops fraudulently removing "Made in Taiwan" stickers and the like, and replacing them with "Made in Alaska." One journalist found a whole village in Bali carving Alaska Native designs out of ivory, whalebone, and other materials sent from Alaska.

Good estimates don't exist of the amount of counterfeit Alaska Native art sold annually, but authorities have put it close to $100 million. That's money taken from Alaska Bush economies where jobs in the cash economy are virtually nonexistent and prices for essentials such as fuel and housing are astronomical. Buying fake Native art is cultural and financial theft from subsistence hunters and fishermen who can least afford it. And besides, who wants

to come home with an Eskimo mask made in Bali?

You can avoid being scammed if you pay attention. Ask questions before you buy. Any reputable art dealer will provide you with a biography of the artist who created an expensive work. Ask specifically if that artist actually carved the piece: Some Native artists have sold their names and designs to wholesalers who produce knockoffs. Price is another tip-off. An elaborate mask is more likely to cost $1,000 than $100. Another indicator is the choice of materials; most soapstone carvings are not made in Alaska. Even less expensive craftwork should bear the name of the person who made it, and the shop owner should be able to tell you how he or she acquired the item.

purchase currently about $500. (Flying is cheaper than the alternatives, driving or taking the ferry and bus.) You can easily pay twice that to fly to an Alaska Bush community. Even the train is expensive, with a one-way fare from Anchorage to Fairbanks (a 350-mile trip) costing $210. A couple ordering a good salmon dinner, appetizers, and wine will usually pay at least $100 in a fine restaurant, plus tip. One reason cruise ships have become such a popular way to visit Alaska is that, for the same quality level, they're less expensive on a daily basis than independent travel, and they offer the chance to see remote coastal areas that can be quite costly to get to for land-based visitors. (See chapter 5 for details on cruising.)

To travel at a standard American comfort level, a couple should allow $175 per person, per day, for room and board. The cost of an activity such as flightseeing, wildlife cruises, or guided fishing typically is $100 to $350 per person per day. Add ground transportation: A car is the best way to see much of the state,

Another caution, for international visitors: Do not buy products made from marine mammals, such as walrus ivory, whale bone, or seal skin. Except for antiques, export of these materials is illegal, so you won't be able to take your purchase home. (You may need a permit to export other wildlife items as well.

The **Alaska State Council on the Arts** (☎907/269-6610) authenticates Native arts and crafts with a **silver hand** label, which assures you it was made by the hands of an Alaska Native with Alaskan materials. But the program isn't universally used, so the absence of the label doesn't mean the work definitely isn't authentic. Other labels aren't worth much: An item could say ALASKA MADE even if only insignificant assembly work happened here. Of course, in Bush Alaska and in some urban shops, you can buy authentic work directly from craftspeople. Buying in Native-owned co-ops is also safe.

Another program covers any item made within the state, both Native and non-Native. The logo of a mother

bear and cub (www.madeinalaska.org) indicates that a state contractor has determined that the product was made in Alaska, when possible with Alaskan materials. Non-Natives produce Alaskan crafts of ceramics, wood, or fabric, but not plastic—if it's plastic, it probably wasn't made here. Again, price is an indicator: As with anywhere else in the United States, the cheapest products come from Asia.

You can learn about and buy authentic work from the **Alaska Native Arts Foundation,** a nonprofit with online shopping at www.alaskanativearts. org and a brick-and-mortar gallery in Anchorage (p. 336). **Sealaska Heritage Foundation** offers a nonprofit website selling work by Southeast Alaska Natives at www.alaskanativeartists.com. Even if you don't buy anything from these sites, taking a look will give you an idea of what real Native art looks like and how much it should cost, so you can be a better shopper when you get to Alaska.

and you won't do much better than $50 a day for an economy model from the major national firms. Weekly rentals generally cost the same as renting for 5 individual days. You also may need train and ferry tickets.

You can trim your costs, however, by cutting your demands. You'll learn more about the real Alaska staying in B&B accommodations than in a standard hotel room. Expect to pay $100 to $125 for a nice room with a shared bathroom, $125 to $150 for one with a private bathroom (much more in a luxury B&B inn). The free breakfast cuts down on food costs, too. And there are plenty of family restaurants where you can eat a modest dinner for two for $50, with a tip and a glass of beer. Traveling in that style will bring down the cost of room and board to about $115 per person, per day, for a couple.

You can save the most money by giving up a private room every night and cooking some of your own meals. Camping is a fun way to really see Alaska and costs only $10 to $20 a night in state and federal government campgrounds. Hostels are available in most towns for around $25 a night.

Don't economize, however, when it comes to activities. Unlike other destinations where relatively inexpensive museums or an interesting street scene take up much of your time, a trip to Alaska is all about getting outside and seeing nature. You can hike for nothing, but to go sea kayaking, whale-watching, or flying out to see bears or to fish in a remote stream, you have to pay. Cut those expenses, and you cut much of the reason for going in the first place.

You can save on activities, however, by traveling in the shoulder season, before and after the peak summer season. Hotel and guided activity prices drop significantly, typically by 25% or more. May and September are solidly in the shoulder season, and sometimes you get bargains as late as June 15 or as early as August 15. Traveling in the winter is a whole different experience, but certainly saves a lot of money—where hotels are open, you'll find their rates typically running a third to a half lower than their high-season levels. For other considerations on off-season and shoulder-season travel, see "When to Go," earlier in this chapter.

Carrying your money need not be a problem, regardless of your style of travel; those from the United States don't need to make any adjustments in their usual habits, and international visitors can expect the same here than in any other U.S. destination. Even Bush hub communities now have ATMs. The only places that don't usually have ATMs these days are remote outdoor destinations such as lodges or parks and tiny Native villages. In the "Fast Facts" section for each town in this book, I'll tell you where to find an ATM.

Every business you'd expect to take credit, charge, or debit cards at home will accept them here. Even bed-and-breakfasts and greasy-spoon diners take cards. Few businesses of any kind will take an out-of-state personal check. Traveler's checks are good just about anywhere, but there's no longer any reason to go through the hassle and expense.

GETTING THERE & GETTING AROUND
By Plane

CARRIERS Anchorage (ANC) is Alaska's main entrance, and is served by numerous major carriers from the rest of the United States. A few flights arrive in Anchorage from Japan, Korea, or Germany, but the vast majority of international travelers arrive in the U.S. in a major city in the contiguous

The Cheapest Way to Alaska

Flying remains the cheapest and by far the simplest way to get to Alaska. Take other means only for the adventure, not for the savings. Round-trip train, ferry, and bus fare between Seattle and Anchorage costs considerably more than a good airfare between the same cities. Driving is expensive, too, when you count rooms, food, and wear and tear on your vehicle. At $3 a gallon, fuel alone for the 4,500-mile drive from Seattle to Anchorage and back would cost $675 in a car that gets 20 miles to the gallon—more than a plane ticket. (Okay, maybe a foursome can do it cheaper than flying if they drive a small car, camp every night, and eat rice and beans.)

states and then take a domestic flight to Anchorage. It's also possible to fly into Fairbanks or Southeast Alaska. Most passengers come into Anchorage through Seattle, but for a bit more you can fly nonstop to Anchorage from various major cities. There are far more choices in summer than in winter. **Alaska Airlines** (℃800/252-7522; www.alaskaair.com) has more flights than all other airlines combined, with as many as 20 nonstops a day from Seattle in summer and daily summer nonstops from many cities around the country. Alaska Airlines is the only jet carrier with more than token coverage anywhere in the state other than Anchorage and has arrangements with commuter lines that fan out from its network to smaller communities.

FARES Alaskans fly so much we tend to talk about airfares the way New Yorkers talk about real estate. Fares vary wildly, especially in these days of economic instability and changing fuel costs. It's almost always cheapest to change planes in Seattle due to the competition on the Seattle-Anchorage route. I hesitate to name sample fares, because the airline industry is changing so rapidly the information will be historic by the time you read it. Prices can double in a single year. However, some rules do apply. Watching for sales can pay off. Summer sales sometimes hit in April. If you can make a last-minute decision, check for Internet specials on the Alaska Airlines website and other airline sites, as there are sometimes bargains to be had you can't get any other way.

BUSH PILOTS To fly to a roadless village, or to fly between most towns without returning to a hub, you will take a small, prop-driven plane with an Alaska Bush pilot at the controls. Small air taxis also charter to fishing sites, lodges, remote cabins, or anywhere else you want to go—even a sand bar in the middle of a river. An authentic Alaskan adventure can be had by taking a Bush mail plane round-trip to a village and back. The ticket price is generally less than a flightseeing trip, and you'll have at least a brief chance to look around a Native village, although don't expect to find any visitor facilities without making arrangements in advance. It's cost effective to take these flights from towns that are relatively close to surrounding villages: Kodiak, Homer, Fairbanks, Nome, Kotzebue, and Barrow fit the bill. You will need to do some research, and not on the Internet; find the name of a local flight service that carries mail from the town visitor center, then call and explain what you have in mind. And wait for good weather.

By Ship

The most popular way to get to Alaska is on a **cruise ship** (chapter 5, "Cruising Alaska's Coast," provides an in-depth look at your options).

For an affordable, independent trip by sea, with a chance to stop as long as you like along the way, take the **Alaska Marine Highway System (☎800/642-0066;** www.ferryalaska.com). It's my favorite form of public transportation. The big blue, white, and gold ferries ply the Inside Passage from Bellingham, Washington, and Prince Rupert, B.C., to the towns of Southeast Alaska, with road links to the rest of the state at Haines and Skagway. In summer, a ferry runs once or twice a month from that system across the Gulf of Alaska to the central part of the state. From there, smaller ferries connect towns in Prince William Sound and the Kenai Peninsula to Kodiak Island and the Aleutian Archipelago. For a complete discussion of the system and its intricacies, see "Getting Around by Ferry: The Alaska Marine Highway," in chapter 6.

By Rail

You can't get to Alaska by train, but you can get close. From the west coast of the U.S. you can take **Amtrak's** Cascades train (☎800/USA-RAIL [872-7245]; www.amtrak.com) to Bellingham, Washington; the dock for the Alaska ferry is quite close to the railroad station. From the east, it makes more sense to use Canada's **Via Rail (☎888/VIA-RAIL** [842-7245]; www.viarail.ca). The transcontinental route starts all the way back in Toronto; you change in Jasper to end up in Prince Rupert, B.C., where you can catch the Alaska ferry north. Of course, it's a long, weary journey, whichever way you go.

By Car

TIME & DISTANCE Figuring how long it takes to drive between various points in Alaska needn't be complicated, but don't trust your computer. A reader checked three different Internet map sites for one trip and came up with drive times ranging from 4 hours 27 minutes to 8 hours 45 minutes. I have included a description of the roads and average speeds you can expect ("Alaska's Highways a la Carte," p. 502). Get the mileage you plan to drive (for that you can trust a website), then divide the distance by the expected speed to get the time it will take. Add some time for stops. For paved highways, you can count on averaging 50 miles per hour. On some roads you can go faster than 50, but you can't often drive at freeway speeds on these two-lane highways. Even when the surface is smooth—not always a given—the roads aren't designed for high speeds and are often clogged in summer with lumbering RVs. Besides, you need to be on the look-out for moose; hit one of those at 75 mph and you both die.

DRIVING TO ALASKA Driving from any of the other states to Alaska is a great adventure, but it requires thousands of miles on the road and plenty of time. Allow at least a week each way. By car, Anchorage is 2,250 miles from Seattle and 3,400 miles from Los Angeles. By comparison, New York to L.A. is 2,800 miles. Traveling at an average of 50 miles per hour, few vacationers will want to cover more than 500 or 600 miles a day, and that's a long day of nothing but driving. On such a plan, Seattle is 4 or 5 days from Anchorage without breaks.

Some of the 1,400-mile **Alaska Highway** is dull, but there are spectacular sections of the route, too, and few experiences give you a better feel for the size and personality of Alaska (and B.C. and Yukon). Putting your car on the ferry cuts the length of the trip considerably, but raises the cost; you could rent a car for 2 weeks for the same price as carrying an economy car on the ferry one-way from Bellingham to Haines. I love riding the ferry up the Inside Passage, but I usually rent a car or bike to get around in the towns on the way. Details on the Alaska section of the Alaska Highway, and other highways, are contained in chapter 10. The ferry is described in chapter 6. *The Milepost* (Morris Communications; $30) contains good maps and mile-by-mile logs of all Alaska highways and Canadian approaches; however, it's not interesting to read and is clogged with advertising masquerading as editorial text.

THE RENTAL OPTION Renting a car is the easiest way to see the Interior and Southcentral parts of the state. All the major national car-rental companies are represented in Anchorage as well as many local operators, who may have lower prices for older cars. In smaller cities and towns, there is always at least one agency; the town descriptions throughout this book provide details on firms in each. Base rates for major rental companies are in the range of $50 a day for an economy car. Weekly rentals equate roughly to 5 days' cost.

One-way rentals between Alaska towns are an attractive way to travel, but you generally pay steep drop-off charges, so a more popular plan is to fly into and out of Anchorage or Fairbanks and pick up and return the car there. A popular circular route from Anchorage or Fairbanks: through Denali and Fairbanks (or Anchorage) on the Parks Highway and back on the Richardson and Glenn highways; an Anchorage circle: to Valdez by ferry from Whittier and back on another part of the Richardson Highway and the Glenn Highway. See chapter 4 for more on routes.

By RV

Touring Alaska in an RV makes a good deal of sense. The home on wheels offers spontaneity by freeing you from hotel reservations, and it gets you out of town and into the countryside, closer to the natural Alaska most visitors come for. At the same time, an RV is more comfortable than a tent in cool, unpredictable weather conditions.

Many retirees drive to Alaska in their motor homes, park the RV by a salmon stream, and spend the summer fishing. Sounds nice, but for most of the rest of us, with limited time, it makes more sense to rent an RV after flying to Alaska. Rental agencies are listed in Skagway (p. 272) and Anchorage (p. 289). The option of shipping your own RV to Alaska is also covered in the Anchorage chapter. Unless you have a large family, an RV rental saves little over traveling with a rental car, staying in hotels, and eating in restaurants (RVs rent for around $1,500 a week, plus gas and possibly mileage charges), so you make this choice to gain advantages, not avoid costs.

Alaska Highway Cruises (☎800/323-5757; www.bestofalaskatravel. com) offer the unique option of traveling one-way on a Holland America cruise ship, then picking up an RV for a land tour. You can choose a package that ends up back at Seattle by road or by air. The tours follow set itineraries with reservations along the way—the service is designed for first-time Alaska travelers

ALASKA BY THE numbers

This chart shows some comparative indicators for 16 of Alaska's most popular destinations. The third column is the best season to visit—months at least part of which have enough going on and weather that is suitable (including weather that's good for winter sports). The fourth column lists modes of transportation to each community—in Alaska you can't drive everywhere.

PLACE	POPULATION	SEASON	TRANSPORTATION
Anchorage	274,003	May–Sept /Jan–Mar	Road, air, rail
Barrow	4,417	June–Sept	Air
Cordova	2,372	May–Sept	Air, ferry
Denali National Park	133	June–Sept	Road, rail
Fairbanks	82,214	May–Sept/Jan–Mar	Road, air, rail
Glacier Bay National Park	438	May–Sept	Air, ferry
Haines	1,715	May–Sept/Nov	Road, air, ferry
Homer	4,893	May–Sept/Mar	Road, air, ferry
Juneau	31,283	May–Sept	Air, ferry
Kenai	7,125	May–Sept	Road, air
Ketchikan	13,548	May–Sept	Air, ferry
Kodiak Island	13,811	May–Sept	Air, ferry
Nome	3,448	June–Aug/Mar	Air
Petersburg	3,060	May–Sept	Air, ferry
Seward	2,733	May–Sept	Road, rail
Sitka	8,891	May–Sept/Nov	Air, ferry
Skagway	845	May–Sept	Road, air, ferry
Unalaska/ Dutch Harbor	4,388	June–Sept	Air, ferry
Valdez	4,060	May–Sept	Road, air, ferry

and RV drivers who don't want to worry about the details—so some spontaneity is sacrificed. You get the security and simplicity of a package without being marched around in a group or cooped up in hotels. A cruise of a week followed by a week-long tour costs around $2,800 per person, double occupancy; a 3-week cruise to Alaska and a drive back (or reverse) is around $4,100 per person. There are various discounts, including for third and fourth passengers. Simple one-way RV rentals to Alaska are available, too, with, for example, an added drop-off fee of $1,000 to $1,200, between Seattle and Anchorage. See p. 289.

ESCORTED TOUR OR DO-IT-YOURSELF?

Hundreds of thousands of visitors come to Alaska each year on escorted package tours, leaving virtually all their travel arrangements in the hands of a single company that takes responsibility for ushering them through the state for a single, lump-sum fee. Many others cut the apron strings and explore Alaska on their own, in the process discovering a more relaxed, spontaneous experience. Each approach has advantages and disadvantages, of course, and which way you choose to visit depends on how you value those pros and cons. Unfortunately, some people make the choice based on expectations that aren't valid, so it's important to know what you're getting into.

An escorted package tour provides security. You'll know in advance how much everything will cost, you don't have to worry about making hotel and ground-transportation reservations, you're guaranteed to see the highlights of each town you visit, and you'll have someone telling you what you're looking at. Often, a package price saves money over traveling at the same level of comfort independently. If there are weather delays or other travel problems, it's the tour company's problem, not yours. Everything happens on schedule, and you never have to touch your baggage other than to unpack when it magically shows up in your room. If you sometimes feel like you're a member of a herd on an escorted tour, you'll also meet new people, a big advantage if you're traveling on your own. Many passengers on these trips are retired, over age 65.

If you're short on time, escorted package tours make the most of it, as they often travel at an exhausting pace. Passengers get up early and cover a lot of ground, with sights and activities scheduled solidly through the day. Stops last only long enough to get a taste of what the sight is about, not to dig in and learn about a place you're especially interested in. On an escorted trip, you'll meet few if any Alaska residents, since most tour companies hire college students from "Outside" (a term Alaskans use to refer to any place other than Alaska) to fill summer jobs. You'll stay in only the largest hotels and eat in the largest, tourist-oriented restaurants—no small, quaint places loaded with local character. For visiting wilderness, such as Denali National Park, the quick and superficial approach can, in my opinion, spoil the whole point of going to a destination that's about an experience, not just seeing a particular object or place.

Studies by Alaska tourism experts have found that some people choose escorted packages to avoid risks that don't really exist. Alaska may still be untamed, but that doesn't mean it's a dangerous or uncomfortable place to travel. Visitors who sign up for a tour to avoid having to spend the night in an igloo or use an outhouse may wish they'd been a bit more adventurous when they arrive and find that Alaska has the same facilities found in any other state. Except for tiny Bush villages that you're unlikely to visit anyway, you'll come across the standard American hotel room almost anywhere you go. The tourism infrastructure is well developed even in small towns—you're never far from help unless you want to be.

It's also possible for an independent traveler to obtain some of the predictability a package tour provides. You can reserve accommodations and activities and control your expenses by using a good travel agent experienced in Alaska travel. Some even offer fixed-price itineraries that allow you to travel on your

3

PLANNING YOUR TRIP TO ALASKA | Escorted Tour or Do-It-Yourself?

Beware of Fraud

In 2003, one of the largest trip planners in Alaska went bankrupt, leaving many visitors with worthless vouchers for pre-paid reservations. It turned out the owner was using clients' credit cards to keep her business afloat. She took her own trip to federal prison in 2005, but by then even worse rip-offs had cropped up on the Internet. Use caution. If you pre-pay large trip expenses to a planner or a provider directly, be certain to use a credit card that will protect you, and buy appropriate travel insurance. Do not buy the insurance from the same entity from whom you bought the trip (see "Travel & Rental-Car Insurance," p. 89).

own (see "Independent Travel Planning," at the end of this section). But independent travelers never have the complete security of those on group tours. Once you're on the road, you'll be on your own to take care of the details, and weather delays and other cancellations can confound the best-laid plans. If you can't relax and enjoy a trip knowing unforeseen difficulties could happen, then an escorted package tour is the way to go.

Large Tour Companies

A single cruise-ship company, Carnival, dominates the Alaska package-tour market operating under various brands. The "vertically integrated" operations allow the company to take care of everything you do while in Alaska with tight quality control. In some popular areas, cruise lines have bought everything in sight, even historic attractions. Holland America and Princess, both owned by Carnival, developed independently as the primary competitors in Alaska and operated independently for years even after the merger. However, the economic downturn led to consolidation, and at this writing it's unclear exactly how separate the companies will remain. For now, each retains its own contact information, but the real differences may become less important. In any event, you can buy tours as short as a couple of hours as an independent traveler or sign up for your whole vacation. All can be booked through any travel agent. Other cruise lines also offer land tours, but typically only for their own passengers. If you will cruise to Alaska and want to add an escorted land tour, check for deals with your own cruise line first.

Holland America Line Tours This giant company offers tours more places than any other, including some excursions—on the Yukon River between Dawson City and Eagle, for example—that are entirely unique. The catalog covers just about anything in the state that could possibly be done with a group. Prices depend on a variety of factors, but in general a tour of a week is about $1,400 per person. The operator of the motorcoach tours is called Gray Line, and the hotels are Westmark. The Westmark hotels, described in the appropriate sections of the book, are sometimes among the best in town, including those in Juneau (called the Baranof) and Fairbanks, while others are unremarkable. You'll find a description of the company's railcars on the Anchorage-Denali-Fairbanks run in chapter 9.

300 Elliott Ave. W., Seattle, WA 98119. ☎**800/544-2206.** www.graylineofalaska.com or www. hollandamerica.com.

Princess Cruises and Tours Princess built Alaska's best chain of hotels, part of the company's superior attention to quality. Two hotels are near Denali National Park, and one each are in Fairbanks, in Cooper Landing (on the Kenai Peninsula), and in Copper Center, near Wrangell–St. Elias National Park. Descriptions of each hostelry can be found in the appropriate chapter. The selection of tours has been more limited than Holland America's and concentrated around Denali and the middle of the state.

800 5th Ave., Ste. 2600, Seattle, WA 98014. ☎800/426-0500. www.princesslodges.com.

Independent Travel Planning

With this guidebook, you can book everything yourself, but for a long trip it can get quite complicated to keep track of all the dates and deposits. If you're using a trusted travel agency to make trip arrangements, our reviews can help you make informed decisions. Read through the book, make your selections, and approach the agent with as detailed a plan as possible, derived from your own research. Then let the agent make the bookings you have chosen. Most agents who don't specialize in Alaska are aware of only the biggest attractions and best-marketed companies. Another option is to use a travel agency or trip-planner based in Alaska. They'll know much more about the place and can help you more in picking out what you want to do. I've listed a few below.

Unfortunately, there are cautions to be offered in using the agencies. They work on commission, which means they're being paid by the establishments you're buying from. A good agent will disregard the size of the commission and really look out for you, but I've encountered too many visitors on poorly planned itineraries not to advise caution. Some travel agents book visitors on trips to far-flung corners of the state in quick succession, so they wind up staying only briefly in expensive places and then zooming off somewhere else, all with little concern for the visitors' true interests. Your best defense is to do enough research so you can actively participate in the planning.

For Coupon Clippers

A coupon book called **The Great Alaskan Tour Saver** (☎907/278-7600; www.toursaver.com), which costs $100, is well worth the price if you plan on traveling as a couple, especially in the Southcentral region. The 140 coupons are freebies or two-for-one deals on some of the best activities, tours, train rides, flightseeing, and lodgings, valuable enough to pay for the book with just a couple of uses. Readers tell me they've saved a lot and it has become quite popular.

Here I've gathered the names of some agencies that book Alaska trips. Expect to pay booking fees and to have the agent collect commissions from the businesses you use. My knowledge of these agencies is limited to contacting them as a journalist, so a mention here is no guarantee; however, all of these have been around for several years, and I remove agencies from the list when I receive justified complaints.

Alaska Bound This Michigan-based agency is the only one I know of in the Lower 48 that specializes in Alaska with a staff of former Alaskans. It started as a cruise planner, working primarily with Holland America, but now plans many independent trips, too, charging a per-person fee that depends on the length of the trip ($100 per person would not be exceptional).

116 Cass St., Traverse City, MI 49684. ☎**888/ALASKA-7** (252-7527) or 231/439-3000. www.alaskabound.com.

Alaska.org This is a deep and well-built website that allows users to shop and customize tour packages or design their own vacations. The company produces an extraordinary amount of video and other material about destinations, so you can get a good idea of what you're buying. Coverage is deepest in the Southcentral-to-Fairbanks region, but extends to much of the rest of the state, too. What I like best is that even after you use all these expensive tools, there is no fee and you don't have to buy through the site. When you've seen enough, book online or call the toll-free number for questions and booking. Or don't. You can use the site just to get information and call the listed businesses yourself, or even to request a referral via email. ☎**888/ALASKA-8** (252-7528). www.alaska.org.

507 E St., Ste. 206, Anchorage, AK 99508. ☎**888/ALASKA-8** (252-7528). www.alaska.org.

Alaska Tour & Travel Started in 1995 and steadily growing, this agency now claims to be the largest custom vacation company in Alaska. The same folks operate the Park Connection shuttle between Denali and Kenai Fjords national parks, and that central part of the state is what they know best and cover deeply. The website is remarkable, including a tool that allows you to build your own itinerary, and a live availability-and-rate calendar for a range of Denali hotels. They also offer photos of destinations and a blog with planning tips.

P.O. Box 221011, Anchorage, AK 99522. ☎**800/208-0200**. www.alaskatravel.com.

AskMatt Alaskan Adventures & Tours Matthew Lowe is an energetic entrepreneur who has turned his encyclopedic knowledge of Southcentral Alaska travel into his own business. His strength is in activities, fishing charters, remote lodges, and winter trips, but he happily books travelers into budget B&Bs as well as more expensive lodges and resorts and charges no up-front fee.

AskMatt Alaskan Adventures & Tours, P.O. Box 110261, Anchorage, AK 99511. ☎**907/868-1786**. www.askmatt.com.

Sport Fishing Alaska Choose this company to plan a fishing vacation. The owner, former lodge operator Sheary Suiter, knows where the fish will be from week to week. That means SFA books clients at fly-in fishing lodges when and where the fishing is hot—a critical piece of information that can be difficult to obtain on your own. She charges a $95 upfront fee. (See "Fishing," later in this chapter.)

9310 Shorecrest Dr., Anchorage, AK 99502. ☎**888/552-8674** or 907/344-8674. www.alaskatripplanners.com.

Viking Travel Entrepreneurs in the small Southeast Alaska town of Petersburg built this agency, initially specializing in independent outdoor trips in their own area. Today, besides offering all the usual services of a travel agency, they plan trips for the whole state and book all the region's ferries without surcharge. Get on their list and they will book your cabins and vehicle reservations on the first day the system makes them available.

P.O. Box 787, Petersburg, AK 99833. ☎**800/327-2571** or 907/772-3818. www.alaskaferry.com.

3

PLANNING YOUR TRIP TO ALASKA | Escorted Tour or Do-It-Yourself?

PLANNING AN OUTDOOR VACATION

Most people visit Alaska to experience wilderness, so it's ironic that so many spend their time in crowded ships, buses, trains, and airplanes, the antithesis of a wilderness experience. You do need technology to get to the wilderness of Alaska, but unless you at least partly let loose of that umbilical cord, you'll never really arrive at your destination.

Every town in Alaska is a threshold to the wild. There's always a way to go hiking, biking, or sea kayaking, or to get on the bank of a stream or the deck of a boat to hook into a furiously fighting wild salmon—and end up in the evening back in a comfortable hotel room. Or take it a step further: Plan to go out overnight, perhaps with a friendly local guide at first, and then go out on your own. I've included lots of details on how to do this throughout the book. Scary? If it weren't a little scary, it would be Disneyland, and that it definitely is not. It's real, and that's why it's worth doing.

Use this section to learn about activities, outfitters, and wilderness lodges. The destination chapters cover outdoor options and practicalities in particular places.

Activities

BACKPACKING Alaska's best country for trail hikes is in **Chugach State Park** near Anchorage (chapter 7), on Chena Hot Springs Road and on the Steese Highway near Fairbanks (chapter 10), and in the **Chugach National Forest** on the Kenai Peninsula (chapter 8). For hiking beyond trails, go to **Denali National Park** or the **Denali Highway** (chapter 9), **Wrangell–St. Elias National Parks,** or the **Dalton Highway** (chapter 10). Alaska trail hikes require the same skills as backpacking anywhere else, plus preparation for cold and damp (see "What to Wear," earlier in this chapter). Hiking beyond the trails is a glorious experience, but you need to know how to cross rivers and find your way—it's best if you have some outdoor experience. Or go with a guide; they're listed below. See "Health & Safety," later in this chapter, for some backcountry safety tips.

Keeping the Wilderness Clean

Human use shows up quickly in wild places. Even small signs can diminish the wilderness experience—trampled vegetation or charred wood from a campfire—and it's disgusting and disheartening to find toilet paper or human waste. The idea of Leave No Trace Camping, encouraged by Alaska's public land managers, is simple: Use the outdoors in such a way that no one would ever know you had been there. It's as important for rural highway driving and for day hikes as for backpacking trips. The key is to plan ahead. For example, bring some kind of digging tool and sealable plastic bags with which you can pack out toilet paper and any other trash. To learn more, see the website of the Leave No Trace Center for Outdoor Ethics, www.lnt.org.

BIKING Most every town in Alaska has a bike-rental agency. There are excellent bike routes all over the state and few restrictions on where you can ride. A bike is a great way into Denali National Park (see chapter 9); Anchorage has an extensive network of paved trails and many mountain-biking routes (see chapter 7); and guided biking is available in Haines and Skagway (see chapter 6). A couple that built an excellent reputation and a large business for more than a decade offering bicycle tours on Alaska's long, rural highways now operates **Alaskabike** (☎907/245-2175; www.alaskabike.com) on their own from a home office. These are terrific vacations for avid cyclists. The 8-day tour over the spectacular Richardson Highway costs $2,995, inclusive. The schedule includes bike and kayak tours, too.

BIRD-WATCHING In Alaska, birders can encounter birds in greater variety and greater numbers than they have seen before and add many new species to their life lists. I have listed birding groups and the best places to go in many of the sections on destinations. Making a "best of" list is difficult, because good bird-watching is found in any Alaska town. For example, I could recommend you go to Haines for the eagle sanctuary, but since you are bound to see eagles in every coastal town, I hesitate to send you on a special trip for that purpose. Weeding out the excellent to mention only the truly exceptional, here are the places I would send birders. For marine birding, consider Sitka, Juneau, Seward (Kenai Fjords National Park), Unalaska, and the Pribilof Islands (chapters 6, 8, and 11, respectively). Migratory bird festivals happen in May in Homer and Cordova; Homer also has handy sea bird colonies, and Cordova has the wetlands of the Copper River Delta, an accessible bird paradise of immense proportions (both in chapter 8). Alaska's two largest cities have parks dedicated to inland birding, and other bird resources as well: See the sections on Anchorage and Fairbanks for details (chapters 7 and 10). For Arctic birding, Nome is probably the best choice thanks to the existence of roads that allow self-guided exploration (chapter 11). The very best bird and wildlife destination in Alaska, and surely among the best in the world, is the Pribilof Islands. You can sign up directly with the island's own Aleut residents for a tour there, described in chapter 11.

Serious birders with money to spend can dedicate an Alaska trip to some of the world's best and most famous remote bird-watching sites (those with milder or budding interest might better choose a less ambitious destination first, or make bird-watching only a part of an Alaska vacation). Learn about trips in birding magazines. *Bird Watcher's Digest* (www.birdwatchersdigest.com) offers good, detailed advice on its website. Group trips are advertised in *Birders' World* (www.birdersworld.com) and *Birding* (www.american birding.org). Among the largest and most reputable operators coming to Alaska is Arizona-based **High Lonesome BirdTours** (☎800/743-2668 or 520/458-9446; www.hilonesometours.com), priding itself on relaxed trips for small groups. All-inclusive tours visit Kenai, Denali, Nome, Gambell, Barrow, Unalaska/Dutch Harbor, Adak, and the Pribilof Islands; and Texas-based **Victor Emanuel Nature Tours** (☎800/328-8368; www.ventbird. com), which counts well-known authors among its leaders.

CANOEING Paddling a canoe on a remote Alaska lake or river is the best way to get into the wilderness without a backpack, a guide, or a great deal of expense. For beginners, it's easy to rent a canoe in Fairbanks (chapter 10)

A Guide to Guide Gratuities

As a general rule, tip fishing guides and outfitters $10 to $20 per person per day. For outings of less than a day, adjust the tip accordingly. At wilderness lodges, which normally have all-inclusive rates, it's often best to add the tip to your final payment when you leave and let the proprietor distribute it to the staff rather than try to do it at each meal. A blanket tip of $15 per person per day is acceptable.

for a day trip. If you're ready to go overnight, the choices of routes are extraordinary, including the rivers of the Interior (chapter 10), the bird-watching country of the Copper River Delta near Cordova, or the supreme lake canoe routes of the Kenai National Wildlife Refuge (both in chapter 8).

CAR OR RV CAMPING Campgrounds are almost everywhere in Alaska, many in extraordinarily beautiful natural places. Public campgrounds outnumber commercial ones. They're usually located where they are because there's something special about the place: a great view or beach, an exceptional fishing stream or trail head. Rarely will you find running water or flush toilets; most are seasonal, with hand pumps for water. (When it's time to wash up, stay at a commercial campground, which I've noted in each town section in the destination chapters throughout this book.) Alaska's public campgrounds fill up only in certain times and places (the Kenai River and Denali National Park campgrounds are among the exceptions), so campers have flexibility other travelers can't share, able to stop when and where they like.

Even if you don't usually consider camping, think about renting a comfortable RV for a tour. One company offers these rentals as add-ons with cruise vacations, taking care of all the details for clients (that and other rental options are under "Getting There & Getting Around," earlier in this chapter).

If you fly to Alaska, car camping can be a bit complicated. Carrying a camp stove on an airplane is forbidden unless there is no attached fuel canister and no odor of fuel; practically, it is best to buy a new stove in Alaska and then give it away or ship it back to yourself at the end of the trip. Also, new baggage fees charged by the airlines make it expensive to bring your bulky gear. Alaska Airlines, the dominant carrier here, charges $15 for the first checked bag, $25 for a second, and $50 for a third, and has fees of $50 to $75 for bags more than 50 pounds or 62 inches (length plus height plus width). Renting sleeping bags and other equipment in Alaska may be cheaper than bringing your own. Rental agencies are listed with large towns in this book. You can also use the mail, sending packages to yourself care of General Delivery at any post office.

I've mentioned some great campgrounds throughout the book, but there are many more than I had space to cover. A free map that lists all the public campgrounds along Alaska's highways is available from the Alaska Public Lands Information Center in Anchorage (p. 292). If you are planning to camp the whole way, get a copy of *Traveler's Guide to Alaskan Camping* by Mike and Terri Church (Rolling Homes Press, $22), which contains detailed reviews of virtually every public and commercial campground in the state.

A salmon PRIMER

In Alaska, it's not so much where you wet your line, but when. The primary catch, Pacific salmon, lives in salt water but spawns in fresh water, with each fish returning to the stream of its birth during a certain, narrow window of time called a "run." When the salmon are running, fishing is hot; when they're not running, it's dead. And the runs change from day to day, typically lasting only a few weeks. (Halibut, on the other hand, are bottom-dwelling ocean fish; you can fish them from a boat every day when the tide is right.) You can fish salmon all over the state in fresh and salt water, but the closer you are to the ocean, the better the fish are. Salmon flesh softens in fresh water and the skin turns dull and red. Salmon right from salt water that haven't started their spawning cycle are called silver bright—when you see one, you'll understand why. No Pacific salmon feeds in fresh water, but kings and silvers, meat eaters at sea, strike out of habit even in the river.

There are five species of Pacific salmon, each preferring its own habitat, and, even when the habitat overlaps, each timing its run differently. Each species has two names.

King (or **chinook**) is the most coveted, best fighting fish, commonly growing to 30 pounds in 5 to 7 years at sea (the sport record, from the Kenai River, was 97 pounds, and the largest ever, taken by commercial fishermen near Petersburg, was 126 pounds). It takes a lot of effort to hook and land a big king, but it's the ultimate in Alaska fishing. You also need a special king stamp on your fishing license from the Alaska Department of Fish and Game, which you can buy at the same time you buy your license. King runs come mostly from late May to early July.

The **silver** (or **coho**) is smaller than the king, typically 6 to 9 pounds, but it fights and jumps ferociously, making it nearly as big a prize. Silvers run mostly in the fall, beginning in August and lasting into October in some streams.

FISHING Fishing in Alaska may spoil you for fishing anywhere else. The world's largest salmon and halibut were caught here in recent years, and Pacific salmon are so plentiful that catching and processing them still provides one of the state's largest sources of employment. Fly fishermen also come for thriving wild stocks of steelhead, cutthroat, and rainbow trout; Dolly Varden and Arctic char; and Arctic grayling.

There's no room here to tell you how to fish in Alaska—the best way is to pick it up from other anglers, most conveniently by going with a guide on your first outing. If you can afford it, a day of guided fly-in fishing to a remote stream is the ultimate (you can do it from virtually any town listed in chapters 6, 7, or 8). You can also study with a book; several are available, the best of which focus on individual areas of the state or particular fishing techniques rather than trying to cover everything.

The best all-around source of information is the **Alaska Department of Fish and Game Sport Fish Division** (www.sf.adfg.state.ak.us). Browse the website for run timing information and hot spots updated weekly, to learn generally about fishing in Alaska, and to obtain particulars about where to wet

Red (or **sockeye**) salmon, so named for their tasty red flesh, are the trickiest to catch. They usually weigh 4 to 8 pounds and can run in any of the summer months, depending on the region and stream. Reds feed primarily on plankton at sea, and when they strike a fly, it's out of an instinct that no one really understands; you need perfect river conditions to catch reds legally, because snagging anywhere but the mouth generally is not allowed in fresh water.

Pinks (or **humpies**) grow to only a few pounds and aren't as tasty as the other three species; their flesh lacks the fat that makes salmon so meaty in flavor, and it deteriorates quickly once the fish enter fresh water. Pinks are so plentiful that Alaska anglers usually view them as a nuisance to get off the line, but visitors often enjoy catching them: There's nothing wrong with a hard-fighting 4-pound fish, especially if you use light tackle, and a sliver-bright pink salmon is tasty if cooked right.

Chum (or **dog**) salmon return plentifully to streams over much of the state but are rarely targeted by anglers. Yet a typical 5- to 10-pound chum hits and fights hard. Chums aren't prized for the table and are mostly used for subsistence by Alaska Natives, who smoke or dry the fish for winter use or freeze it to feed dog teams.

The gear you use depends on the species you are after and the regulations for the area you're fishing. You have to catch the fish in the mouth; snagging is allowed only in special circumstances. On salt water, boats troll for kings and silvers with herring bait and gear to hold it down. Lures, salmon eggs, or flies will work on silvers and kings in the rivers, but regulations vary. Flies work best with reds. Most Alaska fishermen use spinning gear on the larger salmon species—landing such a large fish is iffy with a fly rod.

a line in different parts of the state (select from the menu under "Publications" and then the region you are visiting). You can even buy a fishing license online. If you lack Internet access, the agency also produces printed guides and fields questions from the public, and they record the weekly local updates on telephone hot lines. Contact the office nearest where you will fish; I have listed the phone number for each in the town sections.

If fishing is the primary goal of your trip, think about booking time at a fishing lodge. The remote rivers of the Bristol Bay region have Alaska's most prolific salmon fishing, and the only way out there is to take a floatplane to a remote site. You might find a stream jammed with salmon and with few other anglers around to compete with. But you'll waste your money if you book a date that's not near the peak of the local salmon run (that does happen, as lodge owners hate to admit slow fishing). Consequently, I've listed few river-fishing lodges in this book. (The exceptions: on the Kenai River in Cooper Landing and Kenai-Soldotna, in chapter 8; and ocean fishing in Ketchikan in chapter 6.) Instead, I recommend booking through **Sport Fishing Alaska,** described above under "Independent Travel Planning,"

p. 77. **AskMatt Alaskan Adventures & Tours,** in the same list, also specializes in booking trips to fishing lodges.

FLIGHTSEEING No one should come to Alaska without seeing the scenery at least once from a small plane. The most spectacular rides of all are the Mount McKinley flights from Talkeetna (chapter 9) and the Glacier Bay National Park flights from Haines or other surrounding communities (chapter 6). But just about anywhere you go is worth seeing from the air; only then can you grasp how huge and complex the land is and how little changed it is by mankind. Fixed-wing flights give you the most time aloft for your money, with seats starting for around $100 for a brief flight.

RAFTING Letting an Alaskan river pull you through untouched wild country in a raft provides a unique perspective without the sweat and toil of backpacking. Alaska has many great rivers, virtually all undeveloped and, with few exceptions, never crowded. White-water guides operate on rivers all over the state offering day trips in many towns. Outfitters also lead trips deep into Alaska, using the rivers to visit extraordinary places that can be reached no other way. Many companies offer floats; some are listed below and still others are in the destination chapters throughout this book.

SEA KAYAKING Just about every coastal town, from Kodiak east through Kachemak Bay, Prince William Sound, and the Southeast Panhandle, has at least one kayak outfitter taking visitors on day trips or expeditions. I think it would be a shame for any fit person to come to Alaska and not take a sea-kayaking day trip. It is your best chance to get close enough to really know the wilderness and see whales, sea otters, seabirds, and marine life in an intimate way. Local guides are listed in each town section. Outfitters offering longer trips to a variety of places are listed below.

Outfitters & Outdoor Package Trips

Besides the outfitters and tour guides listed below, I've noted other operators in the destination chapters covering the towns where they are based. Browse through those chapters before deciding on a trip, as a trip with a small-town guide service can be wonderful. There are many other larger operators, too; increasingly, international adventure travel companies bring groups to Alaska, renting equipment or even hiring guides here. Although those trips may be excellent, I've listed mostly homegrown operators who know their territory intimately.

Alaska Discovery A local eco-tourism pioneer, Alaska Discovery was bought out by the famous Mountain Travel Sobek expedition company, but still keeps local staff in Juneau and offers some of the best guided sea-kayaking trips in Southeast Alaska (sales staff is now in California). Glacier Bay and Admiralty Island outings cater to both beginners and the truly rugged. Their inn-to-inn trips are essentially outdoor-oriented package tours, taking groups to the best spots for day activities such as kayaking, rafting, or watching wildlife. Extended river trips float through the Arctic and on the Tatshenshini and Alsek rivers. They also offer outdoor packages for complete vacations. Check the website. A 3-day kayak expedition near Juneau is $995, while 10 days in the Arctic is around $4,695.

P.O. Box 35003, Juneau, AK 99803. **☎800/586-1911.** www.akdiscovery.com.

Alaska Wildland Adventures This company specializes in outdoor vacations for those who want to be comfortable in the evening and aren't seeking strenuous physical challenges. Concentrating on the Kenai Peninsula, where they operate two wilderness lodges, but also going to Denali National Park, most of the company's trips link together a series of outdoor day activities, such as rafting, kayaking, hiking, glacier cruises, or wildlife watching. Groups are small, and they also offer the lodges a la carte. An 11-day group safari is around $5,696; shorter trips, trips for families with kids, fishing trips, and other choices are available, too.

P.O. Box 389, Girdwood, AK 99587. **800/334-8730** or 907/783-2928. www.alaskawildland.com.

Equinox Wilderness Expeditions Karen Jettmar, author of *The Alaska River Guide*, the standard guidebook on floating Alaska's rivers, leads challenging rafting, sea-kayaking, and hiking trips and base-camp wildlife viewing each summer in some of the wildest and most exotic places around the state. Her groups are tiny, with five to eight members, and she offers custom co-ed, family, and women's trips. After 2 decades leading and teaching clients, Jettmar's firm was recently recognized as one of the world's best by *National Geographic Adventure*. A 10-day Arctic float trip costs around $4,000.

2440 East Tudor Rd., Ste. 1102, Anchorage, AK 99507. **604/222-1219.** www.equinox expeditions.com.

Nova These guys started commercial rafting on Alaska's rivers in 1975, but as the industry developed, they expanded only slowly, keeping their base in a tiny village on the Matanuska River, northeast of Anchorage, and primarily employing Alaskan guides. I like the fact that they don't minimize the hazards: They make it clear that these fast, cold waters aren't Disneyland rides. Their catalog covers longer expeditions on some of the state's wildest rivers, but also includes more affordable itineraries of 2 or 3 days. Two-day trips on the Matanuska cost $349; 3 days on the Talkeetna, including the 14-mile-long, Class IV rapids of the Talkeetna Canyon, cost $1,350. Nova offers trips from Copper Center and Hope, as well.

P.O. Box 1129, Chickaloon, AK 99674. **800/746-5753** or 907/745-5753. www.novalaska.com.

St. Elias Alpine Guides When you're ready for a real expedition, these are real professionals in real wilderness. Having given up on McKinley years ago as too crowded, they specialize in trekking, climbing, and floating the deep and rugged wilderness of Wrangell–St. Elias National Park. Theirs is the only trip catalog I know of that offers first ascents as part of the product line; so far, they've taken clients to the tops of previously unclimbed mountains more than 45 times. For details, see p. 561.

P.O. Box 92129, Anchorage, AK 99509. **888/933-5427** or 907/345-9048. www.stelias guides.com.

Multi-Activity Fly-In Wilderness Lodges

Any number of hotels use the word "lodge" in their names, but true wilderness lodges have unique qualities: They lie beyond the road system in places that are hard to get to but that are well worth spending some time in. These qualities also put wilderness lodges beyond most budgets. Getting there is expensive for guests and for operators; also, most lodges are small and have relatively large staffs to offer all-inclusive packages of rooms, meals, and guiding. For reasons explained elsewhere, I've generally excluded fishing lodges, concentrating instead on lodges that offer a variety of outdoor activities. Excellent lodges are described in the sections on Gustavus (p. 256), Homer (p. 425), and Denali National Park (p. 481). Here are three more that are so far from anywhere I had no other place in the book to put them.

Caribou Lodge ★★ There's a lot to love about this place, south of Denali National Park: the location above tree line, on its own alpine lake, miles from any other structure; the unlimited dry tundra hiking and views along the rounded ridge tops; the wildlife and the quiet. But what I love best, and what I suspect will matter most to visitors, is that it's real. This is home to Mike and Pam Nickols, the couple who personally host just three parties at a time, and for more than a decade they've lived out here in true Bush style, year-round, far off the grid. They guide hiking, canoeing on the lake, and watching the wildlife; in the winter, they teach guests to drive a dog team over endlessly rolling hills of snow. Mainly, a visit is a chance to experience another way of life, one that exists in few places. The accommodations are simple but comfortable, each cabin with its own outhouse and a shared shower facility. Access is by small aircraft only, on skis in winter, or floats in summer; in spring and fall, when the ice on the lake is soft, it's just about impossible to get there. For rough figuring, a plane from Talkeetna (p. 491) costs $165 to $210 per person, but inquire to get a more exact cost.

20 miles east of Talkeetna (P.O. Box 706), Talkeetna, AK 99676. ☏/fax **907/733-2163.** www. cariboulodgealaska.com. 3 cabins. $310 per person per day. Rates include all meals and guiding and are based on double occupancy. 2-day minimum. No credit cards. **Amenities:** Restaurant (family style, included in rate); sauna.

Prince William Sound Lodge ★★ This comfortable, casual lodge sits on the beach of Tatitlek Narrows, near the abandoned mining community of Ellamar, in the heart of Prince William Sound. Owner Chris Saal has been here since 1974, and he has built excellent accommodations, but even more important, he has learned to spread an easy-going attitude to help slow guests down to the Sound's proper pace of life, based on the tides. Activities are mostly self-guided or add-ons; you can use the place like a beach house, enjoying walks and the marine environment, or arrange for fishing charters and more active pursuits. The food is terrific, too. A distinct advantage over other lodges: This one lies near the airstrip in the Chugach village of Tatitlek, where you can fly directly on a commercial flight from Anchorage, paying only for your seat rather than chartering the whole plane.

Ellamar (3900 Clay Products Dr., Anchorage, Alaska 99517). ☏**907/440-0909** or 907/248-0909. www.princewilliamsound.us. 5 units. $325 per person per day. Rates include all meals and some guiding. 2-day minimum. No credit cards. **Amenities:** Restaurant (family style, included in rate); boat tours; sauna.

Winterlake ★★★ Among the best of Alaska's remote lodges, Winterlake earned its fame—like other top lodges—thanks to a remarkable couple living there year-round, Carl and Kirsten Dixon. Carl is a classic Alaskan outdoorsman: hearty, cheerful, and most at home when working or traveling on the land. Kirsten is a meticulous innkeeper and a master chef and cookbook author, trained at Le Cordon Bleu, who turns out cuisine, using local ingredients, that is comparable to that at the best urban restaurants. The lodge faces a lake surrounded by mountains northwest of Anchorage and has the Iditarod Trail running through its grounds, at the Finger Lake checkpoint. A dog team is kept for guest instruction, and winter visitors also go snowmobiling and cross-country skiing. In the summer, guests enjoy the lake, float a river, hike trails from the lodge, or use the helicopter that is kept on-site for glacier or mountain-top excursions or remote fishing. Complimentary yoga, massage, and cooking classes are offered every day. The accommodations are in five comfortable but authentic cabins—despite log construction and rustic furniture, they have oil heat and private bathrooms with showers and composting toilets. That's all part of the appealing contradictions of the place: remote, yet with fresh flowers everyday; offering Wi-Fi, but not when all the power is turned off at night. Visitors get to the lodge by air from Anchorage with Rust's Flying Service; the fare is included in the lodge rates listed below, which vary according to how long you stay. I've given just two examples; use of the helicopter is extra.

Mailing address: P.O. Box 91419, Anchorage, AK 99509. (**907/274-2710.** Fax 907/277-6256. www.withinthewild.com. 5 cabins. 2 nights $1,999 per person; 4 nights $3,535 per person. Some guided activities, massage, yoga, and cooking classes included in rate. AE, MC, V. **Amenities:** Restaurant (family style, included in rate); Jacuzzi; sauna.

ENTRY REQUIREMENTS

Coming into the U.S. has become more difficult for almost everyone with new security measures. Even U.S. citizens who pass between the U.S. and Canada must make additional preparations. International visitors can learn of the latest requirements from a travel agent or airline. Another good place to look for help is the U.S. embassy or consulate nearest you www.usembassy.gov.

Passports

U.S. citizens need passports or similar identification to re-enter the United States even from other countries in the Western Hemisphere, a rule which went into effect in 2009. Check www.getyouhome.gov for an explanation of the program. More details are found under "Crossing the Border," p. 546.

For information on how to get a passport, go to **"Passports"** in chapter 12—the websites listed provide downloadable passport applications for each nation as well as the current fees for processing passport applications. *Note:* Children are required to present a passport when entering the United States at airports. More information on obtaining a passport for a minor can be found at http://travel.state.gov.

Visas

A visa is a permit allowing entry to a foreign visitor. Many tourists coming to the United States do not need a visa. Canadian citizens never need visas to enter the U.S. In addition, the U.S. State Department's **Visa Waiver Program** allows citizens of some countries to enter the United States without a visa for stays of up to 90 days, including Andorra, Australia, Austria, Belgium, Brunei, Denmark, Finland, France, Germany, Iceland, Ireland, Italy, Japan, Liechtenstein, Luxembourg, Monaco, the Netherlands, New Zealand, Norway, Portugal, San Marino, Singapore, Slovenia, Spain, Sweden, Switzerland, and the United Kingdom. Citizens of Czech Republic, Estonia, Hungary, Latvia, Lithuania, Malta, Republic of Korea, and Slovakia are soon to be added to the program.

(This list was accurate at press time; for the most up-to-date list of visa waiver countries, consult http://travel.state.gov/visa.) Even though a visa isn't necessary, visitors from countries in the waiver program must register online through the Electronic System for Travel Authorization before boarding a plane or a boat to the U.S. The electronic application asks for basic personal and travel eligibility information. The Department of Homeland Security recommends filling out the form at least 3 days before traveling. Currently, there is no fee for the online application. You may also need an **e-Passport** to enter the U.S. without a visa and will need to present a round-trip air or cruise ticket upon arrival. E-Passports contain computer chips capable of storing biometric information, such as the required digital photograph of the holder. If your passport doesn't have this feature, learn about the issue at **http://travel.state.gov/visa**. Canadian citizens may enter the United States without visas, but they do need to show passports.

Citizens of countries not in the visa waiver program must have a valid passport that expires at least 6 months later than the scheduled end of their visit to the United States, and a tourist visa, which may be obtained from any U.S. consulate. For information on how to get a Visa, go to **"Visas"** in chapter 12. Also check the U.S. State Department website at http://travel.state.gov.

Customs & Border Control
WHAT FOREIGN VISITORS CAN BRING IN

Personal effects, which are items you use yourself, such as clothing, cameras, and fishing rods, are exempt from duties. In addition, every visitor over 21 years of age may bring in the following without paying duties: 1 liter of wine, beer, or hard liquor; 200 cigarettes, or 50 cigars for your own use and another 100 as gifts (but not from Cuba), or 2 kilograms (4.4 pounds) of smoking tobacco; and $100 worth of gifts. To claim these exemptions, you must spend at least 72 hours in the United States and cannot have claimed them within the preceding 6 months. The duty on goods exceeding these exemptions is 3% of the value on the first $1,000 (the flat rate); above that amount, it depends on the item. The flat rate applies only to items for your own use or gifts and can be used only once in 30 days. Importation of most raw food and plant material is prohibited or requires a special license. Foreign visitors may bring in or take out up to $10,000 in U.S. or foreign currency, travelers checks, securities, and so on, with no formalities; larger sums must be declared to U.S. Customs and Border Protection (CBP) on entering or leaving, and paperwork must be filed. For more information, consult CBP's website (www.cbp.gov), contact a U.S. consulate or embassy, or call CBP officials in Anchorage (☎907/271-6855).

Don't think about bringing **firearms** into the United States except for a hunting trip. Unless you are a U.S. citizen or permanent resident alien, you cannot bring in, buy, or even possess a gun without a permit from the **Bureau of Alcohol, Tobacco, Firearms, and Explosives** (☎304/616-4550; www.atf. gov); these take up to 2 months to process (the application, Form 6NIA, is on the ATF website: www.atf.gov/forms/pdfs/f53303d.pdf). The application must be accompanied by a valid hunting license (there are a few narrow exceptions, such as athletes involved in shooting competitions or visitors carrying certain invitations to qualifying events).

The **Alaska Department of Fish and Game** (☎907/465-6085; www. alaska.gov/adfg) sells hunting licenses to non-resident aliens for $300 (tags are that much or more); however, aliens can hunt only with a registered guide. First, find the guide, then let him or her help with all the paperwork, but start many months in advance and be ready to pay.

TAKING HOME WILDLIFE PRODUCTS

Authentic Alaska Native art and crafts made from protected marine mammals are perfectly legal to buy and own under U.S. and Alaska law, even though possessing marine mammal parts is not legal for non-Natives. Alaska Natives have used these materials for thousands of years, and their subsistence harvest is not a danger to the species. But some individual states have more restrictive laws (you may want to check), and generally marine-mammal products you buy made of any threatened or endangered species cannot be taken out of the country unless at least 100 years old. For those items that can legally be taken home, you need a wildlife export permit recognized by the Convention on International Trade of Endangered Species, known as CITES. These permits can be complicated to obtain and take 60 to 90 days for processing. For international visitors, the most practical advice is simply to avoid buying anything made from marine mammals or any other species requiring a CITES permit, including brown or black bear, wolf, lynx, bobcat, or river otter. Before you buy an item, make sure you can legally take it home, then have the shop mail it to you insured, and have them take care of the paperwork. If you carry it with you in your baggage or mail it yourself, perhaps because you bought it from someone who can't handle the paperwork, you'll need to get your own permits. U.S. residents transiting Canada with wildlife products face permitting complications as well; mail the item home to yourself instead. For information, contact the **U.S. Fish and Wildlife Service** in Anchorage (☎907/271-6198; http://alaska.fws.gov/law). Foreign visitors exporting wildlife may need to contact the agency's **Division of Management Authority** in Washington, D.C. (☎800/358-2104; www.fws.gov/international), regarding permit requirements.

TRAVEL & RENTAL-CAR INSURANCE

There are several kinds of travel insurance: for **trip cancellation or interruption,** for **medical costs,** and for **lost or delayed luggage.** Typically they are sold together in a per-trip or annual comprehensive plan. Insurance for trip cancellation or interruption is a must if you have paid the large cash deposits demanded by many Alaska outfitters, fishing guides, wilderness lodges, package tour operators, and cruise companies. A premium of 5% to 7% of the cost of the trip is well worth the protection against the uncertainty of Alaska weather (most deposits are lost in case of weather delays or cancellations) or unexpected crises that might prevent you from being able to depart as planned. Interruption insurance will get you home under covered circumstances. Major insurers such as those listed below offer policy holders access to 24-hour phone assistance to help handle crises. Read the policy carefully to find out when you are covered. Do not buy insurance through the operator holding your deposit, even though the insurer itself is a different entity. Policies may not cover losses related to the company that originally solicited your business. Instead, buy your insurance directly from the insurance company without the involvement of anyone selling you travel products. Medical insurance is covered on p. 92.

Insurance on your baggage is included in most travel insurance plans. If not, consider the pros and cons of a separate policy. Your baggage is often covered under your homeowners' policy or credit card benefits, but that coverage may expose you to high deductibles or sneaky exclusions, so read the fine print carefully and, if relying on a card, make sure to use that card for everything relevant to the coverage. If an airline loses or damages your bags, they are usually responsible for up to $2,500 per passenger on domestic flights or, on international flights, up to approximately $635 per checked bag, excluding expensive items such as jewelry and cameras. Good luck getting an airline to actually pay in a reasonable period of time, however, as it is notoriously difficult. Travel insurance companies pay faster. The simplest course is to leave valuables at home or carry them with you, insuring your baggage only if justified by the worth that you can prove. You would need to establish the value of your lost clothing and such with bills of sale or similar documentation for each item. Various companies sell travel insurance online, including **Travel Guard** (**℡800/826-1300;** www.travelguard.com).

Or look for the best deal around by going to **www.insuremytrip.com**. The site allows travelers to get instant quotes from many insurance companies at once by providing the dates of the trip, amount and type of coverage, and ages of the travelers.

With **rental cars** you face a whole different set of insurance considerations. Most of these are the same as renting a car anywhere, and a few simple preparations will get you through. Before you leave home, check your own auto policy for your liability coverage with a rented car (bringing proof of insurance along is a good idea), and check with your credit card issuer for coverage for damage to a

Using the Internet on the Road

If you decide to bring your laptop, you'll find that many hotels and even B&Bs have wireless Internet access for guests, usually for free, and there are numerous other free hotspots all over the state. If you leave the computer at home, you can stop in at an Internet cafe or the public library when you want to log on. Alaskans are the most Internet-connected population in the country, and there is access even in tiny villages where people live largely by hunting and gathering, so you can always count on finding a way of getting online with a little effort. I have listed Internet access for each Alaska community in the appropriate sections of the book. Coverage for wireless Internet technology, such as your Blackberry or iPhone, spread beyond Alaska's two or three largest cities only in 2006, and you may still hit dead spots in many towns. Check on roaming with your own provider. Voice cellular coverage has spread to smaller communities, but even that remains spotty or non-existent beyond city limits. For more on remote communication, see "Getting Lost/Wilderness Communications," p. 94.

rented car (make sure to use that card when you rent, too). Chances are you are already covered and don't need to buy the unreasonably priced insurance offered by the rental-car company when you rent, but if you are not covered, do buy it: The potential costs you face are even larger than having a crash at home, because they include the rental company's lost business.

One special Alaska consideration: Ask the reservation agent or check the rental contract for rules about driving on unpaved roads, such as the Dalton, Denali, or Steese highways. I have listed two companies in Fairbanks that rent for use on unpaved highways (p. 516), and one in Anchorage (p. 290); very few others allow it. Cars do get damaged on these roads, and you may be setting yourself up for a real headache if you violate the rental contract and that happens. I've suggested alternatives if you want to go to drive the Copper River Highway from Cordova (p. 449) or the McCarthy Road in Wrangell–St. Elias National Park (p. 558).

HEALTH & SAFETY
Crime & Emergency Services

CRIME Sadly, crime rates are not low in Alaska's larger cities, although muggings are rare. Take the normal precautions you'd take at home. You're safe in daylight hours anywhere tourists commonly go, less so late at night leaving a bar or walking in a lonely place. Women need to be especially careful on their own, as Alaska has a disproportionately high rate of rape. This doesn't mean women shouldn't travel alone in Alaska, only that they should be cautious. Most women I know avoid walking by themselves at night, especially in wooded or out-of-the-way areas. The late-night sunlight can be deceiving—just because it's light out doesn't mean it's safe. Sexual assaults occur in towns big and small. Women should never hitchhike alone. If you are a victim of a crime, you can reach police from almost anywhere by calling **☎911,** or, if it is not an emergency, by using the numbers listed under "Fast Facts" in each community section.

MEDICAL EMERGENCIES You'll find modern, full-service hospitals in each of Alaska's larger cities, and even in some small towns that act as regional centers. There's some kind of clinic even in the smallest towns, although they often are staffed by physicians' assistants rather than medical doctors. I've listed the address and phone numbers for medical facilities in each destination under "Fast Facts." Call those numbers, too, for referrals to a dentist or other health professional. In an emergency, call **☎911.**

If health is a particular concern, consider joining **MedicAlert** (**☎800/ ID-ALERT** [432-5378]; www.medicalert.org) and wearing their engraved bracelet, which will inform emergency medical personnel of a primary preexisting medical condition and provide them with access to the organization's response center for your information on file, such as medications and physician and family contacts. The cost is $40 for the first year, then $27 a year.

Health Insurance

Travelers from within the U.S. are often covered under their regular health insurance as long as they remain in the country. Take a minute to check your coverage, making sure it adequately covers emergency medical transportation and treatment, especially if you will be adventuring in remote areas. The cost of a medevac flight can easily be in the five figures. Check the coverage offered by your credit cards or buy a travel insurance policy to cover you just for the trip (p. 89). International visitors should certainly make health insurance arrangements before traveling to the U.S. Doctors and hospitals are expensive and often require proof of coverage before they render services (in an emergency, of course, you'll always get quick treatment regardless of ability to pay). For advice on medical insurance while traveling, visit www.frommers.com/planning.

Outdoors Health & Safety

AVALANCHE When snow sliding down a mountain comes to a stop, it hardens to a consistency that only metal tools can dig through. Avalanche survivors describe the terror of being helplessly locked in this unyielding material hoping for rescue. Understandably, survivors are in the minority. Victims die if not dug out quickly (well before emergency personnel can arrive at a remote slope). No one should go into the snowy backcountry without training in avalanche avoidance and recovery equipment, including locator beacons, probes, and shovels. Go with a guide if you are unsure.

BEARS & OTHER WILDLIFE Being eaten by a bear is probably the least likely way for your vacation to end. More people die from dog bites than bear attacks. But it's still wise to be prepared for bears and to know how to avoid being trampled by a moose, which can be fatal.

The first safety rule for bears is to avoid attracting them. Be tidy with your food and trash when you're camping, putting everything away in sealed containers. When backpacking, you can protect your food by hanging it from a long tree branch or, above tree line, storing it in a bear-resistant canister (for rent or loan in Anchorage or at Denali or Wrangell–St. Elias National Parks; see chapters 7, 9, and 10). Be careful not to spread food odors when you're cooking and cleaning up. Clean fish away from your campsite. Never keep food, pungent items, or clothing that smells like fish in your tent.

Make noise when walking through brush or thick trees to avoid surprising a bear or moose. Call out, sing, or carry on conversation. You might not scare a bear away this way, but at least you won't startle it. At all costs, avoid coming between a bear and its cubs or a bear and food (if a bear wants the fish you just caught, that's his food, too). Moose also are strongly defensive of their young, and a moose on its own can attack if it feels you're getting too close or if it previously has been stressed by contact with people or dogs. People are badly hurt every year trying to sneak by a moose on a trail. I see moose every day when I ski, bike, or run near my house in Anchorage; when the moose wants the trail I either find a way around or go back the other way.

If you see a bear, stop, wave your arms, make noise, and, if you're with others, group together so you look larger to the bear. Avoid running, tempting the bear to chase (unless, of course, you can run a few steps to your car);

depart by slowly backing away, at an angle if possible. If the bear follows, stop. Once in a great while, the bear may bluff a charge; even less often, it may attack. If you're attacked, fall and play dead, rolling into a ball face down with your hands behind your neck. The bear should lose interest. In extremely rare instances, a bear may not lose interest, because it's planning to make a meal of you. If this happens, fight back for all you're worth.

Many Alaskans carry a gun for protection in bear country, but that's not practical for visitors or for anyone not practiced in shooting (a few years ago a greenhorn got flustered and threw his gun at a bear). For most of us, a better alternative is a bear-deterrent spray. These are canisters that you fire to produce a burning fog of capsaicin pepper between you and a threatening bear. While less deadly than a gun, and with limited effectiveness in wind or rain, research shows they have a better overall track record against bear attacks than guns. You can't bring bear-deterrent spray on an airplane, even in your checked baggage, so if you fly you will have to buy it on arrival and get rid of it before you leave, or ship it to yourself in Alaska. The product is easily available at Alaska sporting goods stores for about $45, or order direct from **Counter Assault** (☎800/695-3394; www.counterassault.com). Whatever brand you buy, get a large canister, as this is one product you definitely don't want to run out of—sprays made for personal defense are not large enough. Also be sure to get a holster, as the spray is of no use buried in your backpack. If you do take a gun, it had better be a big one, such as a .300-Magnum rifle or 12-gauge shotgun loaded with slugs. No handgun is big enough to reliably stop a large bear bent on attacking.

BOATING SAFETY Because of the cool temperatures, unpredictable weather, and cold water, going out on the ocean or floating a fast river is more hazardous in Alaska than in most other places, and you should go only with an experienced, licensed operator unless you know what you're doing. There's little margin for error if you fall into the water or capsize in this cold water. Many boating deaths occur when good swimmers who are not wearing life-jackets immediately sink—apparently, the shock of falling in is so intense they shut down and fail to swim. With a life jacket on, you have a few seconds to get used to the cold water, and then, still alive, you can concentrate on getting out. You have 15 minutes to half an hour before cold immobilizes you. Equally important, however, is getting warm and dry after you are out of the water. The body temperature of a wet, cold person can easily sink so far he or she cannot get warm without external heating, a deadly condition called hypothermia. If you're sea kayaking or canoeing, always wear a life jacket; stay close to shore; and use rubberized dry bags (also called float bags) to pack everything you need to quickly warm a person who gets wet (see "Hypothermia," below). Having a way to get help in an emergency is also important (see "Getting Lost/Wilderness Communications," p. 94).

DANGEROUS PLANTS Two shrubs common in Alaska can cause skin irritation, but there is nothing as bad as poison ivy or poison oak. **Cow parsnip,** also called pushki, is a large-leafed plant growing primarily in open areas, up to shoulder height by late summer, with white flowers. The celery-like stalks break easily, and the sap has the quality of intensifying the burning power of the sun on skin. Wash it off quickly to avoid a rash or blisters. **Devil's**

Club, a more obviously dangerous plant, grows on steep slopes and has ferocious spines that can pierce through clothing and cause infections. Also, don't eat anything you can't positively identify, as there are deadly poisonous mushrooms and plants.

DRINKING WATER Unpurified river or lake water may not be safe to drink. Hand-held filters available from sporting-goods stores for around $75 are the most practical way of dealing with the problem. Iodine kits and boiling also work. The danger is a protozoan cyst called *Giardia lamblia,* which causes diarrhea and is present in thousands of water bodies all over the United States, even in remote areas, where it may have been carried by waterfowl. It may not show up until a couple of weeks after exposure and could become chronic. If symptoms show up after you get home, tell your doctor you may have been exposed so that you can get tested and cured.

GETTING LOST/WILDERNESS COMMUNICATIONS Even experienced people get lost outdoors. Hiking off trail or voyaging in a canoe, raft, or kayak, you quickly find that one mountain looks a lot like another. If you are unsure of your navigational skills, maps, or equipment, don't go. Beyond those basics, the most important safety precautions are to go with another person and to make sure someone knows where to look for you if you don't come back. For extended trips (more than a dayhike), leave a written trip plan with a person who will call rescuers if you are late. At the very least, leave a note in your car indicating where you are bound. Cellphones sometimes work near towns and highways, but not reliably, and there is little coverage beyond populated areas.

For serious outdoors people, technology can add an extra safety backup outdoors. Personal Locator Beacons with built-in GPS are the state-of-the-art solution. The beacon is a small device that, when activated, transmits a distress signal and your exact location to an orbiting satellite. Authorities receive the message and find out who you are from a database. After verifying you are really missing, they can then go to the exact spot where the beacon is broadcasting. ACR Electronics' units cost around $600 at stores such as West Marine or REI.

If you don't want to shell out that much money, or if you want a device that also allows you to stay in touch in the wilderness, it is possible to rent an Iridium satellite phone that will work outdoors anywhere on earth. The drawback of this approach is that it is less useful in an emergency than a beacon: You need to know where you are and whom to call, and you have to be able to get the phone to work. I rented one for a 2-week wilderness trip and found it rather finicky; I was always able to make a call, but I wouldn't have wanted my life to depend on doing so quickly. I was happy with the customer service of the firm I rented from, **RoadPost** (☎888/290-1616 or 905/272-5665; www.roadpost.com). Prices start at $9 a day, $1.79 a minute, plus a $35 delivery fee (inbound direct-dial calls and text messages are free). The phone arrives with all needed accessories in an express package, which contains a pre-paid return envelope to send it back.

HYPOTHERMIA A potentially fatal lowering of core body temperature can sneak up on you. It's most dangerous when you don't realize how cold you are, perhaps in 50°F (10°C) weather on a damp mountain hike or rainy boating trip. Dress in material (whether wool or synthetic) that keeps its warmth when wet, choosing layers to avoid chilling perspiration. (See "What to Wear," p. 62.) Eating well and avoiding exhaustion also are important. Among the symptoms of hypothermia are cold extremities, being uncommunicative, displaying poor judgment or coordination, and sleepiness. A shivering victim still has the ability to warm up if better dressed; a lack of shivering means the body has gone beyond that point and warmth must be added from the outside or from warm drinks. Get indoors, force hot liquids on the victim (except if not fully conscious, which could cause choking), and, if shelter is unavailable, apply body heat from another person, skin on skin, in a sleeping bag.

INSECT BITES The good news is that Alaska has no snakes or poisonous spiders. The bad news is that Alaska makes up for it with mosquitoes and other biting insects. West Nile virus has not arrived here, so the mosquitoes are not dangerous, but they can ruin a trip. Effective insect repellent is a necessity, as is having a place where you can get away from them. We use shirts with hoods of netting when the bugs are at their worst. Mosquitoes can bite through light fabric close to the skin, which is one reason why people in the Bush wear heavy, baggy Carhart pants and jackets (made of canvas) even on the hottest days. Benadryl tablets or other antihistamines will often relieve swelling caused by mosquito bites.

RIVER CROSSINGS Hiking in Alaska's backcountry often requires crossing rivers without bridges. Use great caution: It's easy to get in trouble. Often, the water is glacial melt, barely above freezing, and heavy with silt that makes it opaque. The silt can fill your pockets and drag you down. If in doubt, don't do it. If you do decide to cross, unbuckle your pack, keep your shoes on, face upstream, use a heavy walking stick if possible, and rig a safety line. Children should go in the eddy behind a larger person, or be carried.

SEASICKNESS Most summertime visits to Alaska involve boat rides for fishing or sightseeing. Seasickness probably ruins more of these outings than any other cause. Avoid seasickness by abstaining from alcohol the night before, eating a light breakfast, limiting coffee, and sitting low and near the middle of the boat, away from odors and with your eyes on the horizon—no reading. Some people use alternative medicine cures, such as ginger or acupressure, which have no proven benefits, but nonetheless work for many of those who believe in them—a placebo, such as a sugar pill, is 40% effective with seasickness if the patient has faith. My experience and the advice of experts suggests, however, that using seasickness drugs is worthwhile. The very best is the scopolamine skin patch, available only by prescription, which lasts up to 3 days. The main choices for over-the-counter drugs are meclizine (brand names Bonine, Antivert, or Dramamine II) and dimenhydrinate (original Dramamine). Both are drowsiness-inducing antihistamines, but there's less of that side-effect with the newer meclizine. To be effective, the drugs need at least 2 hours to get through your digestive system, so you must take the pill well before you get on the boat. For best effectiveness, take a tablet before bed and another on the morning of the outing. If you've taken nothing and feel yourself getting seasick, there is a last-minute cure that sometimes works: Chew up the tablets but don't swallow them, holding the mush under your tongue or against your cheek. The drug is partly absorbed through the lining of the mouth.

SHELLFISH Don't eat mussels, clams, or scallops you pick or dig from the seashore unless you know they're safe to eat. Generally, that means you need some specific and reliable local knowledge. There is a government program to assure that commercial shellfish areas are safe, but the only easily accessible beaches it affects are on the eastern shore of Kachemak Bay. The risk is paralytic shellfish poisoning, a potentially fatal malady caused by a naturally occurring toxin. It can cause total paralysis that includes your breathing. A victim may be kept alive with mouth-to-mouth resuscitation until medical help is obtained. For more information, check the **Alaska Department of Environmental Conservation** website at www.dec.state.ak.us/eh/fss/seafood/psphome.htm, or go to www.alaska.gov and search for "PSP").

Driving Safety

ROAD REPORTS The Alaska Department of Transportation has centralized highway reports with a handy toll-free phone and Internet system (℡511; http://511.alaska.gov). Even in dry summer conditions, it is worthwhile to make the call or check the site before heading on an inter-city drive, because road construction can cause long delays—at times, workers will close a major highway overnight for work. In winter, checking on conditions is a safety essential. Here are more seasonal tips.

SUMMER Alaska's highways are two-lane except close to Anchorage and Fairbanks. Keep your headlights on all the time to help oncoming vehicles see you. Drivers are required to pull over at the next pull-out whenever five or more cars are trailing them on a two-lane highway, regardless of how fast they're going. This saves the lives of people who otherwise will try to pass. When passing a truck going the other way on a gravel highway, slow down or stop and pull as far as possible to the side of the road to avoid losing your windshield to a flying rock. Always think about the path of rocks you're kicking up toward others' vehicles. Make sure you've got a good, full-size spare tire and jack if you're driving a gravel highway. For remote driving, bring along a first-aid kit, emergency food, a tow rope, and jumper cables, and keep your gas tank full.

WINTER Drivers on Alaska's highways in winter should be prepared for cold-weather emergencies far from help. Take all the items listed for rural summer driving, plus a flashlight, matches, and materials to light a fire; chains, a shovel, and an ice scraper. A camp stove to make hot beverages is also a good idea. If you're driving a remote highway (such as the Alaska Hwy.) between December and March, take along gear adequate to keep you safe from the cold even if you have to wait overnight with a dead car at –40°F (–40°C; see "What to Wear," earlier in this chapter, and add blankets and sleeping bags). Never drive a road marked "Closed" or "Unmaintained in Winter." Even on maintained rural roads, other vehicles rarely come by in winter. All Alaska roads are icy all winter. Studded tires are a necessity. Also, never leave your car's engine stopped for more than 4 hours in temperatures of –10°F (–23°C) or colder. Virtually all vehicles in Alaska have electrical head-bolt heaters installed to keep the engine warm overnight; you'll find electrical outlets everywhere in cold, Interior Alaska areas.

SUGGESTED ALASKA ITINERARIES

Readers ask me about how to fit together their itineraries more frequently than any other travel question. Alaska is unfamiliar territory, and the transportation connections are different from those in most places. You can't get to the capital city of Juneau over land, for example, and the distances seem daunting between the towns that do have roads or rails. If you don't even know how to get around, it seems hard to know where to go or how much time to allow. But don't throw in the towel, like so many visitors who think the only way around these complications is to take a cruise or escorted tour. In fact, these travel issues aren't really that hard. Using a map and the list of transportation modes under "Alaska by the Numbers," on p. 74, you can get a good overview. The "Getting There" section for each destination in the book provides the details.

What's really challenging, and where visitors most commonly make mistakes, is in failing to define their interests and not limiting themselves to covering a reasonable area. Some feel compelled to try to see the entire state. Given that Alaska is defined in part by its enormous size, trying to go everywhere is a fool's errand. A version of the same thing is trying to "do" all the famous wilderness parks, which lie far apart in remote regions: You spend too much time and money getting from place to place. Each of Alaska's regions, by itself, has most of what you're coming to Alaska for—wildlife, mountains, glaciers, historic sites, cute little towns—and you can have a better trip touring one or two regions rather than spending precious time going from region to region. To be specific, travelers with fewer than 10 days to spend should choose to tour either Southeast Alaska or Southcentral and Interior Alaska, but not both.

The other mistake some people make is to focus only on the largest and most famous destinations. Alaska isn't like Europe, with its cathedrals and monuments. Here a goal-oriented style of travel misses the fun and surprises—and may end up missing the whole point. Mount McKinley and Glacier Bay are certainly impressive, but it's perfectly allowable to skip them in favor of memorable places you find on your own that may be just as beautiful, if not as famous. More valuable—and more fundamentally Alaskan—are chance encounters with wildlife or interesting local people, or simply peaceful time alone in the woods.

Finally, remember why you are going to Alaska. Surely it's not to visit museums or tourist attractions, but instead to see one of the most beautiful, unspoiled places on Earth. To do that, you need to get outside. There's only so much you can see and learn through glass. Take a chance on a sea-kayak excursion, a day hike, or a mountain-bike ride. You may never have a better chance to try it.

PREVIOUS PAGE: **Backpacker in Tongass National Forest.**

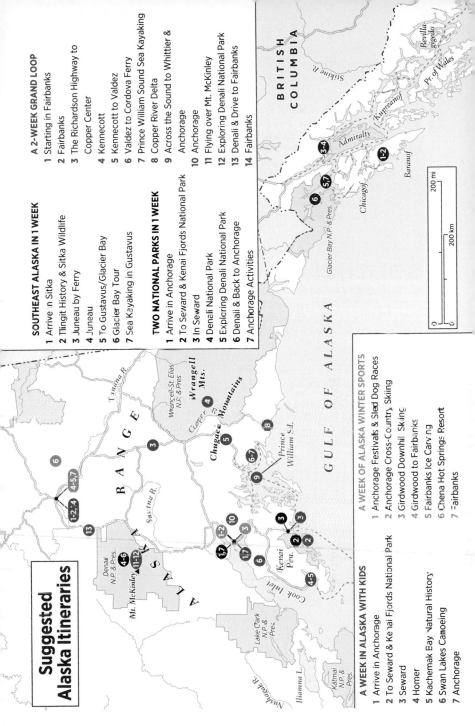

Suggested Alaska Itineraries

SOUTHEAST ALASKA IN 1 WEEK

1 Arrive in Sitka
2 Tlingit History & Sitka Wildlife
3 Juneau by Ferry
4 Juneau
5 To Gustavus/Glacier Bay
6 Glacier Bay Tour
7 Sea Kayaking in Gustavus

TWO NATIONAL PARKS IN 1 WEEK

1 Arrive in Anchorage
2 To Seward & Kenai Fjords National Park
3 In Seward
4 Denali National Park
5 Exploring Denali National Park
6 Denali & Back to Anchorage
7 Anchorage Activities

A 2-WEEK GRAND LOOP

1 Starting in Fairbanks
2 Fairbanks
3 The Richardson Highway to Copper Center
4 Kennecott
5 Kennecott to Valdez
6 Valdez to Cordova Ferry
7 Prince William Sound Sea Kayaking
8 Copper River Delta
9 Across the Sound to Whittier & Anchorage
10 Anchorage
11 Flying over Mt. McKinley
12 Exploring Denali National Park
13 Denali & Drive to Fairbanks
14 Fairbanks

A WEEK IN ALASKA WITH KIDS

1 Arrive in Anchorage
2 To Seward & Kenai Fjords National Park
3 Seward
4 Homer
5 Kachemak Bay Natural History
6 Swan Lakes Canoeing
7 Anchorage

A WEEK OF ALASKA WINTER SPORTS

1 Anchorage Festivals & Sled Dog Races
2 Anchorage Cross-Country Skiing
3 Girdwood Downhill Skiing
4 Girdwood to Fairbanks
5 Fairbanks Ice Carving
6 Chena Hot Springs Resort
7 Fairbanks

Create Your Own Itinerary

If all travelers had the same interests, needs, abilities, and preferences in pacing, they could all follow the same itineraries. Of course, then only the limited number of places that fit on a sample itinerary would receive all the visitors, while the interesting and peculiar places off the beaten path would remain unknown. I hope you use the sample trip plans here as a starting point to design your own individual trip. Substitute different activities or towns, or extend the time in places that are more appealing to you. Do the trips in reverse order or cut and paste portions of two different plans together. Or simply use the itineraries to get a feel for the distances and places, and then build your own plan from scratch after browsing through the rest of the book.

SOUTHEAST ALASKA IN 1 WEEK

This plan takes you to the Southeast's highlights, with whales, glaciers, mountains, totem poles, and Russian American history included. It's fast paced yet still covers less than half of this diverse and fascinating region. If you have more time, this plan would make a much more relaxing 10-day trip. Add a day each in Sitka, Juneau, and Gustavus. There's plenty to do, or not do, in each town. You can extend this itinerary even more by beginning with a flight into Petersburg instead of Sitka. Spend a day or two there sea kayaking, hiking, fishing, or whale-watching before boarding an Alaska Marine Highway System ferry to Sitka and picking up on Day 1 of this plan.

DAY 1: Arrive in Sitka ★

Fly on an **Alaska Airlines** jet to the historic island city of Sitka, once the capital of Russian America. The town layout you see from the air is little changed from historic photographs and paintings. After settling in, take a walk along winding Lincoln Street, taking in the views from **Castle Hill** (p. 207), where the Russians handed over Alaska to the United States in 1867. Look into stately **St. Michael's Cathedral** (p. 206), and visit **The Russian Bishop's House** (p. 204), making sure to take a National Park Service tour of the extraordinary upstairs section.

St. Michael's Cathedral in Sitka.

Dog-sledding in Juneau.

DAY 2: Tlingit History & Sitka Wildlife ★★★

Start the day at the **Sitka National Historical Park** (p. 203) to see an extraordinary collection of historic and contemporary totem poles, meet Tlingit artisans at work, and learn about their culture and history. Now walk through the lovely forested totem park and battlefield sites before continuing to the **Alaska Raptor Center** (p. 206) to see eagles being rehabilitated and learning to fly again after injuries. After lunch, join any one of the half-day **wildlife cruises** that go from the boat harbor to see otters, sea lions, and possibly whales; and, if conditions permit, the **sea bird colony** at St. Lazaria Island (p. 208).

DAY 3: Juneau by Ferry ★★

After a final goodbye to Sitka, board a ferry of the **Alaska Marine Highway System** (p. 72) for a spectacular ride to Juneau that will take much of the day. When you arrive, get a cab from the ferry dock to the airport and rent a car there. If you have time enough left in the day, you can now visit **Mendenhall Glacier** (p. 232) and drive out the road (that's the common local phrase for it) for a lovely and moving walk to the tiny island of **The Shrine of St. Thérèse** (p. 234). Then settle in to your lodgings.

The *Fairweather* ferry.

DAY 4: Juneau ★★

In the morning, take a **helicopter flight** to the **Juneau Icefield** (p. 239) for a walk or even a dog-sled ride and to get a feel for the immensity of the place and to touch glacier ice. If weather isn't promising for that, visit the **Alaska State Museum** (p. 221) or do the **walking tour** downtown (p. 224). In the afternoon, take a **hike** on one of Juneau's beautiful rainforest or mountain trails (p. 235). There are wonderful choices, such as the **Perseverance Trail** near downtown, but since you have a car, you can hike anywhere and get away from any cruise-ship crowds that may wreck the solitude on some of the paths.

DAY 5: To Gustavus/Glacier Bay ★★

Fly a prop from Juneau to Gustavus, the gateway to **Glacier Bay National Park** (p. 248), to arrive early enough to orient yourself and take a walk on the trails around the park headquarters to enjoy the shoreline and mossy forest trails. Or go bicycling on the country roads or explore the long sandy beaches in Gustavus. If you're more ambitious, the waters off Gustavus are among Alaska's best for watching humpback whales, and you'll have time today for a half-day viewing trip. You have two lodging choices here. Check in at the **Glacier Bay Lodge** (p. 253), or stay at a wilderness lodge or country inn in Gustavus (your host will pick you up).

DAY 6: Glacier Bay Tour ★★

The all-day **boat tour ride** (p. 252) leaves from Bartlett Cove and passes through humpback whale areas and other marine mammal grounds far up the bay to where two large glaciers stand like walls at the edge of the water. Be sure to bring binoculars and warm clothing, as the glaciers produce frigid downdrafting winds, even in the height of summer.

Itinerary Add-Ons

This week-long itinerary to two national parks is fast paced. You can have a more relaxing trip and allow for more spontaneity by adding days to the stops that are already planned.

If you've still got more time after slowing down the pace, extend your trip with a visit to **Fairbanks.** Instead of taking the train back to Anchorage on Day 6, take it northward to Fairbanks. There I recommend renting a car to see the sites and perhaps explore the surrounding rural highways for a few days. (See Days 1 and 2 of "A 2-Week Grand Loop," below.) When you're finished, fly home from Fairbanks.

Also consider adding on a **Southeast Alaska** sojourn. When you buy your ticket to Alaska, buy it from Seattle to Anchorage on Alaska Airlines and include a stopover, for a reasonable additional cost, in a Southeast Alaska town—Sitka would be my first choice. Spend time seeing the Russian American history and Tlingit culture there, and getting outdoors (see Days 1 and 2 of "Southeast Alaska in 1 Week," above), before flying on to Anchorage and beginning the itinerary listed at Day 1.

DAY 7: Sea Kayaking in Gustavus ★★★

I've saved some of the best for last. Your Alaska Airlines jet doesn't leave Gustavus until the evening, so you have time today for a **sea-kayaking** outing in the lovely waters of **Bartlett Cove,** where whales frequently visit (p. 256), or, if you are staying in Gustavus, kayak from there (p. 256) into an area where whales are virtually always seen in the summer. You can connect the flight from Gustavus through Juneau onward to home.

TWO NATIONAL PARKS IN 1 WEEK

An itinerary connecting Kenai Fjords National Park, south of Anchorage, and Denali National Park, to the north, is probably Alaska's most popular land trip for first-time visitors. That's because these parks and the area in between offer so much of what visitors come to Alaska to see, and in spectacular places: at Kenai Fjords, waterways full of whales, marine birds, and glaciers; and at Denali, broad swaths of mountain tundra frequented by bears and caribou. This itinerary is set up to do without a car. To save money and have more flexibility, do the same tour with a car rented in Anchorage.

DAY 1: Arrive in Anchorage ★

Fly to Anchorage and move into a room in the walkable downtown area, which is near the train station, from where you will be departing tomorrow.

If the weather is nice, do the **walking tour** (p. 311) to find out what the area is like, or rent a bike and hit the **Tony Knowles Coastal Trail** (p. 328) to see the waterfowl in West Chester Lagoon, the moose in Earthquake Park, and maybe even the beluga whales of Cook Inlet. You can go as far as you want: Anchorage's paved bike trails weave through the entire city on wooded greenbelts. In bad weather, or if you're not up for exercise, spend your time at the **Anchorage Museum at Rasmuson Center** (p. 321), getting oriented to Alaska's history and art, and maybe even catch a planetarium show.

DAY 2: To Seward & Kenai Fjords National Park ★★★

Board an **Alaska Railroad** (p. 359) train to Seward to enjoy some of Alaska's most spectacular scenery along the cliffs and surging ocean waters of Turnagain Arm and through the untouched mountains of the Kenai Peninsula; those who choose to drive get to see similar scenery on a slightly different route (see "Out from Anchorage: Turnagain

Sitka National Historical Park.

Arm & Portage Glacier," in chapter 7, and "The Seward Highway: A Road Guide," in chapter 8). In Seward, board a tour boat to **Kenai Fjords National Park** (see "Kenai Fjords National Park," in chapter 8). Make sure to take a vessel headed all the way into the park so you see the best of the wildlife and get close to a tidewater glacier. Make sure also to take a seasickness remedy such as Dramamine or Bonine 2 hours before getting onboard. If the weather is bad, ask to be switched to a boat tomorrow and do tomorrow's activities instead.

DAY 3: In Seward ★★

After a couple of tiring days, this is a good day to relax in a charming little town. In the morning, join a half-day sea-kayaking paddle from Lowell Point with **Sunny Cove Sea Kayaking** (p. 382). You'll likely see sea otters, birds, intertidal creatures, and maybe spawning salmon. By going in the morning, your chances of smooth water are better. In the afternoon, see the marine life and seabirds you encountered yesterday, up close, at the **Alaska SeaLife Center** (p. 384). Consider joining one of their educational programs to get even closer to the animals.

DAY 4: Denali National Park

Take the comfortable and convenient **Park Connection Motorcoach Service** (p. 463) from Seward straight to Denali National Park, a journey of more than 360 miles. The driver does commentary on the highlights along the route. The bus ride takes almost 10 hours with a couple of long stops. If you drive instead, you can do it in fewer than 7 hours. Arriving in Denali, check into your hotel and stretch your legs, but get to bed promptly to be ready for an early start tomorrow.

Kenai Fjords National Park.

Caribou in Denali National Park.

Tsimshian dancers.

DAY 5: Exploring Denali National Park ★★★

This is the primary day to see Denali and the bears, caribou, and other wildlife there. The park shuttle bus system is the key to your visit. Reserve as far ahead as possible (the previous Dec is not too soon) to get a seat on the earliest bus you can manage (reservation details are on p. 460). Wildlife tends to be more active in the morning. Ride deep into the park, taking along all your food and water, a warm jacket and raincoat, and good hiking shoes. Take a look at the suggestions for cross-country hiking in chapter 9, and then make your route choice according to how the countryside looks to you. This is a remarkable chance for a low-stress, low-cost wilderness experience. When you're ready to head home, just catch another bus on the way back.

DAY 6: Denali & Back to Anchorage ★

Your train back to Anchorage doesn't leave until late afternoon, giving you most of the day to enjoy the Denali park entrance area. The **visitor center** (p. 477) and **Murie Science and Learning Center** (p. 477) should not be missed. The exhibits and programs here will deepen your understanding of the natural places you have already seen. You also have time for a whitewater rafting ride on the Nenana River (p. 480) or a relaxing walk on the nature trails and hiking trails near the visitor center (p. 473). Your train arrives in Anchorage in the evening.

DAY 7: Anchorage Activities ★

If you can arrange for a flight home late in the day, you'll have time for one more activity in Anchorage. Take a shuttle to the **Alaska Native Heritage Center** (p. 323) to meet indigenous people and learn about their cultures in a magnificent facility they built, own, and manage.

UA Museum of the North.

Rika's Roadhouse and Landing.

A 2-WEEK GRAND LOOP

This driving loop includes much of the best of the Interior, Prince William Sound, Anchorage, and Denali National Park. It allows you to end up where you started, saving money on plane tickets and car rental. And you'll see some remote and off-the-beaten-track places. Not many visitors make it to see Childs Glacier on the Copper River Delta, but I think it's the most spectacular accessible glacier in Alaska. Likewise, a trip to Kennecott, in Wrangell–St. Elias National Park, takes you way off the grid, letting you see an amazing historical ghost town and a community of real, backwoods Alaskans.

DAY 1: Starting in Fairbanks ★

Fly to Fairbanks, rent a car, and then check into your hotel. (If you will drive the rented car on gravel roads, such as the McCarthy Rd. on Day 4 or the Copper River Hwy. on Day 8, you will need to rent from one of the few firms that allow this, listed on p. 516.) If time permits, visit the University of Alaska campus and see the magnificent **UA Museum of the North** (p. 512) and, if you are interested in such topics, the **Large Animal Research Station** or the **Georgeson Botanical Garden** (both p. 513).

DAY 2: Fairbanks ★

Take the car to explore the Chena Hot Springs Road and the boreal forest of the **Chena River State Recreation Area** (see "Chena Hot Springs Road," in chapter 10). There are several wonderful trails here with varying difficulty levels. As an alternative, arrange for a canoeing paddle on the Chena. When you've finished hiking or paddling and start thinking about sore muscles, stop at the **Chena Hot Springs Resort** (p. 535) for a soak in the natural mineral springs pond there. At the end of the day, return to Fairbanks for dinner and bed.

DAY 3: The Richardson Highway to Copper Center ★★

Today you will drive approximately 260 miles (driving time: under 6 hr.) through some of Alaska's most spectacular scenery. Drive east from Fairbanks toward Delta Junction; stop there, after about 2 hours, to see the historical park at **Rika's Roadhouse and Landing** (p. 550), and for lunch in the town (see "The Alaska Highway," in chapter 10). Now drive south on the Richardson Highway. The best part of the drive is here, as the highway rises up and over the Alaska Range on open tundra country, along the silver Alaska pipeline, and at the edge of a series of alpine lakes. Stop for the night in the Athabascan village of Copper Center, where there is an exceptional hotel, **Copper River Princess Wilderness Lodge** (p. 555). Be sure to stop in at the **Wrangell–St. Elias National Park Visitor Center** (p. 559) to get oriented to the park before your visit tomorrow.

DAY 4: Kennecott ★★★

Get up early to drive east about 85 miles on the Edgerton Highway to Chitina, arriving there in time for the 8:30am **Backcountry Connection shuttle** (p. 558; reserve in advance) for a ride into the park. It's a rough road over an old railroad line deep into the wilderness park to a copper mine that was abandoned in the 1930s and the ghost town it left behind; by taking the van, you save yourself the driving and the planning necessary for that tough route, and you gain a guide to show you the way (you will have to cross a footbridge at one point). In Kennecott, check into one of two **wilderness lodges** (see "Wrangell–St. Elias National Park & Kennecott," in chapter 10) and join a guided walking tour through the enormous ghost-town buildings.

DAY 5: Kennecott to Valdez ★★

You have time in the morning to relax and wander in the friendly, quiet setting of Kennecott and its funky sister village of McCarthy. If you have the energy, take a half-day guided hike on the glacier that faces the ghost town. In the afternoon, take an air-taxi flight back to **Chitina** (p. 558) to get to your car (if you ride the van back, you will get in too late; besides, the view from the plane will be fantastic). Drive back to the Richardson Highway and then south to Valdez, about 190 miles total (roughly 4 hr.) The mountain scenery is spectacular through Thompson Pass nearing the town. Dine and check into lodgings in **Valdez** (see "Valdez," in chapter 8).

DAY 6: Valdez to Cordova Ferry ★

Today you will be taking your car by ferry for a scenic trip across eastern Prince William Sound to the town of Cordova. Depending on when the ferry leaves, you may have time for a day hike, a museum visit, or another activity in Valdez. In the evening, walk around the quaint, forgotten town of Cordova; if time permits, take a look at the two small **community museums** (see "Cordova: Hidden Treasure," in chapter 8).

Kayaking at Prince William Sound.

Flying onto Kahiltna Glacier, a starting point for Mount McKinley climbers.

DAY 7: Prince William Sound Sea Kayaking ★★★

Join **Cordova Coastal Outfitters** (p. 449) for a sea-kayaking excursion, or, if you are staying at the **Orca Adventure Lodge** (p. 449), you can go with a guide there. Cordova is an exceptional spot for a day's sea kayaking because waters near town are protected and exceptionally rich in marine mammals. You're almost assured of seeing sea otters and sea lions, and very likely to see many birds and other animals as well (see "Cordova: Hidden Treasure," in chapter 8).

DAY 8: Copper River Delta ★★

Drive your car east from Cordova over the gravel Copper River Highway through the Copper River Delta, an immense wetland teeming with wildlife, especially trumpeter swans and other waterfowl. (If your car-rental agency doesn't allow this, you can rent a vehicle for the day in Cordova.) There are several excellent and little-used trails and bird-watching areas along the road. The destination at the far end is the Childs Glacier, an incredible wall of ice that is cut by the Copper River. From a viewing area on the other side of the river, you are remarkably close to the glacier, and in warm weather you can see huge chunks falling off and hear the groan of the moving ice (see "Cordova: Hidden Treasure," in chapter 8). Spend a third night in Cordova.

DAY 9: Across the Sound to Whittier & Anchorage ★

Get back on the ferry for a trip across the sound to Whittier. Again, the scenery is incomparable. Hopefully, you aren't too jaded yet! **Whittier** is a strange little port town built by the military during World War II that is reached only by boat or through a one-lane tunnel almost 3 miles long (p. 371). On the far side of the tunnel, you find yourself on Turnagain Arm about 50 miles from Anchorage. Time permitting, stop in Girdwood for a meal and perhaps a hike or visit to a **historic gold mine** (see "Out from Anchorage: Girdwood & Mount Alyeska," in chapter 7). Finish the day in lodgings in Anchorage.

DAY 10: Anchorage ★

Take in the **Alaska Native Heritage Center** (p. 323) in the morning to meet indigenous people and learn about their cultures in a magnificent facility they built, own, and manage. In the afternoon, visit the **Anchorage Museum at Rasmuson Center** (p. 321), or spend the day outdoors, hiking, mountain biking, fishing, or bird-watching. (See "What to See & Do," in chapter 7.) At the end of this fairly low-key day, eat in one of Alaska's best **restaurants,** of which Anchorage has the broadest selection (see "Where to Dine," in chapter 7).

DAY 11: Flying over Mount McKinley ★★★

Get an early start for the 112-mile drive to Talkeetna (about 2 hr.) so you can be there in time for a morning flight over Mount McKinley before the clouds build up in the afternoon. The flight services that carry mountain climbers to the flanks of North America's tallest peak can also take you there for a landing on a high-elevation glacier (p. 333). This flight may provide the most memorable hours of your visit; I know I'll never forget any of the times I've done it. After lunch and a walk around hip and historic Talkeetna (see "Talkeetna: Back Door to Denali," in chapter 9), drive about 150 miles (roughly 3 hr.) to Denali National Park and check into your lodgings. You should have time to take in the fascinating exhibits at the visitor center, too.

DAY 12: Exploring Denali National Park ★★★

This is the primary day to see Denali and the bears, caribou, and other wildlife there. The park shuttle bus system is the key to your visit. Reserve as far ahead as possible (the previous Dec is not too soon) to get a seat on the earliest bus you can manage. Wildlife tends to be more active in the morning. Ride deep into the park, taking along all your food and water, a warm jacket and raincoat, and good hiking shoes. Take a look at the suggestions for cross-country hiking in chapter 9, and then make your route choice according to how the countryside looks to you. This is a remarkable chance for a low-stress, low-cost wilderness experience. When you're ready to head home, just catch another bus on the way back.

DAY 13: Denali & Drive to Fairbanks ★

The drive from Denali back to Fairbanks is only a couple of hours, so you can take your time at the park. A whitewater rafting ride in the Nenana River would be exciting; a nature walk in the woods from the visitor center might be calming. Also consider an educational program at the **Murie Science and Learning Center** (see chapter 9). Drive to your lodgings in Fairbanks in the afternoon.

DAY 14: Fairbanks

Today you get on a plane and fly back home, but if you have time for a relaxing outing before that, stop off for a stroll in **Pioneer Park** (p. 511) to look at the historic paddle wheeler *Nenana* and the other museums and attractions, and to soak up the small-town ambience.

A WEEK IN ALASKA WITH KIDS

Traveling with children means limiting distances and increasing time for casual fun. The best place to do that is on the Kenai Peninsula south of Anchorage. Despite being a relatively contained area, the peninsula is a microcosm of the whole state, with glaciers, mountains, trails, and rugged coastline like that found over the vast span of Alaska. To make it even easier, I suggest renting an RV, which takes the stress out of having to keep children quiet in restaurants and hotel rooms. If you prefer to tent, rent a car instead; you can even rent most of your camping equipment in Anchorage. You'll have even more flexibility and opportunities for spontaneous fun. If you can, improve on this itinerary by adding days in Homer or on the Swan Lake Canoe Route.

DAY 1: Arrive in Anchorage

Fly to Anchorage and pick up your rented **RV** (p. 290), or pick up your car and rented **camping gear** (see "Equipment," p. 327). After buying your groceries, you can get on your way south on the Seward Highway, stopping at the **Bird Creek Campground** (p. 302) or the **Williwaw** or **Black Bear** campgrounds at Portage Glacier. The children will need to burn off some energy after your flight and drive, and this stretch of the highway has some of Alaska's best hiking trails. They are all covered, along with other sites, in "Out from Anchorage: Turnagain Arm & Portage Glacier," in chapter 7.

DAY 2: To Seward & Kenai Fjords National Park ★★★

Drive the rest of the way to Seward on the Seward Highway and get on a tour boat to see **Kenai Fjords National Park** (see "Kenai Fjords National Park," in chapter 8). Every kid enjoys a boat ride, and on this one you're likely to see whales, glaciers, and lots of seabirds. **Note:** These vessels go into the open ocean, and seasickness is common. Everyone in the family should take a seasickness remedy 2 hours in advance (see "Seasickness," on p. 95). Make sure to take a vessel headed all the way into the park so you see the best of the wildlife and get close to a tidewater glacier. After you get back on land, set up your camp: if in an RV, at **Waterfront Park** (p. 387), or, if tenting, drive out of Seward to the **Primrose Campground** (p. 367).

DAY 3: Seward ★★

You have three choices today, depending on the ages of your children and your interests (consider splitting up, as we often do, so everyone can choose what they enjoy most). (1) Visit the **Alaska SeaLife Center** (p. 384), where you can encounter the marine life and seabirds you saw in the fjords

Touch tanks at the Alaska SeaLife Center.

yesterday up close, and join in educational programs that get you even closer. Allow half a day. (2) Sea kayak for half the day or the whole day with **Sunny Cove Sea Kayaking** (p. 382). You'll likely see sea otters, birds, intertidal creatures, and maybe spawning salmon. (3) Hike the **Caines Head State Recreation Area** (p. 382) to Fort McGilvray to explore the dark corridors of the abandoned World War II installation. (Bring a flashlight and go halfway by water taxi to make the hike more manageable.)

DAY 4: Homer ★

Today you'll drive 135 miles from Seward to the end of the road on the southern Kenai Peninsula and the town of **Homer** (see "Homer & Kachemak Bay: Cosmic Hamlet by the Sea," in chapter 8). Allow 4 hours, with traffic and some stops. In Homer, you can get hookups for the RV on Homer Spit—a fingerlike point into the middle of Kachemak Bay—or in the downtown part of Homer (still near the beach). Tenters have even more choices. Spend the afternoon beachcombing and enjoying relaxed time on the many miles of pebbled shoreline. If it's raining, take in the **Islands and Oceans Visitor Center** (p. 411) or the **Pratt Museum** (p. 416).

DAY 5: Kachemak Bay Natural History ★★★

Join the nonprofit **Center for Alaskan Coastal Studies** (p. 424) for a boat ride to the far side of Kachemak Bay. Their all-day natural history outings take visitors through tide pools to see strange little creatures, through a forest of big trees and wildflowers to learn about ecology, and to an ancient Native archaeological site. Even without the guides and all their knowledge, this would still be an enchanting place to visit, with wide beaches, caves, and plenty of space for a kid's energy and imagination to run free. Bring your own lunch.

DAY 6: Swan Lakes Canoeing ★

Now it's time to start heading back toward Anchorage. Drive about 90 miles to Sterling and stop at **Alaska Canoe & Campground** (p. 408) to rent a canoe you can take down the Swanson River Road to the Swan Lake Canoe Route in **Kenai National Wildlife Refuge** (see "Kenai National Wildlife Refuge," in chapter 8). Spend the rest of the day paddling in this placid network of connected lakes, where you can fish and explore without seeing other people. There are numerous primitive campgrounds for the RV overnight, or, if you are tent camping, you may want to paddle to a campsite among the hundreds on the lakes. If you're thinking this plan will leave you too far from the airport when it's time to fly home tomorrow, fair enough. Skip the canoeing and drive on. There are campgrounds all along the highway to Anchorage, so you can stop wherever you feel comfortable and explore there. See sections 2 and 3 of chapter 8.

DAY 7: Anchorage

From Sterling to Anchorage is about 150 miles and will take more than 3 hours with traffic. You probably won't have extra time after returning the RV or camping equipment before your flight, but if you do, the best way to spend it is at the **Alaska Zoo** (p. 324), where you will be sure of seeing all the most popular Alaska wildlife.

DAYS 8, 9 & 10 (OPTIONAL): Prince William Sound Loop

Another great trip for kids adds 2 or 3 extra days: Instead of returning to Anchorage on Day 7, drive to Whittier and take the Alaska Marine Highway ferry to Valdez. Drive north on the Richardson Highway to Glennallen and west on the Glenn Highway back to Anchorage. An overview of these roads is in "Alaska's Highways a la Carte" (p. 502), and details are included in chapters 8 and 10.

A WEEK OF ALASKA WINTER SPORTS

Winter is when Alaska is at its best. The snow simplifies the scenery and makes it even more beautiful. The outdoor activities are superb: cross-country and downhill skiing, snowmobiling, ice-skating, and dog mushing. The people are especially hospitable, since visitors are rare, and the towns are alive with festivals, sled-dog races, and authentic cultural events—not just tourist stuff. There's also a very good chance you will see the northern lights. One proviso: It's impossible to make up a real itinerary for winter sports without knowing individual interests. Avid downhill skiers should spend most of their time on the slopes, for example. So take the list below as a starting point for ideas.

Fur Rendezvous Festival.

Ice skating at Westchester Lagoon.

DAY 1: Anchorage Festivals & Sled Dog Races ★

To enjoy Anchorage fully, rent a car when you arrive. If you have planned your trip for late February or early March, you can be here when Anchorage is alive with the **Fur Rendezvous Festival,** with its dozens of events and World Championship Sled Dog Race, and the **Iditarod Trail Sled Dog Race** (both p. 293), which starts its journey across Alaska to Nome right after the festival. Local cultural institutions will be busy, too: Visit the **Anchorage Museum at Rasmuson Center** (p. 321) during the day and catch a performance in the evening at the **Alaska Center for the Performing Arts** (p. 314).

DAY 2: Anchorage Cross-Country Skiing ★★

If you've never tried cross-country skiing, Anchorage is an excellent place to give it a go. If you do ski, you can enjoy some of the nation's best trails here in many settings and varying difficulty levels, and with grooming that's world-class—the ski club here sent its groomers to prepare the trails for the winter Olympics in Salt Lake City and Turin. There are no trail fees. The very best trail system is at **Kincaid Park** (p. 334). **Ski rental** is covered under "Equipment," on p. 327. If you don't want to ski, Anchorage also has groomed ice-skating ponds; Westchester Lagoon has more than a kilometer of **skating trails** (p. 334). At the end of the day, drive 40 miles to the **Hotel Alyeska** (p. 349) in Girdwood for the night. You will find two of Alaska's best restaurants to choose from for dinner: the **Seven Glaciers** (p. 350) and **Double Musky Inn** (p. 350).

DAY 3: Girdwood Downhill Skiing ★★★

Spend the day on the slopes of Alyeska Resort, skiing near sea level, but mostly above the tree line, and with extraordinary ocean views from the slopes and lifts. Those who don't want to ski have enough to do: swimming in the saltwater pool at the hotel, visiting the spa or shops, or skating on the outdoor rink at the base of the mountain.

DAY 4: Girdwood to Fairbanks ★

Drive to Anchorage and return the car. Your next destination is Fairbanks, 360 miles north, and I don't recommend driving it unless you are experienced on icy highways and prepared for emergencies. The very best way to go is to take the Alaska Railroad, which runs a single-car train once a week from Anchorage to Fairbanks; it's a spectacular and uniquely Alaskan ride, one of America's last flag-stop trains, but it's unlikely that its infrequent schedule will match yours. The most practical route is to fly from Anchorage to Fairbanks and rent another car when you arrive. That will leave you with most of the day to explore the town. Be sure to stop at the **UA Museum of the North** (p. 512).

DAY 5: Fairbanks Ice Carving ★

If you have timed your visit to see the Fur Rendezvous and Iditarod in Anchorage, you should also be able to see the **World Ice Art Championships** (p. 507) in Fairbanks. This amazing spectacle brings together the best ice carvers to create sculptures from enormous blocks of crystal-clear ice excavated from a Fairbanks pond. Some of the works have been the size of a two-story building. Make a point of going for a dog-sled ride while you're here, too, with **Sun Dog Express Dog Sled Tours** (p. 519) or one of the many other operators giving rides; Fairbanks is a center for the sport, with limitless miles of trails in the hilly boreal forest that extends in every direction.

Doubling Up the Seasons

Here's a little-known approach to experiencing the best of Alaska: Arrive in late March and head to Homer, on the south end of the Kenai Peninsula, as an add-on to the above winter itinerary. The community has lengthy and spectacular cross-country ski trails that usually have plenty of snow all month. At the same time, salmon fishing gets started in March in the waters of Kachemak Bay—there's even a fishing derby joined by hundreds of boats. You can go salmon fishing in the morning and ski in the afternoon! (See "Late March Is Perfect," p. 415.)

DAY 6: Chena Hot Springs Resort ★★

Drive a little more than an hour into the Bush for a visit to the hot springs, a unique resort (for example, one of the buildings is made entirely of ice) nestled in the rounded mountains of winter. **Chena Hot Springs Resort** (p. 535) has its flaws, but the experience of floating in a pond of hot artesian water on a day when the

Chena Hot Springs.

air around is below zero more than makes up for them. If you want to do more than soak, lots of activities are available, including snowmobiling and dog mushing. After dark, step outside for the unsurpassed aurora viewing out here, beyond city lights.

DAY 7: Fairbanks

Today you can take one more swim or ski run before returning your car in Fairbanks and returning home by air.

CRUISING ALASKA'S COAST

by Fran Wenograd Golden
and Gene Sloan

5

Last year Alaska celebrated its 50th anniversary of statehood, with celebrations throughout the state. But cruise lines weren't in a very celebratory mood. The global economic downturn cut into Alaska cruise tourism significantly. And in an attempt to fill ships—and at least try to recover some revenue from onboard sales and shore excursions—the cruise lines cut their fares to the lowest prices ever. A $299 offer from Princess Cruises for weeklong sailing in May even earned a mention in the *Wall Street Journal;* followers of cruise sales wondered, "How low can they go?"

With less demand, added to a $50 per cruise passenger head tax passed by Alaska voters in 2006 (presumably to support the infrastructure at the ports and enforce environmental compliance, but a debatable subject), the cruise lines said enough is enough. Royal Caribbean, Princess Cruises, and Norwegian Cruise Line all announced they were pulling a ship each from the market for 2010, and Holland America also reduced capacity, dropping about 20 Alaska sailings. There will be about 120,000 fewer passengers this year in total, according to the Alaska Travel Industry Association. And there were estimates some businesses in the key cruise towns could see a 25% reduction in sales, depending on whether or not the remaining cruise passengers feel like spending.

That's not necessarily a bad thing for travelers in 2010. Alaska's popularity as a top summer cruise destination is mostly the result of its own natural splendor. Fewer crowds will only highlight that attribute. Still, with less supply, bargain prices may be harder to come by this year.

The number of cruise passengers in the 49th state topped the 1 million mark in 2007 and 2008. It was unclear whether 2009 numbers would reflect a decline or whether those cheap fares would even things out.

The cruise season is dictated by the weather, and generally runs from about mid-May to mid-September.

Especially for first time visitors, a cruise is an excellent way to get the lay of the land and an introduction to Alaska. Cruise passengers visit the towns and wilderness areas of the Southeast (the Inside Passage, also known as the Panhandle) or the Gulf of Alaska by day, and burrow into their ships for effortless travel by night. The lack of roads between towns makes the waters of the Inside Passage the region's de facto highway.

Your options—apart from a somewhat limited airline schedule—are, basically, taking a cruise ship or the Alaska Marine Highway System (the state ferries). You have to be willing to invest more time—both for the actual traveling and for the planning—to utilize the ferries. And you have to be willing to give up the comforts and diversions of the average cruise ship. Then again, the ferry *does*

FACING PAGE: **Royal Caribbean's *Radiance of the Seas*, sailing near Hubbard Glacier.**

give you unlimited stops along the way and a chance to meet Alaskan residents not only in major cruise ports, but also in smaller, less-visited communities. (See "Exploring Southeast Alaska," in chapter 6.) For most people, the luxury of cruise travel is preferable to the rough-and-ready nature of ferry transportation.

No matter how much revenue cruise passengers (and ships' crews) generate for merchants in the ports visited, some locals aren't as welcoming as they might be. Alaskans are known for their hospitality, but they have their limits (don't we all?). The presence of too many cruise passengers has unquestionably spoiled some of Alaska's quaint places. During the height of the cruise season, once-charming streets are transformed into virtual carnival midways jammed wall to wall with vacationers from simultaneous ship landings. As a result, no matter what residents may say, service standards suffer somewhat—especially toward the end of the season when Alaskans have been subjected to a steady stream of strange faces for several months and can get, ahem, a little grumpy.

Some communities feel that the cultural bulldozing brought by cruise ships is not worth the economic benefit and have placed limits on the number of ships that can come in to port in addition to taxes based on passenger count.

The cruise lines have taken the prevailing mood very seriously. Individual lines have appointed community affairs officers with orders to smarten up the public's perception of cruising and cruise operators. And the industry, as a whole, appointed John Binkley, a prominent lifelong political figure (he's a former state senator, gubernatorial candidate, and chairman of the state-run Alaska Railroad) to liaise with both the elected officials in Juneau and the voters who put them in power. Cruise companies reportedly spent $2 million fighting the $50 head tax alone. They have been calling for a repeal—and Carnival Corp. Chairman Micky Arison (whose company owns Carnival, Holland America, and Princess) even hinted in 2009 he might pursue legal action claiming the tax is unconstitutional. Last year, the lines did successfully get a delay in new wastewater dumping regulations that were to take effect this year.

As a visitor, you can avoid much of the human congestion caused by ships by choosing a small-ship cruise that spends more time enjoying the wilderness and the small towns that big ships can't reach. On the small ships you might visit Haines, for instance, or Cordova or Metlakatla and a dozen other places where the big guys don't (or, at least, seldom) go.

On the other hand, riding a megaship is a different kind of fun—the ship itself is an attraction, with far more amenities than any of the towns along the way. If you need to relax and leave all stresses of life at home behind—and if seeing Alaska wilderness isn't the most important part of your trip—a big ship is the way to go. Plus, you can still get a taste of some wilderness areas on shore excursions.

Another way to avoid some of the disadvantages of overcrowding and service problems is to choose an early season cruise—say, the last couple of weeks in May. One other option: You can always travel independently after the cruise to the real Alaska, inland from the cruise ports. (For more on the relative benefits of big versus small cruise ships, see "Weighing Your Cruise Options," below.)

In this chapter, we'll go through the cruise options available in the state, focusing primarily on those that provide a true in-depth experience. For even more information, pick up a copy of *Frommer's Alaska Cruises & Ports of Call* (Wiley Publishing, Inc.).

WEIGHING YOUR CRUISE OPTIONS

Your three main questions in choosing a cruise in Alaska are "When should I go?," "Where do I want to go?," and "How big a ship?"

When to Go

Alaska is very much a seasonal, as opposed to year-round, cruise destination, generally open to cruising from May through September (although some smaller ships start up in late Apr). May and September are considered the shoulder season, and lower brochure rates are offered during these months (and more aggressive discounts as well; watch your local newspaper and check the Internet). Cruising in May can be extremely pleasant—the real, near-gridlock-inducing crowds have yet to arrive, and if you're lucky, the temperatures will already be warm. Locals, coming off what is usually a fairly isolated winter, are friendlier than they are later in the season, when they're tired and, frankly, pretty much ready to see the tourists go home. There is also the statistical fact that May in the Inside Passage ports is one of the driest months in the season. Late September also offers the advantage of fewer fellow tourists clogging the ports. The warmest months are June, July, and August, with temperatures generally around 50° to 80°F (10°–27°C) during the day, and cooler at night. But warmer days can occur as well—and when it gets above 80°F (27°C) in, say, Juneau, you can be sure there will be plenty of local speculation about global warming. Pack a parka, but also pack some T-shirts. You will need to bring along a sweater or two, and a rain slicker is a good idea. June 21 is the longest day of the year, with the sky lit virtually all night. June tends to be drier than July and August, and April and May are drier than September (though in early Apr you may encounter freezing rain and other vestiges of winter). Somebody once said, "Everybody complains about the weather but nobody does anything about it." And that's very much the way it is in Alaska. The simple fact is that, in Alaska, perhaps more than in many other states, the weather is going to do what it's going to do. You may be forced to don a coat, hat, and gloves in July and August—theoretically, the months in which one might expect higher temperatures. On the other hand, we've also been comfortable in short sleeves on deck in Glacier Bay in May and September—when, again, theoretically, it should be a little cooler. You may encounter so much wind-driven rain in Skagway that you'd think the moisture was moving horizontally. But it might also be completely dry and so sunny you have to put on sunblock so you don't burn—and pack a bathing suit because you may even want to take a dip in the ship's pool. In other words, be prepared for anything.

If you are considering traveling in a shoulder month, keep in mind that some shops don't open until Memorial Day, and the visitor season is generally considered over on Labor Day (although cruise lines operate well into Sept).

Inside Passage or the Gulf of Alaska?

The Inside Passage runs through the area of Alaska known as Southeast (which the locals also call "the Panhandle"), that narrow strip of the state—islands, mainland coastal communities, and mountains—that runs from the Canadian border in the south to the start of the Gulf in the north, just above the Juneau/Haines/

Skagway area. The islands on the western side of the area afford cruise ships a welcome degree of protection from the sea and its attendant rough waters (hence the name "Inside Passage"). Because of that shelter, such ports as Ketchikan, Wrangell, Petersburg, and others are reached with less rocking and rolling, and thus less risk of seasickness. Sitka is not on the Inside Passage (it's on the Pacific side of Baranof Island), but that beautiful little community is included in most Inside Passage cruise itineraries.

Southeast encompasses the capital city, **Juneau,** and townships influenced by the former Russian presence in the state (**Sitka,** for instance), the Tlingit and Haida Native cultures (**Ketchikan),** and the great gold rush of 1898 **(Skagway).** It is a land of rainforests, mountains, inlets, and glaciers (including Margerie, Johns Hopkins, Muir, and the others contained within the boundaries of **Glacier Bay National Park**). The region is rich in wildlife, especially of the marine variety. It is a scenic delight. But then, what part of Alaska isn't?

The other major cruising area is the **Southcentral** region's Gulf of Alaska, usually referred to by the cruise lines as the "Glacier Discovery Route" or the "Voyage of the Glaciers," or some such catchy title. "Gulf of Alaska," after all, sounds pretty bland.

The coastline of the Gulf is that arc of land from just north of Glacier Bay to the Kenai Peninsula. Southcentral also takes in the truly spectacular **Prince William Sound;** the **Cook Inlet,** on the northern side of the peninsula; **Anchorage,** Alaska's biggest city; the year-round **Alyeska Resort** at Girdwood, 40 miles from Anchorage; the **Matanuska** and **Susitna** valleys (the "Mat-Su"), a fertile agricultural region renowned for the record size of some of its garden produce; and part of the Alaska Mountain Range.

The principal Southcentral terminus ports are **Seward** or **Whittier** for Anchorage. Ships instead carry passengers from Seward or Whittier to Anchorage by bus or train. (Getting all the way around the peninsula to Anchorage would add a day to the cruise.) Let us stress that going on a Gulf cruise does not mean that you don't visit any of the Inside Passage. The big difference is that, whereas the more popular Inside Passage cruise itineraries run 7 nights round-trip to and from Vancouver or Seattle, the Gulf routing is 7 nights one-way—northbound or southbound—between Vancouver and Seward or Vancouver and Whittier. A typical Gulf itinerary also visits such Inside Passage ports as **Ketchikan, Juneau, Sitka,** and/or **Skagway.**

The Gulf's glaciers are quite dazzling and every bit as spectacular as their counterparts to the south. **College Fjord,** for instance, is lined with glaciers—16 of them, each one grander than the last. On one cruise, Fran saw incredible calving at **Harvard Glacier,** with chunks of 400- and 500-year-old ice falling off and crashing into the water with thunderous sounds every few minutes (worries about global warming aside, the sight was spectacular). Another favorite part of a Gulf cruise, though, is the visit to the gigantic **Hubbard Glacier**—at 6 miles, Alaska's longest—at the head of Yakutat Bay (our all-time favorite, by the way— where the chunks in the water may remind you of ice in a giant punch bowl). Not to raise again the specter of global warming, but, sadly, most of Alaska's glaciers are in retreat, some receding quite rapidly. On a recent visit to Sawyer Glacier, the ice face had gone so far back that the ship was unable to get closer than a mile or so. Not the best way to view a glacier.

Cruisetours combine a cruise with a land tour, either before or after the cruise. Typical packages link the cruise with a 3- to 5-night Anchorage/Denali/Fairbanks tour, a 4- to 7-night Yukon tour (which visits Anchorage, Denali, and Fairbanks on the way), or a 5- to 7-night tour of the Canadian Rockies. Holland America, Princess, and Royal Caribbean/Celebrity lead the big-ship cruisetour market. Cruise West leads by a wide margin in the small-ship category. Even if you book with another cruise line, chances are that at least some portions of your land tour will be bought from one of these operators.

Big Ship or Small?

Imagine an elephant. Now imagine your pet pug dog, Sparky. That's about the size difference between your options in the Alaska market: behemoth modern ships and small, more exploratory coastal vessels.

SMALL SHIPS Just as big cruise ships are mostly for people who want every resort amenity, **small** or **alternative ships** are best suited for people who prefer a casual, crowd-free cruise experience that gives passengers a chance to get up close and personal with Alaska's natural surroundings and wildlife. Small ships offer little in terms of amenities: They usually have small cabins, only one lounge/bar and dining room, and no exercise facilities, entertainment, or organized activities. There are little or no stabilizers on most of these smaller ships, and the ride can be bumpy in open water—which isn't much of a problem on Inside Passage itineraries, since most of the cruising area is protected from sea waves. They are also difficult for travelers with disabilities, as none of the ships in the market have elevators. Despite all of this, they're universally more expensive than the big ships and offer fewer discounts. That's the minus side.

But a big plus, thanks to their smaller size, is that these ships can go places that larger ships can't, such as narrow fjords, uninhabited islands, and smaller ports that cater mostly to small fishing vessels. Due to their shallow draft, they can nose right up to sheer cliff faces, bird rookeries, bobbing icebergs, and cascading waterfalls that you can literally reach out and touch. Also, sea animals are not as intimidated by these ships, so you might find yourself having a rather close encounter with a humpback whale, or watching other sea mammals bobbing in the ship's wake—cruising recently in Misty Fjords, Fran and her fellow passengers on a Cruise West ship watched through binoculars as a shore-side bear stood to its full height, the captain positioning the ship a safe distance from the creature for a good half-hour so everyone could take in the sight. The decks on these ships are closer to the waterline, too, giving passengers a more intimate view than they would get from the high decks of the large cruise ships. Some of these ships stop at ports on a daily basis, like the larger ships, while some avoid ports almost entirely, exploring natural areas instead. Small ships also have the flexibility to change direction as opportunities arise—say, to go where whales have been sighted and to linger awhile once a sighting's been made.

Visitors aboard large ships have access to the real, natural Alaska, too, with frequent whale spottings. But since you are calling mostly at popular ports, to dig further you really need to do some of the more remote (and pricey) shore excursions, so great is the disjunction between the glitzy modern ships and the real world outside. Visitors aboard small ships will have simpler accommodations and not much onboard entertainment, but will get an experience that's more intimate, allowing them to really get in touch with the place they've come to see. Choose your ship accordingly.

BIG SHIPS The **big ships** in the Alaska market fall generally into two categories: midsize ships and megaships. Carrying as many as 2,670 passengers, the **megaships** look and feel like floating resorts. Big on glitz, they offer loads of activities, attract many families and (especially in Alaska) seniors, offer a large number of public rooms (including fancy casinos and fully equipped gyms and spas), and provide a wide variety of meal and entertainment options. And though they may feature 1 or 2 formal nights per trip, the ambience is generally casual (with casual buffet options now available on formal nights and some people not dressing up at all; and we've noticed a trend among those who do—fewer tuxes and ball gowns and more dark suits and cocktail dresses). The Alaska vessels of the Carnival, Celebrity, Princess (with the exception of the *Royal Princess*), and Royal Caribbean fleets all fit in this category, as do Norwegian Cruise Line's *Star* and *Pearl*, and Holland America's *Zuiderdam* and *Westerdam*. **Midsize ships** in Alaska fall into two segments: the ultraluxurious, such as Regent Seven Seas' *Seven Seas Navigator* and Silversea Cruises' *Silver Shadow*, and the modern midsize, such as Holland America's *Veendam, Ryndam, Amsterdam, Volendam, Zaandam,* and *Statendam* of Holland America Line, and the *Royal Princess* of Princess Cruises. In general, the size of these ships is less significant than the general onboard atmosphere. Both the midsize ships and the megaships have a great range of facilities for passengers. Cabins on these ships range from

Sick Ships

Every year, hundreds of cruise-ship passengers and plenty of visitors on shore come down with vomiting and diarrhea caused by a bug now known as the norovirus. The good news is, it's rarer in summer than winter. Still, the illness is no fun. It lasts a day or two and is rarely serious, although some passengers do end up in the hospital because of dehydration. The virus is extremely contagious from the first symptoms until at least 3 days and up to 2 weeks after it clears up. Touching a contaminated handrail and then your face is enough to catch it. To minimize your chances of contracting the virus, wash your hands frequently, drink bottled water, and avoid eating raw food onboard, especially shellfish. The Centers for Disease Control and Prevention (CDC) also recommended in 1998 that passengers 65 and older or those with chronic illnesses check with their doctors before taking a cruise. The CDC website (www.cdc.gov/nceh/vsp) posts sanitation inspection scores for each ship. Type "norovirus" into the search page to find a fact sheet. Most cruise lines now have hand sanitizer stations at the boarding ramp and throughout the ship—including at the entryways to the gangway, buffet area, and the dining rooms. Their use is mostly voluntary, but our advice is—do.

cubbyholes to large suites, depending on the ship and the type of cabin you book. Big dining rooms and a tremendous variety of cuisines are the norm. These ships carry a lot of people and can, at times, feel crowded.

The sizes of these big ships also come with **three major drawbacks** for passengers: (1) They can't sail into narrow passages or shallow-water ports, (2) their size and inflexible schedules limit their ability to stop or even slow down when wildlife is spotted, and (3) when their passengers disembark in a town, they tend to overwhelm it, limiting your ability to get insight into the real Alaska communities. But on the plus side, they offer dozens of excursions at each port so you can get well out of town.

THE BEST CRUISE EXPERIENCES IN ALASKA

Cruise lines are in the business of giving their guests a good time, so they've all got something going for them. Here are our picks for Alaska's best, in a few different categories.

o **The Best Ships for Luxury:** Luxury in Alaska is defined in 2010 by **Regent Seven Seas** and **Silversea.** If you want a more casual kind of luxury (a really nice ship with a no-tie-required policy), the *Seven Seas Navigator* offers just that on an all-suite vessel (most cabins have private balconies) with excellent cuisine. Silversea, on the other hand, represents a slick, Italian-influenced, slightly more formal luxury experience with all the perks—big suite cabins and excellent food, linens, service, and companions. Both lines include fine wine and booze in their cruise fares. For the ultimate Alaska experience in a small-ship setting, check out the yachts of **American Safari Cruises**, where soft adventure comes with luxury accoutrements.

o **The Best of the Mainstream Ships:** Every line's most recent ships are beautiful, but **Celebrity's** *Infinity* is a true stunner, as is its sister ship, *Millennium.* These modern vessels, with their extensive art collections, cushy public rooms, and expanded spa areas, give Celebrity a formidable presence in Alaska. And the late-model *Sapphire Princess* and *Diamond Princess* have raised the art of building big ships to new heights. Both of these vessels will again be in Inside Passage service this year from Vancouver.

o **The Best of the Small Ships:** **Cruise West** is the most prominent of a dwindling number of small-ship players, now that Clipper, Glacier Bay Cruiseline, and Majestic America Line have all vanished from the scene. Our favorite of the ships Cruise West is sending to Alaska in 2010 is the 102-passenger *Spirit of Endeavor* (formerly the *Newport Clipper*), which offers a higher level of comfort for a small vessel.

o **The Best Ships for Families:** All the major lines have well-established kids' programs, with **Carnival, Royal Caribbean,** and **Norwegian Cruise Line** leading the pack in terms of facilities and activities. **Princess** gets a nod for its National Park Service Junior Ranger program to teach kids about glaciers and Alaska wildlife. (They can even earn a Junior Ranger badge.)

- **The Best Ships for Pampering:** It's a toss-up—Celebrity's *Infinity* and *Millennium* offer wonderful AquaSpas complete with thalassotherapy pools and a wealth of soothing and beautifying treatments, and the solariums on **Royal Caribbean's** *Rhapsody of the Seas* and *Radiance of the Seas* offer relaxing indoor pool retreats. We are also fans of the thermal suite (complete with hydrotherapy pool) in the Greenhouse Spas on **Holland America's** *Zuiderdam* and *Westerdam*.

- **The Best Shipboard Cuisine: Regent Seven Seas** is tops in this category. And the expertly prepared and presented cuisine on **Silversea's** *Silver Shadow* must also come in for some props. While this may surprise some, of the mainstream lines, we like the buffet and dining room offerings of **Carnival**—flavorful food, well prepared. The *Carnival Spirit* in Alaska also boasts the Nouveau Supper Club ($30 service charge per person), where you can enjoy just about as fine a meal as you're likely to find anywhere. **Norwegian Cruise Line's** teppanyaki restaurant ($25 per person charge) is also an experience not to be missed—yummy food and a show by knife-wielding chefs.

- **The Best Ships for Onboard Activities:** The ships operated by **Carnival** and **Royal Caribbean** offer a very full roster of onboard activities that range from the sublime (lectures) to the ridiculous (contests designed to get passengers to do or say outrageous things). **Princess's** ScholarShip@Sea program is a real winner, with excitingly packaged classes in such diverse subjects as photography, personal computers, cooking, and even pottery.

- **The Best Ships for Entertainment:** Look to the big ships here. **Carnival** and **Royal Caribbean** are tops when it comes to an overall package of show productions, nightclub acts, lounge performances, and audience-participation entertainment. **Princess** also offers particularly well-done—if somewhat less lavishly staged—shows. **Holland America** has not, historically, been noted for its entertainment package, but the company has improved considerably in the show lounge in recent years, including adding performances by magicians and comedians.

- **The Best Ships for Whale-Watching:** If the whales come close enough, you can see them from all the ships in Alaska—Fran spotted a couple of orcas from her cabin balcony on a recent Holland America cruise, for instance. Smaller ships, though—such as those operated by **American Safari, Lindblad,** and **Cruise West**—might actually change course to follow a whale. Get your cameras and binoculars ready!

- **The Best Ships for Cruisetours: Princess, Holland America,** and the twin-brand Royal Caribbean Cruises (which owns **Royal Caribbean International** and **Celebrity**) are the market leaders in getting you into the Interior of Alaska either before or after your cruise. They own their own deluxe motorcoaches and railcars. Princess and Holland America Line (HAL) also own lodges and hotels. After many years in the business, these two really know what they're doing. Royal Caribbean is a comparative latecomer, but its land company, Royal Celebrity Tours, with some of the finest rolling stock (rail and road) around, has made huge strides. Most of the other lines actually buy their land product components from Princess or HAL. One of Holland America's strengths is its 3- and 4-night cruises combined with an Alaska/Yukon land package. The company offers exclusive entry into the Yukon's Kluane National Park, and they've added another Yukon gem—Tombstone Territorial Park, near Dawson City, a region of staggering wilderness beauty, Native architecture, stunning vistas, and wildlife. Princess is arguably stronger in 7-night Gulf of Alaska cruises in conjunction with Denali/Fairbanks or Kenai Peninsula land arrangements. Princess's Copper River Lodge is by the entrance to Wrangell–St. Elias National Park.

o **The Best Ports:** Juneau and Sitka are our favorites. Juneau is one of the most visually pleasing small cities anywhere and certainly the prettiest capital city in America (once you get beyond all the tourist shops near the pier). It's fronted by the Gastineau Channel and backed by Mount Juneau and Mount Roberts, offers the very accessible Mendenhall Glacier, and is otherwise surrounded by wilderness—and it's a really fun city to visit, too. Recently, an addition to the tourist attraction roster is a drive past the governor's mansion, once the residence of former Governor Sarah Palin. Sitka's Russian architecture, historic totem pole park, and Raptor Rehabilitation Center earn it the nod here, not to mention the fact we've had very pleasant conversations with Sitka locals about topics ranging from the fishing season to local politics—when the first non–locally owned T-shirt shop was railroaded in a couple of years ago, the whole town was abuzz. No town in Alaska is more historically significant than Skagway, with its old buildings so quaint you might think you stepped into a Disney version of what a gold-rush town should look like. But the arrival of so many glitzy, expensive jewelry stores imported from the Caribbean has impacted our impressions of that community. Still, if you can get yourself into the right frame of mind, and if you can recall the history of the place—the gold-rush frenzy that literally put the town on the map—it's easier to capture the true spirit of Skagway. For a more low-key Alaska experience, take the ferry from Skagway to Haines, which reminds us of the folksy, frontier Alaska depicted on the TV show *Northern Exposure* and is a great place to spot eagles and other wildlife. Some ships also stop at Haines as a port of call, usually for a few hours after Skagway.

o **The Best Shore Excursions:** Flightseeing and helicopter trips in Alaska are absolutely unforgettable ways to check out the scenery, if you can afford them. But airborne tours tend to be pretty pricey—sometimes approaching $600 a head. A helicopter trip to a dog-sled camp at the top of a glacier (usually among the priciest of the offerings) affords both incredibly pretty views and a chance to try your hand at the truly Alaskan sport of dog sledding. (Yes, even in summer: If there is not enough snow, the sleds are fitted with wheels.) It's a great way to earn bragging rights with the folks back home. For a less extravagant excursion, nothing beats a ride on a clear day on the White Pass and Yukon Route Railway out of Skagway to Canada—the route followed by the gold stampeders of '98. The railway a couple of years back expanded its rail system so that some of its trains go not just to Fraser at the border, but all the way to Carcross (formerly known as Caribou Crossing) in the Yukon Territory (adding more than 30 miles by rebuilding old track). While you're riding the rails, try to imagine what it was like for those gold seekers crossing the same track on foot! We also like to get active with kayak and mountain-biking excursions offered by most lines at most ports. In addition to affording a chance to work off those shipboard calories, these excursions typically provide optimum opportunities for spotting eagles, bears, seals, and other wildlife. Another, less hectic shore excursion that's become increasingly popular is whale-watching. Recently on an evening excursion from Juneau in May, passengers on one of the whale-watching boats got the thrill of seeing an entire pod of orcas, more than a dozen of the giant creatures frolicking well within view. For wildlife lovers, the Sea Otter & Wildlife Quest tour in Sitka guarantees you'll spot whales, bears, otters, or other impressive wildlife or your money back.

BOOKING YOUR CRUISE

Every cruise line has a brochure full of beautiful glossy photos. You'll see low starting rates on the charts, but look further, and you'll realize those are for tiny inside cubicles; most of the cabins sell for much more. Sometimes the brochures feature published rates that are nothing more than a pie-in-the-sky wish (most customers will pay less). The cruise lines would like you to look at the early-bird savings column and book your cruise early (by mid-Feb for average savings of 25%–30% and sometimes as much as 50%). In 2009, however, if you waited until late March or early April, you saved significantly more. Part of the reason is that travelers' concerns over the economic downturn in general have caused them to book vacations closer to the time they want to travel. Waiting last year meant the appearance of such prices as the crazy $299 in April for May cruises. But keep in mind these kinds of prices are for a limited number of cabins, and getting last-minute airfare is not always that easy. Plus, with less supply in 2010, cruises may actually sell out. So here's our suggestion: Decide what month you want to travel, and keep careful track of what's happening in the market come mid-February into March. You can consult with an experienced cruise travel agent or do the checking yourself online. Check websites that track cruise sales, including Gene's own *USA Today* Cruise Log Blog (www.usatoday.com/travel/cruises). In reality, you may be able to get the cruise for 40% or 50% off, or even a crazy price, such as $299 at the last minute (say in late Apr for a May cruise). But if you don't reserve space early, you could just as easily be left out in the cold. Keep in mind that the most expensive and the cheapest cabins tend to sell out first. The midrange rooms are by and large the last to go. Increasingly aggressive marketing by the cruise lines to previous passengers is adding to the increase in early bookings.

Most people still book their cruises through **travel agents** and, though the **Internet** has knocked some of those agents out of business, many of the remaining traditional travel agencies have created their own websites in an effort to keep pace.

So which is the better way to book a cruise these days? The answer can be both. If you're computer savvy, have a good handle on all the elements that go into a cruise, and have narrowed down the choices to a few cruise lines that appeal to you, websites are a great way to trawl the seas at your own pace and check out last-minute deals, which can be dramatic. On the other hand, you'll barely get a stitch

Shore excursions offered by the cruise lines provide a chance for you to get off the ship and explore the sights close up, taking in the history, nature, and culture of the region—from exploring gold-rush-era streets to experiencing Native Alaskan traditions such as totem carving.

Some excursions are of the walking-tour or bus-tour variety, but many others are activity oriented: Cruise passengers have the opportunity to go sea kayaking, mountain biking, horseback riding, salmon fishing, and even rock climbing or zip-lining through the treetops, and to see the sights by seaplane or helicopter—and maybe even to land on a glacier and go for a walk. Occasionally, with some of the smaller cruise lines, you'll find quirky excursions, such as a visit with local artists in their studios. Some lines even offer scuba diving and snorkeling. The cruise lines vet the operators, so you do get assurance you're dealing with pros.

With some lines, select shore excursions are included in your cruise fare, but with most lines they are an added (though very worthwhile) expense.

of personalized service searching for and booking a cruise online. If you need help getting a refund or arranging special meals or other matters, or deciding which cabin to choose, you're on your own. In addition, agents usually know about cruise and airfare discounts that the lines won't necessarily publicize on their websites. So the best bet, to our way of thinking, is to do your research electronically and, better informed, then visit a travel agent to make the reservation.

Booking a Small-Ship Cruise

The small-ship companies in Alaska—American Safari, Cruise West, and Lindblad Expeditions—all offer real niche-oriented cruise experiences, attracting passengers who have a very good idea of the kind of experience they want (usually educational and/or adventurous, and always casual and small scale). In many cases, a large percentage of passengers on any given cruise will have sailed with the line before. Because of all this, and because the passenger capacity of these small ships is so low, in general you're not going to find the kind of deep discounts you do with the large ships. Still, for the most part, these lines rely on agents to handle their bookings, taking very few reservations directly. All of the lines have a list of agents with whom they do considerable business, and they can hook you up with an agent if you call (or e-mail) and ask for an agent near you.

Booking a Mainstream Cruise

If you don't know a good travel agent already, try to find one through your friends, preferably those who have cruised before. For the most personal service, look for an agent in your local area, and for the most knowledgeable service, look for an agent who has cruising experience. It's perfectly okay to ask an agent questions about his or her personal knowledge of the product, such as whether he or she has ever cruised in Alaska or with one of the lines you're considering. The easiest way to be sure the agent is experienced in booking cruises is to work with a **cruise-only agency** (meaning that the whole agency specializes in cruises), or to find somebody in a more conventional agency who is a **cruise specialist** (meaning he or she handles that agency's cruise business). If you are calling a full-service travel agency, ask for the **cruise desk,** which is where you'll find these specialists. If the agency doesn't have a cruise desk, per se, it might be wise to check elsewhere.

A good and easy rule of thumb to maximize your chances of finding an agent who has cruise experience and who won't rip you off is to book with agencies that are members of the **Cruise Lines International Association (CLIA; ☎754/224-2200;** www.cruising.org), the main industry association. Membership in the **American Society of Travel Agents (ASTA; ☎800/275-2782;** www. travelsense.org) ensures that the agency is monitored for ethical practices, although it does not designate cruise experience.

You can tap into the Internet sites of these organizations for easy access to agents in your area.

The Cost: What's Included & What's Not

However you arrange to buy your cruise, what you basically have in hand at the end is a contract for transportation, lodging, dining, entertainment, housekeeping, and assorted other miscellaneous services that will be provided to you over the course of your vacation. It's important, though, to remember what extras are *not* included in your cruise fare. Are you getting a price that includes port charges, taxes, fees, and insurance, or are you getting a cruise-only fare? Are airfare and airport transfers included, or do you have to book them separately (either as an add-on to the cruise fare or on your own)? Make sure you're comparing apples with apples when making price comparisons. Read the fine print!

Aside from **airfare,** which is usually not included in your cruise fare (see more on air arrangements below), the priciest addition to your cruise fare, particularly in Alaska, will likely be **shore excursions.** Ranging from about $35 for a bus tour to $299 and up (sometimes as high as $600) for a lengthy helicopter or seaplane flightseeing excursion, these sightseeing tours are designed to help cruise passengers make the most of their time at the ports the ship visits, but they can add a hefty sum to your vacation costs.

You'll also want to add to your calculations **tips for the ship's crew.** Tips are given at the end of the cruise, and passengers should reserve at least $10 per passenger per day for tips for the room steward, waiter, and busperson. (In practice, we find that most people tend to give a little more.) Additional tips to other personnel, such as the head waiter or maitre d,' are at your discretion. On small ships, all tips often go into one pot, which the crew divides up after the cruise.

Most ships charge extra for **alcoholic beverages** (including wine at dinner) and for soda. Nonbubbly soft drinks, such as lemonade and iced tea, are included in your cruise fare. (Regent's *Seven Seas Navigator* and Silversea's *Silver Shadow* both include alcoholic beverages in the cruise price.) You'll also want to set some money aside for optional offerings such as spa treatments, fancy dinners in your ship's alternative dining room (which may carry a price tag of up to $30 per person), shipboard photos, Internet access, and other temptations.

Money-Saving Strategies

Cruise pricing is a fluid medium, and there are a number of strategies you can use to save money off the booking price.

EARLY & LATE BOOKING

When you **book in advance,** in a typical year, you can expect to save 25% to 50% off the brochure rate if you book your Alaska cruise by mid- to late February of the year of the cruise. If the cabins do not fill up by the cutoff date, the early-bird rate may be extended. We've seen starting early-bird brochure prices for 2010 as low as $644 for an inside cabin on an early-season weeklong cruise.

If the cabins are still not full as the cruise season begins, cruise lines typically start marketing special deals, usually through their top-producing travel agents. With more limited numbers of ships in the market in 2010, it's our feeling that these last-minute discounts, which can run as high as 50% to 75%, will be less common than in some previous years (and certainly less crazy than in 2009). And keep in mind that last-minute deals are usually for a very limited number of cabins. Planning your Alaska cruise vacation well in advance and taking advantage of early booking discounts is still the best way to go.

SHOULDER SEASON DISCOUNTS

You can save by booking a cruise in the **shoulder months of May or September,** when cruise pricing is lower than during the high summer months. Typically, Alaska cruises are divided into budget, low, economy, value, standard, and peak seasons, but since these overlap quite a bit from cruise line to cruise line, we can lump them into three basic periods:

1. **Budget/Low/Economy Season:** May and September
2. **Value/Standard Season:** Early June and late August
3. **Peak Season:** Late June, July, and early to mid-August

DISCOUNTS FOR THIRD & FOURTH PASSENGERS & GROUPS

Most ships offer highly discounted rates for third and fourth passengers sharing a cabin with two full-fare passengers, even if those two have booked at a discounted rate. It may mean a tight squeeze, but it'll save you a bundle. Some lines offer **special rates for kids,** usually on a seasonal or select-sailings basis, that may include free or discounted airfare.

One of the best ways to get a cruise deal is to book as a **group** of at least 16 people in at least eight cabins. The savings include a discounted rate, and at least the cruise portion of the 16th ticket will be free. Ask your travel agent about any group deals they may offer.

SPECIAL DISCOUNTS

With cruise lines having a difficult time filling their Alaska ships in 2009, they resorted to all sorts of limited-time discount offers. There were two-for-one airfares, free shore excursions, onboard credits (the cruise line gives you, say, $200 per person you can spend any way you please onboard), and offers of cabin upgrades. We can't predict which of these perks will reappear in 2010, or when. But keep an eye out, as they can amount to significant savings.

Booking Air Travel Through the Cruise Line

Except during special promotions, airfare to the port of embarkation is rarely included in the cruise rates, so you'll have to purchase airfare on your own or take advantage of the cruise lines' air add-ons, which is usually a better option. Why? First of all, as frequent customers of the airlines, cruise lines tend to get decent (if not the best) discounts on airfare, which they pass on to their customers. Second, booking air with the cruise line allows the line to keep track of your whereabouts. If your plane is late, for instance, they may hold the boat, though not always. When you book air travel with your cruise line, most lines will include **transfers** from the airport to the ship, saving you the hassle of getting a cab. (If you book the air travel on your own, you may still be able to get the transfers separately—ask your agent about this.) Be aware that once the air ticket is issued by the cruise line, you usually aren't allowed to make changes. It may pay to book your own air transportation if you are using frequent-flier miles and can get your air travel for free, or if you are particular about which carrier route you take. Or you may see a much better deal than the cruise line is offering.

Choosing Your Cabin

Cruise-ship cabins run from tiny boxes with accordion doors and bunk beds to palatial multiroom suites with hot tubs on the balcony. Which is right for you? Price will likely be a big factor here, but so should the vacation style you prefer. If, for instance, you plan to spend a lot of quiet time in your cabin, you should probably consider booking the biggest room you can afford. If, conversely, you plan to be out on deck all the time checking out the glaciers and wildlife, you might be just as happy with a smaller (and cheaper) cabin to crash in at the end of the day. Cabins are either **inside** (without a window or porthole) or **outside** (with), the latter being more expensive. On the big ships, the more deluxe outside cabins may also come with **private verandas.** The cabins are usually described by price (highest to lowest), category (suite, deluxe, superior, standard, economy, and others), and furniture configuration ("sitting area with two lower beds," for example).

Special Menu Requests

The cruise line should be informed at the time you make your reservations about any special dietary requests you have. Some lines offer kosher menus, and all will have vegetarian, low-fat, low-salt, vegan, and sugar-free options available.

Smoking

Cruise lines have recently been reevaluating their smoking policies, and some, including Celebrity Cruises and Regent Seven Seas, have moved to ban smoking in cabins and on cabin balconies (Royal Caribbean does not allow smoking in cabins but does allow it on cabin balconies). Smoking is generally not allowed in shipboard theaters, show lounges, or dining rooms, and may be restricted to certain bars (many ships now have cigar lounges) or even certain sides of the ship (open decks on starboard side only on Royal Caribbean vessels, for instance). If you are a smoker, check with your line in advance. If you are not a smoker, you will no doubt be relieved policies are being enhanced.

THE SMALL-SHIP CRUISE LINES

Small ships allow you to see Alaska from sea level, without the kind of distractions you get aboard the big ships—no glitzy interiors, no big shows or loud music, no casinos, no spas, and no crowds, as the largest of these ships carries only 138 passengers. You're immersed in the 49th state from the minute you wake up to the minute you fall asleep, and, for the most part, you're left alone to form your own opinions. Personally, we feel that despite these ships' higher cost, they provide, by far, the better cruise experience for those who really want to get the feel of Alaska.

Small-ship itineraries can be categorized as **port-to-port,** meaning they mimic the larger ships in simply sailing between port towns; **soft adventure,** meaning they provide some outdoors experiences such as hiking and kayaking, while not requiring participants to be trained athletes; and **active adventure,** meaning the hiking and kayaking will be the real focus of the trip, and may be strenuous.

On all of these types of cruises, the small-ship experience tends toward education rather than glitzy entertainment. You'll likely get **informal and informative lectures** and sometimes video presentations on Alaska wildlife, history, and Native culture. Meals are served in open seatings, so you can sit where and with whom you like, and time spent huddled on the outside decks scanning for whales fosters great camaraderie among passengers.

Cabins on these ships don't generally offer TVs or telephones, and they tend to be very small and sometimes spartan (see the individual reviews below for exceptions). There are no stabilizers on most of these smaller ships, so the ride can be bumpy in rough seas. In general the small ships are not good choices for travelers who require the use of wheelchairs or have other mobility problems.

Note: All average prices listed below are **per night.** Multiply the per-night cost by the number of nights of the cruise for the estimated cost.

American Safari Cruises

3826 18th Ave. W., Seattle, WA 98119. **(888/862-8881.** Fax 206/283-9322. www.amsafari.com.

American Safari Cruises promises an intimate, all-inclusive yacht cruise to some of the more out-of-the-way stretches of the Inside Passage—and it succeeds admirably. The price is considerable—but so is the pampering. The company's three small vessels carry between 12 and 36 guests, guaranteeing unparalleled flexibility, intimacy, and privacy. Once passenger interests become apparent, the expedition leader shapes the cruise around them. Black-bear aficionados can chug off in a Zodiac boat for a better look, active adventurers can explore the shoreline in one of the yacht's kayaks, and slacker travelers can relax aboard ship. A crew-to-passenger ratio of about one to two ensures that a cold drink, a good meal, or a sharp eagle-spotting eye is always nearby on the line's comfortable 120-foot ships. In 2010, the yachts offer 7-night Discoverers' Glacier Bay itineraries and season-beginning and season-ending 14-night Inside Passage cruises as well. The core 7-night itinerary includes an unusual 2 full days in Glacier Bay National Park, in which passengers can hike on glaciers or in the rainforest with a park ranger, as well as stops in more off-the-beaten-path Alaskan areas such as Frederick Sound and Dawes Glacier.

PASSENGER PROFILE Passengers, almost always couples, tend to be more than comfortably wealthy and range from 45 to 65 years of age. Most hope to get close to nature without sacrificing luxury. Dress is always casual, with comfort being the primary goal.

SHIPS More private yachts than cruise ships, the 22-passenger *Safari Quest,* the 12-passenger *Safari Spirit,* and the company's newest, the 36-passenger *Safari Explorer,* look like Ferraris—all sleek, contoured lines and dark glass. Cabins are comfortable, and sitting rooms are intimate and luxurious, almost as if they had been transported whole from a spacious suburban home. A big-screen TV in the main lounge forms a natural center for impromptu lectures during the day and movie-watching at night. A shipboard chef assails guests with multiple-course meals and clever snacks, barters with nearby fishing boats for the catch of the day, and raids local markets for the freshest fruits and vegetables—say, strawberries the size of a cub's paw and potent strains of basil and cilantro. **Sample nightly rates per person:** Lowest-price outside cabin from $699 for the 7-night cruises on *Safari Explorer;* no inside cabins or suites.

Cruise West

2301 5th Ave., Ste. 401, Seattle, WA 98121. **☎800/426-7702** or 206/441-8687. Fax 206/441-4757. www.cruisewest.com.

Cruise West is the largest operator of small ships in Alaska, with four vessels offering itineraries throughout the state that emphasize friendly service and a casual onboard atmosphere. Like all small ships, Cruise West's vessels can navigate in tight areas such as Misty Fjords and Desolation Sound, visit tiny ports such as Petersburg and Haines, and scoot up close to shore for wildlife watching. But these are not adventure cruises. These vacations are for people who want to visit Alaska's coastal communities and see its wilderness areas up close and in a relaxed, comfortable, small-scale environment without big-ship distractions.

The operative words here are *casual, relaxed,* and *friendly.* At sea, the lack of organized activities on the line's port-to-port itineraries leaves you free to scan for wildlife, peruse the natural sights, or read a book. In port—whether one of the large, popular ports or a less-visited one—the line arranges some novel, intimate shore excursions, such as visits with local artists at their homes outside Haines or an educational walking tour led by a Native guide in Ketchikan. All excursions are included in the price.

The company's brochure details a cruise schedule of five different itineraries ranging from a 4-night Glacier Bay cruise out of Juneau, or a 4-night Prince William Sound cruise from Whittier, all the way up to a 10-night Gold Rush Inside Passage voyage that goes one-way between Seattle and Juneau with stops in lots of little Alaska towns.

PASSENGER PROFILE Cruise West passengers tend to be older (typically around 60–75), financially stable, well educated, and independent minded—folks who want to visit Alaska's ports and see its natural wonders in a relaxed, dressed-down atmosphere.

SHIPS The 78-passenger *Spirit of Columbia* and 84-passenger *Spirit of Discovery* are both spartan ships, designed to get passengers into small ports and allow them to see the state up close. The 102-passenger *Spirit of Endeavour* and the 138-passenger *Spirit of Yorktown* (formerly *Yorktown Clipper*), on the other hand, offer high levels of small-ship comfort compared to most small ships in Alaska. **Sample nightly rates per person:** Lowest-price inside cabin $481; lowest-price outside cabin $543; lowest-price suite $974 for 7-night cruise plus 1 hotel night.

Lindblad Expeditions

96 Morton St., 9th Floor, New York, NY 10014. ☎ **800/397-3348** or 212/765-7740. Fax 212/265-3770. www.expeditions.com.

Lindblad Expeditions specializes in environmentally sensitive, soft-adventure vacations that are explorative and informal in nature, what the company calls "respectful tourism." Its programs—operated since 2004 in partnership with the National Geographic Society—are designed to appeal to the intellectually curious traveler seeking a cruise that's ecologically friendly and educational as well as being relaxing. Days aboard are spent learning about life above and below the sea (from National Geographic experts to high-caliber expedition leaders trained in botany, anthropology, biology, and geology), and observing the world either from the ship or during shore excursions, which are included in the cruise package. Educational films and slide presentations aboard ship precede nature hikes and quick jaunts aboard Zodiac boats. Flexibility and spontaneity are keys to the experience, as the route may be altered at any time to follow a pod of whales or school of dolphins.

The Alaska program of its two ships, the nearly identical 62-passenger *Sea Lion* and *Sea Bird,* includes 7-night cruises between Juneau and Sitka from May to August, and an 11-night cruise between Seattle and Juneau (including the San Juan Islands and British Columbia) in April and September.

PASSENGER PROFILE Lindblad Expeditions tends to attract well-traveled and well-educated, professional, 55-and-older couples who have "been there, done that" and are looking for something completely different in a cruise experience—and who share a belief in the need to preserve the environment.

SHIPS The 62-passenger *National Geographic Sea Lion* and *National Geographic Sea Bird* (built in 1981 and 1982, respectively) are nearly identical. Both are well-appointed vessels built to get you to beautiful spots and feature a minimum of public rooms and conveniences: one dining room, one bar/lounge, and lots of deck space for wildlife and glacier viewing. They have the added advantage of being accompanied throughout by historians, anthropologists, scientists, or other such specialist lecturers chosen by the National Geographic Society. Cabins are small and functional, but not inexpensive. **Sample nightly rates per person:** Lowest-price outside cabin $770 for 7-night cruises; no inside cabins or suites.

THE BIG-SHIP CRUISE LINES

The ships featured in this section vary in size, age, and offerings, but share the common thread of having more activities and entertainment options than any one person can possibly take in over the course of a cruise. You'll find swimming pools, health clubs, spas, nightclubs, movie theaters, shops, casinos, multiple restaurants, bars, and special kids' playrooms, and, in some cases, sports decks, virtual golf, computer rooms, martini bars, and cigar clubs, as well as quiet spaces where you can get away from it all. In most cases, you'll find lots and lots of on-board activities, including games, contests, classes, and lectures, plus a variety of entertainment options and show productions, some very sophisticated.

Note: All average prices listed below are **per night.** Multiply the per-night cost by the number of nights of the cruise for the estimated cost.

Carnival Cruise Lines

Carnival Place, 3655 NW 87th Ave., Miami, FL 33178. **℡800/CARNIVAL** (227-6482). Fax 305/471-4740. www.carnival.com.

Carnival is the ultimate fun-in-the-sun warm-weather line, and even in Alaska the Caribbean-focused operator retains its "Fun Ship" philosophy. Sure, you'll be cruising past glaciers and on the lookout for whales, but you'll be doing it with people who like to take in the natural wonders with a multicolored party drink in hand. Drinking and R-rated comedians are part of the scene, as are "hairy-chest contests" and the like.

Entertainment is among the industry's best, with each ship boasting a dozen dancers, a 10-piece orchestra, comedians, jugglers, and numerous live bands, as well as a big casino. Activity is nonstop. Cocktails begin to flow before lunch, and through the course of the day you can learn to country line-dance or ballroom dance; take cooking lessons; learn to play bridge; watch first-run movies; practice your golf swing by smashing balls into a net; or just eat, drink, shop, and then eat again. Alaska-specific naturalist lectures are delivered daily. In port, Carnival offers more than **120 shore excursions,** divided into categories of easy, moderate, and adventure. For kids, the line offers Camp Carnival, an expertly run children's program with activities that include Native arts and crafts sessions, lectures conducted by wildlife experts, and special shore excursions for teens.

Carnival's ship in Alaska cruises the Inside Passage route with round-trip departures out of Seattle.

PASSENGER PROFILE Overall, Carnival has some of the youngest demographics in the industry. But it's far more than age that defines the line's customers. Carnival executives are fond of using the word "spirited" to describe the typical Carnival passenger, and indeed the descriptor is right on target. The line's many fans increasingly come from a wide range of not just ages but occupations, backgrounds, and income levels, but what they share is an unpretentious, fun-loving, and outgoing demeanor. On Carnival you'll find couples, a few singles, and a good share of families, but the bottom line is this is not your average sedentary, bird-watching crowd. Passengers want to see whales and icebergs, but they also want to dance the Macarena.

SHIPS The 2,124-passenger megaship *Carnival Spirit* returns to Alaska in 2010. It offers plenty of activities, great pool and hot-tub spaces (some covered for use in chillier weather), a big ocean-view gym and spa, and more dining options than your doctor would say are advisable. **Sample nightly rates per person:** Lowest-price inside cabin $128, lowest outside cabin $164, lowest suite $192 for a 7-night Inside Passage cruise.

Celebrity Cruises

1050 Caribbean Way, Miami, FL 33132. **℡800/437-3111** or 305/262-8322. Fax 800/437-5111. www.celebritycruises.com.

Celebrity Cruises offers a great combination: a classy, tasteful, and luxurious cruise experience at a moderate price—it's definitely the best in the midpriced category. The line's ships are real works of art; the cuisine is above the norm; the service first-class, friendly, and unobtrusive; and the spa facilities among the best in the business.

A typical day might offer bridge, darts, a culinary art demonstration, a trap-shooting competition, a fitness-fashion show, an art auction, a volleyball tournament, and a not-too-shabby stage show. Resident experts give lectures on the various ports of call, the Alaskan environment, glaciers, and Alaskan culture. For children, Celebrity ships employ a group of counselors who direct and supervise a camp-style children's program. Activities are geared toward different age groups. There's an impressive kids' play area and a lounge area for teens.

Celebrity, like sister company Royal Caribbean, visits the tiny port of Icy Strait Point between Juneau and Glacier Bay; the port offers a prime vantage point for whale- and wildlife watching and easier access to the Alaskan wilderness. The company offers 7-night Inside Passage and 7-night Gulf of Alaska itineraries.

PASSENGER PROFILE The typical Celebrity guest is one who prefers to pursue his or her R&R at a relatively relaxed pace, with a minimum of aggressively promoted group activities. The overall impression leans more toward sophistication and less to the kind of orgiastic Technicolor whoopee that you'll find, say, aboard a Carnival ship. You'll find everyone from kids to retirees.

SHIPS Sleek, modern, and stunningly designed, the 1,896-passenger *Mercury* and the larger, 1,950-passenger *Infinity* and *Millennium* have a lot of open deck space and lots of large windows that provide access to the wide skies and the grand Alaskan vistas. All the ships (but especially *Mercury*) feature incredible spas with hydrotherapy pools, steam rooms, and saunas, plus health and beauty services and exceptionally large fitness areas. **Sample nightly rates per person:** Lowest-price inside cabin $128, lowest outside cabin $150, lowest suite $293 for a 7-night cruise.

Holland America Line

300 Elliott Ave. W., Seattle, WA 98119. **℡800/426-0327** or 206/281-3535. Fax 206/286-7110. www.hollandamerica.com.

Holland America Line (HAL) can be summed up in one word: *tradition*. The company was formed way back in 1873 as the Netherlands–America Steamship Company, and its ships today strive to present an aura of history and dignity, like a European hotel where they never let rock stars register. Thanks to its acquisition over the years of numerous land-based tour operators, Holland America also has positioned itself as Alaska's most experienced and comprehensive cruise company. The company has eight ships in the Alaska market in 2010.

Though most of HAL's Alaskan fleet is relatively young, the ships are designed with a decidedly "classic" feel—no flashing neon lights here. Similarly, Holland America's ships are heavy on more mature, less frenetic kinds of activities. You'll find good bridge programs and music to dance (or just listen) to in the bars and lounges, plus health spas and the other amenities found on most large ships. Service is excellent, delivered by a crew mostly trained at the line's own schools in Indonesia and the Philippines. The line has improved its nightly show-lounge entertainment, adding magicians, comedians, and the like. Alaska Native guides are onboard most Glacier Bay–bound ships, offering their local insight. With fewer kids on these ships than some of the other mainstream lines, the Club HAL children's playrooms are small, but the program is nonetheless big on creative activities. A recently launched "as you wish" dining program allows guests to choose either a set time or anytime dining for dinner. Alaska itineraries include 7-night Inside Passage cruises and 7-night Gulf of Alaska cruises.

PASSENGER PROFILE Holland America's passenger profile used to reflect a much older crowd. Now the average age is dropping, thanks to an increased emphasis on its Club HAL program for children and some updating of onboard entertainment. Still, HAL's passengers in Alaska include a large percentage of middle-aged-and-up vacationers.

SHIPS The 1,266-passenger *Ryndam* and *Statendam* are more or less identical. All cabins have a sitting area and lots of closet and drawer space, and even the least expensive inside cabins run almost 190 square feet, quite large by industry standards. Outside doubles have either picture windows or verandas. The striking dining rooms, two-tiered showrooms, and Crow's Nest forward bar/lounges are among these ships' best features. The somewhat newer, 1,440-passenger *Volendam, Zaandam,* and *Veendam,* and 1,380-passenger *Amsterdam,* are larger and fancier, with triple-decked oval atriums, nearly 200 suites and deluxe staterooms with private verandas, five showrooms and lounges, and an alternative restaurant designed as an artist's bistro, featuring drawings and etchings. The smallest cabin is a comfortable 190 square feet. The *Zuiderdam* and *Westerdam,* two of the newest vessels in the fleet, weigh 82,300 tons and carry 1,916 passengers. These are sophisticated, spacious, yet intimate ships well equipped to support HAL's position as a force in the Alaska market. **Sample nightly rates per person:** Lowest-price inside cabin $128, lowest outside cabin $157, lowest suite $286 for a 7-night cruise.

Norwegian Cruise Line

7665 Corporate Center Dr., Miami, FL 33126. ☎800/327-7030 or 305/436-4000. Fax 305/436-4120. www.ncl.com.

Very contemporary Norwegian Cruise Line (NCL) offers an informal and upbeat onboard atmosphere on two large ships, the *Norwegian Pearl* and *Norwegian Star,* both sailing from Seattle. The line excels at activities, and its recreational and fitness programs are among the best in the industry. NCL recently launched a food upgrade program—the best food is at venues where you pay an extra fee—and has what has become a very popular "freestyle" casual dining policy that allows passengers to have dinner pretty much whenever they want, with whomever they want, dressed however they want.

In Alaska, NCL offers an Alaskan lecturer, wine tastings, art auctions, cooking demonstrations, craft and dance classes, an incentive fitness program, and bingo, among other activities. Passengers can choose from a good selection of soft-adventure shore excursions, including hiking, biking, and kayaking. Entertainment is generally strong and includes Vegas-style musical productions. The top-notch kids' program includes an activity room, video games, an ice cream bar, and guaranteed babysitting aboard, plus sessions with park rangers and escorted shore excursions. The line offers 7-night Inside Passage cruises.

PASSENGER PROFILE In Alaska, the demographic tends more toward retirees than on the line's warmer-climate sailings, but you'll find families as well, including grandparents bringing along the grandkids.

SHIPS One of the first ships built with NCL's trademark "freestyle" cruising in mind, the 2,240-passenger *Norwegian Star* has no fewer than 14 places where people can eat—depending on the time of day. The *Star* also is well equipped for the sports-minded and active vacationer—in addition to the fitness center, there are three heated pools, a jogging/walking track, and a wide array of sports facilities. The 2,394-passenger *Norwegian Pearl* is the line's newest ship in Alaska and has the most bells and whistles (including one of the only bowling alleys at sea!), providing a fun and lively Alaska cruise experience. **Sample nightly rates per person:** Lowest-price inside cabin $107, lowest outside cabin $136, lowest suite from $243 for a 7-night cruise.

Princess Cruises

24305 Town Center Dr., Santa Clarita, CA 91355. **☎800/PRINCESS** (774-6237). Fax 661/753-1535. www.princess.com.

Bringing on several new vessels in recent years, Princess has impressively maintained consistency. Aboard Princess, you get a lot of bang for your buck, attractively packaged and well executed. Although its ships serve every corner of the globe, nowhere is the Princess presence more visible than in Alaska, where it will have seven ships in 2010— almost as many as sister line Holland America. Through its affiliate, Princess Tours, it owns wilderness lodges, motorcoaches, and railcars in the 49th state, making it one of the major players in the Alaska cruise market, alongside Holland America.

Princess passengers can expect enough onboard activities to keep them going morning to night, if they've a mind to, and enough nooks and crannies to allow them to do absolutely nothing, if that's their thing. Kids are well taken care of, with especially large children's playrooms. On shore, the line's shore excursion staff gets big points for efficiency. Passengers have the option of eating dinner at a set time (early and late seating) or can dine in the "anytime dining" room, at any time.

Princess offers the standard 7-night Inside Passage cruises and 7-night Gulf of Alaska cruises, as well as 10-night Inside Passages cruises from San Francisco and 14-night cruises on the small Royal Princess out of Seattle to less-visited places, including Kodiak and Valdez.

PASSENGER PROFILE Typical Princess passengers are likely to be between 50 and 65, and are experienced cruisers who know what they want and are prepared to pay for it. Recent additional emphasis on its youth and children's facilities has begun to attract a bigger share of the family market.

SHIPS Princess's diverse fleet in Alaska essentially comprises seven ships, six of them new since the millennium. The fleet includes the *Diamond* and *Sapphire,* which were completed in 2004; the *Coral* and *Island,* of 2003 vintage; and the *Golden* (2001); the *Sea Princess,* which was built in 1998 and served in the British P & O Cruises fleet until joining Princess after a major refit in 2005; and the smaller and more intimate *Royal Princess,* which was built in 2001 for the now-defunct Renaissance Cruises and later purchased and extensively refurbished by Princess. The ships generally are pretty but not stunning, bright but not gaudy, spacious but not overwhelmingly so, and decorated in a comfortable, restrained style that's a combination of classic and modern. They're a great choice when you want a step up from Carnival, Royal Caribbean, and NCL but aren't interested in the slightly more chic ambience of Celebrity or the luxury of Regent Seven Seas. **Sample nightly rates per person:** Lowest-price inside cabin $92, lowest outside cabin $131, lowest suite $180 for a 7-night cruise.

Regent Seven Seas Cruises

1000 Corporate Dr., Ste. 500, Fort Lauderdale, FL 33334. **☎800/285-1835.** www.theregentexperience.com.

Regent's guests travel in style and extreme comfort. Its brand of luxury is casually elegant and subtle, its cuisine among the best in the industry. That goes for the *Seven Seas Navigator,* which is taking over in Alaska this year for the somewhat larger *Seven Seas Mariner,* which has been deployed there for the last 7 years. The line assumes, for the most part, that passengers want to entertain themselves onboard, so organized activities are limited, but they do include lectures by local experts, well-known authors, and the like, plus facilities for card and board games, blackjack and Ping-Pong tournaments, bingo, big-screen movies with popcorn, and instruction in the fine arts of pompon making, juggling, and such. Bridge instructors are onboard on select sailings. The line has a no-tipping policy and offers creative shore excursions. Room service is about the best you'll find on any ship, and the cuisine is excellent. Regent recently switched to a fleet-wide liquor-inclusive policy on all departures. This year, **Seven Seas Navigator** will sail primarily a 7-night Gulf of Alaska itinerary between June and September, with one interesting 14-day early-season itinerary between San Francisco and Vancouver, B.C., in May.

PASSENGER PROFILE Regent tends to attract passengers in their 40s to 60s who have a household income of more than $200,000 and don't like to flaunt their wealth. The typical passenger is well educated, well traveled, and inquisitive.

SHIPS Cabins on the 490-passenger *Seven Seas Navigator* are all ocean-view suites, all but a handful of which have private verandas. The standard suite is a roomy 301 square feet; some suites can interconnect if you want to book two for additional space. The Seven Seas Lounge is a comfortable, two-tiered showroom in which, despite the space limitations imposed by the ship's mere 30,000 GRT (the Mariner is 50,000 GRT), succeeds in presenting a high level of cabaret, Broadway revue, classical music, and comedian/magic shows. Elsewhere on the ship, Star's Lounge offers dancing to the music of a DJ, from which the less hectic piano bar, Galileo's, is a welcome alternative. The Connoisseur Club is a cushy venue for pre-dinner drinks and after-dinner fine brandy and cigars, and a smallish casino allows guests to indulge their taste for blackjack, roulette, stud poker, craps, and slot machines. The ship's Carita Paris spa, while not as extensive as those of its larger Alaska rivals, is nevertheless well equipped to provide a variety of services using a variety of herbal and water-based therapies. **Sample nightly rates per person:** Per diems for the lowest-priced suites start at $612 for the 7-night cruise, $470 for the season-opening 14-nighter.

Royal Caribbean International

1050 Caribbean Way, Miami, FL 33132. **866/562-7625.** www.royalcaribbean.com.

Royal Caribbean sells a mass-market style of cruising that's reasonably priced and offered aboard informal, well-run ships with nearly every diversion imaginable—craft classes, horse racing, bingo, shuffleboard, deck games, line-dancing lessons, wine-and-cheese tastings, cooking demonstrations, art auctions, and the like—plus elaborate health clubs and spas; covered swimming pools; large, open sun deck areas; and innumerable bars, lounges, and other entertainment centers. The Viking Crown Lounge and other glassed-in areas make excellent observation rooms from which to see the Alaska sights. Royal Caribbean spends big bucks on entertainment, which includes high-tech show productions. Headliners are often featured. Port lectures are offered on topics such as Alaska wildlife, and the line offers dozens of adventurous shore excursions. The line's children's activities are some of the most extensive afloat. The line offers 7-night Inside Passage and Gulf of Alaska cruises.

PASSENGER PROFILE The crowd on Royal Caribbean ships, like the decor, rates pretty high on the party scale, though not quite at the Carnival level. Passengers represent an age mix from 30 to 60, and a good number of families are attracted by the line's well-established and fine-tuned kids' programs (the line's ships are a particularly good bet for tweens and teens, who love such trademark Royal Caribbean decktop offerings as climbing walls and miniature golf).

SHIPS Royal Caribbean owns the largest ships in the world, including the much-ballyhooed, 220,000-ton *Oasis of the Seas,* which set a new record for size when it debuted in December 2009. Although this groundbreaking 5,400-passenger ship—which includes such innovative design features as an open-air Central Park with live trees, an outdoor AquaTheater for water shows, and onboard zip lining—is not in Alaska this year, Royal Caribbean does offer the very up-to-date, 90,000-ton, 2,112-passenger *Radiance of the Seas* sailing Gulf of Alaska cruises between Vancouver, B.C., and Seward. Also returning to Alaska in 2010 is the older (1997) but still up-to-date 1,998-passenger *Rhapsody of the Seas,* a Vision-class ship cruising out of Seattle. **Sample nightly rates per person:** Lowest-price inside cabin on the *Rhapsody,* RCL's least expensive ship, is $95; lowest outside cabin $122; lowest suite $207 for a 7-night cruise.

Silversea

110 E. Broward Blvd., Fort Lauderdale, FL 33301. ℂ **800/744-9966.** www.silversea.com.

Silversea is one of the most luxurious—and pricey—cruise lines in the business, and it's known for exquisite service, gourmet cuisine, and spacious and elegant all-suite accommodations. The line offers an impressive enrichment program with naturalists, well-known authors, and even celebrity chefs mingling with passengers nightly. A Cooking School program allows for cooking lessons at sea. Entertainment is more low-key than on the big ship lines, but the passengers seem to enjoy the cabaret-type acts. The company offers niceties including free alcohol and a fine selection of complimentary wines at lunch and dinner—and probably at breakfast as well, if you're really interested. A friend of Fran's is fond of telling about the time he ordered a late-night hot dog from room service and it came elaborately presented on a silver tray. For Alaska, the line offers 7- to 12-night Gulf of Alaska cruises between Los Angeles, San Francisco, Vancouver, and Seward, Alaska.

PASSENGER PROFILE Look for the 60-something set, well heeled, well educated, and knowing what to look for when they lay out the kind of money it takes to get a place on one of this company's ships.

SHIPS While Silversea has a growing fleet of six ships, it sends just one to Alaska, the 382-passenger *Silver Shadow.* There are no rock-climbing facilities, but there are two alternative restaurants, one of which doubles as the breakfast and lunch buffet room, and there's a small casino—there is no children's program; it's not a ship for kids. **Sample nightly rates per person:** Least expensive suite is $628 for a 7-night cruise.

6

SOUTHEAST ALASKA

Rich, proud people have lived in Southeast Alaska for thousands of years, fishing the region's salmon and hunting in its primeval forests, where the tree trunks grow up to 10 feet thick. In canoes, they explored the hundreds of misty, mossy, enchanted islands where animals, trees, and even ice had living spirits. The salmon lived under the sea in human form, becoming fish in the summer to swim in seething masses up the rivers and streams as a gift of food to feed their kin, the people. In return, the people treated the salmon with respect and ceremony, allowing their spirits to return to human form under the sea to live another year. So blessed, the Tlingit and Haida built great, carved houses and poles, fought wars, owned slaves, traded with faraway tribes, and held rich contests of giving called potlatches, where they passed on the stories that still help explain their mysterious world. Even for a modern non-Native walking in the grand quiet of the old-growth rainforest, it's easy to find yourself listening for the spirits of the trees speaking their mysteries.

Discovery subsists on mystery, and Southeast Alaska is still being discovered. A honeycomb of limestone caves under Prince of Wales Island wasn't found until 1987. Explorers continue to map its endless miles of caverns, finding the bones of extinct animals, the artifacts of some of North America's earliest prehistoric people, bear dens, strange eyeless shrimp that live nowhere else, and even underground streams that host spawning salmon. The caves network at every step into passages that lead straight up or down or off to either side, some only wide enough to allow a cool wind to pass through. The unfathomable intricacy is exhilarating but also a bit disquieting, like a breath of the supernatural, for it is proof of the unknowable.

Southeast Alaska unfolds like this intricate, hidden world below the tree roots. On a map, this land of ice and forest may not look as large as other parts of Alaska, but the better you know it, the bigger it becomes, until you have to surrender to its immensity. You don't need to go underground to experience the sensation—you can feel it by gazing from a boat at the fractal geometry of the endlessly folded, rocky shoreline. On a cruise through the Inside Passage, you'll marvel at all the little beaches and rocky outcroppings you pass, hundreds of inviting spots each day. If you were to stop at random on any one of those uninhabited beaches in a skiff or kayak, you'd find you could spend a day surveying just a

PREVIOUS PAGE: **Humpback whale breaching in Frederick Sound.**

few acres of rocks, the overhanging forest, and the tiny pools of water left behind by the tide. And if you gazed down into any one of those pools, you'd find a complex world all its own, where tiny predators and prey live out their own drama of life in the space of a few square feet. The discoveries you make in Southeast Alaska depend only on how closely you look.

The region stands apart from the rest of Alaska, and not only because most of it can't be reached by road. No other part of the state shares the mysterious, spirit-laden quality of the coastal rainforest. No other area has such mild weather, more akin to the climate of the Pacific Northwest than to the heart of Alaska. Certainly no other area in Alaska gets as much rain, nor do many other places on earth. The traditional Native people here differed from other Alaska Natives, too: They were far richer and left behind more physical artifacts. The Tlingit, Haida, and Tsimshian exploited the wealth nature gave them and amplified it by successfully trading with tribes to the south and over the mountains in today's British Columbia and Yukon Territory. In their early contact, the Tlingits even briefly defeated the Russian invaders in the Battle of Sitka, and after white dominance was established, managed to save many of their cultural artifacts and stories.

Along with its other riches and complexities, Southeast Alaska also has many charming small towns and villages that seem to have grown organically from the mountainsides bordering the fjords and channels of the islands. With economics that pre-date Alaska's oil boom, they developed slowly, their fishermen building houses to hand down to their children. The smaller towns remain completely exempt from the American blight of corporate sameness. Real, old-fashioned main streets are prosperous with family businesses where the proprietors know their customers by first name.

Sunset on Douglas Island.

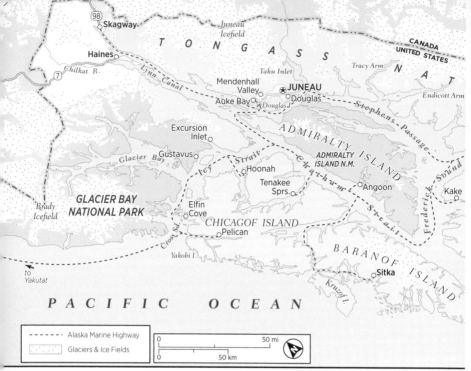

EXPLORING SOUTHEAST ALASKA

A unique and inviting aspect of travel in Southeast Alaska is that no roads connect most of the communities. People are forced to get out of their speeding cars and ride on boats, where they can meet their fellow travelers and see what's passing by—slowly. The islands of the region form a protected waterway called the **Inside Passage,** along which almost all of the region's towns are arrayed. Thanks to the **Alaska Marine Highway** ferry system, it's not too expensive to travel the entire passage, hopping from town to town and spending as much time in each place as you like. And if you're short on time, air service is frequent, with jets to the major towns and commuter planes to the villages.

Getting Around by Ferry: The Alaska Marine Highway

The state-run **Alaska Marine Highway System** (☎800/642-0066 or 907/465-3941; www.ferryalaska.com) is a subsidized fleet of big, blue-hulled ferries connecting many of Alaska's roadless coastal towns. Call for a free schedule or download it from the website.

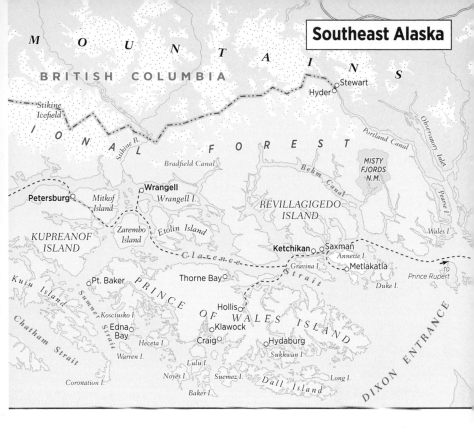

Southeast Alaska

PROS & CONS The ferry system's strengths are its low cost, frequent summer sailings, inexpensive stopovers, exceptional safety, and the fact that kids love it. In the summer, Forest Service guides offer interpretive talks on board in Southeast's Inside Passage and in Prince William Sound. The system's weaknesses are crowding during the July peak season, the fact that if they're late they can be many hours late (although they're usually on time), and a shortage of cabins, which means that most people have to camp on deck or in chairs during overnight passages. An added problem is that schedules and service can change from year to year, undercutting my ability to give advice and making it even more important to get on the Internet early for planning.

ROUTES The system mostly serves Southeast Alaska, though it does cover most of coastal Alaska, with a sailing or two a month (the *Kennicott*) connecting Southeast Alaska with the Southcentral region nearer Anchorage. The smaller Southcentral ferries link communities all the way out the Aleutian chain (see chapters 8 and 11).

In the Southeast, the large, mainline ferries serve the Inside Passage. Some begin their run in British Columbia's Prince Rupert and travel about 30 hours north to Haines and Skagway. Less frequent sailings start in Bellingham, Washington, travel 37 hours nonstop to Ketchikan, then continue up to Skagway and Haines. Each of these four towns is connected to the rest of the world by roads, but none of the towns in between are. In the summer, the large ships stop approximately daily (although sometimes in the middle of the night) in Ketchikan, Wrangell, Petersburg, Juneau, Haines, and Skagway. Sitka is on the west side of Baranof Island, off the Inside Passage, and in the current, changeable arrangement is served from Juneau by some mainline ferries and by a newer fast ferry, the *Fairweather,* which travels at up to 45 mph.

Smaller ferries belonging to the state system and to other operators connect the larger towns to tiny villages up and down the coast. They mostly take local residents back and forth to their villages, so they're rarely crowded. Those routes are definitely off the beaten track, offering the cheapest and easiest way to absorb the real wilderness of the Alaska Bush. The small ferries don't have cabins.

View of the landscape approaching Cordova.

CONNECTING TO THE FERRY **From the south:** The appeal of taking the Alaskan Marine Highway ferry to Alaska from Bellingham, Washington is obvious, but it is not cheaper than flying, and it takes 2 days just to get to Ketchikan. The popular alternative is to board the ferry in Prince Rupert, B.C. You can get to Prince Rupert by rail or road (this is covered under "Getting There & Getting Around," in chapter 3). Another option is to get to Prince Rupert by riding the **BC Ferries** system (✆888/223-3779 or 250/386-3431; www.bcferries.bc.ca). This is quite a trek and requires you to have a car. First you have to take a ferry to the southern end of British Columbia's Vancouver Island, then drive the island's length to its northern end, then take another ferry from Port Hardy to Prince Rupert. That ferry docks next to the Alaska ferry. You can get to Vancouver Island's southern end from the mainland from two directions. BC Ferries goes to Nanaimo from near the city of Vancouver. **Black Ball Transport** (✆360/457-4491; www.cohoferry.com) operates a ferry from Port Angeles, Washington, to Victoria. U.S. citizens need a passport to get back into the country after traveling through Canada (see "Crossing the Border," p. 546).

To the north: The northern end of the Inside Passage Alaska ferry system rejoins the road system in Skagway and Haines. Haines is a bit closer to the rest of the state. Both towns have Avis car-rental outlets, and Skagway also has an RV-rental business. (See the Haines and Skagway sections of this chapter.) Most summers it is also theoretically possible to take a bus from Skagway to Whitehouse and there catch another bus to travel onward on the Alaska Highway, but I wouldn't recommend spending a vacation that way, and arrangements are so changeable I cannot provide details. The **Skagway Convention and Visitors Bureau Center** (☎**907/983-2854;** www.skagway.com) should know the latest.

By air: By flying to your starting point, you can save time and reduce the chance of having to spend the night sleeping in a chair on board. Long hauls on the ferry can be uncomfortable and don't save you much money over flying, but the ferry is much less expensive and more appealing for connecting nearby towns within the Southeast region. Fly into Juneau, Sitka, or another sizable town and plan a ferry trip from there, stopping at various places before catching a plane home.

STOPPING OVER Buying ahead or booking round-trip tickets saves you nothing on the ferry, and stopovers of any length add little to the cost of your passage. Use the ferry system to explore the towns along the way, grabbing the next ferry through to continue your journey. If you travel without a vehicle, you generally don't need reservations (with the possible exceptions of the Bellingham sailings and passages across the Gulf of Alaska). Bring along a bike, or even a sea kayak, to have total freedom in exploring Southeast. Port calls usually are not long enough to see the towns; if the boat is running late, they may not let you off at all.

WALK-ON FARES Fares change every year, so don't count on these, but they may help for planning. The adult walk-on fare from Prince Rupert to Skagway is $171. Bellingham to Ketchikan is $239, Bellingham to Skagway $363. Juneau to Sitka is $45. All fares for children 6 to 11 are roughly half-price, and children 5 and under ride free. Off-season only, October through April, the driver of a vehicle rides free, and other fare sales sometimes go in effect. Check the website for specials.

Ferry System Booking

The **Alaska Marine Highway** (www.ferryalaska.com) has an online booking system that makes figuring out a trip far easier than using its inscrutable timetables. Just be sure to make vehicle and cabin reservations as early as possible

If you need to talk to a real person for advice or to change reservations, the system has a toll-free number (☎800/642-0066), but there can be waits to talk to someone. One way around the state's reservation system is to call **Viking Travel,** in Petersburg (☎800/327-2571 or 907/772-3818; www.alaskaferry.com), which will accept your booking before the official

reservation system opens, then reserve it the first day the system becomes available; likewise, if your preferred date is booked, they'll monitor the system for cancellations to grab you a spot. They can also take care of all your air and tour connections, lodgings, activities, travel insurance, and so on.

You can sometimes avoid crowds on the boats with careful scheduling. Ferries are crowded northbound in June and southbound in August and both ways in July. If you're planning to fly one way and take the ferry the other, go against the flow.

BRINGING VEHICLES In the summer, you often need a reservation for any chance of taking your vehicle on the ferry, and you should reserve as soon as you know your travel dates. Some routes book up quickly after they become available, particularly the vehicle spots on the ferries from Bellingham and Prince Rupert. Fares vary according to the size of the car as well as your destination; a passage from Prince Rupert to Haines for a typical 15-foot car is $356; the passage from Bellingham to Haines is $797. You also have to buy a separate ticket for each person on the ferry. Renting a car at your destination will probably save money and enhance your trip because you will have more flexibility in your stopovers. You can carry a kayak, canoe, or bike on the ferry (without a car) quite inexpensively.

CABIN RESERVATIONS Sometimes you can snag a cabin from the standby list when you sail (board quickly and approach the purser immediately), but generally you must reserve ahead for the summer season. Cabins from Bellingham book many months ahead. A two-berth outside cabin (one with a window) with a bathroom is under $75 on most town-to-town hops, $178 from Prince Rupert to Haines, and $393 from Bellingham to Haines, plus the cost of your ticket. The great majority of the cabins are small and spartan, coming in two- and four-bunk configurations, but for a premium you can reserve a more comfortable sitting-room unit on some vessels. Most cabins have tiny private bathrooms with showers. Try to get an outside cabin so that you can watch the world go by. Cabins can be stuffy, and the windowless units can be claustrophobic as well.

DO YOU NEED A CABIN? If you do a lot of layovers in Southeast's towns, you can arrange to do most of your ferry travel during the day, but you'll probably have to sleep on board at least once (unless you make that hop by air). You can't sleep in your vehicle. One of the adventures of ferry travel is finding a chair to sleep in or setting up a tent on deck with everyone else. The patio-furniture lounge chairs on the covered outdoor solarium, on the top deck, are the best public sleeping spot on board, in part because the noise of the ship covers other sounds. A camping pad will make it much more comfortable. If you're tenting, the best place is behind the solarium, where it's not too windy. On the *Columbia* that space is small, so grab it early. The *Kennicott* has hardly any outdoor deck space and the fast ferries essentially none. Bring duct tape to secure your tent to the deck in case you can't find a sheltered spot, as the wind over the deck of a ship in motion blows like an endless gale. The recliner lounges are comfortable, too, but can be stuffy. Bring a pillow. If the ship looks crowded, grab your spot fast to get a choice location. **Showers** are available, although there may be lines. Lock any valuables and luggage you don't need in the **coin-operated lockers.** If all that sounds too rugged, or if you have small children and no tent, reserve a cabin. It offers a safe and private home base and a good night's rest, and there's a certain romance to having your own compartment on a public conveyance.

FERRY FOOD If you can, bring at least some of your own food on the ferry. Ferry food can get boring after several meals in a row and, during peak season, lines are sometimes unreasonably long. We usually bring a cooler or picnic basket. Even if you're traveling light, you can pick up some bagels and deli sandwiches on a stopover or long port call.

THE BEST RUNS Going to Sitka through **Peril Straits,** the ferry fits through extraordinarily narrow passages where no other vessel of its size ventures; the smooth, reflective water is lovely, and you may see deer along the shore. The **Wrangell Narrows,** between Petersburg and Wrangell, is also an incredible ride, day or night, as the ship accomplishes a slalom between shores that seem so close you could touch them, in water so shallow the schedules must be timed for high tide. **Frederick Sound,** between the Narrows and Wrangell, is prime for whale sightings. Approaching Skagway through the towering mountains of the **Lynn Canal** fjord also is impressive.

Getting Around by Air & Road

BY AIR Air travel is the primary link between Southeast's towns and the rest of the world. Several towns without road access have jet service, provided by **Alaska Airlines** (☎800/252-7522; www.alaskaair.com), the region's only major airline. Juneau is Southeast Alaska's travel hub. Ketchikan and Sitka each have a few flights a day, while Wrangell, Petersburg, and Yakutat each have one flight going each direction daily. Gustavus is served from Juneau once daily during the summer. Some of these "milk runs" never get very far off the ground on hops between small towns: On the 31-mile Wrangell-to-Petersburg flight, the cabin attendants never have time to unbuckle. Haines and Skagway, which have highway connections, don't receive visits from jets, but all the towns and even the tiny villages have scheduled prop service.

Like the ferries, the planes can be quite late. Each of the airports in Southeast has its own challenges caused by the steep, mountainous terrain and the water. In bad weather, even jet flights are delayed or they "overhead"—they can't land at the intended destination and leave their passengers somewhere else. Your only protection against these contingencies is

Seeing Southeast From Above

If you can possibly afford it, take a **flightseeing** trip at some point during your trip. The poor man's way of doing this is to fly a small prop plane on a scheduled run between two of your destinations instead of taking the ferry. If you ask, the pilot may even go out of his or her way to show you the sights; if not, you'll still gain an appreciation for the richness and extreme topography of the region. Each flight service also offers flightseeing tours in addition to scheduled runs between destinations. Flightseeing costs as little as $100 for a brief spin. Flight services are listed in each town section. You can also potentially see more by booking puddle-jumper flights on the Alaska Airlines jets rather than the higher-flying nonstops. If you're lucky with weather and a window seat, you may see some amazing terrain. That's really the only way to see the mind-blowing mountain and glacial area between Yakutat and Cordova, which a single north and south jet flies over each day (flights 61 and 66 btw. Anchorage, Juneau, and Seattle). You will need a good seat. Northbound, get a window seat on the right side of the plane, southbound on the left.

travel insurance, a schedule that allows plenty of slack in case you're significantly delayed, and low blood pressure.

BY ROAD Three Southeast Alaska communities are accessible by road: Haines, Skagway, and the village of Hyder, which lies on the British Columbia border east of Ketchikan and is accessible from the gravel Cassiar Highway through Canada (although beyond the scope of this book, that's an interesting way-off-the-beaten destination with good bear viewing). If you're driving the Alaska Highway, passing through Haines and Skagway adds 160 miles of very scenic driving to the trip, as well as a 15-mile ferry ride between the two towns (they're separated by 362 road miles). This ferry route is not as heavily booked as the routes heading between either town and Juneau, but it's still a good idea to reserve ahead. You also can rent a car from Haines or Skagway for travel to the rest of the state at the end of a ferry journey (Haines saves just 60 miles over Skagway). If you're driving the highway in winter, you should be prepared for weather as cold as 40°F below zero (–40°C). Alaska winter driving information is under "Health & Safety" in chapter 3.

Bikes make a lot of sense for getting around Southeast's small towns, which tend to be compact. You can rent one almost anywhere you go, or bring your own on the ferry. The networks of abandoned or little-used logging roads on some islands offer limitless routes for mountain biking. Elsewhere, Forest Service hiking trails are often open for riding.

Getting Outside in the Tongass National Forest

Nearly all of Southeast Alaska, stretching 500 miles from Ketchikan to Yakutat, is in Tongass National Forest. The towns sit in small pockets of private land surrounded by 17 million acres of land controlled by the U.S. Forest Service—an area nearly as large as the state of Maine, and considerably larger than any other national forest or national park in the United States. The majority of this land has never been logged, and the rate of logging has dropped dramatically in recent years, preserving one of the world's great temperate rainforests in its virgin state. It's an intact ecosystem full of wildlife, and mostly free of human development. Indeed, you quickly forget it *is* the Tongass National Forest. Since it always surrounds you when you're in this region, it's simply the land.

FOREST SERVICE CABINS

One of the best ways to get into Southeast's wilderness is by staying at one of the scores of remote Forest Service Public Recreation Cabins. These are simple cabins without electricity or running water where you can lay your sleeping bag on a bunk and sit by a warm woodstove out of the rain. You need to bring everything with you, as if camping, but it's a good deal more comfortable than a tent. And you will probably find yourself in a stunningly beautiful spot, perhaps with your own lake and a boat for fishing. Cabins are located along canoe trails, on beaches best reached by sea kayak, on high mountain lakes accessible only by floatplane, and along hiking trails. We've done this many times with our family by boat or canoe or on foot. I've learned three critical lessons to pass on: Do your research, pack carefully (take all the essentials, but little more), and spend at least 3 nights to make all the effort pay off with real relaxation.

Tongass National Forest.

GETTING CABIN INFORMATION In this chapter, I've listed a few of the cabins in the sections devoted to the town that they're closest to, but for complete information, check the Tongass website (**www.fs.fed.us/r10/tongass**) or contact the visitor centers and ranger offices listed with each town section in this chapter. The main contact point for recreation information for the whole forest is the **Southeast Alaska Discovery Center,** 50 Main St., Ketchikan, AK 99901 (☏907/228-6220).

You'll need a good map to figure out where the cabins are, and an idea of how to get there and how much travel will cost—generally, the cost of transportation will be many times larger than the cabin rental fee of $25 to $45 a night. Few cabins can be reached without a boat or aircraft, and for all but large groups, flying is the most economical way to go. A flight service can help you choose a cabin according to your interests and how far you can afford to fly. You may be able to rent the gear you need, but you'll have to reserve that ahead, too. The solution to these puzzles is different for each town; I've listed where to find help in the town sections later in this chapter.

RESERVING A CABIN OR CAMPSITE The cabins and some campgrounds are reserved through a national system. Don't rely on the reservations operators or website for advice or cabin information—they're in upstate New York—instead, pose your questions to the ranger station nearest where you plan to go. The rangers are friendly and have probably stayed in the cabin you're interested in. When you're ready to book, the easiest way is to use **www.recreation.gov**, where you can check availability dates at various places. By telephone, contact the **National Recreation Reservations Service** at ☏877/444-6777. The phone lines are open March through October daily 10am to midnight eastern time, November through February 10am to 10pm. The system accepts payment only by credit or debit card: American Express, Discover, MasterCard, or Visa. Cabins and campsites are available for reservation on a first-come, first-served basis, starting 180 days ahead. For the most popular cabins, you need to be online the minute reservations become available to have a chance.

KETCHIKAN: ON THE WATERFRONT

Had they known about it, the film noir directors of the 1950s would have chosen the Ketchikan (*Ketch*-e-kan) waterfront for Humphrey Bogart to sleuth. The black-and-white montage: A pelting rain drains from the brim of his hat, suspicious figures dart through saloon doors and into the lobbies of concrete-faced hotels, a forest of workboat masts fades into the midsummer twilight along a shore where the sea and land seem to merge in miles of floating docks. Along Creek Street, salmon on their way to spawn swim under houses chaotically perched on pilings beside a narrow boardwalk; inside, men are spawning, too, in the arms of legal prostitutes. Meanwhile, the faces of totem poles gaze down on the scene disapprovingly, mute holders of their own ancient secrets.

In fact, a 1954 B-movie crime drama, "Cry Vengeance," did film in Ketchikan. Locals watched a video to see how the city once looked. Today, the director hoping to re-create that scene would have his work cut out for him removing the T-shirt shops and jewelry stores with bright street-front signs that seek to draw in throngs of cruise passengers to buy plastic gewgaws. Not so long ago, Ketchikan was a rugged and exotic intersection of cultures built on the profits of logging Southeast's rainforest, but in 15 years it has transformed itself into a tourist center, softening its rough edges while selling their charm to visitors. Southeast Alaska's last major timber mill—the Louisiana Pacific pulp plant in Ward Cove, north of town—closed in 1997 due, in part, to environmental concerns. A major portion of the mill was blown up in 1999; they sold tickets to see who would get to press the button on the explosives, but the occasion was less than festive, as former employees saw the scene of their work lives disappear into dust. The idea of a smaller, more labor-intensive operation, intended to replace the lost pulp mill jobs with jobs sawing lumber and making veneer, had a rocky time getting off the ground. In the meantime, the economy had moved on.

On summer days, the white cruise ships tower above the town like huge new buildings on the dock facing Front Street, the downtown's main drag. Each morning their gangways disgorge thousands of visitors, clogging the streets and, for a few hours, transforming the town into a teeming carnival. On their short visits, the passengers explore the closest of the twisting streets, see the museum at the Southeast Alaska Discovery Center, or take a tour to one of the totem pole parks. Then evening comes, the streets empty, and the cruise ships slide off quietly on the way to their next port.

That is when a sense of the old, misty, mysterious Ketchikan starts to return. Visitors with a little more time to spend, and the willingness to explore beyond the core tourist areas, can drink in the history and atmosphere of the place. Stay in a quaint old hotel; hike a boardwalk path through the primeval rainforest; and visit the museums, clan house replicas, and totem pole parks that make Ketchikan a center of Tlingit and Haida culture.

Ketchikan also makes a great jumping-off point for some spectacular outdoor experiences, including a trip to **Misty Fjords National Monument** (p. 164). As the state's fourth-largest city, Ketchikan is the transportation hub for the southern portion of Southeast Alaska. (The nicknames "Gateway City" and "First City" refer to its geographical location and transportation function.) Seaplanes based on docks along the waterfront are the taxis of the region, and a big inter-agency visitor

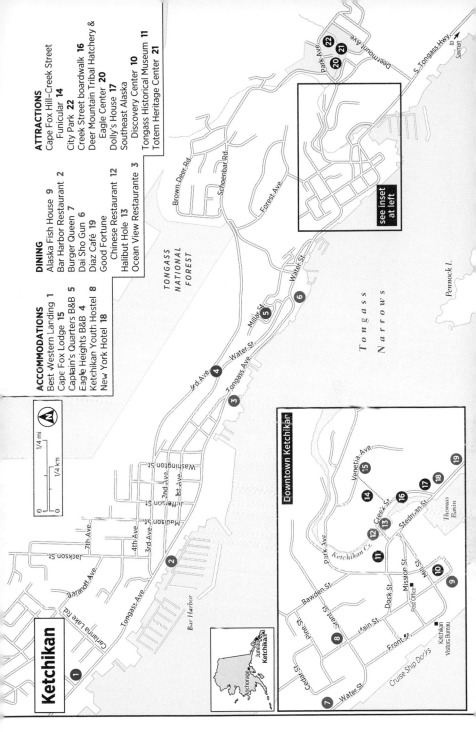

Ketchikan

ACCOMMODATIONS
Best Western Landing **1**
Cape Fox Lodge **15**
Captain's Quarters B&B **5**
Eagle Heights B&B **4**
Ketchikan Youth Hostel **8**
New York Hotel **18**

DINING
Alaska Fish House **9**
Bar Harbor Restaurant **2**
Burger Queen **7**
Dai Sho Gun **6**
Diaz Café **19**
Good Fortune
  Chinese Restaurant **12**
Halibut Hole **13**
Ocean View Restaurante **3**

ATTRACTIONS
Cape Fox Hill–Creek Street
  Funicular **14**
City Park **22**
Creek Street boardwalk **16**
Deer Mountain Tribal Hatchery &
  Eagle Center **20**
Dolly's House **17**
Southeast Alaska
  Discovery Center **10**
Tongass Historical Museum **11**
Totem Heritage Center **21**

Downtown Ketchikan

center can get you started on your explorations of the area. Ketchikan is one of the wettest spots on earth, with rain measured in the hundreds of inches; quality rain gear is requisite for any activity, in the wilds or in the streets of town.

Essentials

GETTING THERE

BY AIR Alaska Airlines (☎800/252-7522; www.alaskaair.com) jet service connects Ketchikan south to Seattle nonstop and north to Petersburg, Wrangell, Sitka, Juneau, and Anchorage. Commuter lines run wheeled planes and floatplanes from Ketchikan to the neighboring communities, and also offer fishing packages and flightseeing.

The airport is on Gravina Island, to which there is no bridge (perhaps you've heard of the famous "Bridge to Nowhere" Congressional scandal—the Ketchikan airport is its destination). A ferry runs each way every half-hour (more frequently at peak times). Believe the airline when it tells you when to catch the ferry for your plane. The fare is $5 for adults, $2 ages 6 to 12, and free under 6. Returning the same day is free. The fare for cars is $6 each way, no matter how soon you come back. Carts are available to move your luggage onto the boat. See "Getting Around," below, for how to get from the airport ferry dock to town and for a water taxi right from the airport (a fun option).

BY FERRY The dock is 2½ miles north of downtown. **Alaska Marine Highway** ferries (☎800/642-0066; www.ferryalaska.com) run 6 hours north to Wrangell and 6 hours south to Prince Rupert, B.C. The walk-on fare from Prince Rupert is $54, from Wrangell $37. Call the local terminal at ☎907/225-6182 or 907/225-6181 for a recording of updated arrival and departure times.

ORIENTATION

Ketchikan is on huge **Revillagigedo Island,** popularly known as **Revilla Island.** The downtown area, pretty much taken over by tourism, is quite compact and walkable, but the whole of Ketchikan, including a second commercial area used by locals, is long, strung out between the Tongass Narrows and the mountains. A waterfront road goes under various names through town—Front Street, Water Street, Tongass Avenue—becoming North Tongass Highway as it stretches about 16 miles to the north. Saxman is 2½ miles to the south of downtown on the 14-mile South Tongass Highway.

GETTING AROUND

You can spend a day seeing the downtown sights on foot, but you will need transportation to get to the totem pole parks or airport.

BY TAXI The local taxis, mostly minivans, are convenient and usually easy to flag down on the single main road through town. Try **Sourdough Cab** (☎907/225-5544). **Alaska Cab** (☎907/225-2133) is another taxi company in Ketchikan. Taking a cab to the airport terminal is costly because of time that runs up on the meter waiting for and riding the ferry to Gravina Island. A better choice is to take the cab to the ferry and then walk on, using a cart to move your luggage on the ferry. On the far side, you will have to go up a hill to the airport terminal. If this doesn't sound practical, ask about a shuttle or take a cab. For years airport shuttles operated in Ketchikan, but none are in business as of this writing.

BY WATER TAXI Only in Ketchikan could you take a boat from the airport to your hotel. **Tongass Water Taxi** (☎ 907/225-8294) also happens to be reasonably priced and quick. The six-passenger boat runs back and forth from near the airport ferry dock to downtown all day. The first person is $19 and each additional person $8. It also crosses the same route as the airport ferry (without going on to downtown) for $8. Several hotels are right on the water, so the water taxi can take you almost to your door. The operator holds up a sign in the baggage claim area to meet arriving flights, or you can call to arrange a pick-up.

BY BUS The least costly way to the airport or ferry dock is the **Ketchikan Gateway Borough bus** (☎ 907/225-8726). To get downtown or points south from the airport costs $1. Buses come every half-hour. Your luggage must fit under the seat.

BY RENTAL CAR Budget has locations at the airport or in town (☎ 800/527-0700 reservations, 907/225-6004 at the airport, 907/225-8383 in town; www.budget.com). **Alaska Car Rental** (☎ 800/662-0007 or 907/225-5000; www.akcarrental.com) also has offices at the airport or in town.

VISITOR INFORMATION

The **Southeast Alaska Discovery Center,** 50 Main St., Ketchikan, AK 99901 (☎ 907/228-6220; www.fs.fed.us/r10/tongass), is much more than a visitor center. Housed in a large, attractive building of big timbers and cedar, and located a block from the cruise-ship dock, the center is the best museum in the region when it comes to illustrating the interaction of the region's ecology and human society, including both traditional Native and contemporary uses. An auditorium shows a selection of films. Admission to these facilities in summer costs $5, free ages 15 and under, with a $15 family maximum; in winter it's free. Without paying, you can get guidance about planning your time and activities in the outdoors. An information kiosk is located near the entrance, and downstairs you'll find a luxurious bookstore decorated like an explorer's private den with room to relax. The center is open May through September daily from 8am to 5pm, October through April Tuesday through Friday noon to 4pm and Saturday 10:30am to 4:30pm.

The **Ketchikan Visitors Bureau,** 131 Front St., Ketchikan, AK 99901 (☎ 800/770-3300 or 907/225-6166; fax 907/225-4250; www.visit-ketchikan.com), has two offices on the docks. The main office on downtown cruise ship Berth 2 offers town information and booths where tourism businesses sell their wares, including tickets for tours. A satellite is located on Berth 3, just north of the downtown tunnel, where the town has also built a large new public restroom. The bureau is open daily in the summer from 8am to 5pm and when cruise ships are in town; weekdays only in winter.

Special Events

There's a detailed events calendar at www.visit-ketchikan.com.

The **Festival of the North** brings art to Ketchikan audiences for the entire month of February, including theater, ballet, live music, poetry readings, and a wearable art show the first weekend of the month that is a highlight of the winter.

The festival is sponsored by the Ketchikan Area Arts and Humanities Council, 716 Totem Way (☎907/225-2211; www.ketchikanarts.org).

King Salmon Derby, a 60-year-old tradition, takes place at the end of May and the beginning of June.

The Fourth of July celebration is huge, with a long parade on Front Street attended by mobs of locals and visitors. Don't miss the legendary **pie sale** at St. John's Church at 423 Mission St., where a slice, ice cream, and beverage is $5. Fireworks are at 11pm on Gravina Island, best viewed from the cruise-ship dock.

Twice weekly through July, the **First City Players** (☎907/225-4792) perform the melodrama "Fish Pirate's Daughter," as they have for more than 40 years, and serve a crab feed at the Civic Center.

The crowd-pleasing **Great Alaskan Lumberjack Show** goes on all summer near the cruise-ship pier and Alaska Discovery Center (☎888/320-9049 or 907/225-9050; www.lumberjacksports.com). Canadian and U.S. professional teams of lumberjacks—highly skilled and cute, too, according to my friend Charlotte—compete three or more times daily, mostly to an audience of cruise-ship passengers. The show is charming and intentionally a little goofy. The setting is attractive and comfortable. Tickets are $34 adults, $17 ages 3 to 12—not cheap for a show that lasts 1 hour, but the great majority of clients leave happy.

The Blueberry Arts Festival, held the first weekend of August, has booths, music, and food, and is put on by the Ketchikan Area Arts and Humanities Council, mentioned just above as the sponsor of the Festival of the North. Check with the council for the **Monthly Grind** coffeehouse variety show, as well, which happens in the Saxman Tribal House every third Saturday from September to May, and the **Torch Night Performing Series,** which brings in well-known musicians for shows in Ketchikan.

Log rolling competition at the Great Alaskan Lumberjack Show.

[FastFACTS] KETCHIKAN

Banks A bank with an ATM is at 306 Main St.; grocery stores and the visitor center also have ATMs.

Hospital Ketchikan General Hospital is at 3100 Tongass Ave. (☎907/225-5171).

Internet Access SeaPort Cyberstations (☎907/247-4615; www. seaportel.com) is at the ship dock on the second floor at 5 Salmon Landing. The public library at 629 Dock has two free guest terminals with a 15-minute limit.

Police Call ☎907/225-6631 for nonemergencies.

Post Office 3609 Tongass Ave.; a more convenient downtown substation is 2 blocks from the cruise-ship dock at 422 Mission St.

Taxes Sales tax is 6% within city limits, 2.5% outside. Room taxes add another 7% to each sales tax.

Exploring Ketchikan.

Pick up a copy of the **Official Historic Ketchikan Walking Tour Map,** available all over town, which has three routes to follow and loads of information about sites of both great and modest interest on the way. In 2008 the town also posted handy directional signs and maps at intersections all over the downtown area.

Many motorized tours of the town vie for customers, getting the majority of their clients from the cruise ships but welcoming independent travelers when space is available. Tickets are for sale at the visitor center on the dock. Besides riding a tour bus through town, you can go into the woods in a Hummer or on a motorcycle, or even drive from the streets into the harbor in an amphibious vehicle. That one, painted bright yellow and called **The Duck** (☎866/341-DUCK [341-3825] or 907/225-9899; www.akduck.com), is a favorite of kids. It costs $38 adults and $24 children, and lasts 90 minutes.

One of the longest-established tour guides caters only to five visitors at a time—not ships full of clients. Schoolteacher Lois Munch, of **Classic Tours** (☎907/225-3091; www.classictours.com), has a fun personality and neat concept: She wears a poodle skirt to drive visitors around in her '55 Chevy. A 2-hour tour to the Saxman totem poles is $109; a 3-hour tour adds a natural history stop and costs $139. Rates are per person and include the admission to Saxman.

TLINGIT, HAIDA & TSIMSHIAN CULTURAL HERITAGE

The Ketchikan area has two totem pole parks and a totem pole museum, as well as a wealth of contemporary Native art displayed all over town. Notable pieces stand at Whale Park at Mission and Bawden streets and at the Cape Fox Lodge. Most of what you see in Southeast Alaska is Tlingit—the Haida and Tsimshian generally live to the south and east in British Columbia—but Ketchikan is near the boundary between the three peoples' areas, so their similar cultures mix here.

Totem Bight State Historical Park ★★★ The park presents poles and a clan house carved beginning in 1938 by Natives working with traditional tools to copy fragments of historic poles that had mostly rotted away. The project, funded by the New Deal's Civilian Conservation Corps, helped save a Tlingit and Haida culture that had been essentially outlawed until that time. The setting,

Totem Bight State Historical Park.

purportedly the site of a traditional fishing camp, is a peaceful spot on the edge of Tongass Narrows, at the end of a short walk through the woods, so the experience is both aesthetic and educational. The park also stands out for its excellent interpretive signs, a printed guide, and an interpretive website. There's a small park bookstore.

10 miles out of town on N. Tongass Hwy. Ketchikan Area State Park Office, 9883 N. Tongass Hwy. **907/247-8574.** www.alaskastateparks.org (click on "Individual Parks"). No admission fee. Park always open.

Totem Heritage Center ★★ Located near City Park, the center contains the largest collection of original 19th-century totem poles in existence. The poles, up to 160 years old, are displayed indoors, mostly unpainted, many with the grass and moss still attached from when they were rescued from the elements in villages. Totem poles were never meant to be maintained or repainted—they generally disintegrate after about 70 years, and were constantly replaced—but these were preserved to help keep the culture alive. A high ceiling and muted lighting highlight the spirituality of the art. The museum also shows changing exhibits by contemporary masters of Tlingit art. Well-trained guides are on hand to explain what you're looking at, and there are good interpretive signs.

601 Deermount St. **907/225-5900.** Admission $5 in summer, free in winter. Summer daily 8am–5pm; winter Mon–Fri 1–5pm.

Saxman Native Village Totem Pole Park ★ Saxman's park has artifacts similar to those at Totem Bight park, but with an added attraction: You can see carvers at work in the building to the right of the park, including Nathan Jackson, perhaps Alaska's greatest contemporary artist, who has even been honored by a postage stamp. Cape Fox Corp. hosts visitors at the park, catering mainly to cruise-ship passengers with its 2-hour tour, which includes entry to the clan house and a demonstration of traditional dance and song by the Cape Fox Dancers. The tour schedule is different each day, depending on the ships. Buy tour tickets in the gift store on the right as you enter the park. If you're not interested in the tour and just want to see the poles, Totem Bight is a better stop—it has a more inspiring location and better interpretive materials. On the other hand, the carving studio at Saxman is remarkable, and you can sneak in there on your own without the tour by paying the $3 park fee.

In Saxman, 2½ miles south of Ketchikan on the S. Tongass Hwy. **☎907/225-4846** for tour times and tickets. www.capefoxtours.com. Tour $35 adults, $18 children 12 and under; unguided visits $3. Park always open. No tours Oct–Apr.

DOWNTOWN ATTRACTIONS

Ketchikan's best downtown attractions are all within walking distance of one another. See Creek Street, then walk up Park Avenue past the Ketchikan Creek fish ladder and up to lovely **City Park,** site of the Totem Heritage Center, described above. The park is among my favorite places in Ketchikan. The creek splits into a maze of ornamental pools and streams once used as a hatchery, with footbridges, a fountain, and large trees with creeping roots.

The **Creek Street** boardwalk starts at the Stedman Street bridge, running over the tidal creek. It was Ketchikan's red-light district until not that long ago; now it's a quaint tourist mall. Prostitution was semi-legal in Alaska until 1952, recent enough to survive in local memories but distant enough to have made Creek Street historic and to transform the women who worked there from outcasts to icons. Dolly Arthur, who started in business for herself on the creek in 1919 and died in 1975, lived through both eras, and her home became a commercial museum not long after her death. **Dolly's House** (**☎907/225-6329**) is amusing, mildly racy, and a little sad. Admission is $5; it's open from 8am to 4pm during the summer and when cruise ships are in town.

Creek Street has some interesting shops, described below, but it's also fun just to walk on the creekside boardwalk, into the forest above, and over the "Married Men's Trail"—once a discreet way for married men to reach the red-light district. The **Cape Fox Hill–Creek Street Funicular** (known as "the tram"), a sort of diagonal elevator, runs 211 feet from the boardwalk up to the Cape Fox Lodge on top of the hill. Take it up and then enjoy the walk down through the woods. The summertime fare is $2, but if no one is around, just press the "up" button and go.

Avoiding the Crowds

Ketchikan is overrun with as many as 10,000 cruise-ship passengers every day May through September, far more than the small visitor attractions or even the streets can comfortably handle. Independent travelers can avoid the crush by planning to visit popular spots in the afternoon. Spend the morning on an outdoors activity instead. Ships usually leave the town in early evening.

Deer Mountain Tribal Hatchery and Eagle Center ★★ This remarkable nonprofit center combines one of Alaska's best hatchery tours and a great place to see a bald eagle close up. The wooden buildings stand over Ketchikan Creek. You can see fish climbing against the current up into pools where they are sorted before being cut open to complete their biological purpose (salmon die when they spawn anyway). The hatchery tours are special for letting you get so close, right in the action, where you can feed the growing salmon fry yourself. The hatchery produces king and silver salmon and steelhead trout. Visitors can also walk right through the eagle enclosure. Remarkably, the resident pair of injured, flightless bald eagles have mated for life and built a nest where they lay eggs each year. They hunt salmon swimming naturally through their enclosure. No glass stands between you and this activity, only a few feet away.

1158 Salmon Rd. **☎800/252-5158** or 907/228-5530. Admission $9; ages 12 and under free. May-Sept daily 8am-4:30pm; winter by arrangement.

Tongass Historical Museum This one-room museum is where Ketchikan talks back to itself, with well-executed revolving exhibits that have always held my interest. A small permanent area shows Native artifacts. In the same building, the attractive Ketchikan Public Library is a great place to recharge, especially in the children's section downstairs, where big windows look out on Ketchikan Creek's falls.

629 Dock St. **☎907/225-5600.** Admission $2 summer; free winter. Summer daily 8am-5pm; winter Wed-Fri 1-5pm, Sat 10am-4pm, Sun 1-4pm.

Shopping

The Ketchikan art scene is one of Alaska's liveliest, thanks in part to the Ketchikan Arts and Humanities Council, whose helpful staff operates the **Mainstay Gallery,** at 330 Main St. (www.ketchikanarts.org). Shows change monthly.

Ray Troll is Alaska's leading fish-obsessed artist. His small gallery, **Soho Coho,** at 5 Creek St., is worth a visit even if you aren't a shopper. It shows Troll's

Creek Street boardwalk.

Soho Coho gallery.

own work and that of other Ketchikan artists from the same school of surreal rainforest humor. In Troll's art, subtle ironies and silly puns coexist in a solidly decorated interior world. T-shirts are his most popular canvas; "Spawn Till You Die" is a classic. Troll's incredible work-of-art website delves far into his strange mind (and sells shirts), at www.trollart.com. The gallery is open in summer daily from 9am to 6pm; in winter Wednesday through Saturday from noon to 5:30pm; or order at **☎800/888-4070.**

Adjacent to Soho Coho, **Alaska Eagle Arts** is a serious gallery featuring the bold yet traditional work of Native artist Marvin Oliver. Upstairs, **Parnassus Books** is a pleasing little cubbyhole with Alaskana, art, cooking, and popular fiction. Down the boardwalk at 18 Creek St., craftspeople carve and interact with visitors at **Hide-A-Way Gifts.** At 716 Totem Way, check out the **Forget-Me-Not Sweater Shop,** which carries imported woolens from around the world and locally made furs by Haida Roger Alexander, who makes gloves, hats, teddy bears, and custom pieces.

Back toward the town's center, at 633 Mission St., **Exploration Gallery** is owned by local artist Diane Naab and framer Anna Annicelli and shows original work from all over the region, and antique maps and prints. Moving nearer the waterfront, **Arctic Spirit Gallery of Ketchikan,** 310 Mission St., shows some very impressive Alaska Native art, including large carved pieces from this region.

Note: Ketchikan is a shopping and art destination, but if you want something authentically Alaskan you have to be careful. For some important tips, see "Native Art: Finding the Real Thing," in chapter 3.

Getting Outside

There's a lot to do outdoors around Ketchikan, but most of it will require a boat or plane; drive-by attractions are limited. In any event, your first stop should be the trip-planning room at the Southeast Alaska Discovery Center (see "Visitor

Ward Lake Recreation Area.

Information," near the beginning of the Ketchikan section) for details on trails, fishing, and dozens of U.S. Forest Service cabins.

BEAR VIEWING Salmon returning to a fish hatchery on a creek south of town have long attracted black bears. A local business, **Alaska Rainforest Sanctuary** (☎877/847-7557; www.alaskarainforest.com), takes advantage of the viewing opportunity by hosting visitors on well-made trails with guides. A tour also includes captive reindeer and an owl and bald eagle as well, and a Native carving demonstration. It's a good variety of experiences, and the tour is the right length. Most guests come from cruise ships, affecting times, so call to check for availability and scheduling. The price is $80 for adults, $50 children 12 and under, which I consider high. But you may be able to watch the same bears from public property for free, without a guide. Drive about 10 miles south of town, beyond Saxman on the South Tongass Highway, to the Herring Cove Bridge. From here you have a viewpoint of the same estuary owned by the sanctuary and just as good a chance of seeing black bears. Bears may be present June through September, and sightings are most likely in July and August.

For more of a wilderness experience, Ketchikan is a good place to get on a floatplane, soar over water and wooded islands, and land where bears are gathering at streams where the salmon are running. Depending on where the bears are and the flight service you choose, it costs $329 to $495 per person. **Promech Air** (☎800/860-3845 or 907/225-3845; www. promechair.com) and **Island Wings Air Service** (☎888/854-2444 or 907/225-2444; www.islandwings.com) offer this service; both are described in "Majestic Misty Fjords," p. 164.

CABIN TRIPS The U.S. Forest Service maintains more than 50 **cabins** around Ketchikan; all are remote and primitive, but at $25 to $45 a night, you can't beat the price or the settings. This is a chance to be utterly alone in the wilderness; many of the lake cabins come with a boat for fishing and exploring. For details and descriptions of all the cabins, contact the **Southeast Alaska Discovery Center** (☎907/228-6220; www.fs.fed.us/r10/tongass). The reservations system to use when you're actually ready to book a cabin is described in "Getting Outside in the Tongass National Forest" on p. 150.

If you stay in a cabin, you'll need all your camping gear except a tent, including sleeping bags, a camp stove, your own cooking outfit and food, a lantern, and so on. The easy way to handle this is to contact **Alaska Wilderness Outfitting and Camping Rentals,** 3857 Fairview St. (☎907/225-7335; www.latitude56.com/camping/index.html), which has been supplying cabin trips for more than 15 years. They rent almost everything you need, including small outboards and life jackets for the skiffs, and deliver directly to the air taxi or water taxi.

The cabins are remote. You can hike or take a boat to some of them, but most are accessible only by floatplane (and unless you have loads of stuff, flying is probably the cheapest way to go). Expect to pay around $1,000 to $1,500 round-trip for three to five passengers. Obviously, it makes sense only if you will stay for a while—we never go for less than 3 nights. For recommended carriers, see "Majestic Misty Fjords," p. 164.

FISHING The **Alaska Department of Fish and Game** produces a 24-page fishing guide to Ketchikan with details on where to find fish in both fresh and salt water, including a list of 17 fishing spots accessible from the roads. Get it from the local office of the **Alaska Department of Fish and Game,** 2030 Sea Level Dr., Ste. 205, Ketchikan, AK 99901 (☎907/225-2859), or download it from www.alaska.gov/adfg (click "Sport Fish" then the Southeast region on the map). More fishing ideas are under "Hiking," below, and "Cabin Trips," above.

As is generally true in Southeast Alaska, most fishing takes place from boats in saltwater, for which you need guided charters. **Ketchikan Charter Boats** (☎800/272-7291 or 907/225-7291; www.ketchikancharterboats. com) has a lot of experience in these waters. You can also find links to charter companies on the Visitor Bureau's website (www.visit-ketchikan.com) or contact them for a referral. The going rate for a daylong charter for salmon or halibut is around $300 per person, half-day about $160.

HIKING Eight miles out the North Tongass Highway, the **Ward Lake Recreation Area** covers a lovely patch of rainforest, lake, and stream habitat and has a picnic area, several trails, and campgrounds. Ward Creek has steelhead and cutthroat trout, Dolly Varden char, and silver salmon; check current regulations before fishing. The wide, gravel **Ward Lake Nature Trail** circles the placid lake for 1⅓ miles among old-growth Sitka spruce large enough to put you in your place. For a more challenging hike, **Perseverance Lake Trail** climbs through forest with steps and boardwalks from the Three Cs Campground, across the road from Ward Lake, to a lake 2¼ miles away that can be reached no other way. There's a good bit of climbing to get there, but the trail is extraordinarily well maintained, without mud even in wet weather. To reach the recreation area, turn right off the highway on Revilla Road and follow the signs.

MAJESTIC MISTY FJORDS

In Punchbowl Cove, south of Ketchikan in Misty Fjords National Monument, sheer cliffs rise 3,150 feet straight up from calm water, as high and smooth as those in the Yosemite Valley. Misty is more than twice Yosemite's size, but there isn't a single car here; there isn't so much as a mile of road; in fact, there are hardly any trails. It's something like a great national park before the people arrived.

Visits to the monument are by tour boat, floatplane, or, for the hardy, sea kayak. It isn't a cheap place to go, and you don't see much wildlife. By boat, you don't see glaciers, although glaciated mountains are a spectacular feature of the flights. Unlike Glacier Bay, Tracy Arm, or Kenai Fjords—all places with more wildlife and more glaciers at sea level—the experience at Misty is pure geology. You go for the scenery.

Two companies currently offer boat tours to Misty's Punchbowl Cove, Rudyerd Bay, and back, with both including meals in the price. Sitka-based **Allen Marine** (☎877/686-8100 or 907/225-8100; www.allenmarinetours.com) has some distinct advantages. The fast, quiet boat makes the round-trip in 4½ hours. All seats face forward. A knowledgeable naturalist interprets the scenery. Adult passengers can peruse regional books while children work with craft boxes and activities. Tickets are $159 adults, $109 children. Sailings

every day in the summer coordinate with the cruise ships' dockings. A Misty Fjords tour operated by **Alaska Travel Adventures,** doing business as Alaska Cruises (☎800/323-5757 or 907/247-5295; www.bestofalaskatravel.com), offers the opportunity see the fjords from above by floatplane and return to Ketchikan by water for $329 adult, $289 child; taking the boat both ways is $158 adult and $105 child.

I prefer seeing the fjords on an extended floatplane flight (and I certainly recommend it for those susceptible to seasickness). Flying over the scenery is amazing, but it's the floatplane landing that really blows your mind, because then you get a sudden sense of the scale of everything you've seen from the air. The cliffs are magnified while you shrink to a speck. Go in the late afternoon when the light is pretty and the swarms of planes carrying cruise-ship passengers are gone. Several air-taxi operators in

Deer Mountain Trail, right behind downtown, is a steep but rewarding climb through big, mossy trees up to great views. You can walk from City Park to the trail head, half a mile and 500 feet higher on steep Fair Street and Ketchikan Lakes Road, but if you take a cab you will save energy for the trail. The first mile rises 1,000 feet to a great ocean view south of Tongass Narrows, and the next mile and 1,000 feet to another great view, this time of Ketchikan. The alpine summit, at 3,000 feet, comes near the 3-mile mark. A public shelter (first-come, first-served) is a bit farther, and the trail continues to another trail head 10 miles away. Pick up a trail guide sheet from the Forest Service at the Southeast Alaska Discovery Center (p. 155).

her was among the most memorable of the many I've taken around Alaska. She flew with a choice of music on the iPod as background to her impromptu commentary about the fjords. We soared with Van Morrison while Michelle told us about her favorite places down below. The landing was as long as anyone needed to soak in the awesome surroundings. It felt like an outing with old friends. Masden charges $249 for a seat on a six-passenger DeHavilland Beaver for a 2-hour flight that includes 45 minutes on the ground at the fjords. She also flies guests to Forest Service cabins (many of them in Misty), places she knows intimately, and she will take the time to help you choose one that suits your interests and budget. Take a look at her informative website for a good start.

Ketchikan take flightseeing day trips to Misty Fjords or drop clients at remote cabins. **Promech Air** (☎800/860-3845 or 907/225-3845; www.promechair. com) is a large one with many years' experience, charging about $200 for a 75-minute flight including about 10 minutes on the water.

But I like best a smaller company, **Island Wings Air Service** (☎888/854-2444 or 907/225-2444; www.island wings.com). The owner and pilot is Michelle Masden, and my flight with

Visiting the fjords by kayak is a real expedition, advisable only for those who already know they enjoy this mode of travel, but I can think of few more spectacular places to paddle. **Southeast Exposure** (☎907/225-8829; www. southeastexposure.com) does guided paddles there, and has for 20 years, earning a good reputation. Their 4-day trip is $800 per person.

SEA KAYAKING The islands, coves, and channels around Ketchikan create protected waters rich with life and welcoming exploration by kayak. **Southeast Sea Kayaks** (☎800/287-1607 or 907/225-1258; www.kayakketchikan. com) rents kayaks and guides day trips and overnights. They specialize in taking small groups of independent travelers, not big mobs from the cruise ships. The guides do a terrific job. The half-day trips start with a boat ride to real wilderness with only six paddlers along. Those are $159 adults, $139 children, including food and drink. A 2½-hour paddle is $94 adults, $64 children. Children's rates are for age 15 and younger; kids need to be at least 6 to go along. The shop is a mile from the cruise-ship dock at 1621 Tongass Ave. They have multiday Misty Fjords expeditions, too.

Alaska Rainforest Sanctuary canopy tour.

ZIP-LINE TOURS The sport of zooming through the tree tops in a harness attached to a cable has become a popular visitor attraction in Southeast Alaska, but no more so than in Ketchikan, where there are three choices. **Southeast Exposure** (☎907/225-8829; www.southeastexposure.com) offers the new **Rainforest Ropes and Zipline,** which is like a giant jungle gym, with eight spans, suspended logs, and rope bridges. It happens at three regular morning sessions, costs $99, and is only for ages 11 and older. The same folks who do the Alaska Rainforest Sanctuary bear-viewing experience, described above, have a family-oriented zipline at that site, with a mountain slide and a more challenging set-up at the end of an all-terrain-vehicle ride. The tours each cost $179 and last 3½ hours. Book with **Alaska Canopy Adventures** (☎907/225-5503; www.alaskacanopy.com).

Where to Stay

In addition to the hotels and B&Bs listed below, the **Ketchikan Reservation Service,** 412 D-1 Loop Rd., Ketchikan, AK 99901 (☎800/987-5337 or ☎/fax 907/247-5337; www.ketchikan-lodging.com), books many bed-and-breakfasts and outfitted apartments, and has online availability and reservations. **Alaska Travelers Accommodations LLC** (☎800/928-3308 or 907/247-7117; www.alaskatravelers.com) is a Ketchikan-based service of long standing that handles lodgings here and in Juneau.

Here are a couple of single-unit rentals in pleasant residential settings that I can recommend, each with cooking facilities: **Soaring Eagle Vacation Rental** (☎907/247-1710; www.vrbo.com/162011), a luxurious, brand-new suite for $135 double; and **Stormy Seas Bed & Breakfast** (☎907/617-1997; www.stormyseasbb.com), a great choice for a small family, in a lovely location, for $125 double.

EXPENSIVE

Best Western Landing ★★ This hotel offers rooms in bright colors with granite bathroom counters, some with 9-foot ceilings and big opening windows and equipped with high-quality beds, cherry wood furniture, and the latest technology. Service is warm and efficient, and the entire place is kept immaculately. The competition wins only in the category of charm, as an excellent but corporate-feeling place may not be what you want in historic Ketchikan. The location, right across from the ferry dock, is distant from the downtown sights, so you'll need to rent a car or use the courtesy van that the hotel offers.

The **Landing Restaurant,** a fountain and grill with lots of chrome, is a local favorite and very kid friendly. Food is consistently good year after year. Try the fresh halibut sandwich or Salisbury steak with real mashed potatoes. Lunch and dinner range from $7.25 to $25. You can order from that same steak and seafood menu upstairs, at **Jeremiah's** bar, which also serves sandwiches, pizza, and good pasta in a sumptuous room.

3434 Tongass Ave., Ketchikan, AK 99901. ☎800/428-8304 or 907/225-5166. Fax 907/225-6900. www.landinghotel.com. 107 units. High season $200–$215 double, $210–$235 suite; low season $125–$142 double, $145–$162 suite. AE, DC, DISC, MC, V. Covered parking. **Amenities:** Free airport transfers; 2 restaurants; bar; exercise room; limited room service. *In room:* TV, fridge, hair dryer, microwave, Wi-Fi.

Cape Fox Lodge ★★ This is Alaska's most beautiful hotel. It stands on a wooded pinnacle above downtown, reached from Creek Street by a funicular. The sheer drop-off and tall rainforest trees create the lofty feeling of a tree house in the rooms and restaurant. Perfectly proportioned buildings are executed in extraordinarily good taste. Warm wood frames complement the stunning views out of the double hung windows. The Cape Fox Native corporation built the hotel, and the lobby and parking area are a museum of Tlingit art masterpieces, adding to the peace and rainforest spirit. Rooms are large and airy, appointed in rich-toned wood, and all but a dozen share a view of Ketchikan and the sea and islands beyond (rooms on the opposite side are $10 less). Each room has an attractively tiled bathroom. The hotel and furniture are showing a little age, but the place is well kept. There's a good coffee shop off the lobby.

The **Heen Kahidi** restaurant has one of Alaska's most attractive dining rooms, a tall, narrow rectangle of windows with a fireplace. The furniture is notably attractive and comfortable. The setting is worth going for a meal. The food is generally quite good, but prices are higher than other choices in town. Lunch ranges from $9 to $24; dinner main courses range from $20 to $60, with most around $30. The dining room is open from 7am to 9pm daily.

800 Venetia Way, Ketchikan, AK 99901. ☎800/325-4000 or 907/225-8001. Fax 907/225-0286. www.westcoasthotels.com. 72 units. High season $209–$229 double, $300 suite; low season $99–$109 double, $229 suite. AE, DC, DISC, MC, V. **Amenities:** Restaurant; bar; limited room service. *In room:* TV w/pay movies and Nintendo rental, hair dryer, Wi-Fi.

Salmon Falls Resort ★★ If fishing is your goal, a stay at this big on-island lodge has several advantages. First, there's the incredible setting, on island-dotted Clover Pass next to a waterfall where 10,000 pink salmon spawn. Next is the cost savings of a road-accessible lodge, since you don't have to fly there. Finally, you're not trapped in the middle of nowhere if one of you doesn't want to fish— the attractions of Ketchikan are a 17-mile drive down the road. The resort itself is comfortable and flawlessly managed by new owners who took over in 2008, improving on already good facilities, including refreshing the large, up-to-date bedrooms and adding a spa. Rooms in the upper building are slightly preferable and cost the same. Some 40 lodge-operated boats tie at the dock. Rates are inclusive of food at the excellent restaurant.

The **restaurant** and bar are in a massive log octagon held up in the center by a section of the Alaska pipeline, with great views. Dinner here is well worth the drive out the road, even if you aren't staying at the resort (but make reservations). Meals from the menu of steak and seafood, ranging in price from $22 to $33, are generous and deftly prepared, service is excellent, and children are well treated. The kitchen gladly cooks guests' own catch. It is open 5 to 9:30pm.

16707 N. Tongass Hwy. (P.O. Box 5700), Ketchikan, AK 99901. **℡800/247-9059** (reservations) or 907/225-2752. Fax 907/225-2710. www.salmonfallsresort.com. 52 units. 3-day minimum includes all meals. $2,150 per person double occupancy for a 3-day stay with 2 days on the water with guide; $1,460 per person without guide; $880 room and board only. AE, MC, V. Closed Sept 21–May 15. **Amenities:** Restaurant; bar; inclusive guided fishing; outdoor Jacuzzi; massage; spa. *In room:* TV.

MODERATE

Black Bear Inn ★★★ 🛏 This is a luxury inn on a large waterfront lot with extensive gardens and a trail to a private beach. The main building shows the owners' attention to detail and exquisite taste—wood floors, exceptional tile, fireplaces, the best fabrics, leather furniture, Alaskan art originals, satellite TV and radio, and so on. Each of the five units has its own covered porch, and there is a large outdoor hot tub and barbecue area, shielded from the wind and with space heaters. A cabin in a refurbished cannery building overlooks the water, with walls of whitewashed red cedar and floors of slate and porcelain. The hosts, Nicole and Jim Church, offer unusual services as well: They'll lend a crab pot or teach a guest to smoke fish, and they make every effort at environmental sustainability. Breakfasts are self-served from a shared guest kitchen; a suite and the cabin have their own cooking facilities. The location is near the ferry terminal and airport, 4 miles north of downtown.

5528 N. Tongass Hwy., Ketchikan, AK 99901. **℡907/225-4343.** www.stayinalaska.com. 6 units. $169–$189 double; $210 suite; $194 cabin. Extra person $50. Rates include self-serve breakfast from stocked kitchen. AE, MC, V. Children by arrangement only. **Amenities:** Jacuzzi; fish cleaning and freezing facilities. *In room:* TV/DVD, gas fireplace, fridge, Wi-Fi.

The Narrows Inn ★ The motel buildings sit above the water, where fishing charters and floatplanes collect guests for outings. The rooms, done in an outdoors theme, are fresh and nicely decorated, with wallpaper borders. My only complaint is that they are too small—the TV is mounted on the wall. The bathrooms are large. Rooms with balconies rent for $10 more. The location is 4 miles from downtown; they have a shuttle that takes guests to the airport, ferry terminal, and sites within city limits. For flexibility, however, you may want to rent a car if staying here.

A skilled chef and good service at the **Narrows Inn Restaurant (℡907/ 247-5901)** makes this dining room a favorite with local families, serving consistently excellent meals. Try the crab cakes. Breakfasts are generous, well-prepared, and reasonably priced. The comfortable seating has a water view.

4871 N. Tongass Hwy. (P.O. Box 8296), Ketchikan, AK 99901. **℡888/686-2600** or 907/247-2600. Fax 907/247-2602. www.narrowsinn.com. 47 units. High season $135–$150 double, $220–$235 suite; low season $99–$115 double, $160–$185 suite. Extra person $10. AE, DC, DISC, MC, V. **Amenities:** Free airport transfers; restaurant; bar; marina. *In room:* TV, fridge, hair dryer, microwave, Wi-Fi.

INEXPENSIVE

Captain's Quarters Bed & Breakfast ★ 🗡 These big, spotless rooms with sweeping views of the city and ocean are a remarkable value. Those who prefer hotels to B&Bs will be happy saving here, as well, as the self-serve breakfast setup allows as much privacy as you want—socialize with hostess Toni Bass, a gregarious school secretary, or come and go without seeing anyone. A charming nautical theme carries through the building. One room has a full kitchen. The house is perched in a mountainside neighborhood just north of the tunnel, where half the streets are stairs or wooden ramps. It's a significant but doable walk from downtown.

325 Lund St., Ketchikan, AK 99901. **☎907/225-4912.** www.captainsquartersbb.com. 3 units. High season $105–$115 double; low season $75 double. Extra person $15. Rates include continental breakfast. MC, V. *In room:* TV, hair dryer.

Eagle Heights Bed & Breakfast ★ 🎁 A house with treetop views of the waterfront shows exceptional craftsmanship and taste in large, airy guest rooms and a comfortable common room. Two of the units are large suites, and all three are equipped with many amenities, including refrigerators stuffed with goodies and pre-stocked with continental breakfast. Hostess Cherry Ferry keeps the place as immaculate as the day it was built. She even washes guests' laundry. Every room has a private entrance, there's plenty of parking, and the downtown sites are about 20 minutes away on foot.

1626 Water St., Ketchikan, AK 99901. **☎800/928-3308** or 907/225-1760. www.eagleheightsbb.com. 3 units. $105–$135 double. Extra adult $25. MC, V. *In room:* TV/VCR, stocked fridge, hair dryer, microwave.

New York Hotel/The Inn at Creek Street ★★ 🗡 The same family operates two sets of lodgings in the center of the most historic area. The original portion is the hotel, a funny little 1924 building with a tiny lobby and charming, antique-furnished rooms. It is on the National Register of Historic Places, and the owners have done a good job of adding modern comfort consistent with its pedigree. Four rooms look out on a small boat harbor, while five, with less street noise, face the garden. None are large, but all are a good value, and are constantly upgraded and refreshed. The newer part of the business, the inn, consists of spacious, modern individual suites above the shops on the Creek Street boardwalk. These units are downright luxurious, with kitchens, excellent amenities, and great privacy, and they sit on pilings over the flowing creek. The hotel offers a courtesy van to the airport, ferries, and hiking trails. Note that those who have trouble with stairs shouldn't consider either of these properties.

The Ketchikan Coffee Company, in a storefront in the hotel (**☎907/225-1803**), is one of the town's best places to eat breakfast or lunch: inexpensive; hip and friendly; and with healthy, delicious food, including many vegetarian choices, such as the black bean burrito, hummus plate, or terrific soups. It's a small, bright dining room with historically appropriate furniture, including a long mahogany bar where guests order; occasional long lines to order and noisy crowds are the only down-sides of the restaurant.

207 Stedman St., Ketchikan, AK 99901. **☎866/225-0246** or 907/225-0246. Fax 907/225-1803. www.thenewyorkhotel.com. 14 units. High season $129–$149 double, $189–$229 suite; low season $89 double, $119 suite. AE, DISC, MC, V. **Amenities:** Free airport transfers; restaurant. *In room:* TV, hair dryer, Wi-Fi.

A HOSTEL & CAMPING

Three Forest Service campgrounds with a total of 47 sites are located at **Ward Lake** (see "Special Places," p. 190). A salmon stream runs through the middle of the lakeside Signal Creek Campground, which, along with the Last Chance Campground, can be reserved through the national system described in "Getting Outside in the Tongass National Forest," on p. 150. The camping fee at either place is $10.

Eighteen miles out on North Tongass Highway, the **Settler's Cove State Park** includes a sandy beach (a good place to watch whales, beachcomb, or even swim); a disabilities-accessible path to a spectacular waterfall; and a short coastal trail. There are 14 campsites, half of which will take rigs of up to 30 feet, without hookups. Camping costs $10 a night. For information, contact the **Alaska Division of Parks,** 9883 N. Tongass Hwy. (☎907/247-8574).

If you need hookups for an RV, try **Clover Pass Resort,** about 15 miles north of the ferry terminal on North Point Higgins Road (☎800/410-2234 or 907/247-2234; www.cloverpassresort.com). They charge $31 to $36 a night.

Ketchikan Hostel This downtown hostel in the First United Methodist Church offers utilitarian male and female dorms and allows guests use of the church kitchen, although the hostel is independent of the church. Bring a sleeping bag or rent bedding from the hostel. It is open only June through August; office hours are from 7 to 9am and 6 to 11pm.

400 Main St. (P.O. Box 8515), Ketchikan, AK 99901. ☎907/225-3319. $17 per person. Closed Sept–May.

Where to Dine

Besides these restaurants, see the Best Western Landing, Narrows Inn, Salmon Falls Resort, Cape Fox Lodge, and New York Hotel, all above, for other choices, which are among the best in town.

There are several good stops for light meals or snacks. The Smith family's **Alaskan Surf Fish and Chips** booth comes back to the dock every summer to the delight of locals and cruise-ship crew members who line up at lunchtime. The fish is halibut with beer batter, and they also serve shrimp and great clam chowder. Picnic tables are handy for seating on a sunny day.

Halibut Hole, 7 Creek St., on the deck of the Eagles Club (☎907/225-5162), serves some of the best fried fish in town, including halibut, salmon, clams, and shrimp in crispy batter, with fries and hush puppies. It's open daily 11am to 4pm in the summer and accepts cash only.

The **Alaska Fish House,** at the end of Main Street on the waterfront (☎907/225-4055, ext. 122; www.alaskafishhouse.com), serves delicious seafood takeout, fried or grilled, from a stylish building that looks like a cannery; you can eat outdoors or in a cedar booth in a dining room on pilings just behind the fish house.

Burger Queen ♟AMERICAN Restaurants with the word *burger* in the name don't often get full write-ups in travel guidebooks, and this place looks unlikely for special treatment as well, but Debbie and Shawn Rahr have turned their four-table restaurant into a Ketchikan institution by doing simple food right. You certainly won't go wrong ordering a burger and milkshake here, but also consider the grilled chicken (teriyaki or barbecue), the cornmeal-breaded halibut, or the Asian grilled chicken salad—teriyaki grilled chicken, loads of veggies, crispy noodles, and homemade tangy soy sauce–flavored dressing. The portions are so large most adults will get plenty to eat ordering from the children's section of the menu. Since the dining room is so small, having your meal delivered for no extra charge makes sense, or get takeout and eat in the park across the street.

518 Water St. ☎907/225-6060. Lunch and dinner $6–$17. MC, V. High season Mon–Sat 11am–7pm; low season Wed–Sat 11am–3pm.

Diaz Cafe ★ 🎁 FILIPINO Many Alaskan towns have strong, cohesive Filipino communities, created over decades by large, close families drawn across the ocean one by one for cannery work. In Ketchikan, the heartbeat of the Filipino community has beat in this bright little diner since the early 1950s as ownership passes generation to generation in the same family. The place is so well-loved among all ethnicities in Ketchikan that its current owner is unable to change the slightest detail—she even faced an insurrection when she tried to change the color of the menus—so everything remains today as it was half a century ago: the Formica, worn from wiping, and the yellow and red walls. (They had to change the facade in 2009 when heavy snow knocked the old one off the building.) If you haven't had Filipino food, this is the place to try it. The spicy chicken adobo, a huge, delicious half chicken bathed in gravy with rice, is $12. The sweet and sour halibut is memorable, too. Regulars order the "Large guy," a bowl of sweet and sour rice mixed with meat, which arrives instantly and costs $5.25. You can also get sandwiches, burgers (also served with rice), and Chinese food.

335 Stedman St. ☎907/225-2257. Lunch and dinner $8–$20. No credit cards. Tues–Sat 11:30am–2pm, 4–8pm; Sun noon–7:30pm.

Good Fortune Chinese Restaurant CHINESE This restaurant stands on pilings in Creek Street, with small upstairs and downstairs dining rooms. The food is consistently good, without change through the years. A varied menu allows you to choose by style of cuisine—Cantonese, Szechuan, and so on. The broccoli beef is a classic and not to be missed.

4 Creek St. ☎907/225-1818. Lunch $6.25; dinner $12–$19. DISC, MC, V. Mon–Sat 11am–9pm; Sun noon–9pm. Closed Mon in winter.

Ocean View Restaurante ★ 🎁 MEXICAN This lively, festive family restaurant is loud even on an off-season weeknight—in fact, the dining room can be deafening —but few tourists know about it or make the drive a mile from downtown. The menu is long and reasonably priced, with separate columns of Mexican and Italian cuisine (and an occasional Greek item slipped into the Italian column); a page of seafood and sautéed entrees; plus chicken, veal, steak, pasta, and pizza. Variety is a common technique used by small-town restaurants to make it through the winter, as is consistent, basic cooking. The food here is inexpensive and predictable—nothing that will surprise you for good or bad. The pizza, delivered free, is the best in town. The restaurant's popularity may require dining early on weekends to get a table, call ahead.

1831 Tongass Ave. ☎907/225-7566. Reservations recommended. Lunch $7–$9; dinner $6–$20. MC, V. Daily 11am–11pm.

WRANGELL

Wrangell, valued for its position near the mouth of the Stikine River, began as a Tlingit stronghold and trading post and became the site of a Russian fort built in 1834. The British leased the area from the Russians in 1840, and their flag flew until the U.S. purchase of Alaska in 1867. Over the balance of the 19th century, Wrangell experienced three gold rushes and the construction of a cannery and sawmill.

Then time pretty much stopped.

While the world outside changed, Wrangell stayed the same from the mid–20th century on. It even moved backward. Elsewhere, Wal-Mart and shopping malls were invented and small-town main streets deflated. Then people noticed what they had lost and tried to bring back their communities. Not out here, beyond the road system. With little incentive for anyone to visit, Wrangell stayed as it was after a 1952 fire burned the downtown: a burly, blue-collar American logging town, simple and conservative. Wrangell cut trees, processed them, and shipped them. The bars stayed busy, and no one thought of opening a health food restaurant. As long as there were trees to saw into lumber, the future was safe in the past.

Or so it seemed until environmental and economic issues closed the mill in 1994. Some feared the town would die, too. Sawing lumber had sustained the local economy for more than 100 years, and a third of the paychecks in town came from that one plant. But it hasn't been so simple. The logging industry survived, off and on, and on a much smaller scale. The town grew quieter. The population declined, some trailer houses disappeared, and stores closed, but the lights didn't go out.

Wrangell worked to improve on its positive qualities. Residents show an endearing eagerness to please. A new museum was completed in 2005, and ecotourism operators offer kayaking paddles. Tour boats take guests up the wild Stikine River, out on the water for Southeast's great salmon fishing, and over to

A carving at Petroglyph Beach.

the mainland to see hordes of black bears at the Anan Wildlife Observatory. The U.S. Forest Service maintains gravel roads that lead to some spectacular places.

The community even built a golf course to attract visitors, and **Muskeg Meadow** (℡907/874-4653; www.wrangellalaskagolf.com) is truly spectacular. The townspeople are so proud of it you'll find it difficult to turn down a round ($20–$40 per day; clubs are for rent).

The town has a nonthreatening, small-scale feel that allows a family to wander comfortably and make friends. We were invited home to dinner by another family we had just met. With so little crime, there is no fear of strangers. We picnicked in a totem pole park, hiked in the rainforest, and looked at ancient art strewn across Petroglyph Beach. We were sorry to have to leave. On the ferry back to Juneau, a class of Wrangell sixth-graders sat next to us. They talked with excited innocence of all the new things they hoped to experience in the state capital, the most electrifying of which seemed to be the prospect of eating for the first time at McDonald's. Wrangell, I thought, still has a long way to go to catch up with the rest of the world, and that is a condition much to be envied.

Essentials

GETTING THERE Alaska Airlines (℡800/252-7522; www.alaskaair.com) serves Wrangell once daily with a jet flying 28 minutes north from Ketchikan and another 19 minutes south from Petersburg, a flight that skims treetops the entire way.

Wrangell is on the main line of the **Alaska Marine Highway System** (℡800/642-0066; www.ferryalaska.com). The voyage through the narrow, winding **Wrangell Narrows** north to Petersburg is one of the most beautiful and fascinating in Southeast Alaska. It's quite a navigational feat to watch as the 400-foot ships squeeze through a passage so slender and shallow the vessel's own displacement changes the water level onshore as it passes. The route, not taken by cruise ships, which approach through larger waterways, is also a source of delays, as the narrows are deep enough for passage only at high tide. The walk-on fare is $37 from Ketchikan, $33 from Petersburg. The terminal is downtown (℡907/874-3711), a block from the Stikine Inn.

VISITOR INFORMATION The city's **Wrangell Visitor Center** is in the Nolan Center, along with the Wrangell Museum, on the water in the heart of town at 296 Campbell Dr. (℡800/367-9745; www.wrangell.com). Staff from both the Nolan Center and the U.S. Forest Service are on hand to answer questions.

The Forest Service's **Wrangell Ranger District Office** is at 525 Bennett St. (P.O. Box 51), Wrangell, AK 99929 (℡907/874-2323; www.fs.fed.us/r10/tongass), located on the hill behind town. Forest Service personnel here and at the visitor center have local knowledge of the logging roads and fishing holes, offer printed information on each Forest Service cabin and path, and, for $10, sell a detailed Wrangell Island Road Guide topographic map, which is printed on waterproof material. The district office is open Monday through Friday from 8am to 4:30pm.

ORIENTATION The main part of town is laid out north to south along the waterfront on the northern point of Wrangell Island. **Front Street** is the main

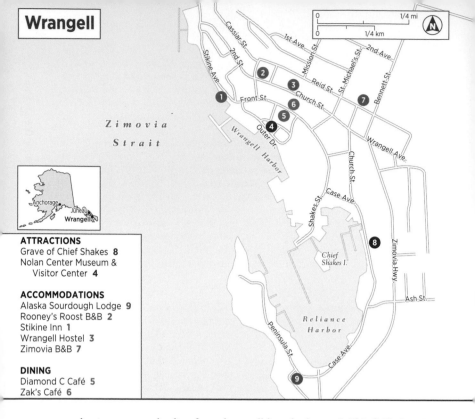

Wrangell

business street, leading from the small-boat harbor and **Chief Shakes Island** at the south to the city dock and the ferry dock at the north. Most of the rest of the town is along **Church Street,** which runs parallel to Front Street a block higher up the hill. **Evergreen Avenue** and **Bennett Street** form a loop to the north that goes to the airport. The only road to the rest of the island, the **Zimovia Highway,** heads out of town to the south, paved for about 12 miles, then connects to more than 100 miles of gravel logging roads built and maintained by the Forest Service, most of which are usable by two-wheel-drive vehicles in the summer.

GETTING AROUND You can do the town on foot, but you will need wheels for the airport or Zimovia Highway. **Practical Rent A Car** is located at the Wrangell Airport (☎907/874-3975). **Northern Lights Taxi** is at ☎907/874-4646.

SPECIAL EVENTS The **Garnet Festival,** held the third week of April, marks the arrival of the sea lions, hooligans (a smelt also known as eulachon), shorebirds, and a great concentration of bald eagles on the Stikine River Delta, a spring tornado of wildlife in the region's largest coastal marshes. Community activities take place in town, while jet boat tours traverse the delta. **The Wrangell King Salmon Derby,** the last half of May and first half of June, started in 1953. Contact the Wrangell Chamber of Commerce for details (☎907/874-3901; www.wrangellchamber.org). Wrangell also puts on a classic small-town **Independence Day** celebration.

[FastFACTS] WRANGELL

Bank Wells Fargo is at 115 Front St., with an ATM. There's also a **First Bank** ATM across from the Stikine Inn.

Hospital Wrangell Medical Center is at 310 Bennett St. (☎ **907/874-7000**).

Internet Access At the **Nolan Center,** 296 Campbell Dr. (☎ **907/874-3770**), access is $5 for the first 20 minutes, $10 an hour. It's free at the public library on Church Street ([tel **907/874-3535**).

Police For non-emergency calls, dial ☎ **907/874-3304.**

Post Office At 105 Federal Way, across from the Stikine Inn.

Taxes Sales tax is 7%. Rooms are taxed at 13%.

Exploring Wrangell & Environs

Before white settlers arrived, the Tlingit had already warred for centuries over this strategic trading location near the mouth of the Stikine River. The first Chief Shakes was a successful conqueror who enslaved his enemies, then handed down power through the female line, in the Tlingit tradition, for seven generations. Charlie Jones was recognized as Chief Shakes VII, the last of the line, at a potlatch in 1940, but the position had long since lost most of its status. The decline began after the Alaska purchase, in 1867. Word came of the Emancipation Proclamation, which theoretically freed a third of the residents of the coast's Tlingit villages. Chief Shakes VI sent his slaves in canoes to dry halibut; they kept paddling home to Puget Sound, never looking back. (An excellent pamphlet, "Authentic History of Shakes Island and Clan," by F. L. Keithhahn, sells for $4 at the Nolan Center Museum, described below.)

Chief Shakes Island, a tiny islet in the middle of the small-boat harbor, is the site of a Tlingit clan house and collection of totem poles constructed by

Chief Shakes Island.

Native workers, using traditional tools, in the Civilian Conservation Corps during the 1930s. Unlike some CCC clan house replicas in the region, which mix Tlingit styles, this house is an exact, scaled-down copy of the house in which Chief Shakes VI lay in state in 1916. The inside of the clan house is fascinating, both in the sense it gives of the people's ways, and for some extraordinary artifacts. A community fundraiser is underway to repair major rot that impairs the building. Along with that effort, the Native owners of the house have set up a website and plan a regular schedule when visitors can see the clan house, which previously had been open somewhat unpredictably. Those hours will be posted around town, or on the site www.shakesisland.com. Admission is $5. Otherwise, you can pay a $25 minimum to have someone come down and show you around. Great-granddaughters of Chief Shakes VII open the house: Tis Peterman (☎907/874-3097), or, if you can't reach Tis, Carol Snoddy (☎907/874-3538). Even if you can't arrange to get in, visit the island to see the totem poles and the charming setting (and, with extra time, visit the grave of Chief Shakes V, on Case Ave. just across the harbor). You can often see an otter near the island's footbridge.

The carved house posts in the clan house are replicas of the mid-18th-century originals protected by the local museum. These are probably the oldest and certainly the best-preserved Tlingit house posts in existence, still bearing the original fish-egg and mineral paints, and a gash where, during a potlatch, a chief hacked off an image that a visitor admired and gave it to him—a gesture that demonstrated the extent of his wealth then, and still does.

The **Nolan Center Museum,** 296 Campbell Dr. (☎907/874-3770), is an impressive building, with galleries devoted to natural history, logging and fishing,

A carving at Petroglyph Beach.

and Native culture. The museum owns many important early Alaska Native pieces, and a lot of just plain old stuff telling the story of Wrangell, one of Alaska's most historic towns. Admission is $5 adults, $3 seniors, $2 children ages 6 to 12; family admission is $12. The museum is open May 1 to September 30 Monday through Saturday 10am to 5pm, the rest of the year Tuesday through Saturday 1 to 5pm, or by appointment. Don't miss the shop, which has an extraordinary collection of books on Alaska and authentic Native crafts for bargain prices.

The museum helped preserve an impressive set of petroglyphs that lie on the beach a mile north of town. The 50 carvings at **Wrangell Petroglyph Beach State Historic Park** probably represent the work of forgotten indigenous people pre-dating the Tlingit and were made over a long period of time. The images, chipped into rocks, are of animals and geometric forms. Their purpose is lost to time. Walk north on Evergreen Avenue and follow the signs down to the beach (don't go within an hour of high tide). Replicas of the petroglyphs were carved so that visitors who want to take rubbings will not destroy the originals; also try not to step on them. The great pleasure here is simply to search for the carvings—they're just lying out there, and it takes some looking—and to wonder at their meaning and age.

Getting Outside

ON THE ISLAND Wrangell Island's network of gravel roads, maintained by the Forest Service, leads to places of awesome beauty rarely visited by non-Alaskans. There are a few day-hike trails, some lovely campsites, and paths to remote shelters and fishing lakes you can have to yourself. There are also a couple of calm and scenic places to start a kayak paddle.

There's only one way out of town: south on the **Zimovia Highway** along narrow Zimovia Strait. The Forest Service map (see "Visitor Information," above) is helpful for anything you might want to do along this route. The first potential stop is **City Park,** just south of town. Besides having a picnic area on the shore among big trees, it's a fine **tide pooling** spot. Go a couple of hours before a good low tide.

Five miles out on Zimovia Highway, you reach the **Shoemaker Bay Recreation Area,** with a small boat harbor, campground, and picnic sites (see "A Hostel & Camping," later in this chapter). Continuing south, **Eight Mile Beach** is a good stop for a ramble, and don't miss **Nemo Point,** a high, oceanside overlook from which you can see more than 13 miles along Zimovia Strait all the way back to town. There are eight gorgeous campsites, and a plank walking trail (described under "Hiking," below) along the road leads down to the beach.

All the way across the island, about 45 minutes from town, **Earl West Cove** gives access to the protected wilderness waters on the Eastern Passage. There's a campsite there, too.

OFF THE ISLAND Wrangell provides a stepping-off point for vast, rich wild lands and remote fishing, rafting, sea kayaking, or wildlife watching. I've described two of the main off-island destinations below—the Stikine River and the Anan Wildlife Observatory—but there are many more, too many to mention. The guides I've listed can give ideas, or look into the Forest Service cabins for rent to the public, many of which provide exclusive access

Stop in for a Swim

Every time I visit Wrangell I end up envying the people living there. **The Wrangell Municipal Pool** helps cause that reaction. It's also a good stop for visitors on rainy days (which are plentiful here). The facility, at 321 Church St., next to the high school (℡**907/874-2444**), has a weight room, sauna, racquetball and basketball courts, and the pool itself, which during open swim contains a giant inflatable dinosaur that drives children gaga. General admission costs all of $2.50 for adults, and court fees are similarly very inexpensive, and towels are for rent. It's open Monday to Friday 6:30am to 8pm, Saturday noon to 4pm.

to exceptional fishing. To get beyond the island, you need a boat or floatplane. You can go independently, hiring a water taxi for $200 to $260 an hour; it costs more than $500, one-way, to get to a remote Forest Service cabin by boat. That service is offered by various operators (see "Gearing Up," below). If you prefer to go by air, **Sunrise Aviation** (℡**800/874-2311** or 907/874-2319; www.sunriseflights.com) is a Wrangell-based operator offering charters and glacier flightseeing.

GEARING UP For a lift over the water, a guide, or rental equipment, there are several long-established businesses. **Alaska Waters,** with a desk in the Stikine Inn, 107 Stikine Ave. (℡**800/347-4462** or 907/874-2378; www.alaskawaters.com), rents equipment and offers various marine services, including fishing and tours. Check the website for monthly specials and other useful information. **Alaska Vistas,** at the city dock where the cruise ships land (℡**866/874-3006** or 907/874-3006; www.alaskavistas.com), started as a sea-kayaking business, but now offers water taxis; guided hiking and rafting; rental of canoes, kayaks, and rafts; and other services. You can stop in at their office on the dock for advice, books and maps, gear, and espresso. Both companies are listed below under the appropriate headings. There are other excellent charter businesses in town as well.

OUTDOOR ACTIVITIES NEAR WRANGELL

FISHING Anglers can dip a line in various streams and lakes on Wrangell Island reachable by car or a drive and short hike. The Forest Service provides a list, and the **Alaska Department of Fish and Game** (℡**907/874-3822;** www.adfg.state.ak.us, click "Sport Fish" then the Southeast region) publishes an extensive *Petersburg/Wrangell Sport Fishing Guide,* available online or in print. May and June are the prime months for king salmon fishing, silvers start in July, and halibut are available all summer. **Alaska Waters** (see "Gearing Up," above) offers a long day of saltwater fishing for $250 per person; they're professional and knowledgeable. They also rent skiffs with outboard motors for self-guided fishing. Many other charter boats are available at the harbor; ask at the visitor center. You can often arrange to use part of the day on the boat for sightseeing and wildlife watching, too.

HIKING Across the road from the Shoemaker Bay Recreation Area, the **Rainbow Falls Trail** climbs steeply for just under a mile (and 500 ft. in elevation gain) on a boardwalk with steps, up a ridge between two creeks, forested with big, mossy Sitka spruce and western hemlock. The falls seem to tumble down between the branches. From that point, you can continue another 2.7 miles and another 1,100 feet higher into open alpine terrain on the **Institute Creek Trail** to the Shoemaker Overlook, where there are great views, a picnic area, and a shelter. An additional section of the trail continues from there another 8 miles across the island.

Besides Rainbow Falls, various other walks start from the logging roads—the Forest Service can point the way. The **Nemo Saltwater Access Trail** is a well-built ½-mile plank walk leading to the beach near Turn Island, near a wonderful stand of red cedar and the Turn Island Campsite, with two wooden platforms, picnic tables, and dry firewood. An easy 1-mile **trail to Thoms Lake** was reconstructed in 2008, starting from the Nemo–Skip Loop Road (Forest Rd. 6267). Another good choice is the **Salamander Ridge Trail,** which leads a mile to subalpine terrain, where you can go off-trail hiking. The trail begins 27 miles from Wrangell on Salamander Road, also known as Forest Road 50050. The **Long Lake Trail** leads over a half-mile boardwalk to a public shelter and rowboat on the lake, on Forest Road 6271 (you'll need a map).

SEA KAYAKING Alaska Vistas (see "Gearing Up," above) offers kayaking day-trip paddles starting from the boat harbor, longer day tours to lovely Earl West Cove on the east side of the island, or guided trips of many days.

THE STIKINE RIVER

The Stikine's gray, glacial waters rush all the way from the dry Interior of British Columbia to a broad, shallow delta in the rainforest a few miles from Wrangell. It's among the fastest free-flowing navigable rivers in North America, and in early

Touring glaciers by floatplane.

A boat tour of Shakes Creek.

gold-rush years was a route through the Coastal Range. Tours that sometimes go as far as Telegraph Creek, B.C., speed against the current with the roar of high-powered engines that send a jet of water out from under their shallow, metal bottoms. On still water, the jet boats can go as fast as a car on the highway.

The shallow delta is an exceptionally rich wildlife-viewing area, a habitat of grasslands, braided channels, and marshes populated by sea lions, eagles, and many other species of birds. In late April and early May, when the hooligan run, more than 1,500 bald eagles congregate, and some two million other birds rest on their West Coast migration. Later in the year, when summer's salmon are running, you can see them thrashing in their spawning pools. Farther upriver, tours encounter Sitka black-tailed deer, moose, brown and black bears, mountain goats, river otters, and beavers.

Why the Garnet Stands?

In the streets of Wrangell you sometimes encounter kids selling garnets the way children other places sell lemonade. The gems come from the Garnet Ledge, near the mouth of the Stikine River, a mine that is still productive recreationally 130 years after its discovery. A visit to the mine isn't worth the effort for most travelers, but the story is interesting. The ledge was mined commercially from 1907 to 1936 by the first all-woman corporation in the nation, a group of investors from Minneapolis. Its current ownership is unusual, too: A 1962 deed gave the mine to all the children of Wrangell, which is interpreted to mean that only children have the right to remove the stones. You can get a water taxi out there, but take a Wrangell child along if you intend to take garnets. Of course, it's easier simply to buy garnets from a kid at a card table in the street.

Traveling upriver, tours usually stop at the **Shakes Glacier** and **Shakes Lake,** where there are 3,000-foot cliffs and some 50 waterfalls. Among others, Alaska Waters and Alaska Vistas offer these outings (see "Gearing Up," above). Some trips stop at the Forest Service–owned **Chief Shakes Hot Springs,** where there's an indoor and an outdoor tub for public bathing. Alaska Waters goes all the way to Telegraph, B.C., 160 miles upriver, bringing travelers to a remote homestead lodge. Commentary on all their trips includes natural history and Tlingit cultural traditions and legends. A 4-day, 3-night package is $1,499. The going rate for a 5-hour jet-boat tour from Wrangell to the glacier, delta, and hot springs is $150 to $180.

Rafting the Stikine offers fast water, expansive scenery, and the potential for a remote, many-day journey. Alaska Vistas offers these guided trips, lasting about 9 days, for an inclusive price of around $2,600 per person. Alaska Vistas also rents rafts and other gear for floating the Stikine. (See "Gearing Up," above.)

ANAN WILDLIFE OBSERVATORY

When the pink salmon are running in July and August (peak is mid-July to Aug 20), a population of about 60 black **bears** and 10 brown bears gather near a waterfall on Anan Creek, on the mainland southeast of Wrangell Island, often walking close to a platform where visitors stand watching. Don't visit outside the time of this salmon run, however, unless you have it on good authority that bears are actively using the creek. Forest Service interpreters are on duty during the bear months; visitors must also follow safe bear behavior (they'll brief you when you arrive; also see "Outdoors Health & Safety," in chapter 3). Most visitors will enjoy a guided day trip from Wrangell more than going on their own. Both **Alaska Waters** and **Alaska Vistas** go by boat (see "Gearing Up," above). Expect to pay $200 to $250 per person for the hour-long run from Wrangell and at least a few hours with the bears. Both are good companies. Alaska Vistas particularly emphasizes the long day they spend with the bears and their guides' biology and game-management experience.

It's also possible to go to the Anan observatory without a guide, but you will need a pass issued by the Forest Service **Wrangell Ranger District Office,** 525 Bennett St. (P.O. Box 51), Wrangell, AK 99929 (☎ **907/874-2323;** fax 907/874-7595; www.fs.fed.us/r10/tongass/districts/wrangell). Check the website for an explanation of the system, a calendar showing the number of permits available each day, and application forms. A total of 60 passes are allocated for each day of the period from July 5 through August 25, with 12 held back until 3 days before the

Brown bear at Anan Wildlife Observatory.

visit. Passes are given out first-come, first-served by mail, fax, e-mail, or in person and cost $10. There's a Forest Service cabin for rent, too, in very high demand during the bear-viewing season. The walk to the observatory is a half-mile from the shore where you land, on a good trail. **Sunrise Aviation** (☎800/874-2311 or 907/874-2319; www.sunriseflights.com) offers charters to Anan for prices competitive with going by boat.

Where to Stay

Besides the accommodations listed in detail, families and fishing groups will enjoy **Grand View Bed & Breakfast,** Mile 2, Zimovia Hwy. (☎907/874-3225; www.grandviewbnb.com), with lots of room, cooking facilities, well-equipped new rooms, and breakfast cooked to the guests' specifications. Rates are $115 double, and the B&B does not accept credit cards. You'll also find clean but basic budget rooms at **Diamond C Hotel,** 225 Front St. (☎907/874-3322; www.diamondchotel.com), for $95 per room, regardless of number of guests, year-round.

Alaskan Sourdough Lodge ★ For-mer mayor Bruce Harding runs this hotel in the style of a fishing lodge, renting the rooms alone or as packages with trips to the Anan Bear Observatory, Stikine River tours, fishing, kayaking, rafting, and other outdoor activities. The attractive building with a wraparound porch is immaculately kept. It stands in a waterfront area about a mile from the ferry dock, but Harding will drive you there or wherever else you want to go. The lodge is decorated on an outdoors theme. Most rooms are small, and some have shower stalls rather than tubs. The suite is huge and has a Jacuzzi tub. Fresh seafood dinners are served nightly, family style (you eat what they cook). Dinner prices are $19 to $24 per person; nonguests by reservation only.

1104 Peninsula (P.O. Box 1062), Wrangell, AK 99929. ☎800/874-3613 or 907/874-3613. Fax 907/874-3455. www.akgetaway.com. 16 units. $124 double; $209 suite. Rates include continental breakfast. AE, DC, DISC, MC, V. **Amenities:** Free airport transfers; bike rental; fish freezing; sauna. In room: TV, high-speed Internet.

Rooney's Roost Bed & Breakfast A warm family has offered this old downtown house with dormer windows to guests for many years. Antiques rest on the hardwood floors in the common areas, and the four rooms, while small, are decorated according to cute themes. All have private bathrooms and four-poster beds with thick mattresses, comforters, and oversize pillows. In the summer, elaborate breakfasts with local ingredients, such as seafood or berries, are served in a sunny dining room at the guests' convenience.

206 McKinnon (P.O. Box 552), Wrangell, AK 99929. ☎907/874-2026. Fax 907/874-4404. www.rooneysroost.com. 4 units. $115 double. Extra person $25. Rates include full breakfast. MC, V.

Stikine Inn ★ The waterfront hotel has been a center of community activity for decades, and attentive owners have worked at upgrading and remodeling it a little at a time for several years. The public spaces had terrific improvements in 2008, including a coffee bar and lounge, The Stik, with dark hardwood floors and a fresh but classic look. Also new, a women's salon and spa, The Parlor (☎907/874-3595; Mon–Sat 10am–5pm), occupies a bright, tiled space with ocean views. The rooms are comfortable and clean and have been kept up, but I hope new furniture fits in the next round of hotel improvements. For guests, the convenience of the location can't be better, close to the ferry dock and right on the water's edge. Rooms sharing superb water views carry an $11 to $12 premium. You can watch the sunset on the ocean and hear water lapping the shore.

The **Stikine Inn Restaurant** offers pleasant casual meals in a dining room that is noticeably clean and bright and has a terrific view. Simple local specialties, such as the halibut and chips, are done quite well and priced reasonably for the region. The salads also are very good. The restaurant serves lunch and dinner year-round. Prices range from $9 to $35.

107 Stikine Ave. (P.O. Box 662), Wrangell, AK 99929. (**888/874-3388** or 907/874-3388. Fax 907/874-3923. www.stikineinn.com. 35 units. $114–$140 double/quad; $131–$160 suite. Rates constant all year. AE, DC, DISC, MC, V. **Amenities:** Restaurant; airport/ferry courtesy van. *In room:* TV, Wi-Fi ($7 a day).

Zimovia Bed & Breakfast ★★ 🏚 The cedar-shingled house 2 blocks above Front Street contains a pair of extraordinary hand-crafted rooms—one with a boat's door on the closet, garnets in the tiles, and a cedar-walled sauna, the other decorated with hand-fused glass tiles and a glass sink atop a display of coral, sand, and glass fish. Nor is the beauty skin deep. Both rooms are encased in 10-inch-thick soundproofed walls and have heated floors, and the linens and beds are sumptuously first-rate. Each unit has a private entrance from a riotously blooming garden outside. The hospitality of hostess Barb Rugo—with her wonderful baking—matches the attention to excellence that has been poured into creating the place. She even picks up guests on arrival and gives them a town tour.

319 Weber St. (P.O. Box 1424), Wrangell, AK 99929. (**866/946-6842** or 907/874-2626. www.zimoviabnb.com. 2 units. $100 double. MC, V. Rates include continental breakfast. *In room:* Satellite TV/VCR, stocked fridge, kitchenette, Wi-Fi.

A HOSTEL & CAMPING

Wrangell Hostel is at the First Presbyterian Church, 220 Church St. (P.O. Box 439), Wrangell, AK 99929 (**907/874-3534**). They're open Memorial Day through Labor Day, the rate is $20 a night, and there is no daytime lock-out period.

There are several attractive campgrounds in Wrangell. I've never seen another campground in a spot like the mountaintop **Nemo Point Forest Service Campground** (see "Getting Outside," earlier in this section), but it's more than a dozen miles out of town. Five miles south of town, the **Shoemaker Bay Recreation Area** has sites by the road overlooking the boat harbor, right across from the Rainbow Falls Trail. There are free tent sites and RV sites with electric hookups for $25 a night, $15 without electric; the camping fee includes use of the town pool and its showers (see "Stop in for a Swim," above). Contact the **Wrangell Recreation and Parks Department** (**907/874-2444**) for information. They also manage **City Park,** right at the edge of town on Zimovia Highway, where camping is permitted with a 1-night limit.

For a full hookup RV site, try **Alaska Waters'** small park, 241 Berger St. (**800/347-4462**). They charge $25 a night for rigs up to 35 feet, $30 over that length.

Where to Dine

The two hotels (see "Where to Stay," above) also offer some of Wrangell's best dining. **Alaskan Sourdough Lodge** serves meals to guests, and to others by reservation. It's a family style dinner without a menu. The **Stikine Inn Restaurant** is a popular spot, with excellent simple meals.

You have other choices for deli sandwiches or a simple meal, including the **Diamond C Coffee Shop,** 223 Front St. (☎ 907/874-3350), next to the cafe of the same name, described below. It's a typical coffee and espresso shop, with good daily sandwich specials for lunch, such as the halibut panini served the day we visited. The deli at **Bob's IGA,** 223 Brueger St. (☎ 907/874-2341), produces good sandwiches and also sells ice cream. It is open Monday through Saturday 9am to 6pm.

Diamond C Cafe ★ DINER This is a clean, reliable diner offering speedy, friendly service and well-done food from the grill. Indeed, it produces some of the most consistently satisfying meals in town. On our latest visit, the day's fresh halibut, perfectly and simply grilled, came with a generous salad and garlic bread, all for $11. The pies are delicious, too. The menu is lengthy, but all prices are reasonable and the food familiar and done right.

215 Front St. ☎ **907/874-3677.** Breakfast $5.50–$12; lunch $7.50–$14. AE, MC, V. Mon–Sat 6am–3pm; Sun 6am–2pm.

Zak's Café ★ SEAFOOD Options are few in the evening, but this is a good one. The owners started it partly out of frustration with the lack of fine dining in Wrangell, and their dinner menu of halibut, salmon, steaks, pasta, poultry, and stir fry could come from many a traditional restaurant in a larger town. For lunch they serve salads, wraps, burgers, and sandwiches. We've found the cuisine sometimes excellent, other times too heavy or not perfectly executed, but the hospitality is always wonderful from the fascinating owners, James and Katherine, who staff the kitchen and dining room, respectively. On our last visit they were cooking with donated food and giving the proceeds from dinner to Heifer International.

316 Front St. ☎ **907/874-3355.** Reservations recommended for dinner. Lunch $6.25–$10; dinner $13–$25. MC, V. Mon–Sat 11am–8pm.

PETERSBURG: UNVARNISHED THRESHOLD TO THE OUTDOORS

Petersburg is the perfect small town, the sort of prosperous, picturesque, quirky place that used to be mythologized in Disney films. Except that Petersburg would never let Disney in the door. People here are too smart for that, and too protective of a place they know would be spoiled by too much attention. For the same reason, Petersburg's residents are just as glad the big cruise ships can't enter their narrow harbor. The town is unspoiled by the ships' throngs of tourists and seasonal gift shops. Instead, locals spend the money that keeps Nordic Drive, the main street, thriving with family-owned grocery and hardware stores, a fish market, and other businesses. Wooden streets over Hammer Slough still serve utilitarian purposes, making them far more appealing than if they were prettied

Homes in Petersburg reflected in the waters of the Inside Passage.

up as tourist areas. As you walk along Sing Lee Alley and check out the stylish little bookstore, you rarely see others like yourselves—instead, you see Norwegian fishermen in pickup trucks and blond-haired kids on bikes.

Because Petersburg is insular and authentic, the sublime outdoor opportunities nearby remain little used. There are wonderful trails, mountain-biking routes, and secret places. On the water, the humpback whale–watching is as reliable as anywhere in Alaska and largely undiscovered. There's a glacier to visit, terrific fishing, and limitless sea-kayaking waters. The in-town attractions are few—a day is plenty for simple sightseeing—and little attempt has been made to accommodate lazy gawkers. But Alaska's best is waiting for those willing to spend the effort to look.

Petersburg is named for its founder, Peter Buschmann, who killed himself after living here for only 4 years. But that shouldn't be a reflection on the town, which is in an ideal location and has flourished since that inauspicious beginning. In 1898, or thereabouts (historians differ), Buschmann founded a cannery on Mitkof Island facing the slender, peaceful Wrangell Narrows in what was to become Petersburg. The stunning abundance of salmon and halibut and a nearby source of ice—the LeConte Glacier—made the site a natural. Buschmann had emigrated from Norway in 1891 and, as a proud old son of Norway told me, he always hired Norwegians. Any Norwegian who came to him, he hired. In a few years, the cannery failed. Perhaps an excessive payroll? My suggestion was met with an icy glance and a change of subject. Teasing aside, Buschmann's mistake was merging his cannery with a firm trying to challenge a monopolistic canning operation, and they went down together.

Buschmann's suicide followed his financial reverses, but the promise of Petersburg remained. The Norwegians stayed and slowly built a charming town of white clapboard houses with steeply pitched roofs, hugging the water. Their living came from the sea, as it still does. Appropriately, the downtown area doesn't stop at water's edge. Roads, boardwalks, and buildings continue over the smooth waters of Wrangell Narrows, out to the cannery buildings that survive on long wooden piers, and into the boat harbors, which branch out in a network far more extensive than the city's streets.

Today the town's economy is based on fishing and government work. The Stikine Ranger District of the Tongass National Forest is headquartered here. That makes for a wealthy, sophisticated, and stable population.

Essentials

GETTING THERE Petersburg has the most welcoming **ferry terminal** in the system (☎907/772-3855), with a grassy lawn and a pier from which to watch the boats and marine animals. It's about a mile to the town center. The **Alaska Marine Highway** (☎800/642-0066; www.ferryalaska.com) connects to Juneau directly (an 8-hr. run), or by way of Sitka, far to the west; the details of the schedule are complicated and have changed in recent years, so your best source of information is the website. The fare is $33 from Wrangell (3 hr.), $45 from Sitka (8 hr.), and $66 from Juneau (10 hr.).

Petersburg is served by **Alaska Airlines** jets (☎800/252-7522; www. alaskaair.com) once north and once south each day, with the nearest stops on the puddle jumper being Juneau and Wrangell. From the airport, call **Metro Cab** (☎907/772-2700) or **Midnight Rides** (☎907/772-2222) for a taxi into town.

VISITOR INFORMATION The Petersburg Chamber of Commerce **Visitor Information Center,** at the corner of 1st and Fram streets (P.O. Box 649), Petersburg, AK 99833 (☎866/484-4700 or 907/772-4636; www.petersburg. org), offers guidance on outdoor opportunities, boats, lodgings, and Forest Service cabins; distributes trail guides, maps, and natural history publications; and sells useful books. The center is open in summer Monday through Saturday from 9am to 5pm, Sunday from noon to 4pm; winter Monday through Friday from 10am to 2pm.

The full-service **Viking Travel** agency, corner of Nordic Drive and Sing Lee Alley (☎800/327-2571 or 907/772-3818; www.alaskaferry.com), also specializes in booking local guides for tours, kayaks, whale-watching, flights, fishing charters, bear viewing, and other activities. Owners Dave and Nancy Berg are knowledgeable and helpful.

ORIENTATION Petersburg is on Mitkof Island, divided from the much larger Kupreanof Island by the long, slender channel of the Wrangell Narrows. There are three small-boat harbors and so many docks, boardwalks, and wooden streets that the town seems to sit on the ocean. **Nordic Drive** is the main street, running from the ferry dock through town, then becoming **Sandy Beach Road** as it rounds Hungry Point to the north. At Sandy Beach, you can circle back, past the airport, which stands above the town, to **Haugen Drive,** which meets Nordic again near **Hammer Slough,** right in town. To the south, Nordic becomes the **Mitkof Highway,** which runs to the undeveloped balance of the island.

ATTRACTIONS
Clausen Memorial Museum **11**
Eagle's Roost Park **13**
Fishermen's Memorial Park **4**
Sons of Norway Hall **5**

ACCOMMODATIONS
Alaska Island Hostel **12**
Bumbershoot B&B **14**
Das Hagedorn Hans B&B **10**
Scandia House **7**
Sea Level B&B **14**
Tides Inn Motel **9**

DINING
Helse **3**
Java Hus **7**
Joan Mei Restaurant **1**
Papa Bear's Pizza **8**
Rooney's Northern Lights **2**
Tina's Kitchen **6**

Wrangell Narrows

North Boat Harbor

Dolphin St.
Visitor Info. Center
Excel St.
N. Fram St.
Gjoa St.

Sing Lee Al.

Haugen Dr.
Ira II St.
Kiseno St.

Alaska Ferry Dock

South Boat Har.

Odin St.

Petersburg

0 ——— 1/4 mi
0 ——— 1/4 km

Anchorage
Juneau
Petersburg

GETTING AROUND You can walk downtown Petersburg, but you'll need wheels or a boat to get to most outdoor activities. The **Tides Inn Motel** and **Scandia House** (see "Where to Stay," later in this chapter) both rent cars, but not many are available in town, so book well in advance for summer.

A **bike** is a great way to get around town and explore the island. A shop called **Zoom,** across from the Tides Inn at 400 Nordic Dr. (✆**907/772-2546**), rents mountain bikes for $25 for 24 hours. It is open April through October Monday through Friday 9am to 5pm.

A boat opens more of the area than any other mode of transportation, allowing exploration of Wrangell Narrows, the trails on the far side, and the opportunity for inexpensive self-guided fishing. **Doyle's Boat Rentals,** in North Harbor (✆**877/442-4010** or 907/772-4439; www.doylesboatrentals. com), offers 18-foot skiffs and a 21-foot runabout with a top, with quality outboards and trolling motors, for $135 and $300 a day, respectively, including a crab pot. The firm also rents fishing and shrimping gear. The Scandia House also rents small boats.

SPECIAL EVENTS The **Little Norway Festival,** which celebrates the May 17, 1814, declaration of independence of Norway from Sweden, is an occasion for Petersburg to go wild. The 4-day schedule of events includes a street fair,

[FastFACTS] PETERSBURG

Banks There are two banks, both with ATMs, at the intersection of Nordic Drive and Fram Street.

Hospital Petersburg Medical Center is at 2nd and Fram streets (☎907/772-4291).

Internet Access Free at the public library, at Nordic and Haugen drives (☎907/772-3349).

Police Find them on Nordic Drive near Haugen; nonemergencies ☎907/772-3838.

Post Office Near the airport on Haugen Street. **Trading Union Grocery Store,** 401 N. Nordic (☎907/772-3881), sells stamps and has a postal drop box.

Taxes Sales tax is 6%. The tax on accommodations totals 10%.

food and craft booths, a luncheon and bunad-style show (a bunad is a traditional embroidered Norwegian costume), street music and dancing, and a salmon bake on the beach. The celebration is held on the third full weekend of May. The **King Salmon Derby** offers $30,000 in prizes over Memorial Day weekend. **July 4th** is a very big deal in Petersburg and lasts 2 days. The **Canned Salmon Classic** lasts from July 1 to August 15, with a first prize of up to $4,000 going to the person who guesses how many cans of salmon will be packed in Petersburg during the season. The **Festival of Lights** begins the day after Thanksgiving with an evening candlelight parade, the lighting of the Community Christmas Tree, and caroling. **Julebukking,** a Norwegian tradition, happens on Christmas Eve, when merchants offer food and drink to their customers and the streets fill with people under twinkling white lights.

For information on any of the above events, contact the **Petersburg Chamber of Commerce** (☎866/484-4700 or 907/772-4636; www. petersburg.org).

Exploring Petersburg

A walk around Petersburg should include the boardwalk streets of **Hammer Slough,** the tidal mouth of a creek that feeds into the waterfront. **Sing Lee Alley** leads from North Nordic Drive at the charming center of town, passing by several interesting little shops, including **Sing Lee Alley Books,** at no. 11 (☎907/772-4440), where there's a good collection on natural history and local culture. Petersburg has so many thriving little shops because of its isolation and healthy economy—so far, it's been too small to attract the predation of Wal-Mart and other chains.

Sing Lee Alley turns from solid ground to wooden dock before you reach the **Sons of Norway Hall,** a town center where a large model Viking ship used in the Little Norway Festival is often parked. Next door, also on pilings, is the **Fishermen's Memorial Park.** Plaques memorialize Petersburg mariners lost at sea under a bronze statue of Bojer Wikan, a fisherman and lifelong resident.

Across the street, on the outboard side, **Tonka Seafoods** (☎888/560-3662 or 907/772-3662; www.tonkaseafoods.com) is a specialty fish processor with a shop and mail-order operation; they will process your sport-caught fish, too.

Continue on to Nordic Drive and turn left, crossing back over the slough to **Birch Street,** which follows the slough's bank on pilings upstream past old, weathered houses that hang over the placid channel. Many have one door for the road and another for the water. It's a charming, authentic place. Step out of the way of cars on the one-lane dock/street.

Back down at the waterfront, stroll the harbor floats to see the frenetic activity of the huge commercial fishing fleet in the summer, then continue north on Nordic Drive to **Eagle's Roost Park,** where there is a grassy area to sit and a stairway that leads down to the water. At low tide an interesting but rugged beach walk starts here. You're almost guaranteed to see eagles, which congregate for the fish waste from the nearby cannery. Look in the tops of the trees. (In fact, you can see eagles almost anytime and anywhere along the water in Petersburg.) Another nice walk leads you on a boardwalk a third of a mile over muskeg swamp from the uphill side of the elementary school, at 4th Street.

The **Clausen Memorial Museum,** at 2nd and Fram streets (☏**907/772-3598;** www.clausenmuseum.org), interprets Petersburg and its history for the people who live here. It has a living, community feel, like being invited into the town's collective memory. On one visit a portfolio of old photographs was on display with notes for visitors to write down the names of anyone they could identify. No doubt the local fishermen are fascinated by the obsolete fishing gear, rugged old nautical equipment, and a model fish trap, outlawed in 1959 when Alaska became a state. The world's record king salmon is mounted here—126.5 pounds—landed by a Petersburg commercial fisherman. It is almost 30 pounds heavier than the record sport-caught king, in Soldotna. The museum is open in

Large model Viking ship next to the Sons of Norway Hall.

summer Monday through Saturday from 10am to 5pm; call for hours in the winter. Admission is $3 for adults, free for children 12 and under.

There are some interesting gift and art shops in town. **Wild Celery Framing Studio and Eclectic Gifts,** 400 N. Nordic, carries a distinctive collection of art and jewelry, as well as gifts and linens, and has Norwegian carvings and turnings. **Seaport Gallery and Gifts,** 219 Nordic Dr. (www.petersburg.org/businesses/gift.html#seaport), concentrates on fine art, offering ceramics, prints, oils, and locally made jewelry by Sue Savage that is sold all over Alaska.

Getting Outside

I have listed only a few highlights from Petersburg's wealth of outdoor opportunities. For other choices, many of them just as good as those I've written about here, or for the detailed trail and backcountry information you'll need, contact the U.S. Forest Service at the **Petersburg Ranger District** offices at 12 N. Nordic Dr. (P.O. Box 1328), Petersburg, AK 99833 (☎**907/772-3871;** www.fs.fed.us/r10/tongass/districts/petersburg).

Some of the best places to go around Petersburg require a boat. **Viking Travel** (see "Visitor Information," above) books most of the dozen or so small charter boats that operate from the harbor at any one time, allowing them to consolidate small groups into 6- to 15-person boatloads for whale-watching, sightseeing, glacier viewing, or fishing. See p. 187 for the option of renting your own boat.

A few operators have made a specialty of natural history and environmentally responsible tours. Barry Bracken, a marine biologist, offers these kinds of trips on his 28-foot vessel. Contact **Kaleidoscope Cruises (☎800/TO-THE-SEA** [868-4373] or 907/772-3736; www.petersburglodgingandtours.com). You can also set up a package with Bracken for a multiday stay in a lovely waterfront guesthouse. To get to remote cabins by air, or for flightseeing, contact **Pacific Wing Air Charters (☎907/772-4258**).

SPECIAL PLACES

SANDY BEACH The beach at City Park is an easy bike ride or a longish walk 1½ miles up Nordic Drive, around Hungry Point at the northern tip of the island, then along Sandy Beach Road to the beach and picnic area. Return by way of the airport, coming back into town on Haugen Drive. The beach itself is coarse sand and fine gravel, and you can't swim in the frigid water, but it's a lovely spot, facing Frederick Sound on the east side of Mitkof Island.

If you go at high tide, you can beachcomb and bird-watch—a great blue heron was hanging around on one visit—but a better plan is to time your visit at low tide (free tide books are widely available, or ask at the visitor center). At tides of 1 foot or lower, you can see the outlines of ancient fish traps built on the beach beginning 2,000 years ago. They look like V-shaped rows of rocks, and at times you can see stakes. The indigenous people who built them knew how to create channels that would corral salmon at high tide, leaving them stranded to be gathered up when the water receded. These ancient people presumably also created the petroglyphs on rocks near the traps, which may depict the traps or could have something to do with the sun. Finding the traps and petroglyphs isn't easy—it's best if you can get someone to lead you, perhaps by joining the occasional Forest

Service walks that you can ask about at the Ranger District office. But, if you have the time and inclination to explore, walk out to the left from the picnic area, to the edge of the lagoon near the house with the greenhouse. A major petroglyph is on a black bedrock face, visible when you are looking back toward the picnic area, and the traps are just offshore from there. Please be sensitive to the delicate artifacts so they can last another 2,000 years, being especially careful of the fish trap stakes, which are not obvious and can be trampled.

RAVEN TRAIL & RAVEN'S ROOST CABIN About 4 miles up the steep but spectacular Raven Trail, which begins behind the airport off Haugen Drive roughly a mile from town, the Raven's Roost Forest Service cabin sits atop a mountain with a sweeping view of the town and surrounding waters and islands. It's the sort of place that inspires artists and poets. Allow 3 to 4 hours for the climb along a boardwalk, then up a steep muddy slope, then along a ridge, with an elevation gain of more than 1,000 feet. To stay at the cabin you'll need sleeping bags, cooking gear, lights, and food. Reserve the cabin through the national system described in under "Getting Outside in the Tongass National Forest," and check there for information sources on the other 19 cabins in the area, most of which are reached by plane or boat.

MITKOF ISLAND The Mitkof Highway, leading south from Petersburg, opens access to most of Mitkof Island, with its king salmon fishing; views of swans, fish, and glaciers; hiking trails; lakes; and many miles of remote roads for mountain biking. The town's swimming hole and ice-skating pond are out the road, too. Anyone can enjoy a day's sightseeing drive over the island, and if you like hiking and the outdoors, you'll find days of fun. Pick up the $9 *Forest Service Mitkof Island Road Guide* map at the visitor center or ranger office; it shows what you'll find along the way.

Black-tailed deer at Sandy Beach.

The **Three Lakes Loop Road** intersects with the highway twice, once 10 miles from Petersburg and again 20 miles from town. From the north intersection, the one closest to town, it's 15 more miles to the level, 4.5-mile boardwalk and dirt **Three Lakes Trail,** which circles four small lakes, each of which contains trout, and three of which have Forest Service rowboats for public use. A three-sided shelter at the smallest lake makes a good rest or camping spot. Besides the fish, the area is abundant with wildflowers and berries, and you may see deer, beavers, bear, and many birds, including seasonal sandhill cranes.

Fourteen miles down Mitkof Highway from Petersburg, a quarter-mile wheelchair-accessible boardwalk leads across the damp, hummocky

Mitkof Island.

ground of the rainforest muskeg to **Blind River Rapids,** a peaceful spot with a three-sided shelter where you can watch and fish for king salmon in June and silvers in September, and sometimes see eagles and bears feeding on the fish. A half-mile-long loop leads farther into the forest and muskeg.

At 17 miles, somewhat hidden in the trees on the right, a bird-watching blind looks out on **Blind Slough,** where trumpeter swans winter. Swans normally will be gone by mid-March, but later in the year you can see bear, salmon, and eagles.

At 18 miles you'll reach the **Blind Slough Recreation Area,** where locals go to swim in amber water in the summer. Water warms in the narrow slough, more than 5 miles from Wrangell Narrows. In the winter much of the town congregates here for ice-skating and bonfires.

At 20½ miles from Petersburg, the popular **Man Made Hole** picnic area and swimming pond has foot bridges and a pathway; it is accessible to people with disabilities.

At 22 miles you reach the **Ohmer Creek campground** ($6 camping fee in summer), with a 1-mile trail, a floating bridge over a beaver pond, and trout and some salmon in late summer. The road continues from here along the south shore of Mitkof Island, with great ocean views, to its end at mile 32.

PETERSBURG CREEK The lovely, grassy Petersburg Creek area could offer either an afternoon frolic among the meadows of wildflowers that meet the water, or could be the start to a challenging 21-mile, multiday hike into the **Petersburg Creek-Duncan Salt Chuck Wilderness.** The fishing is exceptional: The creek contains four species of salmon and two of trout. You'll need a skiff or sea kayak, or get a charter to drop you off, as the creek is on Kupreanof Island, across Wrangell Narrows from town; the state maintains a dock there. Sea-kayaking up the creek makes a wonderful day trip, which you can do on your own or with a guide (see "Sea Kayaking," below). A trail reaches two Forest Service cabins, at Petersburg Lake and East Salt Chuck, each with a boat for public use (reservations are required). The trail to the lake is not difficult, but continuing on to East Salt Chuck is tougher going, including wading some beaver ponds. At the lake you can fish for trout, and odds are good of seeing ducks, geese, loons, trumpeter swans, bald eagles, or black bears. The Kupreanof dock also provides access to the 3-mile, 3,000-foot trail that climbs Petersburg Mountain, a challenging hike that has spectacular views from the top.

ACTIVITIES

FISHING Besides the ocean fishing mentioned below, there are various fishing streams and lakes that you can reach on the roads, for cutthroat and rainbow trout and Dolly Varden char—several are mentioned above, under "Mitkof Island"—and many more lake and stream fishing opportunities are accessible by boat or plane. Check at the visitor center, or contact the **Alaska Department of Fish and Game** (☎907/772-5231; www.alaska. gov/adfg). They produce an informative *Petersburg/Wrangell Sport Fishing Guide*, available on the website (click on "Sport Fisheries," then the Southeast region and the Wrangell/Petersburg area). The site also contains updated fishing reports, run-timing calendars, and other useful information. You can request a printed version of the guide as well.

The boat harbor has a couple dozen licensed charter fishing boats, mostly six-passenger vessels. As elsewhere, halibut and salmon are usually the target. You can get a list of operators at the visitor center, or book through **Viking Travel** (see "Visitor Information," earlier). Half-day salmon charters cost around $175 per person, while halibut charters or longer salmon charters are $225 to $280 per day. You can rent your own boat and gear for much less, without a guide. See "Getting Around," p. 187.

SEA KAYAKING The waters of Wrangell Narrows are protected and interesting, with plenty to see. On longer trips of 3 days to a week, you can get out among the glaciers, Stikine River Delta, and even the whales—there's as much variety here, among these rainforest islands, as anywhere in the region. It's possible to set up a kayak trip linking some of the Forest Service cabins, too, or to use one as a base camp for a few days of exploration. (Get a copy of the free handout "Paddling the Petersburg Ranger

Takeout Lunch & Take-Home Fish

The counter at **Coastal Cold Storage**, at Excel Street and Nordic Drive (☎907/772-4177; www. coastalcoldstoragealaska.com), is a good stop for seafood or panini sandwiches, fried halibut and shrimp, king crab, or chowder, and, for breakfast, a bunch of choices, including eggs, kielbasa, or smoked salmon. At the same place they sell seafood from freezers and live from tanks, offer mail order through their website, and process anglers' catches to take home. Hours are Monday through Saturday 7am to 2pm, and the entire menu is served at all times.

Humpback whales feeding off Frederick Sound.

District" from the district office, or download it from their website.) **Tongass Kayak Adventures** (☎907/772-4600; www.tongasskayak.com) offers guided and unguided versions of each of these adventures (they rent equipment, too). Their 4-hour paddle crosses Wrangell Narrows from the harbor and penetrates Petersburg Creek, where they stop for a snack and often see bear and deer. No experience is required. They charge $85; reserve through Viking Travel, listed under "Visitor Information," above. A 3-night base camp tour costs $930 per person and an 8-night version begins at $1,980; reserve those trips directly with Tongass Kayak.

WHALE-WATCHING Most summers, Petersburg's **Frederick Sound** is one of the best places in the state to see humpbacks feeding. Whale-watching charters can go any day from May 15 to September 15, but the height is mid-summer. You may see stunning bubble-net feeding, when the whales confine a school of fish in a circle of bubbles, then lunge upward to scoop them up, bursting through the surface in a great swoosh. Whales have even been known to spy hop, poking their heads as high above the surface as possible in order to look down into the boats that are watching them. In summer 1995, a humpback jumped right into one of these boats, presumably accidentally. (No one was injured, but a few people fell into the water.) Several charter operators offer trips in small, six-passenger boats. Some, including Kaleidoscope Cruises (p. 190), have hydrophones on board, so you may be able to hear the whales' vocalizations while waiting for them to surface, if their feeding behavior and the water conditions are right. Book trips through Viking Travel or directly with one of the operators. Trips usually leave around 8am and stay out 6 to 10 hours, with several hours among the whales. Prices are $150 to $210 per person. Viking Travel's conference room (at the corner of Nordic Dr. and Sing Lee Alley) houses the Petersburg Marine Mammal Center (www.psgmmc.org), where you can use a computer or talk to interns to learn more about whales.

Where to Stay

There are lots of places with character to stay in Petersburg, more than I have room to describe in full. Besides those listed below, I also recommend **Das Hagedorn Haus,** right downtown at 400 2nd St. N. (☎907/772-3775; www. dashagedornhaus.com), where a wonderfully hospitable couple rents a full apartment in their historic home for $80 in high season, including amenities such as Wi-Fi, free laundry machines, and a full breakfast cooked to order. They do not take credit cards.

Bumbershoot Bed & Breakfast ★ 🎁 The industrious and delightful Gloria Ohmer, who also owns the Tides Inn Motel (see below), has opened her extraordinary waterfront home on Frederick Sound to guests as well. The rooms are large, decorated with quilts she made, and Gloria will happily show off beadwork, woodwork, sewing, stained glass, stone cutting and engraving, a fish-cleaning room, and deck barbecue. The place is brimming with Gloria's enthusiasm for life. Some rooms have water views, and the water is only barely beyond your reach. For $185 a night, you can rent the entire downstairs apartment, with two bedrooms, a kitchen, and a large living room with a fireplace.

901 Sandy Beach Rd. (P.O. Box 372), Petersburg, AK 99833. ☎907/772-4683. Fax 907/772-4627. 4 units, 2 with shared bathroom. $80–$90 double. Rates include continental breakfast. No credit cards. **Amenities:** Free airport transfers. *In room:* TV/VCR, hair dryer.

Scandia House ★★ Built in the town's distinctive Norwegian style, this building's solid simplicity puts it in a class by itself. White rooms with blonde-wood trim are blessed with natural light. They have various configurations of comfortable beds, including rooms with kitchenettes and a magnificent fourth-floor suite with towering ceilings. Most units have only one bed, and a few have shower stalls, not tubs. The hotel has an elevator and is barrier-free. The rooms are some of the cleanest I've ever seen, over various visits. A continental breakfast is served from 6 to 9:30am, including fresh homemade muffins. Book well in advance for the busy summer season. The owners offer skiff rentals and car rentals, and a hair salon is off the lobby.

110 Nordic Dr. (P.O. Box 689), Petersburg, AK 99833. ☎800/722-5006 or 907/772-4281. Fax 907/772-4301. www.scandiahousehotel.com. 33 units. $100–$130 double; $150 double with kitchenette; $185–$195 suite. Extra person 13 and older $10. Rates include continental breakfast. AE, DC, DISC, MC, V. **Amenities:** Free airport transfers; boat rental; courtesy van. *In room:* TV.

Sea Level Bed & Breakfast ★ 🎁 This remarkable building stands on pilings over the water, creating a sense of being at sea when you look out the big picture windows. At high tide you can fish from the front deck. It's perfect Petersburg, like many of the town's historic marine buildings, which reach to the sea as if unsatisfied with their land-bound fate—but the B&B is brand new, built for its purpose. Hostess Jean Ellis made it this way. She's a lifelong resident deeply rooted here, and a legislative staffer, full of stories and interesting political talk. There are two rooms, both well equipped and tastefully decorated with soft colors and floral quilts. She serves breakfast to order in the smaller room; the other unit has a full kitchen and living area, and Jean stocks it with self-service food. Each room has one bed and rents to no more than two adults, although kids are welcome without charge. The B&B does not accept credit cards.

N. Nordic Dr. (P.O. Box 1068), Petersburg, AK 99833. **☎907/772-3240.** www.sealevelbnb.com. 2 units. High season $110–$140 double; low season $90–$120 double. No credit cards. *In room:* TV, Wi-Fi.

Tides Inn Motel ★ ⚓ Few hotels in Alaska have such good rooms at such affordable prices. The kitchenette rooms are a particular bargain. The biggest difference among the rooms is the views, as all are well maintained. Those in the older part of the motel face the other building, while nonsmoking units in the front of the new section get a sweeping view. I watched bald eagles doing aerobatics less than 50 feet from my front window. The motel management is efficient and committed to quality, and they keep the motel in clean, attractive condition. Besides, it's one of the friendliest places I've ever stayed—the staff makes life easy. The hotel has an Avis car-rental franchise.

307 N. 1st St. (P.O. Box 1048), Petersburg, AK 99833. **☎800/665-8433** or 907/772-4288. Fax 907/772-4286. tidesinn@alaska.net. High season $90–$120 double; low season $65–$85 double. Extra person $10. Rates include light continental breakfast. AE, DC, DISC, MC, V. **Amenities:** Free airport transfers; Internet access. *In room:* TV, Wi-Fi.

Waterfront Bed & Breakfast The attraction here is the location, on pilings over the Wrangell Narrows near the ferry dock and steps from Emily's Bakery. Rooms have Mission-style oak beds with excellent mattresses and down comforters. Each unit has individual heat control. Bathrooms have shower stalls, not tubs. Four of the rooms have one bed—two with a queen and two with a double—and one has two double beds. The communal living room is cozy and has a great view.

1004 S. Nordic Dr. (P.O. Box 1613), Petersburg, AK 99833. **☎866/772-9301** or 907/772-9300. Fax 907/772-9308. www.waterfrontbedandbreakfast.com. 5 units. $100–$120 double, $10 each additional adult. Rates include full breakfast. MC, V. **Amenities:** Covered outdoor Jacuzzi.

A HOSTEL & CAMPING

Friendly little **Alaska Island Hostel,** 805 Gjoa St. (**☎877/772-3632** or 907/772-3632; www.alaskaislandhostel.com), has male and female dorm rooms with four beds in each and a family room with four beds. The $25 nightly rate includes room tax and Internet access. They're open regularly from June 1 to August 31. Check-in and office hours are 5 to 7pm or by arrangement.

The closest natural camping is found 22 miles out the Mitkof Highway at **Ohmer Creek** (see "Special Places: Mitkof Island," above). **Twin Creek RV Park** is 7½ miles out the highway (**☎907/772-3244**) and charges $28 for full hookups, $15 for tent camping. Showers are $3 extra.

Where to Dine

Emily's Bakery, 1000 Nordic Dr. (**☎907/772-4555**), is one of those inspired bakeries people write home about (or at least text about). If I didn't mention Emily's here, someone in Petersburg would tell you about it. The bakery produces truly memorable whole-grain pastries, cookies, bars, and cakes, as well as quiche that will fill you with longing until the day you return. Also for lunch, a loaf of whole wheat bread with a swirl of cheese and sautéed vegetables baked inside. Hours are Monday through Friday 8am to 4pm. The bakery itself has no seating, but Emily's Bakery items are sold along with good coffee at **Java Hus,** by Scandia House at 110 N. Nordic Dr. (☎907/772-2626), a bright, comfortable spot, open summer Monday through Saturday 6am to 6pm, Sunday 7am to 5pm; winter closing an hour earlier each day.

For terrific takeout pizza or calzone, burgers, fried fish, or other casual choices, try **Papa Bear's Pizza** (☎907/772-3727; www.papabearspizza.com), above Coastal Cold Storage at Excel Street and Nordic Drive. The owners are fanatics in search of the perfect pizza, and it shows. The pizzeria is open in summer Monday through Saturday 11am to 9pm, Saturday and Sunday 3 to 8pm (in winter Mon–Sat 11am–8pm; closed Sun). It is one of the better bets in town.

Helse, 13 Sing Lee Alley (☎907/772-3444), is a popular lunch spot serving soup, salads, and specials. The stir-fry is a good choice here. It is open summer Monday through Friday 8am to 5pm, Saturday 10am to 3pm; winter Monday through Saturday 11:30am to 3:30pm.

Joan Mei Restaurant ★ CHINESE This is a good choice for dinner. The whole family works together in a large, bright dining room, serving familiar Americanized Chinese cuisine and an appealing salad bar. Service is friendly and the food satisfying. Ask about the nightly specials. The menu also includes American items such as burgers and fried fish, well done, I'm told, and a few Mexican selections. Locals come here for a nice dinner out.

1103 S. Nordic Dr., across from the ferry dock. ☎907/772-4222. Lunch $7.50–$15; dinner $10–$25. MC, V. Mon–Tues and Thurs–Sat 11am–2pm and 4–8:30pm; Sun 8am–2pm and 4–8:30pm. Closed mid-Jan to mid-Feb.

Rooney's Northern Lights ★ SEAFOOD You couldn't find a much better site for a restaurant than this one, sitting on pilings in Hammer Slough, overlooking a boat harbor. Locals pack in for nicely prepared fried halibut and shrimp, salads, and sandwiches. In the evening you can order steaks as well, or pick from inexpensive Mexican selections or burgers. Healthy choices augment the heavy selections, and the restaurant has a good children's menu. Breakfast is done well, with big skillets or eggs Benedict. Call ahead to reserve one of the tables at the window or on the deck, where you can see Kupreanof Island, the fishermen working in the harbor, a cannery, and often waterfowl, seals, or a sea lion.

203 Sing Lee Alley. ☎907/772-2900. Lunch $7–$12; dinner $7–$30. MC, V. Mon–Sun 6am–9pm.

Tina's Kitchen ★ FAST FOOD On a sunny summer day, this booth in an empty lot next door to the Scandia House is *the* place for a quick and tasty lunch or dinner. Picnic-style dining is outdoors or in a heated tent. The menu includes Korean, Japanese, Mexican, and American choices, all for reasonable prices. Our halibut tacos were fresh and flavorful, and the mood of the happy teens and friendly staff were infectious.

104 N. Nordic Dr. ☎907/772-2090. All items $4.50–$11. No credit cards. Mon–Sat 10am–8pm; Sun 11am–7pm. Closed Oct to mid-Apr.

SITKA: RICH PRIZE OF RUSSIAN CONQUEST

If I could visit only one Alaska town, it would probably be Sitka. Sitka preserves the Russian legacy of Alaska's initial European invasion and, more deeply, the story of the cultural conflict between Alaska Natives and the newcomers, and the Natives' resistance and ultimate accommodation of the new ways. Here, 18th-century Russian conquerors who had successfully enslaved Aleuts to the West met their match in battle against the rich, powerful, and sophisticated Tlingit. A visit to Sitka reveals the story of that war, and also the cultural blending that occurred in the uneasy peace that followed under the influence of the Russian Orthodox church—an influence that remained even after the Russians sold Alaska to the U.S. in 1867 (that exchange also happened here), and continues today.

Sitka's history is Alaska's richest, and there's more of real interest in this town than any other you might visit. The fact is, most Alaska towns haven't been on the map long enough to have accumulated much history. Those that have been around for a while often have been wiped out a time or two, leaving little to remind you of the distant past. There's usually a small museum and a few gold rush sites that can be seen in half a day. Not so in Sitka. Historic photographs bear a surprising resemblance to today's city. The National Park Service protects buildings and grounds of major historic significance—places where the pioneers spoke Russian, with ways much more European than those of the rest of the American West. Even a superficial exploration of the attractions takes a day, and that's without time for the out-of-the way points of interest or the outdoors.

In 1799, the Russians chose these protected waters on Sitka Sound, on the ocean side of Baranof Island, for a new fort as part of a strategy of pushing their sea otter hunting operations and territorial claims east and south along the west coast of North America. The Tlingit understandably considered this to be an invasion, and in 1802 they attacked the Russians' redoubt and killed almost everyone inside. The Russians counterattacked in 1804 with the cannons of the ship *Neva* and a swarm of kayaking Aleut warriors, eventually forcing the Tlingit battle leader, Katlian, to withdraw. But the Russians never rested easy in their new capital, named New Archangel, and the hostility of the proud and dangerous Tlingit long remained. Some Russian laborers intermarried and essentially adopted Tlingit culture, but the bureaucrats and naval officers sent to run the colony for the czar tended to view Alaska as purgatory and left as soon as they could. Under their ineffective and uninterested control, the Russians

Thank You. No, Thank *You.*

In 1867, Russia's Czar Alexander feared that he couldn't hold the unprofitable colony of Alaska and saw a political advantage in doing his American allies the favor of selling it to them. Ironically, the Americans thought they were doing Russia a favor by buying it. Congress balked at paying the $7.2 million price that Secretary of State William Seward had negotiated for this worthless waste, relenting more than a year later partly out of fear of offending the czar. Americans didn't change their dim view of "Seward's Folly" until gold discoveries decades later.

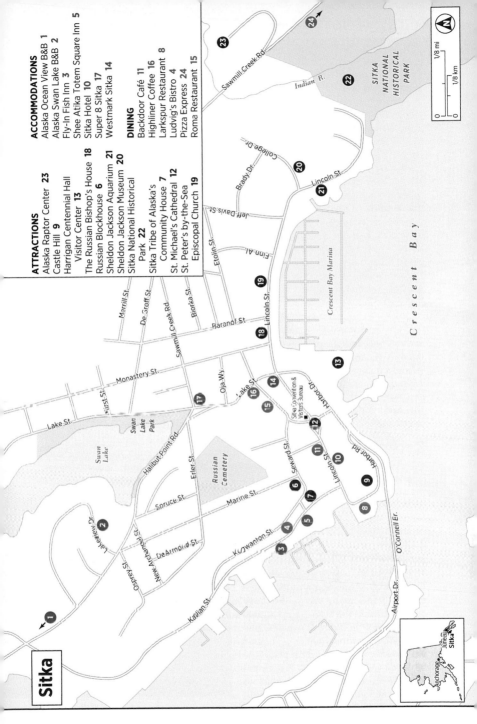

Sitka

ACCOMMODATIONS
Alaska Ocean View B&B **1**
Alaska Swan Lake B&B **2**
Fly-In Fish Inn **3**
Shee Atika Totem Square Inn **5**
Sitka Hotel **10**
Super 8 Sitka **17**
Westmark Sitka **14**

DINING
Backdoor Café **11**
Highliner Coffee **16**
Larkspur Restaurant **8**
Ludvig's Bistro **4**
Pizza Express **24**
Roma Restaurant **15**

ATTRACTIONS
Alaska Raptor Center **23**
Castle Hill **9**
Harrigan Centennial Hall
    Visitor Center **13**
The Russian Bishop's House **18**
Russian Blockhouse **6**
Sheldon Jackson Aquarium **21**
Sheldon Jackson Museum **20**
Sitka National Historical
    Park **22**
Sitka Tribe of Alaska's
    Community House **7**
St. Michael's Cathedral **12**
St. Peter's by-the-Sea
    Episcopal Church **19**

made surprisingly little impression on the great mass of Alaska. They failed to explore the Interior and held only tenuous control of the vast coastline, never fully subduing the Tlingit chiefs or removing their war-making ability.

The departing Russians rushed home, leaving only three significant towns—Unalaska, Kodiak, and Sitka—of which only Sitka retains more than a single Russian building. During their century of rule, the Russians had nearly wiped out the sea otter and the culture of the Aleuts, but both would eventually bounce back. The Russian Orthodox church stood as Russia's only lasting cultural gift to Alaska. Thanks to the efforts of one extraordinary cleric, Bishop Innocent Veniaminov, Alaska Natives were able to worship in their own languages, winning for the Russian Orthodox church many villages' continuing loyalty over less tolerant Protestant churches that came under American rule.

Besides its historic significance, Sitka is also fun to visit. Somehow it has retained a friendly, authentic feel, despite the crush of thousands of visitors. Perhaps because cruise-ship travelers must ride shuttle boats to shore, or because Sitka is a slightly inconvenient, out-of-the-way stop on the Alaska Marine Highway's main-line ferry routes, the city's streets haven't been choked by solid rows of seasonal gift shops, as has occurred in Ketchikan, Skagway, and a large part of Juneau. It remains picturesque, facing Sitka Sound, which is dotted with islands and populated by feeding eagles. Tourism is important here, but Sitka's own residents remain the center of the business and cultural world. The process of being "spoiled" hasn't begun, and they seem alert to its hazards. The town recently voted down a proposal to build a new cruise-ship dock.

Even beyond the town and its rich history, Sitka is a gateway to a large, remote portion of Southeast Alaska, in the western coastal islands. This area contains some of Tongass National Forest's least-used outdoor opportunities. The ocean halibut and salmon fishing are excellent, and the bird- and wildlife watching is exceptional.

Essentials

GETTING THERE Sitka sits on the west side of Baranof Island, a detour from the Inside Passage for the **Alaska Marine Highway System** (☎800/642-0066; www.ferryalaska.com). Of late, the fast ferry *Fairweather* has run frequently to Juneau, cutting the 9-hour journey to less than 5; however, the system seems to change every year. On any of the ships, the ride through narrow Peril Straits into Sitka is definitely worth the trip. The shore seems close enough to touch, and if you look closely you can sometimes see deer. The fare from either Juneau or Petersburg (10 hr. away by conventional ferry) is $45, and a two-berth cabin is $58 more. The ferry dock (☎907/747-3300) is 7 miles out of town.

Alaska Airlines (☎800/252-7522; www.alaskaair.com) links Sitka daily to Juneau, Ketchikan, and Seattle; northbound flights continue to Anchorage.

To get to town from the airport or ferry dock, the **Sitka Tours** (☎907/747-8443) bus charges $8 one-way, $10 round-trip. No reservations are needed, just climb aboard and pay the driver. **Nina's Taxi** (☎907/738-1931) and **Sitka Cab** (☎907/747-5001) are among five taxi companies in town; the ride from the ferry dock is around $18. See Hank's Cab on p. 203.

VISITOR INFORMATION A kiosk in the city-operated **Harrigan Centennial Hall,** 330 Harbor Dr., next to the Crescent Boat Harbor (☎907/747-3225), is a handy walk-in information stop. It is staffed 9am to 4pm daily in the summer, and you may be able to ask questions of hall staff other times. The hall is open Monday through Friday from 8am to 10pm, Saturday and Sunday 8am to 5pm. The town's professional visitor organization is the **Sitka Convention and Visitors Bureau,** P.O. Box 1226, Sitka, AK 99835 (☎907/747-5940; fax 907/747-3739). They maintain a very useful website at **www.sitka.org.**

The **Sitka National Historical Park Visitor Center,** 106 Metlakatla St., Sitka, AK 99835 (☎907/747-0110; www.nps.gov/sitk), run by the National Park Service, which maintains key historic sites in Sitka, is an essential stop to gather information and learn about what happened here. The center is open daily from 8am to 5pm in summer, and Monday through Saturday from 8am to 5pm in winter. Also see "Exploring Sitka," below, for more on the park.

ORIENTATION Sitka, on the west side of Baranof Island, has only a few miles of road. The **ferry terminal** is located at its north end, 7 miles out, on **Halibut Point Road;** the site of an abandoned pulp mill is at the south end, roughly the same distance out on **Sawmill Creek Road.** The town faces Sitka Sound. Across Sitka Channel is **Japonski Island,** with the **airport** (don't worry, it only looks as if your plane is going to land in the water). **Lincoln Street** contains most of the tourist attractions.

GETTING AROUND The airport has branches of **Avis** (☎800/230-4898 or 907/966-2404; www.avis.com) and **North Star Rent-a-Car** (☎800/722-6927 or 907/966-2552; www.northstarrentacar.com).

The Visitor Transit Bus operated by the **Sitka Tribal Tours** (see "Exploring Sitka," below) makes a continuous circuit of the sites from May to September when large cruise ships are in town. The fare is $5 round-trip or $10 all day.

Bike rental makes a good deal of sense in Sitka. **Yellow Jersey Cycle Shop,** 329 Harbor Dr., right across from the Centennial Hall downtown (☎907/747-6317; www.yellowjerseycycles.com), rents quality bikes for $25 a day.

[Fast FACTS] SITKA

Banks Three banks are at the center of downtown, around 300 Lincoln St., with ATMs, which are also found at local grocery stores.

Hospital Sitka Community (☎907/747-3241) is at 209 Moller Dr.

Internet Access Try **Highliner Coffee,** on Lake Street near Seward Street, or the downtown post office.

Police Call ☎907/747-3245 for nonemergency business.

Post Office At 338 Lincoln St.; it is open Saturday.

Taxes Sales tax is 5% October through March, 6% April through September. The tax on rooms totals 11% and 12%, respectively.

SPECIAL EVENTS The **Starring Ceremony,** January 7, marks Russian Orthodox Christmas with a procession through the streets and song and prayer at the doors of the faithful. Call St. Michael's Cathedral for information (☎907/747-8120).

The **Sitka Salmon Derby** occurs at the end of May and beginning of June, when the kings are running; contact the Sitka Sportsman's Association (☎907/747-3469) for information.

The **Sitka Summer Music Festival,** a chamber-music series that began in 1972, is one of Alaska's most important cultural events, drawing musicians from all over the world for 3 weeks in June. Performances take place Tuesdays, Fridays, and Saturdays, as well as other events all week. Contact the festival office for information (☎907/747-6774; www.sitka musicfestival.org).

Alaska Day, October 18, commemorating the Alaska Purchase, is a big deal in this former Russian capital city; the **Alaska Day Festival** lasts 4 days leading up to the big event. The Convention and Visitors Bureau has information. The **Sitka Grind,** a music and arts celebration at varying sites around town, takes place the third Saturday of each month from October to March.

The **Sitka WhaleFest** (☎907/747-7964; www.sitkawhalefest.org) takes place over a weekend in early November, during the fall and early winter period when humpback whales congregate in Sitka Sound to feed before migrating to Hawaiian waters. Experts come from around the world to present a 3-day symposium on marine mammal research, and there are whale-watching tours, concerts, a craft show, local food and music, a run, and other community events.

New Archangel Dancers.

The Singing Cabbie

Hank Moore, of **Hank's Cab** (☎907/747-8888; www.hankstours. com), can drive you around, like any taxi driver, but, if you ask, he offers something more. For $35 to $35 per person he offers a tour of Sitka's Russian and natural history, including a stop at a lakeside waterfall where he pulls out his guitar and performs. Hank's a good blues/folk musician with two CDs out, and he can really sing.

Exploring Sitka

The **Sitka Tribe of Alaska**'s Community House is a good starting point, where you can watch Tlingit dance performances (see below), join walking or bus tours, or sign up for kayaking or other outdoor activities, including trail hikes. A 2-hour walking tour includes the town and national historic park. The house is at 200 Katlian St. (☎888/270-8687 or 907/747-7290; www.sitkatours.com). **Sitka Tours** (☎907/747-8443) also offers tours, taking more of the Russian perspective. Prices for each choice of tour range from about $20 for a brief downtown tour to $66 for a longer town tour that includes most of the attractions and dancing; the type of dancing—Native or Russian—depends on which firm you go with. See "Sitka Tribe Dance Performances," p. 206, for a description of the Alaska Native choice. Russian folk dance is performed by the women of the **New Archangel Dancers** (☎907/747-5516) in the Harrigan Centennial Hall at 330 Harbor Dr., next to the Crescent Boat Harbor. Performances are scheduled when cruise ships are in town, and most of the audience comes from Sitka Tours, but walk-ins are welcome.

SITKA'S TLINGIT & RUSSIAN HERITAGE

Sitka National Historical Park ★★★ In 1799, the Russian American Company, led by Alexander Baranof, landed from their base in Kodiak, established Redoubt St. Michael (today the **Old Sitka State Historic Site**, 7½ miles north of town—just a grassy picnic area with interpretive signs), and claimed the Pacific Northwest of America for Russia. The Tlingit, sophisticated traders who had already acquired flintlocks, attacked with knives, spears, and guns, and destroyed the redoubt in mid-June 1802, killing almost all of the Russians. The Natives immediately began building fortifications on the site now within the national historical park, anticipating a Russian counterattack, which came in 1804. Baranof returned with an attacking force of a Russian gunship and a swarm of Aleut kayaks, which towed the becalmed vessel into position to begin the bombardment. The Tlingits withstood

Sitka National Historical Park.

the siege for 6 days, then vacated their fort at night after a canoe delivering gunpowder exploded, leaving them short of ammunition. The Russians founded and heavily fortified the town of New Archangel, and in 1808 it became their administrative capital. But the Tlingit name is the one that stuck: Shee Atika, since contracted to Sitka.

The historic significance of the battle site was recognized early. Pres. Benjamin Harrison, a friend of Alaska missionary Sheldon Jackson, set the land aside as a public park in 1890. In 1902 and 1905, a collection of totem poles from around Southeast was brought here, and in 1910 the site was designated a national monument. The park visitor center and grounds emphasize the Native perspective. There is no better place to learn about Tlingit art and history. A naturally lit hall with a 30-foot ceiling displays the original poles (reproductions stand outside) in startlingly good condition despite their age. The artistic power of these poles is overwhelming, and their age and value for the Tlingit and Haida cultures only adds to the impact. Moreover, the art still lives. Extraordinary poles by current Native artists stand outside, and within the building artisans of the Southeast Alaska Indian Cultural Center work in a series of windowed work-shops creating traditional crafts of metal, wood, beads, textiles, and woven grass. Visitors are invited to enter the workshops and ask questions. A free 12-minute video provides a good historical overview.

The outdoor totem loop trail and the site of the battle and of the fort also must not be missed. The totems stand tall and forbidding along a pathway through massive spruce and hemlock, where misty rain often wanders down from an un-seen sky somewhere above the trees. The shoreside battle site and the nearby fort site—only a grassy area now—are along the trail. While plenty of imagination is needed to place a desperate fight in this peaceful setting, it is easy to feel deep down what the Tlingits were fighting for when you stand among the trees and totems and hear the lapping sea and raven's call.

Though they lost the battle for this ground, the Tlingit won the war—they're still here. In 1996, a gathering of clans erected a major new pole in front of the center to explain their story back to mankind's arrival in North America. It took quite a bit of debate to settle the story the pole would tell. For example, the crests of the eagle and raven tribal moieties are traditionally never shown on the same pole, but they had to be to tell the whole history of the Tlingits. In 1999, another new pole rose at the site of the battle to commemorate that story. At the bottom of the pole is a carving of the raven helmet worn by Katlian, the Tlingit's leader in the battle of Sitka. You can see the helmet itself in the Sheldon Jackson Museum (see below). Contrary to the popular phrase "low man on the totem pole," the po-sition shows the strength with which Katlian led and supported his people.

106 Metlakatla St. (**907/747-0110.** Admission $4. Visitor center open summer daily 8am–5pm; winter Mon–Sat 8am–5pm. Park open summer daily 6am–10pm; winter daily 7am–8pm.

The Russian Bishop's House ★★★

Bishop Innocent Veniaminov, born in 1797, translated scriptures into Tlingit and other Native languages and trained deacons to carry Russian Orthodoxy back to their Native villages. Unlike most of the later Protestant missionaries led by Sitka's other historic religious figure, Sheldon Jackson, Veniaminov and his followers allowed parishioners to use their own language, a key element to saving Native cultures. When the United States bought Alaska in 1867, few Russians stayed behind, but thanks to Veniaminov's

Sheldon Jackson Museum.

work, the Russian Orthodox faith remains strong in Native Alaska; today there are 89 parishes, primarily in tiny Native villages. In 1977, Veniaminov was canonized as St. Innocent in the Orthodox faith.

From 1842 to 1843, the Russian American Company constructed this extraordinary house for Veniaminov as a residence, school, and chapel. It may have survived many years of neglect in part because its huge beams fit together like a ship's. In 1972, the National Park Service bought and began restoring the building, which is the best of only three surviving from all of Russian America (the others are in Kodiak and at 206 Lincoln St. in Sitka, most recently occupied by a gift store). The Bishop's House is Alaska's most interesting historic site. Downstairs is a self-guided museum; upstairs, rangers lead tours of the bishop's quarters, which are furnished with original and period pieces. It's an extraordinary window into an alternate stream of American history, from a time before the founding of Seattle or San Francisco, when Sitka was the most important city on North America's Pacific Coast. The tour concludes with a visit to a beautiful little chapel with many of the original icons Innocent imported from Russia.

Lincoln and Monastery sts. No phone; call Sitka National Historical Park Visitor Center (☎907/747-0110). Admission $4 per person, $15 per family (family admission covers both facilities). Summer daily 9am–5pm, by appointment in winter.

Sheldon Jackson Museum ★★ Sheldon Jackson, a Presbyterian missionary with powerful friends in Washington, was Alaska's first General Agent for Education, a paternal guardian of the welfare, schooling, and spiritual lives of Alaska's Natives. His benevolent aim was to defend Natives from exploitation and abuse and bring them into American civilization as equals. Tragically, his strategy to accomplish this goal was to erase indigenous cultures and replace them with Protestantism, causing deep, lasting harm to people over a broad swath of Alaska. As a side hobby during his travels from 1888 to 1898, Jackson gathered an omnivorous 5,000-piece collection of Native art and everyday cultural objects. That collection, the best in Alaska, has been displayed for more than a century in a concrete building on the campus of a college that bore Jackson's name, but that closed its doors and currently stands vacant. The museum is a jewel box; the overwhelming wealth is displayed by Alaska state museum curators in ingenious ways that avoid a feeling of clutter. Many drawers open to reveal more displays. Don't miss Katlian's helmet, worn by the Kiksadi clan's war leader in the Battle of Sitka in 1804; raven-shaped, it is that rare piece of great history that's also great art. Native artists demonstrate their skill on summer days, and the gift shop contains almost exclusively authentic Native arts and crafts. Authentic Native art pieces cost more than tourist trinkets: Plan to spend more than $100 except for small, simple items. (If you're already here, take time for the aquarium, mentioned under "Walking Downtown," below.)

104 College Dr. ☎907/747-8981. www.museums.state.ak.us. Admission $4 adults, free for ages 18 and under. Mid-May to mid-Sept daily 9am–5pm; mid-Sept to mid-May Tues–Sat 10am–4pm.

St. Michael's Cathedral ★★ The first Orthodox cathedral in the New World stands grandly in the middle of Sitka's principal street, where it was completed in 1848. Bishop Veniaminov (see "The Russian Bishop's House," above) designed it and oversaw construction. The cathedral contains several miraculous icons, some dating from the 17th century. The St. Michael, the farthest right of six on the front screen, was bound for Sitka aboard the *Neva* in 1813 when the ship went down some 30 miles out. Thirty days later the icon, in its crate, washed ashore undamaged and was recovered by Sitka's townspeople. The original building burned down in a 1966 fire that started elsewhere and took much of Sitka's downtown, but almost all the contents were saved by a human chain in the 30 minutes before the building was destroyed. One man lifted down the huge central chandelier, which later took six men to carry. Orthodox Christians all over the United States raised the money to rebuild the cathedral exactly as it had been, using a Russian architect who could interpret Veniaminov's original plans. It was completed in 1976. A knowledgeable guide is on hand to answer questions or give talks when large groups congregate. Sunday services are sung in English, Church Slavonic, Tlingit, Aleut, and Yupik. Right across Lincoln Street, stop in at the cathedral's well-stocked Archangel Michael Icons, Books and Gift Shop for souvenirs, music CDs, books, and even children's books.

Lincoln and Cathedral sts. ☎**907/747-8120.** $2 donation requested. Generally summer Mon–Fri 9am–4pm; however, hours change and are extended due to cruise-ship calls. Call ahead. Also call for winter hours.

Sitka Tribe Dance Performances ★ The Sheet'ka Kwaán Naā Kahidi, Sitka's community house, on the north side of the downtown parade ground, is a modern version of a Tlingit Clan House, with an air handling system that pulls smoke from the central fire pit straight up to the chimney. The magnificent house screen, a carved wall at the front of the hall, installed in 2000, is the largest in the Pacific Northwest. Performances last 30 minutes, including dances and a story. It's entirely traditional and put on by members of the tribe. You can also sign up for tours and activities in the lobby.

200 Katlian St. ☎**888/270-8687** or 907/747-7290. www.sitkatours.com. Admission $8 adults, $5 children. Call for times.

OTHER ATTRACTIONS IN TOWN

Alaska Raptor Center ★★ This nonprofit center takes in injured birds of prey (mainly bald eagles, but also owls, hawks, and other species) for veterinary treatment and release or, if too badly injured, for placement in a zoo or as part of the collection of

Giant house screens at Sitka's community house.

20 that live on-site. Visitors get to see the impressive birds up close in a lecture setting, through the glass wall of the veterinary clinic, and in outdoor enclosures, but the highlight is an extraordinary flight-training center, built in 2003 at a cost of $3 million. This enormous aviary is where recuperating birds learn to fly again, and visitors can walk its length behind one-way glass, watching them preen, feed, and take to the air in a peaceful setting simulating their natural habitat. Watching these giant birds fly from so close is awesome. The center's grounds also include a pleasant nature trail (accessible for travelers with disabilities) that leads down to a salmon stream where healthy eagles can sometimes be seen feeding.

1000 Raptor Way (off Sawmill Creek Blvd.). ☎ 800/643-9425 or 907/747-8662. www.alaskaraptor. org. Admission $12 adults, $6 ages 12 and under. Summer daily 8am–4pm. Call for winter hours.

WALKING DOWNTOWN The grassy park at Lincoln and Katlian was the site of the Russians' barracks and parade ground. Just north on Marine Street is a replica of a **Russian Blockhouse;** across Lincoln Street to the south and up the stairs is **Castle Hill,** a site of historic significance for the ancient Tlingits, for the Russians, and for contemporary Alaskans. The first American flag raised in Alaska was hoisted here in 1867. There are historic markers and cannons. As you walk east past the cathedral and Crescent Harbor, several quaint historic buildings are on the left. My favorite is **St. Peter's by-the-Sea Episcopal Church,** a lovely stone-and-timber chapel with a pipe organ, consecrated in 1899.

At the east end of the harbor is a **public playground** and the **Sheldon Jackson Aquarium,** in the Sage Building on the ocean side of Lincoln Street. All the tanks contain local marine life. It's eye-opening to realize what's down below. Best of all are the large touch tanks where visitors can handle animals from three different seafloor habitats. The aquarium and associated fish hatchery were part of a college of the same name that closed. Sitka donors and volunteers are struggling to keep it alive. Admission is free, but donations are appreciated, and hours cannot be predicted reliably.

Shopping

There are some good shops and galleries in Sitka, mostly on Lincoln and Harbor streets. Several are across the street from St. Michael's Cathedral. **Fairweather Prints,** 209 Lincoln St., has a fun, youthful feel; it is large and has a diverse selection, including wearable art (including T-shirts), watercolors, prints, ceramics, and cute, inexpensive crafts. Continue west on Lincoln to **Old Harbor Books,** 201 Lincoln St., a good browsing store with an excellent selection of Alaska books. Back in the other direction, the **Fly Away Fly Shop,** at Lake and Lincoln, under the Westmark Sitka Hotel (www.flyawayflyshop.com), carries a creative array of clothing (including distinctive fleece or leather jackets), jewelry, pottery, and kites, as well as fly-fishing supplies. Near the Crescent Harbor dock, the **Sitka Rose Gallery** occupies a Victorian house at 419 Lincoln St., featuring higher-end work, mostly local: sculpture, original paintings, engraving, and jewelry. The **Sheldon Jackson Museum Gift Shop,** 104 College Dr., is an excellent place to buy Alaska Native arts and crafts with assurance of their authenticity. Artists, or those who want to buy a gift for one, should stop in at the beautiful **Visions: Framing and Art Supplies,** 110 American St., which carries craft kits and other fun items along with the high-end paints and materials.

Getting Outside: On the Water

The little islands and rocks that dot Sitka Sound are an invitation to the sea otter in all of us; you must get out on the water.

SIGHTSEEING & WILDLIFE TOURS

When conditions allow, tour boats visit **St. Lazaria Island,** a bird colony where you can expect to see tufted puffins, murres, rhinoceros auklets, and other pelagic birds. Storm petrels show up by the hundreds of thousands at dawn and dusk for those who charter a boat to stay overnight at the rookery. The volcanic rock drops straight down into deep water, so even big boats can come close, but in rough weather even they won't go to the exposed location of the island. Even then, there's plenty to see in protected waters. Humpback whales show up in large groups in the fall and are often seen by the half dozen in the summer. There are so many bald eagles that you're pretty well guaranteed to see them even from shore. But the lowly sea otter is the most common and, in my experience, most amusing and endearing of marine mammals, and you'll certainly see them from a tour boat. The public tubs at **Goddard Hot Springs,** 17 miles south of town, are another possible stop for charters.

The **Sitka Wildlife Quest,** operated by Allen Marine Tours (☎888/747-8101 or 907/747-8100; www.allenmarinetours.com), runs a popular marine tour with well-trained naturalists to explain the wildlife. You have a good chance of encountering humpback whales and sea otters. Tours visit St. Lazaria Island when sea conditions permit. A 2-hour cruise Tuesday and Thursday at 6pm costs $59 adults, $39 children. A 3-hour cruise Saturday at 9am costs $79 adults, $49 children. The boat leaves from the Crescent Harbor Visitors Dock late May through early September. Buy tickets on board. These are different excursions from the ones offered to cruise-ship passengers. Allen Marine, which also builds vessels, has a long-standing reputation for the quality of its offerings.

For $120 per person, you can charter a six-passenger boat for a 3-hour tour to St. Lazaria Island for whale-watching and to learn about the Sound with a married couple who are both former wildlife biologists, Kent Hall and Beverly Minn, at **Sitka's Secrets** (☎907/747-5089; www.sitkasecret.com). They do fishing charters, too.

Friendly Davey Lubin of **Ester G Sea Taxi** (see "Forest Service Cabins," below) also offers educational small-boat marine tours.

Sea Life Discovery Tours (☎877/966-2301 or 907/966-2301; www. sealifediscoverytours.com) offers a chance to see the rich underwater life of Sitka Sound from an extraordinary boat with big windows 4 feet below the waterline; it's really cool. They charge $86 for a 2-hour tour; call for times.

SALTWATER FISHING

Many charter boats are available for salmon or halibut. The Sitka Convention and Visitors Bureau (see "Visitor Information," earlier) keeps a detailed charter boat list online. Using the grid view (www.sitka.org/grid.html), you can compare boats, rates, and services, and link to the vessel's own home page. Or book through **Alaska Adventures Unlimited** (☎907/747-5576), which has set up charters in Sitka since 1982. If you can handle your own boat, skiffs rent for $95 half-day and up from BJ's Boat Rentals (☎907/752-6375).

Tide pools at St. Lazaria Island.

SEA KAYAKING

Sitka's protected waters and intricate shorelines are perfect for sea kayaking. You're almost sure to see sea otters, seals, sea lions, and eagles, and could see whales. A locally owned firm, **Sitka Sound Ocean Adventures** (**☎907/752-0660;** www.kayaksitka.com), offers day paddles of various lengths. A 2½-hour outing is $69 for adults and $49 for children ages 6 to 12, or $149 and $109 for a half-day paddle. Make contact at the blue bus in the parking lot of the Harrigan Centennial Hall.

Getting Outside: Onshore
FRESHWATER FISHING

Anglers should pick up the *Sitka Area Sport Fishing Guide,* which has lots of tips on streams, lakes, and fishing methods in the area. You can download the guide from the **Alaska Department of Fish and Game** at www.alaska.gov/ adfg (the URL for the guide itself is long; to find it, click on "Sport Fish" and then the Southeast region, the Sitka area, and finally on "Additional Information"). The site also has weekly fishing updates during the summer months. The local Fish and Game office is at 304 Lake St., Room 103, Sitka, AK 99835 (**☎907/747-5355**).

FOREST SERVICE CABINS

The **Sitka Ranger District,** 204 Siginaka Way, Sitka, AK 99835 (**☎907/747-6671;** www.fs.fed.us/r10/tongass/districts/sitka), maintains two dozen wilderness cabins on Baranof, Chichagof, and Kruzof islands, in sea-kayaking coves and on remote fishing lakes, where rowing skiffs are generally provided. The cabins and their facilities are described in a Forest Service handout or on their website. One cabin is accessible by road from Sitka (see "Camping," below).

You will need camping gear to use any of the cabins, and a boat or floatplane to all but that one, a much greater cost than the nightly rental of $35 to $50. For cabins on salt water near Sitka, the most affordable way may be a water taxi, such as **Esther G Sea Taxi** (☎907/747-6481 or 907/738-6481 cell; www.puffinsandwhales.com). Operator Davey Lubin also offers educational marine wildlife tours and kayak drop-offs to remote shores. Ken Bellows' of **Air Sitka** flying service (☎907/747-7920) has been flying anglers, hunters, and cabin visitors out to remote spots around Sitka for many years. He also does half-hour flightseeing spins for $250. His helpful office person is on duty Monday through Friday from 8am to noon, at 485 Katlian St., under the Fly-In Fish Inn. Either way, allow time in your schedule in case bad weather prevents backcountry travel. Information on researching and reserving a cabin is under "Getting Outside in the Tongass National Forest," earlier in this chapter.

HIKING

Sitka is a great hiking area, with trails threading all over the mountains behind the town. There are a dozen U.S. Forest Service hiking trails accessible from the roads around Sitka and another 20 rough trails you can get to by plane or boat. A beautifully made little book, *Sitka Trails* (Alaska Geographic, $8), covers each trail with a detailed description and fine-scale color topographic map. If you need further advice, contact the ranger district office (see the preceding paragraph).

From downtown, the 4-mile (one-way) **Indian River Trail** is a relaxing rainforest walk rising gradually up the river valley to a small waterfall. Take Indian River Road off Sawmill Creek Road just east of the downtown. For a steeper mountain-climbing trail to alpine terrain and great views, the **Gavan Hill-Harbor Mountain Trail** is near the end of Baranof Street, which starts near the Russian Bishop's House. It gains 2,500 feet over 3 miles to the peak of Gavan Hill, then continues another 3 miles along a ridge to meet Harbor Mountain Road. The **Sitka Cross Trail** connects these trails and neighborhood streets, allowing you to start almost anywhere.

 One Halibut Per Customer

For years, ever more charter boats carried visitors to Southeast Alaska in pursuit of halibut, all chasing the same resource of fish. Although anglers take far fewer halibut than the commercial fishing industry, they have repeatedly overrun the annual limits set on their total catch. Consequently, federal fishery managers invoked a one-fish-per-day bag limit starting in 2008. Charter captains sued, and a court set aside the rule for a year, but it was firmly in effect in 2009. In other parts of Alaska, the limit continued at two halibut per day, but conservation problems exist in Southcentral Alaska as well, so the new rule may spread. If you enjoy fishing, the limit shouldn't stop you. A single 50-pound fish should be enough for anyone, and you can keep fishing and throwing back halibut until you decide to land and kill one. Or book a charter, in season, to fish halibut and salmon on the same day.

At the north end of Halibut Point Road, 7½ miles from downtown, several wonderful trails loop through the **Starrigavan Recreation Area.** On the right, the **Estuary Life Trail** and **Forest Muskeg Trail,** totaling about a mile, are well developed and accessible to anyone, circling a grassy estuary rich with birds and fish. The pleasant **Mosquito Cove Trail,** starting from within the bayside loop picnic area on the left, circles 1.3 miles along the shore to the secluded gravel beach of the cove, returning over boardwalk steps through the old-growth forest.

TIDE POOLING & SHORE WALKS

Halibut Point State Recreation Area, 4½ miles north of town on Halibut Point Road, is a great place for a picnic, shore ramble, and tide pooling. The Mosquito Cove Trail (above) is also promising. To find the best low tides, check a tide book, available all over town. It's best to go at the lowest tide possible, arriving on the shore an hour before the low. To identify the little creatures you'll see, pick up a plastic-covered field guide at a bookstore.

WHALE-WATCHING

Humpback whales stop to feed in Sitka Sound on their way south in the winter migration. During October, November, December, and March, you can watch from shore—the local government has even built a special park for the purpose. At the fun **Whale Park,** just south of town on Sawmill Creek Road, spotting scopes are mounted on platforms along a boardwalk and at the end of staircases that descend the dramatic, wooded cliffs. Excellent interpretive signs, located near surfacing concrete whales in the parking lot, explain the whales. The Sitka WhaleFest, in November (see "Special Events," earlier), is the best time for whale enthusiasts, as then you can watch whales in the company of cetacean scientists. For summertime whale-watching, take a boat: Choices are above under "Sightseeing and Wildlife Tours."

Where to Stay

In addition to the places below, you'll find super-clean rooms with many amenities in a quiet, landscaped building downtown at the **Super 8 Sitka,** 404 Sawmill Creek Blvd. (☎800/800-8000 for reservations, or 907/747-8804; www. super8.com). The 24-hour laundromat is open to the public, too. I also like the **Cascade Inn,** 2½ miles from downtown on Halibut Point Rd. (☎800/532-0908 or 907/747-6804; www.cascadeinnsitka.com), with 10 light, waterfront rooms over Sitka Sound, for reasonable prices, next to a gas station and liquor store.

The town has several good B&Bs. The **Sitka Convention and Visitors Bureau** (☎907/747-5940; www.sitka.org) has links to many on its website, and can send you a printed list as well. Among them is **Alaska Swan Lake Bed & Breakfast,** 206½ Lakeview Drive (☎907/747-3917; www.sitka.org/swanlake/index.htm), with rooms with private bathrooms for $100 a night in a big, white house above the lake just a half-mile from the downtown area.

Alaska Ocean View Bed & Breakfast ★★★ Ebullient Carole Denkinger and her husband, Bill, have a passion for making their bed-and-breakfast one you'll remember. They've thought of everything—the covered outdoor Jacuzzi where you can watch the eagles, a Nintendo Wii setup, a laptop to borrow, an open snack counter, and HEPA air cleaners in each room for people with allergies, just to name a few items. Rooms are soft and plush, and guests are pampered. The exceptional hospitality extends to Carole's big, organic breakfasts, which she cooks to suit guests' dietary preferences—for vegans, dieters, those with special sensitivities, etc. The couple also strives to reduce the B&B's environmental footprint, and it has been certified "green." The house is on a residential street with a view of the water about a mile from the historic district.

1101 Edgecumbe Dr., Sitka, AK 99835. **☎907/747-8310.** Fax 907/747-3440. www.sitka-alaska-lodging.com. 3 units. High season $139–$229 double; low season $85–$139 double. Extra person $40. Rates include full breakfast. AE, DC, DISC, MC, V. **Amenities:** Outdoor Jacuzzi; free media library. *In room:* TV/VCR and DVD, CD player, fridge, hair dryer, microwave, MP3 docking station, Wi-Fi.

Fly-In Fish Inn ★★ This is a classy little boutique hotel right on the water a bit off the beaten path north of the town center. The spacious rooms, with entrances off covered walkways, have simple, elegant decoration, in sage, gold, and burgundy. High-quality mattresses are covered with down pillows and cotton comforters. Each unit has a small wet bar with a sink, microwave, and coffeemaker, stocked with snacks and supplies. Rooms renting for a $20 premium enjoy wonderful views, as does the beautifully appointed waterfront bar downstairs, with a fireplace and a mosaic behind the bar and a deck over the harbor. The included breakfast is served in the bar, cooked to order for each guest. The hotel is only a few years old, and everything has been kept so clean it's as if you're the first guest. The name comes from the air taxi service that's on-site and that leaves from the dock.

485 Katlian St., Sitka, AK 99835. **☎907/747-7910.** www.flyinfishinn.com. 10 units. High season $159–$179 double, $388 suite; low season $99 double, $199 suite. Extra person no charge. Rates include full breakfast. MC, V. **Amenities:** Bar. *In room:* TV, hair dryer, microwave, Wi-Fi.

An Otter's Cove Bed & Breakfast ★ A custom-built house contains three large, well appointed bedrooms and an attractive common room right on the ocean, with stunning views and a covered outdoor seating area, on Halibut Point Road, north of town. Newly constructed, the building has elaborate stonework and landscaping, and even the fish cleaning area is a work of art, divided off by a stained glass window. Guest quarters take up the entire downstairs and are entered from the far side from the family's quarters, helping create the B&B's overall sense of privacy and peace. Hostess Cheryl Jordan cooks full breakfasts and keeps the place like new.

3211 Halibut Point Rd., Sitka, AK 99835. **☎907/747-4529.** www.ottercovebandb.com. 3 units. High season $130–$150 double; low season $89–$109 double. Extra person 13 and older $20–$25. MC, V. **Amenities:** Barbecue; fish cleaning/freezing facility; Internet. *In room:* TV/DVD, hair dryer, Wi-Fi.

Shee Atika Totem Square Inn ★★ This is the best large hotel in town. Owned by the local Native corporation and standing across the street from the community house, it makes full use of their Tlingit motifs and colors in its decoration—red, black, white, and earth—and employs many Natives on its staff. The service was uniformly excellent on both our recent visits and the housekeeping spotless. The building makes use of the ocean view in two directions, and the rooms are well thought out and nicely equipped, with comfortable beds and large flatscreen TVs. Continuous upgrading for several years has kept it all like new. Common rooms include a light, spacious breakfast room, where a generous continental breakfast is served; fast, free computer terminals in the lobby; and snacks for guests available at all hours. A dock for tour and fishing charter boats is attached. The downtown location allows walking to some of the attractions, although the national historic site is a long walk.

201 Katlian St., Sitka, AK 99835. **866/300-1353** or 907/747-3693. Fax 907/747-2839. www.totemsquareinn.com. 67 units. High season $139–$169 double; low season $49–$119 double. Extra person $15. AE, DC, DISC, MC, V. **Amenities:** Free airport transfers; exercise room; Internet. *In room:* Fan, TV, hair dryer, Wi-Fi.

Sitka Hotel 💎 An old building facing the parade ground right downtown contains some large, attractive rooms with large TVs and good beds for bargain rates. But the hotel is a budget choice and has its rough edges, including noisy heat and thin walls—not for the light sleeper—and service that was far from attentive on our last visit. The rooms vary, with those in the older section at the front relatively small and creaky, and the newer rooms, in the back of the building, larger, and with added amenities, such as coffeemakers. Overall, it's a good place to save money, and has always been clean on our many visits.

  Victoria's Restaurant, with about a dozen tables in the storefront downstairs, tries for a high Victorian feel, but in actuality it's more of a friendly small-town diner, with hearty breakfasts and lunches in winter and an inexpensive fine-dining dinner menu added in the summer. The hotel has a small bar, too.

118 Lincoln St., Sitka, AK 99835. **907/747-3288.** Fax 907/747-8499. www.sitkahotel.com. 60 units, 46 with private bathroom. High season $105 double with private bathroom; low season $70 with private bathroom. Extra person $5. AE, DISC, MC, V. **Amenities:** Restaurant. *In room:* TV, Wi-Fi.

Westmark Sitka ★ This hotel, above Crescent Harbor in the heart of the historic district, contains many standard rooms with sweeping views of Sikta Sound. Remodeled in 2009 with granite countertops, rooms have mission-style oak furniture and all the amenities expected in a corporate hotel. The lobby is done up with leather furniture, the walls decorated with mounted fish. The hotel is recently under new management, and we found it had some kinks to work out on our last visit, including inattentive service.

  The **Raven Dining Room** restaurant shares the hotel's view and outdoorsy decorative theme, with numerous mounted animal heads on the walls. Dark blue tablecloths accent mahogany furniture. They serve a long menu of seafood and beef. The food is not memorable, and the service was poor on our last visit.

330 Seward St., Sitka, AK 99835-7523. **800/544-0970** for reservations, or 907/747-6241. Fax 907/747-5486. www.westmarkhotels.com. 101 units. High season $159 double; low season $99 double. Extra person no charge. AE, DC, DISC, MC, V. **Amenities:** Restaurant; bar. *In room:* TV, high-speed Internet, hair dryer.

CAMPING

The Forest Service's **Starrigavan Recreation Area** contains excellent campsites and a cabin at the north end of Halibut Point Road, 7½ miles from town and ¾ mile from the ferry dock. There are three loops. The Backpackers' Loop has six hike-in sites. The Estuary Loop (which joins the Estuary Life Trail), on the right, has 25 sites for RVs or tents, which are widely separated under huge trees. The Bayside Loop, at the water's edge, is the last left on the highway. Three of its sites are situated on the edge of Starrigavan Bay, creating the feeling that you're way out in the wilderness. Fees are $12 to $30 a night, or $50 for the new Starrigavan Creek Cabin, a rare road-accessible Forest Service cabin that is also fully usable by people with disabilities. Twenty-one sites and the cabin can be reserved on the national system (see "Reserving a Cabin or Campsite," p. 151). The recreation area is open all year, but vehicle access is restricted in the winter. May through mid-September, access gates are locked from 10pm to 7am.

There are two RV parks, each with water and electric hookups only, and each charging under $22: City-run **Sealing Cove RV Park** (☎907/747-3439) is near the airport and a free dump station, and **Sitka Sportsman's Association RV Park** (☎907/747-6033) is near the ferry dock.

Where to Dine

In addition to the restaurants described here, and in the Sitka Hotel and Westmark Sitka, a Subway sandwich shop is at Seward and Lake streets, behind the Westmark.

The Channel Club ★★ STEAK For 5 decades, the Channel Club was among Alaska's most famous restaurants for its perfectly grilled steaks and unbelievable salad bar, but the ultra-casual, ultra-masculine formula ultimately wore thin, and it closed several years ago. In its new incarnation, the club has kept the best of the old restaurant—the rich, various salad bar is still mind-blowing—but with an updated dining room and improved service that create a lovely, calming place to eat, enjoy company, and take in the ocean view. Now the restaurant's look is simple, elegant, and spotless. The menu includes salmon, halibut, and cod, which are done well, but it's a steakhouse, and the specialty is seasoned beef grilled right. The location, several miles out of town, requires you have a car or take the restaurant's free shuttle.

2906 Halibut Point Rd. ☎907/747-7440. www.sitkachannelclub.com. Reservations recommended. Lunch $6–$24; dinner $16–$48. MC, V. Daily 11am–10pm year-round.

Larkspur Cafe ★ CAFE Below Sitka's public Raven Radio, in the historic cable house building on the water, this is a happening coffee shop that also serves sophisticated, handcrafted food. The dining room has a small collection of funky, mismatched antique tables on a painted wood floor, and there's more seating outside with ocean views. That's where you'd go if you wanted to get away from the live music and the loud voices in the festive atmosphere inside. The menu changes daily with the availability of local food, but includes items such as cold smoked lox on rye toast with cream cheese and capers, or marinated black cod with brown rice and baby bok choy. Influences are eclectic, with the common element the owners' enthusiasm and the positive scene they've created.

2 Lincoln St. ☎907/966-2326. http://larkspurcafe.blogspot.com. All items specials; prices vary, but around $5–$15. MC, V. Mon–Tues 11am–3pm; Wed–Sun 11am–10pm.

Ludvig's Bistro ★★ MEDITERRANEAN This tiny dining room and its chef-owner, Colette Nelson, offer Sitka's first-rate cuisine, and it's a very pleasant place for a meal. She's taken a formerly grungy concrete space and filled it with charm and warmth, with Mediterranean colors, wine bottles, and whimsical art. The restaurant is too small to serve many meals a night, so each one is carefully crafted, coming from a changing menu intended to stretch the chef and

Quick Eats & Coffee in Sitka

A cool couple owns **The Backdoor Café,** in the back half of Old Harbor Books at 104 Barracks St. (☎907/747-8856), the kind of place that develops a following among the local poets, musicians, and the like. Besides coffee and the owners' own homemade bagels and fantastic pies, the cafe serves fresh pastries for breakfast and a single special for lunch (which can run out). It's open Monday through Friday from 6:30am to 5pm, Saturday 6:30am to 2pm. Credit cards are not accepted.

Highliner Coffee, on Lake Street just above Seward Street (☎907/747-4924), is a fancier place, with free Wi-Fi (or use their computer for $2 for the first 15 minutes).

A "highliner" is a top commercial fisherman; the name here is a bit of a boast for its fisherpeople owners, who hope to educate customers about their way of life as well as roasting Sitka's coffee. It's open Monday through Saturday from 5:30am to 6pm, Sunday from 7am to 5pm.

For something a bit more traditional, and sweeter, stop at **Harry's Soda Shop** in the Harry Race Pharmacy at 106 Lincoln St. (☎907/747-8006), a real old-fashioned soda fountain serving sundaes, floats, cones, and shakes. It's open Monday through Saturday 9am to 6pm and accepts MasterCard and Visa.

introduce the small-town clientele to new tastes. A recent menu included grilled marinated lamb chops, a wild mushroom ragout, and calamari. The food is truly memorable. For lunch, catch their chowder cart downtown. The only complaint about Ludvig's is that it operates inconsistently —locals complain they don't know when it is open.

256 Katlian St. ☎**907/966-3663.** Reservations recommended. Dinner main courses $17–$27. MC, V. Daily 4–10pm.

Pizza Express ✦ MEXICAN Despite the name, this is primarily a Mexican place that also bakes pizza pies. But the pizza is good. It's where Sitka families dine. Come here when you want a filling, inexpensive meal or to take out and get a pizza without a delivery fee. The dining room is in strip mall a long walk from downtown, near the Raptor Center and across from the historical park. The menu is very lengthy and produced by Mexican-American owners who know their stuff. Take-out pizza is sold somewhat later than the dining room hours listed below.

1321 Sawmill Creek Rd. ☎**907/966-2428.** Main courses $8.50–$19. MC, V. Mon–Sat 11am–9pm; Sun noon–9pm.

Roma ☺ ITALIAN This is a traditional family restaurant with a long list of familiar dishes kids love, such as fettuccini alfredo, meat lasagna, and, of course, pizza. They're especially good at making that. The "Climax," with Italian sausage and pesto, was terrific. The dough is flash fried in oil before being baked, creating a crisp outside and fluffy inside. The dining room, with about 15 tables, has russet walls painted with Italian village scenes, and there are a few outdoor tables, too. Service is fast and enthusiastic.

327 Seward St. ☎**907/966-4600.** Reservations recommended. Lunch $9.50–$13; dinner $12–$25. MC, V. Tues–Fri 11am–9pm; Sat–Sun noon–9pm.

JUNEAU: FOREST CAPITAL

Juneau (*June*-oh) hustles and bustles like no other city in Alaska. The steep downtown streets echo with the mad shopping sprees of cruise-ship passengers in the summer tourist season and the whispered intrigues of politicians during the winter legislative session. Miners, loggers, and eco-tourism operators come to lobby for their share of Southeast's forest. Lunch hour arrives, and well-to-do state and federal bureaucrats burst from the office buildings to try the latest restaurant or to brown-bag on one of the waterfront wharves, the sparkling water before them and gift store malls behind. The center of town becomes an ad hoc pedestrian mall as the crush of people forces cars to creep.

My Juneau is close at hand, but very different. As a child, at a magical age, I lived here with my family in a house on the side of the mountains above downtown. My Juneau is up the 99 steps that lead from the cemetery to the bottom of Pine Street—the way I walked home from school—and then to the top of residential Evergreen Avenue, where the pavement gives way to a forest trail among fiddlehead ferns and massive rainforest spruces. That trail leads to the flume (a wooden aqueduct that used to bring water down from the mountains), upon which we would walk into the land of bears and salmon, the rumbling water at our feet. It's still a short walk from the rackety downtown streets to a misty forest quiet, where you can listen for the voices of trees.

Juneau is Alaska's third-largest city (Anchorage and Fairbanks are larger), with a population of 30,000, but it feels like a small town that's just been stuffed with people. Splattered on the sides of Mount Juneau and Mount Roberts along Gastineau Channel, where there isn't room for much of a town, its setting is picturesque but impractical. Further development up the mountains is hemmed in by avalanche danger; beyond is the 1,500-square-mile **Juneau Icefield,** an impenetrable barrier. Gold-mine tailings dumped into the Gastineau created the flat land near the water where much of the downtown area now stands. The Native village that originally stood on the waterfront is today a little pocket several blocks from the shore. There's no road to the outside world, and the terrain discourages building one. Jets are the main way in and out, threading down through the mountains to the airport.

Gold was responsible for the location; it was found here in 1880 by Joe Juneau and Richard Harris, assisted by the Tlingit chief Kowee, who told them where to look. All three men are buried in the Evergreen Cemetery. Their find started Alaska's development. The territory's first significant roads and bridges and its first electrical plant were built in the mountains here, which were carved with miles of hard rock tunnels well before the Klondike gold rush began. In a few years these mines removed more gold than the United States paid for all of Alaska, as attested to by a photograph in the State Museum showing comparative piles. There's plenty of gold left, but mining died out with World War II; efforts to start again have repeatedly faltered in the face of environmental controls and economics. There are several interesting gold mining sites to visit.

In 1900, Congress moved the territorial capital here from Sitka, which had fallen behind in the flurry of gold-rush development. Alaskans have been fighting over whether or not to keep it here for many decades since, but Juneau's economy is heavily dependent on government jobs, and it has successfully fought off a series of challenges to its capital status. The closest call came in the 1970s, when

Juneau.

the state selected a wilderness site near Willow for a whole new city to house the capital—a necessity since neither Anchorage nor Fairbanks, which have their own rivalry, would support the move if it meant the other city got to have the capital nearby. Juneau defeated that move by pushing through an initiative that required voter approval of the full cost of any move. When the price tag became public, the electorate turned down building a brand new city.

In 2002, voters turned down a petition initiative to move only the legislature by a two-to-one margin. In 2005, Juneau attempted to cement its place as the capital city by launching a drive to build a new capitol building, but the ploy backfired when the public panned the futuristic design city leaders selected. A new threat arrived in 2006 with the election of Governor Sarah Palin, who preferred to spend time at her home in Wasilla, near Anchorage, and who allowed other officials to move their offices to Anchorage. In 2007, she held the state's first special legislative session outside Juneau, in Anchorage. But her resignation in 2009 seemed to give Juneau another reprieve. Still, Juneau remains vigilant to the threat of an incremental movement of government functions that could outflank its best defense, that 1970s law that remains on the books requiring a vote on the full costs of moving.

There's plenty to see in Juneau, and it's a good town to visit because the population of government workers supports restaurants and amenities of a quality not found elsewhere in Southeast. Alaska's most accessible glacier, the Mendenhall, is in Juneau, and many businesses have set up tours, including visits to the fish hatchery, the brewery, and an abandoned mine. Juneau is also a starting point and travel hub for outdoor activities all over the northern Panhandle: You'll likely pass through on your way to Glacier Bay or virtually anywhere else in the region. The outdoors is always close at hand in Juneau. You can start from the capitol building for a hike to the top of Mount Juneau or Mount Roberts, or up the Perseverance Trail that leads in between. Sea-kayaking and whale-watching excursions are nearby, as well as some of Alaska's most scenic tide pooling and beach walking.

Downtown, the crush of visitors can be overwhelming when many cruise ships are in port at once. The streets around the docks have been entirely taken over by shops and other touristy businesses. Many of these are owned by people from outside Alaska who come to the state for the summer to sell gifts made outside Alaska. But only a few blocks away are quiet mountainside neighborhoods of houses with mossy roofs, and only a few blocks farther are the woods and the mountains, populated by bear, eagles, and salmon.

Essentials

GETTING THERE

BY AIR Jet service is available only from **Alaska Airlines** (☎**800/252-7522;** www.alaskaair.com), with several daily nonstop flights from Seattle and Anchorage and from the smaller Southeast Alaska towns. Many of the region's commuter and air-taxi operators also maintain desks at the airport and have flights out of Juneau. Among the best is **Wings of Alaska** (☎**907/789-0790;** www.ichoosewings.com).

BY FERRY All the main-line ferries of Southeast's **Alaska Marine Highway System** (☎**800/642-0066;** www.ferryalaska.com) stop at the terminal in Auke Bay (☎**907/789-7453,** or 907/465-3940 recording), 14 miles from downtown, and the fast ferry, *Fairweather,* is based here, too. It cuts sailing times in half. The conventional ferries take 5 hours to make the run to Haines or Skagway. The passenger fare is $37 to Haines, $50 to Skagway.

GETTING INTO TOWN FROM THE AIRPORT & FERRY TERMINAL An airport shuttle may be operating when you visit. Ask at the visitor desk in the baggage claim area.

An express **Capital Transit** city **bus** (☎**907/789-6901**) normally comes to the airport at 11 minutes past the hour on weekdays from 7:11am to 5:11pm and costs $1.50; your luggage has to fit under your seat or at your feet. The service stopped in 2009 due to construction, but is due to recommence. Ask the driver for the stop closest to your hotel. Generally, you can walk from there.

The Cruise Ship Dock: Where Do You Get Off?

Cruise-ship passengers disembark in Juneau's attractive **Marine Park** waterfront area, where a kiosk dispenses information and tour operators sell their services. Downtown shops and attractions are close by. Among the most popular sights is one right at the dock, the statue of a small dog facing the ships as they come in. This is *Patsy Ann,* a bull terrier that in the 1930s always seemed to know when a steamer was arriving and faithfully stationed herself on the dock to meet the disembarking passengers. There's also a spotting scope in the park for watching mountain goats on Mt. Juneau. For a quiet break, visit the beautiful library at the top of the parking garage at the south end of the dock.

Flying to Juneau

Juneau's mist-shrouded airport, wedged between ocean and mountain, has a special verb: *to overhead.* That means that when you try to fly to Juneau on a foggy day, you could end up somewhere else instead (although this now happens less frequently thanks to new navigational technology). Planes overhead other Southeast towns, too, but more frequently in Juneau, since it is the region's travel hub, with many flights a day. The airline will put you on the next flight back to Juneau when the weather clears, but they won't pay for hotel rooms or give you a refund. Your only protection is travel insurance and a loose itinerary. This situation is such an ingrained part of Juneau's way of life that a channel on the cable TV system broadcasts the view toward the airport 24 hours a day, showing the weather over the Gastineau Channel (it's called the Channel Channel, 19 on the dial). Residents know the view so well they can tell from the silent image if they'll get out that day.

Shuttles sometimes operate from the ferry dock downtown in the summer, but the arrangements are changeable. Ask when you arrive, or call ahead to the visitor center (below). A cab downtown from the airport will cost you $22, from the ferry dock $33. One taxi company is **Capital Cab** (℡907/586-2772), which also offers tours for $55 an hour.

ORIENTATION

Juneau has three main parts: downtown, the Mendenhall Valley, and Douglas. Downtown Juneau is a numbered grid of streets overlying the uneven topography like a patchwork quilt over a pile of pillows. As you look at Juneau from the water, Mount Juneau is on the left and Mount Roberts on the right; Mount Roberts is a few hundred feet taller, at 3,819 feet. **Franklin Street** extends south of town 5½ miles to good hiking trails and the hamlet of Thane. When the city outgrew its original site downtown, housing spread to the suburban **Mendenhall Valley,** about a dozen miles north out the Egan Expressway or the parallel, two-lane Glacier Highway. The glacial valley also contains the Juneau International Airport, University of Alaska Southeast, and the **Auke Bay** area, where the ferry terminal is located. The road continues 40 miles to a place known as **"The End of the Road."** Across a bridge over the Gastineau Channel from downtown Juneau is Douglas Island. Turn left for the town of **Douglas,** mostly a bedroom community for Juneau, and turn right for the North Douglas Highway, which leads to the ski area and some beautiful rocky beaches.

GETTING AROUND

BY RENTAL CAR A car is a hindrance in compact downtown Juneau, but if you're going to the Mendenhall Glacier or to any of the attractions out the road or on Douglas Island, renting a car for a day or two is a good idea. Hertz, Avis, Budget, Alamo, and National are based at the airport.

[FastFACTS] JUNEAU

Banks Wells Fargo, 123 Seward St. (☎**907/586-3324**), is one of the many banks and stores that have ATMs.

Hospital Bartlett Regional, 3260 Hospital Dr. (☎**907/796-8900**), is 3 miles out the Glacier Highway from downtown.

Internet Access Computers are easy to find downtown at coffeehouses and businesses such as **Copy Express,** 230 Seward St. (☎**907/586-2174**). In the Mendenhall Valley, try **Electronic Adventures,** 9109 Mendenhall Mall Rd. (☎**907/790-3658**).

Police The police station is at 6255 Alaway Ave. (☎**907/586-0600** for nonemergencies).

Post Office Downtown in the federal building, 709 W. 9th St.; and in the Mendenhall Valley at 9491 Vintage Blvd., near Carr's/Safeway supermarket. A postal contract station handier to the cruise-ship docks is at 145 South Franklin St.

Taxes Sales tax is 5%. You pay 12% tax on rooms.

BY BIKE If you can handle hills, bikes make good sense in Juneau, where separated paths parallel many of the main roads and downtown traffic is slow. The 24-mile round-trip to Mendenhall Glacier keeps you on a bike path almost all the way. Bikes are for rent at the **Driftwood Lodge,** 435 Willoughby Ave. (☎**800/544-2239** or 907/586-2280; www.driftwoodalaska.com), for $25 a day, $15 for a half-day.

VISITOR INFORMATION

The **Visitor Information Center** is in the Centennial Hall at 101 Egan Dr., near the State Museum (☎**888/581-2201** or 907/586-2201; fax 907/586-6304; www.traveljuneau.com). Operated by the Juneau Convention and Visitors Bureau, the center distributes a *Juneau Guide & Travel Planner,* online or on paper, that contains exhaustive listings of hotels and B&Bs, charter boats, tours, and other services. On-site you can use a touch-screen kiosk for information and reservations. The center is open in summer Monday through Friday from 8:30am to 5pm, and Saturday and Sunday from 9am to 5pm; in winter Monday through Friday from 9am to 4pm. The bureau also operates **information desks** at the airport, near the door in the baggage-claim area, and at the Auke Bay ferry terminal. During the summer, centers are staffed at the cruise-ship terminal and at Marine Park.

The office of the **Tongass National Forest Juneau Ranger District** is at 8510 Mendenhall Loop Rd., Juneau, AK 99801 (☎**907/586-8800;** fax 907/586-8808; www.fs.fed.us/r10/tongass).

SPECIAL EVENTS

An events calendar is posted on the visitors' bureau website: www.traveljuneau.com/discover.

The **Alaska Folk Festival** (☎**907/463-3316;** www.alaskafolkfestival.org) is the state's biggest annual coming together of musicians, at Centennial Hall. Musicians take over the town and can be found jamming in every bar and coffeehouse, or wherever a crowd gathers. The 36th annual festival is April 5 to 11, 2010.

Native Parade at Celebration.

The Juneau Jazz & Classics Festival (☎907/463-3378; www.jazzand classics.org), May 21 to 30, 2010, presents concerts and workshops in many styles of music—blues, jazz, classical, rock—at various venues, even on a boat, and at many prices—free to $60 a ticket. Most evening performances are around $25.

The simply named **Celebration,** sponsored by the Sealaska Heritage Institute (☎907/463-4844; www.sealaskaheritage.org), is among Alaska's largest cultural gatherings. Alaska Natives gather from every corner of the state to share dance and art, sell crafts, meet, and, well, celebrate. Book well ahead if you will be in Juneau at this time, as rooms will be in short supply. It happens only every other year, with the next meeting due June 3 to 5, 2010.

The Golden North Salmon Derby (☎907/789-2399; www.goldennorth salmonderby.org), held annually since 1947, targets kings and silvers, normally the first weekend in August. Unlike some other such fishing contests around the state, this isn't just a tourist thing— it brings out as many as 3,000 local fishermen and is even covered live on the radio.

Exploring Downtown

Alaska State Museum ★★★ The museum contains a large collection of art and historical artifacts, but it doesn't seem like a storehouse at all because the objects' presentation is based on their meaning, not their value. Come here to put the rest of your visit in context. A clan house in the Alaska Native Gallery contains authentic art in the functional places where it would have been used in a memorial potlatch. The Lincoln Totem Pole is here, carved by an artist who used a picture of the president as his model to represent his clan's first encounter with whites. Superb artifacts from Native cultures from around the state are presented to illustrate the lifestyle of those who made them. The ramp to the second floor wraps around the natural history display, with an eagle nesting tree, and at the top a state history gallery uses significant pieces to tell Alaska's story. The children's area is exceptionally fun, with a ship that the kids can play in. In 2009, the museum installed "Science on a Sphere," a huge interactive globe for displaying earth science concepts, sponsored by the National Oceanic and Atmospheric

Haida Indian mask at the Alaska State Museum.

Administration. Allow at least 2 hours for the museum; half a day would not be out of line. The shop off the lobby is also well worth a look. Although small, it carries lots of quality Alaska Native art and books (there's a branch at 124 Seward St.). 395 Whittier St. **☏907/465-2901.** www.museums.state.ak.us. Admission mid-May to mid-Sept $5 adults, free for ages 18 and under; mid-Sept to mid-May $3 adults, free for ages 18 and under. Mid-May to mid-Sept daily 8:30am–5:30pm; mid-Sept to mid-May Tues–Sat 10am–4pm.

The Juneau-Douglas City Museum ★ This fun museum displays artifacts and photographs from the city's pioneer and mining history and Tlingit culture, and impressive special art exhibits that change annually. It's quite well done and holds real interest. There are gorgeous stained-glass windows, a 600-year-old fish trap found in a local river, and a hands-on history area that will interest children, allowing them to dress up in period costume. Curators have fit an extraordinary amount of information into a small space, creating a sense of immersion in Juneau's past. Interactive kiosks contain stories produced by local students and a 26-minute video on Juneau's gold-mining history shows each half-hour. The tiny bookshop is stocked with handy information for your visit to Juneau, including the historic hike guide booklet, free historic walking-tour map, and maps of the Evergreen Cemetery and the old Treadwell Mine. In the summer, the museum leads historic walking tours Tuesday, Thursday, and Saturday at 1:30pm. The cost is $10 adults, $7 age 18 and under.

At the corner of 4th and Main sts. **☏907/586-3572.** www.juneau.org/parkrec/museum. Admission $4 adults (free in winter), free for ages 18 and under. Summer Mon–Fri 9am–5pm, Sat–Sun 10am–5pm; winter Tues–Sat 10am–4pm.

The Last Chance Mining Museum and Historic Park ★ 🎁 On the site on forested Gold Creek where gold was first discovered in Juneau, the museum preserves old mining buildings and some of their original equipment, including an

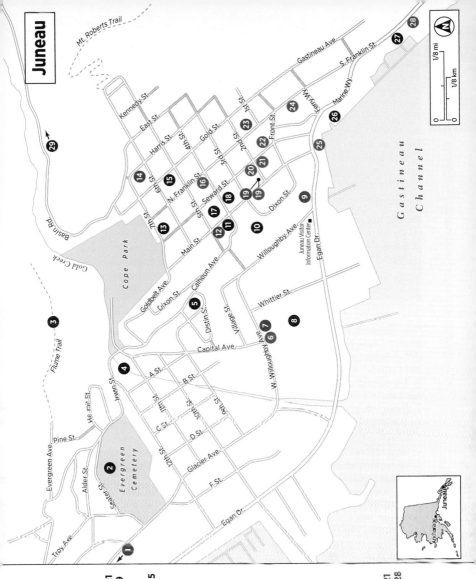

Juneau

ATTRACTIONS
Abandoned wooden flume **3**
Alaska State Capitol **17**
Alaska State Museum **8**
Evergreen Cemetery **2**
Gold Creek **4**
Governor's Mansion **5**
Juneau-Douglas City Museum **11**
Last Chance Mining Museum **29**
Mount Roberts Tramway **27**
Patsy Ann statue **26**
St. Nicholas Orthodox Church **15**
State Courthouse **18**
State Office Building **10**
The Wickersham House
State Historic Site **13**

ACCOMMODATIONS
Alaska's Capital Inn **12**
Baranof Hotel **23**
Breakwater Hotel **1**
The Driftwood Lodge **7**
Goldbelt Hotel Juneau **9**
The Historic Silverbow Inn **19**
Juneau International Hostel **14**

DINING
The Hangar **25**
Heritage Coffee Co. & Café **24**
Pizzeria Roma **25**
Rainbow Foods **16**
Sandpiper Café **6**
Silverbow Bakery **19**
Tarantino's Italian Restaurant **21**
Twisted Fish Co. Alaskan Grill **28**
Valentine's Coffee House &
Pizzeria **22**
Zephyr Restaurant **20**

immense 1912 air compressor and a layered glass map of the tunnels. This was once a nerve center for one of the world's biggest hard-rock mines. The highlight is its energetic and learned guide, Renee Hughes, who lives above the compressor with her husband Gary Gillette. Both are leaders of the Gastineau Channel Historical Society. Ask Renee about the cave-in of the Treadwell Mine to hear her riveting storytelling. The entrance to the site—which contains relics and buildings spread over several acres—is a bridge across the creek, which leads to a steep trail up to the buildings.

1001 Basin Rd. ☎907/586-5338. Admission $4. Daily 9:30am–12:30pm and 3:30–6:30pm. Closed Oct to mid-May. From downtown, take Gold St. up the hill to its end, then join Basin Rd., continuing 1 mile up the valley to the end of the road.

Mount Roberts Tramway ★ The tram takes only 6 minutes to whisk passengers from tourist-clogged Franklin Street to the clear air and overwhelming views at the tree line (1,760 ft.), a destination that used to require a day of huffing and puffing to witness. The tram can be crowded; it's once you're up there that the beauty hits you. The Alaska Native owners seem to understand that, and they have built a network of alpine paths that take advantage of the views. If you're energetic, you can start a 6-mile round-trip hike to Mount Roberts's summit (at 3,819 ft.), or you can hike the 2½ miles back to downtown. At the top you'll also find a film on Tlingit culture, a gift shop, and a bar and grill serving lunch and dinner. I would choose something else to do on a day when fog or low overcast obscures the view, however, especially considering the high price.

490 S. Franklin St., at the waterfront near the cruise-ship dock. ☎888/461-8726 or 907/463-3412. www.mountrobertstramway.com. Full-day pass $27 adults, $14 children ages 6–12, free age 5 and under; tax included. May–Sept daily 9am–9pm. Closed Oct–Apr.

WALKING TOUR: JUNEAU

START & FINISH: **Alaska State Capitol, 4th and Seward streets.**

TIME: **1 hour (1 mile) for standard tour; 2½ hours (2½ miles) for the extended tour, with minimal stops.**

1 The Alaska State Capitol

This structure fills the block between 4th and 5th and Main and Seward streets. Except for the marble portico on the 4th Street side, it is a nondescript brick box, probably the least impressive state capitol in the most beautiful setting in the nation. Legislators hanker for a larger, grander building, but the still-simmering desire of some politicians to move the capital nearer the state's population center has defeated plans to build here (see the section introduction, earlier in the chapter, for more on the capital move debate). The federal government built the Capitol in 1931, when Alaska was still a territory. Inside, some of the old-fashioned woodwork and decorative details are interesting, and the public is free to walk through. During the summer, free tours are offered. Check at the desk in the lobby, or call ☎907/465-3800 for information. The legislature is in session from January to April.

The bear statue in front of the State Courthouse.

Across 4th is the:

2 State Courthouse

The statue of a bear in front defines official Alaskan taste in art: It replaced a hated abstract steel sculpture called *Nimbus* that was removed by an act of the legislature and that finally came to rest in front of the state museum a few blocks away.

On the opposite, northwest corner is the:

3 Juneau-Douglas City Museum

Stop in here now to buy the Evergreen Cemetery map if you plan to include that in your walk, or get the *Historic Downtown Juneau Guide* to learn more on the whole walk. (The museum is described on p. 222.) Even if you don't stop in, take a look at a rare American flag out front. This small plaza is where the 49-star U.S. flag was first raised in 1959 —they didn't make many of those, as Hawaii was admitted as the 50th state within a year, but you'll still find one flying here.

On the southwest corner of Main and 4th is the:

4 State Office Building

This building is built into the edge of a cliff that forms a major barrier through the downtown area; if you're headed for the lower land, where the State Museum and Centennial Hall are located, you can avoid eight flights of steps in between by taking the building's elevator down. In any event, visit the towering atrium, with its great views and a 1928 movie theater pipe organ that's played on Fridays at noon. The historical collections of the Alaska State Library are housed here (www.library.state.ak.us/hist), and a stop to view historic photographs and artifacts on display is well worth the effort. Visitors are welcome to browse, too; or do it from home, as a thousands of pieces have been digitized at http://vilda.alaska.edu.

On sunny days, the patio off the atrium is a warm place for a picnic, with a fabulous view.

Leaving again through the door that you entered, turn left and follow Calhoun Street around the curve. An outdoor staircase here leads down to the flat area of town below (but you know about taking the elevator). Those lowlands originally were mostly underwater and this embankment stood just above the shoreline, which continued along Front and South Franklin streets. The land you see below you is made of mine tailings that were dumped in the Channel. Continue on Calhoun; the governor uses the pedestrian overpass (which we walk under) to cross Calhoun to get to the Capitol from the white, neoclassical:

5 Governor's Mansion

Located on the left, the mansion was built by the federal government in 1912 for $40,000. It isn't normally open for public tours. Its current occupant is Sean Parnell, the former lieutenant governor who moved in when Governor Sarah Palin resigned from office in the summer of 2009. She reputedly didn't care for this grand, old-fashioned house and spent little time here, living normally in her own lakeside house in Wasilla. As this is written, it's unknown whether she will run for president in 2012 or otherwise capitalize on her celebrity (see "Alaska's Political Earthquake," in chapter 2). Parnell has until the primary election in August and the general election in November 2010 to prove he is worthy of the position. He will have plenty of opponents. Parnell doesn't have his predecessor's charisma. He unsuccessfully ran for Congress in 2008 and did poorly, earning the nickname "Captain Zero" from his opponent for his lackluster campaigning. Meanwhile, the corruption investigation of Alaska's Republican old guard has taken a strange turn, as revelations of prosecutorial misconduct led to U.S. Attorney General Eric Holder to call for the release of already convicted and imprisoned legislators. Stay tuned.

Shortcut: If you don't mind missing the next stop (Gold Creek), you can save yourself some hill-climbing by continuing on Calhoun, turning

The Governor's Mansion.

right on Goldbelt Street, climbing past some beautiful houses to 7th, then picking up the tour at the Wickersham House.

Continuing down Calhoun, you'll come to:

6 Gold Creek

Juneau's founders made their gold strike in this stream in 1880. Trace it upstream through peaceful **Cope Park,** past the playground and tennis courts to the unique ball field, which is bounded by the stream's forested canyon walls. (To continue this walk to Evergreen Cemetery and up to the top of the town and through the woods on the flume—a long, strenuous hike—return to Calhoun St. and continue in the direction you were going. That route is covered below under "The Extended Walk.")

Go all the way to the right side (that's left field, on your right) of the baseball diamond to find a lovely path and public stairway through the woods running steeply up to 7th Street. Seventh runs along a narrow ridge between downtown Juneau and the creek. Across the street from the top of the stairway is:

7 The Wickersham House State Historic Site

This white, 1898 frame house, at 213 7th St. (**907/586-9001;** www.alaskastateparks.org, click "Individual Parks"), was the retirement home of Judge James Wickersham, who was revered by Alaskans for bringing law to the gold rush in Eagle, Nome, and Fairbanks; for exploring the Denali area and helping to make it a national park; for helping convince the federal government to build the Alaska railroad and found the state university; and for winning Alaska's right to make its own laws when he represented the territory as a non-voting delegate in Congress. The house was in the family from 1928 until the state bought it in 1984, so it still contains many of Wickersham's belongings, including an Edison cylinder gramophone he took to Fairbanks, and his written assignment to go to Alaska, which is signed by Theodore Roosevelt. The house badly needed repair when a renovation project funded in part by the National Park Service began several years ago. Although work continues, the first floor is open during the summer months from 9am to 3pm.

Continue on 7th to Gold Street, turn right, and follow it downhill to 5th, site of the:

8 St. Nicholas Orthodox Church

This small structure is a significant architectural and historic landmark. The octagonal building was built in 1893–94 by Serbian miners and Tlingits. Many Tlingits chose the Russian Orthodox faith in the late 19th century when government-sponsored Protestant missionaries arrived with authority to force Christianity on Alaska Natives. The Protestants' civilizing program entailed wiping out Native languages and culture, but the Orthodox allowed people to worship in Tlingit and to continue more of their own customs. Bishop Innocent Veniaminov had translated sacred texts into Tlingit 50 years earlier when the Russians were still in Sitka (learn more under "The Russian Bishop's House," p. 204). Today, Alaska Natives make up the bulk of Russian Orthodox congregations in Alaska, and St. Nicholas still has an active Tlingit parish. There is no admission, but a donation is requested. There is a small gift shop and museum.

Walk 1 block down and 2 blocks to the right to the start/finish point.

The Extended Walk

This walk, totaling 2½ miles, includes some steep stairways and streets. Follow the walking tour until you reach Gold Creek (see number 6, above).

Cross the creek and stay on the same road (which goes under various names), bearing right as it becomes Martin Street. On the left is:

9 The Evergreen Cemetery

The cemetery slopes toward the ocean, opening a wonderful vista over the clear green lawn. One reason the view is so broad and open is that the markers are flush with the ground. The old Alaska Native graves are in the wooded portion on the far side. Joe Juneau and Richard Harris, the city's founders, are buried near the cross at the top end of the cemetery, close to where you arrive on the walk.

Across the road from the cross, Hermit Street reaches a little way into the mountainside. Follow the steep public stairs next to house no. 430 up to the bottom of Pine Street. This is the walk I described in the introduction. The views get better and better as you rise to the top of Pine Street, then go right on Evergreen Street, following the road to where it dissipates into a trail among shadowy spruce and western hemlock.

Continue on the peaceful forest trail among the ferns and evergreens up the valley, coming to the:

10 Abandoned Wooden Flume

Once the town's aqueduct, the flume now is maintained as a boardwalk into the forest. Since it carried water, it's nearly level, but watch your step in wet weather, as it crosses some high trestles over gullies.

At the end of the flume, cross over the valley to Basin Road and continue upstream. Stop to see:

11 The Last Chance Mining Museum

The museum is described on p. 222.

To the left is the Perseverance Trail, which continues up between the mountains; the Perseverance also leads to the trail head for a challenging hike up Mount Juneau (both hikes are covered below).

To get back to town, follow Basin Road 1 mile back down the valley. Taking the first right will put you at the top of Gold Street. Descend a block to 7th and pick up the walking tour at stop seven (the Wickersham House is a block down 7th) or continue down Gold to St. Nicholas Orthodox Church, stop eight on the tour.

Shopping

The shops near the dock cater primarily to cruise-ship passengers. After around 500 summer port calls, many close their doors. The year-round community and more local shops tend to be farther up the hill. If you're looking for authentic Alaska Native arts and crafts, be warned that counterfeiting is widespread. For buying tips, read "Native Art: Finding the Real Thing" in chapter 3.

The Raven's Journey, 435 S. Franklin (℃**907/463-4686;** www.ravens journeygallery.com), shows Tlingit and other Northwest coast Indian carvings and masks, totemic silver jewelry, and whalebone, ivory, basketry, and fossil ivory carvings and jewelry from the Yup'ik and Iñupiat of western and northern Alaska. Works are displayed with biographical placards of the artists.

Juneau Artists Gallery, in the Senate Building at 175 S. Franklin (℃**907/ 586-9891;** www.juneauartistsgallery.com), is staffed by a co-op of local artists and shows only the members' work: paintings, etchings, photography, jewelry, fabrics, ceramics, and other media. Much of it is good and inexpensive, and the way it is displayed creates a panorama of artistic visions.

Juneau's Rie Muñoz is one of Alaskans' favorite artists for her simple, graphic, generally cheerful watercolors of coastal Alaskan communities and Native people, among other subjects. Her prints, silkscreens, note cards, and the like are shown downtown at the **Decker Gallery,** 233 S. Franklin (℃**907/463-5536**), and in the Mendenhall Valley at the **Rie Muñoz Gallery,** 2101 Jordan Ave., across from the Nugget Mall (℃**800/247-3151** or 907/789-7449; www.rie munoz.com), where you'll also find her original watercolors and stained glass.

For gifts, try **Annie Kaill's** fine arts and crafts gallery at 244 Front St. It's a little out of the cruise ship shopping area and gets business from locals. The shop has a rich, homey feeling, with local work at various price levels. The long-established **Ad Lib,** 231 S. Franklin St., is also a fun little shop.

Hearthside Books (www.hearthsidebooks.com) is a cubbyhole of a bookstore at the corner of Franklin and Front streets, but has a good selection for its size, especially of Alaskan books and maps. (A larger branch, with a good toy

Avoiding Cruise-Ship Crowds

On the busiest days of the summer, cruise ships bring more than 10,000 passengers and another 4,000 crew members to the docks on Juneau's Franklin Street. That's simply too many for these narrow old streets; downtown becomes a solid crush of people, and attractions are packed, spoiling the experience for everyone. The crush is largely unavoidable, with some ships in port every day of the summer, but of late the heaviest days have been midweek, with Fridays and weekends quieter. If you can plan your Juneau sightseeing then, you may find somewhat less crowding; also, the farther you go from the dock, the less crowding you encounter. For a current schedule of ships, which shows the number docking on each day of the summer, go to www. juneau.org and search for "Cruise Ship Schedule."

department, is in the Mendenhall Valley's Nugget Mall, 8745 Glacier Hwy., a 5-min. walk from the airport.)

The most unexpected shop in Juneau is **The Observatory,** 299 N. Franklin St. (☎907/586-9676; www.observatorybooks.com). This browser's paradise specializes in rare maps and books about Alaska, with a large collection of antique engravings. Among the items I've seen here were huge charts drawn by the first 18th-century explorers to trace Alaska's coastline. To get the full effect you must strike up a conversation with the shop's owner, Dee Longenbaugh. She is a fellow of the Royal Geographical Society and member of the Antiquarian Booksellers Association. One question will start a fascinating tour of Alaska history. **The Urban Eskimo,** 217 Seward St. (☎907/796-3626; www.urbaneskimo.com), also specializes in history, focusing on the gold-rush era with photographs, books, and ephemera, and carrying regional art and antiques.

Bill Spear sells his own brightly colored enamel pins and zipper pulls from his studio, hidden upstairs at 174 S. Franklin (☎907/586-2209; www.wmspear. com). Alaskans collect the vividly executed fish, birds, airplanes, dinosaurs, vegetables, and many other witty, provocative, or beautiful pins, which cost from $5 to $20 each.

Taku Store, 550 S. Franklin, across the parking lot from the tram station (☎800/582-5122 or 907/463-3474; www.takustore.com), is worth a stop if you're nearby, even if you're not in the market for the pricey seafood in the case: It's interesting to watch workers fillet, smoke, and pack salmon through large windows, and to read the explanatory signs about what they're doing. They'll ship fish anywhere in the U.S.

Attractions Beyond Walking Distance

Mendenhall Glacier Transport (☎907/789-5460; www.mightygreattrips. com) does a 2½-hour town and Mendenhall Glacier tour for $30, or you can ride their "Blue Bus Express" to the glacier for $15. Generally, it runs every half-hour both directions, from the waterfront visitor center to the glacier and back, daily 9am to 6pm in summer. Otherwise, take a rented car or, for vigorous people, bike 24 miles out to the Mendenhall Glacier and back. I've listed these sites by distance from downtown with directions starting from there.

Alaskan Brewing Company Beer lovers and aspiring capitalists will enjoy the tour of Alaska's most popular craft brewery. Now too big to be called "micro," the brewery started small in 1986 when Geoff and Marcy Larson had the idea of bringing a local gold rush–era brew back to life. It worked, and now Alaskan Amber and several other brews are everywhere in Alaska and many places down the West Coast, and the brewery has won a long list of national and international awards for its brews. The short, free tour, which starts every half-hour, is fairly interesting, with views of the brewing equipment behind glass and an amazing worldwide beer bottle collection, but it's the tasting that makes it fun. They serve a wide variety of free samples, often creating an impromptu party in the lobby. Identification is required.

5429 Shaune Dr. ☎907/780-5866. www.alaskanbeer.com. May–Sept daily 11am–6pm; winter Thurs–Sun 11am–5pm. Last tour starts at 4:30pm winter and 5:30pm summer. Turn right from Egan Dr. on Vanderbilt Hill Rd., which becomes Glacier Hwy., then right on Anka St., and right again on Shaune Dr.

Juneau Beyond Downtown

0 — 2 mi
0 — 2 km

N

Mendenhall Glacier

Mendenhall Lake

Nugget Cr.

Lake Cr.

Heintzleman Ridge

Mendenhall Valley

Montana Cr.

Mendenhall R.

Mendenhall Loop Rd.

Auke Bay

Auke L.

Auke Bay

Glacier Hwy.

TONGASS NATIONAL FOREST

Lemon Cr.

JUNEAU INT'L. AIRPORT

Blackerby Ridge

Salmon Creek Res.

Fritz Cove

Salmon Cr.

Gastineau Channel

N Douglas Hwy.

Egan Dr.

see downtown Juneau map

Juneau

DOUGLAS ISLAND

West Juneau

TONGASS NATIONAL FOREST

Douglas

ATTRACTIONS
Alaskan Brewing Company **7**
Glacier Gardens **6**
Macaulay Salmon Hatchery **8**
Mendenhall Glacier Visitor Center **4**

ACCOMMODATIONS
Alaska Wolf Lodge **9**
Pearson's Pond Luxury Inn & Adventure Spa **3**
Frontier Suites Airport Hotel **5**

DINING
Chan's Thai Kitchen **2**
Hot Bite **1**

Glacier Gardens This is the place to see the rainforest if you have mobility problems. The heart of the hour-long tour is a ride in vehicles similar to golf carts up a steep mountainside, past a stream and pools, to a platform with a view of the Mendenhall Valley. They mainly get groups from the cruise ships, but the staff will take just a few independent travelers at a time for a ride, explaining the forest flora in as much detail as you wish. Gardeners will especially enjoy the extraordinary hanging baskets and other bright and ingenious plantings in the lower area—weddings of cruise-ship passengers are held here almost every day in the summer. The gardens' trademark is upside-down trees whose roots, way up in the air, are planted with trailing flowers. An eagle nest on the grounds has been active in recent years. All good, but as much as I like the place, I have to point out it is priced as a guided tour, not a botanical garden. The garden has a hiking trail for those who don't want to ride on the vehicles, but hikers have plenty of rainforest trails to choose from without fees.

7600 Glacier Hwy. **☎ 907/790-3377.** www.glaciergardens.com. Admission $22 adults, $16 ages 6–12, free 5 and under. Summer daily 9am–6pm. Closed Oct–Apr. Near the Fred Meyer store about 1 mile from the airport.

Macaulay Salmon Hatchery ★ The hatchery, known by locals as DIPAC (Douglas Island Pink and Chum, Inc.), was ingeniously designed to allow visitors to watch the whole process of harvesting and fertilizing eggs from outdoor decks. From mid-June to October, salmon swim up a 450-foot fish ladder, visible through a window, into a sorting mechanism, then are "unzipped" by workers who remove the eggs. Guides and exhibits explain what's happening. During that period you can often see seals and other wildlife feeding on the returning salmon just offshore from the hatchery. Inside, large and realistic saltwater aquariums show off the area's marine life as it looks in the natural environment. The tour is less impressive in May and June, before the fish are running. At that time visitors see the immature salmon before their release and sometimes get to feed them. The tours don't take long; allow 45 minutes for your entire visit.

2697 Channel Dr. **☎ 877/463-2486** or 907/463-5114. www.dipac.net. Admission $3.25 adults, $1.75 children ages 12 and under. Summer Mon–Fri 10am–6pm, Sat–Sun 10am–5pm; winter call ahead. 3 miles from downtown, turn left at the first group of buildings on Egan Dr.

Mendenhall Glacier ★★★ This is easily Juneau's best attraction, and one of the most rewarding in the state, with Alaska's easiest access to both a glacier and to bear viewing. Read on.

Mendenhall Glacier.

At the head of Mendenhall Valley, the glacier glows bluish white, looming above the suburbs like an Ice Age monster that missed the general extinction, a truly impressive sight. The parking and an adjacent shelter have a great view across the lake 1 mile to the glacier's face, and a wheelchair-accessible trail leads close to the water's edge. The land near the parking lot shows signs of the glacier's recent passage, with little topsoil, stunted vegetation, and, in many places, bare rock that shows the scratch marks of the glacier's movement. The glacier, currently retreating about 500 feet a year, covered what is now the visitor area in 1935. Atop a bedrock hill, reached by stairs, a ramp, or an elevator, the Forest Service visitor center contains a glacier museum with excellent explanatory models, computerized displays, spotting scopes, and ranger talks.

Beginning in August and lasting into September, the area has an extraordinary added attraction: the most accessible bear-viewing opportunity you're likely to find anywhere. Red and silver salmon spawn in **Steep Creek,** just short of the visitor center on the road, making an easy source of bear food. Around 10 female and juvenile black bears congregate to catch and feast on the fish, all within a few yards of viewing platforms. Unlike other bear-viewing sites that require use of permit systems and expensive plane rides, anyone can come here at any time for free. One viewing platform is off the first parking lot on the left as you arrive at the area; the other is at the far end of the short Steep Creek Trail, next to the parking lot nearest the visitor center. The unique situation developed beginning around 2005, when bears got used to humans being on the new boardwalks, which had been built to view fish, not bears. This group of females apparently uses the human crowds as a shield against dangerous males, which stay away because of all the people. Despite the bears' apparent docility and interest in their dinner, remember they are dangerous wild animals. Stay on the trail and give them space. Don't bring food. Back away from a bear that is on the trail, but never run.

There are several hiking trails at the glacier, including two fairly steep hikes, one on each side of the glacier. At the visitor center and a booth near the parking lot, the Forest Service distributes a brochure which includes a trail map. The **East Glacier Loop Trail** is a beautiful 3.5-mile round-trip hike leading through the forest to a view of a waterfall above the glacier about half a mile from its face, and to parts of an abandoned rail tram and an abandoned dam on Nugget Creek; the trail has steep parts but is doable for school-age children. You can park at the visitor center and start from there. The **West Glacier Trail,** 7 miles round-trip, is more challenging, leaving from 300 yards beyond the Skaters' Cabin and following the edge of the lake and glacier, providing access to the ice itself for experienced climbers with the right equipment. You will need wheels to get to the trailhead. Take the Mendenhall Loop Road to Montana Creek Road, turn right, and then turn right again on Skaters' Cabin Road.

The granite Skater's Cabin is also the starting point for a groomed cross-country-ski loop on Mendenhall Lake in front of the glacier. Don't go beyond the orange safety markers near the glacier's face.

At the head of Glacier Spur Rd. (right from Egan Dr. on Mendenhall Loop to Glacier Spur). Visitor center admission summer $3 adults, free children under 16; winter free. Visitor center (☎907/789-0097) open daily in summer 8am–7:30pm; winter Thurs–Sun 10am–4pm.

What to See & Do "Out the Road"

On sunny summer weekends, Juneau families get in the car and drive "out the road" (northwest along the Glacier Hwy., as it's officially known). The views of island-stippled water from the paved two-lane highway are worth the trip, and there are also several good places to stop. To use this road guide, set your trip odometer to zero at the ferry dock (which is 14 miles from downtown Juneau).

The **Auke Village Recreation Area** is a mile beyond the ferry dock and is a good place for picnics and beach walks. Less than a mile farther is a Forest Service campground.

The **Shrine of St. Thérèse** ★ (☏907/780-6112; www.shrineofsaint therese.org), 9 miles beyond the ferry dock (23 miles from downtown), rests on a tiny island reached by a foot-trail causeway. The wonderfully simple chapel of rounded beach stones, circled by markers of the 15 stations of the cross, stands peaceful and mysterious amid trees, rock, water, and the cries of the raven and eagle. It is the most spiritual place I know. The vaguely Gothic structure was built in the late 1930s of stone picked up from these shores and dedicated by Alaska's first Catholic bishop to St. Thérèse of Lisieux, who died in 1897 at the age of 24. Sunday liturgy services are held from June to September at 1:30pm. The shrine is part of a large retreat maintained by the Juneau Catholic Diocese, which includes a log lodge on the shore facing the island as well as several cabins for rent as lodgings. The shrine's island is a good vantage from which to look upon **Lynn Canal** for marine mammals or, at low tide, to go tide pooling among the rocks. The website covers the shrine's history and gives information on the facilities, as well as a labyrinth, a columbarium, gardens, and trails at the shrine.

Shrine of St. Thérèse.

Eagle Beach, 14 miles beyond the ferry dock, makes a good picnic area in nice weather, when you can walk among the tall beach grass or out on the sandy tidal flats, watch the eagles, or go north along the beach to look for fossils in the rock outcroppings.

The road turns to gravel, then comes to **Point Bridget State Park,** 24 miles beyond the ferry dock (✆907/465-4563; www.alaskastateparks.org, click on "Individual Parks"). A flat 3.5-mile path leads through forest, meadow, and marsh to the shore, where you may see sea lions and possibly humpback whales. Three public-use cabins rent for $35 or $45 a night, depending on the season; for rental information, see "State Parks Cabin Reservations," p. 360. The road ends 26 miles from the ferry dock at pretty **Echo Cove.**

Getting Outside: Onshore

BIRD-WATCHING Bald eagles are as common as pigeons in Juneau. Years ago, one of them made off with a tourist's Chihuahua, starting a statewide debate about whether it was funny or horrible. Eagles are most common on the shoreline, especially where fish are plentiful, such as at the hatchery. For more variety, visit the **Mendenhall Wetlands State Game Refuge,** which encompasses 3,800 acres of tidal estuaries in the Gastineau Channel near the airport. More than 100 species of birds use the refuge, mainly during the April and May migrations. Access points are on either side of the channel, including a viewing platform on the downtown-bound side of Egan Drive, at mile 6.

FRESHWATER & SHORELINE FISHING Juneau isn't known particularly for its stream fishing (boat charter fishing is covered below under "Getting Outside: On the Water"). But there are a few places on the road system where you can find good fishing in freshwater or even in the ocean. The advice you need is in the free *Juneau Sportfishing Guide* available in print or online from the Alaska Department of Fish and Game, 1255 W. 8th St. (P.O. Box 115526), Juneau, AK 99811-5526 (✆907/465-4320; www.alaska.gov/adfg, click on "Sport Fish," then on the Southeast region on the map).

For a remote fly-in experience with fly or spinning gear, contact **Alaska Fly 'N' Fish Charters,** 9604 Kelly Court (✆907/790-2120; www.alaska byair.com). A guided 5-hour trip is $550 per person, with a two-person minimum. The same reputable guy (Butch Laughlin) also does flightseeing and bear-viewing flights. **Bear Creek Outfitters** (✆907/723-3914; www. juneauflyfishing.com) specializes in catch-and-release fly fishing only, with all gear and hand-tied flies provided. The aircraft drops off a guide with no more than five anglers for an 8-hour full day, for $625 per person.

HIKING I've mentioned several good hikes at Mendenhall Glacier and out the road, above. More than two dozen are described in a nicely made book with detailed topographic maps of each, *Juneau Trails* (www.alaskageographic. org; $8), which you can find at visitor centers. *In the Miner's Footsteps,* a guide to the history behind 14 Juneau trails, is available for a nominal price from the Juneau–Douglas City Museum. The Juneau city and borough **Department of Parks and Recreation** (✆907/586-5226; www.juneau.org/ parksrec) leads hikes (and other activities) through the year; check the website or call the 24-hour hike line at ✆907/586-0428.

Gearing Up for Juneau's Outdoors

You can rent the gear you need for outings on the water or to equip Forest Service cabin visits from Alaska Boat and Kayak, at the Auke Bay Harbor (☎907/789-6886; www.beyondak.com). Besides camping gear, they rent sea kayaks ($50 a day for a single, $70 double, with multiday discounts), and will deliver the boat anywhere on Juneau's road system, to outlying areas, or to Admiralty Island. Rent skiffs with outboard motors that you can use for fishing or exploring from Panhandle Powerboats (☎907/789-5767; www.panhandle powerboats.com). Prices range from $195 to $400 a day. See "Getting Around," earlier in this section, for bike rentals.

The **Perseverance Trail** climbs up the valley behind Juneau and into the mining history of the area it accesses. It can be busy in summer. The trail head is about 1½ miles from town on Basin Road. The trail is 4 miles of easy walking on the mountainside above Gold Creek to the Perseverance Mine, at the Silverbow Basin, a mining community from 1885 to 1921. Use caution on icy patches, as there are steep drop-offs. A well-documented historic pamphlet is for sale at the Juneau–Douglas City Museum.

Two trails start from points along the Perseverance Trail. The challenging **Mount Juneau Trail** rises more than 3,500 feet over about 2 miles from a point 1 mile along the trail from the Perseverance trail head. Go only in dry weather to avoid disastrous falls. The **Granite Creek Trail,** starting 2 miles in on the Perseverance Trail, climbs 1,200 feet over 1½ miles to an alpine basin. Both are quieter than the Perseverance Trail.

Another hike right from downtown climbs **Mount Roberts**—just follow the stairway from the top of 6th Street in a neighborhood called Star Hill. The summit is 4½ miles and 3,819 vertical feet away, but you don't have to go all the way to the top for incredible views and alpine terrain. At the 1,760-foot level, you come to the restaurant at the top of the Mount Roberts tram, mentioned on p. 224. Of course, it's easier to take the tram up and hike down. A third choice: Start from the tram and hike to the summit.

The **Treadwell Mine Historic Trail,** on Douglas Island, is a fascinating hour's stroll through the ruins of a massive hard-rock mine complex that once employed and housed 2,000 men. Since its abandonment in 1922, big trees have grown up through the foundations, intertwining their roots through rails and machinery and adding to the site's exceptional power over the imagination. A well-written guide to numbered posts on the trail is available from the Juneau–Douglas City Museum. This is a great hike for kids. To find the trail head, take 3rd Street in Douglas, bearing left at the Y onto Savikko Street, which leads to Savikko Park, also known as Sandy Beach Park. The trail starts at the far end of the park.

Another great family outing is to the **Outer Point Trail,** 1⅓ miles on a forest boardwalk to a beach with good tide pooling, lots of eagles, and possible whale sightings. Many different kinds of loveliness present themselves over the short walk: The mossy rainforest, the stunted muskeg swamp, a glassy little creek, and the pebbled beach and bedrock ocean pools. From there, on the western point of Douglas Island—the opposite side from Juneau—you can see Auke Bay to the east, Admiralty Island to the west, and the tiny islands of Stephens Passage before you. The trail's only drawback is crowding, especially when tour groups tromp through; avoid them by going early or late. To get there, drive over the bridge to Douglas, then right on North Douglas Highway 12 miles to the trailhead.

SKIING For **downhill skiing,** the city-owned **Eaglecrest Ski Area (☎907/790-2000;** www.skijuneau.com) is the large, steep hill home of Olympic silver medalist Hillary Lindh, Juneau's favorite daughter (her father helped choose the site in the 1970s). A chair goes almost to the top of Douglas Island, with expansive views and 640 acres of skiing terrain. The four lifts serve 31 runs with a total vertical drop of 1,400 feet, rated 40% expert, 40% intermediate, and 20% novice. It's only 12 miles from downtown on North Douglas Highway. An all-day lift ticket is $43 for adults. Even among Alaskans, Eaglecrest is little known, despite being second in size and ski lift development only to Alyeska Resort, near Anchorage.

Eaglecrest has 8km of **cross-country-skiing** trail, offering the most reliable track skiing in town. Generally, Juneau's warm, damp winters don't provide enough snow for good cross-country skiing at lower elevations. Many of the hiking trails into the mountains become winter backcountry routes, however, and snow does stick up there. Before going out, always check with the Forest Service (see "Visitor Information," earlier) for advice on your route and on avalanche conditions. Several of the Forest Service cabins also serve as winter warm-up houses during the day, and make good skiing destinations. If conditions permit, a network of trails is set around the Mendenhall Glacier, with parking and access from the Skaters' Cabin off Montana Creek Road (see "Mendenhall Glacier," above)

ZIP-LINE TOURS A zip line is a cable strung between two high points from which a passenger hangs on a wheeled runner, zipping from one end to the other. Once thought the province of Special Forces training and the like, riding a zip line (with a safety harness) is now considered a cruise activity and is billed as a way of seeing the rainforest. I'm aware of six tours, in Ketchikan, Juneau, and at the Icy Strait cruise-ship stop, but this one, on Juneau's Douglas Island, caters primarily to independent travelers, with less stratospheric prices. **Alaska Zipline Adventures (☎907/321-0947;** www. alaskazip.com) with a tour of seven rides near the Eaglecrest Ski Area. The 3½-hour tour costs $139 adults, $99 children 12 and under, including a snack and transfer to the site. Clients must be 10 and older, fit, not pregnant, and between 70 and 250 pounds. Wear pants and shoes with closed heels and toes.

Getting Outside: On the Water

SALTWATER FISHING Many charter boats are available for fishing excursions from Juneau. Some will also include whale-watching on a trip. Juneau **Sportfishing and Sightseeing,** 2 Marine Way, Ste. 230 (☎907/586-1887;** www.juneausportfishing.com), is one of the largest operators. They charge $395 per person for a full day fishing for salmon, $425 for halibut and salmon; or $205 for 4 hours fishing salmon. They charge $125 for a 2½-hour whale-watching trip. See other whale-watching choices below.

SEA KAYAKING The calm waters around Juneau appeal to sea kayakers, and the city is a popular hub for trips on the water farther afield. Besides the sublime scenery, you'll likely see eagles and sea birds, and you may encounter porpoises, seals, and possibly humpback whales. **Alaska Travel Adventures** (☎800/323-5757; www.bestofalaskatravel.com) offers 3½-hour kayak trips (half that time on the water) in Auke Bay for $89 adults, $59 children 6 to 12. The tour includes orientation for beginners, a snack, and transportation from downtown. A business that rents and delivers kayaks is listed under "Gearing Up for Juneau's Outdoors" (p. 236).

WHALE-WATCHING As close as I've come to a humpback whale—I almost touched it—was the first of many times I've seen them, as a child on a family friend's boat returning to Juneau. Whale-watching is reliable near Juneau, and many small boats are available for trips, offering a chance to experience the whales closely. You've got good chances of encountering humpback and killer whales, Steller sea lions, harbor seals and, perhaps most exciting, Dalls

A DAY TRIP TO tracy arm

The fjords of the Tracy Arm–Fords Terror Wilderness (part of Tongass National Forest) are relatively unknown outside the area, but the scenery and wildlife viewing easily rival those of Glacier Bay National Park. And for those not riding a cruise ship, Tracy Arm has a significant advantage over Glacier Bay: It costs less than half as much and is easier to get to. A Tracy Arm tour takes about 8 hours; going to Glacier Bay from Juneau is an exhausting day trip—it's wiser to overnight there, though that adds more to the cost.

The Tracy Arm fjord is a long, narrow, twisting passageway into the coastal mountains, with peaks up to a mile high that jut straight out of the water, waterfalls tumbling thousands of feet down their sides. At its head, Sawyer Glacier and South Sawyer Glacier calve ice into the water with a rumble and a splash. Whales and other wildlife usually show up along the way. And, as at Glacier Bay, John Muir paid a visit. No second-best here!

Adventure Bound Alaska, 76 Egan Dr., across from the Goldbelt Hotel (☎800/228-3875 or 907/463-2509; www.adventureboundalaska.com), is a family business operating a 56-foot single-hull boat to Tracy Arm every day in the summer, with deck space all the way around. The boat leaves from the downtown Marine Park by 8am (you have to be on board at least 15 min. earlier). They charge $150 adults, $95 ages 5 to 17; children must be at least 5 to go.

Another way to visit to Tracy Arm is to charter your own boat. Although it may cost twice as much or more per person, you can decide when and where to linger with the animals or ice. Check with the visitor center for a referral, or with **Juneau Sportfishing and Sightseeing** (☎907/586-1887), listed in this section under "Saltwater Fishing."

Dog-sledding in Juneau Icefield.

porpoises, which shoot through and over the water in packs. The Juneau Convention and Visitors Bureau maintains a list of businesses, and their website has links to each. **Harv & Marv's Outback Alaska** (☎866/909-7288 or 907/209-7288; www.harvandmarvs.com) is run with six-passenger boats by a couple of lifelong Juneau residents with decades of experience, each of whom go by their high school nicknames (really they're Jay and Pete), and who are known as characters doing fun, personal whale-watching trips. They charge $142 per person for a half day, but prices vary by group size. **Orca Enterprises** (☎800/SEE-ORCA [733-6722] or 907/789-6801; www.alaskawhalewatching.com) is a larger whale-watching firm, with four good-sized vessels, offering 3½-hour tours and free transfers from your hotel. The cost is $114 adults, $84 ages 5 to 12, and $54 ages 4 and under.

Getting Outside: On the Ice

More than 36 major glaciers around Juneau flow from a single ocean of ice behind the mountains, the 1,500 square-mile **Juneau Icefield.** You can land on it in a helicopter just to touch the ice or to take a nature hike or dog-sled ride. It's expensive, but there are few other places to see, let alone explore, the kind of ice sheet that carved North America in the last ice age. From the air, glaciers look unreal, like creations by a graphic artist, their sinuous lines of blue and white ice striped with darker gray gravel debris. Only standing on the ice, which on closer inspection resembles the crusty compressed snow of springtime snow berms, do you get a clear sense of this entirely unfamiliar kind of terrain.

It's worth noting that these tours have had some major mishaps. While the accidents represent a tiny fraction of all the safe flights, they're a reminder that flying a helicopter to a glacier is not like flying an airliner.

Era Helicopters (☎800/843-1947 or 907/586-2030; www.eraflightseeing.com) is a respected operator. Their 1-hour flight over four glaciers with a 20-minute landing on Norris Glacier costs $279 per person. They also offer a program of **dog-sled rides** on the ice, a chance to try a winter sport in the summer. That excursion includes the 4-glacier overflight and adds about an hour at a sled-dog camp on a glacier with a ride behind the dogs. It costs $489 per person.

One caveat: Poor or even overcast weather makes it difficult to see the ice clearly, but if you wait for a sunny morning all seats will likely be booked. They have a 48-hour cancellation policy, so you have to gamble to some extent on good viewing conditions. Of course, they don't fly in unsafe conditions.

NorthStar Trekking (☎907/790-4530; www.northstartrekking.com), another company with its own helicopters, specializes in hiking and teaching about glaciers. Their small groups (a maximum of 12, with two guides) go on ice hiking excursions of up to a few miles, with the speed determined by the group. Various tour lengths are offered, with 1 to 3 hours spent on the ice. The 4¼-hour trip, which includes 2 hours on the ice and 30 minutes in the air (the balance is getting to the helicopter and gearing up), costs $399 per person.

Wings Airways (☎907/586-6275; http://wingsairways.com) offers glacier overflights by floatplane and flightseeing tours to the remote Taku Lodge, where they land for salmon for brunch, lunch, or dinner. It's a great opportunity to see bears, which snoop around the lodge.

Getting Outside: On Admiralty Island

Beyond Douglas Island from Juneau, near the entrance to Gastineau Channel, is 1 million-acre Admiralty Island, one of the largest virgin blocks of old-growth forest in the country. The vast majority of the island is the protected **Kootznoowoo Wilderness.** Kootznoowoo, Tlingit for "fortress of bears," is said to have the highest concentration of brown bears on earth. Despite the town of Angoon on the western side of the island, there are more bears than people on Admiralty. The island's **Pack Creek Bear Viewing Area** is the most famous and surefire place to see bears in Southeast. The area has been managed for bear viewing since the 1930s, when hunting was outlawed. Visitors come to see bears up close as they feed on salmon spawning in the creek in July and August. Peak viewing occurs in the middle of that period. The bears generally pay no attention to the

Bear cub on Admiralty Island.

watchers, who mostly gather on a gravel bar with no barriers between people and bears. There's good bird-watching here, too, with an extraordinary abundance of bald eagles.

Only 25 miles from Juneau, Pack Creek is so popular that the Forest Service uses a permit system to keep it from being overrun during the day (from 9pm–9am, no humans are allowed). The great majority of people go for only a few hours. There are no facilities in this wilderness area, and you can't even camp without some kind of water craft to get to a designated area. The easiest way to go is with a tour operator who has permits. The Forest Service District Ranger Office can give you a list of guides.

Alaska Fly 'N' Fish Charters (☎907/790-2120; www.alaskabyair.com) has permits for its naturalist-guided 5½-hour fly-in Pack Creek visits, which cost $600 per person, with everything you need included. **Alaska Discovery** (☎800/586-1911; www.alaskadiscovery.com) offers 2-night Pack Creek sea-kayak trips, camping out near the creeks with more time to see the bears and appreciate the scenery. It costs $995 per person.

Twelve permits per day go to the commercial operators and 12 to people who go without any guide; eight of those 12 private permits can be booked in advance with the Forest Service beginning on March 1, and the other four are available 3 business days before the date on which they're good, the previous Friday for Tuesday and Wednesday, at 9am at the Juneau Ranger District Office. In the peak season, July 5 to August 25, permits cost $50 for adults, $25 for those ages 16 or under or 62 and over. Lower prices and easier availability prevail outside the peak, but then you might not see any bears. After you have the permit, you'll still need a way to get there, plus your own gear (including rubber boots and binoculars). The Forest Service lists air taxi operators on its website (see the next paragraph).

Protected **Seymour Canal,** on the east side of the island, is good for canoeing and kayaking, and has two other sites besides Pack Creek where bears often show up: Swan Cove and Windfall Harbor. For information on the island, its 15 Forest Service cabins, and an excellent $4 map, contact the **Admiralty Island National Monument,** 8510 Mendenhall Loop Rd., Juneau (☎907/586-8800; www.fs.fed.us/r10/tongass/districts/admiralty).

Where to Stay

Lodging rates are high and room reservations tight in Juneau. The Juneau Convention and Visitors Bureau's *Juneau Guide & Travel Planner* and website contain listings of the hotels and B&Bs with links (☎888/581-2201; www.traveljuneau.com).

Besides those places listed below in detail, here is another good choice. **Alaska Wolf Lodge,** 1900 Wickersham Dr., Juneau, AK 99801 (☎888/425-9653 or 907/586-2422; www.alaskawolflodge.com), overlooks Gastineau Channel just off the Glacier Highway a half-mile beyond the edge of Juneau's core area. A lot of dark woodwork contributes to a masculine wilderness lodge atmosphere—there's even a wolf pelt draped over the couch. The host presents guests with a pint of Guinness on arrival. There's also a massage cabin out back and a full-time masseuse. Summer rates $129 to $199; winter $95 to $139.

Near downtown, but a long walk from the sights, try the **Breakwater Hotel** (☎800/544-2250 or 907/586-6303; www.breakwaterinn.com), a rectangular building overlooking the boat harbor with clean standard rooms for $150 double in the high season.

VERY EXPENSIVE

Alaska's Capital Inn ★★★ This scrupulously restored 1906 mansion offers constant surprises in its fascinating detail: the shining potbellied stove and 1879 pump organ in the parlor, the Persian rugs, the original (electrified) gas lamps, period wallpaper, and even those old-fashioned push-button light switches. It took owners Linda Wendeborn and Mark Thorson 3 years to bring the house back to its former glory. They poured effort and expense into making details so authentic that no one will ever notice. Fortunately, the house was worth it, with many large rooms with high ceilings, good views, fireplaces, claw-foot tubs, and real elegance. The best asset of all, however, may be the warmth and fun of the inn. The common rooms are conducive to socializing, and the hosts love to connect with guests and strive to accommodate their needs. A Scotty dog patrols throughout. An elaborate breakfast is served at 8:30am.

113 W. 5th St., Juneau, AK 99801. ☎**888/588-6507** or 907/586-6507. Fax 907/586-6508. www. alaskacapitalinn.com. 7 units. High season $259–$339 double; low season $139–$259 double. Extra person $25. Rates include full breakfast. AE, DC, DISC, MC, V. Off-street parking. Children under 11 are not permitted. **Amenities:** Shared computer with Internet access; Jacuzzi. *In room:* TV, Wi-Fi.

Pearson's Pond Luxury Inn and Adventure Spa ★★★ This sensual retreat of superbly appointed rooms, packed with every conceivable amenity, is on grounds that create the illusion of being in a fairyland somewhere in the Alaska wilderness—there's even a private pond with a rowboat—although it really lies in a residential subdivision near the Mendenhall Glacier. The inn hosts business travelers—there's a well-stocked snack room, and all units have Ethernet ports and access to a wireless LAN (and they'll lend you a laptop, too)—but it's really a place for couples. Rooms are elaborately decorated, some have wonderful bathing facilities, and all are heavily sound-proofed for nights of passion. The inn offers massage and daily yoga classes, as well, and the well-trained staff keeps everything immaculate. Staff also plan custom tour packages, if you want them to set up your whole vacation (see the sample itineraries on the website). The hostess, Diane Pearson, is a wedding commissioner and marries many guests here on the grounds or even on the glacial ice. Having thought of everything, she also lends all the equipment needed to make photo disks from the pictures. Book their Web specials to save something on the high rates.

4541 Sawa Circle, Juneau, AK 99801. ☎**888/658-6328** or 907/789-3772. Fax 907/789-6722. www.pearsonspond.com. 5 units. High season $299–$499 double; low season 149–$299 double. Extra person $50. AE, DC, DISC, MC, V. Rates include full breakfast summer, continental winter. **Amenities:** Concierge; health club; 2 outdoor Jacuzzis; massage; free loan of kayak, rowboat, paddleboat, fishing gear, bike, or laptop computer. *In room:* TV/VCR and DVD, CD player, hair dryer, kitchenette, Wi-Fi.

EXPENSIVE

Goldbelt Hotel Juneau ★★ This is a solidly built business hotel on the waterfront amid the sights downtown. It is the only place in town that has a covered entry where guests can be dropped off out of the rain and enter a full lobby, filled with superb Tlingit art presented by the Goldbelt Native Corporation, which owns the hotel. The clean, geometrical lines of the building are carried throughout, including large rooms with high ceilings and bold fabrics. There's a special feeling of privacy here, perhaps because even those units facing the busy street on the water side are noticeably quiet. All smell and look immaculate. Rooms with the water view cost $10 more. The best in the house are on the corners, with even more space and light.

The restaurant off the lobby, **Zen,** is among the best in town. The dining room is beautifully decorated in a fully realized Asian theme in shades of green. Tables are widely separated. The Asian fusion cuisine includes items such as ginger halibut and black cod, $24 to $29, as well as steaks and other American dishes.

51 W. Egan Dr., Juneau, AK 99801. **☏888/478-6909** or 907/586-6900. Fax 907/463-3567. www. goldbelttours.com. Summer $189–$199 double; winter $114–$169 double. Extra person $15. AE, MC, V. **Amenities:** Restaurant; lounge; airport shuttle. *In room:* TV, Wi-Fi.

The Historic Silverbow Inn ★★ This quirky little downtown hotel has an oddly pleasing style and warm, casual hospitality. The 1914 building, with wood floors, bare brick, and stained glass, is decorated with a stylish, contemporary mode that nonetheless captures the warmth of a B&B. The cozy rooms come with extras such as lollipops and popcorn, among other original and considerate touches that show up repeatedly—for example, the shelf of supplies you may have forgotten, the answering machines on the direct-line phones, and the sack breakfast if you have to leave too early for the free full breakfast in the bakery. That bakery, also called The Silverbow, is a popular local gathering place, with terrific bagels, spreads, and hearty sandwiches. That space, and the lounge, where the proprietors and staff have a free wine tasting for guests in the summer months and show films and other cultural events in the winter, adds to the sense when you stay here that you've been adopted into a friendly community scene.

120 2nd St., Juneau, AK 99801. **☏800/586-4146** or 907/586-4146. Fax 907/586-4242. www. silverbowinn.com. 11 units. High season $149–$208 double; low season $88–$148 double. Extra person $20. $20 surcharge for 1-night stays in high season. Rates include full breakfast. AE, DISC, MC, V. **Amenities:** Restaurant. *In room:* TV, hair dryer, Wi-Fi.

MODERATE

Baranof Hotel ★ The Baranof is the only lodging in Alaska with the pedigree and style to pull off the role of the old-fashioned grand hotel. Built of concrete in 1939, it served for decades as an informal branch of the state capitol. In 2007 and 2008, its history gained a chapter with the FBI surveillance of legislators taking bribes from oil industry executives in suite no. 604. The structure feels historic, in part, because the concrete construction limits modernization—bathrooms and many bedrooms will always be small. In some places, past efforts at renovation have made the most of the classic features, retaining glass doorknobs and pressed-tin hallway ceilings, while in other spots the building is pretty typical of an older urban hotel. Floors 7, 8, and 9 have the best rooms, with great views on the water side. There's a discount on the second floor, which lacks a view, and the rates are reasonable for this market.

The Art Deco **Gold Room ★★** restaurant is Juneau's most traditional fine-dining establishment, and among its best. The dining room combines intimacy and grandeur in a showplace of shining brass, frosted glass, and rich wood. A recent menu included scallops in pomegranate butter sauce and macadamia nut halibut, as well as lamb, duck, and veal selections. Most entrees are above $30.

127 N. Franklin St., Juneau, AK 99801. ☎800/544-0970 or 907/586-2660. Fax 907/586-8315. www.westmarkhotels.com. 196 units. High season $149–$189 double; low season $129–$139 double. Extra person no charge. AE, DC, DISC, MC, V. **Amenities:** 2 restaurants; bar; fitness room; limited room service. *In room:* TV, hair dryer, kitchenettes in some rooms, Wi-Fi.

Frontier Suites Airport Hotel ★ 🏷 A rambling group of four-story buildings among spruce trees provide a good option for those who want to stay in a standard room in the Mendenhall Valley, near the airport. Rooms are large, all have full kitchens, and the rates are low compared to comparable hotels in Juneau. They're decorated with Alaska art and bedspreads and kept up to date, and there are a variety of options to match your needs. A courtesy van serves the airport, ferry terminal, and a 5-mile radius, which will get you to basic shopping, but to visit the town's attractions you will need a car. Pizza and pasta restaurants are on-site, as well as outdoor recreation areas, including a playground and basketball court.

9400 Glacier Hwy., Juneau, AK 99801. ☎800/544-2250 or 907/790-6600. Fax 907/790-6612. www.frontiersuites.com. 104 units. Summer $129–$179 per room; winter $119. Extra person no charge. AE, DISC, MC, V. **Amenities:** 2 restaurants; courtesy van; exercise room; room service. *In room:* TV, hair dryer, Internet, full kitchen.

INEXPENSIVE

The Driftwood Lodge 🏷 This downtown motel, next door to the State Museum, is popular with families, and houses legislators and aides in the winter in its apartment-like kitchenette suites. Although the building can't hide its cinder-block construction and old-fashioned motel exterior, small bathrooms, or lack of elevators, the rooms are comfortable and well maintained. The management has held prices low while making improvements, so for a rate that won't get you in the door at most Juneau hotels ($125), you can put four people in a two-bedroom suite with a full kitchen. Don't expect luxury, just a basic, clean motel room for a good price. The round-the-clock courtesy van saves big money to the airport or ferry, and the rental bikes will cover your transportation needs downtown.

435 Willoughby Ave., Juneau, AK 99801. ☎800/544-2239 or 907/586-2280. Fax 907/586-1034. www.driftwoodalaska.com. 63 units. High season $94–$100 double, $110–$125 suite; low season $68 double, $98 suite. Extra person $10. AE, DC, DISC, MC, V. **Amenities:** Courtesy van; bikes. *In room:* TV.

A HOSTEL

Juneau International Hostel 🛏 The historic yellow house among the downtown sights is a showplace of custom cabinetry and big, light common rooms. It's a volunteer-operated nonprofit with the mission of uniting people; guests pay little, but are expected to pitch in with chores. Men and women sleep in a number of small separate dorm rooms, and there is one private room for families with children, which is in high demand. Office hours are from 7:30 to 9am and 5pm to midnight in the summer, 8 to 9am and 5 to 10:30pm in the winter, with lockout during the day. Internet access, Wi-Fi, and local calls are free. Reservations must be prepaid by mail or phone for a 5-night maximum stay; if there is space available, you can stay up to 7 days. Alcohol, drugs, and pets are not allowed, and shoes are removed at the door.

614 Harris St., Juneau, AK 99801. **☎907/586-9559.** www.juneauhostel.net. 47 beds. $10 per adult; $5 children ages 6–17 with parent; free 5 and under. $2 premium for credit card payment. MC, V. Closed intermittently Nov–Mar; check website. **Amenities:** Lockers; Wi-Fi.

CAMPING

Juneau has two exceptional Forest Service campgrounds open from mid-May to mid-September. For information, call the Juneau Ranger District (**☎907/586-8800;** www.fs.fed.us/r10/tongass); for reservations, see "Reserving a Cabin or Campsite," p. 151. **The Mendenhall Glacier Campground,** overlooking the lake and glacier and next to the Mendenhall River, is the best built public campground in the state, with granite block construction. The bathrooms have showers and flush toilets, and there is a half-mile wheelchair-accessible nature trail. The 69 sites are huge and broadly separated; nine have full RV hookups and another nine have electricity and water. Tents and RVs are segregated. To get there, turn north on Montana Creek Road from Mendenhall Loop Road. Tent sites are $10, RV sites $26 and $28. The 11-site **Auke Village Campground,** 1¾ miles north of the ferry dock, is in an extraordinary place, with sites among large trees along an ocean beach, looking out on the islands of Auke Bay. The campground, reconstructed in 2006, has vault toilets and running water. Sites are $10 per night.

   Spruce Meadow RV Park, 10200 Mendenhall Loop Rd. (**☎907/789-1990;** www.juneaurv.com), has the good qualities of a public campground, with wooded and open sites in a forested area near the glacier, and offers extras such as cable and free Wi-Fi. Full hookups are $32, tenting $20. Reserve ahead.

Where to Dine

Juneau has a number of excellent restaurants. Besides those detailed below, see two superb choices above, the Gold Room, in the Baranof Hotel, on p. 243 and Zen, in the Goldbelt Hotel Juneau, p. 242.

   For breakfast or lunch, try the **Sandpiper Cafe,** near the State Museum at 429 Willoughby Ave. (**☎907/586-3150**), with an immaculate dining room recalling a sun-faded beach-front eatery. The short menu includes tasty comfort foods, sandwiches, and breakfast all day. A hamburger is $10; besides ground beef, you can have one made of caribou or Tibetan yak. It's open daily 6am to 2pm.

   Pizzeria Roma, on the waterfront across the hall from the Hangar at 2 Marine Way (**☎907/463-5020**), produces some of the best pizzas and calzones in town in a small dining room. Hours are daily 11am to 10pm summer, closing a half-hour earlier in winter.

Chan's Thai Kitchen ★★ 📷 THAI The small, overlit dining room in a half-basement sees few tourists, but I've heard locals brag about how long they were willing to stand in the small entrance area to get a table. When I went I became a believer, too—the authentic Thai food is that good and the atmosphere, if lacking in polish, is conducive to a good time. You will need a car, as the location is 20 minutes from town across from the Auke Bay boat harbor. Reservations are not accepted, and they do not have a liquor license.

11820 Glacier Hwy. **☎907/789-9777.** Reservations not accepted. Main courses $11–$14. MC, V. Tues–Sat 4:30–8:30pm; Sun 4:30–8pm.

The Hangar ★ GRILL Situated in a converted airplane hangar on a wooden pier with large windows, this bar and grill has great views and a fun atmosphere; even off season, it's packed. It's a fine place to drink beer (with 24 brews on tap), listen to live music, or play at one of the three pool tables. Service is quick and professional. What's surprising is that the food is usually good, too (although I did have a disappointing meal recently). The seared ahi sashimi appetizer, raw inside, has a pleasant texture and taste, and the jambalaya, a huge portion for $13, is spicy but balanced. The fish chowder is very thick and has a pleasing, slightly smoky flavor. Although the menu's steaks and such range up to $30, plenty of choices are under $15.

2 Marine Way. ☎907/586-5018. www.hangaronthewharf.com. Reservations recommended. Main courses $13–$30. AE, MC, V. Daily 11am–10pm.

Island Pub ★ PIZZA Across the bridge from Juneau, this is where local people go for a fun night out. The food is good and far from boring—I had a steak salad, which consisted of rare, well-seasoned slices of grilled steak on a bed of lettuce with a load of bleu cheese dressing and caramelized onions. The specialty is pizza with creative ingredients. The delicious scent of the brick oven hangs in the air. The dining room, dating from the 1930s, is historic by Alaskan standards and comes by its pub ambience honestly. It looks out on the Gastineau Channel through picture windows; at times customers watch killer whales from the bar (they have the photos to prove it). The pub is easy to find. Drive across the bridge to Douglas, turn left, and after entering the town turn left on E Street.

1102 2nd St., Douglas. ☎907/364-1595. www.theislandpub.com. Main courses $10–$12; pizza $13–$19. AE, DC, DISC, MC, V. Daily 11:30am–10pm.

Quick Bites in Juneau

The **Silverbow Bakery,** 120 2nd St. (☎907/586-4146; www.silverbowinn.com), is a happening spot for bagels or hearty sandwiches. It's open daily 6am to 8pm. The **Rainbow Foods** natural food grocery, an organic hang-out in a former church at the corner of Franklin and 4th streets (☎907/586-6476; www.rainbow-foods.org), is the best picnic-packing place downtown, making sandwiches and salads at the deli and with a buffet and salad bar. It's also a good place to network with a socially con-scious crowd and is a Wi-Fi hot spot.

Hot Bite, at the Auke Bay boat harbor, is a local secret, serving charcoal-broiled hamburgers, halibut burgers, and mind-blowing milkshakes from a run-down little house. Take out or sit at one of six indoor tables.

Downtown Juneau's young, professional population sup-ports several good coffeehouses. **Valentine's Coffee House and Pizzeria,** 111 Seward St. (☎907/463-5144), serves light, hot meals in an authentic old-fashioned storefront. **Heritage Coffee Co. and Café,** 174 S. Franklin St. (☎907/586-1087; www.heritagecoffee.com), and 216 2nd St. (☎907/586-1752), has two trendy, comfortable coffeehouses good for watching people or using the Internet, either wireless or on their terminals. They also roast famous coffee.

Tarentino's ★ ITALIAN This is a traditional family restaurant, located on a corner downtown, for a filling, familiar meal and quick service. The restaurant has an up-to-date and casual atmosphere, and is decorated in warm tones with lots of booths, but it's still a couple of steps up from a basic pizzeria. The sausage lasagna is very generous and nicely presented for a reasonable price, like all the main courses—for lunch, it was $11 with bread and soup or a salad.

140 Seward St. **☎907/523-0344.** Lunch $9–$15; dinner $12–$20. MC, V. Mon–Thurs 11am–9pm; Fri 11am–9:30pm; Sat noon–9:30pm.

Twisted Fish Co. Alaskan Grill ★★ SEAFOOD Overlooking the water at the cruise-ship dock, in the same building as Taku Smokeries, the dining room is magnificent, with high ceilings and an entire wall of windows on the Gastineau Channel, a fireplace of beach rock, lots of hardwood, and, to keep it from being too grand, cartoonlike fish hanging down. The quality and range of the food brings locals to a tourist zone they would otherwise avoid: items such as salmon on a cedar plank or in pastry, halibut or salmon tacos, and also little pizzas, burgers, and terrific desserts. The service is fast and attentive, but the dining room makes you want to stay long after you are done eating.

550 S. Franklin St. **☎907/463-5033.** http://twistedfish.hangaronthewharf.com. Reservations recommended. Lunch $7–$15; dinner main courses $18–$30. AE, DISC, MC, V. Summer daily 11am–10pm. Closed Oct–Apr.

Zyphyr Restaurant ★★★ MEDITERRANEAN The dining room, once an old-fashioned grocery store, was remodeled with restraint and a magnificent sense of style, using its wooden floors, very high ceilings, and huge storefront windows to create the illusion of elegance passed down for generations rather than only since late 2006. Tables robed in linen of dark rust are set so far apart that diners feel they are alone, and on the winter evening I first ate here, the darkness outside contributed to the velvety intimacy. The service— fast, courteous, but with character—lives up to the setting. Dishes are from the traditional fine dining palette of colors: calamari, pasta puttanesca, or bouillabaisse, for example. Each meal I've had was memorable and flawless. On my most recent visit, the dayboat scallops, seared with a soft-cooked egg and romesco sauce, were wonderfully flavored and textured. The generous portion of tender duck was perfectly complimented by a dusky sauce. Deserts are excellent, too. Save this place, one of Alaska's best restaurants, for a special romantic meal or a treat at the end of the day.

200 Seward St. **☎907/780-2221.** Reservations recommended. Main courses $13–$32. MC, V. Summer Tues–Sun 5–9:30pm; winter Tues–Sat 5–9:30pm.

Nightlife

Alaska Travel Adventures has offered its **Gold Creek Salmon Bake** (**☎800/323-5757** or 907/789-0052) for more than 30 years. It's touristy, yes, but fun, with marshmallow roasting, music, and other entertainment— great for families (I'd avoid it in the rain, however). The cost is $39 for adults, $26 for children.

For more substantial performances, try to catch a show by Juneau's **Perseverance Theatre,** Alaska's largest professional theater. The winter season, starting in September and lasting until early June, includes Alaska's best cutting-edge drama, including serious homegrown work. Paula Vogel was here when she wrote *How I Learned to Drive,* which later won the Pulitzer Prize. Summer offerings are limited to youth theater and workshops. To find out what's playing, contact the theater's office at 914 3rd St., Douglas (☎907/ 364-2421), or check the website at www.perseverancetheatre.org.

A political scandal or two put a damper on some of the infamous legislative partying that once occurred in Juneau, far away from home districts, but good places to go out drinking and dancing still exist. The **Red Dog Saloon,** 278 S. Franklin St., is the town's most famous bar, with a sawdust-strewn floor, a slightly contrived but nonetheless infectious frontier atmosphere, and walls covered with Alaska memorabilia. Locals hang across the street at **The Alaskan Bar,** 167 S. Franklin, which occupies an authentic gold-rush hotel with a two-story Victorian bar room. Boisterous parties and music go on there all year. **The Hangar,** listed above under "Where to Dine," is the place for beer drinkers. They have a big-screen TV and live music Friday and Saturday nights, as well as pool and darts.

GLACIER BAY NATIONAL PARK

Glacier Bay is a work in progress; the boat ride to its head is a chance to see creation unfolding. The bay John Muir discovered in a canoe in 1879 didn't exist a century earlier. Eighteenth-century explorers had found instead a wall of ice a mile thick where the entrance to the branching, 65-mile-long fjord now opens to the sea. Receding faster than any other glacier on earth, the ice melted into the ocean

and opened a spectacular and still-unfinished land. The land itself is rising 1½ inches a year as it rebounds from the weight of now-melted glaciers. As your vessel retraces Muir's path—and then probes northward in deep water where ice stood in his day—the story of this new world unravels in reverse. The trees on the shore get smaller, then disappear, then all vegetation disappears, and finally, at the head of the bay, the ice stands at the water's edge surrounded by barren rock, rounded and scored by the passage of the ice but not yet marked by the waterfalls cascading from the clouds above. And there, still doing their landscape-shaping work, are the great, blue glaciers, the largest among them the awesome Grand Pacific Glacier.

Glacier Bay, first set aside as a national monument by Calvin Coolidge in 1925, is managed by the National Park Service, which has the difficult job of protecting the wilderness, the whales, and the other wildlife while serving the huge public visiting the park. This

Grand Pacific Glacier.

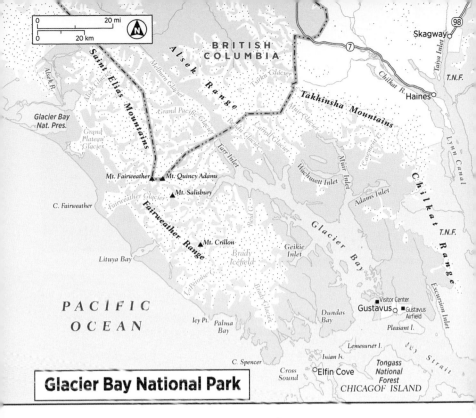

Glacier Bay National Park

rugged land the size of Connecticut cannot be seen by car, only by boat or plane, and the presence of too many boats threatens the wilderness experience and may disturb the wildlife. The whales appear to be sensitive to the noise of vessels and, since the 1970s, when in some years hardly any whales returned, the park service has used a permit system to limit the number of cruise ships and other vessels that can enter the bay. Any boat sees several other vessels on a day's journey up the bay, but how much they bother the whales and other wildlife is difficult to measure precisely, and, with 90% of visitors arriving on cruises, political pressure pushed to allow more huge ships. In response to legislation passed by Alaska's pro-development Congressional delegation, the park service increased the number of cruise ships entering the bay, but in 2001 environmentalists won a court ruling that briefly reduced the number and held off a further increase pending study. In 2003, the Park Service completed an Environmental Impact Statement on the issue. It allowed an increase from 139 cruise ships during the summer season to as many as 184, depending on an annual decision by the Park Superintendent, and added a scientific advisory board to monitor the effect on the whales and other park resources. The Superintendent allowed 153 ships, a figure that could be called a compromise between the cruise lines and environmentalists. Scientific results from the board's study are due in 2010, but are unlikely to settle the issue once and for all. To read more about the park's vessel management plan, go to www.nps.gov/glba/parkmgmt/planning.htm.

A breaching humpback whale in Glacier Bay.

On my longest visit, I saw humpback whales breaching (leaping all the way out of the water) every day. I saw orcas, too. One day, while fishing for halibut from a small boat in foggy Icy Strait, just outside the park, I heard a sound like thunder not far off. Like thunder, the sound was repeated, growing closer, but its source remained hidden behind the white circle of fog that surrounded us. Then the smooth water suddenly bulged and a huge, barnacled creature shot upward and crashed down with a sharp clap and a splash that rocked the boat. And then it happened again. The whale went on performing for most of an hour. A day later, I encountered the same spectacle while sea kayaking in the park's Bartlett Cove.

Leaping whales and falling glaciers are hard to beat. But the park also has major drawbacks to consider. Sightings aren't guaranteed, so there's a risk that you'll spend a lot of money and not see any whales. And even though this is a huge wilderness, the ways to see it are limited, so most people never get away from crowds. The lone concessionaire-operated tour boat into the bay costs $193 per person and is usually full of people. The large cruise ships that bring most visitors to the park view the scenery without getting up close to the shore or wildlife and miss the shore-based attractions. Smaller ships see more, with smaller groups and more chances to get outdoors. Independent travelers can spend a few days in some of Alaska's most attractive remote accommodations, in Gustavus, with great fishing, hiking, sea kayaking, and tour boat rides into the park. But the only way to see the heart of the park in true solitude is on a boat you charter for yourself (out of range of most budgets) or on a rugged multiday sea-kayaking adventure.

As an alternative, consider the other places to see Alaska's glaciers and whales that are easier and less expensive to visit. If you're in Juneau, consider a day trip to Tracy Arm instead. In Southcentral Alaska, plan a day trip from Whittier to see the glaciers of western Prince William Sound or from Seward to see Kenai Fjords National Park. There are other places in Southeast rich with marine wildlife, as well. Still, Glacier Bay beats them all—and just about anyplace on earth—for the combination of lots of whales and lots of big glaciers.

Essentials

GETTING THERE

Most visitors get to the park on cruise ships that pass through the bay without landing, so those readers can skip the material below (although you may be interested in the introduction, above). Others begin their visit to the park at the headquarters area at Bartlett Cove. But once at Bartlett Cove, you're only at the edge of a park with no roads. To go onward into the park, you need some kind of boat. That's covered below under "Activities in the Park."

BY AIR Gustavus, covered in the next section of this chapter, is the gateway to Glacier Bay National Park, lying 10 miles by road from the Bartlett Cove headquarters. The only practical way to Gustavus is by air. That information is covered in the next section. Getting from the Gustavus airstrip to Bartlett Cove is easy. Vans meet planes, charging $15 adult, $8 children 8 and under (both including tax), and carry passengers to Bartlett Cove. It's free if you are traveling with a package tour; also, most of the inns and lodges in Gustavus offer free transfers to the park. **TLC Taxi** (☎907/697-2239) also offers rides from the airstrip to the park.

BY WATER A summer passenger ferry, the fast catamaran *Fairweather Express II*, is operated by the park concessionaire, Glacier Bay Lodge and Tours (☎888/BAY-TOUR [229-8687]; www.visitglacierbay.com), connecting Juneau's Auke Bay harbor directly to Bartlett Cove. The boat starts from Bartlett Cove Friday and Sunday at 4pm, leaves from Auke Bay at 7:30pm, and arrives again at Bartlett Cove at 10:30pm. The fare is $75 one-way for adults, half-price for children 3 to 12 years old.

VISITOR INFORMATION

Contact the **Glacier Bay National Park and Preserve** at P.O. Box 140, Gustavus, AK 99826 (☎907/697-2230; www.nps.gov/glba). The park service interprets the park mainly by placing well-prepared rangers on board most cruise and tour vessels entering the bay. The park also maintains a modest visitor center with displays on the park on the second floor of the lodge at wooded Bartlett Cove. Pick up the park map and handy guide, the *Fairweather*. Nearby are the park's offices, a free campground, a backcountry office, a few short hiking trails, a dock, sea-kayak rental, and other park facilities. During the summer, rangers lead a daily nature walk and present an evening program.

Activities at the Park

HIKING AT BARTLETT COVE There are three short hiking trails through the rainforest of Sitka spruce and western hemlock at Bartlett Cove. Each weaves through the cool, damp quiet created by these huge trees and the moss on the forest floor. Some wet spots are often crossed by boardwalks with railings. A map is included in the *Fairweather* visitor guide.

The **Forest Loop** is an easy trail about 1 mile long, beginning at the lodge and passing through the woods and past some park buildings to the cove's pebble beach. The **Bartlett River Trail** is a 4-mile round-trip leading to the Bartlett River Estuary, a good bird-watching spot, especially during migrations. The **Bartlett Lake Trail** branches off the Bartlett River

Trail after about ¼ mile for a 3.8-mile one-way forest hike to the lake.

BOAT TOURS Bartlett Cove is nowhere near the park's highlights. Most independent travelers take a day boat to see the vast majority of Glacier Bay. The boat is operated by a park concessionaire called **Glacier Bay Lodge and Tours,** a joint venture of ARAMARK and Huna Totem, with offices at 241 North C St., Anchorage, AK 99501 (**☎888/229-8687** or 907/264-4600; fax 907/258-3668; www.visitglacierbay. com), or, locally, in the summer only, at P.O. Box 179, Gustavus, AK 99826 (**☎907/697-4000;** fax 907/697-4001). The boat leaves from the dock in Bartlett Cove at 7:30am and returns at 8pm, sailing to the fjords' very head and the Grand Pacific Glacier. The

Bartlett Cove.

voyage is too long for many children. There's a snack bar, and a simple lunch is provided. Bring binoculars, good rain gear, and layers of warm clothing. A park service employee does the commentary, so you can count on accuracy and an educational approach missing from most commercial tours. The fare is $193 for adults, half price for children 2 to 12; lunch included.

CHARTERING A BOAT Local family operators based in Gustavus take visitors up the bay in comfort, with the spontaneity and intimacy of boating with friends. If you have a group, you can have a boat and guide to yourself. Mike Nigro, a former backcountry ranger and longtime resident, takes groups of four to six for $1,800 per day on a 42-foot yacht, the *Kahsteen.* His **Gustavus Marine Charters** can be reached at **☎907/697-2233** or www. gustavusmarinecharters.com.

KAYAKING IN THE PARK You won't forget seeing a breaching humpback whale from a sea kayak, sitting just inches off the water. It happens around here. When we breathlessly told our innkeepers about the experience, they smiled politely. They hear the same descriptions all the time. Inexperienced paddlers should choose a guided trip. **Glacier Bay Sea Kayaks,** based in Gustavus (**☎907/697-2257;** www.glacierbayseakayaks.com), offers half-day and all-day paddles in Bartlett Cove good for beginners. Although the trips go nowhere near the glaciers, the paddlers stand a good chance of seeing whales, sometimes quite close up. Any fit person can enjoy it. A half-day costs $95, full day $150, including a lunch. The same folks rent kayaks for day trips in the cove. These self-guided outings begin with a briefing, and novices are welcome. The cost is $30 half-day, $40 full day. Experienced kayakers ready for an overnight in the wilderness up the bay can rent equipment, too, and get dropped near the glaciers for $222 round-trip. Do your planning and decide what to bring before you leave for the park, as you may not be able to buy or rent what you need once there. Check the gear list and other advice on the Glacier Bay Sea Kayaks website. Before starting off on an overnight, you also will have to attend a park service briefing and get a backcountry permit from the headquarters. The company operates May 1 to September 15.

Alaska Discovery (☎800/586-1911; www.alaskadiscovery.com) offers 5-day guided expeditions in Glacier Bay. Although I wouldn't recommend this to someone who hasn't tried kayaking before (what if you hate it?), those who do will find this the most intimate and authentic way to experience this wilderness. A 5-day trip, with 4 days of kayaking, 3 days of camping, and 1 day at an inn, costs around $2,390 from Gustavus.

FLIGHTSEEING One spectacular way to get into the park is by flightseeing. Gustavus-based **Air Excursions** (☎907/697-2375; www.airexcursions. com) offers air tours in float or wheeled planes. Other operators fly from various nearby towns, including Haines and Skagway (covered later in this chapter). You'll see the incredible rivers of ice that flow down into the bay, and you may even see wildlife. What you give up is the sense of scale from ground level.

Where to Stay, Camp & Dine

Glacier Bay Lodge ★ This is the only place to stay in the park. The park visitor facilities are in the central lodge building, where there's also a rock fireplace around which visitors sit on a rainy day, and big windows on the cove—a good, old-fashioned national park space. The wood-paneled bedrooms are kept in good shape—the concessionaire put in new mattresses in 2009—but they're aged and frankly drab, without much art or decoration. The buildings are set in the soothing quiet of large rainforest trees, and 12 units that rent for a $25 premium have water views, but essentially guests just get a comfortable bed in a special place for their money. Meanwhile, in Gustavus, 10 miles down the road, you'll find some of the most attractive accommodations in Alaska.

The **restaurant** has huge windows looking onto Bartlett Cove. The staff and menu change each year, so it's impossible to offer an up-to-date review. In the past the menu has included a wide variety of dishes, including fresh fish. It's fun to have nachos and beer on the deck, where campers and lodge guests watch for whales all summer. The restaurant serves breakfast from 6 to 9:30am, lunch 11:30am to 2pm, and dinner 5:30 to 10pm.

The lodge also provides public showers and laundry facilities for the free park service **campground,** about ¼ mile away. The campground lacks running water but has a warming hut, firewood, and bear-resistant food caches. You have to cook in a fire ring in the intertidal zone and observe other bear-avoidance rules the rangers will explain. Get a camping permit at the ranger station when you arrive; the campground is almost never full.

Bartlett Cove (P.O. Box 179), Gustavus, AK 99826. ☎888/229-8687 or 907/697-4000. Fax 907/258-3668 or 907/697-4001. www.visitglacierbay.com. 48 units. $171–$196 double. Extra person $20. AE, DC, DISC, MC, V. Closed mid-Sept to late May. **Amenities:** Restaurant, bikes; fishing gear rental.

GUSTAVUS: COUNTRY INNS & QUIET

Gustavus (Gus-*tave*-us) remains an undiscovered treasure—or at least it succeeds in feeling that way. Although wonderfully remote and easily accessible only by air, the town has a selection of comfortable and even luxurious inns and lodges, plus several days' worth of outdoor activities, excellent salmon and halibut fishing, sea kayaking, nearly surefire whale-watching, close access to Glacier Bay National Park, and places for casual hiking and bicycle outings. Large cruise ships cannot land here, leaving the roads free of their throngs of shoppers. Miraculously, the 450 townspeople have been smart enough to value what they've got and build on it. Even the gas station is a work of art. Walking, biking, or driving down the quiet roads, everyone you pass—every single person—waves to you.

The buildings, mostly clapboard houses and log cabins, are scattered widely across an oceanfront alluvial plain. Several of the founding homesteads were farms, and the broad clearings of sandy soil wave with hay and wildflowers. The setting is unique in Alaska, and when I had a choice to go anywhere in the state for a 4-day trip with extended family, this is the place I chose. Each of us took something lasting from the trip. My older son, then 8, learned what it was like to be able to bike anywhere at will, making discoveries in the woods and friends on the quiet lanes without his parents reining him in. My parents, in their 60s, glowed when they returned from kayaking among the breaching humpback whales in the park's Bartlett Cove. I often reminisce about a day at the beach when I built dams and sand castles with the children, looking up to see a family of orcas romping just offshore. My cousin won't forget the huge platters of Dungeness crab that came for dinner one night at the inn.

The problem with Gustavus is the expense (and the dampness, but you get used to that). The best outdoor activities involve charters or rentals, which can add more than $250 a day per person to the cost of your trip. Most accommodations have all-inclusive plans, which include great meals but come with price tags of $200 per person per night or more. Less expensive B&Bs exist, but the choice of restaurants for dinner is limited.

Town Without a Downtown

The town looks like the country. Houses, cabins, and a few businesses are spread far apart along gravel roads. Services are limited. On Dock Road, the Bear Track Mercantile sells necessities. Gustavus also has a gas station and a liquor store. Bring whatever else you will want with you, and reserve all accommodations in advance. The local government, founded in 2004, imposes a 2% sales tax on goods and a 4% tax on accommodations.

Essentials

GETTING THERE It's currently possible to take a passenger ferry called *Fairweather Express II* only two evenings a week in summer from Juneau's Auke Bay to Bartlett Cove, 10 miles by road from Gustavus (p. 251). The primary mode of transportation to Gustavus is air. During the summer, **Alaska Airlines** (**☎800/252-7522;** www.alaskaair.com) flies a jet once a day from Juneau to

An old-time gas station in Gustavus.

Gustavus and back in the early evening. An advance fare is about $200, round-trip.

For more frequent service by prop from Juneau to Gustavus, at roughly the same fare as Alaska Airlines, use Gustavus-based **Air Excursions** (☎ 907/697-2375; www.airexcursions.com), which flies many times a day on demand, or **Wings of Alaska** (☎ 907/789-0790 reservations, or 907/697-2201 in Gustavus; www.ichoosewings.com).

VISITOR INFORMATION The traditional way to plan a trip to Gustavus is to contact a lodge and, once you're comfortable with them, allow your hosts to advise you and book your activities. You can look up information from the **Gustavus Visitor Association** at www.gustavusak.com. A local travel agency, **Alaska's Glacier Bay Travel** (☎ 907/697-2475; www.glacierbay travel.com), run by the same folks as the TLC Taxi (see below), can also help with choices and reservations. Be certain to reserve a place to stay before showing up in Gustavus.

GETTING AROUND There are just a few roads. The main one starts at the airport and runs about 10 miles to **Bartlett Cove,** the Glacier Bay National Park base of operations. **Dock Road** branches off to the left, at the gas station, and leads to the ocean dock and sandy beach. There's a map and list of businesses posted near the gas station, and most businesses will give you one to take along for exploration by bicycle. Many inns and B&Bs have courtesy vans and free bicycles; ask about transportation when you reserve. **TLC Taxi** (☎ 907/697-2239) offers transportation between the airport, Bartlett Cove, and points in between, with flat fees depending on the destination. Reserve ahead. A van can accommodate groups, gear, and kayaks. **Bud's Rent a Car** is at ☎ 907/697-2403.

Exploring Gustavus

Everything to do in Gustavus involves the outdoors. I've listed the activities here in the order of importance.

WHALE-WATCHING & FISHING Whales keep their own schedule, but you're almost certain to see them on a whale-watching excursion here, where the swirling current of Icy Strait creates such a rich feeding ground that humpbacks come back every summer without fail. The big tour boat in the national park (see the previous section) frequently sees whales, but Icy Strait, outside the park, is even more prolific. Currently there are two options. Since arrangements change annually, it's wise to call ahead or get advice from your lodge or B&B host.

Cross Sound Express (☎888/698-2726 or 907/766-3000; http://taz.gustavus.com) takes two viewing trips a day with up to 23 passengers aboard the *TAZ*, which is also used for kayak drop-offs and other marine transportation. The cost is $120 per person, $60 children 4 to 6, and free for those 3 and younger. The park concessionaire, **Glacier Bay Lodge and Tours** (☎888/229-8687 or 907/264-4600; www.visitglacierbay.com), offers a whale-watching dinner cruise on Thursday and Saturday at 5:30pm. The cost is $138 adults, $69 ages 2 to 12.

Gustavus has superb charter boat fishing for halibut and salmon (if salmon are running). The waters are protected and seasickness less likely than in many places. Your inn host in Gustavus can make the arrangements. A boat typically charters for $300 to $350 per person for a full day, plus the cost of having your fish professionally packed and shipped home to you. Half-days are rarely available because the boats are fully booked. If you do a fishing charter, and the others on board agree, you can take some of the time for whale-watching.

SEA KAYAKING Gustavus-based **Spirit Walker Expeditions** (☎800/KAY-AKER [529-2537] or 907/697-2266; www.seakayakalaska.com) has a good reputation locally. They lead guided day trips to the whale-watching grounds and overnight expeditions as long as a week. **Alaska Discovery** (☎800/586-1911; www.alaskadiscovery.com) offers an easy 3-day, 2-night kayaking expedition among the whales for $995 per person. They take a boat to a base camp, then kayak among the whales from there. The outing is suitable for fit beginners and older children.

HIKING & BICYCLING There are few cars in Gustavus, but most inns provide bikes. The roads are fun to explore, and the sandy beaches, accessed from the town dock, are great for a walk and a picnic and to watch eagles and other birds and wildlife. You can go many miles, if you are of a mind, for a run or long walk, but we saw little reason to go far before stopping to play and picnic on a broad sand beach undisturbed by any other human footprint.

Where to Stay

Gustavus contains some of Alaska's best remote accommodations, more than I have room to describe here. Most accommodations are "Gustavus style," which means they charge a daily per-person price for rooms; breakfast; dinner served family style; brown-bag lunches; bicycles and some other outdoor equipment and transfers; and they book and charge for fishing, sea kayaking, hiking, and Glacier Bay tours. It's expensive, but it's a carefree way to visit. Another set of accommodations charges less, but leaves you on your own for lunch and dinner. Before choosing that less costly, a la carte approach, consider your dining options, which are covered below. Except as noted, rooms in Gustavus don't have phones. Some of the inns do not have licenses to serve alcohol; if that's a consideration, be sure to ask before you book your stay. There's a liquor store with limited hours, or you can bring it with you.

Besides the lodgings described in full, I can also recommend **Homestead Bed & Breakfast,** near the center of Gustavus at 17 Faraway Rd. (**907/697-2777;** www.homesteadbedbreakfast.com), where a family opens two bedrooms and a comfortable common room to guests hoping to visit on a relative budget. A full breakfast is included in the summer rate of $135 double, and the Homeshore Cafe or Gustavus Inn (both below) are nearby for other meals.

Annie Mae Lodge ★ This rustic, post-and-beam lodge in the woods, near the Good River, provides a more flexible way to stay in Gustavus, with relatively reasonable rates and a good place to eat dinner—but you don't have to eat at the lodge. Although kept fresh and bright, the atmosphere is of a cozy, old-fashioned place, with antiques and reproductions, local art, and quilts. Rooms are on the small side but nicely decorated. The lodge books activities, loans bikes, and takes care of transfers. The lodging rate includes breakfast—either continental or cooked to order—while dinner consists of a pair of entree choices, a starter, and dessert, for $35 per diner. One choice is always local seafood, the other an entree such as prime rib or baked chicken. Reports on the food are consistently excellent. I emphasize the point, because this is a good place to come if you are staying elsewhere and need a place to eat breakfast or dinner. Breakfast is served 6 to 9am; dinner is at a single sitting, at 6:30pm, and reservations are required.

2 Grandma's Farm Rd. (P.O. Box 80), Gustavus, AK 99826. **800/478-2346** or 907/697-2346. Fax 907/697-2211. www.anniemae.com. 11 units, 9 with private bath. High season $185–$200 double; low season $125 double. Extra person 13 and older $50. AE, DISC, MC, V. **Amenities:** Free airport transfers; bike loan. In room: Wi-Fi.

Blue Heron Bed and Breakfast at Glacier Bay ★ Stay here if your budget doesn't allow a pricey all-inclusive package, and you'll still get many of the same comforts in fresh, bright rooms with features such as DVD players, comforters, and superior linens. The hosts, longtime residents, are enthusiastic about their guests and serve large, gourmet breakfasts. If you rent one of the cottages, you can cook your own evening meal; the rooms have access to microwaves and refrigerators in the sunroom dining area, and a country store and deli are a few minutes' walk away. The location is among the wildflowers and marshland near the Gustavus waterfront.

Off Dock Rd. (P.O. Box 77), Gustavus, AK 99826. **907/697-2337.** Fax 907/697-2293. www.blue heronbnb.net. 2 units, 2 cottages. $145 double; $185 double cottage. Extra adult $80. Discounts for children. Rates include full breakfast. No credit cards. **Amenities:** Free airport transfers; free bike loan; Internet access. In room: TV/DVD, free movie loan, hair dryer.

Glacier Bay's Bear Track Inn ★★★ Six miles from Gustavus, this extraordinary log building faces its own field of wildflowers, which, if you walk half a mile across it, leads to the shore. You look out on this scene from a lobby with a huge fireplace, a ceiling 28 feet high, and a wall of windows. The immense logs of the walls and the isolation give the place the feeling of a wilderness lodge, but the rooms are as good as those of any upscale hotel, and have the advantage of large dormer windows with sweeping views. Objectively, it's the best place in Gustavus, and one of the best remote lodges in Alaska, but which place you prefer depends on your taste. I also like the funky, quaint atmosphere of the rest of the town, which is absent at the more perfect Bear Track. Another difference compared to other lodges and inns: Meals here are cooked to order from a menu. Those not staying here can buy dinner, too. The inn serves beer and wine.

255 Rink Rd. (P.O. Box 255), Gustavus, AK 99826. **☎888/697-2284** or 907/697-3017. Fax 907/697-2284. www.beartrackinn.com. 14 units. $604 per person per night, double occupancy; discounts for additional nights. Rates include round-trip air from Juneau, transfers, and all meals. DISC, MC, V. Closed Oct–Apr. **Amenities:** Free airport transfers; restaurant; free bike loan; concierge; limited room service. *In room:* Hair dryer.

Gustavus Inn at Glacier Bay ★★★ This is the original and still my favorite of the Gustavus full-service inns. By objective standards of modern luxury, imitators have surpassed the old homestead farmhouse, but no one could duplicate the extraordinary hospitality of the Lesh family, honed over 40 years of running the inn. Dave and JoAnn know how to make guests feel immediately a part of the place. The site is unsurpassed, too, standing at the center of the community amid blowing grass and with a huge vegetable garden that provides much of the wonderful food, which is in the foreground of views from the newly expanded dining room and deck. Dave, the chef, has published a cookbook, and his ginger sablefish is now widely copied. He serves beer and wine with the sushi appetizers and big platters of food. Before going, talk over what you want to do with JoAnn or Dave, and let them book everything.

1 Gustavus Rd. (P.O. Box 60), Gustavus, AK 99826. **☎800/649-5220** or 907/697-2254. Fax 907/697-2255. www.gustavusinn.com. 13 units. $205 per person per night. Half price for children 11 and under. Rates include all meals. AE, MC, V. Closed Sept 16–May 15. **Amenities:** Free airport transfers; restaurant; bike loan; fishing rods (bring your own tackle). *In room:* Wi-Fi ($5 fee).

Where to Dine

Even if you do not stay at one of the full-service inns, I recommend taking at least some of your meals there. Annie Mae Lodge offers breakfast and dinner to nonguests. The food at Gustavus Inn at Glacier Bay is famous (I still try to copy some of the flavors prepared by Dave Lesh). Make reservations; you can't just show up and eat. The other choice for fine dining is the Glacier Bay Lodge, which serves three meals a day—but it's 10 miles away at the park's Bartlett Cove headquarters. Otherwise, the dining choices in Gustavus are very few and fairly basic.

The **Homeshore Cafe,** at Gustavus's central intersection on Wilson Road (**☎907/697-2822**), serves meals all year in a dining room with about 40 seats next door to an art gallery. The menu includes pizza, calzones, sandwiches, salads, and the like, and beer and wine; a large pizza is $20 to $25, sandwiches $10. Summer hours are Tuesday through Saturday 11:30am to 2pm and 5 to 8pm; winter Tuesday through Friday 11:30am to 1:30pm and 4:30 to 6:30pm, staying open Friday until 7:30pm. The cafe accepts Visa and MasterCard. Internet access on a terminal is $5 for a half-hour, and they have Wi-Fi.

HAINES: EAGLES & THE UNEXPECTED

For years we always just passed through Haines on the way from the ferry up the highway. I didn't know what I was missing until I stopped and took a couple of days to really investigate. Now Haines is one of my favorite Alaska towns.

Haines is casual, happy, and slightly odd. It waits for you to find it, but, once found, it unveils wonderful charms. If you're looking for the mythical town of Cicely from television's *Northern Exposure*, you'll get closer in Haines than anyplace else I know (in fact, the producers scouted here before choosing to shoot in Roslyn, Washington). As I walked down a sidewalk, I saw a sign in a storefront that said to look in the big tree across the street. I looked, and there was an eagle peering back at me. At the Alaska Indian Arts Native cultural center, seeking an office or a ticket window or someone in charge, I wandered into a totem pole studio where a carver was completing a major commission. He gladly stopped to talk. It turned out there wasn't anyone in charge. Issues that are a big deal in some other towns just aren't in Haines.

Haines's dominant feature, the 1904 **Fort William H. Seward,** gives the town a pastoral atmosphere. The fort is a collection of grand white-clapboard buildings arranged around a 9-acre parade ground, in the middle of which stands a Tlingit clan house—out of place, yes, but wonderfully symbolic of Haines. The town is a friendly, accessible center of Tlingit culture as well as a retired outpost of seemingly pointless military activity.

And Haines has **bald eagles**—always plenty of bald eagles, and in the fall, a ridiculous number of bald eagles. More, in fact, than anywhere else on earth. The chance to see the birds draws people into the outdoors here. There are well-established guides for any activity you might want to pursue, all cooperating and located together. There are some excellent hiking trails right from town, and sea kayaking is just as handy. Also, it's worth noting that because of its location in the flow of weather, adjacent to the drier Interior, Haines is not quite as rainy as towns farther south.

The big controversy of local politics concerns how firmly Haines should embrace tourism. Some want Haines to remain friendly, funky, and forgotten, while others hope new recognition the town has recently received for its attraction to visitors will help start an economic boom. Neither has too much to worry about. Haines is a healthy, energetic little town and not likely to be spoiled soon.

Fort Seward.

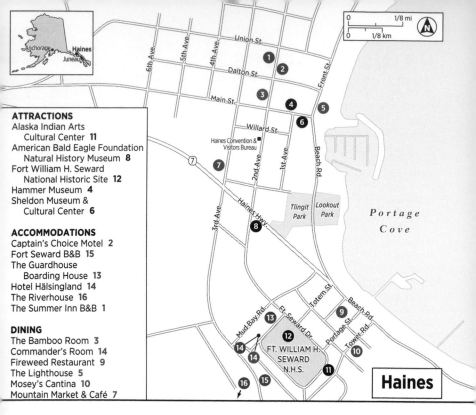

ATTRACTIONS
Alaska Indian Arts
   Cultural Center **11**
American Bald Eagle Foundation
   Natural History Museum **8**
Fort William H. Seward
   National Historic Site **12**
Hammer Museum **4**
Sheldon Museum &
   Cultural Center **6**

ACCOMMODATIONS
Captain's Choice Motel **2**
Fort Seward B&B **15**
The Guardhouse
   Boarding House **13**
Hotel Hälsingland **14**
The Riverhouse **16**
The Summer Inn B&B **1**

DINING
The Bamboo Room **3**
Commander's Room **14**
Fireweed Restaurant **9**
The Lighthouse **5**
Mosey's Cantina **10**
Mountain Market & Café **7**

Essentials

GETTING THERE The **Alaska Marine Highway System** (☎**800/642-0066,**
or 907/766-2111 locally; www.ferryalaska.com) is how most people get to
Haines, and the cruise on the Lynn Canal fjord from Juneau or Skagway
is among the most beautiful in the Inside Passage. The conventional ferry
takes almost 5 hours from Juneau, the fast ferry about half that. The Ju-
neau-Haines fare is $37. The trip from Skagway takes an hour and the fare
is $31. The dock is 5 miles north of town. No taxi is operating in town at this
writing, so ask about getting a ride when you reserve your lodgings. Both of
the hotels in town offer courtesy shuttles.

    You may be able to take a fast private boat to or from Skagway, landing
in town, so you don't need a ride out to the ferry dock. **Haines-Skagway
Fast Ferry** (☎**888/766-2103** or 907/766-2100; www.hainesskagwayfast
ferry.com) charges $35 one-way, $68 round-trip. It runs daily during the
summer and carries passengers only, not vehicles.

    If you're driving, the **Haines Highway** leads 155 miles to Haines
Junction, Yukon Territory, an intersection with the Alaska Highway (you
must pass through Canadian Customs—see the "Alaska Highway" section
in chapter 10 for rules). The road runs along the Chilkat River and the bald
eagle preserve, then climbs into spectacular alpine terrain. Anchorage is
760 driving miles from Haines and Fairbanks is 644.

Several air services offer scheduled prop service, air taxis, and flight-seeing tours to surrounding communities from Haines. **Wings of Alaska** (☎907/789-0790 reservations, or 907/766-2030 in Haines; www.ichoose wings.com) has plenty of flights, charging $218 round-trip from Juneau.

VISITOR INFORMATION The small but well-staffed and -stocked **Haines Convention and Visitors Bureau Visitor Information Center,** 2nd Avenue near Willard (P.O. Box 530), Haines, AK 99827 (☎800/458-3579 or 907/766-2234; www.haines.ak.us), is operated by the local government, which also sends out a vacation-planning packet. It's open summer Monday through Friday from 8am to 6pm, Saturday and Sunday from 9am to 5pm; in winter, hours are Monday through Friday from 8am to 5pm.

ORIENTATION Haines sits on the narrow Chilkat Peninsula near the north end of the Southeast Alaska Panhandle. Highways run north and east on either side of the peninsula; the one on the east side goes to the ferry dock, 5 miles out, and ends after 11 miles at **Chilkoot Lake.** The other is the **Haines Highway,** which leads to the Canadian border, the Alaska Highway, and the rest of the world. The town has two parts: the sparsely built downtown grid and, a short walk to the west down Front Street or 2nd Avenue, the Fort William Seward area.

GETTING AROUND Bikes are available from **Sockeye Cycle,** just uphill from the Port Chilkoot Dock on Portage Street in the Fort William Seward area (☎907/766-2869; www.cyclealaska.com), for $14 for 2 hours or $35 for 8 hours.

Rent cars at the Captain's Choice Motel or Hotel Hälsingland (see "Where to Stay," below).

[Fast FACTS] HAINES

Bank First National Bank of Alaska, which has an ATM, is at Main Street and 2nd Avenue.

Hospital The **Haines Medical Clinic (☎907/766-6300)** is on 1st Avenue, near the visitor center.

Internet Access The gorgeous **Haines Borough Library,** 111 3rd Ave. S. (☎907/766-2545; www.haineslibrary.org), has eight public terminals.

Police Reach city police in nonemergencies at ☎907/766-2121. Outside

city limits, call the **Alaska State Troopers** at ☎907/766-2552.

Post Office At 55 Haines Hwy., just west of Fort Seward.

Taxes The local sales tax is 5.5%. Tax on accommodations totals 9.5%.

SPECIAL EVENTS The 160-mile **Kluane Chilkat International Bike Relay** (www.kcibr.org) is held the third Saturday in June, heading steeply up and down the Haines Highway from Haines Junction, with more than 1,300 entrants riding solo or in teams of two, four, or eight.

The **Southeast Alaska State Fair (☎907/766-2476; www.seakfair. org)** is the biggest event of the summer, held for 4 days in late July; it's a regional small-town get-together, with livestock, cooking, a logging show, a parade, music, and other entertainment. Buildings constructed for the filming of the movie *White Fang* in 1990 were donated to the fair, and form the nucleus of a retail area. One stop of interest here, at any time, is the local microbrewery, **Haines Brewing Co. (☎907/766-3823)**, which offers samples and informal tours.

The **Alaska Bald Eagle Festival** (**☎907/766-3094;** www.baldeagle festival.org) offers seminars and special events to mark the annual eagle congregation. Held over 5 days in mid-November.

Southeast Alaska State Fair.

Exploring Haines

Haines is Alaska's center of odd or unusual museums and attractions, each somehow reflecting the character and contributions of local personalities.

You can't miss **Fort William H. Seward National Historic Site,** the collection of large, white, wood-frame buildings around sloping parade grounds overlooking the magnificent Lynn Canal fjord. (Get the informative *History Walking Tour* brochure of the National Historic Site from the Haines Convention and Visitors Bureau to learn about each building.) The fort led a peaceful life, for a military installation. By the time the U.S. Army built it, in 1904, the Klondike gold rush was over, and there's no evidence it ever deterred any attack on this little peninsula at the north end of the Inside Passage. It was deactivated at the end of World War II, when it was used for training.

In 1947 a group of World War II veterans from the Lower 48 bought the fort as surplus with the notion of forming a planned community. That idea didn't quite work out, but one of the new families from Outside helped spark a Chilkat Tlingit cultural renaissance in the 1950s. The Heinmillers, who still own a majority of the shares in the fort, formed a youth group that evolved into the Chilkat Dancers. A pair of elders led the group in construction of a Tlingit tribal house on the parade grounds. The **Alaska Indian Arts Cultural Center (☎907/766-2160)** grew from the same movement. Lee Heinmiller, a member of the family's second generation, still manages the arts center, where you can see totem carving and silversmithing practiced. It is open from 9am to 5pm Monday through Friday. The center occupies the old fort hospital on the south side of the parade grounds. Check out the coffee shops, small galleries, and smoked salmon shop while walking around the area.

In the downtown area, the **Sheldon Museum and Cultural Center,** 11 Main St. (**☎907/766-2366;** www.sheldonmuseum.org), contains an upstairs gallery of well-presented Tlingit art and cultural artifacts; downstairs is a collection on the pioneer history of the town. There's a uniquely personal feel to the Tlingit objects, some of which are displayed with pictures of the artisans who made them and the history of their relationship with the Sheldons, for whom the

American Bald Eagle Foundation Natural History Museum.

museum is named. The museum also has a new gallery hosting traveling exhibits and contemporary work by local artists. It's open in summer Monday through Friday 10am to 5pm, Saturday and Sunday 1 to 4pm; in winter, it's open Monday through Saturday from 1 to 4pm. Admission is $3 for adults, free for children 11 and under.

The entirely unique **American Bald Eagle Foundation Natural History Museum,** at 2nd Avenue and Haines Highway (✆907/766-3094; www.baldeagles.org), is essentially a huge, hair-raising diorama of more than 180 eagles and other mounts of Alaska wildlife. At this writing, a falconer had just joined the staff, and the museum planned construction of a mew, a facility for keeping live birds of prey for exhibit. Admission is $5 adults, $2.50 ages 9 to 12, free 8 and under; children need to be with an adult. It's open summer Monday through Friday from 10am to 6pm, Saturday and Sunday from noon to 4pm; closed during the winter.

Hammer Museum.

You'll recognize the **Hammer Museum,** 108 Main St., across from the bank (✆907/766-2374; www.hammermuseum.org), by the 19-foot-long hammer out front. Longshoreman Dave Pahl created his collection of hammers over a couple of decades of building a homestead and added to it using the Internet. He found the prize of his collection, an 800-year-old Tlingit war hammer, while digging up the foundation of the museum itself. More than 1,800 hammers from all over the world, old and new, exotic and ordinary, fill the four rooms (Pahl has another 4,000 in storage). The fun part is guessing what each is for. The museum gained front-page coverage in the *Wall Street Journal* in October, 2007, over a trademark dispute with the Hammer Museum at UCLA (an art museum founded by industrialist Armand Hammer). It is open summer Monday through Friday 10am to 5pm, closed off season. Admission is $3 adults, free for children 12 and under.

Getting Outside

GEARING UP A fraternity of wilderness guides with few equals operates in Haines, and you can make contact with many of them through **Alaska Backcountry Outfitters,** 111 2nd Ave. (tel] **907/766-2876;** www.alaskanaturetours.net), which books outings to ski, climb, kayak, raft, or fly, as well as the company's own Alaska Nature Tours, described below. The shop carries gear and clothing for birding, camping, climbing, hiking, skiing, snowboarding, pedaling, skate boarding, and paddling. Bike rental is covered above, under "Getting Around."

EAGLE VIEWING Haines is probably the best place on earth to see bald eagles. The **Chilkat Bald Eagle Preserve** protects 48,000 acres of river bottom along the Chilkat River. From October to mid-December, peaking around Thanksgiving, up to 3,000 eagles gather in the cottonwood trees (also known as western poplar) on a small section of the river, a phenomenon known as the Fall Congregation. (A healthy 200–400 are resident the rest of the year.) The eagles come for easy winter food: A very late salmon run spawns here into December in a 5-mile stretch of open water known as the Council Grounds. During the Congregation, dozens of eagles stand in each of the gnarled, leafless cottonwoods on the riverbanks, occasionally diving for a fish. The best places to see them are pull-outs, paths, and viewing areas along the Haines Highway from miles 18 to 21. Don't walk on the flats, as that disturbs the eagles. The preserve is managed by **Alaska State Parks** (www.alaskastateparks.org, click on "Individual Parks"). Contact the local ranger at (**907/766-2292;** the headquarters is at 400 Willoughby, 3rd Floor, Juneau, AK 99801.

Two bald eagles.

Cruise passengers often see the river on noisy, high-powered jet boats, which environmentalists maintain are damaging the preserve; if you want a more sensitive way of visiting the eagles, many options are available. Local guides offer trips by raft, bicycle, or bus. Most tours happen in the summer, when the eagles are fewer but visitors more numerous. **Chilkat Guides,** based at Mile 1, Haines Hwy. along Sawmill Road (☎888/292-7789 or 907/766-2491; www.raftalaska.com), does a rafting trip several times a day during the summer down the Chilkat to watch the eagles. The water is gentle—if it's too low, there's a chance you'll be asked to get out and push—and you'll see lots of eagles, mostly at a distance. The 3½-hour trip, with a snack, costs $89 for adults, $62 for children ages 7 to 12.

Serious bird-watchers, photographers, and others who want an in-depth tour should join **Alaska Nature Tours** (☎907/766-2876; www.alaska naturetours.net), whose naturalists lead 3-hour wildlife-viewing tours by bus for $65 year-round. The company also offers longer tours, including all-day guided hikes, for $115, and cross-country skiing in and around the preserve. **Sockeye Cycle,** directly below, visits the eagle preserve on tours, too.

BIKING **Sockeye Cycle,** 24 Portage St., near the dock (☎907/766-2869; www. cyclealaska.com), leads a variety of guided trips—a couple of hours, half or full day, or even a 10-day trek along gold rush routes. A 3-hour ride costs $75, and could include various sites around town. Or you can rent your own bicycle for $35 a day. The area is quite conducive to biking.

FISHING There are several charter operators in Haines for halibut and salmon fishing, and guided freshwater fishing for silver or sockeye salmon, Dolly Varden, and cutthroat trout. The **Haines Convention and Visitors Bureau,** 2nd Street near Willard (P.O. Box 530), Haines, AK 99827 (☎800/458-3579 or 907/766-2234; www.haines.ak.us), can help you find a guide or fishing lodge through the links on their website or the list of operators they keep at the office. For self-guided fishing advice and weekly summer updates of what's running, contact the local office of the Alaska Department of Fish and Game (☎907/766-2625; www.alaska.gov/adfg, click on "Sport Fish," then the Southeast region on the state map).

FLIGHTSEEING This is one of Alaska's best places to go flightseeing. The Inside Passage is beautiful, and one mountain away is Glacier Bay National Park; the ice field and the glaciers spilling through to the sea are a sight you won't forget. It's possible to land on an immense glacial ice field and see the sun slicing between the craggy peaks. **Alaska Mountain Flying and Travel,** 132 2nd Ave. (☎800/954-8747 or 907/766-3007; www.flyglacierbay.com), offers these flights—or, as owner Paul Swanstrom says, adventures. He is known for his glacier and beach landings and offers commentary to make flights fully guided experiences. Prices range from $149 to $499 per person, and reservations are recommended. Other flight services offer these tours, too; ask at the visitor center.

HIKING There are several good trails near Haines, ranging from an easy beach walk to a 10-mile, 3,650-foot climb of **Mount Ripinsky,** north of town (it starts at the top of Young St.). Get the *Haines Is for Hikers* trail guide from the visitors bureau. The easiest for families is the 2-mile **Battery Point**

Trail, which goes along a beach decorated with wild iris. The trail starts at the end of Beach Road, which leads southeast from the Port Chilkoot cruise-ship dock. **Mount Riley** is south of town, with three trail routes to a 1,760-foot summit that features great views and feels much higher than it is; get the trail guide or ask directions to one of the trail heads. **Seduction Point Trail** is 7 miles long, starting at Chilkat State Park at the end of Mud Bay Road south of town and leading to the end of the Chilkat Peninsula. It's a beach walk, so check the tides; they'll give you a tide table at the visitors bureau. For a guided hike, rock climbing, or even a multiday glacier trek, check with Alaska Mountain Guides, directly below. Their mountaineering programs cost $180 per day.

SEA KAYAKING Alaska Mountain Guides (☎800/766-3396 or 907/766-3366; www.alaskamountainguides.com) offers instruction, short guided trips, longer expeditions, and rentals ($50 a day for a single). A half-day guided paddle is $85, including a snack; a full day, including lunch, is $125.

Where to Stay

Lodging prices are reasonable in Haines, and choices include many friendly little places with lots of charm. Besides those described in detail below, here are two more reliable places to stay: **Fort Seward Bed and Breakfast** (☎800/615-6676; www.fortsewardalaska.com) in the fort surgeon's quarters, overlooks the parade grounds and the Lynn Canal. Operating since 1981, it offers 7 rooms, some with high ceilings, fireplaces, and wonderful cabinetry. **The River House** (☎907/766-3849; www.riverhousehaines.com), a rental cottage in a spectacular spot at the mouth of the Chilkat, a mile from town, can be rented in whole or in two individual units.

The Guardhouse Boardinghouse 🍴 Situated on the edge of Fort Seward nearest downtown, a block from the waterfront, this B&B offers inexpensive, central lodgings in an atmosphere that's like being houseguests of a friendly couple. Phyllis Sage and Joanne Waterman, lifelong Alaskans, and their ever-present spaniel, share light-filled living quarters as common rooms, including the computer, six-person Jacuzzi hot tub, and the deck out back with a barbecue and a great view. Rooms have attractive country decor and lots of Alaskan art. One has a kitchenette and large bathroom; the least expensive room has a private bath that is not attached to the room. Despite the name "boardinghouse," only a continental breakfast is served.

15 Seward Dr. (P.O. Box 853), Haines, AK 99827. ☎866/290-7445 or 907/766-2566. www.alaska guardhouse.com. 3 units. $85–$115 double. Extra person age 12 or older $15. MC, V. Rates include continental breakfast. **Amenities:** Jacuzzi. *In room:* TV, hair dryer, Wi-Fi.

Captain's Choice Motel ★ Many towns have a lot of chainlike hotels and only one or two unique places with character. In Haines, the situation is reversed, and these trim, red-roofed buildings are the one exception to the general eccentricity. The standard rooms contain all the anticipated amenities, yet the motel still has a certain amount of charm (and a small resident dog in the lobby). The room decor is on the dark side, with paneling, and is somewhat out-of-date, but it's quite clean, and many of the rooms have good views on a large sun deck. They're in the process of adding a lounge with a full bar and finger foods.

108 2nd St. N. at Dalton St. (P.O. Box 392), Haines, AK 99827. ☎800/478-2345 or 907/766-3111. Fax 907/766-3332. www.capchoice.com. 39 units. High season $129 double; low season $116 double; year-round $146–$182 suite. Extra person $5. Rates include continental breakfast. AE, DC, DISC, MC, V. **Amenities:** Free airport transfers; limited room service. *In room:* TV, fridge, hair dryer, microwave, Wi-Fi (fee).

Hotel Hälsingland ★ 🏊 This grandly rambling hotel has always been the most interesting place in town to stay. The group of buildings, designated a National Historic Landmark, served as the Commanding Officer's Quarters for Fort William Seward during both World Wars. You can almost hear well-shined boots on the wood floors, echoing off high ceilings and old-fashioned woodwork. Today it's well-kept, but rooms vary widely, so it's a good idea to take a look before checking in. Some share bathrooms and some of those with private bathrooms have only shower stalls, while others have claw-foot tubs. The hotel also books tours, offers Avis car rental, and has an RV park out back.

The **Commander's Room** restaurant, open for dinner only, offers a short menu of well prepared dishes in continental styles, and prices for main courses in the $22 to $28 range. The small bar has craft brews on tap. While the town's most formal dining room, it's still a friendly, low-key place in the evening.

Fort William Seward parade grounds (P.O. Box 1649), Haines, AK 99827. ☎800/542-6363 or 907/766-2000. Fax 907/766-2060. www.hotelhalsingland.com. 50 units, 45 with private bathroom. $69 double without bathroom; $89–$119 double with private bathroom. AE, DC, DISC, MC, V. Closed mid-Nov to mid-Mar. **Amenities:** Free airport transfers; restaurant; bar. *In room:* TV, Wi-Fi.

The Summer Inn Bed & Breakfast This lovely old clapboard house downtown has a big porch and a living room decorated in whites and pale, lacy fabrics, just like grandma's house. The five rooms are cozy but small, and share three bathrooms among them (bathrooms were immaculate when we visited). The house was built by a reputed former member of Soapy Smith's gang in 1912 (see the Skagway section for more on Soapy), and the big claw-foot tub is said to be the first in the history of Haines's upstairs bathtubs. No smoking or drinking are allowed.

117 2nd Ave. (P.O. Box 1198), Haines, AK 99827. ☎/fax 907/766-2970. www.summerinnbnb.com. 5 units, none with private bathroom. High season $110 double, $130 suite; low season $100 double, $120 suite. Extra adult $20, child $15. Rates include full breakfast. MC, V.

A Quick Side Trip to Juneau from Haines or Skagway

Without changing your lodgings, you can travel from Skagway or Haines for a tour of Juneau's highlights and a sightseeing day cruise of the Lynn Canal. **Alaska Fjordlines'** high-speed catamaran (☎800/320-0146 or 907/766-3395; www.alaskafjordlines.com) carries passengers for half a day in Juneau, with wildlife sightings on the way. The fare is $155, including a narrated bus tour of Juneau and Mendenhall Glacier, with time for shopping and dining downtown. The whole excursion is about 12 hours.

Where to Dine

Haines has a few consistently good restaurants—which is a few more than most other Alaska towns this size—and you can also eat well during the summer at the Hotel Hälsingland (see "Where to Stay," above).

There are lots of places for a casual meal, as well. Among the best lunch places is the **Mountain Market & Café ★**, a natural food store and cafe at 3rd Avenue and the Haines Highway (☎907/766-3340). A primary town hangout and the best espresso stop, it serves hearty and reasonably priced sandwiches, tortilla wraps, soups, and many fresh-baked goods. Pick up a picnic, or stop by for coffee, roasted in-house, or breakfast. The liquor store carries organic wine.

The Bamboo Room ★ DINER The building started as a French restaurant during the gold-rush era and then became a brothel and speakeasy before the Tengs family got it in 1953. The history is on the back of the menu. In the current generation the food has taken center stage from the bar. The two parts are divided off by attractive etched glass, but both are smoke-free. The diner serves burgers, wraps, salads, pasta, and lots of seafood. A wide variety of food and prices should suit everyone, including a good children's menu. The halibut and chips is celebrated.

2nd Ave. near Main St. ☎907/766-2474. www.bamboopioneer.net. Lunch $8–$16; dinner $10–$35. AE, DC, DISC, MC, V. Summer daily 6am–11pm; winter daily 6am–2pm.

Fireweed Restaurant ★ PIZZA A historic building in Fort Seward was remodeled into the most attractive dining room in Haines using salvaged wood from other old buildings: Natural tones, hand-crafted wood, and local art and photography create a softly aesthetic setting. With only seven tables, the place can get a bit crowded and noisy, but the popularity attests to the quality of the casual food. The menu includes pasta dishes, hero sandwiches, and burgers, but the specialty is pizza, around $25 for a large pie with a few ingredients of your choice. The calzone also is noteworthy.

Historic building #37, Blacksmith Rd. ☎907/766-3838. Lunch $8–$14; dinner $11–$20. MC, V. Summer Tues–Sat 11am–11pm; Apr and Sept Tues–Sat 4:30–9pm. Closed Oct–Mar.

The Lighthouse ★ SEAFOOD This is the place to go for a traditional seafood dinner or steak in a light, stylish dining room with a spectacular water view (don't let the saloon exterior scare you away). The menu includes local seafood simply prepared—not all fired, as is often the case—and it's a favorite of locals and visitors alike. The restaurant is open year-round and serves a good, traditional American breakfast and a lunch of burgers and sandwiches as well as a few entrees. Service is quick and professional. The attached bar is smoky.

Main and Front sts. ☎907/766-2442. Lunch $7–$18; dinner $15–$30. AE, DC, DISC, MC, V. High season daily 8am–10pm; low season daily 11:30am–9pm.

Mosey's Cantina ★ 👜 MEXICAN/SOUTHWEST A couple gave up river guiding on the Grand Canyon for Alaskan floats, then settled in Haines and began serving the cuisine they brought with them, which is re-energized with annual chile-buying trips to New Mexico. The food is authentic and well prepared. For lunch, the green chile burrito is huge and delicious, for $9; for dinner, the enchiladas chicken mole hits a perfect mix of spice and sweetness, for $17. At lunch you order at the counter, while a server comes to the table in the evening.

The atmosphere, in a gray house with a big porch, is fun, bright, and loud. As the dining room is small and the restaurant popular, calling ahead is a good idea. It's walking distance from downtown, just south of Fort Seward off Tower Road.

1 Soap Suds Alley. ☎**907/766-2320.** Reservations accepted. Lunch $6–$15; dinner $9–18. MC, V. Mon–Sat 11:30am–2:30pm and 5:30–9pm. Closed Oct–Feb.

SKAGWAY: AFTER THE GOLD RUSH

It's only been 110 years since white civilization came to Alaska. There were a few scattered towns in Southeast before that—Juneau, Sitka, and Wrangell, for example—but until the Klondike gold rush, the great mass of Alaska was populated only by Natives who had never seen a white face. Then, in a single year, 1898, the population exploded. That year still stands as the greatest in Alaska's short but eventful history, for the influx of those people set the patterns of development ever since.

In the rush years of 1897 and 1898, Skagway and its ghost-town twin city of Dyea were the logical places to get off the boat to begin the trek to the gold fields near the new city of Dawson City, Yukon Territories. (See "Dawson City & Eagle: Detour into History," p. 544.) Skagway instantly grew from a single homestead to a population of between 15,000 and 25,000. No one knows exactly how many, partly because the people were flowing through too quickly to count and partly because there was no civil authority to count them. This was a wide-open boomtown, a true Wild West outpost that in its biggest years was completely without law other than the survival of the meanest.

Gold Rush monument.

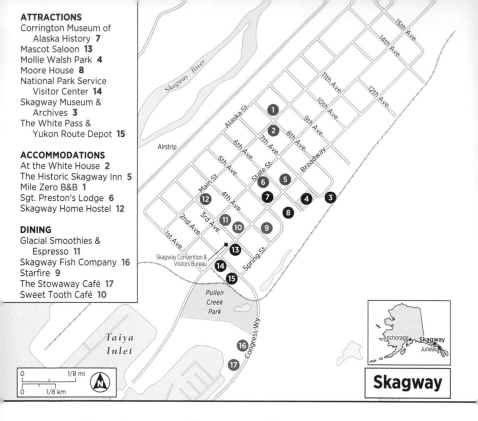

Skagway

Then, almost as quickly as it started, the rush ended and the town deflated.

But Skagway survived by showing off where it all happened. In 1896 there was a single log cabin in Skagway, in 1897 the word of the Klondike strike made it to the outside world, and in 1898 Skagway was a huge gold-rush boomtown. In 1899 the gold rush was ending, and in 1903, 300 tourists arrived in a single day to see where the gold rush happened. By 1908, local businessmen had started developing tourist attractions, moving picturesque gold-rush buildings to Broadway, the main street, to create a more unified image when visitors arrived on the steamers. By 1920, tourism had become an important part of the economy. By 1933, historic preservation efforts had started. Today, more money and more than 20 times as many visitors come through in a year as made the trip to the Klondike during the gold rush.

With 862 residents and more than 900,000 visitors annually, the "real" town has all but disappeared, and most of the people you'll meet are either fellow visitors or summer workers brought north to serve them. Most of the tourists are from cruise ships—it's not unusual for several ships to hit town in a single morning, unleashing as many as 9,000 people at once up the wharf and into the one historic street. There are plenty of highway and ferry travelers, too, and outdoor enthusiasts come to do the Chilkoot Trail, just as the stampeders did.

Is it worth all those visits? Skagway, spared from fire and recognized so long ago for its history, may be the best-preserved gold-rush town in the United

States. What happened here in a 2-year period was certainly extraordinary, even if the phenomenon the town celebrates is one of mass insanity based on greed, inhumanity, thuggery, prostitution, waste, and, for most, abject failure. While Canada was well policed by the Mounties, Skagway was truly lawless—a hell on earth, as one Mountie described it. Soapy Smith ruled this scam-pire with a team of con artists and toughs who milked the suckers for every dollar available. Half of the stories about Soapy are probably lies, but here's one too good not to repeat: He set up a telegraph office for suckers to wire their money home, but with no telegraph line. Such was his influence and high repute in the newspapers he controlled that the governor offered to put Smith officially in charge as a territorial marshal and rode with him in the 1898 Independence Day parade. Four days later, Smith was shot dead in a gunfight with Frank Reid, who led a vigilante committee upset over one of Smith's thefts. Reid died of wounds sustained in the shootout, too, but Soapy Smith's gang was broken. Of course, the gold rush was about to end anyway.

In 1976, the National Park Service began buying many of Skagway's best old buildings for the **Klondike Gold Rush National Historic District,** and now it owns about 15, having completed restoration in 1999. Broadway is a prosperous, freshly painted 6-block strip of gold-rush era buildings. A few that look like real businesses turn out to be displays showing how it was back then. Other buildings restored by the park service are under lease to gift shops and such. Sadly, those historic businesses not preserved by the Park Service have been lost to the onslaught of cruise ship–oriented shopping: A curio shop operating since the gold rush was converted a few years ago, and in 2002 the longest-operating hotel in Alaska, which dated from the earliest days, became a T-shirt shop.

Captain William Moore Bridge on the Klondike Highway.

Essentials

GETTING THERE The **Alaska Marine Highway System** (☎800/642-0066, or 907/983-2941 locally; www.ferryalaska.com) connects Skagway daily with Haines and Juneau. The fare is $31 from Haines, $50 from Juneau. If you're headed to Haines without a vehicle, consider the private **Haines-Skagway Fast Ferry** (p. 260). Haines is 15 miles away by boat but more than 350 miles by road.

Since 1978, **Klondike Hwy.** 2 has traced the route of the stampeders through the White Pass into Canada, a parallel route to the Chilkoot Trail. The road runs 99 miles, then meets the Alaska Highway a dozen miles southeast of the Yukon capital of Whitehorse. The border is at the top of the pass, 14 miles from Skagway. (Information on requirements to cross the border is in chapter 10 in the Alaska Highway section, p. 543.) This is one of the most spectacular drives anywhere in Alaska, with views basically equivalent to those from the White Pass and Yukon Route railway (but a lot cheaper). The road is a well-maintained two-lane highway with wide shoulders. Do it in clear weather, if possible, as in cloudy weather all you'll see is whiteout.

Car rentals in Skagway are available from **Avis,** in the Westmark Hotel at 3rd and Spring streets (☎800/230-4898 or 907/983-2247; www.avis.com).

Riding the ferry to Skagway and then heading inland **in a rented RV** is an attractive option. Expect to pay around $230 a day, plus many required extras (it's not a cheap option). **Alaska Motorhome Rentals** (☎800/323-5757; www.bestofalaskatravel.com) rents RVs one-way to Anchorage with a drop-off fee of $795 to $995, plus the cost of the rental, mileage, and gas. The same company, under a different name, also offers structured RV tours from Skagway as add-ons to cruise vacations; that's covered in chapter 3 under "Getting There & Getting Around."

Traveling **by bus** between Skagway and Anchorage or Fairbanks is not a practical option for most visitors. It's a marginal business to be in, and operators change annually. At best, the journey takes a couple of days. If taking the bus is your goal, contact the Skagway Convention and Visitors Bureau (below) for the latest advice. They can help you figure out how to get to Whitehorse, summer only, by tour bus or on the White Pass & Yukon Route railway by train and bus (p. 277), and there to catch another bus to Alaska. Do plan all the details ahead, as otherwise you could be stranded for days.

Several air taxi operators serve Skagway. A round-trip from Juneau costs $238 on **Wings of Alaska** (☎907/789-0790 reservations, or 907/983-2442 in Skagway; www.ichoosewings.com).

VISITOR INFORMATION Located in the restored railroad depot, the **National Park Service Visitor Center,** 2nd Avenue and Broadway (P.O. Box 517), Skagway, AK

The Slow Season

Skagway is a seasonal community. After September and before May, almost none of the commercial tourist attractions are open, and hardly any lodgings or restaurants. Many residents close their businesses and leave in the fall. This section focuses on what you can do in the summer, and you can assume that most of what I describe is not available in the winter.

99840 (☎907/983-9223; www.nps.gov/klgo), is the focal point for activities in Skagway. Rangers answer questions, give talks, and show films, and five times a day lead an excellent guided walking tour. The building houses a small museum that lays the groundwork for the rest of what you'll see. The park service's programs are free. The visitor center is open early May through late September daily from 8am to 6pm; the rest of the year the museum is open Monday through Friday from 8am to 5pm.

The **Skagway Convention and Visitors Bureau Center,** 245 Broadway (P.O. Box 1029), Skagway, AK 99840 (☎907/983-2854, fax 907/983-3854; www.skagway.com), occupies the historic Arctic Brotherhood Hall, the building with the driftwood facade. The website contains links to lodgings and activities, or you can request the same information on paper (and/or at ☎888/762-1890) Stop in especially for the handy and informative *Skagway Walking* **Tour Map** of historic sites. The center is open summer daily from 8am to 6pm, winter Monday through Friday from 8am to 5pm.

GETTING AROUND Skagway is laid out on a simple grid, with streets branching off from Broadway. The main sights can be reached on foot. For places you can't walk, try the **Dyea Dave Shuttle** (☎907/612-0290) which operates like a taxi. Skagway also has a bus, called SMART (☎907/983-3743), which runs a circuit around town for $2 a ride, or out of town to sites such as the Klondike Gold Dredge for $5, leaving on the hour from 7th Hall and 7th Avenue and Spring Street. A bike is fun and practical transportation in Skagway. **Sockeye Cycle,** on 5th Avenue off Broadway (☎907/983-2851; www.cyclealaska.com), rents good mountain bikes for $14 for 2 hours and leads guided day trips (see "Getting Outside," below).

[FastFACTS] SKAGWAY

Bank Wells Fargo, at Broadway and 6th Avenue, has an ATM.

Hospital The Dahl Medical Clinic, staffed by a physician's assistant, can be reached at ☎907/983-2255 during business hours.

Internet Access Mr. Mike's Cruiseship Services, charging $4 an hour, is at 2nd Avenue and State Street (☎907/983-3398).

Police For nonemergency business, call ☎907/983-2232. The station is located off State Street, just south of 1st Avenue.

Post Office On Broadway between 6th and 7th Avenues.

Taxes Sales tax is 5%. The bed tax total 8%.

SPECIAL EVENTS The springtime **Buckwheat Ski Classic,** in the deep snow of the White Pass, is as much for fun as it is for Nordic skiing competition. Various events for adults and kids range from 5 to 50km. Racers often wear costumes and carry libations, and spectators carve open shelters from the snow to drink beer and soak up the warm spring sun. A dinner and dance follow. It happens in late March. **Skagway's July 4th Parade and Celebration,** organized by the chamber of commerce and featuring lots of small-town events, has been a big deal since Soapy Smith led the parade in 1898. **The**

Klondike Road Relay, a 110-mile overnight footrace over the pass, brings hundreds of runners in teams of 10 from all over the state in mid-September. Contact the visitor center for information on any of these events.

Exploring Skagway

You can see most of Skagway on foot, and everything by bike. Many companies also offer car, van, or bus tours, too. No one goes to greater lengths to give visitors a unique experience than the **Skagway Street Car Company** (☎907/983-2908; www.skagwaystreetcar.com), which uses antique touring vehicles and costumed guides performing "theater without walls." The amusing, historical 2-hour streetcar tour, based on a tour originally given to President Harding in 1923, is $42 for adults and $21 for children 12 and under. Book the tour at least 2 weeks in advance, as they're frequently sold out.

TOURING THE HISTORIC PARK

The main thing to do in Skagway is to see the old buildings and historic gold-rush places. Do it with the *Skagway Walking Tour Map,* or join a fascinating National Park Service guided walking tour (see "Visitor Information," above).

Start with a visit to the **museum** at the National Park Service Visitor Center and in the building next door. It helps put everything else in context. Of greatest interest is a collection of food and gear similar to the ton of supplies each prospector was required to carry over the pass in order to gain entry into Canada, a requirement that prevented famine among the stampeders, but made the job of getting to Dawson City an epic struggle.

While they prepared to go over the pass, gold-rush greenhorns spent their time in Skagway drinking and getting fleeced in the many gambling dens and brothels. Law didn't mean much in the town's heyday with the lack of civil authority. It's hard to picture at times, because everything looks so orderly now, but

Mannequins at the Mascot Saloon.

the park service has tried. For example, the **Mascot Saloon,** at Broadway and 3rd Avenue, has mannequins bellying up to the bar. It's open daily from 8am to 6pm; admission is free.

The Park Service walking tour ends at the **Moore House,** near 5th Avenue and Spring Street, open from 10am to 5pm during the summer. Ten years before the gold rush happened, Capt. William Moore brilliantly predicted it and homesteaded the land that would become Skagway, knowing that this would be a key staging area. He built a cabin in 1887, which stands nearby. But when the rush hit, the stampeders simply ignored his property claims and built the city on his land without offering compensation. Years later, he won in court.

A block east, on 6th Avenue, is **Mollie Walsh Park,** with a good children's play area, public restrooms, and phones. A sign tells the sad story of one of Skagway's first respectable women, a lady who chose to marry the wrong man among two suitors and was killed by him in a drunken rage. The other suitor—who'd previously killed another rival for her affections—commissioned the bust of Walsh that stands at the park.

The **Gold Rush Cemetery** is 1½ miles from town, up State Street. Used until 1908, it's small and overgrown with spruce trees, but some of the charm and mystery of the place is lost because of the number of visitors and the shiny new paint and maintenance of the wooden markers. The graves of Soapy Smith and Frank Reid are the big attractions, but don't miss the short walk up to Reid Falls. The closely spaced dates on many of the markers attest to the epidemics that swept through mobs of stampeders living in squalid conditions. Remember, there was little sanitation for the tens of thousands who passed this way in 1898.

About 10 miles northwest of Skagway is the ghost town of **Dyea,** where stampeders started climbing the Chilkoot Trail. It's a lovely coastal drive or bike ride: From Skagway, go 2 miles up Klondike Hwy. 2 and then turn left, continuing 8 miles on gravel road. Dyea is a lot more ghost than town. Little remains other than boards, broken dock pilings, a single false front, and miscellaneous iron debris. On a sunny day, however, the protected historical site is a perfect place for a picnic, among beach grasses, fields of wild iris, and the occasional reminder that a city once stood here. The National Park Service leads an interesting guided history and nature walk here daily in summer at 10am and 2pm; check at the visitor center. (See "Getting Outside," below, for more on going to Dyea.)

The little-visited **Slide Cemetery,** in the woods near Dyea, is the last resting place of many of nearly 100 who died in an avalanche on the Chilkoot Trail on Palm Sunday, April 3, 1898. No one knows how many are here, or exactly who died, or how accurate the wooden markers are. In 1960, when the state reopened the Chilkoot Trail, the cemetery had been completely overgrown and the markers were replaced. But somehow the mystery and forgetting make it an even more ghostly place, and the sense of anonymous, hopeless hardship and death it conveys is as authentic a gold-rush souvenir as anything in Skagway.

MUSEUMS & ATTRACTIONS

Jewell Gardens ★ Early Skagway promoters planted big, showy gardens to impress the tourists and named the town "Garden City of Alaska." Jim and Charlotte Jewell revived this tradition using grounds originally planted by gold-rush stampeder Henry Clark and maintain some of his original 1898 plantings, including fruit trees and a 4-foot-tall rhubarb. Besides the organic show garden, with a

Jewell Gardens.

boardwalk and model train, the Jewells also produce food here, and offer visitors lessons on composting and growing in cold conditions. Artists demonstrate their work in a glass-blowing studio, and their whimsical creations decorate the trails. Stop in the greenhouse for English tea or a meal. The restaurant, Poppies at Jewell Gardens, serves some of the best meals in town, including local seafood and the garden's produce, for lunch and dinner. A full lunch is $15, and dinner main courses are in the $15 to $25 range. The garden is at the far end of the town from the waterfront; you can buy a SMART bus ticket with your admission ($18, or $21 as a package with lunch included). Cruise-ship tours are heaviest Tuesday through Thursday, so avoid those days.

Mile 1.5, Klondike Hwy. ☎907/983-2111. www.jewellgardens.com. $12 adults, $6 children 12 and under. Early May to late Sept daily 9am–5pm.

Klondike Gold Dredge Tours Gold mining never happened in Skagway; it was only a transit point. But more gold-rush tourists come here than anywhere else, so promoters brought a dredge to where the people are. The 1937 rig, weighing 350 tons, dug up and sorted gravel to remove gold first in Idaho, then near Dawson City, and finally near the border on the Top of the World Highway. A 2-hour visit includes a 10-minute video, costumed guides who spice up the tour with humor, and gold panning in heated water. If you will visit Dawson City or Fairbanks, you can see larger dredges in authentic historic settings, but if not, this stop can satisfy your mechanical curiosity and fever to pan for gold.

Mile 1.7, Klondike Hwy. ☎907/983-3175. www.klondikegolddredge.com. $45 adults, $35 children 11 and under. Summer Sun–Fri 8:30am–4:30pm; full tours 9:30am and 1:30pm.

Skagway Museum and Archives ★ The museum contains a fine collection of gold-rush artifacts and other items reflecting Skagway's colorful history. The building is the town's most impressive, and one of the state's most dignified architectural landmarks, with crisp granite walls and a high pitched roof standing among tall shade trees on the edge of town. It began life as a short-lived gold rush–era college and later became a federal courthouse and jail. The city hall and museum

have occupied the building since 1961 except for a brief hiatus for renovations.
7th and Spring sts. ℂ907/983-2420. Admission $2 adults, $1 students, free for children 12 and under. Summer Mon–Fri 9am–5pm; Sat 10am–5pm; Sun 10am–4pm. Winter hours vary; call ahead.

The White Pass and Yukon Route ★★ A narrow-gauge railroad line that originally ran to Whitehorse, the White Pass was completed after only 2 years in 1900. It's an engineering marvel and a fun way to see spectacular, historic scenery from a train inching up steep tracks that were chipped out of the side of the mountains. Some of the cars are historic, as well—originals more than 100 years old. The railroad "recommends" you don't get out of your seat, but it's a long ride on a slow train, and most people get up and socialize; however, you cannot move from car to car while the train is moving. The trick is to go in clear weather. When the pass is socked in, all you see are white clouds. Tickets are expensive, however, and you have to reserve ahead. Take the gamble: Cancellation carries only a $10 per person penalty, and you can change dates for no charge. Also, try to go on a weekend, when fewer cruise ships are in town taking up all the seats; weekend trains can be booked as little as a week ahead, while midweek excursions can book up months ahead. The summit excursion—which travels 20 miles with an elevation gain of 2,865 feet, then turns back—takes about 3 hours and costs $103 for adults. All fares are half price for ages 3 to 12 (except for Chilkoot Pass hiker's fares; see "Backpacking," below).

For a longer journey, trains travel to Carcross, Yukon, with a stop for a hot meal at Lake Bennett. That costs $170. But the biggest treat for a train lover is a steam-powered trip. Friday and Sunday afternoons, steam trains go over the pass to Fraser Meadows, 6 miles beyond the pass, and return. The fare is $133. In either case, bring your passport, as the train will go into Canada. Other choices are available, too; check the website.

These days, the line operates only as a tourist attraction, May through September.
2nd Ave. depot, Skagway. ℂ800/343-7373 or 907/983-2217. www.wpyr.com. For the entire schedule and fares, see the website.

Getting Outside

The **Mountain Shop,** 355 4th Ave. (ℂ907/983-2544), rents and sells the equipment you need for backpacking or other outdoor activities in Skagway. The owner leads guided day hikes, backpacking trips, and kayaking and float trips under the name **Packer Expeditions** (ℂ907/983-3005; www.packerexpeditions.com) at the same address. **Alaska Mountain Guides,** on 4th between Main and Broadway (ℂ907/983-3365; www.alaskamountainguides.com), offers half-day rock climbing in Skagway for $85 and 5-day Chilkoot Pass hikes for $890 per person.

BACKPACKING The National Park Service and Parks Canada jointly manage the famous **Chilkoot Pass Trail,** publishing a trail guide and offering information at their offices in Skagway and Whitehorse. Some 20,000 stampeders used the trail to get from Dyea—9 miles from Skagway—to Lake Bennett, 33 miles away, where they could build and launch boats bound for Dawson City. Today about 3,000 people a year make the challenging hike, taking 3 to

5 days. The Chilkoot is not so much a wilderness trail as an outdoor museum, but don't underestimate its difficulty, as so many did during the gold rush.

To control the numbers, **Parks Canada,** 205–300 Main St., Whitehorse, Yukon Y1A 2B5, Canada (☎ **800/661-0486** or 867/667-3910; fax 867/393-6701; www.pc.gc.ca/chilkoot), allows only 50 hikers with permits per day to cross the summit. You should reserve ahead. To buy permits, call with a Visa, American Express, or MasterCard; the date you plan to start; and the campsites you will use each night. Permits are C$54 for adults, C$27 ages 16 and under, plus a C$12 per person reservation fee. You pick up the permit at the Trail Centre in Skagway; that's also where 8 of the 50 daily permits are held for walk-ins, to be distributed along with any no-shows. The reservation fee is non-refundable, and the permit fee is refundable only until a month before the hike.

Once over the pass, you're on Lake Bennett, on the rail line 8 miles short of the road. You can walk to the road (stay safely off the tracks), or get back to Skagway on the White Pass and Yukon Route railway (p. 277) at 2pm daily except Saturday. The one-way fare to Frasier, B.C., is $50, and the scenic 3-hour ride to Skagway is $95. The railroad requires tickets be purchased in advance, as well as meals at Lake Bennett, if you choose to eat there. You will also need a passport to get back into the United States.

BIKING Sockeye Cycle, on 5th Avenue off Broadway (☎ **907/983-2851;** www.cyclealaska.com), leads bike tours, including one that takes clients to the top of the White Pass in a van and lets them coast down on bikes; the 2½-hour trip is $79. Going up on White Pass and Yukon Route railroad and riding back down brings the price to $179. Riders must be at least 12 years old.

Miners making their way up Chilkoot Pass during the gold rush of 1897-1899.

The company also leads a 3-hour tour of the quiet ghost town site of Dyea for $79, going over in a van. I rode to Dyea from Skagway on my own over the hilly, 10-mile coastal road—a very pleasant, scenic ride.

FLIGHTSEEING Skagway, like Haines, is a good place to choose for a flightseeing trip, as Glacier Bay National Park is just to the west. The flightseeing operators listed in the Haines and Gustavus sections offer flights from Skagway, too (p. 253 and 265). **Temsco Helicopters (☎866/683-2900** or 907/983-2900; www.temscoair.com) takes 80-minute tours near Skagway with half that time spent on a glacier (not in Glacier Bay); those flights cost $289. A 90-minute helicopter and dog-sled tour, including an hour at a dog camp on Denver Glacier, is $479.

HIKING A *Skagway Trail Map* is available from the visitor center, listing 10 hikes around Skagway. An easy evening walk starts at the footbridge at the west end of the airport parking lot, crossing the Skagway River to **Yakutania Point Park,** where pine trees grow from cracks in the rounded granite of the shoreline. Across the park is a shortcut taking a couple of miles off the trip to Dyea and to the **Skyline Trail and A.B. Mountain,** a strenuous climb to a 5,000-foot summit with great views. On the southeast side of town, across the railroad tracks, a network of trails heads up from Spring Street between 3rd and 4th avenues to a series of mountain lakes, the closest of which is **Lower Dewey Lake,** less than a mile up the trail.

Where to Stay

The accommodations in Skagway are within close walking distance of the historic district, except as noted.

At the White House ★ 🏠 The Tronrud family essentially rebuilt a burned 1902 gable-roofed inn, which has dormer and bow windows and two porticos with small Doric columns. They made the rooms comfortable and modern while retaining the authentic gold-rush style of the original owner, Lee Guthrie, a successful gambler and saloon owner of the early years. The inn has hardwood floors and fine woodwork. Bedrooms vary in size, but all have quilts and other nice touches, including ceiling fans.

Corner of 8th and Main sts. (P.O. Box 41), Skagway, AK 99840-0041. ☎907/983-9000. Fax 907/983-9010. www.atthewhitehouse.com. 10 units. High season $125 double; low season $85 double. Extra person $10. Rates include continental breakfast. AE, DISC, MC, V. *In room:* TV, fridge, Wi-Fi.

Chilkoot Trail Outpost ★ These beautifully crafted log cabins contain comfortable, modern lodgings with carpeted floors and log interior walls, some in the form of two-room suites, with many amenities, but no phones. The hiker's suite consists of two rooms in a duplex with bunk beds that rent for $145 double, including breakfast. The location, in Dyea near the Chilkoot Trail and Taiya River, puts you in quiet, natural surroundings away from the carnival atmosphere created by the crush of tourists in Skagway proper. In good weather, the hosts have a nightly campfire and provide supplies for s'mores. You can barbecue in a screened gazebo, or buy a dinner of steak or local seafood in a remarkable log building with a vaulted ceiling for $25. There's a full bar, too. The included breakfast consists of a buffet with various choices, including one hot selection.

Mile 7, Dyea Rd. (P.O. Box 286), Skagway, AK 99840. ☎**907/983-3799.** Fax 907/983-3599. www.chilkoottrailoutpost.com. 11 units. $145 double in duplex; $175 double-occupancy cabin. Extra adult $25; extra child 2–11 years $13. MC, V. Rates include full breakfast. Closed off-season. **Amenities:** Bike loan. *In room:* TV/VCR, fridge, hair dryer, microwave, no phone, Wi-Fi.

The Historic Skagway Inn ★ An 1897 building that served as a gold-rush brothel was moved to this site in 1902 and added onto until the 1950s. The inn's country decoration, wallpaper, and period antiques make for homey, pleasant accommodations, and the place is loaded with character, each room named after a prostitute who may have once worked there. But prostitutes lived in small rooms, and the bathrooms created from converted closets are tiny. Also consider "At the White House," above, which does the historic thing well for lower rates. A full breakfast is included in the rate, served in the dining room of **Olivia's,** an on-site restaurant serving gourmet dinners. It draws for produce on the inn's own large and luxurious garden, which is also open for tours.

7th Ave. and Broadway (P.O. Box 500), Skagway, AK 99840. ☎**888/SKAGWAY** (752-4929) or 907/983-2289. www.skagwayinn.com. 10 unites. High season $189 double, $199 suite; low season $99 double, $169 suite. Extra person 16 and older $30. AE, DISC, MC, V. Rates include full breakfast. **Amenities:** Courtesy van, Internet access. *In room:* Hair dryer, Wi-Fi.

Mile Zero Bed & Breakfast ★ This building was designed to be a B&B, and it shows in details such as the soundproofing and the back doors to every room—guests can access the common rooms through one door or go outside through French doors leading to the porch. The design makes the B&B more like a motel in its privacy and convenience. Rooms, all with private bath, have satellite TV and iPod docks. There are barbecue facilities on-site. The inn is a few blocks from the historic area.

9th Ave. and Main St. (P.O. Box 165), Skagway, AK 99840. ☎**907/983-3045.** Fax 907/983-3046. www.mile-zero.com. 6 units. High season $145 double; low season $85 double. Extra person $25. Rates include continental breakfast. MC, V. **Amenities:** Internet station. *In room:* Satellite TV, Wi-Fi ($5 fee).

Sgt. Preston's Lodge ★ Three buildings sit on a landscaped lawn just steps off Broadway, Skagway's main historic street, at 6th Avenue and State Street. U.S., Canada, and Alaska flags fly out front, underlining the theme—along with the tan, red, and green paint scheme—of the tidy image of the Royal Canadian Mounted Police. Once inside, you will find typical, modern motel rooms, the best choice in town for those who simply want a comfortable place to sleep for a reasonable rate. Ten rooms have only shower stalls—no tubs. The lobby, recently fixed up in 2009, has a computer station and shelves of books.

370 6th Ave. (P.O. Box 538), Skagway, AK 99840. ☎**866/983-2521** or 907/983-2521. Fax 907/983-3500. www.sgtprestonslodge.com. 38 units. High season $85–$120 double; low season $80 double. Extra person age 12 and over $10. AE, DISC, MC, V. **Amenities:** Courtesy car; Internet access. *In room:* TV/DVD, fridge, microwave.

A HOSTEL & CAMPING

A primitive **National Park Service Dyea Campground** has 22 well-separated sites along a river at the ghost town site 9 miles from Skagway. The campground has pit toilets and no water. RVs more than 27 feet are not allowed. The fee is

$10. The **Pullen Creek RV Park** (☎800/936-3731 or 907/983-2768) is near the small-boat harbor, with coin-operated showers. RV sites with power, water, and dump station use are $32, car camping sites are $24, tenting with no vehicle $16.

Skagway Home Hostel For more than 20 years, Frank Wasmer and Nancy Schave have opened up their historic home to hostellers, sharing their meals, refrigerator, bathrooms, laundry machines, and hospitality side by side with guests. The atmosphere is like off-campus shared housing at college, except the house is nicer and better kept. Bunks are in separate male, female, or co-ed dorms, except for the single private room. To reserve, use the website, as they don't return long-distance calls. In winter, reservations are required, as Frank and Nancy might otherwise not be there. Summer registration hours are from 5:30 to 10:30pm. No pets, alcohol, or smoking.

3rd Ave. near Main St. (P.O. Box 231), Skagway, AK 99840. ☎907/983-2131. www.skagwayhostel. com. 1 private room, 3 dorms. $15–20 per bunk; $50 double private room. MC, V. **Amenities:** Computer; shared kitchen and TV.

Where to Dine

Restaurants go out of business and open up faster in Skagway's entirely seasonal economy than anywhere else I know. It's not unusual for a third of the restaurants to be new each year. Asking around for a current recommendation may pay off.

Restaurants that stay open year-round tend to be better for two reasons: They can keep their staff, and they have to be good or they wouldn't make it through the winter in a town with fewer than 1,000 residents. The **Sweet Tooth Café,** 315 Broadway (☎907/983-2405), is a good, year-round diner, open for breakfast and lunch. **Glacial Smoothies and Espresso,** 336 3rd Ave., off State Street (☎907/983-3223), has built a year-round clientele by serving good coffee, bagels, and wraps. It's a fun little place for a light meal where the kids can play Monopoly or Hungry Hungry Hippos while you sip.

A seasonal place good for quick seafood lunch or dinner and a beer is **Skagway Fish Company,** on the boat harbor at 210 Congress Way (☎907/983-3474), with a casual, noisy dining room and a water view. You should also consider Olivia's, at the Historic Skagway Inn, and Poppies, at Jewell Gardens, mentioned above and earlier in the chapter; and Skagway Brewing Co., below.

Starfire ★ THAI The specialty here is spicy Thai cuisine— stir fries, curries, soups, and salads. The pad Thai came in a large portion with a cabbage salad and was cooked and seasoned just right. You can also choose from French dishes and local seafood cooked in basic Alaskan styles. The small, 10-table dining room is the restaurant's most memorable aspect, with dark hues and art that create an intimate and relatively upscale experience despite the paper napkins and tight quarters. Service is helpful and speedy, and the menu is clearly presented to help those not used to the food to order intelligently.

4th Ave. btw. Spring St. and Broadway. ☎907/983-3663. Reservations recommended. Lunch or dinner $14–$19. MC, V. Summer Mon–Fri 11am–10pm; Sat–Sun 4–10pm. Closed winter.

The Stowaway Cafe ★★ SEAFOOD Housed in a bright blue building overlooking the boat harbor, a 5-minute walk from the historic sites, this little restaurant has, for several years, turned out many of Skagway's best meals. Grilled and blackened salmon and halibut anchor the menu, but you can also get either fish with various creative preparations—salmon with a wasabi panko crust or with a green apple chipotle sauce, or even grilled halibut with Jamaican jerk spice and a cranberry chutney garnish. Another part of the attraction is the restaurant's hand-made charm, with a tiny dining room decorated in a mermaid theme that will keep your attention almost as well as the harbor view. They have a beer and wine license.

End of Congress Way near the small boat harbor. **☎907/983-3463.** Reservations recommended. Lunch $8–$15; dinner $16–$29. V. Summer daily 10am–10pm. Closed winter.

Nightlife

Incredibly, the ***Days of '98 Show*** has been playing since 1927 in the Fraternal Order of Eagles Hall No. 25, at 6th Avenue and Broadway (**☎907/983-2545**). Jim Richards carries on the tradition each summer with actors imported from all over the United States, doing at least two shows a day (10:30am and 12:30pm) during the summer, and sometimes as many as four. If you can catch an evening show, you can check out an hour of mock gambling at a casino run by the actors before the curtain. The actual performances, which last 1 hour, include sing-ing, cancan dancing, a reading of Robert Service's humorous period poetry, and the story of the shooting of Soapy Smith. Daytime shows are $20, evening $22. Children 12 and under are charged half price.

The **Red Onion Saloon,** at 2nd Avenue and Broadway, plays up its gold-rush history with costumed waitresses wearing corsets. It was a brothel origi-nally—what wasn't in this town?—and mock madams offer $5 tours of a "brothel museum" upstairs. The saloon often has live acoustic music. It closes in winter.

The **Skagway Brewing Company,** at 7th Avenue and Broadway, is a brew pub serving many beers made on site as well as a long menu of sandwiches, soup, and bar food. Happy hour is popular here, as is the local beer, and the attractive barroom with high tables and pub chairs has a well-stocked bar.

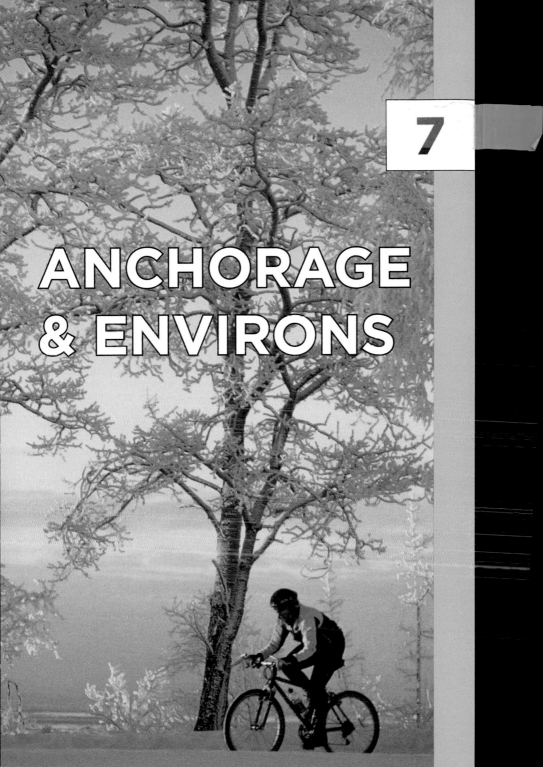

ANCHORAGE & ENVIRONS

7

A
s teenagers living in Anchorage, my cousin and I got a job painting the lake cabin of a family friend. He flew us out on his floatplane and left us there, with paint, food, and a little beer. A creek that ran past the lake was so full of salmon that we caught one on every cast until we got bored and started thinking of ways to make it more difficult. We cooked the salmon over a fire, then floated in a boat on the lake under the endless sunshine of a summer night, talking and diving naked into the clear, green water. We met some guys building another cabin one day, but otherwise we saw no other human beings. When the week was over, the cabin was painted—it didn't take long—and the floatplane came back to get us. As we lifted off and cleared the trees, Anchorage opened in front of us, barely 10 minutes away.

The state's largest city, Anchorage—where 40% of Alaska's population resides— is accused crushingly of being just like a city "Outside," not really part of Alaska at all. It's true that the closer you get to Anchorage, the more the human

PREVIOUS PAGE: **Biking in winter;** ABOVE: **A seaplane landing at Lake Hood Seaplane Base, the world's busiest, in Anchorage.**

development reminds you of the outskirts of Anytown, USA, with fast-food franchises, occasional traffic jams, and the ugly big-box retail development inflicted everywhere by relentless corporate logic. You often hear the joke, "Anchorage isn't Alaska, but you can see it from there," and writers piously warn visitors to land in Anchorage but move on as soon as possible, as if it's catching.

When I hear that advice, I think of the many great experiences I've had here—like painting that cabin, years ago. Anyone in Anchorage with a few hundred dollars for a floatplane can be on a lake or river with the bears and salmon in a matter of minutes, in wilderness deeper than any you could find in the Lower 48. **Chugach State Park** is largely within the city limits, but it's the size of Rocky Mountain National Park and has similar alpine terrain, with the critical difference that most of it is virtually never visited. Yet you can be climbing those mountains after a half-hour drive from your downtown hotel. **Chugach National Forest,** the nation's second largest, is less than an hour down the road. In downtown's **Ship Creek,** people catch 40-pound salmon from under a freeway bridge. Within

A fisherman drags away his catch after a day on Ship Creek.

the city's urban neighborhoods you can bike dozens of miles along the coast or through wooded greenbelts, or ski one of the nation's best Nordic skiing parks.

Anchorage is indeed a big American city, with big-city problems of crime and pollution, but it's also entirely unique for being surrounded by pristine and spectacular wild lands. Anywhere else, Anchorage would be known not for its shortcomings, but as one of America's greatest cities for outdoor enthusiasts.

Anchorage Yesterday & Today

Anchorage isn't old enough to have a sharp identity as a city. The first mayor to be born here, Mark Begich, was elected only in 2003, when he was barely 40 (now he is a U.S. Senator). The city started as a tent camp for workers mobilized to build the Alaska Railroad in 1915. A few houses and businesses went up to serve the federal employees who were building and later running the railroad, as Steve McCutcheon's father was. McCutcheon, a noted photographer who died in 1998, remembered a remote, sleepy railroad town enlivened by a couple of large World War II military bases, but never more than strictly functional. As one visitor who came in the early 1940s wrote, the entire town looked like it was built on the wrong side of the tracks.

Anchorage

Knik Arm

mud flats

Tony Knowles
Coastal Trail

Earthquake
Park **6**

7 L. Hood

TED STEVENS
ANCHORAGE
INTERNATIONAL
AIRPORT

DeLong
Park

DeLong L.

Sand L.

Jewel L.

Emerald
Hills Park

Campbell Lake

see downtown
Anchorage map

E 3rd Ave.
1
2
3 E 5th Ave.
E 6th Ave.
4

MERRILL
FIELD

5 W 15th Ave.
E 15th Ave.

Sitka
Street
Park

C. Smith
Mem.
Park

Chester Cr.

W Fireweed Ln.
E Fireweed Ln.
18
19
W Northern Lights Blvd.
16 **17**
E Northern Lights Blvd.
15
22 E Benson
W Benson Blvd.
14

24

W 36th Ave.
20 **21**
23
E 36th Ave.

13
12
10 **11**
9
Spenard
Lake
8 W Int'l. Airport Rd.

E Tudor Rd.

25

Connors
Lake Park

Connors L.

26

Dowling Rd.

Raspberry Rd.

New Seward Hwy.

Old Seward Hwy.

Taku L.

27

E Dimond Blvd.
28

W Dimond Blvd.

29

Lake Otis Pkwy.

Campbell Cr.

0   1 mi
0   1 km

Wisconsin St.
Hood Cr.
Spenard Blvd.
Minnesota Dr.
Arctic Blvd.
C St.
Gambel St.
Ingra St.
Jewel Lake Rd.
Westchester Lagoon

ATTRACTIONS
Alaska Aviation Heritage
  Museum **7**
Alaska Botanical Garden **25**
Alaska Museum of Natural
  History **2**
Alaska Native Heritage Center **1**
The Alaska Zoo **29**
Earthquake Park **6**

ACCOMMODATIONS
Alaska Backpackers Inn **3**
Courtyard by Marriott **8**

Dimond Center Hotel **28**
Elderberry B&B **27**
Holiday Inn Express **11**
Lake Hood Inn **10**
Lakeshore Motor Inn **12**
Millennium Alaskan Hotel
  Anchorage **9**
Residence Inn by Marriott **24**
Spenard Hostel International **13**

DINING
Arctic Roadrunner **18, 26**
Bear Tooth Theatrepub & Grill **16**

Cafe del Mundo **22**
Campobello Bistro **21**
City Diner **14**
The Greek Corner **19**
Jens' Restaurant **20**
Kaladi Brothers **15**
The Lucky Wishbone **4**
The Moose's Tooth Pub &
  Pizzeria **23**
New Sagaya's City Market **5**
Spenard Roadhouse **17**

McCutcheon looked out the picture window from his living room on a placid lake surrounded by huge, million-dollar houses, each with a floatplane pulled up on the green front lawn, and he recalled the year people started to take Anchorage seriously. It was the year, he said, when they started thinking it would be a permanent city, not just an encampment where you went for a few years to make money before moving on—the year they started building Anchorage to last. That year was 1957. Oil was discovered on the Kenai Peninsula's Swanson River, south of here. It was around that time that McCutcheon built his own house all by itself on a lake, far out in the country. At that time, you could homestead in the Anchorage bowl. Those who had the opportunity but chose not to—my wife's family, for example—gave it a pass only because it seemed too improbable that the flat, wet acreage way out of town would ever be worth anything.

Oil fueled Anchorage's growth like nitrogen fertilizer poured on a shooting weed. Those homesteads that went begging in the 1950s and early 1960s now have shopping malls and high-rise office buildings on them. Fortunes came fast, development was haphazard, and a lot was built that we'd all soon regret. I had the bizarre experience of coming home from college to the town I'd grown up in and getting completely lost in a large area of the city that had been nothing but moose browse the last time I'd seen it. Visitors found a city full of life but empty of charm.

In the last 20 years, that has started to change. Anchorage is slowly outgrowing its gawky adolescence. It's still young, prosperous, and vibrant—and exhausting when the summer sun refuses to set—but now it also has some excellent restaurants, a good museum, a large Native cultural center, a nice little zoo, and culture in the evening besides the tourist melodramas you'll find in many Alaska towns. People still complain that Anchorage isn't really Alaska—in Fairbanks, they call it "Los Anchorage" (and in Anchorage, Fairbanks is known as "Squarebanks")—yet the great wilderness around the city remains intertwined with its streets. Along with a quarter million people, Anchorage is full of moose—so many, they're considered pests and wintertime hazards. The urban area is home to an estimated 250 black bears and 65 brown or grizzly bears. Since three urban bear attacks in the summer 2008, some commentators have said we should somehow get rid of them, but no one has suggested how to stop more from coming back if such a plan succeeded, since the city is surrounded by prime bear habitat. Wildlife of all kinds infiltrates a system of parks, greenbelts, and bike trails that brings the woods into almost every neighborhood.

Anchorage stands on broad, flat sediment between the Chugach Mountains and the silt-laden waters of upper Cook Inlet. At water's edge, mud flats not yet made into land stretch far offshore when the tide is at its low point, as much as 38 vertical feet below high water. There's a **downtown area** of about 8 by 20 blocks, near Ship Creek where it all started, but most of the city lies on long commercial strips. Like many urban centers built since the arrival of the automobile, the layout is not particularly conducive to any other form of transportation. But the roads go only so far. Just beyond, wilds beckon in the Chugach, along the trails of Turnagain Arm, at Alyeska Ski Resort in Girdwood, in Prince William Sound, and in the Matanuska and Susitna valleys. You'll find ways to that wilderness, and the urban pleasures by its side, throughout this chapter.

ESSENTIALS
Getting There

BY PLANE You'll probably get to Anchorage at the start of your trip by air, as the city receives by far the most flights linking Alaska to the rest of the world, on many airlines. The **Ted Stevens Anchorage International Airport** is a major hub (on the subject of Senator Stevens's recent travails, see "Alaska's Political Earthquake," p. 32). Seattle has the most frequent flights connecting to Anchorage, with numerous domestic carriers flying nonstop all day. (See "Getting There & Getting Around," in chapter 3, for more details.) Within Alaska, most flights route through here, even for communities that are much closer to each other than they are to Anchorage. **Alaska Airlines** (℡800/252-7522; www.alaskaair.com) is the dominant carrier for Alaska destinations, and the only jet operator to most Alaska cities.

Various commuter carriers link Anchorage to rural destinations not served by jet, offering a convenient, time-saving alternative to driving to communities such as Homer, Kenai, or Valdez. **Era Aviation** (℡800/866-8394 or 907/266-8394; www.flyera.com), one of the largest for Southcentral Alaska destinations, was recently sold to a Fairbanks operator, **Frontier Flying Service** (℡907/450-7250; www.frontierflying.com). For the present, Era is operating separately, but changes are expected. In any event, tickets also can be booked through Alaska Airlines.

Unless your hotel has a courtesy van or you rent a car, a taxi is probably the best way to get downtown from the airport. A **taxi ride** downtown from the airport runs $18 to $20. Try **Alaska Yellow Cab** (℡907/222-2222). Shuttle vans serve the airport, with arrangements changing frequently. Ask at the visitor information desk in the baggage claim area. The **People Mover** city bus connects the airport and the downtown transit center hourly. Take Spenard Route 7A (every other Route 7 bus on weekdays). For finding schedules and other details on using the People Mover, see "Getting Around," below.

BY CAR There's only one road to the rest of the world: the Glenn Highway. It leads through the Mat-Su Valley area and Glennallen to Tok, where it meets the Alaska Highway, 330 miles from Anchorage. Thirty miles out of Anchorage, the Glenn meets the Parks Highway, which leads to Denali National Park and Fairbanks. The only other road out of town, the Seward Highway, leads south to the Kenai Peninsula. See "Alaska's Highways a la Carte" (p. 502) in chapter 10 for a review of all the roads. For more on driving to Alaska, see chapter 3.

BY BUS Alaska/Yukon Trails (℡800/770-7275; www.alaskashuttle.com), a van and mini-bus service, runs between Anchorage and Fairbanks, with a stop at Denali National Park and Talkeetna. From Fairbanks, they run tours to Dawson City and Whitehorse. In Anchorage they stop at the airport, hostels, and downtown. A one-way ticket to Denali costs $75 and to Fairbanks $99. Various other van and bus services offer transportation to and from Seward, Homer, Talkeetna, Denali National Park, Fairbanks, and other points; options are listed in the sections on each of those places.

BY RV A recreational vehicle is a popular way to explore the region. Renting an RV in Anchorage for a tour is covered below under "Getting Around."

Downtown Anchorage.

Driving an RV to Alaska is covered in chapter 3. It's also possible to come to Alaska with your own RV without making the time-consuming return trip by shipping your RV back from Anchorage to Tacoma, Washington, and flying to meet it (since southbound ships are relatively empty, you get a special rate). Contact **Totem Ocean Trailer Express** (☎800/234-8683 in Anchorage, or 800/426-0074 in the Lower 48; www.totemocean.com).

In addition, some firms offer one-way rentals beginning or ending in Anchorage. **Alaska Motorhome Rentals** (☎800/323-5757; www.bestof alaskatravel.com) offers several city pairs, allowing visitors to drive one-way from Seattle, to rent after riding the ferry partway, or to rent between Anchorage and Fairbanks. Sample rates. Skagway to Anchorage carries a drop-off fee of $795 to $995, plus the cost of the rental, $209 to $249 a day in the high season, plus mileage (or pay $35 a day for unlimited mileage), gas (budget generously), and tax. Check the website for discounts. The same company has another operation, **Alaska Highway Cruises** (☎800/323-5757), that provides packages to cruise one-way, tour Alaska in an RV, and fly home. For more on that option and on one-way rentals from the balance of the Lower 48, see chapter 3.

BY RAIL The **Alaska Railroad** (☎800/544-0552 or 907/265-2494; www.alaskarailroad.com) connects Anchorage with Seward and Whittier to the south and Fairbanks, Denali National Park, and Talkeetna to the north. It's a fun way to travel, with expert commentary in the summer, good food, and clean, comfortable cars. However, the train is priced as a tourism excursion and costs more than ordinary transportation. Most trains run only in the summer, but a snowy 12-hour odyssey to Fairbanks runs once a week all winter. The summer fare to Fairbanks is $210 one-way; the winter fare is $150 one-way, $131 for Alaska residents. See chapter 9 on Denali National Park and sections on other destinations for fares and service details.

Orientation

Many visitors never make it beyond the **downtown** area, the old-fashioned grid of streets at the northwest corner of town where the high-rise hotels and gift shops are located. Street numbers and letters work on a simple pattern, and navigation is easy. Beyond downtown, most of Anchorage is oriented to commercial strips, and you'll need a map to find your way. It's easy to orient yourself, because you can always see the huge Chugach Mountains on the east side of the Anchorage bowl. Some parts of greater Anchorage are in distinct communities outside the bowl, including **Eagle River** and **Eklutna,** within half an hour on the Glenn Highway to the northeast, and **Girdwood** and **Portage,** on the Seward Highway, 45 minutes to the south. The suburban **Matanuska and Susitna valleys** (known as Mat-Su) lie an hour north of the city on the Glenn and Parks highways.

Getting Around

BY RENTAL CAR Driving is the most practical way for most independent travelers to tour the main part of Alaska, and the location of Anchorage at the hub of transportation networks makes it the handiest place to start. A car improves a visit to Anchorage, too, as the city is spread out and public transportation and taxi service are far less practical. Most major car-rental companies operate in Anchorage, largely from the car-rental facility next to the main terminal at the airport. A compact car for $50 a day, with unlimited mileage, is a fair deal. The airport adds a 10% concession fee plus a $4-a-day facility fee, which you can avoid by renting off-site from **Avis,** at 5th Avenue and B Street (☎ 800/230-4898 or 907/277-4567; www.avis.com), or several other firms. The city charges an 8% rental-car tax, and the state adds an additional 10% tax. Including the airport fees, taxes total well over a third of the rental price. Cars can sell out in summer, so reserve ahead.

BY RENTAL RV Several large RV-rental agencies operate in Anchorage (see "Getting There," above). High-season rates for a mid-sized unit are around $1,500 to $1,800 a week, plus the large amount of fuel RVs use and taxes; a truck camper (the kind of unit that is on a pickup truck) rents for closer to $100 a day. Recently, off-season discounts and sales have lowered these prices, and last-minute renters may be able to dicker for a good price if the operator has extra units that aren't rented. **ABC Motorhome Rentals,** 3875 Old International Airport Rd.

Car Wheels on Gravel Roads

Contracts for most car-rental agencies do not allow vehicles on gravel roads, and none of the name-brand companies' agreements do. Pavement will get you to all the major places tourists go, but some magnificent back roads are unpaved, such as the Denali Highway or Mc-Carthy Road (covered in chapters 9 and 10, respectively). Violating the rental contract places you at risk of paying out of pocket for repairs and the rental agency's lost business if the car is damaged. In Anchorage, **High Country Car and Truck Rental (** 888/685-1155 or 907/562-8078; www.highcountryanchorage.com) does rent for use on gravel highways (although not the Dalton Hwy.). I've also located a couple of agencies in Fairbanks that offer the service (p. 516).

Blking the Tony Knowles Coastal Trail.

(☎800/421-7456 or 907/279-2000; www.abcmotorhome.com), charges no mileage fee. See chapter 3 for more on this option.

BY BUS In a city as spread out as Anchorage, city buses will always be a slower and less convenient choice than cabs or rental cars, but the **People Mover** system (☎907/343-6543; www.peoplemover.org) is well-run and perfectly practical for destinations that are served by direct routes from downtown. A new website (http://bustracker.muni.org/infopoint) uses a map to track the exact location of each bus and the actual time it will arrive at any stop, making the system easy to use for a novice. Bus fares all over town are $1.75 for adults; $1 for ages 5 to 18; 50¢ for those over age 60, with disabilities, or with a valid Medicare card; free ages 4 and under. The transit center bus depot is at 6th Avenue and G Street. Buses generally come every half-hour, hourly on weekends; you will need to go online and figure out your route and timing in advance.

BY BIKE The network of bike trails is a great way to see the best side of Anchorage, but not a practical means of point-to-point transportation for most people. The **Tony Knowles Coastal Trail** starts right downtown (see "Getting Outside," later in this chapter). Good street bikes are usually for rent near Elderberry Park downtown, at the start of the Coastal Trail, from **Pablo's Bike Rental**, a booth at the corner of 5th and L (☎907/250-2871; www.pablobicyclerentals.com). Rates are $15 for 3 hours, $30 for a day.

A bike-rental shop with a wide choice of equipment is in the blue 4th Avenue Marketplace at 4th and C: **Downtown Bicycle Rental** (☎907/279-5293; www.alaska-bike-rentals.com). Rates start at $16 for 3 hours, $4 each additional hour; max $32 per day. The shop also carries tandems, kids' bikes, and trailers, as well as clip-in shoes and pedals for advanced cyclists. The shop also offers a hikers' shuttle to the Glen Alps parking lot, the trail head for Flattop Mountain (p. 329).

Visitor Information

The **Anchorage Convention & Visitors Bureau,** 524 W. 4th Ave., Anchorage, AK 99501-2212 (℡**907/276-4118;** fax 907/278-5559; www.anchorage.net), offers information on the city and the entire state at its centers and extensive website (the site even has a feature to allow visitors to ask questions of staffers by email). The main location is the **Log Cabin Visitor Information Center,** downtown at 4th Avenue and F Street (℡**907/274-3531;** open daily June–Aug 7:30am–7pm, May and Sept 8am–6pm, Oct–Apr 9am–4pm). If it's crowded, go to the storefront office right behind it. You'll also find visitor information desks at the airport: in the baggage-claim area in the C concourse and in the international terminal.

The **Alaska Public Lands Information Center,** 605 W. 4th Ave. (across the intersection from the log cabin at 4th and F), Ste. 105, Anchorage, AK 99501 (℡**866/869-6887** or 907/644-3661; www.alaskacenters.gov; daily 9am–5pm in summer, Mon–Fri 10am–5pm in winter), can help anyone planning to spend time outdoors anywhere in Alaska. Exhibits in the grand room with high ceilings—the building was a 1930s post office and federal courthouse—orient visitors to Alaska's geography and outdoor activities, and make an excellent starting point for your trip. When you're ready for details, you will find all the land agencies represented by rangers whose advice is based on personal experience. Be sure to pick up the free booklets they distribute on the highways and parks you will be visiting, and select from an excellent selection of trail and field guides at the bookstore. Even if you have no need for information, stop in for free films, presentations, and children's programs. The center is well worth passing through the federal security checkpoint at the entrance.

Alaska Public Lands Information Center.

[FastFACTS] ANCHORAGE

Banks A bank is rarely far away, and all grocery stores and gas stations also have **ATMs.** Downtown, **Wells Fargo** (☎ **907/263-2016**) has a branch in the 5th Avenue Mall (5th Ave. and D St.), with a foreign exchange desk and wire transfer services.

Hospitals **Alaska Regional Hospital** is at 2801 DeBarr Rd. (☎ **907/276-1131**; www.alaskaregional. com), and **Providence Alaska Medical Center** is at 3200 Providence Dr. (☎ **907/562-2211**; www. providence.org).

Internet Access & Business Services Downtown, the **UPS Store,** at 645 G St., next to City Hall (☎ **907/276-7888**), has computers with high-speed connections for $1 per 5 minutes, or $10 an hour, as well as other services. Across 6th Avenue, half a block north, the **Kaladi Brothers** coffee shop offers computers in a fashionable setting.

Police The **Anchorage Police Department** has main offices at 4501 Elmore Rd., south of Tudor Road; for a nonemergency,

call ☎ **907/786-8500.** For nonemergency police business outside the city, call the **Alaska State Troopers,** 5700 E. Tudor Rd. (☎ **907/269-5511**).

Post Office Downtown, it's downstairs in the 4th Avenue Marketplace at D Street.

Taxes There's no **sales tax** in Anchorage. The **room tax** is 12%. **Car-rental taxes** amount to more than a third of the price between the state and local taxes and airport fees.

Special Events

For more events, and online calendars, see "The Performing Arts," later in this chapter.

The **Anchorage Folk Festival** (☎ **907/529-7383**; www.anchoragefolk festival.org), January 14 to 24, 2010, imports musicians and shows off local talent in free concerts, workshops, and jam sessions, as well as four guest musician dances that raise money for the festival. Check the website for times and venues.

The **Anchorage Fur Rendezvous Festival** (☎ **907/274-1177**; www.fur rondy.net), February 26 through March 7, 2010, is a winter celebration marking its 75th anniversary, recently rejuvenated with creative, youthful events such as the exciting and funny Running of the Reindeer, an event like the Pamplona Running of the Bulls but far safer for all involved, since reindeer are notably gentle animals. The MultiTribal Gathering and Native Arts Market should not be missed, and there are many community events, as well: a parade, fireworks, a carnival, craft fairs, snowshoe softball, dog-sled rides, and so on. The Rondy's traditional centerpiece (global warming permitting) is the speedy **World Champion Sled Dog Race,** a 3-day sprint event of about 25 miles per heat. In addition, the last weekend of the festival coincides with the start of the **Iditarod Trail Sled Dog Race** (☎ **907/376-5155**; www.iditarod.com). The Iditarod, long Alaska's biggest winter event, brings in a flood of visitors who link seeing the race with winter sports and festivals in Anchorage and Fairbanks. On the weekend of the start, the streets of Anchorage fill with foreign languages, as European visitors come in disproportionate numbers. The Iditarod begins from Anchorage the first

Fur Rendezvous Festival.

Saturday in March (in 2010, Mar 6) and then proceeds in trucks to re-start the next day in the Mat-Su Valley for the 1,000-mile run to Nome (see the section on Nome in chapter 11 for more details).

The **Anchorage Market & Festival** is a big street fair and farmer's market held every weekend from mid-May through mid-September at 3rd Avenue and E Street (✆907/272-5634; www.anchoragemarkets.com).

The stocked salmon runs in Ship Creek, which runs right through downtown Anchorage, produce one of the town's most popular summer activities (see "Roadside Fishing," p. 332). The **Slam'n Salm'n Derby** (✆907/646-4846; www.shipcreeksalmonderby.com), in early June, adds the possibility of winning money and prizes for catching king salmon. One-day tickets are $10, or $20 for the entire derby, and benefit the Downtown Soup Kitchen; they are available at the derby headquarters in the Alaska Railroad plaza near the creek.

The **Alaska State Fair** (✆907/745-4827; www.alaskastatefair.org), which culminates a 12-day run on Labor Day each year, is the biggest event in the area. It takes place in Palmer, 40 miles north of Anchorage on the Glenn Highway. In most ways, it's a typical state fair, with rides, booths, exhibits, contests, fireworks, and live music. Not typical are the vegetables. The good soil and long days in the Matanuska Valley around Palmer boost their growth to massive size, the stuff of childhood nightmares. Cabbages are the size of bean-bag chairs. A mere beach-ball-sized cabbage would be laughed off the stage. And it's not just the 100-pound cabbages. Imagine a 19-pound carrot, 35-pound broccoli, 43-pound beet, 63-pound celery, or 76-pound rutabaga (all records from the fair, among others you can check out on the website). The flower gardens are amazing, too, although not in the same way. Note that on the weekends the fair ties up traffic between Palmer and Anchorage, so it's wise to go mid-week if possible.

The **Carrs/Safeway Great Alaska Shootout basketball tournament** (✆907/786-1250; www.goseawolves.com), hosted by the University of Alaska

Anchorage, brings college men's and women's teams from all over the nation to the Sullivan Arena over Thanksgiving weekend and the preceding week.

The **Anchorage International Film Festival** (www.anchoragefilmfestival. org) has grown in a decade into a major event, with as many as a dozen screenings a day over a 2-week period in mid-December. The films come from every corner of the world, and include the obscure and bizarre as well as the profound.

WHERE TO STAY

A decent hotel room under $150 a night is almost unknown in Anchorage in mid-summer. To visit economically, choose a B&B or small inn. I've searched for such places, choosing those with character and reasonable prices. There are hundreds more, many of them just as good. Dozens of B&Bs are listed on a website maintained by the cooperative **Anchorage Alaska Bed and Breakfast Association** (www.anchorage-bnb.com). You can search by area of town or preferred amenities, or browse alphabetically. Links go directly to the B&Bs' own sites. Many have online availability calendars. Without a computer, call the association's hotline (**888/584-5147** or 907/272-5909), which is answered by hosts at member properties to offer referrals to places that meet callers' requirements.

Downtown

VERY EXPENSIVE

Besides the Hotel Captain Cook, described in full below, three other high-rise ho tels downtown offer a similar level of service without as much character or quite as many amenities. **Hilton Anchorage,** 500 W. 3rd Ave. (**800/HILTONS** [445-8666] or 907/272-7411; www.hilton.com), is a large conference hotel right at the center of downtown activities. The **Sheraton Anchorage,** 401 E. 6th Ave. (**800/478-8700** or 907/276-8700; www.sheratonanchoragehotel.com), is comparable to the Hilton, but in a slightly less attractive area a few blocks away. The **Anchorage Downtown Marriott,** 820 W. 7th Ave. (**888/236-2427** or 907/279-8000; www.marriotthotels.com), has a nice pool and fabulous views from rooms with wall-size picture windows.

Hotel Captain Cook ★★★ This is Alaska's great, grand hotel, where royalty and rock stars stay. Former Gov. Wally Hickel built the first of the three towers after the 1964 earthquake, and now the hotel fills a city block and anchors the downtown skyline. Inside, the earth tones and dark wood decor contribute to a fully realized (maybe a little excessive) nautical theme, with art memorializing Cook's voyages and enough teak to build a square-rigger. The regularly renewed rooms are decorated in a rich, sumptuous style using exquisite fabrics, unique pieces of custom-built furniture, and lots of varnished trim. Rooms are comfortable in size, but not as large as those in modern upscale chains, and all have a choice only of a king or two twin beds. Lots of custom tile, mirrors, and granite make up for the relatively small size of the bathrooms. There are great views from all sides, and you don't pay more to be on a higher floor. The pool, spa, and fitness facilities in the below-ground lower lobby are among the best in town.

Sophisticated food and superb service justify the high prices at The **Crow's Nest ★★★**, the city's most traditional fine-dining restaurant, on the hotel's top floor. Most tables have stupendous views, and high-backed booths lend intimacy

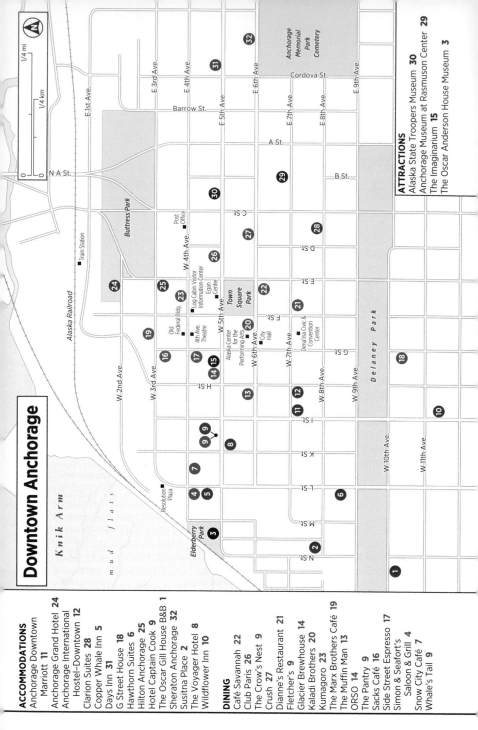

Downtown Anchorage

Knik Arm

mud flats

Elderberry Park

Buttress Park

Town Square Park

Delaney Park

Anchorage Memorial Park Cemetery

Resolution Plaza

Alaska Railroad

Train Station

Post Office

Old Federal Bldg.

Log Cabin Visitor Information Center

Egan Center

4th Ave. Theatre

Alaska Center for the Performing Arts

City Hall

Dena'ina Civic & Convention Center

N A St.

E 1st Ave.

E 3rd Ave.

E 4th Ave.

Barrow St.

E 5th Ave.

Cordova St.

E 6th Ave.

E 7th Ave.

E 8th Ave.

E 9th Ave.

A St.

B St.

C St.

D St.

E St.

F St.

G St.

H St.

I St.

J St.

K St.

L St.

M St.

N St.

W 2nd Ave.

W 3rd Ave.

W 4th Ave.

W 5th Ave.

W 6th Ave.

W 7th Ave.

W 8th Ave.

W 9th Ave.

W 10th Ave.

W 11th Ave.

1/4 mi

1/4 km

ACCOMMODATIONS

Anchorage Downtown Marriott **11**
Anchorage Grand Hotel **24**
Anchorage International Hostel–Downtown **12**
Clarion Suites **28**
Copper Whale Inn **5**
Days Inn **31**
G Street House **18**
Hawthorn Suites **6**
Hilton Anchorage **25**
Hotel Captain Cook **9**
The Oscar Gill House B&B **1**
Sheraton Anchorage **32**
Susitna Place **2**
The Voyager Hotel **8**
Wildflower Inn **10**

DINING

Café Savannah **22**
Club Paris **26**
The Crow's Nest **9**
Crush **27**
Dianne's Restaurant **21**
Fletcher's **9**
Glacier Brewhouse **14**
Kaladi Brothers **20**
Kumagoro **23**
The Marx Brothers Café **19**
The Muffin Man **13**
ORSO **14**
The Pantry **9**
Sacks Café **16**
Side Street Espresso **17**
Simon & Seafort's Saloon & Grill **4**
Snow City Café **7**
Whale's Tail **9**

ATTRACTIONS

Alaska State Troopers Museum **30**
Anchorage Museum at Rasmuson Center **29**
The Imaginarium **15**
The Oscar Anderson House Museum **3**

for a romantic dinner. The cuisine draws on many influences without being trendy and looks wonderful on the plate. Main courses range from $32 to $50. The wine list is voluminous, with just a few bottles under $40. **Fletcher's,** off the lobby, is an English pub serving good Italian-style pizza, pasta, and sandwiches. **The Pantry** is an above-average hotel cafe, with interesting entrees in moderate serving sizes. The **Whale's Tail** serves light meals, coffee, and cocktails amid overstuffed chairs and big TVs. It's a good place for a drink without feeling like you're in a bar.

939 W. 5th Ave. (P.O. Box 102280), Anchorage, AK 99510. ☎**800/843-1950** or 907/276-6000. Fax 907/343-2298. www.captaincook.com. 547 units. High season $255–$265 double, $265–$1,500 suite; low season $155–$165 double, $165–$1,500 suite. Extra person $20. AE, DISC, MC, V. **Amenities:** 4 restaurants; 3 bars; concierge; concierge-level rooms; separate men's and women's health clubs with racquetball, Jacuzzi, steam room and sauna; massage; indoor pool; 24-hr. room service. *In room:* TV w/pay movies, fridge, hair dryer, Wi-Fi.

EXPENSIVE

Here are a few chain-hotel options downtown for those who prefer national brands: **Days Inn,** 321 E. 5th Ave. (☎**800/DAYS INN** [329-7466] or 907/276-7226; www.daysinn.com), which has a courtesy van to the airport and rail depot; **Clarion Suites,** 325 W. 8th Ave. (☎**888/389-6575** or 907/274-1000; www. clarionsuites.com), an all-suite building across from the Federal Building, with a small pool; and **Hawthorn Suites,** 1110 W. 8th Ave. (☎**800/527-1133** or 907/222-5005; www.hawthorn.com), with similar facilities as the Clarion Suites, plus a Benihana Restaurant on-site.

Anchorage Grand Hotel ★★ This all-suite hotel has a rare combination of advantages: a superb, central location; solid rooms, fully equipped kitchens in every unit with house wares, dishwashers, and automatic ice makers; generous amenities; and rates competitive for this area of town. The hotel lacks much of a lobby, as the main entrance and wheelchair-accessible entrance lead directly into a stairway or hallway; that's because it is a reincarnation of an old, concrete apartment building. But the rooms and tiled bathrooms are quite large, decorated in a trim, subdued style with fine cabinetry, and immaculate. Despite the full kitchens, I've never noticed odors in the many rooms I've checked on several occasions, which is remarkable. Also despite the kitchen, they serve a free continental breakfast in the morning (and deliver the newspaper). Every unit has a bedroom and a queen-size sofa sleeper in the living room. Ask for a room on the quiet street side if you might be disturbed by railroad noise from the station facing the back of the building (although those rooms have better views).

505 W. 2nd Ave., Anchorage, AK 99501. ☎**888/800-0640** or 907/929-8888. Fax 907/929-8899. www.anchoragegrand.com. 31 units. Summer $205 double; winter $105 double. Extra person over age 13 $20. Rates include continental breakfast. AE, DISC, MC, V. *In room:* TV, hair dryer, kitchen, Wi-Fi.

Copper Whale Inn ★★ A pair of clapboard houses overlook the water and Elderberry Park right on the Coastal Trail downtown, with attractive rooms of various shapes and sizes, all redone in 2006 and 2008 with fashionable tans and browns, comfortable new beds, huge nature photographs and Alaskan art, and granite countertops in the bathrooms and common areas. The small upstairs rooms in the main building have wonderful views and funny angles; two of these share a bathroom. Lower-level rooms open onto a patio. The rooms in the newer building, nearer the water, have high ceilings on the upper level, and are larger, although none is very large. The staff is more than hospitable, creating the homey feeling of a country inn right in the urban core. They serve a large continental breakfast in the common area, which is comfortable for relaxing but not well suited for meals.

440 L St., Anchorage, AK 99501. ☎866/258-7999 or 907/258-7999. Fax 907/258-6213. www. copperwhale.com. 14 units, 12 with private bathroom. High season $185 double with shared bathroom, $210 double with private bathroom; low season $85 double with shared bathroom, $110 double with private bathroom. Extra person $20. Rates include continental breakfast. AE, DISC, MC, V. **Amenities:** Bike rental; concierge; access to health club; Internet. *In room:* TV, hair dryer, iron, Wi-Fi.

The Voyager Hotel ★★ This small hotel's emphasis on understated quality and central location have created a loyal clientele. The large, light rooms are equipped with fine linens and memory-foam mattresses, and thoughtfully designed kitchenettes. Business travelers will appreciate the well-equipped desks, with speaker phones, free wired and wireless broadband, and extra electrical outlets. Housekeeping is exceptional. The pick of the rooms are three on the northwest corner, which have an added meeting or sitting room but cost the same as the units that have only the bedroom; however, they're in high demand and often unavailable. There's nothing ostentatious or outwardly remarkable about the hotel, yet experienced travelers return again and again. Note that the hotel is nonsmoking.

501 K St., Anchorage, AK 99501. ☎800/247-9470 or 907/277-9501. Fax 907/274-0333. www. voyagerhotel.com. 40 units. High season $209 (up to 3 people per room); low season $109 (up to 3 people per room). Extra person $10. AE, DC, DISC, MC, V. **Amenities:** Restaurant; access to nearby health club with $7 day pass. *In room:* A/C, TV, hair dryer, kitchenette, Wi-Fi.

INEXPENSIVE

Hotel rooms reliably meeting most readers' standards are not available downtown for a price I can bring myself to call "inexpensive," but there are several small inns or B&Bs where you can save money and may also have a warmer, more rewarding visit. Besides those described in full below, the **Downtown Guest House,** 1238 G St. (☎907/279-2359; www.downtownguesthouse.com), is a two-bedroom apartment, beautifully decorated and with many amenities, for only $150 double in the summer. The owner is one of Alaska's most noted photographers.

G Street House Bed & Breakfast ★ 🏷 This appealingly traditional family home lies within easy walking distance of the downtown sights, in one of the city's oldest intact residential neighborhoods. Trim, understated guest rooms have private bathrooms and are priced reasonably. Among the B&B's chief attractions is the knowledgeable and charming host, Pam Tesche, an expert on local history, a gourmet cook, and an energetic community volunteer. The garden out back features a cigar court, and common rooms are open to all. You can book through the website.

1032 G St., Anchorage, AK 99501. ☎907/276-3284. Fax 907/279-8253. www.gstreethouse.com. 3 units. $115 double. Rates include full breakfast. AE, MC, V. Free parking. **Amenities:** Internet access. *In room:* Wi-Fi.

The Oscar Gill House Bed & Breakfast ★★ On the Delaney Park strip, just a few blocks from downtown, this is truly the oldest house in Anchorage—it was built in 1913, in Knik, before Anchorage was founded, and moved here on a barge a few years later. Oscar Gill was an early civic leader. The house was to be torn down in 1982, but was moved to storage by a historic preservation group; Mark and Susan Lutz saved it in 1993, transferring it to its present location and, with their own labor, restoring it authentically as a cozy bed-and-breakfast. Now it's on the National Register of Historic Places. Appropriate antiques sit on plank floors in rooms sized in those more modest times. With the period decoration, it's like visiting your grandmother's house when it was brand new. The outgoing Lutzes create a warm, social setting. Book early, as rooms fill up; you can check availability and select a room on their website.

1344 W. 10th Ave., Anchorage, AK 99501. ℓ/fax **907/279-1344.** www.oscargill.com. 3 units, 1 with private bathroom. High season $115 double with shared bathroom, $135 double with private bathroom; low season $75 double with shared bathroom, $85 double with private bathroom. Extra person $25 (except infants). Rates include full breakfast. AE, MC, V. **Amenities:** Babysitting by arrangement. *In room:* TV, hair dryer, Wi-Fi.

Susitna Place ★★ 🍴 Just a few blocks from the downtown core, where a narrow residential street reaches a quiet end, a nondescript door under a carport leads into a rambling house of rooms ranging from comfortable and inexpensive to grand. It turns out the street side is really the back of the house, which sits at the top of a high bluff facing an unobstructed view of Cook Inlet and Mount Susitna beyond, a view so unlike most urban vistas it is easy to forget you are right in town. A large, gracious common room and breakfast area and an adjoining balcony command this extraordinary view. Remodeling completed in 2007 filled the house with new furniture. The suite is quite luxurious, but the four rooms that share two bathrooms are the rarer find: Cozy and very clean, sharing this prime location, they allow travelers to save money without compromise. The hosts, successful journalists, are hospitable Alaskans.

727 N St., Anchorage, AK 99501. ℓ**907/274-3344.** Fax 907/272-4141. www.susitnaplace.com. 9 units, 5 with private bath. High season $105–$110 double with shared bath, $135–$140 with private bath, $165–$195 suite; low season $65–$70 double with shared bath, $80–$85 with private bath, $95–$115 suite. Extra person $15. Rates include continental breakfast. AE, DISC, MC, V. Free covered parking. *In room:* TV w/HBO, Wi-Fi.

Wildflower Inn ★ 🍴 The clapboard house behind a picket fence is across from the community's favorite gourmet grocery and casual eatery, New Sagaya's City Market. The B&B offers attractive, well-equipped two bedroom suites for only $139 double, with full bathrooms with tubs. They're decorated in Mission style. The enthusiastically friendly hosts keep the place immaculate, warm, and cozy, and they serve a fancy hot breakfast from 7 to 9:30am. The walk downtown is a little longer than from the other choices here, an easy half-mile. The bus stops right in front of the house. The same folks also rent apartment-like units off-site for very reasonable prices.

1239 I St., Anchorage, AK 99501. ℓ**877/693-1239** or 907/274-1239. Fax 907/222-3061. www.alaska-wildflower-inn.com. 3 units. High season $129–$139 suite; low season $79 suite. Extra person over age 6 $15. Rates include full breakfast. MC, V. **Amenities:** Computer/Internet access. *In room:* TV/VCR, hair dryer, Wi-Fi.

HOSTELS

Choose from two hostels downtown and another nearer the airport (described in the next section). **Anchorage International Hostel—Downtown,** 700 H St. (☎**907/276-3635;** www.anchoragehostel.org), occupies a centrally located concrete building with an urban feel. A coin-op laundry, kitchen, and storage are available, and they have Wi-Fi in some areas. Dorm rooms are small, with just a few bunks each, totaling 96 beds. A bunk is $25, a private room $65. Dorms close between 10am and 4pm daily. The curfew is midnight and checkout is 10am.

A much homier hostel that lies in a slightly seedy area just east of the downtown core, although still walkable, is **Alaska Backpackers Inn,** 327 Eagle St. (☎**907/277-2770;** www.alaskabackpackers.com), which opened in 2007. The atmosphere is friendly and vibrant in rooms with murals painted on the floors and walls and large, well-equipped gathering places, bathrooms, and kitchen. Bikes are for rent, and the hostel offers Internet access and a coin-op laundry. There is no curfew, but only guests with key cards can enter the building and the rooms. Smoking and alcohol are not allowed. A total of 94 beds and bunks fill 37 guest rooms, renting for $25 a bunk or $60 for a private room for two.

Beyond Downtown

These lodging choices are spread across Anchorage, with its long, wide, commercial strips. Like most residents, you need a car to stay here. On the other hand, by leaving downtown you can sometimes find larger, newer rooms for less, and you avoid downtown parking problems.

VERY EXPENSIVE

Dimond Center Hotel ★★ ⓘ This hotel is unique in several ways. Owned by the Seldovia Native Association, its primary clientele is rural Alaska residents coming to the big city for shopping and entertainment. That explains the location, on the south side of town, far from downtown sites, in a huge parking lot near a Wal-Mart store, a large shopping mall, and a bus transit center. Strange as it sounds, however, the location makes sense for many visitors: Chugach State Park, the zoo, and the Seward Highway and its many attractions are closer than from anywhere else you could stay. Since the owners built the hotel for themselves, the attention to comfort and detail are impressive. The common areas are stylish and decorated with Native art, and the rooms are grand: high ceilings, granite counters, attractive modern furniture, 42-inch flatscreen TVs, and pillow-top beds with comforters. The bathrooms are elaborate, with large shower areas and separate soaking tubs that can connect to the bedroom by opening wooden shutters.

700 E. Dimond Blvd., Anchorage, AK 99515. ☎**866/770-5002** or 907/770-5000. Fax 907/770-5001. www.dimondcenterhotel.com. 109 units. Summer $250–$300 double; winter $130–$179 double. Extra person $10. AE, DC, DISC, MC, V. Rates include continental breakfast. **Amenities:** Breakfast room; bar; free airport shuttle; access to nearby health club. *In room:* TV, fridge, hair dryer, microwave Wi-Fi.

Residence Inn By Marriott ★ Families who can afford it should stay here, and many business travelers would find it convenient, too. All units are suites with cooking facilities, and most have full kitchens. They're big enough to provide family members with privacy and sanity breaks, and save money over renting adjoining rooms in an ordinary hotel and dining out for all meals. Room decoration is light and hotel-typical; common areas have an Alaska Native motif reflecting the Native corporation management of the hotel. The clapboard building, with a gabled roof and stone accents, stands in a parklike enclave in the midtown commercial area, next to a high-rise office building and walking distance from a large Fred Meyer grocery and department store. The hotel offers a daily breakfast in a common area, and light evening meals with beer and wine Monday through Thursday, included in the room rate. Get driving directions, as it's a little tricky.

1025 35th Ave., Anchorage, AK 99508. **☎877/729-0197** or 907/729-0197. Fax 907/563-9636. www.residenceinn.com. 148 units. Summer $239–$299 suite; winter $169–$205 suite. Rates apply for any number of guests in unit. Rates include full breakfast. AE, DC, DISC, MC, V. **Amenities:** Free airport transfers; fitness room; pool; spa; outdoor basketball and mini–tennis courts; Wi-Fi. *In room:* TV w/pay movies, broadband Internet, kitchenette or full kitchen.

EXPENSIVE

Lake Hood Inn ★★ 📶 Pilot Bill Floyd built this place right next to his floatplane slip (he flies a Cessna 180) and filled it with fascinating aviation stuff: photographs, propellers, and even rows of seats from a Russian airliner. The guestbook is an aircraft log book. On the comfortable balconies, headphones are at the ready to listen to radio traffic between the tower and the aircraft you can see taxiing on the lake in front of you. Floyd invested in commercial-quality construction, and the rooms have the feel of a solid, upscale hotel room, not a family B&B; they are decorated in cool, muted shades with Berber carpet, light flooding in through big windows. The bathrooms have large shower stalls. Beds can be configured as two twins or as one king. Two front rooms have their own balconies and cost $20 more; the two back rooms have access to a shared balcony and are smaller. All four rooms are up a flight of stairs.

4702 Lake Spenard Dr., Anchorage, AK 99509. **☎866/663-9322** or 907/258-9321. www.lakehoodinn.com. 4 units. $169–$189 double. Extra person over age 16 $20. Rates include continental breakfast. AE, DISC, MC, V. **Amenities:** Fish freezer; guest kitchen. *In room:* TV/VCR, fridge, hair dryer, high-speed Internet.

INEXPENSIVE

Elderberry Bed & Breakfast 📶 If you want to make new friends, stay at this bed and breakfast, where visitors mingle in the residents' living quarters like houseguests. Linda and Norm Seitz, brimming with old-time Alaskan hospitality, enjoy telling about their experiences as long-time residents. The house, across from a large apartment complex, is a typical middle-class subdivision home, surrounded by flowers and, inside, immaculate and full of memorabilia. Located near the airport, it makes a good first stop on a trip—the Seitzes take pride in orienting their guests and letting them in on local secrets. The three rooms are small but charming, with floral and nautical themes. Two have bathrooms attached, and one has a private bathroom across the hall.

8340 Elderberry St., Anchorage, AK 99502. **☎907/243-6968.** www.elderberrybb.com. 3 units. Summer $95–$115 double; winter $75 double. Extra person $15. Rates include full breakfast in summer, continental breakfast winter. MC, V. **Amenities:** Internet access. *In room:* TV/VCR.

A HOSTEL

Spenard Hostel International, 2845 W. 42nd Ave. (☎907/248-5036; www. alaskahostel.org), is a friendly place near the airport, with free phones, inexpensive bike rental, storage, Internet access, and laundry machines. It feels more like communal housing than an impersonal hostel. There are three lounges for different activities and three kitchens. The owner has installed heat exchangers in the bedrooms to keep the air fresh. You can come and go 24 hours a day. The office is open daily from 9am to 1pm and from 7 to 11pm in summer, only 7 to 11pm winter. Beds are $25 by cash or check, $27 if you use a credit card (Visa or MasterCard).

CAMPING

Anchorage is a big city, and to find natural camping I recommend going beyond the urban area. The two closest state park campgrounds to Anchorage are at Bird Creek, to the south of town, and Eagle River, just to the north. The **Bird Creek Campground** is one of my favorites. It sits next to Turnagain Arm and the salmon-filled creek. A paved pathway passes by under the large spruce trees. There are 28 sites, and the fee is $15 per night. From Anchorage drive 25 miles south on the Seward Highway to milepost 101. The 57-site **Eagle River Campground** sits in a thickly wooded riverside spot, and it's well developed with paved roads and large sites with lots of privacy. It costs $15 a night, and sites can be reserved

 Rooms Near the Airport

Good, inexpensive standard motel rooms near the airport are rare to the vanishing point, although up-scale rooms and B&Bs are readily available. The prize winner in my search for reasonably priced hotel rooms with consistently high quality is the **Lakeshore Motor Inn** (☎800/770-3000 or 907/248-3485; www.lakeshoremotorinn.com). The rate of $159 a night double, at peak season, includes a continental breakfast, Wi-Fi, and use of a 24-hour courtesy van. Don't be deterred by the older concrete building: The rooms inside are inviting.

Two good chain hotels stand near the airport, with higher rates: **Courtyard by Marriott** (☎800/314-0782 or 907/245-0322; www. marriott.com/anccy), with many amenities and a pool, at $199 to $299 double in summer; and the **Holiday Inn Express**

(☎800/HOLIDAY [465-4329] or 907/248-8848; www.hiexpress. com), at $269 double in the summer.

A large, full-service hotel stands lakeside near the airport, **Millennium Alaskan Hotel Anchorage** (☎800/544-0553 or 907/243-2300; www.millenniumhotels.com/ anchorage). It might be a huge fishing and hunting lodge judging by the large lobby, with its warm colors and fly rods and animal mounts on display, but the rooms, on long corridors in a wooden building, are loaded with comfort and amenities. The hotel has two restaurants and offers many services. High season rates are $239 to $319 double.

I also recommend Lake Hood Inn (p. 301), Elderberry Bed & Breakfast (p. 301), and Spenard Hostel International (below), all of which are handy to the airport.

in advance. Book up to a year ahead at ☏800/952-8624 or 907/694-7982 (www. lifetimeadventures.net). They also have a couple of tents with cots for rent. Take the Glenn Highway 12 miles north from Anchorage and exit at Hiland Road. Both Bird Creek and Eagle River tend to fill up, so it's wise to arrive early in the day, especially for weekends; the next closest public campgrounds to the south are at Portage Glacier (p. 345) and to the north at Eklutna Lake (p. 331).

If you seek a place to hook up your RV in town, **Anchorage Ship Creek RV Park** (☏800/323-5757; www.bestofalaskatravel.com) is nearest to downtown. The site is in an industrial area a short drive away but a little too far to walk to the attractions. Sites with water, sewer, and power are $46 in the summer.

WHERE TO DINE
Downtown
EXPENSIVE

Club Paris ★★ STEAK Coming from a bright spring afternoon into midnight darkness, under a neon Eiffel Tower and past the bar, I sat down at a secretive booth for two, and felt as if I should lean across the table and plot a shady 1950s oil deal with my companion. And I would probably not have been the first. In contrast to Sullivan's Steakhouse, across the street, which contrives a masculine, retro feel, Club Paris is the real thing, decorated with mounted swordfish and other cocktail-era decor. The club is the essence of old Anchorage boomtown years, when the streets were dusty and an oil man needed a classy joint in which to do business. Steak, of course, is what to order, and rare really means rare. It's consistently voted the best in town. Ask for the blue cheese stuffing; the stuffed filet is worth the years it probably takes off your coronary arteries. They have a full bar.

417 W. 5th Ave. ☏907/277-6332. www.clubparisrestaurant.com. Reservations recommended. Lunch $7–$15; dinner $18–$44. AE, DC, DISC, MC, V. Mon–Thurs 11:30am–2:30pm and 5–10pm; Fri–Sat 11:30am–2:30pm and 5–11pm; Sun 4–9pm.

The Marx Brothers Cafe ★★★ NEW AMERICAN A restaurant started by three friends back when gourmet food was an exotic hobby in Anchorage long ago became the standard of excellence in the state. Treatments of Alaska seafood that began here as cutting-edge creative cuisine now turn up in many of the best restaurants, yet chef Jack Amon's signature macadamia nut–encrusted halibut is nowhere done better. He still presides in the kitchen of the cottage downtown, one of the city's first houses, while maître d' Van Hale manages the front, preparing his famous Caesar salad at tableside, a ritual that allows him to schmooze with anyone he chooses in the tiny dining rooms. His attitude mirrors the casual elegance of the entire evening, where those wearing ties are in the minority. I've labeled the cuisine "New American" because I had to choose from a list, but the cookery is truly eclectic, ranging from Asian to Italian to uncategorizeable, although always turned out flawlessly. The changing menu is not long, but the wine list is the size of a dictionary, winner of many awards, but potentially intimidating. A meal is an experience that takes much of the evening, and most entrees are more than $30. Save room for the exceptional desserts.

627 W. 3rd Ave. ☎907/278-2133. www.marxcafe.com. Reservations required. Main courses $28–$36. AE, DC, MC, V. Summer Tues–Sat 5:30–10pm; winter Tues–Thurs 6–9:30pm, Fri–Sat 5:30–10pm.

ORSO ★★ MEDITERRANEAN This restaurant is unique in Anchorage for serving interesting food even though it is large and oriented to the downtown tourist trade. The warm colors of the ornate dining room are lightened with big, modern paintings. Bold flavors amp up a long menu full of surprises. The mushroom ravioli, with a generous dose of smoked salmon, was rich and strongly flavored. Service is professional but not stuffy, and the food comes fast enough not to use up the entire evening. Generally, the prices are reasonable for this kind of food, and the bar offers "Bear Bites," discounts on appetizers before 6 and after 9pm. We also enjoy the bar for a drink and dessert at the end of an evening out (it's open an hour later than the dining room and stays open through the afternoon).

737 W. 5th Ave. ☎907/222-3232. www.orsoalaska.com. Reservations recommended. Lunch $10–$15; dinner pasta or main course $12–$33. AE, MC, V. Summer Sun–Thurs 11:30am–4pm and 5–10pm, Fri–Sat 11:30am–4pm and 5–11pm; winter Tues 11:30am–2:30pm and 5–9:30pm, Wed–Thurs 11:30am–2:30pm and 5–10pm, Fri 11:30am–2:30pm and 5–11pm, Sat 5–11pm, Sun 5–9:30pm, closed Mon.

Sacks Cafe ★★★ INTERNATIONAL This is the most fashionable restaurant in town, and also one of the best. The storefront dining room, in warm Southwest colors and sharp angles, resembles a showcase for the food and diners, who can sit at tables or at a tapas bar. The cuisine defies categorization, but is consistently interesting and creative, frequently with Thai influences. The menu changes, but one consistent offering was chicken with scallops, shiitake mushrooms, snow peas, udon noodles, ginger cream sauce, and black bean salsa. Vegetarians do as well as meat eaters. For lunch, the sandwiches are unforgettable, with choices such as shrimp and avocado with herb cream cheese on sourdough. Do not fail to try the tomato soup with Gorgonzola. The beer and wine list is extensive and reasonably priced. They serve brunch Saturday and Sunday 10am to 2:30pm.

The Best Takeout in Town

Anchorage has great takeout food (as my family's continued survival attests). Downtown, **The Muffin Man,** 817 W. 6th Ave. (☎907/279-6836), produces some of the best meals eaten at the city's desks, including the memorably delicious smoked red salmon and cream cheese sandwich. You can eat in the sunny, tiled dining room, too, and they serve wine and local beer.

The best, most original burgers are at **Arctic Roadrunner,** with locations on Arctic Boulevard at Fireweed Lane and on Old Seward

Highway at International Airport Road. Try the Kodiak Islander, which has peppers, ham, onion rings, and God knows what else on top.

We get carry-out Chinese from **New Sagaya's City Market** (☎907/274-6173; www.newsagaya. com) at the corner of 13th and I streets. It's also a wonderful gourmet grocery and community meeting place, and has a good deli and Italian-style brick-oven pizza. Pack a picnic here, or eat at the enclosed or sidewalk dining areas.

328 G St. **☎907/274-4022.** www.sackscafe.com. Reservations recommended. Lunch $5–$15; dinner main courses $18–$34. AE, MC, V. Mon–Fri 11am–2:30pm and 5–9:30pm (until 10:30pm Fri); Sat 10am–2:30pm and 5–10:30pm; Sun 10am–2:30pm and 5–9:30pm.

Simon and Seafort's Saloon and Grill ★★ GRILL Simon's, as it's known, is a jolly beef and seafood grill where voices boom off the high ceilings. On sunny summer evenings, the rooms, fitted with brass turn-of-the-20th-century saloon decor, fill with light off Cook Inlet, down below the bluff; the views are magnificent. The food is consistently good. Besides a nightly list of specials, the restaurant boasts of its macadamia nut-stuffed halibut, but most of the cuisine is simpler—prime rib, for example. Service is warm and professional, and quick enough to allow time for other evening activities. Children are treated well. To enjoy the place on a budget, order a sandwich and soup for lunch in the well-stocked bar; it's open until 11pm every night. Getting a table in the restaurant at a reasonable hour requires advance planning in peak season or on off-season weekends; call a couple of days ahead.

420 L St. **☎907/274-3502.** Reservations recommended. Lunch $7.50–$18; dinner main courses $16–$42. AE, DISC, MC, V. Summer Mon–Fri 11am–2:30pm and 4:30–10pm, Sat–Sun 4:30–10pm; winter Mon–Thurs 11:00am–2:30pm and 5–9:30pm, Fri 5–10pm, Sat 4:30–10pm, Sun 4:30–9pm.

MODERATE

Cafe Savannah ★★ SPANISH Right across from town square, this storefront restaurant is stylish, relaxing, and serves interesting and delightful food. The specialty is tapas, and a popular way to dine is to order many plates and then share them. Selections under $7 include items such as *hongo relleno con chorizo* (stuffed portobello mushroom caps with Spanish chorizo and manchego cheese) or cold *gambas embueltas con jamón* (shrimp with cilantro sauce wrapped with prosciutto). I learned a lot eating here! For a simpler lunch, the grilled sandwiches and soups are spicy and satisfying. The dining room has tables and a bar decorated with colored stones and bent flatware under a hard, clear surface. Monthly art shows hang on the walls. Don't choose to dine here if you're in a rush, or if you're looking for warm Alaskan hospitality; although I enjoyed the waiter's classy attitude, we didn't become buddies.

508 W. 6th Ave. **☎907/646-9121.** All items $4–$29. AE, DC, DISC, MC, V. Mon–Thurs 11am–3pm and 5–10pm, Fri–Sat 11am–3pm and 5–11pm.

Crush ★★ BISTRO Situated in the city's small upscale shopping area, across from Nordstrom's, the elegant, spare dining room occupies an appealing space in a small brick building with a curved facade. The bistro presents itself as a wine bar that also serves food, and nearly 30 choices are available by the glass, but the cooking is terrific, too, and there's no reason to stay away even if wine holds no interest. Besides special entrees, priced from $16 to $21, the dinner menu largely consists of inexpensive plates of noshes and delicacies to pass around the table. For lunch, all selections are $10: wonderful salads or sandwiches, which are served with soup or a salad. In the morning, the restaurant serves coffee and pastries, and it also has a limited menu from 2:30 to 5:30pm. Even if trendy, it's a place for a low-stress, reasonably priced meal with food as good as at the most ponderous sit-down restaurants in town.

343 W. 6th Ave. **☎907/865-9198.** www.crushak.com. Lunch $10; dinner $7–$14. AE, DC, MC, V. Mon–Thurs 8am–11pm; Fri 8am–midnight; Sat 5pm–midnight.

Glacier Brewhouse ★ BREW PUB An eclectic and changing menu is served in a large dining room with lodge decor, where the pleasant scent of the wood-fired grill hangs in the air. It's a lively place to see others and be seen. A glass wall shows off the brewing equipment, which produces eight or more hearty beers, and also turns out spent grain for bread that's then set out on the tables with olive oil. An advantage for travelers is the wide price range—a pizza with feta cheese, sundried tomato pesto, and roasted garlic is $11; crab legs are $37. The food is usually quite good. Choose this place for a boisterous meal with quick, casual service that will get you out in time to do something else with the evening. Do reserve ahead, however, as waits can be long.

737 W. 5th Ave. ☎**907/274-BREW** (274-2739). www.glacierbrewhouse.com. Reservations recommended. Lunch $8–$15; dinner $9–$34. AE, DC, DISC, MC, V. High season daily 11am–11pm; low season Mon 11am–9:30pm, Tues–Thurs 11am–10pm, Fri–Sat 11am–11pm, Sun 4–9:30pm.

Kumagoro ★ JAPANESE Anchorage has several good, authentic Japanese restaurants, but this one, right on the main tourist street downtown, has the most convenient location. Among my favorite lunches anywhere is their lunch box ($16), a large sampler of many dishes, including sushi, sashimi, and other tasty things, always a little different, that I can't always identify. The dining room is pleasantly low-key, with tables in rows, so you may have the opportunity to meet those seated next to you. The restaurant serves beer and wine.

533 W. 4th Ave. ☎**907/272-9905.** Lunch $8–$16; dinner main courses $16–$42. AE, DC, DISC, MC, V. Summer daily 11am–10:30pm; winter Mon–Sat 11am–9:45pm.

INEXPENSIVE

Dianne's Restaurant ✦ CAFE This sandwich shop is my first choice for a quick, healthful, inexpensive lunch downtown. Located off the lobby of a tall, glass building, Dianne's cafeteria line fills with well-dressed office workers seeking the hearty freshly baked bread, soups, sandwiches, and specials turned out for the lunch hour. The atmosphere is bright and casual, and you don't waste your day eating. On a sunny day, choose a table in the courtyard. The restaurant does not have a liquor license.

550 W. 7th Ave., Ste. 110. ☎**907/279-7243.** www.diannesrestaurant.com. Main courses $4.75–$10. AE, DISC, MC, V. Mon–Fri 7am–4pm.

Snow City Cafe ★ CAFE This is the happening spot downtown for breakfast or lunch. What started as a smaller, granola-crowd place grew on the basis of hearty, tasty food and a friendly young waitstaff into a large, busy restaurant with lots of life, energy, and a diverse clientele. It's especially popular in the morning, when you'll rarely do better than the salmon cakes and eggs or omelets. Breakfast is served all day. Lunch, starting at 11am, includes comfort food such as mac and cheese or meat loaf, but also unusual sandwiches, such as roast beef and blue cheese, or the delicious portobello. The dining room is light and colorful, with a clean feel, and with tables out in the open amid lots of movement. The restaurant offers free Wi-Fi. As it's busy, consider calling 45 minutes ahead to get on the wait list. Small monthly art shows begin with artist receptions every first Friday, a pattern shared with all the downtown galleries. They serve beer and wine.

1034 W. 4th Ave. ☎**907/272-CITY** (272-2489). www.snowcitycafe.com. Breakfast and lunch $8–$12. AE, DISC, MC, V. Daily 7am–4pm (espresso counter only after 3pm on weekdays).

Beyond Downtown

EXPENSIVE

Jens' Restaurant ★★★ INTERNATIONAL Chef Jens Hansen is truly gifted. His restaurant is for the kind of diner who loves exciting food, surprises, and beautiful plates of new tastes and textures; the meals are about the food, sharing bites, and saying "Wow," and "How did he do that?" The cuisine is highly eclectic, but I won't call it experimental, because these dishes work far more often than any experimentalist has a right to expect. There's often only one item on the changing menu that isn't unusual or challenging: the superb pepper steak. Like everything, even that dish has a sauce, and it is complex and memorable. The wine list is exceptional but manageable and reasonably priced, and you can sip your selection while dining inexpensively on appetizers in a pleasant bar area; try the incredible spinach ravioli with Gorgonzola, for example. Desserts are sublime. The dining room is uncluttered and decorated with modern art. Service is highly professional, with each formally attired waiter assigned to just a few tables, and they earn their keep as well by helping diners learn about food and wine they have probably never tried.

701 W. 36th Ave. (**907/561-5367.** www.jensrestaurant.com. Reservations recommended. Lunch $9–$34; dinner main courses $18–$39. AE, DC, DISC, MC, V. Mon–Fri 11:30am–2pm; Tues–Sat 6–10pm; wine bar serves appetizers starting at 4pm. Closed Jan.

Coffeehouses

There are coffeehouses all over the city to get a cup of java and a pastry, and to meet people and engage in conversation. My favorite is **Side Street Espresso**, on G Street between 4th and 5th, a gathering place for artists, activists, and anyone who wants to trade ideas, sometimes with live acoustic music in the evening. **Cafe del Mundo**, at Northern Lights and Denali midtown, gathers an older crowd of businesspeople, yuppies, stay-at-home parents, and those looking for a comfortable meeting spot. **Kaladi Brothers** has several locations with Internet access, including the classy space in the back corner of the Alaska Center for the Performing Arts downtown, at 6th Avenue and G Street. Their location in the shopping center on Northern Lights Boulevard between Arctic and Minnesota is extremely popular, sharing space with the huge Title Wave used book store and just down from the essential REI sporting goods store.

MODERATE

Bear Tooth Grill ★★ 🥘 SOUTHWESTERN Food of this quality rarely comes for prices this low. Dishes such as the soy grilled halibut are sophisticated and nicely done, but take up only a small part of a menu that goes on and on with Mexican choices, sandwiches, and other selections inexpensive enough to make the restaurant fit for an after-work impulse—most main courses are under $11. The partners who own the restaurant started in business by making beer and then opened a pizzeria to sell the beer (see the Moose's Tooth, below); next they opened a theater-pub (see "Anchorage Nightlife," later in this chapter); the grill, in the same building, was the final addition. Eat tacos, wraps, or pizza watching a movie or at tables in the movie theater lobby, a loud, free-flowing setting perfect for kids and open for lunch Monday to Friday at 11am, and serving the full menu until the late-night closing. The grill is in a separate, calmer, and more confined dining room, best for couples and parties of four or fewer. The food comes more slowly, as befits the atmosphere. Tables are more comfortable than booths, but at peak times you have to take what you can get, often with a wait, so try to dine here early or late. Besides the beer, they have a full bar serving many margaritas and 20 wines by the glass.

1230 W. 27th Ave. ☎**907/276-4200.** Reservations not accepted. All items $6–$20. AE, DC, DISC, MC, V. Mon–Fri 11am–11pm; Sat–Sun 4–11:30pm.

Campobello Bistro ★★ NORTHERN ITALIAN BISTRO This quiet little midtown restaurant is amazingly like stepping into northern Italy, except for the Alaska seafood. Even the service has the quality of jocular professionalism I remember from Italy. The same priceless pair of waiters has developed a following over a decade in the restaurant. Unlike most of Anchorage's best restaurants, the bistro doesn't try to reinvent the cookbook. Most of the menu consists of recognizable dishes, such as veal Marsala or Italian sausage and polenta. Meals are bold, highly flavored, and entirely satisfying. The seafood crepe is fantastic. Those seeking the bland tomatoes and cheese of a typical Italian family restaurant should go elsewhere (Sorrento's and Romano's, both on Fireweed Lane, each do that tried-and-true formula well). The wine and food are reasonably priced.

601 W. 36th, Ste 10. ☎**907/563-2040.** Lunch $10–$13; dinner main courses $15–$25. DC, MC, V. Mon 11am–2:30pm; Tues–Fri 11am–2:30pm and 5–9pm; Sat 5–9pm.

City Diner ★ DINER In 2007, a pair of well-known local chefs opened this chrome and neon diner out of a Hollywood movie set. Standing at the corner of busy Benson Boulevard and Minnesota Drive (on the route downtown from the airport), the building is unmistakable and nearly irresistible, with its big clocks labeled "Time to Eat" and shiny metal siding. The counter, booths, and finishes inside carry the theme to its conclusion. It's all bigger, cleaner, and more contrived than any "real" diner, but fun anyway, and the food is better than you would expect. The grilled Reuben is probably the best I've had—and that's saying something. The menu includes many classic sandwiches, including an open-faced meatloaf, for non-classic prices (the meatloaf is $15). Entrees, including seafood and steak, are reasonably priced under $20. Six beers are on tap, including craft brews. Service is quick.

3000 Minnesota Dr. ☎**907/277-CITY** (277-2489). All main courses $7–$19. AE, DISC, MC, V. Daily 6am–11pm.

The Greek Corner ★ GREEK/ITALIAN When we need a relaxed place for a three-generation family meal, this place always seems to come to the top of the list. The dining room is sunny, spacious, and informal (one reason we feel comfortable taking the children here). The hospitality of the service is sincere and, when the place isn't too busy, it can feel as if you've been adopted by the wait staff. Food comes fast. I usually order the lamb chops, which are tender and seasoned and cooked just right, and come with perfectly prepared asparagus and baby potatoes. A dozen authentic traditional Greek dishes are on the menu, mostly priced around $15, or you can order from a list of old Italian favorites such as spaghetti or lasagna. They serve pizza, too, and reasonably priced lunches—a gyro with soup or a salad is $9.

201 E. Northern Lights Blvd. ☎907/276-2820. Lunch $5.50–$10; dinner main courses $10–$20. MC, V. Mon–Fri 11am–10pm; Sat noon–10pm; Sun 4–10pm.

Spenard Roadhouse ★ AMERICAN Anchorage has grown up enough to have a restaurant that celebrates the kitschy frontier culture of the 1970s with loving irony, displaying old license plates on the wall and offering TV dinners as specials. But the owners, a team who started two of the city's coolest restaurants individually (Sacks and Snow City Cafe), know the younger clientele who

Downtown Anchorage at 4th Avenue.

have made this part of Spenard newly hip don't mainly want the chocolate milk and macaroni and cheese on the menu, so they serve a broad range of choices, including a sumptuous blackened ahi tuna with yellow Thai curry, rice noodles, and pineapple salsa, as well as steaks, chops, sandwiches, pizza, and lots of small plates to share. The full bar makes good strong drinks and specializes in small batch and single barrel bourbons. It's a fun, social place to eat.

1049 W. Northern Lights Blvd. **☎907/770-7623.** www.spenardroadhouse.com. Lunch and dinner $9-$20. AE, DISC, MC, V. Daily 11am-11pm.

INEXPENSIVE

The Lucky Wishbone ★ 🎒 DINER This Anchorage institution of more than half a century (in high school we called it "The Bone") is where the real pioneer Alaska meets families out for a delicious, not-too-greasy fried chicken dinner and famous milkshakes (try the hot fudge) and other delights from the fountain. It is our children's favorite. One section of the counter is reserved for discussion of aviation and golf. When the beloved owners outlawed smoking years ago, it made the front page of the newspaper. It's authentic, not a tourist trap; indeed, the walk to most downtown hotels is too far to this location, among the car dealerships at the extreme east end of downtown. They have a drive-thru window.

1033 E. 5th Ave. **☎907/272-3454.** All items $3.50-$12. MC, V. Mon-Thurs 10am-10pm; Fri-Sat 10am-11pm.

The Moose's Tooth Pub and Pizzeria ★★ ☺ PIZZA The best pizza and beer in Anchorage undoubtedly come from this fun and friendly place. The microbrewery came first, but the pizza really is the greater accomplishment. It has a soft, light crust like Italian pizza but the oomph of American pizza. They offer many ingenious toppings, but not just to dump on: The combinations really work. The ambience is youthful, casual, and loud; the high energy means kids aren't out of place. The dining room, although handsomely built, still looks from top to bottom like a college town pizzeria. The only drawback is the restaurant's popularity, which can make for long waits at peak times. Also, the menu has few choices for anyone in your party who doesn't want pizza.

3300 Old Seward Hwy. **☎907/258-2537.** www.moosestooth.net. Large pizza $13-$25. AE, DC, DISC, MC, V. Summer Mon-Thurs 10:30am-midnight, Fri 10:30am-1am, Sat 11am-1am, Sun 11am-midnight; winter Mon 10:30am-11pm, Tues-Thurs 10:30am-midnight, Fri 10:30am-1am, Sat 11am-1am, Sun 11am-11pm.

WHAT TO SEE & DO

I've arranged this section starting with a self-guided walking tour through downtown Anchorage, followed by details on the downtown museums and then attractions that are farther afield. If you'd prefer to tour by bus, **Gray Line of Alaska's** Anchorage Highlights Tour (**☎800/544-2206;** www.graylineofalaska.com) takes 3 hours to visit downtown and the Ship Creek area, the Anchorage Museum, and the Alaska Native Heritage Center. It spends an hour at the center; not as long as I like to stay. The tour costs $49 for adults, half price for children 12 and under, including admission to the center.

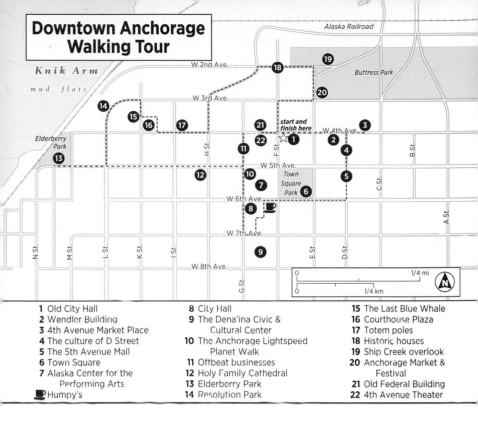

Downtown Anchorage Walking Tour

Knik Arm

mud flats

Alaska Railroad

W 2nd Ave.

Buttress Park

W 3rd Ave.

W 4th Ave.

start and finish here

W 5th Ave.

Town Square Park

W 6th Ave.

W 7th Ave.

W 8th Ave.

Elderberry Park

1/4 mi

1/4 km

1 Old City Hall	**8** City Hall	**15** The Last Blue Whale
2 Wendler Building	**9** The Dena'ina Civic &	**16** Courthouse Plaza
3 4th Avenue Market Place	Cultural Center	**17** Totem poles
4 The culture of D Street	**10** The Anchorage Lightspeed	**18** Historic houses
5 The 5th Avenue Mall	Planet Walk	**19** Ship Creek overlook
6 Town Square	**11** Offbeat businesses	**20** Anchorage Market &
7 Alaska Center for the	**12** Holy Family Cathedral	Festival
Performing Arts	**13** Elderberry Park	**21** Old Federal Building
☕ Humpy's	**14** Resolution Park	**22** 4th Avenue Theater

WALKING TOUR **DOWNTOWN ANCHORAGE**

START & FINISH: **4th Avenue and F Street.**

TIME· **2 hours (use the shortcuts noted for a briefer tour).**

Start at the **Log Cabin Visitor Information Center** at 4th Avenue and F Street. Outside is a sign that shows the distance to various cities and a 5,114-pound jade boulder put on display by Stewart's Photo Shop, an Anchorage institution that is just across the street.

Walk east, toward the mountains, to:

1 Old City Hall (1936)

The building is on the right of 4th Avenue as you approach E Street. The lobby contains a fun and illuminating free display on city history, including dioramas of the early streetscape, old photographs, and the fire bell and fire pole that once were used in this building.

Crossing E Street, notice on the left side of 4th Avenue that all the buildings are modern—everything on that side from E Street east for several blocks collapsed in the 1964 earthquake. The street split in half, lengthwise, with the left side ending up a dozen feet lower than the right. That land was later reinforced with a gravel buttress by the U.S. Army Corps of Engineers, and the slope below forever set aside as open space because of the earthquake risk. This stretch of 4th Avenue is where the **Iditarod Trail Sled Dog Race** and the **Anchorage Fur Rendezvous World Championship Sled Dog Race** start each year in March and February, respectively.

Continue walking east. At 4th Avenue and D Street is the:

2 Wendler Building (1915)

The old Club 25 is among the oldest buildings in Anchorage. The bronze statue of the dog commemorates the sled-dog races that start here. Across D Street is a mural that depicts a map of coastal Alaska and British Columbia, with the Iditarod Trail faintly marked.

Cross 4th Avenue to the north side to see:

3 4th Avenue Market Place

On the north side of 4th, a shopping center was converted into a Native arts and crafts mall and entertainment center, collecting together Alaska Native businesses in the heart of downtown. The Two Spirits Gallery, owned by the Cook Inlet Tribal Council, presents carvers and artists working on-site every day. Alaska Natives cultural groups are scheduled to perform in the common area daily in the summer. On the eastern end of the building, take

Map mural across D Street.

Cyrano's Off-Center Playhouse.

in large, interesting graphics about the 1964 earthquake and other historic topics. Don't miss the exhibit of the complete collection of prints by a painter respected as capturing the colors of the Arctic like no other, the late Fred Machetanz. If you want to take the time, the Alaska Experience Theater is housed here, too: It presents a dizzying large-format film called *Alaska the Greatland* and an interactive earthquake exhibit. Call ☎**907/272-9076** for showtimes. The Rusty Harpoon (p. 336) is a good craft and gift shop in the yellow building next door.

Cross back to the south side of 4th and retrace your steps to D Street, taking it south to see:

4 The Culture of D Street

This 1-block street contains two of the city's most interesting cultural outlets. First on the left, at 4th and D, is **Cyrano's Off-Center Playhouse** (☎**907/274-2599;** www.cyranos.org), home of its own theater company. They really are good; the tiny theater can cause quite a stir in town and has won many awards. They also have poetry readings and the like, and you can stop in the cozy little cafe for a glass of wine or beer on performance days. Tickets are sold through CenterTix (☎**907/263-ARTS** [263-2787]; www.centertix.net) and 2 hours before shows at the box office. A little farther on the left, the **International Gallery of Contemporary Art** (www.igcaalaska.org) is the community's nonprofit forum for the art that is happening right now. Typically, the gallery is given over to a single artist or theme. Hours are on p. 337.

Cross 5th Avenue at the end of D Street and enter:

5 The 5th Avenue Mall

This grand, four-story shopping center is Alaska's fanciest mall, with Nordstrom and JCPenney as its anchor stores. A large, airy food court is on the top floor. Take a look, or walk straight through to the doors on the opposite side. (Just a block east are the Anchorage Museum at Rasmuson Center and the Alaska State Troopers Museum, described below.)

Cross the mall to the doors opposite, exiting onto 6th Avenue. Turn right, walk a block, and cross E Street to:

6 Town Square

In the early '90s, the community raised money for improvements to the square by collecting donations of $40 each for the granite bricks, with an inscription

Town Square.

of the contributor's choosing. There are 13,344 (bet you can't find mine). This created controversy recently when the city wanted to redo the square and the bricks were in the way (most survived). On the east side of the square, behind you, the huge whale mural was painted freehand by Wyland in 1994. He painted similar whale murals in cities all along the West Coast. The mural's days are numbered, as a new shopping center will take the place of the parking lot in front of it. The building on the northeast corner of the square is one of the city's oldest and was saved from demolition when the park was created; it contains a charming gift and candy shop with a bakery and coffee shop in the back.

On the west side of the square is the massive, highly decorated, dominating:

7 Alaska Center for the Performing Arts

The center was completed in 1988 amid controversy about its design, among other things—it's either clever and bold or garish and busy. You decide. The lobby is usually open, and whatever your opinion of the decor, a look inside will spark a discussion. Alaskans have gotten used to it, and now we think of the building mostly as a focal point of our cultural life. Tours are held Wednesday at 1pm; a $1 donation is requested (reach the center's administrative offices at ☎907/263-2900; www.myalaskacenter.org). Thespians believe the building is haunted by the ghost of painter Sydney Laurence, who makes lighting mysteriously vary and elevators go up and down with no one in them. An auditorium demolished to make room for the center was named for Laurence. Check the box office for current performances in the three theaters and rehearsal hall, Alaska's premier performance venues (and see "The Performing Arts," later in this chapter).

☕ Take a Break

From the performing arts center, cross 6th Avenue at the F Street light and turn right (west) to **Humpy's** (☎**907/276-2337**), a popular tavern on the south side of 6th with a huge selection of microbrews, live music, and good casual meals.

The square green office building next door to Humpy's is:

8 City Hall

Turn left through the pedestrian walkway between Humpy's and City Hall. A large mural showing a timeline of the history of Anchorage faces the parking lot. An artistically superior mural, by Duke Russell, is on the wall in Humpy's outdoor seating area on the near side of the parking lot.

Cross the parking lot to 7th, where you face:

9 The Dena'ina Civic & Convention Center

The center's name honors the indigenous people of the area, as the Alaska Federation of Natives acknowledged to huge applause at the first meeting ever held here, in the fall of 2008. The airy lobby facing 7th and the corridors on either side contain several spectacular pieces of public art, and the views from the top floor windows and the deck on the southeast corner are well worth a ride up the escalator.

☕ Take a Break

I realize you've walked only half a block from the last tavern, but **McGinley's** (☎**907/279-1782**), at the corner of 7th and G Street, provides an excellent excuse

Duke Russell mural at Humpy's.

Anchorage Lightspeed Planet Walk.

for another pint, if only because of the identity of its owner: Anchorage's mayor, Dan Sullivan, elected in 2009, whose father, George Sullivan, was also mayor, from 1967 to 1981.

From 7th and G walk north, past McGinley's, cross 6th Avenue, and proceed north to 5th Avenue. In the plaza on the southeast corner of 5th and G, note an enormous, 3-ton model of the sun, at the start of:

10 The Anchorage Lightspeed Planet Walk

The sun you see here is just the beginning of a scale model of the solar system in which you walk at the speed of light. The inner planets are along 5th Avenue toward the water, where you will be going in a moment. Earth is about 8 minutes' walk away, at 5th and K (it takes light 8 min. to get from the sun to Earth). The walk continues down the Tony Knowles Coastal Trail and all the way to Pluto, in the parking lot at Kincaid Park, 5½ hours away, although you can go warp speed on a bike. High school student Eli Menaker designed the walk, which the Anchorage Rotary Club completed in 2005. Since then, the scale model planets and their informative signs have been a little molested by vandals, although several are off in the coastal trails' quiet woodlands. This first site, in the plaza, also has an interactive video kiosk. Learn more about the project at www.anchorageplanetwalk.org.

Before following more of the planet walk, take a detour 1 block farther on G Street, between 5th and 4th avenues, where you'll find some of the downtown's best:

11 Offbeat Businesses

First comes **Aurora Fine Arts,** an attractively cluttered arts and crafts shop with plenty to see. Next are: **Darwin's Theory,** a friendly, old-fashioned bar with character that shows up in an Indigo Girls song ("Cut It Out" from the 1997 album *Shaming of the Sun*); **Suzi's Woollies** (www.suziswoollies.net), a Celtic shop carrying imported sweaters, jewelry, and scarves, and with live Irish music most Saturday afternoons and the first Friday of the month; and **Side Street Espresso,** where you can get into a lively discussion on art or politics and make contact with thinking people. On the opposite side of the street, at 423 G St., the light-filled storefront of the **Alaska Glass Gallery Downtown** (www.alaskaglassgallery.com) exhibits fanciful and dramatic glass sculptures by glassblower and gallery director Cynthia England and by other artists from all over the United States and Canada.

Shortcut: You can cut an hour off the tour here by continuing north on G Street to 4th, then turning right and walking 1 block to the starting point at F Street.

Backtrack to 5th and G, then proceed west (away from the mountains) on 5th. Crossing H Street, you'll see the:

12 Holy Family Cathedral

This concrete Art Deco church is the seat of the Roman Catholic archbishop. The interior is unremarkable.

Keep going toward the water, crossing L Street and going down the hill to:

13 Elderberry Park

The yellow-and-brown house in the park is the Oscar Anderson House Museum, described under "Downtown Museums," below. Besides good playground equipment, the park offers the easiest access point to the Tony Knowles Coastal Trail (see "Walking & Biking," later in this chapter). The trail tunnels under the Alaska Railroad tracks from the bottom of the park, where you can see the muddy shores of Cook Inlet up close, and perhaps spy some waterfowl.

Now hike back up the hill to L Street and turn left. At 3rd Avenue is:

14 Resolution Park

The bronze Captain Cook Monument stands on a large wooden deck, but he's gazing out to sea—the opposite of

Captain Cook Monument at Resolution Park.

the way he was facing when he explored Cook Inlet in 1778 aboard *HMS Resolution*. Cook didn't personally come as far as the future site of Anchorage, instead sending a boat with his ship's master, William Bligh (later the Capt. Bligh who inspired mutiny aboard the *HMS Bounty*). Failing to find a shortcut to the Northwest Passage here, Cook considered his 2 weeks in the inlet a waste of time, grousing in his journal, "Nothing but a trifling point in geography has been determined," and left it unnamed. Ironically, the British Admiralty chose this body of water to honor Cook after he died in Hawaii months later, naming it Cook Inlet. The park's informative signs, powerful mounted binoculars, and commanding vantage point make this a rewarding stop for gazing out at the water and the mountains beyond. The waters you see are ferocious, with whirlpool currents and a tidal range of almost 40 vertical feet. The shore across the inlet, about 2 miles away, is virtually uninhabited, but for how much longer? It is the destination of a famous $700-million "Bridge to Nowhere" partially funded by Alaska's Congressional delegation, which is still in the planning stages.

Follow 3rd Avenue east (back toward the mountains) 1 block and turn right on K Street. On the right is:

15 The Last Blue Whale

Joseph Princiotti's huge 1973 bronze of combat between a whale and whalers in small boats shows the whale's point of view.

Cross K Street to walk through the:

16 Courthouse Plaza

The plaza frames the Nesbett State Courthouse; the sinuous shapes of the plaza's concrete walkways are supposed to suggest both the flow of people through the court system and a braided glacial river. The metal "Grizzly Bear and Cub," by Homer sculptor Mike Sirl, was installed in 2004; local and state law require projects to construct public buildings to set aside 1% of their budget for art, and this work is one result.

Cross the plaza to 4th Avenue, cross I Street, and take a look at the two:

17 Totem Poles

Carved of red cedar by Lee Wallace, of Ketchikan, and erected in 1997, they represent the eagle and raven moieties of the Tlingit people, intended to symbolize the balance of justice. A Tlingit creation story tells of how raven stole the moon and stars and brought them to mankind; here, the moon and stars are the stars of the Alaska flag.

Walk around past the courthouse on 4th Avenue and turn left onto H Street. Follow H as it crosses 3rd Avenue and becomes Christensen Drive. Descend the hill on Christensen and turn right on 2nd Avenue, toward the mountains. Look around at the:

Totem poles carved by Lee Wallace.

18 Historic Houses

The old wooden houses along 2nd are mostly attorneys' offices now, but once this was one of the better residential areas in town. Several houses are marked, and a kiosk at 2nd and F relates some town history. If you imagine houses like this over much of downtown, you'll know what Anchorage looked like before oil.

Continue east on 2nd Avenue to F Street, where you will find:

19 A Ship Creek Overlook with a Monument to President Eisenhower

The bust commemorates Alaska's 1959 admission to the Union (in fact, Eisenhower was a major barrier to statehood). More interesting than the statue is the overlook. You can see the Alaska Railroad yards from here, and part of the port of Anchorage and the neighborhood of Government Hill across the Ship Creek river bottom. This is where the tent city of Knik Anchorage, later shortened to Anchorage, was set up in 1914. An informative set of signs on the overlook explains the history. The Alaska Railroad, which helped build Anchorage, still has its headquarters in a modern brick building that stands by the creek. The nearer concrete building is the railroad's stately depot. The restored steam engine on the pedestal in front was used in construction of the Panama Canal, then worked in the yard here as a switch engine. The creek itself is full of salmon in June and August (see "Fishing," later in this chapter), and a walkway that crosses a dam just upstream from here is a good place to watch the fish and to feed ducks. But the walk down the stairs to the river bottom and back is strenuous.

Walk up the hill on E Street to 3rd Avenue. The extensively landscaped parking lot on the left becomes the:

20 Anchorage Market & Festival

This street fair, held every weekend from mid-May to mid-September, draws hundreds of vendors and thousands of shoppers. You can buy everything from local vegetables to handmade crafts to tourist junk. There are food booths and music, too.

Bust of President Eisenhower.

Turn right on 3rd Avenue, then left on F Street. F Street Station, on the left, is a fun bar with an after-work crowd. Proceed to 4th Avenue, and you're back at the Log Cabin Visitor Information Center, but don't stop. Turn right on 4th Avenue. On the right side is the:

21 Old Federal Building

This grand, white, Depression-era structure now contains the Alaska Public Lands Information Center, with interesting displays and lots of information about the outdoors (p. 292). Don't let the security check point deter you—go in and look around. At the celebration for Alaska's admission to the union in 1959, a huge 48-star flag covered the front of the building. While Anchorage watched, the Fur Rendezvous queen climbed a fire truck ladder to pin on the 49th star for Alaska. Hawaii became the 50th state later that year.

Across the street is Anchorage's most attractive historic building, the:

22 4th Avenue Theater (1947)

The theater was built by Cap Lathrop, Alaska's first business magnate, who created it as a monument to the territory and the permanence of its new society, an old-fashioned movie palace with the bas-relief murals and a blinking Big Dipper on the ceiling. It flourished for decades, but began losing money when one-screen, downtown movie theaters became obsolete in the

1980s. Saved from destruction in 1991 and made a tourist attraction by a local businessman with a sentimental attachment to the building, the theater again closed its doors in 2006 and now faces doom at the hands of developers who would put a parking garage in its place. Voters balked at paying to buy the building, and it became a political football among city leaders. At this writing, its fate remains uncertain.

Downtown Museums

Alaska State Troopers Museum This charming little museum has more than one way into the heart. For law enforcement people, the appeal is obvious (the official name is the Fraternal Order of Alaska State Troopers Law Enforcement Museum). Others may enjoy perusing a trove of law enforcement insignia, equipment, a 1952 Hudson Hornet patrol car, and old Alaska memorabilia—even a grinning mug shot of Steve McQueen, who was picked up in 1973 spinning doughnuts in city streets in an Olds Toronado. The whole place conveys the positive spirit of pioneer Alaska.

245 W. 5th Ave. **☎800/770-5050** or 907/279-5050. www.alaskatroopermuseum.com. Free admission. Mon–Fri 10am–4pm; Sat noon–4pm.

4th Avenue Theater.

Anchorage Museum at Rasmuson Center ★★★ The state's largest museum has been under construction for years with a $106-million expansion project that is planned for completion in 2010. You can't miss the new entrance on C Street, in a series of vertically lined reflective rectangles that look like pinstriped ice cubes. (I guess no one told the British architect, David Chipperfield, that we already have plenty of icy surfaces in Alaska.) As I write this, interior work goes on, so I cannot describe the museum's content, but the source of ingredients is promising. A gallery will show 600 traditional Alaska Native objects returned here from the Smithsonian; another new gallery will show contemporary Alaska Native art from the museum's unequalled collection; and a popular children's science museum called the Imaginarium will move in to become a center within the larger museum, with interactive exhibits. The expansion also includes a small planetarium. Formerly called the Anchorage Museum of History and Art, the museum's strength had been to tell Alaska's story in many ways; the expansion comes with new management, new governance, and a new, broader mission, and only time will tell where it will find its strengths.

A swanky new restaurant, Muse, opened in the expanded museum—again, after my deadline. It is operated by the locally famous gourmets who own the Marx Brothers Cafe, described earlier, who plan to offer such treats as tea-smoked duck spring rolls and ahi nachos, as well as creative cocktails from a full bar. The restaurant has a large dining room and a patio.

625 C St. ☎907/929-9200. www.anchoragemuseum.org. Admission $15 adults; $7 children age 3–12. Alaska residents $10 adults; $8 over age 65, students, or military. Mid-May to mid-Sept daily 9am–6pm; mid-Sept to mid-May Tues–Sat 10am–6pm, Sun noon–5pm.

The Oscar Anderson House Museum This house museum, moved to a beautiful site in Elderberry Park over the water, shows how an early Swedish immigrant lived. Although far from grand, the house is quaint, surrounded by a lovely little garden, and dates from the city's founding in 1915. The 45-minute guided tour provides a good explanation of Anchorage's short history. In those small-town days, Anderson found success in the meat, coal, and aviation businesses. He died in 1974, and the house contains many of the family's original belongings, including a working 1909 player piano around which the structure was built. If you come at Christmas, don't miss the Swedish Christmas tours, the first 2 weekends in December.

420 M St. ☎907/274-2336. Admission $3 adults, $1 children 5–12. Summer Mon–Fri noon–5pm. Closed in winter.

Sights Beyond Downtown

Alaska Aviation Heritage Museum ★★ Alaska's late development meant it skipped a technological step: Travel and mail went straight from dogsleds and riverboats to airplanes, without the intervening development of a significant road or rail network. One day towns were separated from the outside world by perilous journeys that could last a month; the next day, people could come and go in hours. But the peril remained. In the early days, Alaska aviators crossed vast wilderness without proper maps, landmarks, weather reports, or even formal airstrips. This museum on the shore of the Lake Hood floatplane base contains five hangars of their planes, most of them beautifully restored (you can sometimes watch restoration work in progress and they fly some of the vintage planes at an annual July 4 fundraiser). The galleries contain exhibits and artifacts from Alaska's eventful military history, films, and a flight simulator for guest use. Aviation enthusiasts shouldn't miss it, and anyone can get a strong feeling for that pioneering time. There's an aviation-themed gift store, of course. The museum's entrance faces the lake, not the road.

4721 Aircraft Dr. ☎907/248-5325. www.alaskaairmuseum.org. Admission $10 adults, $8 seniors, $6 children ages 5–12. Summer daily 9am–5pm; winter Wed–Sun 9am–5pm. The museum is near the international airport; driving toward the airport on International Airport Rd., turn right toward Postmark Dr., then right again on Heliport Dr., and right again on Aircraft Dr.

Alaska Botanical Garden 👫 The garden is a pleasant place to walk and learn about native flora and some of the garden flowers and herbs that grow in this region. The plantings are in a few small clearings connected by gravel paths on thickly wooded grounds at the edge of a large wildland park. The quiet, shady setting of the boreal forest sets a muted tone. Gardeners will be interested in the two perennial gardens, the small rock garden, and the formal herb garden. The

Alaska Aviation Heritage Museum.

placards on the wildflower trail will help you identify plants you see on Alaskan hikes. The Lowenfels Family Nature Trail is a 1-mile loop with a guide brochure that is pitched at an unusually thoughtful level. Along the walk is a chance to see salmon in Campbell Creek. Those without strong interest in gardening or native plants may find other attractions more deserving of limited time, however, especially considering the drive from downtown, which is 20 minutes without traffic, and possibly twice that at rush hour. The garden is open during daylight hours year-round, but the gardens are worth viewing mid-May to mid-September (the gift shop is open June–Aug 11am–4pm).

Campbell Airstrip Rd. (off Tudor Rd.). **☎907/770-3692.** www.alaskabg.org. Admission $5 per person, $10 per family. Summer daily daylight hours. Guided tours June–Aug daily 1pm. From downtown, drive out New Seward Hwy. (Gambell St.) to Tudor Rd., exit to the east (left), turn right off Tudor onto Campbell Airstrip Rd., and park at the Benny Benson School.

Alaska Museum of Natural History This young museum 3 miles east of downtown focuses on paleontology with a permanent exhibit of Alaskan fossils belonging to the Bureau of Land Management, including interactive features that children especially enjoy. Alaska's Arctic once was warm and humid, and now is a hot spot for dinosaur-bone hunters. Temporary annual exhibits have been good, too.

201 N. Bragaw St. **☎907/274-2400.** www.alaskamuseum.org. $5 adult, $3 ages 5–12. Summer Mon–Sat 10am–5pm; winter Tues–Sat 10am–5pm.

Alaska Native Heritage Center ★★★ Alaska Natives built this extraordinary center to bring their cultures to visitors. It's Alaska's best Native cultural attraction. What makes it so is not the graceful building or the professional and informative displays, but Native people themselves, who often create a personal connection with visitors and rarely come across as practiced or distant. The three main parts of the center take half a day to absorb. First, there's a hall where storytellers, dancers, and Native athletes perform, with three 30-minute programs rotating through the day. Next is a gallery of educational displays with a theater showing short films and a series of workshops, where artisans practice and show off traditional crafts and often teach crafts to visitors. Finally, there's a pond surrounded by six traditional Native dwellings representing each cultural group, hosted by a member of those cultures. A snack bar and grill serves soup, sandwiches, and other meals, and a gift shop carries inexpensive items and real Native art and crafts for sale by the center or on consignment from artisans. Getting to the center requires wheels. The center offers a free shuttle from various points around town. Call for details on where and when to catch it.

From the Glenn Hwy., take the North Muldoon exit. ☎800/315-6608 or 907/330-8000. www.alaskanative.net. Admission $25 adults, $21 seniors and military, $17 children 7–16; Alaska residents $10 adult, $7 children. Discounts in winter, for families, or for joint admission to Anchorage Museum at Rasmuson Center. Summer daily 9am–5pm; call for winter hours.

The Alaska Zoo ★★ ☺ Don't expect the variety of a big-city zoo, but what the Alaska Zoo lacks in size it makes up with a charm all its own. Anchorage residents have developed personal relationships with the animals, naming many of them. The zoo's best feature is the opportunity it affords to see familiar Alaskan animals up close. I enjoy watching the polar bears, Ahpun and Lyutyik, play and swim underwater (you can check that out on a webcam, too). Gravel paths meander through the woods past enclosures with natural flora for bears, wolves, seals and otters, musk oxen, Dall sheep, moose, caribou, and waterfowl. If you want to pass yourself off as a master wildlife photographer, crop out the Bactrian camels, snow leopards, and a few other northern creatures that don't normally live in Alaska. Two-hour naturalist tours take place every day at noon, and include some backstage stops, for $25 adults, $15 children 12 and under. A snack bar serves basic meals, and there is a gift shop. The zoo is a 20-minute drive from downtown, without traffic; if you don't have a car, it's possible in the summer to take a People Mover bus to the Dimond Mall transit center and then take a shuttle to the zoo (call for details).

4731 O'Malley Rd. ☎907/346-3242. www.alaskazoo.org. Admission $12 adults, $9 seniors and military, $6 ages 3–17, free under 3. May–Aug daily 9am–6pm, until 9pm Tues and Fri Memorial Day to Labor Day; summer educational programs most Tues at 7pm, live music most Fri at 7pm. Off-season open daily at 10am; closing time varies depending on the time of sunset. Drive out the New Seward Hwy. to O'Malley Rd., then turn left and go 2 miles.

Earthquake Park The 1964 Good Friday earthquake was the biggest ever in North America, registering at 9.2 on the Richter Scale, killing 131 people, and flattening much of the region. Downtown Anchorage and the Turnagain residential area, near the park, suffered enormous slides that turned neighborhoods into chaotic ruins. A simple sculpture and interpretive signs commemorate and explain the event, but you can't see much through the trees that have grown up since the quake. If you are up for a walk in the woods, however, descend into the park on the paved coastal trail; then explore the dirt paths that branch from it. Those quiet ways climb over the strange topography of hummocks and small ponds created when the ground went liquid. This also is a good access point to the Coastal Trail and a likely place to spot birds and moose. Early in the summer the mosquitoes can be horrendous. Continue west on the Coastal Trail or Northern Lights Boulevard to outlooks at Airport Park and Point Woronzof, within 2 miles of Earthquake Park, where Mount McKinley is visible in clear weather.

Spirit houses at Eklutna Historical Park.

West end of Northern Lights Blvd. Free admission. Always open. From downtown, take L St. (which becomes Minnesota Dr.) to Northern Lights Blvd. and turn right. The park is on your right after 2 miles, beyond the residential area.

Eklutna Historical Park ★ The Native village of Eklutna has a fascinating old cemetery, still in use, in which each grave is enclosed by a highly decorated spirit house the size of a large dollhouse. These little shelters excite the imagination in a way no ordinary marker would. The unique practice evolved from the melding of Athabascan and Russian Orthodox beliefs. There are two small Russian Orthodox churches on the site, including the **St. Nicholas Orthodox Church.** Built north of here of logs sometime before 1870, it is among the oldest buildings in the state. Tour guides offer an orientation talk before leading visitors through the site and both churches. Given the drive from Anchorage of at least half an hour, it makes sense to call ahead. If you go, wear mosquito repellent, and also take the time to see Thunderbird Falls, described below under "Hiking & Mountain Biking." Also note that the diocese operates a tiny museum with a coffee and gift shop downtown, at 605 A St., across from the Anchorage Museum at Rasmuson Center (**☎907/276-7257**).

About 26 miles out the Glenn Hwy. **☎907/688-6026.** Admission $5 adults, $3 ages 10–18, free under 10. Summer Mon–Fri 10am–4pm; Sat–Sun noon–4pm. Closed winter. Take the Glenn Hwy. 26 miles to the Eklutna exit, then go left over the overpass.

Spectator Sports

Most big events in Anchorage happen at the **Sullivan Arena,** at 16th Avenue and Gambell Street (sometimes known as the Sully, it is named after a former Mayor Sullivan who is the current Mayor Sullivan's father). The ticket agency is Ticketmaster (**☎800/745-3000;** www.ticketmaster.com), which also sells through local Fred Meyer grocery stores.

BASEBALL Anchorage has two semi-pro baseball teams—the **Anchorage Glacier Pilots** (☎907/274-3627; www.glacier pilots.com) and the **Anchorage Bucs** (☎907/561-2827; www. anchoragebucs.com)—with college athletes playing in a six-team Alaska league during June and July. Cool summer nights under the natural light at tiny Mulcahy Stadium bring the game close: the sound, smell, and rhythm. The quality may be uneven, but exceptional players grow up in this league, and dozens are currently in the majors. Famed alumni in-clude Mark McGwire, Rick Aguil-era, Tom Seaver, Dave Winfield, Barry Bonds, Wally Joyner, Randy Johnson, and Jason Giambi. Check the *Anchorage Daily News* or the websites above for game times. Mulcahy is at 16th Avenue and A Street, a long walk or a short drive from downtown. Tickets are around $5. Dress warmly for evening games; a blanket is rarely out of order. A weekend day game is warmer, but then you won't get to see baseball played at night without lights.

Alaska Aces.

BASKETBALL The University of Alaska Anchorage hosts an NCAA Division I preseason basketball tournament, the **Carrs/Safeway Great Alaska Shootout** (☎907/786-1250; www.goseawolves.com), in late November. The noted men's tournament takes place at the Sullivan Arena over Thanksgiving weekend. The women's tournament is held on the 2 days prior to Thanksgiving. The Seawolves, themselves in Division II, play the regular season at the Well Fargo Sports Complex, on campus on Providence Drive.

HOCKEY Anchorage is a hockey town. The biggest headline I've ever seen on the local newspaper is when the minor league hockey team won the national ECHL championship in the spring of 2006. The team, the **Alaska Aces** (☎907/258-2237; www.alaskaaces.com), competes at the Sullivan Arena. The western division that Alaska faces regularly includes cities such Las Vegas and Phoenix. The season lasts from October to May.

Most years, the **University of Alaska Anchorage Seawolves** (☎907/786-1250; www.goseawolves.com) get plenty of attention all winter. They play NCAA Division I hockey at the Sullivan, a notoriously noisy and raucous venue for opposing teams.

GETTING OUTSIDE

Anchorage is unique in Alaska (and anywhere else I know) for the number of places right in and near town to hike, bike, ski, and otherwise get into the wild. I've broken the options down by activities below. In town, the city's bike trails connect through greenbelts that span the noisy, asphalt urban core with soothing creekside woods. Kincaid Park and Far North Bicentennial Park are both on the trail system within the city, and encompass thousands of acres and scores of miles of trails for Nordic skiing, mountain biking, and horseback riding. The Chugach Mountains, which form the backdrop to the town, offer tundra hiking, backpacking, mountain biking, and climbs that range from easy to technical. More trails and streams, only slightly farther afield, are covered in the "Out from Anchorage" sections later in this chapter. Many cruises, tours, fishing charters, and sea-kayaking trips leave from nearby **Whittier,** easily managed as a day trip; see "Whittier: Dock on the Sound," in chapter 8, for details.

INFORMATION The **Alaska Public Lands Information Center** (p. 292; ℂ907/ 644-3661; www.alaskacenters.gov) offers guidance for all these recreation areas and more throughout Alaska. For information on the bike trails, parks, swimming, and other city recreation, contact **Anchorage Parks & Recreation** (ℂ907/343-4355; www.muni.org/parks). Cross-country skiers can get information from the **Nordic Ski Association of Anchorage** (ℂ907/276-7609; www.anchoragenordicski.com).

Get information specific to **Chugach State Park** from the public lands center or directly from the park at ℂ907/345-5014 (www.alaskastateparks. org; click on "Individual Parks"). **Chugach National Forest** can be reached at ℂ907/743-9500 or www.fs.fed.us/r10/chugach.

The best trail guide to the entire region is John Wolfe, Jr., and Helen Nienhueser's **55 Ways to the Wilderness,** 5th edition (The Mountaineers, $17), available in any bookstore in the area. Two excellent trail maps are widely available: "Chugach State Park" by Imus Geographics, covers the entire park, while "Anchorage & Vicinity," by Alaska Road & Recreation Maps, covers the park's southern portion as well as the entire Anchorage bowl, and is at a finer scale than the Imus map. You can find either at sporting-goods stores or information centers.

EQUIPMENT You can rent most anything you need for outdoor activities. For bike rentals, see "Getting Around," p. 291. Get advice, buy gear, and rent cross-country skis, snowshoes, bear-proof containers, and mountaineering equipment at **Alaska Mountaineering and Hiking,** 2633 Spenard Rd. (ℂ907/272-1811; www.alaskamountaineering.com). It's a small shop where the staff takes the time to help you plan a trip. A block away, at 1200 W. Northern Lights Blvd., **REI** has a larger store (ℂ907/272-4565; www. rei.com) that rents a wide range of gear, including lightweight canoes and touring kayaks with car-top carriers, camping gear, packs, tents, sleeping bags, and cross-country skis (but not bikes or ice-climbing gear). It is the best-stocked place in town to buy outdoor athletic clothing as well. (For Arctic cold weather gear and where to buy it, see "What to Wear" on p. 62.)

Walking & Biking

Anchorage has an award-winning network of paved **bike trails** spanning the city along wooded greenbelts. You rarely see a building and almost always cross roads and rail lines through tunnels and over bridges, so you're never in traffic. Here are two of the best.

TONY KNOWLES COASTAL TRAIL
★★★ Leading 10 miles from the western end of 2nd Avenue along the shore to **Kincaid Park,** the coastal trail is among the best things about Anchorage. It's a unique pathway to the natural environment from the heart of downtown. I've ridden parallel to beluga whales swimming along the trail at high tide and encountered as many as six moose on a single ride. (Don't approach moose or bear or try to slip by; wait at a safe distance for them to go their own way.) The most

Westchester Lagoon.

popular entrance is at **Elderberry Park,** at the western end of 5th Avenue. **Westchester Lagoon** (a pond) is 10 blocks south of Elderberry Park. From downtown, the lagoon is a good destination for a lovely stroll and a fine place to picnic and feed the ducks, which nest on small islands.

LANIE FLEISCHER CHESTER CREEK TRAIL ★ Starting at an intersection with the Coastal Trail at Westchester Lagoon, this trail runs about 4 miles east along the greenbelt to **Goose Lake,** where you can swim in a cool woodland pond at the end of a bike ride and perhaps buy ice cream—still, improbably enough, in the middle of the city. South from the lake, a wooded trail leads through the university campus and, with some navigation, to miles more riding. The paved bike trails, including the Fleischer, stay well back in the trees, so you rarely see a building, and tunnels and bridges span all road and railroad crossings, so you're never in traffic.

Hiking & Mountain-Biking

Besides these hikes and bikes in Anchorage proper, more excellent, nearby options are along Turnagain Arm and in Girdwood, covered in sections 8 and 9 of this chapter.

KINCAID PARK ★★ Covered in more detail below, Kincaid Park is an idyllic summer setting for mountain-biking and day hikes. Moose sightings are a common daily occurrence on wide dirt trails that snake for about 40 miles through the birch and white spruce of the park's hilly 1,500 acres of boreal forest, often with views of the sea and mountains beyond, including McKinley. Trails open to bikes around June 1, or as soon as they dry, and a mountain-bike race series runs through the summer. On the busiest summer day, however, there is plenty of room for relaxed, solitary rambling or cycling. Within the park, wooded Little Campbell Lake is a picturesque spot for family canoeing and fishing for stocked trout; there is no lifeguard. There's also an 18-hole Frisbee golf course. **Note:** The park gates are locked at 10pm, so get your car out before then or park in one of the lots outside the gates.

FAR NORTH BICENTENNIAL PARK/CAMPBELL TRACT ★ A rectangle totaling 4,730 acres of city park and Bureau of Land Management land brings wilderness into the city on the east side of town, a habitat for bears, moose, and spawning salmon. People use it for dog mushing and skiing in winter, and for exceptional mountain-biking and day hiking in summer. The Alaska Botanical Garden, listed above, and the Hilltop Ski Area, below, are both within the park's boundaries. A good place to start a hike or ride through the woods is the **Campbell Creek Science Center** (☎907/267-1247; www.blm.gov/ak/sciencecenter), an educational facility operated by the BLM. Staff are often on hand to answer questions, and you can consult books and maps and look at an aquarium of native fish. To get to the science center from downtown, take Gambell Street (it becomes New Seward Hwy.) south to Dowling Road, go east (toward the mountains), turn right on Lake Otis Road, turn left on 68th Avenue, and follow 68th to its end; then go left at the BLM Campbell Tract entrance sign.

FLATTOP MOUNTAIN & THE GLEN ALPS TRAILHEAD ★★★ There are many ways to reach the alpine tundra, intoxicating fresh air, and cinematic views in the Chugach Mountains behind Anchorage, but the easiest and best developed portal is the Chugach State Park Glen Alps Trailhead. Even those who aren't up to hiking should go for the drive and a walk on a short, paved loop with incredible views and interpretive signs. If you are ready for a hike, you can start at the trail head for trips of up to several days, following the network of trails or taking off across dry, alpine tundra by yourself, but usually within mobile phone range. Camping is permitted anywhere off the trails.

Flattop Mountain is the most popular hike from Glen Alps and a great family climb, if a bit crowded on weekends. It's a steep afternoon hike, easy for fit adults and doable by school-age children. There's a bit of a scramble at the top, easiest if you stick to the painted markers on the rocks. Dress warmly and don't go in the rain, when slick rocks at the top could cause a fall.

For a longer or less steep hike or a mountain-biking trip, follow the broad gravel trail that leads up the valley from the Glen Alps Trailhead to

Far North Bicentennial Park/Campbell Tract.

several other great routes. Trails lead all the way over the mountains to Indian or Bird Creek, on Turnagain Arm, up some of the mountains along the way or to round alpine lakes in high, rocky valleys. You're always above the tree line, so you don't need to follow a trail if you have a good map. This is wonderful backpacking country.

To get to the trail head, take New Seward Highway to O'Malley Road, head east toward the mountains, and then turn right on Hillside Drive and left onto Upper Huffman Road. Finally, turn right on the narrow, twisting Toilsome Hill Drive. Don't forget to bring cash or a check for the self-service day-use fee of $5 (not required if you are going only to the overlook and park in the designated spaces). A shuttle runs to Glen Alps May through October afternoons daily at 1pm, returning at 4:30pm, from **Downtown Bicycle Rental** at the 4th Avenue Marketplace downtown (p. 291) when enough passengers sign up. The fare is $22 adults, $15 ages 6 to 12, $5 under 5. Call ☎907/279-3334 to sign up (www.hike-anchorage-alaska.com).

EAGLE RIVER VALLEY ★★ The **Eagle River Nature Center,** at the end of Eagle River Road, 12 miles up Eagle River Valley from the Glenn Highway exit (☎907/694-2108; www.ernc.org), resembles a public wilderness lodge, with hands-on nature displays about the area and daily nature walks in the summer and weekends year-round (2pm weekends, call for other times). Operated by a nonprofit concessionaire for Chugach State Park, it's open June through August daily from 10am to 5pm, May and September from 10am to 5pm daily except Monday; October through April Friday to Sunday from 10am to 5pm. There's a $5 parking fee.

The .8-mile **Rodak Nature Trail,** with interpretive signs, leads to viewing platforms over a beaver pond. The **Albert Loop Trail** is a 3-mile route; a geology guide from the center matches with numbered posts on the way. Both trails have good bird- and wildlife watching. The 25-mile **Crow Pass Trail,** a portion of the historic Iditarod Trail, continues up the valley into the mountains along the river. You can make a day-hike loop of 6 miles or less by returning on the **Dew Mound Trail.** Continuing, the Crow Pass Trail eventually surmounts the Chugach in alpine terrain and passes near Raven Glacier before descending into Girdwood (p. 346). There are campsites with fire rings along the way, and a mile up the trail the center rents

Bears in the City

Most cities don't have this problem, but during the summer of 2008, two serious brown-bear attacks occurred in one of Anchorage's city parks—Far North Bicentennial—and one more on a suburban street. The maulings were rare events in unusual circumstances. Fear of bears shouldn't keep anyone indoors in Alaska. To be safe, stay off closed trails, don't go running or biking in thick woods or late at night, and follow the advice in chapter 3 under "Outdoors Health & Safety," p. 92. If you're really worried, the staff at the information centers listed earlier in this section can answer your questions.

Thunderbird Falls.

out a public-use cabin for $65 a night. A yurt on the Crow Pass Trail and another on the Albert Loop rent for the same price. Reserve well ahead for weekends. Availability is shown on the website.

THUNDERBIRD FALLS & EKLUTNA LAKE
★★ The hike to Thunderbird Falls is an easy, 1-mile forest walk with a good reward at the end. You can see the falls without the steep final descent to their foot. Take the Glenn Highway north to the Thunderbird Falls exit, 25 miles from Anchorage. Continuing 10 miles up the Eklutna Lake Road, you come to an appealing state parks campground ($10 a night, $5 day-use fee) and the glacial lake for canoeing, hiking, and exceptional mountain biking. The Lakeside Trail leads 14 miles to Eklutna Glacier; you can camp on the way, stay at the state park's Yuditna Creek Cabin at 3 miles, or stay in the communal Serenity Falls hut at 13 miles. Advance reservations are required for the cabin or hut. See, "State Parks Cabin Reservations," p. 360. For the hut, you can reserve in person only. Rental bikes, kayaks, and other equipment, and guided kayak and bike tours, are offered by **Lifetime Adventures,** with a booth at the trail head of the Lakeside Trail (☎907/746-4644; www.lifetimeadventures.net). For $75 you can kayak 8 miles to the other end of the lake and pick up a bike there to ride back.

Bird-Watching

The Anchorage bowl contains varied bird habitat that is easily accessed and close at hand: lakes, streams, marshes, seashore, woodlands, and mountains. Visiting birders can see species they don't encounter at home (Pacific loons, Hudsonian godwits, boreal chickadees) and familiar birds in breeding plumage unique to these northern latitudes (a red-necked grebe that actually does have a red neck, for example). Local birders have recorded more than 225 species in the city. You will need the help of a rental car or at least a bike. Potter Marsh is a superb freshwater birding area (see "Out from Anchorage: Turnagain Arm & Portage Glacier," later in this chapter). Salt marshes and mud flats lie along much of the Tony Knowles Coastal Trail (see above). Right downtown, Ship Creek provides a river habitat. Glen Alps, described above, is the place to go for alpine birding. You can join field trips and network with local birders through the **Anchorage Audubon Society** (www.anchorageaudubon.org). The site contains an updated log of unusual sightings, which you can also check on a recorded hotline

(☎ **907/338-BIRD** [338-2473]), and a way to purchase the local chapter's birding map of the city ($10).

A terrific booklet, *Anchorage Wildlife Viewing Hot Spots,* published by the Alaska Department of Fish and Game, is sold for $6 at the Alaska Public Lands Information Center. It has more places to go than I can include here, detailed directions, and helpful information. Learn more about wildlife viewing around Alaska at www.wildlifeviewing.alaska.gov.

Fishing

There are hatchery salmon in several of Anchorage's streams, and stocked trout, salmon, or char in 28 lakes, so you need not leave town to catch a fish. The **Alaska Department of Fish and Game,** 333 Raspberry Rd., Anchorage, AK 99518-1599 (☎ **907/267-2218;** www.sf.adfg.state.ak.us), publishes informative booklets on the Web and on paper and an online fishing report updated weekly in season. There's also a recorded information line (☎ **907/267-2503**) with what's hot and lots of other advice. See chapter 3 for general guidance and license information, and information for planning a fishing vacation, and see chapter 8 for the famous fishing opportunities on the Kenai Peninsula.

ROADSIDE FISHING Although the setting (under a highway bridge in an industrial area) might not be the wilderness experience you've dreamed about, the 25- to 40-pound king salmon you pull from **Ship Creek** may make up for it. From downtown, just walk down the hill to the railroad yard. A couple of shacks sell and rent gear in the summer. Fishing for kings is best in June and for silvers in August and September. Fish only on the rising tide, when the fish come into the creek. Fishing near the end of the rising tide will mean crossing less mud, but one successful angler I know insists it's the start of the tide that's best. Either way, you'll need rubber boots, preferably neoprene chest waders, for the muddy banks, but don't go too far out, as the mud flats are dangerous and several times every summer the fire department has to rescue stuck fishermen.

Campbell Creek, a more natural urban stream, is stocked with silver salmon that make good fishing in August and September, and rainbow trout and Dolly Varden char are in the creek year-round. The creek runs along a greenbelt across the city through residential and industrial neighborhoods; the adjacent bike trail is a good access route. You can join the trail on Dimond Boulevard east of Jewel Lake Road, or where C Street crosses the creek just north of Dimond, among other places; or ask for directions and tips at the Public Land Information Center.

Bird Creek, 25 miles south of Anchorage on the Seward Highway (see "Out from Anchorage: Turnagain Arm & Portage Glacier," later in this chapter), is known for hot silver salmon fishing in the late summer and fall. Pinks run from late June to early August during even-numbered years. Other creeks along the Arm have similar but smaller runs.

FLY-IN FISHING ★★★ Serious anglers will use Anchorage as a base from which to fly to a remote lake or river with more fish and fewer people. Such a flight can be an unforgettable experience for those who are less than enthusiastic about fishing, too. The plane lifts off from Anchorage's Lake Hood floatplane base and within half an hour smoothly lands on a lake or river. You climb out and watch as the plane lifts off and disappears, leaving behind the kind of silence unique to true wilderness. It's on these trips that avid anglers are made—or spoiled. I've heard people complain of how sore their arms got from pulling in too many salmon.

Several companies offer fly-in trips; the best-established is **Rust's Flying Service** (☎800/544-2299 or 907/243-1595; www.flyrusts.com). It's a family-owned company with a strong safety ethic. They can take you out guided or on your own, for the day or for a longer stay in a cabin or lodge. If you fly to a lake, they'll provide a boat. They can't make fish appear if none are running, but they will try to take you to the hot spots. You can bring your own gear, or they can provide it. Prices for an unguided day trip start at around $240 per person, with a two-person minimum; guided, $485. Pick-up from most hotels is included, but not fishing licenses.

Other Summer Activities

FLIGHTSEEING/BEAR VIEWING Small planes are the blood cells of Alaska's circulatory system, and Anchorage its heart. There are several busy airports in Anchorage, and Lake Hood is the world's busiest floatplane base. If you will travel to Talkeetna, Denali National Park, Juneau, Glacier Bay National Park, or Ketchikan, you may want to save your flightseeing splurge for those extraordinary places, which are closer to famous attractions. Likewise, for bear-viewing flights, Katmai National Park, Homer, Kodiak, Juneau, and Wrangell may be closer to the action. (All those places are covered in this guide with the details for flights; check the table of contents or index.) On the other hand, plenty of spectacular territory is near Anchorage, and, if time is short, you can see bears or Denali in an afternoon. I recommend Rust's Flying Service (see "Fly-In Fishing," directly above), a reliable operator that has designed a menu of choices around visitors' most common interests. They can take you on a floatplane ride for as little as $100. A flight to see Mount McKinley is $365 and takes 3 hours. An all-day bear-viewing tour from Anchorage is $585 to $785 per person. The exact destination—Lake Clark or Katmai national parks, or somewhere else, depends on where bears are active when you are traveling.

RAFTING There are several white-water rivers within a 90-minute drive of Anchorage. **Nova Raft and Adventure Tours** (☎800/746-5753 or 907/745-5753; http://novalaska.com) has more than 30 years of experience offering trips all over the state, and five different half-day floats near Anchorage. Various rafting trips are available, ranging from the relatively easygoing Matanuska and Kings rivers, north of town, to the Class IV and V white water of Six-Mile Creek, which begins with a required instructional swim and includes fun optional swims, a 90-minute drive south of the city. White-water rafting always entails risk, but Nova's schedule allows you to calibrate how wild you want to get. Call to reserve, and let them guide you to the float that fits you best. The company also offers add-ons for self-paddling, helicopter flightseeing, or glacier hiking. The half-day trips range in price from $75 to $135. Children 5 to 11 can go on the calmer Matanuska River float for $45. Other trips are suitable only for older children and adults. You'll need your own transportation to the river and may need to bring your own lunch.

Rafting at Six-Mile Creek.

Chugach Outdoor Center (☎866/277-**RAFT** [277-7238] or 907/277-RAFT; www.chugachoutdoorcenter.com) also offers several rafting options south of Anchorage. The company has two daily choices on Six-Mile Creek, and floats in Turnagain Pass and in Seward's Resurrection River.

SEA KAYAKING Except at Eklutna Lake (see above), kayaking day trips from Anchorage go through Whittier, on Prince William Sound (see "Whittier: Dock on the Sound," in chapter 8, for complete details).

Winter Activities

The best downhill skiing and snowmobile tours are covered in the Girdwood section, p. 346.

ICE-SKATING **Westchester Lagoon,** just 10 blocks from downtown (see "Walking & Biking," above), is a skating paradise in the winter. When the ice gets thick enough, usually by mid-December, the city clears a large rink and more than a mile of wide paths that wind across the pond, mopping the ice regularly for a smooth surface. Skaters gather around burn barrels, well stocked with firewood, to socialize and warm their hands, and on weekends vendors often sell hot chocolate and coffee. More than a dozen lakes and outdoor rinks are maintained in the city, so you're never far from a place to skate; for information and current conditions, check with **Anchorage Parks & Recreation** (☎907/343-4355; www.muni.org/parks). Ice skates rent for $10 a day at **Champions Choice,** a hockey shop in the University Center Mall at Old Seward Highway and 36th Avenue (☎907/563-3503).

SKIING **Kincaid Park** is one of the best **cross-country skiing** areas in the country, with the first World Cup–certified trails in the U.S. About 65km of trails are geared to every ability level, but mostly intermediate and expert.

Besides the superb trails, it's a beautiful place to ski, through rolling hills of open birch and spruce, with views of the mountains and ocean. Most trails are expertly groomed for skating and classical techniques, with two loops reserved for classical only. Sixteen kilometers are lighted, an important feature on short winter days. The **Kincaid Park Outdoor Center** (☎907/343-6397) is open daily from 10am to 9:45pm, shorter hours on holidays. The gate closes at 10pm, so park at one of the lots outside it if you will be skiing later. Skiing usually lasts well into March and sometimes into April. Big races come in late February and early March (see "Only-in-Alaska Events," in chapter 3). **Far North Bicentennial Park** also has some excellent trails—32km total, 7km lighted—and a slightly longer season because of a hillside location. Start at Hilltop Ski Area. Many other parks and the bike trails have lengthy skiing routes, too, some lighted. See "Equipment," on p. 327, for information on where to rent skis. For current trail conditions, check www.anchoragenordicski.com and www.crosscountryalaska.org/trails.

Anchorage has several **downhill ski areas.** The best, **Mount Alyeska,** in Girdwood, is described on p. 347. **Hilltop Ski Area,** in Bicentennial Park in town, is a great place to learn to ski, with one long beginner slope, at 7015 Abbott Rd. (☎907/346-2167; www.hilltopskiarea.org). One-day lift tickets are $22 to $30, and ski package rentals essentially the same price.

Anchorage also is a great starting point for **backcountry skiing.** Non-experts should go with a guide (you can find one through Mount Alyeska). Experts can get ideas from some of the folks mentioned under "Equipment," p. 327. The key safety consideration is, of course, avalanche awareness and preparation. I've described that on p. 92, but if you are turning to this book to learn how to backcountry ski, you are not ready to go without a

Skiing at Mount Alyeska.

guide. An avalanche hotline is available for the Chugach National Forest near Anchorage (☏907/754-2369); for much more information, including updated avalanche forecasts, maps, and educational material, check www. cnfaic.org.

SHOPPING

Some of the most interesting shops are mentioned earlier, in the walking tour of downtown, where most galleries and gift shops are located.

NATIVE ARTS & CRAFTS Many downtown shops in Anchorage carry Alaska Native arts and crafts. Before making major purchases, know what you're buying (see "Native Art: Finding the Real Thing," in chapter 3).

Don't miss the **4th Avenue Market Place** if you have any interest in Native Art. The mall at 4th between C and D streets contains several shops, including a Native-owned nonprofit, and stages demonstrations and performances during the summer (p. 312). Right next door, in a bright yellow building, **The Rusty Harpoon,** 411 W. 4th Ave., has authentic Native items, Alaskan jewelry, less expensive crafts, and reliable, longtime proprietors who only buy directly from Native artists they know. Locals shop here.

The **Alaska Native Arts Foundation Gallery,** 6th Ave. and E St. (www.alaskanativearts.org), is a nonprofit promoting the best work of indigenous artists, both in traditional and contemporary forms. The gallery hosts shows dedicated to individual artists in a light, open space; another area shows a mix of pieces. The website is well worth a visit and has an online shopping function.

Nowhere else will you find a business like the **Oomingmak Musk Ox Producers' Co-operative** (☏888/360-9665 outside Alaska or 907/272-9225; www.qiviut.com), located in the house with the musk ox on the side at 6th Avenue and H Street. Owned by 250 Alaska Native women living in villages across the state, the co-op sells only scarves and other items they knit of *qiviut* (ki-vee-ute), the light, warm, silky underhair of the musk ox, which is collected from shedding animals. Each village has its own knitting pattern. They're expensive—adult caps are $130 to $180—but the quality is extraordinary. The website contains the women's fascinating correspondence and links to a few of the rural knitters' own pages. When I bought a piece for my wife a few years ago, one of the knitters sent me a thank-you card. As an aside, if you are driving north from Anchorage, you may also want to stop at the **Musk Ox Farm** (☏907/745-4151; www.muskoxfarm. org), just north of Palmer on the Glenn Highway, where you can see the strange-looking creatures close up (summer daily 10am–6pm; admission $8 adults, $7 seniors, and $6 ages 5–12). Musk oxen also are at the Alaska Zoo (covered earlier in this chapter) and are easy to see in the wild near Nome (see "Nome: Arctic Frontier Town," in chapter 11).

Anchorage also has several small shops and local secret places to find authentic Native artwork. The **Yankee Whaler,** in the lobby of the Hotel Captain Cook, at 5th Avenue and I Street, is a small but well-regarded shop carrying Native arts and other Alaskan-made gifts. At the **Anchorage**

Museum at Rasmuson Center, 6th and C streets (p. 321), check out the gift shop for a tastefully selected and beautifully displayed array of Alaska Native art.

If you can get beyond the downtown area, you can shop at among the best places for Native crafts in Alaska, the **Hospital Auxiliary Craft Shop** in the Alaska Native Medical Center, off Tudor east of Bragaw (☎907/729-1122), where everything is made by the indigenous people eligible to use the hospital and the staff are all volunteers. The work you find here is all authentic and entirely traditional, and it's possible to stumble on artistic masterpieces. The shop is open Monday through Friday from 10am to 2pm and the first and third Saturday of each month from 11am to 2pm. They don't accept credit cards. There's exceptional Native art to see on the walls of the hospital, too.

FURS If you're in the market for a fur, Anchorage has a wide selection and no sales tax. **David Green Master Furrier,** 130 W. 4th Ave. (www.davidgreenfurs.com), is an Anchorage institution. Others are nearby.

GIFTS There are lots of places to buy both mass-produced and inexpensive handmade crafts other than Alaska Native items. If you will be in town on a weekend during the summer, be sure to visit the **Anchorage Market and Festival** street fair, in the parking lot at 3rd Avenue and E Street, with food, music, and hundreds of miscellaneous crafts booths. You won't have any trouble finding gift shops on 4th. Our favorite is the relatively classy **Cabin Fever,** 650 W. 4th. The **Kobuk Coffee Company,** 5th Avenue and E Street, next to the town square, occupies one of Anchorage's earliest commercial buildings; it's a cozy candy, coffee, and collectibles shop.

FINE ART Downtown has several galleries, including those mentioned under "Alaska Native Arts and Crafts," above, and others in the 4th Avenue Market Place. Openings are coordinated to happen on the first Friday of each month, allowing for an evening of free party hopping and art shopping.

The **International Gallery of Contemporary Art,** 427 D St. (www.igcaalaska.org), is a nonprofit space dedicated to artists. Come here for an in-depth look at just a few artists' work and to meet people who really care about art. Since it is run on contributions by volunteers, hours are short

Oomingmask Musk Ox Producers' Co-operative.

and changeable; currently: Tuesday through Sunday, noon to 4pm; closed Monday. They're also open for first Friday, 5:30 to 7:30pm.

Artique, 314 G St., is Anchorage's oldest gallery and has a large selection. Half of the gallery is given over to big oils and other impressive originals; the other half is chock-full of prints, less-expensive ceramics, and some mass-produced stuff. At 5th and G, **Aurora Fine Arts** carries pottery, prints, and gifts. Directly across G is a gallery showing only glass sculpture.

ANCHORAGE NIGHTLIFE
The Performing Arts

WHAT'S PLAYING The primary arts season begins in the fall and ends in the spring, but in the summer you can catch traveling performers, music festivals, and live music at the nightclubs and coffeehouses. To find out what's happening, check Friday's edition of the *Anchorage Daily News,* which has a section called "Play" that includes reviews and listings information in grid format. The website (www.adn.com/play) includes an exhaustive event calendar. The free weekly *Anchorage Press,* given away in racks all over town, also offers extensive event coverage aimed at a younger audience. See "Special Events" above for some major happenings.

BUYING TICKETS Ticketmaster (℡800/745-3000; www.ticketmaster.com) handles the Sullivan Arena and the convention centers, and sells tickets at Fred Meyer grocery stores. The Alaska Center for Performing Arts, 631 W. 6th Ave. (www.myalaskacenter.com), operates its own ticket agency, **CenterTix** (℡907/263-ARTS [263-2787] or www.centertix.net), and also sells tickets for many of the smaller venues and less mainstream artists. The call center and box office in the center are open Monday through Friday 9am to 5pm, Saturday noon to 5pm, and evenings prior to events.

PRESENTERS The **Anchorage Concert Association** (℡907/272-1471; www.anchorageconcerts.org) offers a fall-through-spring schedule of classical music, theater, dance, and other performing arts. **Whistling Swan Productions** (www.whistlingswan.net) promotes folk and acoustic alternative performers in intimate venues all year. The **Anchorage Symphony** (℡907/274-8668; www.anchoragesymphony.org) performs during the winter season. Anchorage also has lots of community theater and opera, and limited professional theater, including the experimental **Out North Contemporary Art House** (℡907/279-3800; www.outnorth. org), which produces local shows and imports avant-garde performers. Downtown, **Cyrano's Off Center Playhouse** (℡907/274-2599; www. cyranos.org), at 4th Avenue and D Street, is a tiny theater with its own semiprofessional repertory company.

Nightclubs & Bars

I've mentioned some fun downtown bars in the walking tour, including Humpies, Darwin's Theory, and F Street Station. The hippest downtown club is **Bernie's Bungalow Lounge,** 626 D St. (℡907/276-8808), which grew from a little bungalow into a large, artsy playground with a backyard patio enclosed by a hedge.

You can sometimes find foreign films, poetry readings, and similar cultural fare here, and, more often, you can socialize with people interested in such things.

Blues Central/Chef's Inn, 825 W. Northern Lights Blvd. (☎907/272-1341), long a showcase of the best blues performers available, now also presents imported rock acts, with live music virtually every night. Major blues names and up-and-coming national performers come through on a regular basis. Shows start at 9:30pm. They're also known for their beef.

The most famous bar in Anchorage, with the slogan, "We cheat the other guy and pass the savings on to you," is the huge **Chilkoot Charlie's,** at Spenard Road and Fireweed Lane (☎907/272-1010; www.koots.com). It has two stages, three dance floors, and 10 bars with different themes, including a historic old dive from the Seward Highway called the Bird House that was picked up and moved into the building. The place is huge and full of entertainment, like an adult Disneyland, but I find it claustrophobic when crowded, with its low ceilings and confusing layout. It's open every day of the year from 10:30am until after 2am. If you do go there late, avoid conflict and use caution when leaving, as it can be a wild crowd and rough neighborhood.

The Movies

A movie at the **Bear Tooth TheatrePub,** 1230 W. 27th Ave. (☎907/276-4200; www.beartooththeatre.net), is a chance to sit back with a big glass of craft-brewed beer and a plate of nachos or a full dinner —it feels a lot like watching at home except for the big screen and the other people around you in the dark. (Well, our home is usually a bit cleaner, but our cooking isn't as good.) The films tend to be second run Hollywood output, but Monday is art house night, and film festivals and special events come through. They also put on concerts monthly: Check the website. The dining choices include gourmet tacos, pizzas, and other hand-held selections. Everything is quite good. And now the fine print. Even bad movies sell out, and there's often a crush. Unless you reserve and pay extra for a booth (a few days ahead for weekend shows), you must arrive quite early to find parking, get your ticket and seat, order your food and beer, and finish waiting in various lines before the movie starts. The staff brings the meal to you in the theater. Eating here without taking in a movie is covered under "Bear Tooth Grill" on p. 308.

There are several multiplexes in Anchorage playing all the current Hollywood output; check the sources at the beginning of this section for listings and reviews. **Century 16,** 301 E. 36th Ave. (☎907/770-2602; www.cinemark.com), is an attractive, modern multiplex a reasonable cab ride from downtown.

SIDE TRIPS TO TURNAGAIN ARM & PORTAGE GLACIER

One of the world's great drives starts in Anchorage and leads roughly 50 miles south on the Seward Highway to Portage Glacier. It's the trip, not the destination, that makes it worthwhile. The two-lane highway along Turnagain Arm, chipped from the foot of the rocky Chugach Mountains, provides a platform to see a magnificent, ever-changing, mostly untouched landscape full of wildlife. I've listed the sights in the style of a highway log, for there are interesting stops all the way along

Turnagain Arm.

the road. It will take at least half a day round-trip, and there's plenty to do for an all-day excursion. Use your headlights for safety even in daylight, and be patient if you get stuck behind a summertime line of cars—if you pass, you'll just come up behind another line ahead. Mileage markers count down from Anchorage. Continue with this highway log on to the Kenai Peninsula and Seward in chapter 8, starting on p. 361. Car rental is covered in "Getting Around," earlier in this chapter. Bus tours follow the route and visit Portage Glacier. **Gray Line of Alaska** (☎800/544-2206 or 907/277-5581; www.graylineofalaska.com) offers a 7-hour trip that includes a stop in Girdwood and a boat ride on Portage Lake for $72 adults, $36 children 12 and under, twice daily in summer.

You can also see this incredible scenery—and more—from a train, although, of course, without stopping along the Arm for hikes or wildlife viewing. The **Alaska Railroad** (☎800/544-0552 or 907/265-2494; www.alaskarailroad. com) operates summer trains to Whittier and Seward that trace Turnagain Arm on the way (you can book the train and a Prince William Sound day boat with one call).

Definitely also consider the railroad's day-trip tour to the glaciated interior of the Kenai Peninsula, beyond Turnagain Arm where no road extends. That unique tour, called the "Glacier Discovery Train to Grandview," begins in Anchorage, Girdwood, Whittier, or Portage; if starting from Anchorage, the return from Portage is by bus. The tour costs $110 adults from Anchorage or Girdwood, $85 from Portage or Whittier, and roughly half price for children. There are several choices of what to do on your day in the backcountry: Take a hike led by a Forest Ranger at Spencer Glacier, go white-water rafting, or even use the whistle stop service for your own, self-guided hike or expedition. The railroad and Forest Service are working on ambitious plans for a backcountry network of trails, campsites, public cabins, and rail stations, which will take a number of years to complete but parts of which are already usable.

POTTER MARSH (Mile 117) Heading south from Anchorage, the Seward Highway descends a bluff to cross a broad marsh formed by water impounded behind the tracks of the Alaska Railroad. The marsh has a boardwalk from which you can watch a huge variety of birds. Salad-green grasses grow from sparkling, pond-green water.

POTTER SECTION HOUSE (Mile 115) Located at the south end of Potter Marsh, the section house was an early maintenance station for the Alaska Railroad. Today it contains the offices of Chugach State Park, open during normal business hours, and, outside, a few old train cars and interpretive displays. Just across the road is the trail head for the **Turnagain Arm Trail.** It's a mostly level path running down the arm well above the highway with great views breaking now and then through the trees. Hike as far as you like and then backtrack to your car; or, if you can arrange a one-way walk with a ride back from the other end, continue 4 miles to the McHugh Creek picnic area and trail head, or 9 miles to Windy Corner.

MCHUGH CREEK (Mile 111) Four miles south of Potter is an inviting and memorable state park picnic area, perched on terraced rock above the ocean and bisected by a series of crashing rapids and waterfalls. Above the picnic area starts a challenging day hike with a 3,000-foot elevation gain to Rabbit Lake, which sits in a tundra mountain bowl, or to the top of 4,301-foot McHugh Peak. You don't have to climb all the way; there are spectacular views within an hour of the road. The trail branches from the Turnagain Arm Trail: Hike west (back toward Anchorage) to where it heads uphill.

On the highway, you will find that from this point onward most of the stops are on the right or ocean side of the road: Plan your stops on the outbound trip, not on the return when you would have to make left turns across traffic.

Old train at Potter Section House.   Turnagain Arm.

tidal **WAVE**

Tides in Turnagain Arm rise and fall over a greater range than anywhere else in the United States, with a difference between an extreme high and low of more than 41 feet. When the tide is rising, the water can grow deeper by as much as 7 feet an hour, or a foot of water every 8½ minutes. If your foot gets stuck in the mud, it takes less than an hour to drown. (Yes, that has really happened.) Amazing as that speed is, the tide here can go even faster. A breathtaking wall of water up to 6 feet tall called a bore tide can roar up Turnagain Arm twice a day. To see the ocean do such a thing is so unfamiliar it looks almost like science fiction, as the wide arc of foam rushes ahead of a noticeably deeper sea. You can (theoretically) predict the bore tide. Get a tide-table book or look up the tide change on the Web (start at

http://tidesandcurrents.noaa.gov and pull down "Products"). Note the size of the tidal range for the day you are visiting: The bore tide will be most noticeable during periods of large tides. (The magnitude of tides varies on the lunar cycle.) Find the time of low tide in Anchorage. Now add the following intervals to the time of the Anchorage low for a prediction of when the bore tide will pass each of these spots on the highway:

- Beluga Point (Mile 110): 1 hour 15 minutes
- Bird Point (Mile 96): 2 hours 15 minutes
- Twentymile River (Mile 80): 4 hours
- The best viewing is Beluga Point to Bird Point; at the latter wayside, a set of signs explains the tides, and tide tables are posted to predict the tidal bore.

BELUGA POINT (Mile 110) The state highway department probably didn't need to put up scenic overlook signs on this pull-out, 1½ miles south of McHugh Creek—you would have figured it out on your own. The terrain is simply awesome, as the highway traces the edge of Turnagain Arm, below the towering cliffs of the Chugach Mountains. If the tide and salmon runs are right, you may see beluga whales, which chase the fish toward fresh water. Sometimes they overextend and strand themselves by the dozens in the receding tide, farther along, but they usually aren't harmed. The pull-out has spotting scopes to improve the viewing. The farther right-hand pull-outs over the next few miles have interpretive signs about the 1895 gold rush in this area and other topics.

WINDY POINT (Mile 106) Be on the lookout on the mountain side of the road for Dall sheep picking their way along the cliffs. It's a unique spot, for the sheep get much closer to people here than is usual in the wild; apparently, they believe they're safe. Windy Point is the prime spot, but you also have a good chance of seeing sheep virtually anywhere along this stretch of road. If cars are stopped, that's probably why; get well off the road and pay attention to traffic, which will still be passing at high speeds.

You may also see windsurfers in the gray, silty waters of the Arm. They're crazy. The water is a mixture of glacial runoff and the near-freezing ocean. Besides, the movement of water that creates the huge tides causes riverlike currents, with standing waves like rapids.

INDIAN VALLEY (Mile 104) Up the road by the Turnagain House restaurant is the **Indian Valley** trail head, a gold rush–era trail that ultimately leads 24 miles to the other side of the mountains. The path, while often muddy, rises less steeply than other trails along the Arm.

BIRD RIDGE TRAIL (Mile 102) This is a lung-busting climb of 3,000 vertical feet in a little over a mile. It starts with an easy, accessible trail, then rises steeply to views that start at impressive and get more amazing as you climb. With the southern exposure, it's dry early in the year.

BIRD CREEK (Mile 101) The excellent state campground on the right side of the highway, over the water, is described on p. 302, and the productive salmon fishing in the creek is described on p. 332. If you stop, use the lot on the left side of the road before you reach the creek. There is also a short trail, interpretive signs, an overlook, and a platform that makes fishing easier for people with disabilities. Pink salmon run from late June to mid-August, silver salmon mostly in August. A scenic bike trail starts here and runs 10 miles to Girdwood, much of it on an older highway alignment.

BIRD POINT (Mile 96) The remarkable wayside here is not to be missed. A paved pathway rises up to a bedrock outcropping with a simply wonderful view— all the severity of the Turnagain Arm, but framed by the soft green of a freshwater wetland with a beaver lodge. Take a look at the fascinating interpretive signs on many subjects. A $5 day-use fee is charged for each vehicle at a self-service kiosk.

THE FLATS (Miles 96–90) At Bird Point the highway descends from the mountainside to the mud flats. Several pull-outs on the right side of the highway have interpretive signs. At high tide, water comes right up to the road. At low tide, the whole Arm narrows to a thin, winding channel through the mud. The Arm is not practically navigable, and navigational charts are not even available. Few have ever tried to navigate it other than gold prospectors in rowboats a century ago or today's occasional death-defying canoeist or kayaker. The first to try was Capt. James Cook, in 1778, as he was searching for the Northwest Passage on his final, fatal voyage of discovery (he was killed by Hawaiians later that year). He named this branch of Cook Inlet Turnagain Arm because the strength of the currents and shoals foiled the boat he sent to check it out. Cook believed the Inlet was a river and left well before reaching its head; but when his ships got back to England, geographers believed his report left open the possibility that this could be a route to the Northwest Passage, requiring another expedition led by George Vancouver to come and make sure. Vancouver noted in disappointment that another day of work by Cook could have saved him immense effort.

TURNOFF TO GIRDWOOD (Mile 90) The attractions of Girdwood, covered below, are worth a visit, but the shopping center here at the intersection is not chief among them. Stop for a simple meal or a restroom break (the convenience store has large public restrooms), or to fill your gas tank for the last time for many a mile.

TWENTYMILE RIVER (Mile 80) Three species of salmon and a small smelt, the eulachon, known locally as the hooligan, spawn in this river. In the spring you can see Native families dip-netting the hooligan. There is good bird-watching here and from turnouts farther on, but venturing out on Turnagain Arm's tidal mud carries the real risk of getting stuck in quicksandlike mud and drowning in the tide. Don't do it.

FROM TOP: **Bird Point; Alaska Wildlife Conservation Center.**

OLD PORTAGE (Mile 80) All along the flats at the head of Turnagain Arm are large marshes full of what looks like standing driftwood. These are trees killed by salt water that flowed in when the 1964 quake lowered the land as much as 10 feet. On the right, ¾ mile past the Twentymile River and across from the rail depot, a few ruins of the abandoned town of Portage are still visible, more than 45 years after the great earthquake.

ALASKA WILDLIFE CONSERVATION CENTER (Mile 79) The nonprofit center, developed with visitors in mind, gives homes to injured and orphaned deer, moose, owls, elk, bison, musk ox, bear, fox, and caribou (☎907/783-2025; www.awcc.org). Visitors drive through the 200-acre compound to see the animals in fenced enclosures as large as 110 acres—you can often get a close look at the animals, but the larger enclosures give them natural vegetation and the ability to get away from view if they want to. There's no need to visit both here and the Alaska Zoo (p. 324). The zoo has more kinds of animals and it's a fun place to stroll, but the cages there are much smaller and often seem constricting. Here the animals' settings are more natural and perhaps more humane, but viewing is car-based. A big, log gift shop and outdoor snack bar are at the end of the tour. Admission is $10 for adults; $7.50 for military, seniors, and children 4 to 12, with a maximum of $30 per vehicle. Summer hours are daily 8am to 8pm (last vehicle in at 7:30pm); off-season hours vary, but in the spring and fall are at least daily 10am to 5pm.

PORTAGE GLACIER (Take the 5½-mile spur road at Mile 78) The named attraction has largely melted, receding out of sight of the visitor center. (The glacier you *can* see is Burns.) When the center was built in 1985, it was predicted that Portage Glacier would keep floating on its 800-foot-deep lake until 2020. Instead, it withdrew to the far edge of the lake in 1995. Today the exhibits in the lakeside **Begich-Boggs Visitor Center** focus on the Chugach National Forest as a whole, rather than just the glacier, and they're worth an hour or two to become oriented to the area's nature, history, and lifestyles. Children and adults find much to hold their interest here. To see Portage Glacier itself, take the road toward Whittier that branches to the left just before the visitor center and stop at a pullout beyond the first (toll-free) tunnel; or take the boat mentioned below.

Several short trails start near the center. Check at the center for rangers-led nature walks. The Moraine Trail is an easy, paved quarter mile. Another trail leads less than a mile to Byron Glacier, in case you're interested in getting up close to some ice. Always dress warmly, as cold winds are the rule in this funnel-like valley.

A **day boat** operated by **Gray Line of Alaska** (☎800/478-6388, 907/277-5581 for reservations, or 907/783-2983 at the lake; www.grayline ofalaska.com) traverses the lake to within a few hundred yards of Portage Glacier on hour-long tours, ice conditions permitting. It costs $29 adults,

---

Gone but Not Forgotten

The **Begich-Boggs Visitor Center** at Portage Glacier is named for Hale Boggs, who was U.S. House majority leader, and Rep. Nick Begich, then Alaska's lone congressman, who disappeared together in a small plane during Begich's 1972 reelection bid. The most likely theory is that the wings iced up in Portage Pass, causing a crash into Prince William Sound just beyond the mountains. No trace was ever found—as with many other Alaskan planes that have simply flown off into oblivion. Begich was reelected anyway. His opponent, Republican Don Young, later won a special election and continued more than 36 years as Alaska's only congressman, winning reelection again in 2008 despite ethics charges that led both houses of Congress to ask the FBI to investigate him. Boggs' wife, Lindy, served out her husband's term and was elected to eight more. Boggs' daughter, Cokie Roberts, is the famous broadcast journalist. Begich's son, Mark, served as mayor of Anchorage from 2003 to 2008, when he was elected to the U.S. Senate.

$15 ages 12 and under, and goes five times daily in summer, every 90 minutes starting at 10:30am. If this is your only chance to see a glacier in Alaska, it's a good choice, but if your itinerary includes any of the great glaciers in Prince William Sound, Kenai Fjords National Park, or the like, you won't be as impressed by Portage. Sandwiches and other simple meals are sold at a cafeteria near the visitor center called the **Portage Glacier Lodge** (☎907/783-3117).

There are no lodgings in Portage, but two **Forest Service campgrounds** are on the road to the visitor center, with 72 sites between them (more details are in the Chugach National Forest section in chapter 8). At the Williwaw Campground, there's also a place to watch red salmon spawning in mid-August, but no fishing.

SIDE TRIPS TO GIRDWOOD & MOUNT ALYESKA

Girdwood, 37 miles south of Anchorage, is proof that a charming little town can coexist with a major ski resort, as long as the resort goes undiscovered by the world's skiers. Girdwood still has a sleepy, offbeat character. Retired hippies, ski bums, and a few old-timers live in the houses and cabins among the big spruce trees in the valley below the Mount Alyeska lifts. They all expected a development explosion to follow the construction of an international resort here a number of years ago, but it never happened. That may not have been good news for the Japanese investors who finally sold the resort in 2006, but it is for skiers and other visitors who discover this paradise. They find varied, uncrowded skiing through long winters, superb accommodations, and an authentically funky community.

The primary summer attractions are the hiking trails, the tram to the top of Mount Alyeska, and the Crow Creek Mine, described below. In winter, it's skiing. Mount Alyeska doesn't have the size of the famous resorts in the Rockies, but it's more than large and steep enough. Half the mountain is above the tree line, and the snow lasts a long time. Olympian Tommy Moe trained here, the Alpine national championships have raced down these slopes many times, most recently in 2009. The national extreme skiing and snowboarding competition was here in 2008. Skiers used to tamer, busier slopes rave about the skiing here, with long, challenging downhills, few lift lines, and stunning views of the Chugach Mountains and glistening Turnagain Arm below.

A wealthy skiing enthusiast bought the ski resort in 2006 from owners that had paid it little attention for several years. He pledged to make many welcome improvements on the mountain and at the skiing facilities. Developments have begun to materialize, so be aware that changes may affect the information you find here.

ESSENTIALS A **rental car** is the most practical means for getting to Girdwood. If you will only ski, however, you may be able to take a shuttle; call the resort before you come. The **Girdwood Chamber of Commerce** maintains a website at **www.girdwoodalaska.com**. For more guidance, check the Anchorage visitor information listed under "Essentials," earlier in this chapter.

Exploring Girdwood

Crow Creek Mine ★ This mine, opened in 1896, is still operated, mostly as an attraction for visitors, by the pioneering Toohey family. They use the paths and eight small original buildings to show off the frontier lifestyle and teach about gold mining. Rabbits and ducks wander around, and weddings are held in the pleasant compound. A bag of dirt, guaranteed to have some gold in it, is provided for gold panning, and you can dig and pan to get more if you have the patience for it. Crow Creek Road, off the Alyeska Highway, is only partly paved and can be quite rough and muddy in the spring. Camping is $5 a night, with portable toilets.

Crow Creek Rd. (off the Alyeska Hwy.). ☎907/278-8060. www.crowcreekmine.com. $5 adults, free for children. Gold panning $15 adults, $10 seniors and active military, $5 children 11 and under (includes admission). May 15–Sept 15 daily 9am–6pm.

Mt. Alyeska Tram ★ The tram isn't cheap, but I think it's worth it for anyone who otherwise might not make it to high alpine tundra during an Alaska trip. (In winter, ride on your lift ticket; in summer, ride free with a meal at the Seven Glaciers Restaurant at the top, p. 350.) The tram takes 7 minutes in summer to get to the 2,300-foot level, where it stops at a station containing both the Seven Glaciers and an attractive but pricey cafeteria, the Glacier Express. Whether or not you eat here, the tram presents an opportunity for everyone, no matter how young, old, or infirm, to experience the pure light, limitless views, and crystalline quiet of an Alaskan mountaintop. Take the opportunity to walk around and enjoy it. Dress very warmly.

At the Hotel Alyeska (see below). $18 adults ($14 Alaska residents), $15 ages 60 and older, $15 ages 8–17, $9 ages 4–7, free 3 and younger. Summer daily 9am–9pm; winter, when lifts operate (call to check as hours vary).

Activities

Here I have covered activities right in Girdwood. In nearby Whittier (p. 371), you can go ocean fishing, sea kayaking, or take a glacier and wildlife cruise. See "Side Trips to Turnagain Arm & Portage Glacier," above, for information on sightseeing along Turnagain Arm, hiking and other summer activities, and how to take the train into the mountainous backcountry for hiking or white-water rafting.

SKIING Mount Alyeska, at 3,939 feet, has 1,000 acres of skiing, beginning from a base elevation of only 250 feet and rising 2,500 feet. The normal season is from late November to April, and it's an exceptional

Mt. Alyeska Tram.

Ski Conditions

The rainforest of Girdwood and the dry Anchorage bowl often have different weather, despite being within the same municipality. Before heading down the road for a day of skiing, check out the conditions. Call ☎907/SKI-SNOW (754-7669) for snow, weather, and visibility conditions, or check that information online at www. alyeskaresort.com. For visibility from below, check out the cam at www.chairfive.com.

year when there isn't plenty of snow all winter (although the warming climate has brought some late-starting ski seasons). The average snowfall is 721 inches, or 61 feet. Because it's near the water, the weather is rarely very cold. Light is more of an issue, with short days in midwinter. There are 27 lighted trails covering 2,000 vertical feet on Thursday, Friday, and Saturday evenings from mid-December to mid-March, but the best Alaska skiing is when the days get longer and warmer in the spring.

Alyeska has ten lifts, including the tram. Two chairs serve beginners, with a vertical drop of around 300 feet. The other 89% of the mountain is geared to intermediate to expert skiers. The biggest drawback for less experienced skiers is a lack of runs in the low-intermediate ability range. After graduating from the primary beginners' lift, Chair 3, skiers must jump to significantly more challenging slopes. That explains the long lines in busy periods on Chair 3 (it is the only lift on the mountain with real lines). More confident skiers like the mountain best. Most of it is steep, and the expert slopes are extreme. Helicopter skiing goes right from the resort's hotel as well.

An all-day lift ticket costs $55 for adults, $40 for ages 14 to 17 or 60 to 69, $35 for ages 8 to 13, and $10 for ages 7 and under or over 70. Private and group instruction are available, and you can save a lot by buying your lessons, lift ticket, and equipment rental at the same time. A basic rental package costs $35 a day for adults, $27 for ages 13 and under or over 60; high performance and demo packages (at the hotel rental location only) are $45 to $75. There are groomed **cross-country trails** as well, and gear for rent at the hotel, but the best Nordic skiing is in Anchorage.

The resort's utilitarian **day lodge** is a large, noisy building with snack and rental counters, located at the front of the mountain. The relatively cozy **Sitzmark Bar and Grill,** nearby, has long been a more comfortable place for a meal (burgers are around $10). **The Hotel Alyeska** (below) is on the other side of the mountain, connected to the front by the tram to the top and beginner-level chair 7 (you can ski right from the door). It makes a quieter and more genteel starting point for day-trippers as well as guests, with the same equipment-rental prices as the day lodge, plus higher-priced demo rentals. There are several dining choices here and at the top of the tram (see "Where to Stay," below).

HIKING There are a couple of great Chugach National Forest trails starting in Girdwood.

Among the best trails in the region for a family hike is the **Winner Creek Trail,** which begins behind the Hotel Alyeska and leads to a roaring gorge where Winner Creek and Glacier Creek meet; a hand-operated tram crosses the water. The trail is essentially level and a good length for an afternoon:

The round-trip to the gorge is about 4.5 miles. A winter ski trail takes a separate route, through a series of meadows, to the same destination.

The **Crow Pass Trail** is more ambitious. The route rises into the mountains and continues all the way over to Eagle River, after a 26-mile hike that can take a couple of days. But with less expenditure of time you can make a strenuous day hike of it going just up to the pass, where you can see the glaciers, wildflower meadows, and old mining equipment. The Forest Service's A-frame Crow Pass public use cabin makes an excellent destination for an overnight from Girdwood; it lies on a lake at 3,500 feet of elevation, half a mile from the pass. The trail head is up Crow Creek Road, off the Alyeska Highway. For more information on the national forest and cabin reservations, see "Chugach National Forest: Do-It-Yourself Wilderness," in chapter 8.

Hand-operated tram at Winner Creek Trail.

SNOWMOBILING Glacier City Snowmobile Tours (☎877/783-5566 or 907/783-5566; www.snowtours.net) operates out of the Great Alaskan Tourist Trap gift shop in the shopping center on the Seward Highway. Guides suit up clients—most of whom have never been on a snowmobile—and drive them to a promising site, determined according to snow conditions. At best, the winter tours make it all the way to Spencer Glacier. Groups are no larger than six and the attitude is casual: After a brief introduction, you are driving your own machine, using your own judgment. The entire outing lasts as long as 6 hours, with 3½ hours riding. The cost is $240 per person.

Where to Stay

Besides the resort hotel, there are plenty of condos and B&Bs in town. **Alyeska Accommodations,** on Olympic Mountain Loop (☎888/783-2001 or 907/783-2000; www.alyeskaaccommodations.com), offers rooms, condos, cabins, and luxurious houses.

I highly recommend **Hidden Creek Bed & Breakfast** (☎907/783-5557; www.hiddencreekbb.com), a beautiful craftsman-style inn built among huge spruce and hemlock trees by a pair of outgoing corporate drop-outs who came to Alaska on vacation and fell in love with Girdwood. Each of the three well-equipped rooms is stylish and finely crafted in its own way, and the hostess, a culinary school graduate, serves full breakfasts. Summer rates are $175 to $225, winter $145 to $175.

Hotel Alyeska ★★★ This hotel is among Alaska's best. The beauty of the building alone separates it from the competition, as does its location in an unspoiled mountain valley among huge spruce trees. Studded with dormers and turrets, it impresses on first sight. Inside, sumptuous cherrywood and rich colors unite the welcoming common rooms and elegant guest rooms. Although not large, rooms have every convenience. The saltwater swimming pool is magnificent, with a cathedral ceiling and windows by the whirlpool overlooking the mountain. A full-service spa offers all the latest pampering. A few days spent here skiing, swimming, and relaxing make the rest of life seem too drab. Now for the bad news. On weekends and school holidays in the winter, the hotel is overrun by partying families from Anchorage who overtax the facilities and destroy the peaceful ambience. Children run wild, the pool becomes impossibly crowded, and service deteriorates to an unacceptable level. Avoid these times for a skiing vacation.

Six dining options vie for attention. **The Seven Glaciers,** 2,300 feet above the lobby by tram on Mount Alyeska, serves trendy and beautifully presented dinners in a sumptuous dining room floating above the clouds. Service is warm and highly professional. Meals are expensive, especially since the small servings make it desirable to order several courses. The restaurant opens only on the weekends in the winter. A mountaintop cafeteria is right next door (great views, limited choices). At the base level, choices include a teppanyaki and sushi place, a hotel cafe, a bar and grill, and a casual cafe.

1000 Arlberg Ave. (P.O. Box 249), Girdwood, AK 99587. ☏**800/880-3880** or 907/754-1111. Fax 907/754-2200. www.alyeskaresort.com. 304 units. Summer and Christmas $275–$360 double, $400–$1,500 suite; winter $145–$240 double, $300–$1,500 suite. Extra adult $25. Children stay free in parent's room. AE, DC, MC, V. **Amenities:** 6 restaurants; 2 bars; babysitting; bike rental; children's programs; concierge; health club; massage; indoor pool; limited room service; spa; Wi-Fi. *In room:* TV w/pay movies, fridge, hair dryer, Internet.

Where to Dine

Also see directly above for restaurant options at the Hotel Alyeska.

Chair 5 Restaurant ★ ☺ AMERICAN This is where Girdwood locals meet their friends and take their families for dinner, and it's also one of our favorites after skiing or on a drive to the Kenai Peninsula. The casual feeling is enhanced by the relaxed, sunlit bar at the front of the restaurant, often occupied by ponytailed guys sipping microbrews and sharing a game of pool. The dining rooms are small and quiet, but the nicely funky atmosphere continues throughout. A lengthy menu offers choices pleasing to each family member, including pizza, burgers, fresh fish, steaks, and even game. The food and service are consistently good.

5 Lindblad Ave., in the New Girdwood Town Square. ☏**907/783-2500.** www.chairfive.com. Lunch $9–$13; dinner $18–$28; large pizza $16–$23. AE, DC, DISC, MC, V. Daily 11am–11pm (bar until 2am).

Double Musky Inn ★★★ CAJUN The ski-bum-casual atmosphere and rambling, cluttered dining room among the trees match the wonderful Cajun and New Orleans food in a way that couldn't have been contrived—it's at once too improbable and too authentic. Service is as relaxed and friendly as at a greasy spoon. Food takes a long time to arrive, but when it does, every dish is flawless. I love the jambalaya, and the steaks are famous (by which I mean, really famous—Food Network chose this as one of the 10 best restaurants in America). The Double Musky isn't to everyone's taste, however; your senses can feel raw after the noise, highly spiced food, and crowds, and parking can be difficult. Loud groups will enjoy it more than couples, and families don't really fit. Since the restaurant doesn't take reservations, here's an important tip: Grab seats in the bar and dive into your meal there with appetizers and drinks rather than simply waiting.

Mile 3, Crow Creek Rd., Girdwood. **☎907/783-2822.** Reservations not accepted. www.double muskyinn.com. Main courses $18–$37. AE, DC, DISC, MC, V. Tues–Thurs 5–10pm; Fri–Sun 4:30–10pm. Closed Nov.

SIDE TRIPS TO THE MATANUSKA & SUSITNA VALLEYS

On a longer visit to Anchorage, you may want to spend a day or two in the suburbs to the north, known as the Mat-Su Valley. Perhaps you're curious for insight into the formative influences of Alaska's celebrity politician, former Governor Sarah Palin, who lives here and exemplifies the area in many ways. The lifestyle, made famous during her vice-presidential run, attracted a flood of similar families since the early 1980s, enough people to drive rapid, unplanned development. Reached by the Glenn Highway about 40 miles from Anchorage, Mat-Su is a bedroom community for the city superimposed on a former frontier farming region. Folks commute an hour or more each way to live out here, gaining space to run snow machines and all-terrain vehicles, and for lower-priced land, low taxes, and a less restrictive local government. In the well-populated central valley, where Palin lives, migrants with these goals transformed lovely meadows into commercial sprawl, with little to interest a visitor who already knows what parking lots, big-box stores, and fast-food franchises look like. But the entire Matanuska-Susitna Borough is the size of West Virginia, and beyond the suburban blight, vast wild lands of unspoiled mountains, glaciers, and rivers remain relatively close at hand.

If you are driving anywhere north from Anchorage, especially toward Denali National Park or Fairbanks, you will pass through this area. There are some

Mat-Su Valley.

Independence Mine State Historical Park.

interesting places to stop if you have the time. In this summary I've covered a few highlights in the central area. Some of the best attractions are covered in other parts of the book. **The Alaska State Fair,** held before Labor Day, is covered under "Special Events," near the beginning of this chapter. The **Musk Ox Farm** is under "Shopping," above. Funky Talkeetna, a gateway to Denali National Park, is in chapter 9. The Matanuska Glacier area (on the Glenn Hwy.), with its great canyon views and late-season cross-country skiing and snowmobiling, is in chapter 10.

You can learn more about visitor attractions, lodging, and the area's greatest strengths, its hiking, fishing, and skiing, from the **Mat-Su Visitors Center,** 7744 E. Visitors View Court, Palmer, AK 99645 (☏907/746-5000; www.alaskavisit. com). The center is open mid-May to mid-September, 8:30am to 6:30pm. To find it, take the Trunk Road exit from the Parks Highway near the intersection with the Glenn Highway.

Through Hatcher Pass

If you're headed north to Denali National Park or Fairbanks, the winding road through Hatcher Pass to Willow makes a glorious alpine detour around the least attractive part of your drive. Note, however, that past the mine and skiing area the road is unpaved, open only in summer, and not suitable for large RVs. From the Parks Highway, just after it branches from the Glenn Highway, exit to the right on the Trunk Road and keep going north when you reach Palmer-Fishhook Road, which becomes Hatcher Pass Road. From the Glenn Highway near Palmer, take Palmer-Fishhook just north of town.

Even if you're not headed north, a trip to Hatcher Pass combines one of the area's most beautiful drives, access to great hiking and Nordic skiing, and interesting old buildings to look at. The **Independence Mine State Historical Park ★★** (☏907/745-2827 or 907/745-3975; www.alaskastateparks.org, click on "Individual Parks," then "Matanuska and Susitna Valleys") takes in the remains of a hard-rock gold mine that operated from 1938 to '51. Some buildings have been restored, including an assay office that's a museum and the manager's house that's a welcoming visitor center, while a big old mill, towering on the hillside, sags and leans as a picturesque ruin. A visit is interesting even if you don't go inside, using the interpretive panels and map on a self-guided tour. The paved trails are easily navigable by anyone, and the rugged, half-mile Mill Trail leads up to that building's ruins. The setting, in a bowl of rock and alpine tundra, is spectacular. The day-use fee is $5 per vehicle. A guided tour is an additional $5 per person and leaves at 1:30 and 3:30pm weekdays, plus 4:30pm weekends. Tours depend on staffing and may be increased or decreased from these hours. The visitor center is open from 10am to 7pm daily in the summer, closed off-season.

Leave some time for a summer ramble in the heather if you visit the mine. In the winter, the Nordic or telemark skiing is exceptional, with a few kilometers of groomed trail and miles of open country to explore. (See the Hatcher Pass Lodge, below, for more details.) There are four hiking trails and two mountain-biking routes in the area—ask at the visitor center. The **Gold Cord Lake Trail** is less than a mile. The **Reed Lakes Trail** is spectacular for its mountain scenery and waterfalls; starting from the Archangel Road, it gains 3,000 feet over 4.5 miles to Upper Reed Lake. Another challenging hike is the **Gold Mint Trail,** which starts across the road from the Motherlode Lodge on Hatcher Pass Road and leads 8 miles to the Mint Valley.

The park maintains two campgrounds along Hatcher Pass Road, charging a $10 fee. Backcountry camping is allowed without a permit, but fires are prohibited outside of campground fire rings.

On the Parks Highway

The **Museum of Alaska Transportation and Industry** ★, off the Parks Highway at mile 47 on Museum Drive, west of Wasilla (☎907/376-1211; www. museumofalaska.org), is a paradise for gearheads and tinkerers. The volunteers have gathered every conceivable machine and conveyance—14 airplanes, 13 fire trucks, 7 locomotives, and 2 steam cranes, for example—and fixed up to running order as many as they can. An indoor museum displays their finished masterpieces, while the 20 acres outside are crammed with deteriorated treasures—trains, tractors, fishing boats, mining equipment, even a barn—all grist for memories and imagination. It's open May 1 to September 30 daily 10am to 5pm, winter by appointment. Admission is $8 for adults; $5 for students, seniors, and military with military ID; $18 for families.

Where to Stay & Dine

See the accommodations described below for some good places to eat in the Valley. In addition, there are unlimited fast-food spots and roadhouse burger places. One place of note is **Vagabond Blues,** in Palmer at 642 S. Alaska St. (☎907/745-2233), a coffeehouse and cafe offering sandwiches, wraps, baked goods, homemade bread and soup, and music. The food is great, and the music is exceptional: A steady stream of national folk and alternative acoustic acts that come to Anchorage also make a pilgrimage to this small-town venue; many are booked by Whistling Swan Productions, whose website lists dates (p. 338). The coffeehouse is open Monday through Saturday 6am to 8pm, Sunday 8am to 6pm.

Two good, down-home places to eat—popular with the locals—allow you to escape franchise food: the **Windbreak Cafe** (☎907/376-4484; www. windbreakalaska.com), on the Parks Highway in Wasilla, and **Colony Kitchen** (☎907/746-4600), on the Glenn Highway in Palmer.

HATCHER PASS

Hatcher Pass Lodge ★ 🏕️ A charming family presides at this tiny mountain lodge 3,000 feet high in a treeless alpine bowl near the Independence Mine State Historic Park. Out on the open snowfield in winter, or the heather in summer, the nine cabins and A-frame lodge seem far more remote than they really are, just 90 minutes from Anchorage. There is a phone in the main lodge for emergencies but no TV. Our family goes for Nordic skiing vacation weekends here, with as many as 12 of us from three generations, all enjoying having nothing to divert us but snow, a warm cabin, and good meals. The cabins are nicely set up but basic, with chemical toilets and drinking water from an urn. Guests go to the main lodge for showers, meals, and drinks; the family produces surprisingly good meals there. Stay in summer for a taste of the real Alaska with doorstep access to wonderful alpine hiking.

Hatcher Pass Lodge.

P.O. Box 763, Palmer, AK 99645. ☎907/745-5897. www.hatcherpasslodge.com. 9 cabins, 3 lodge rooms. $165 cabin for 2; lodge rooms $100 double. Extra person $15. AE, DC, DISC, MC, V. **Amenities:** Restaurant; bar; sauna.

WASILLA

Best Western Lake Lucille Inn ★ This attractive hotel in Wasilla sits on the same lake as former Governor Palin's house. It offers the best standard rooms in the valley. They're large and well appointed, and those facing the lake have balconies and a grand, peaceful view. The hotel helps arrange some local activities. You'll have to take meals off-site, which will most likely require a drive.

1300 W. Lake Lucille Dr., Wasilla, AK 99654. ☎800/528-1234 or 907/373-1776. Fax 907/376-6199. www.bestwesternlakelucilleinn.com. 54 units. High season $169–$224 double, $299 suite; low season $89, $175 suite. Extra person $20. Rates include continental breakfast. AE, DC, DISC, MC, V. **Amenities:** Exercise room; Jacuzzi; sauna. *In room:* TV, hair dryer, fridge, Wi-Fi.

PALMER

Colony Inn ★ 🍴 This classic country inn occupies a restored teacher's dormitory from the New Deal Colony Project, right in the middle of Palmer. The rooms are attractively old-fashioned, although a little worn in spots, with rockers and comforters but also Jacuzzi bathtubs in most rooms. A large sitting room and a dining room downstairs are decorated with historic photographs that help tell the building's story. Meals are served here at the **Inn Cafe** (☎907/746-6118): lunch Monday through Friday and a popular Sunday brunch. Guests check in at the comparatively down-scale Valley Hotel, which has a cafe open around the clock, at 606 S. Alaska St. (☎907/745-3330), as there often is no innkeeper onsite to let you in or help with problems.

325 E. Elmwood, Palmer, AK 99645. ☎907/745-3330. Fax 907/746-3330. 12 units. $100–$120 double; $180 suite. AE, DISC, MC, V. **Amenities:** Restaurant. *In room:* TV/VCR, fridge, Wi-Fi.

THE KENAI PENINSULA & PRINCE WILLIAM SOUND

8

The Gulf of Alaska arcs at its northern edge, forming the rounded northern shore of the Pacific Ocean, a zone of great collisions. This is where the earth's tectonic plates collide, spewing forth froths of hot lava from dozens of volcanoes and fracturing and folding the mountains with titanic earthquakes. Here the ocean's wildest weather hits peaks jutting miles high from the sea, growing immense prehistoric ice sheets and glaciers that carve the rock into long, deep, intricate fjords. The sea proffers prodigious biological wealth on these shores, including the salmon it unleashes into the rivers in furious swarms of life that climb over the mountains and into the Interior to spawn. Nature seems giant and superabundant along this magnificent arc of land and water.

Geography endowed this one stretch of coast with several of the world's great natural places. On the east, near Cordova, the **Copper River's** immense, entirely unspoiled delta is one of the largest contiguous wetlands in the Western Hemisphere. On a day trip, you're immediately alone with flocks of rare, graceful waterfowl that congregate on shallow ponds surrounded by miles of waving grass. **Prince William Sound** is a vast protected sea of wooded mountains and mammoth glaciers. This is our family's favorite place, where we go each summer to camp among the otters and eagles on tiny islands out of contact with the rest of mankind. **Kenai Fjords National Park** takes in bays off the open ocean where the mountains soar a mile straight up from the water. Boats travel here among humpback, gray, and orca whales; spot otters, seals, and sea lions; and visit swarming colonies of puffins and other seabirds. The **Kenai River** harbors the world's biggest salmon, on the western side of the Kenai Peninsula; and on its southern tip, **Kachemak Bay** is like a miniature Prince William Sound, but with people. The bay's shores are dotted by tiny towns with lodges, art galleries on pilings, and some of Alaska's best restaurants.

The whole region is exceptionally accessible, by Alaska standards. The Kenai (*Keen*-eye) Peninsula, in particular, is easy to get to without the expense and exhausting travel that can make much of the state difficult. Most of what you're looking for in Alaska lies along a few hundred miles of blacktop, within reach of a rental car and perhaps a tour-boat ticket: glaciers, whales, legendary sportfishing, spectacular hiking trails, interesting little fishing towns, bears, moose, and high mountains.

People from Anchorage go to the peninsula for the weekend to fish, hike, dig clams, paddle kayaks, and so on, and certain places can get crowded. There's a

PREVIOUS PAGE: **Hiker overlooking Portage Lake.**

special phrase for what happens when the red salmon are running in July on the Kenai and Russian rivers: *combat fishing.* At hot times in certain places, anglers stand elbow to elbow on the bank, each casting into his or her own yard-wide slice of river, and still catch plenty of hefty salmon. The peninsula also exerts a powerful magnetic force on RVs, those road-whales that you find at the head of lines of cars on the two-lane highways. During the summer, the fishing rivers, creeks, and beaches on the west side of the peninsula and the end of Homer Spit can become sheet-metal cities of hundreds of Winnebagos and Airstreams parked side by side. Often some local entrepreneur will be selling doughnuts or newspapers door-to-door.

Yet the decision is yours as to whether you spend time in the company of tourists. If the roadside fishing is hairy, hiking a little farther down the bank usually means you can be by yourself. In this chapter, I'll describe some towns of unspoiled charm, where you can kayak virtually from your room. Being alone is easy. You can paddle among otters in Resurrection Bay; tramp over the heather in Turnagain Pass; and hike, bike, or ski one of the many maintained trails in Chugach National Forest. And, when you're ready to come back to the comforts of civilization, you'll find that some of the state's best restaurants and most interesting lodgings are here, too.

EXPLORING THE KENAI PENINSULA & PRINCE WILLIAM SOUND

The Towns

Kenai, on Cook Inlet on the west side of the Kenai Peninsula, is the largest town in the region. Ten miles up the Kenai River, **Soldotna** is Kenai's twin. Together with their neighboring communities, these two form a unit with almost half of the Kenai Peninsula's population of 53,000. They're also the least interesting of the peninsula's towns. **Homer,** at the southern end of the peninsula, has wonderful art and character and lots of ways to get out on the water. **Seward,** on the east side, is smaller and quieter, a charming gateway to Kenai Fjords National Park.

There are three towns on Prince William Sound. **Valdez** is an oil town at the southern terminus of the trans-Alaska pipeline where tankers are loaded. **Cordova** is more attractive, a historic community on the eastern side of the Sound, with outdoor activities close at hand. **Whittier** is a grim former military outpost, but a convenient gateway to the protected fjords and glaciers of the western Sound.

Getting There & Getting Around

BY CAR Highways connect all the region's large towns, except Cordova, which is reached only by air or water. Like all of Alaska's main highways, these are paved two-lane roads. The Seward Highway runs south from Anchorage to the Kenai Peninsula. That route is described below. A road built in a railway tunnel connects Whittier, on Prince William Sound, to the Seward Highway. The Glenn and Richardson highways reach from Anchorage to Valdez through Alaska's Interior. Stops along that route are described in chapter 10, and all of Alaska's highways are summarized on p. 502.

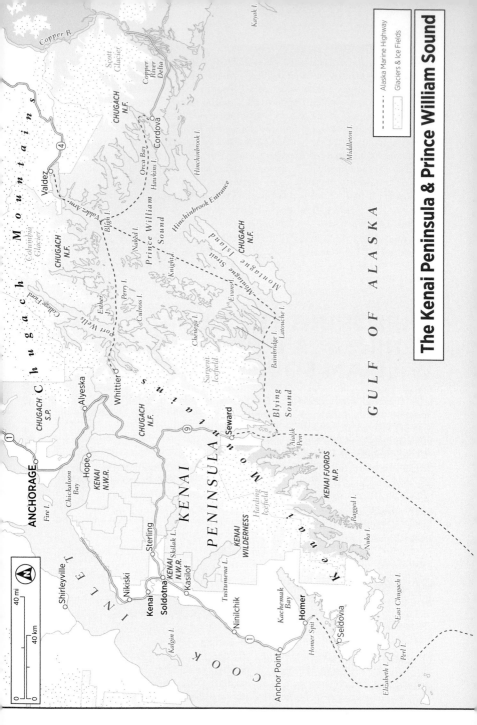

The Kenai Peninsula & Prince William Sound

BY FERRY The ferry system connects Whittier with Valdez and Cordova via the fast ferry *Chenega*. Driving from Anchorage to Whittier, taking the ferry to Valdez, then driving back to Anchorage (or north to Fairbanks) makes a great loop (see chapter 4). The ferry *Tustumena* (the *"Tusty"*) connects Homer to Kodiak Island and the Aleutian Archipelago (covered in chapter 11), and also runs from Homer to Seldovia. The schedule is not convenient for Seldovia, however; for that trip, it's easier to take one of the private passenger ferries that serve the towns and remote sites around Kachemak Bay from Homer. A U.S. Fish and Wildlife Service ranger offers programs on the *Tusty*. For more on the ferry system, see "Exploring Southeast Alaska," in chapter 6; call **800/642-0066;** or visit www.ferryalaska.com.

BY AIR Commuter aircraft connect Anchorage to Kenai, Homer, Valdez, and Cordova. You can also fly between Anchorage and Cordova on an Alaska Airlines jet once a day in each direction (the northbound originates in Seattle). Scheduled and air-taxi services use these smaller towns as bases for the villages, carrying passengers, mail, and cargo, and flying to remote lodges and cabins for fishing or other outdoor activities. Valdez, Cordova, and Anchorage operators serve the Prince William Sound region. Kenai and Anchorage companies cover Cook Inlet and remote public lands such as Lake Clark National Park. Homer is the base for villages around Kachemak Bay and lower Cook Inlet bear-viewing sites.

BY TRAIN The **Alaska Railroad** (**800/544-0552** or 907/265-2494; www.alaskarailroad.com) runs from Anchorage south to Seward or Whittier and back daily in the summer.

Visitor Information

For information on the peninsula as a whole, contact the **Kenai Peninsula Tourism Marketing Council,** 35477 Kenai Spur Hwy., Ste. 205, Soldotna, AK 99669 (**800/535-3524** or 907/262-5229; www.kenaipeninsula.org), which

Portage Lake.

distributes a vacation planner with information on businesses and trip planning in the area (order through the website). The staff will answer inquiries during normal business hours.

Getting Outside

The towns of the region are like beads strung along the laces of the highways; everything else is wilderness. You can find all the activities and isolation you seek here, yet the presence of the towns means that comfort is closer at hand than in other parts of Alaska.

Chugach National Forest takes in all of Prince William Sound and most of the eastern Kenai Peninsula. At 5.3 million acres, it's more than double the size of Yellowstone National Park. Anywhere else but Alaska it would be a national park, and one of the largest and most spectacular, with some of the best sea kayaking, hiking, backpacking, wildlife watching, and scenery anywhere. General

State Parks Cabin Reservations

Alaska's state parks rent remote public cabins such as the famous Forest Service cabins (see "Chugach National Forest: Do-It-Yourself Wilderness"), but they're usually newer, larger, and easier to get to. Most are in Southcentral Alaska—in this chapter, they're mentioned near Homer, Seward, and Valdez. Like the Forest Service cabins, it takes a hike, boat ride, or air taxi to get to the state cabins, and you need cabin equipment, such as a cookstove and sleeping bags, but once there you can experience the real Alaska all by yourself.

Some of these cabins book up the minute they become available and, since Alaska residents get a jump on the reservation system, visitors are unlikely to be able to use the most popular cabins at peak periods. But if you can be flexible about where you go, or if you can travel out of the peak season, you can probably find a cabin. Alaska residents can reserve 7 months ahead, non-residents 6 months ahead; however, reservations do not initially open on weekends or holidays, only at 10am

Alaska time on the following business day. Once a date opens on the system, it stays open 24-hours a day until someone takes it.

The easiest way to reserve is by using the online system with a MasterCard or Visa, but you can also reserve in person, by mail, or by fax (you can ask questions by phone, but not apply). The staff is friendly and will guide you around the system, and help you find a cabin where you can get a permit, even if it's not your first choice. The main information and reservations desk is the **Department of Natural Resources Public Information Center— Anchorage,** 550 W. 7th Ave., Ste. 1260, Anchorage, AK 99501-3557 (**☎907/269-8400,** or 907/269-8411 TDD; fax 907/269-8901; www.alaskastateparks.org). The website is the best source of information about the cabins, with a picture and description of each and a real-time availability calendar. The center is open Monday through Friday 10am to 5pm. Cabins rent for $25 to $75 a night, with fees highest for popular cabins at peak periods.

information, camping, and ideas on remote areas in the Chugach are covered in "Chugach National Forest: Do-It-Yourself Wilderness," while details about national forest areas near towns are in the appropriate town sections.

Kenai Fjords National Park ("Kenai Fjords National Park") protects the outer edge and ice cap of the Kenai Peninsula's southern side. The park is incomparable in its remoteness, stark beauty, and abundance of marine wildlife. Access is through Seward ("Seward: Gateway to Resurrection Bay & Kenai Fjords").

On the peninsula's western side, **Kenai National Wildlife Refuge** ("Kenai National Wildlife Refuge") has Alaska's most accessible wilderness lake and river canoeing as well as extraordinary fishing, with access from roads near Soldotna ("Kenai/Soldotna & Sterling: Giant Salmon").

Kachemak Bay State Park offers good sea-kayaking waters and wilderness hiking not connected to any road. The **Alaska Maritime National Wildlife Refuge** protects the wildlife habitat of remote islands and seashores around the state. Both are covered in "Homer & Kachemak Bay: Cosmic Hamlet by the Sea," later in this chapter, on Homer.

VISITOR INFORMATION The region's best and most central place to get outdoor information is the **Alaska Public Lands Information Center,** 605 W. 4th Ave., Ste. 105, Anchorage, AK 99501 (☎866/869-6887 or 907/644-3661; www.alaskacenters.gov). You'll be able to ask guidance of residents who have spent time in the places you'll be visiting, and there are exhibits on the wildlife and outdoor opportunities in the region—even maps showing where to find various species of fish. Land agencies present information on the whole state, and the bookstore is well stocked with maps, field guides, and such. Summer hours are daily from 9am to 5pm, winter Monday through Friday from 10am to 5pm. Visitor centers for particular areas are covered in the appropriate sections.

THE SEWARD HIGHWAY: A ROAD GUIDE

The Kenai Peninsula's lifeline is the road down from Anchorage, a 127-mile drive to Seward on a good two-lane highway, most of it through public land without development or services. Hwy. 1, commonly known as the Seward Highway, is more than scenic—it's really a wonderful attraction in itself, designated a National Scenic Byway and an All-American Road. A detailed booklet about the highway with maps and mile-by-mile descriptions, *The Seward Highway: Alaska's All-American Road,* is distributed by the Alaska Public Lands Information Center in Anchorage (p. 292). There are excellent campgrounds and hiking trails all along the way in the Chugach National Forest, which I've covered in "Chugach National Forest: Do-It-Yourself Wilderness," later in this chapter.

The mileposts start in Seward. Here we count backward, since you'll likely start from Anchorage.

MILE 127-79 The highway begins at the south end of Anchorage, the only way out of town in that direction, and runs along Turnagain Arm 48 miles to the Portage Glacier. I've written about that spectacular portion of the drive in chapter 7 under "Out from Anchorage: Turnagain Arm & Portage Glacier."

Turnagain Pass.

MILE 79–75 Beyond the Portage Glacier turnoff, the road traverses the salt marshes to the south side of the Arm. These wetlands are good bird-watching grounds. The dead trees on the flats are left over from before the 1964 earthquake. The area was inundated in the quake, when the entire region shifted—including the Kenai Peninsula and Prince William Sound—lowering this area 12 feet and raising areas to the east as much as 30 feet. Everything moved laterally, too. Besides being the second strongest earthquake ever recorded, the '64 quake moved more land than any other. People who were here tell of their surprise when the tide came far higher than they had ever seen it before in the days after the earthquake, until finally they realized that the land itself had sunk. Large parts of Homer, Hope, and Seldovia disappeared under the waves at high tide. Seward, Whittier, Valdez, and Kodiak were swept by destructive tsunami waves.

MILE 75–68 The highway steeply climbs through the spruce forest to the fresh, towering alpine terrain of the 1,000-foot-elevation **Turnagain Pass.** The vistas here are stupendous year-round.

MILE 68 If you find the meadow and tundra hard to resist for a walk, go ahead. Park at the pull-out with the toilets on the right side at the pass summit and follow the path, or just amble off into the wildflowers (assuming the ground is dry when you're there). In the winter and spring, this is a backcountry skiing and snowmobiling paradise. Skiers go on the left (east) side of the road and snowmobilers on the right. Always check with the Chugach National Forest (see "Chugach National Forest: Do-It-Yourself Wilderness," below) for avalanche conditions first. Avalanches have taken lives here more than once.

MILE 68–57 The pass forms a divide; crossing it, Granite Creek flows down toward the south. The road follows, falling back below the tree line of stunted spruce and then popping back up into sweeping views. Arcing to the northwest after the Granite Creek Campground, the highway follows another north-flowing river, Sixmile Creek.

MILE 57 & HOPE HIGHWAY The Hope Highway divides off to the north and west along Sixmile Creek while the Seward Highway continues south. Rafting companies based in Anchorage use this wild stretch of water for some of their most challenging rides (see chapter 7).

MILE 57–46 The Seward Highway climbs steeply from the Hope Highway intersection, up the canyon of Canyon Creek, before leveling out above the tree line at about 1,400 feet of elevation. Next comes a series of alpine lakes in a narrow mountain valley.

MILE 46 Upper Summit Lake lies smooth and reflective in a steep alpine valley. On the far side is the Tenderfoot Creek Campground, a calming spot warmed by sun off the water (p. 370). On the near side is a traditional highway stopping place without neighbors for miles in any direction, the **Summit Lake Lodge,** at mile 45.5 (☎907/244-2031; www.summitlakelodge.com). The main building is a traditional log roadhouse that's been updated to house a modern restaurant. Meals can take some time, so eat here only if you're not in a rush. Even if you don't want dinner, however, the location can't be beat for a driving break. You can enjoy an ice cream from the counter in the log gift shop while you stroll near the lake. The lodge rents six motel rooms with private bathrooms, but without TVs or phones.

MILE 46–37 The highway continues through similar mountain terrain before descending into the trees again and branching at **Tern Lake.** This is a stirringly beautiful spot year-round, and a good place to get out and taste the fresh mountain air and watch for moose, waterfowl, and other birds. A 13-site picnic area is to the right at the intersection, at mile 37 of the Sterling Highway, which then leads to Cooper Landing, Soldotna, Kenai, and Homer.

MILE 36 Look on the right to turn for the luxurious **Inn at Tern Lake** (☎907/288-3667; www.ternlakeinn.com), a family-operated lodge surrounded by mountains and hiking opportunities with four airy, well-made rooms overlooking a pond. The inn has many amenities—even a tennis court. It's a place to spend a few days of quiet, as you'd be too sorry to leave if you stopped only overnight. Summer rates are $175 to $200 double, winter $100.

Tern Lake.

MILE 32 Moose Creek has a viewing platform to watch thousands of spawning salmon, in season; half a mile on, the Trail Lake Fish Hatchery sits on the edge of Upper Trail Lake. This is the first of a string of sparkling mountain lakes that the road will follow for the next 15 miles.

MILE 30 The community of Moose Pass, with a population of about 200, sits on the shore of Upper Trail Lake.

MILE 18-0 Down among the big spruces of the coastal forest, the highway comes to Seward.

CHUGACH NATIONAL FOREST: DO-IT-YOURSELF WILDERNESS

I've lived near the Chugach National Forest all my life, but it wasn't until well into adulthood that I had seen all its parts and appreciated its vastness and variety. Still, I doubt I'll ever really know this seemingly infinite land. **Prince William Sound,** just one of the national forest's three parts, has 3,500 miles of shoreline among its folded islands and deeply penetrating fjords and passages. It would take a lifetime to really know all those cove beaches, climb all the island mountains, and explore to the head of every narrow bay under big rainforest trees.

A SIDE TRIP TO hope

If you want a break, you'll find **Hope** at the end of the scenic 17-mile Hope Highway. It's a charming gold rush-era village and the starting point for some great hikes (see the Resurrection Pass Trail, p. 367, and Porcupine Campground, p. 370). A few white frame buildings remain from the days when Hope was a gold-mining boom-town after a strike in 1894. Before the 1964 earthquake, the rest of the town used to stand where the creek gives way to a tidal meadow. Hope's year-round population today is about 150. Walking the town's gravel roads, you'll find many quaint spots and friendly people. Locals have been gathering at one cafe since 1896 (it shows). Here, far off the beaten track, time seems to have stopped. In fact, the place is so relaxed, clocks would seem superfluous.

For information, contact the **Hope-Sunrise Community Library** (☎907/782-3121), which is open daily in summer from 11am to 4pm, when volunteer manpower allows. You can also find Hope information online at www.advenalaska.com/hope.

The **Hope and Sunrise Historical and Mining Museum** (☎907/782-3740)

has a one-room log cabin displaying historic objects and photographs and a collection of pioneer buildings that are fun to poke around in—a barn, blacksmith's shop, miner's bunkhouse, and old-time school—which hardly seem out of place in contemporary Hope. Volunteers keep the museum open Memorial Day to Labor Day daily noon

The **Copper River Delta** is another world entirely. Unlike the musty secrets of the Sound's obscure passages, the delta opens to the sky like a heavenly plain of wind and light, its waving green colors splashed by the airiest brushstrokes. It's another huge area: Just driving across the delta and back from Cordova takes most of a day. Finally, there's the western part of the national forest, on the **Kenai Peninsula.** This is largely an alpine realm. The mountains are steep, their timber quickly giving way to rock, tundra, and wildflowers up above. It's got remote, unclimbed peaks, but also many miles of family hiking trails, accessible fishing streams, and superb campgrounds. This is where you go in Alaska for multiday trail hikes.

The Chugach is managed primarily for recreation and conservation. President Theodore Roosevelt created it in 1907. After he left office in 1909, a fight over conservation of coal lands in the forest led to a split between Roosevelt and his hand-picked successor, William Howard Taft, with the result that Roosevelt ran against Taft as the Bull Moose Party candidate in 1912. Democrat Woodrow Wilson won the three-way race. The next historic moment for the national forest came with the 1989 *Exxon Valdez* oil spill, which also evolved into a story of conservation politics, when environmentalists demanded Exxon pay to stop large-scale logging on private lands that threatened further damage in the Sound. Logging had never occurred on national forest lands in the Sound.

to 4pm. Right across from the museum, **Sweet Mo's Simple Pleasures Ice Cream** is a cute place to buy a cone and a souvenir in the town's old post office. It's operated by the same warm and enthusiastic couple who have the best restaurant and lodgings in town, **Bowman's Bear Creek Lodge and Dinner House**

(✆ **907/782-3141;** www.bowmansbearcreeklodge.com), which is on the right side of the Hope Highway as you approach the village. The compound of cabins, the restaurant, and the family's home are arrayed around a placid pond where a canoe drifts. The dining room is tiny, its country decoration charming and authentic. The little bar serves craft-brewed beer. Entrees range from $22 to $26. Cabins are cozy, with firewood stacked for the wood stove and the sound of a nearby creek always in the background. Guests use an attractively tiled shower house. Cabins are $150 double summer, $100 winter. The restaurant is open summer Tuesday through Sunday 4 to 10pm, winter Thursday through Sunday the same hours.

Ultimately, Exxon was forced to pay $1 billion to a recovery fund, half of which government trustees spent to buy back timber rights in the Sound and beyond, protecting the trees. Here and elsewhere in the spill region the newly purchased protected lands include 1,419 miles of coastline and almost as much land as is in all of Yosemite National Park.

Essentials

GETTING THERE & GETTING AROUND There are many ways to the Chugach National Forest. For Prince William Sound, use Whittier, Valdez, or Cordova as gateways; for the Copper River Delta, go through Cordova. Trails and campgrounds on the Kenai Peninsula generally meet the Seward or Sterling highways, or spur roads from the highways. The individual town listings later in this chapter provide details on how to get there and into that part of the national forest. "The Seward Highway: A Road Guide," above, describes the Seward Highway.

VISITOR INFORMATION The most central place for information on the national forest is the Alaska Public Lands Information Center in Anchorage (p. 292). You can download a 16-page guide to the forest at www.alaskageographic. org (click "Trip Planning"). For general forest inquiries, you can also contact the **forest headquarters,** 3301 C St., Ste. 300, Anchorage, AK 99503 (✆907/743-9500; www.fs.fed.us/r10/chugach). The national forest also has three ranger district offices, where you can get up-to-date local information and personal advice: **Glacier Ranger District,** 145 Forest Station Rd., near the Seward Highway off Alyeska Road, in Girdwood (✆907/783-3242); **Seward Ranger District,** 334 4th Ave. (at Jefferson St.), in Seward (✆907/224-3374); and **Cordova Ranger District,** 612 2nd St. (at Browning St.), in Cordova (✆907/424-7661). You can't reserve campground sites and remote cabins through these local offices—for that you must use the national system listed below under "Where to Stay"—but you can call them with questions.

Getting Outside

HIKING, MOUNTAIN-BIKING & BACKPACKING

Alaska's best long trails lead through the mountain passes of Chugach National Forest, including historic gold-rush trails and portions of the original Iditarod trail (the race doesn't use these southern portions). The Forest Service maintains **public cabins** on many of these trails, and in other remote spots reachable only with a boat or small plane. If the nights you need are available, you can use the cabins instead of a tent on a backpacking trip. Or make a cabin your destination and spend a few days there hiking or fishing. I've covered trails near Cordova under "Cordova: Hidden Treasure," later in this chapter, and some shorter hikes are mentioned below with the campgrounds under "Where to Stay." In addition, the superb Winner Creek Trail and Crow Pass Trail, from Girdwood, are described on p. 348. Two excellent trail guides cover the peninsula. **55 Ways to the Wilderness,** 5th edition, by Helen Nienhueser and John Wolfe (The Mountaineers, $17), is the most complete, with detailed coverage in readable prose. The newer **Kenai Trails,** for $8 (✆866/257-2752; www.alaska geographic.org), includes an extremely detailed topographic map along with each trail description. **Trails Illustrated** publishes excellent plastic recreation maps of the region (☎800/962-1643; www.natgeomaps.com).

CARTER LAKE TRAIL An excellent day hike starts from mile 33 of the Seward Highway, a few miles east of Tern Lake (p. 363), rising about 1,000 feet over 2 miles to alpine views and Carter Lake, which is stocked with rainbow trout. Continuing another 1⅓ miles brings you to the east end of Crescent Lake.

JOHNSON PASS TRAIL The 23-mile trail climbs to a pair of lakes above the tree line at the 1,450-foot Johnson Creek Summit, tracing impressively narrow mountain valleys. The route, part of the Iditarod National Historic Trail, leads from near the Trail Lake Fish Hatchery, at mile 32 of the Seward Highway, to near the Granite Creek Campground, on the highway at mile 63. Plan to do the trail as an overnight and have transportation ready at each end.

LOST LAKE TRAIL & PRIMROSE TRAIL With their fields of alpine wildflowers and small lakes, these connected trails offer one of the most beautiful hikes in the area. Snow lasts until late in the season up at the top. The upper, northern trail head is at the 10-site Primrose Campground, on vast Kenai Lake, 17 miles from Seward off the Seward Highway on Primrose Road. The trail rises through hemlock past a waterfall about 2 miles up (look for the spur to the right when you hear water), past an old mining cabin, and then through ever smaller trees and above the tree line. A Forest Service cabin is on a 2-mile spur about 11 miles along the 16-mile route. Strong hikers can do the whole trail in a long day, but it makes more sense to hike in and out on the upper end, or to spend the night along the way. The lower, Lost Lake trailhead is in a subdivision near Seward; ask for directions at one of the visitor centers to find it.

RESURRECTION PASS TRAIL This gold-rush trail begins 4 miles above the town of Hope (mentioned above in the preceding section on the Seward Hwy.) and runs over the top of the Kenai Peninsula to Cooper Landing (covered in "Cooper Landing: Road Meets River," later in this chapter). It's a beautiful, remote, yet well-used trail for hiking, mountain biking, Nordic skiing, or snowshoeing; it rises through forest, crosses the alpine pass, and then descends again to a highway trail head where you'll need to have transportation waiting. The 39-mile trail has eight public-use cabins, available for $35 to $45 a night. (See "Where to Stay," below, for reservation information.) The cabins are well spaced to cover the trail in an easy 5 days, and those on lakes have boats for fishing. Cabins book up well ahead of time in winter and summer, but there are lots of good camping spots, too. The **Devil's Pass and Summit Lake trails** cut off from the Resurrection to the Seward Highway south of Summit Lake, shortening the route. The difficulty of doing the whole trail, by any of the entrances, is that you either need two cars or someone willing to drive you back to your starting point.

RUSSIAN LAKES TRAIL This trail begins in Cooper Landing (covered in "Cooper Landing: Road Meets River," later in this chapter), near the end of the Resurrection Pass Trail, and leads to three remote cabins and a series of lakes. There's excellent fishing and wildlife viewing (bears are common). It's less than 3 miles with little elevation gain to Lower Russian Lake and the cabin there, or you can make a backpacking trip over the entire 21 miles.

Resurrection Pass Trail.

FISHING

The national forest contains some of the most famous, and crowded, fishing banks in Alaska, including the **Russian River,** near Cooper Landing, with its incredible run of red salmon in July and good fishing lasting into September. Easiest access is at the Russian River Campground, just west of the village. There are plenty of other roadside salmon streams and remote fishing rivers and lakes in the national forest where you can lose sight of other anglers. Some remote lakes have Forest Service cabins for rent on their shores, with rowboats. The Forest Service publishes information on these opportunities. See chapter 3 for other information sources.

SEA KAYAKING & BOATING

A variety of Prince William Sound tour boats are listed in the Whittier, Valdez, and Cordova sections of this chapter. Whittier offers the greatest number of boats and the most impressive scenery, with big glaciers that come right to the water. It's also possible to rent your own boat there.

All three communities also have operators offering sea-kayak rentals and guided outings of various lengths. The best sea kayaking is near Cordova or east of Whittier. The long fjords reached from Whittier feature calving glaciers, narrow passages, and Forest Service cabins, but to get out there you need a boat ride first—the waters right around Whittier aren't as interesting—and that is expensive. The local sea-kayaking operators can help you arrange drop-off service. Cordova has more interesting waters right near town, so you can paddle from the boat harbor. Those who haven't done much sea kayaking should consider only a guided trip; if it's your first time, start with a guided day trip rather than an overnight.

Where to Stay

CABIN & CAMPSITE RESERVATIONS

Some campsites in the Chugach can be reserved in advance, and public-use cabins are available only by reservation. **The National Recreation Reservation Service** works well, but it is operated from upstate New York, so reservation agents are not the best people to ask for information about which remote cabin or campground is right for you. Instead, use the Chugach National Forest website (www.fs.fed.us/r10/chugach) and follow up on questions with the ranger stations (p. 366). The easiest way to reserve a cabin or campsite is online at **www.recreation.gov**, because the availability calendars allow you to shop for open days at various places. To reserve by phone, call **☎877/444-6777.** The phone lines are open March through October daily 10am to midnight Eastern Standard Time, November through February 10am to 10pm. The system accepts payment by bank card only: American Express, Discover, MasterCard, or Visa. All reservations open 180 days ahead on a first-come, first-served basis.

REMOTE CABINS

There are no more authentic Alaska accommodations than a pioneer cabin with a woodstove—a place to give you a better feel for the soul of a wild place. Chugach National Forest maintains more than 40 remote recreation cabins for rent to the public. This is simple shelter: Cabins don't have electricity or plumbing; you bring your own sleeping bags, cooking equipment, and other gear; and the cabin is only as clean as the last user left it. But no other room you can rent has a better location or greater privacy. Some cabins are along hiking and skiing trails, others on shores where boats and kayaks can pull up, and others on remote fishing lakes accessible only by floatplane. You can stay up to a week in most, with a summer limit of 3 days in the Resurrection Trail cabins.

The Forest Service produces descriptions of each cabin online or in printed form. You will also need a trail guide and detailed map (see "Getting Outside," above). Some cabins rent for $35 a night, most for $45 a night. Typically, the price of the cabin itself is not your major expense: You'll need a way to get there, either by plane, by boat, or by having a vehicle to drive to a trail head and then hiking. If you're flying, contact flight services in the nearest town (listed in the sections later in this chapter) to find out the cost before you book the cabin. Flight time is several hundred dollars an hour. You can rent the camping equipment you'll need at the businesses listed in the Anchorage chapter on p. 327, but you should talk to a ranger first to get details about access and what to take. And start planning early. For summer dates, many cabins book up the second they become available on the reservation system, 6 months prior. This is not an exaggeration. Reservation details are above.

CAMPGROUNDS

Forest Service campgrounds mostly have pit toilets and water from hand pumps, and roads usually are not paved. But some of these places are truly spectacular. I've listed them in order of distance from Anchorage, counting in reverse direction on the Seward Highway mileposts. For information on campgrounds below mile 60, call the Seward Ranger District; for the others, call the Glacier Ranger District, in Girdwood (p. 366 for phone numbers). Sites in a few of the following campgrounds, as noted, take reservations through the national system explained above. RVs and cars can access and park at all of the campgrounds, but Williwaw is the only campground intended primarily for RVs.

Williwaw & Black Bear These two campgrounds are next to each other near Portage Glacier, along a creek where you can watch spawning red salmon in mid-August (no fishing is allowed). Williwaw is one of the more developed campgrounds in the national forest, with paved roads and pumped water, and is intended primarily for RVs.

Mile 4, Portage Glacier Rd. (turn at mile 78.9 Seward Hwy.). Williwaw: 60 sites. Reservations accepted with additional fee. $13 single site per night, $20 double site per night. Black Bear: 12 sites. $11 per night.

Bertha Creek This one's in the high country.

Mile 65.5, Seward Hwy. 12 sites. $11 per night.

Granite Creek Near the Johnson Pass trail head.

Mile 63, Seward Hwy. 19 sites. $11 per night.

Porcupine This campground near the gold-rush village of Hope (p. 364) is among the most beautiful in the Chugach National Forest. The widely separated sites are on a mountainside overlooking Turnagain Arm, five with sweeping ocean views. Thick trees make for privacy, but also mosquitoes. Bring repellent. Two good day hikes leave from the campground: The level 5-mile trail to **Gull Rock** makes a good family ramble, and with some effort you can scramble down to remote beaches along the way, where we've enjoyed a picnic. The **Hope Point Trail** is a stiff climb that rises 3,600 feet to expansive views.

At the end of the Hope Hwy. 24 sites. $11 per night.

Tenderfoot Creek This pleasant campground lies across Summit Lake from the Seward Highway as it passes through a narrow mountain valley above the tree line. Campsites look out on the water from a peaceful, sunny hillside. The nearby Summit Lake Lodge, described on p. 363, offers meals and is the only business on the Seward Highway for many a mile.

Mile 46, Seward Hwy. 27 sites. $11 per night.

Ptarmigan Creek & Trail River Near the tiny towns of Moose Pass and Crown Point, the Ptarmigan Creek campground is at the start of the trail to Ptarmigan Lake, 4 miles away with only 500 feet in elevation gain—a good place for a picnic or fishing for Dolly Varden char and rainbow trout. Trail River campground is a mile away and on the other side of the highway.

Mile 23, Seward Hwy. Ptarmigan Creek: 16 sites. Reservations accepted with additional fee. $11 per night. Trail River: 91 sites. Reservations accepted with additional fee. $11 single site per night, $17 double site per night.

Primrose Another favorite, this lovely campground lies on the edge of Kenai Lake and at the base of the Primrose Trail to Lost Lake, one of the area's most beautiful (see "Getting Outside," above). This campground is the closest to Seward that has a sense of natural isolation.

Mile 17, Seward Hwy. 10 sites. $11 per night.

Russian River This large, well-developed campground mainly serves fishermen pursuing red salmon on the river. When the fishing is good, the campground overflows and can be noisy. Overnight parking is $6. Reserve ahead.

Mile 52, Sterling Hwy., just west of Cooper Landing. Reservations accepted, with additional fee. 84 sites. 3-day limit. Flush toilets. $14 single site per night, $22 double site per night.

Cooper Creek The campground has two halves bisected by the highway right in Cooper Landing. Ten sites are on the Kenai River and the balance across the road and somewhat better screened and separated.

Mile 50.7, Sterling Hwy. Reservations accepted. 26 sites. $11 single site per night, $17 double site per night.

Quartz Creek Thickly wooded sites stand well separated a bit off the highway, many right on Kenai Lake and others with good mountain views. There is a boat ramp in the campground and a lodge nearby.

Quartz Creek Rd., at mile 45 Sterling Hwy. 45 sites. Reservations accepted. Flush toilets, boat launch. $14 single site per night, $22 double site per night.

Crescent Creek This campground is quieter and more secluded than others near Cooper Landing, at the Crescent Lake trail head. The 6.5-mile trail leads to the Crescent Lake Forest Service Cabin, where renters have a boat for grayling fishing.

Mile 3 Quartz Creek Rd., at mile 45 Sterling Hwy. 9 sites. $11 per night.

WHITTIER: DOCK ON THE SOUND

Whittier is Anchorage's portal to Prince William Sound. Although Anchorage itself is on Upper Cook Inlet, that muddy, fast moving water is little used for recreational boating. Whittier, on the other hand, stands on the edge of a long fjord in the northwest corner of the Sound, whose clear waters are full of salmon, orcas, and otters, and bounded by rocky shores, rainforests, and glaciers. The only land access to Whittier is a railway tunnel that has been paved for cars, making it also North America's longest highway tunnel. And one of the most inconvenient to use. The tunnel has only one lane to be shared among traffic and trains in both directions, and in between trips the tunnel often must be aired out, so vehicles have to wait their turn, sometimes for an hour or more.

Whittier certainly has major advantages for visitors seeking to get out on the water. The ocean is calmer here than on excursions to Kenai Fjords National Park, so seasickness is rare, and the glaciers are even more numerous. One company's selling point is a "26-glacier cruise," all done in a day trip from Anchorage by rail and large tour boat (see "Phillips Cruises and Tours," below). Prince William Sound boats also see otters and sometimes whales; Kenai Fjords tours, on the other hand, more often see whales and see more birds. Sea kayakers also have great places to go from Whittier. Almost all of Prince William Sound is in Chugach National Forest, with its public-use cabins in lovely, remote spots on the shores (see the previous section).

There's little other reason to go to Whittier, unless you're on a quest to find the oddest towns in America. Most of the roughly 180 townspeople live in a single 14-story concrete building with dark, narrow hallways. The grocery store is on the first floor and the medical clinic on the third. The rest of the people live in one other building. **The Begich Towers,** as the dominant structure is called, was built during the 1940s, when Whittier's strategic location on the Alaska Railroad and at the head of a deep Prince William Sound fjord made it a key port in the defense of Alaska. Today, with its barren gravel ground and ramshackle warehouses and boat sheds, the town maintains a stark military-industrial character. The pass above the town is a funnel for frequent whipping winds, it always seems to rain, and the glaciers above the town keep it cool even in summer. As one young town ambassador told me once when I was on a visit, "You're thinking, 'Thank God I don't live here,' right?" The official boosters look more on the bright side: Having everyone live in one building saves on snow removal in a place that gets an average of 20 feet per winter. Kids don't even have to go outside to get to school—a tunnel leads from the tower to the school.

Essentials

GETTING THERE By Car: Take the Seward Highway to the Portage Glacier Road, at mile 78.9 (48 miles from Anchorage). The road through the 2¾-mile-long World War II rail tunnel to Whittier is only one lane and also accommodates trains, so you'll have to wait your turn. Get the schedule through the tunnel's website (http://tunnel.alaska.gov), through its phone recording (☎877/611-2586 or 907/566-2244), or by tuning to 1610AM in Portage or 530AM in Whittier. Checking the schedule helps you avoid a wait of an hour or more if you miss the opening, but you can also wait if you arrive just on time at peak hours, when there may be too many vehicles in line to get through during one open period. Typically, the crowding comes in the summer around 6 to 7pm Friday through Sunday. The tunnel closes altogether at night. In summer the first opening from Whittier is at 5:30am and the last

Whittier's boat harbor.

Be Prepared

Whittier lacks a bank, large stores, or downtown businesses. Bring what you need. But if you forget something, there is a little harbor store, which is amazingly well stocked.

to Whittier is at 11:15pm. Winter hours are shorter and changeable, so check ahead. The toll is $12 for cars; $20 for RVs, cars with trailers, or large vans. It is charged only going toward Whittier. Special permits are required for really huge vehicles (over 14 ft. high or 10 ft. wide). Parking in Whittier is $10 a day. As I mentioned in the introduction, Whittier really isn't worth the trouble unless you are going out on the water.

By Train: If you plan to take a day trip on the Sound from a base in Anchorage (or Girdwood)—the way most people use Whittier—you can leave the car behind and take the train. The large tour operators will book it for you when you buy your boat ticket. The **Alaska Railroad** (☎800/544-0552 or 907/265-2494; www.alaskarailroad.com) runs a daily train timed to match the schedules of Prince William Sound tour boats. Unless you have planned an activity or tour on the water, however, you'll find the 6-hour stay in Whittier is too long to just hang around. The round-trip fare is $80, one-way $65, half price ages 2 to 11. The train ride is scenic and fun, but a rental car will take about half as long and save money if there is more than one of you along.

By Bus: Boat tour operators have buses that can save time and money over the train. Reserve when you buy your boat cruise ticket.

By Ferry: Ferries of the **Alaska Marine Highway System** (☎800/642-0066; www.ferryalaska.com) connect Whittier, Valdez, and Cordova. The fast ferry *Chenega* has dramatically cut travel times and increased sailings in the summer. A ride across the Sound can be over by lunchtime. Passenger areas are enclosed, quiet, and smooth– hardly like being on a boat at all. The fare from Whittier to either Valdez or Cordova is $89 for an adult, half price ages 6 through 11, free under 6. A 15-foot car costs $105 to take along. The Whittier-Valdez run creates the opportunity for a wonderful loop tour of a couple days or more: Drive Anchorage to Whittier, take the ferry to Valdez, then return to Anchorage via the Glenn Highway or continue up the Richardson Highway to Fairbanks and drive back to Anchorage on the Parks Highway. See chapter 4 for a complete loop itinerary.

Whittier is the system's main port connecting Southeast and Southcentral Alaska via the oceangoing ferry *Kennicott*. The ship's route spans the state, from Prince Rupert, B.C., to Juneau, across the Gulf of Alaska to Whittier, around the Kenai Peninsula to Homer and out to Kodiak. The entire loop takes 2 weeks. The fare for the 2-day voyage between Whittier and Juneau is $221 for adults, $508 for a 15-foot vehicle, and roughly $200 to $350 for a cabin. See "Exploring Southeast Alaska," in chapter 6, for information about the system. A Chugach National Forest ranger interprets the scenery for passengers on the Prince William Sound ferry in the summer.

VISITOR INFORMATION There is no visitor center, but you can contact the **Whittier Chamber of Commerce** (☎907/677-9448; www.whittieralaskachamber.org), which includes a business directory with links on its website.

The people at the harbormaster's office are helpful and maintain public toilets and showers; it's the two-story building at the harbor (☎907/472-2327, ext. 115; www.whittieralaska.gov).

SPECIAL EVENTS Whittier has an event that I'm quite sure you won't find anywhere else: The **Walk to Whittier,** through the 2¾-mile tunnel, June 13, 2010. Entertainment and shopping specials in Whittier reward those who complete the trek, then buses carry everyone back. The town also holds a summer-long halibut derby and fall silver salmon derby. Contact the chamber of commerce, mentioned above, for information on any of the events. The town also has an old-fashioned Fourth of July celebration.

Getting Out on the Sound

Whittier is the entrance to western Prince William Sound, at the end of one of many long, deep fjords where marine mammals and eagles are common. Glaciers at the heads of many of the fjords dump ice in the water for the tour boats that cruise from Whittier.

LARGE TOUR BOATS

Several companies with offices in Anchorage compete for your business for day-trip tours to the Sound's western glaciers. Besides having incredible scenery, the water is calm, making seasickness unlikely—for the queasy, this is a much better choice than Kenai Fjords National Park. Each operator times departures to coordinate with the daily Alaska Railroad train from Anchorage, described above, which means they have up to 6 hours for the trip. Some try to see as much as possible, while others take it slower to savor the scenery and wildlife sightings. Between the train and boat fare, expect to spend around $250 per person for this day's outing, leaving Anchorage at 10am and returning at 9:30pm. You can save $30 a person and up to 3 hours by taking a bus the tour boat arranges instead of the train. If you have two or more people, you can save by renting a car and driving. You will be able to buy meals on board or one will be provided.

Phillips Cruises and Tours The 26-glacier cruise travels the Sound on a fast three-deck catamaran, covering many miles of scenery and counting the glaciers as they go. The boat ride is 4½ hours, so if you use their bus you cut the total time from Anchorage to under 8½ hours. The boat has a snack bar and bar, and a hot lunch is provided with the fare.

519 W. 4th Ave., Anchorage, AK 99501. ☎800/544-0529 or 907/276-8023. www.26glaciers.com. 4½-hour cruise $139 adults, $79 children under 12; fees and fuel surcharge $15 per passenger.

Major Marine Tours This company operates a smaller, 149-passenger vessel at a slower pace than Phillips—they hit a mere 10 glaciers, but spend more time waiting for them to calve. Another important feature: The tour is narrated by a Chugach National Forest ranger, not the company. The route goes up Blackstone Bay. There's an emphasis on food, which costs extra; the salmon and prime rib buffet is $19 for adults, $9 for children. It's quite good. Time on the water is 5 hours. Check on prices, as they are expected to change.

411 W. 4th Ave., Anchorage, AK 99501. ☎800/764-7300 or 907/274-7300. www.majormarine. com. $107 adults, $53 children ages 11 and under.

SMALL BOAT TOURS

Instead of getting on a giant tour boat with a crowd of people, you can go on a small boat with a local whom you'll get to know as he shows off favorite places and lands on beaches to picnic and walk. If you see a whale or other point of interest, you stay as long or as short a time as you like. However, you give up the comfort of a large vessel, you pay more, and most small boats have a four-person minimum.

Sound Eco Adventures Beloved Gerry Sanger is a retired wildlife biologist who spent years researching the waterfowl and ecology of Prince William Sound. Now he carries up to six passengers at a time on whale, wildlife, and glacier sightseeing and photography tours from his speedy 30-foot aluminum boat, which has a landing craft–like ramp perfect for pulling up on gravel beaches and suitable for wheelchairs. Gerry's success rate at finding whales is better than 90% since 1999, and he has gone years without missing once. His shorter, 5-hour tours usually do not encounter whales. Fares include snacks, but bring your own lunch. Gerry is considering retiring again, so grab the chance to spend a day with him.
P.O. Box 707, Whittier, AK 99693. ☎888/471-2312 or 907/472-2312. www.soundecoadventure. com. 10-hr. whale and wildlife cruise $232–$258 per person; 8-hr. glacier and wildlife $190; 5-hr. sightseeing $155.

Honey Charters A family runs three sturdy aluminum boats built for these waters, specializing in personal tours, water transportation, and kayaker drop-offs. They operate with a minimum of four passengers; by paying the four-person minimum, you can have a boat to yourself. For larger groups, their *Qayaq Spirit* carries up to 30 passengers for kayaking or sightseeing cruises. Bring your own food.
On the Whittier waterfront (P.O. Box 708), Whittier, AK 99693. ☎888/477-2493 or 907/472-2493. www.honeycharters.com 3-hr. cruise $139 per person; 6-hr. $189 per person.

FISHING

About 30 charter fishing boats operate out of Whittier, the closest saltwater fishing to Anchorage, mostly targeting halibut but also getting salmon at certain times.

The Sound by Yacht

I came across the *Discovery* one evening in a secret little cove in the remote southwestern corner of Prince William Sound's Knight Island. Briefly pulled from my rough camping existence, I suddenly found myself sitting on a soft couch in a sumptuous mahogany lounge, eating a delicious chocolate dessert, and sipping wine. The *Discovery* is a classic old wooden vessel, and accommodations are nautical and yachtlike, not as fancy even as a small cruise ship. But it's comfortable, groups are only about a dozen per trip, and the owner and skipper know the Sound well, taking passengers to its most intimate and beautiful spots—places such as that cove that hardly anyone knows about. It's like a first-class wilderness lodge afloat. A 7-day itinerary, including 5 nights aboard and 2 at a B&B in Anchorage, starts at $3,800 per person, double occupancy. Contact **Discovery Voyages** (☎800/324-7602; www.discoveryvoyages.com).

Contact the Whittier Chamber of Commerce or the Whittier Harbormaster (see "Visitor Information," above) for a list of operators. **Bread N Butter Charters** (**☏888/472-2396** or 907/472-2396; www.breadnbuttercharters.com) has been around for many years. They charge $285 per person for a day of halibut fishing and have an office on the waterfront. Honey Charters, listed above under "Small Boat Tours," has a similar service.

You can also rent your own boat for fishing, camping, or even sleeping on board, from **Whittier Boat & Tackle Rentals** (**☏907/632-1188**; www.whittierboatrentals.com). The company carries quality equipment, including boats suitable for an extended trip. Full-day rentals range from $300 to $725.

SEA KAYAKING

Whittier is a popular starting point for kayak trips to beautiful and protected western Prince William Sound. Day trips for beginners paddle along the shore near Whittier, often visiting a bird rookery, or take a boat 5 miles from the harbor to Shotgun Cove and paddle back. Longer multiday trips go by boat to even more interesting waters where you can visit glaciated fjords and paddle narrow passages. Several businesses compete in Whittier. **Alaska Sea Kayakers** (**☏877/472-2534** or 907/472-2534; www.alaskaseakayakers.com) offers 3- and 5-hour day trips, for $79 to $175; paddles at Blackstone Glacier that begin and end with a charter boat ride, for $300; and extended trips. Guides are well trained and they occasionally offer weekend instructional clinics (check the website for times). Offices are at each end of Whittier Harbor. They rent to experienced paddlers, too. **Prince William Sound Kayak Center** (**☏877/472-2452** or 907/472-2452; www.pwskayakcenter.com) offers guided half-day trips starting at $80 as well as full days and other options, and rents kayaks. They've been in business since 1981.

Most self-guided kayakers charter a boat to drop them off among the islands beyond the long, deep fjord in which Whittier is located. Honey Charters, listed above under "Small Boat Tours," offers a drop-off service. There are six Forest Service cabins in this idyllic area, which must be reserved 6 months ahead. Flat sites suitable for a tent are not plentiful on these rocky shores, which dropped in the 1964 earthquake, so do some research with the Forest Service or Alaska Public Lands Information Center in Anchorage before you go (the tent platforms at Surprise Cove State Marine Park make an excellent remote base camp). For information and cabin reservations, see "Chugach National Forest: Do-It-Yourself Wilderness."

Where to Stay & Dine

Most meals served in Whittier are for people grabbing a sandwich or fish and chips while waiting for a boat or otherwise passing through. Several such restaurants are in the triangle at the east end of the harbor where you can conveniently check them all out before making a choice. For something a bit fancier, there's a beautiful craftsman-style inn at the west end of the harbor, which you can't miss. At this writing, however, it was not in business. A new owner hoped to get it going by 2010.

June's Whittier Bed and Breakfast Condo Suites ★ These 12 condo units are on the top two floors of the Begich Towers, the concrete building that dominates Whittier, allowing guests to live as Whittier people do, with narrow corridors and a small elevator leading to rooms with breathtaking views and hummingbirds feeding at the high-rise windows. Rather than a traditional B&B, you are essentially renting an equipped apartment for the night. All units have full kitchens and some have big living rooms that are the equivalent of a nice family home. Housekeeping is first rate. The friendly hostess, June Miller, and her husband, Ken, also have a fishing charter and sightseeing business, Bread N Butter Charters, listed above; you check in at their harborside office.

P.O. Box 715, Whittier, AK 99693. **☎888/472-2396** or 907/472-2396. Fax 907/472-2503. www. breadnbuttercharters.com. 10 units. $145–$450 double; extra adult $15. AE, MC, V. **Amenities:** Harbor shuttle. *In room:* TV/DVD, Internet, kitchen.

SEWARD: GATEWAY TO RESURRECTION BAY & KENAI FJORDS

Located by the broad fjord of Resurrection Bay, Seward's main reason to exist has always been its ocean dock. The agreeable little town started life as a place to fish and to get off boats arriving in Alaska, then continued as a place for Alaskans and visitors to get *on* boats and see the bay and Kenai Fjords National Park (described in "Kenai Fjords National Park," later in this chapter). With the growth of the cruise industry, Seward again is a place to get off the boat. Many cruises that cross the Gulf of Alaska start or end here, with their passengers taking a bus to or from the airport in Anchorage. The minority of those cruise passengers who spend any time in town find a mountainside grid of streets lined with old wood-frame houses and traditional businesses operating in historic store fronts. The community has a lot of pride, and wonderful murals appear on the side of many buildings. Increasing tourism has brought more traffic and development, but Seward certainly isn't spoiled yet.

Seward's history is among the oldest in Alaska. The Russian conquistador Alexander Baranof stopped here in 1793, named Resurrection Bay, and built a ship, which later sank, perhaps because Baranof's workers didn't have proper materials. Gold prospectors blazed trails from here to finds on Turnagain Arm starting in 1891, and in 1907 the army linked those trails with others all the way to Nome, finishing the Iditarod Trail. Today that route is discontinuous south of Anchorage, but you can follow it through Seward and hike a portion of it on the Johnson Pass Trail north of town (p. 367). More relevant for current visitors and the local economy, the federal government took over a failed railroad-building effort in 1915, finishing the line to Fairbanks in 1923. Until the age of jet travel, most people coming to the main part of Alaska arrived by steamer in Seward and then traveled north by rail. The train ride to Anchorage, daily during the summer, is still supremely beautiful.

Seward's in-town highlight is the Alaska SeaLife Center, a research aquarium that's open to the public. Combined with Seward's excellent ocean fishing, the national park, the wonderful hiking trails, and the unique and attractive town itself, the center helps make Seward well worth a 2-day visit.

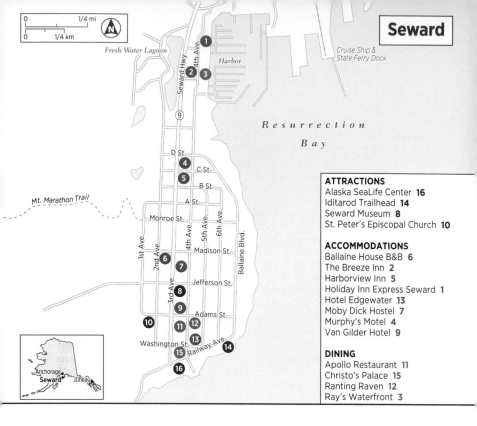

Scale: 0 to 1/4 mi, 0 to 1/4 km

Seward

Fresh Water Lagoon

Harbor

Cruise Ship &
State Ferry Dock

Resurrection

Bay

Mt. Marathon Trail

D St.

C St.

B St.

A St.

Monroe St.

Madison St.

Jefferson St.

Adams St.

Washington St.

Railway Ave.

Seward Hwy.

4th Ave.

1st Ave.

2nd Ave.

3rd Ave.

4th Ave.

5th Ave.

6th Ave.

Ballaine Blvd.

Anchorage
Seward
Juneau

ATTRACTIONS
Alaska SeaLife Center **16**
Iditarod Trailhead **14**
Seward Museum **8**
St. Peter's Episcopal Church **10**

ACCOMMODATIONS
Ballaine House B&B **6**
The Breeze Inn **2**
Harborview Inn **5**
Holiday Inn Express Seward **1**
Hotel Edgewater **13**
Moby Dick Hostel **7**
Murphy's Motel **4**
Van Gilder Hotel **9**

DINING
Apollo Restaurant **11**
Christo's Palace **15**
Ranting Raven **12**
Ray's Waterfront **3**

Essentials

GETTING THERE By Car: See "The Seward Highway: A Road Guide," earlier in this chapter, for how to make the spectacular 127-mile drive down from Anchorage. All major car-rental agencies are represented in Anchorage.

By Bus: The **Seward Bus Line** (☎907/224-3608 in Seward or 907/563-0800 in Anchorage) makes a round-trip from Seward to Anchorage and back daily, year-round (except Sun Oct–Apr); the fare is $50 one-way, $95 round trip. They'll pick up and drop off passengers anywhere en route and, for an extra $5, take you to the airport.

The **Park Connection Motorcoach Service** (☎800/266-8625 or 907/245-0200; www.alaskatravel.com/bus-lines) connects Seward with Anchorage, Talkeetna, and Denali National Park twice daily in summer in each direction with big, comfortable coaches. The fare is $55 between Seward and Anchorage, $145 between Seward and Denali, half off under age 12. Passengers going to Anchorage get a free pass to the Anchorage Museum at Rasmuson Center.

By Train: The train Coastal Classic route between Anchorage and Seward is one of miraculous beauty. The **Alaska Railroad** (☎800/544-0552 or 907/265-2494; www.alaskarailroad.com) offers passenger service from Anchorage and back daily in summer. The route is even prettier than the highway, passing close by glaciers and following a ledge halfway up the narrow, vertical Placer River gorge, where it ducks into tunnels and pops out at bends in the river. The landscape looks just as it did when the first person beheld it. The railroad's young guides are well trained. The fare for basic service is $75 one-way, $119 round-trip; children ages 2 to 11 half price. Or choose Gold Star Service, on double-decker cars with white tablecloth dining, taking those cars one-way and coming back at the regular class, for $187 adults. A rental car will almost always be cheaper, but the train ride is unforgettable. The railroad also offers packages with lodging and activities in Seward. Don't try to do it in 1 day from Anchorage—the 16-hour marathon is too much.

GETTING AROUND You can easily cover downtown Seward on foot, although a little help is handy to get back and forth from the boat harbor. If it's not raining, a bike may be the best way. **Seward Bike Shop** (☎ **907/224-2448**), in a railcar near the depot at the harbor, rents high-performance mountain bikes and models good for just getting around town, plus accessory equipment. A cruiser is $12 half day, $19 full day; a mountain bike $18 or $30. **PJ's Taxi** (☎ **907/224-5555**) is one of the cab companies in Seward.

VISITOR INFORMATION The **Seward Chamber of Commerce,** P.O. Box 749, Seward, AK 99664 (☎ **907/224-8051**; www.seward.com), has a visitor center, on the right side of the Seward Highway as you enter town, that's open year-round (summer daily 8am–6pm; winter Mon–Fri 9am–5pm). The chamber can give business information and last-minute help in finding a room. In addition to these town information sources, the **Kenai Fjords National Park Information Center** is covered in "Kenai Fjords National Park," later in this chapter. For contacts for the Chugach National Forest, see "Chugach National Forest: Do-It-Yourself Wilderness."

Coastal Classic train route.

[FastFACTS] SEWARD

Bank **Wells Fargo** is at 908 3rd Ave., with an ATM.

Hospital **Providence Seward Medical Center** is at 417 1st Ave. (**☎907/224-5205**).

Internet Access Free at the **Seward Public Library,** 5th and Adams.

Police For nonemergency situations, call the **Seward Police Department** (**☎907/224-3338**) or,

outside the city limits, the **Alaska State Troopers** (**☎907/224-3346**).

Post Office At 5th Avenue and Madison Street.

Taxes Sales tax is 7%. The **room tax** totals 11%.

SPECIAL EVENTS The **Fourth of July** is the biggest day of the year in Seward, when the whole town explodes with visitors, primarily from Anchorage. Besides the parade and many small-town festivities, the main attraction is the 3¼-mile **Mount Marathon Race,** run every year since it started as a bar bet in 1915. The racers go from the middle of town straight up rocky Mount Marathon to its 3,022-foot peak, then tumble down again, arriving muddy and bloody at the finish line in town. Strong binoculars allow you to see the whole thing from town, including the pratfalls of the runners on their way down.

The huge **Silver Salmon Derby** starts the second Saturday of August, although the peak of silver season comes later. The chamber of commerce visitor center can provide tickets and rules.

Getting Outside

Here I've described things to do out of Seward other than visiting the national park, which includes the fjords and Exit Glacier. See "Kenai Fjords National Park," later in this chapter, for that information. Although this is listed in alphabetical order, fishing and other marine activities are the main event in Seward.

DOG MUSHING & GLACIER FLIGHTS

When Mitch Seavey won the Iditarod Trail Sled Dog Race in 2004, many agreed it couldn't have happened to a nicer guy. He had made a lot of friends over the years offering rides with his dogs. It's a family business, including the four boys (one is a Junior Iditarod champ), making use of their kennel on Old Exit Glacier Road off Herman Leirer Road. They offer summer rides in Seward and in winter in Sterling (near Soldotna). The summer ride uses a wheeled sled and a full, 12-dog team—not the real thing (no snow), but you'll get a feel for the dogs' power and intelligence. The 90-minute tour costs $59 for adults, $29 for children 11 and under. Husky puppies are available for cuddling, too. They call their company **IdidaRide** (**☎800/478-3139** or 907/224-8607; www.ididaride.com).

Those willing to spend much more should consider mushing on snow at the height of summer by joining a helicopter tour to Godwin Glacier from the Seward Airport with **Godwin Glacier Dog Sled Tours** (**☎888/989-8239** or 907/224-8239; www.alaskadogsled.com). A chopper lands at a camp of 100 dogs, where guests take a ride in the dogsled, or even drive it themselves. The company also offers overnight camping on the ice. For the mushing program they charge

Mount Marathon Race.

$450 adults, $430 children 12 and under; the overnight is $520 per person; or just fly up to the glacier for $290.

FISHING

Seward is renowned for its saltwater silver salmon fishing. The silvers start showing up in the bay in mid-July and last through September. You can catch the fish from shore, from Lowell Point south of town, or even near the boat harbor, but your chances of success are far greater from a boat. I prefer small, six-passenger boats because you can get to know the skipper better and can learn more about fishing. If your party has the whole boat, you can control where it goes, perhaps adding whale-watching or sightseeing to the day. Larger boats add more comfort and stability in the waves. The going rate for a guided charter, with everything provided, is around $175 per person, or $245 to go for salmon and halibut on the same day. Andrew Mezirow, a marine biologist and maritime instructor, operates two boats, including a 12-passenger vessel and a six-passenger boat custom-built for fishing salmon in Resurrection Bay year-round. Besides day fishing, he takes guests on multiday fishing expeditions to extremely remote and beautiful places. His business is **Crackerjack Sportfishing Charters** (☏800/566-3192 or 907/224-2606; www.crackerjackcharters.com). The office is on the boardwalk at the top of the harbor ramps.

There are many other fishing charter companies, mostly booked through central charter agencies, which make life simpler for visitors. **The Fish House** is the largest charter-fishing agency in Seward, located at the Small Boat Harbor. The store also sells and rents ocean-fishing and spin-casting gear, and carries some fly-fishing supplies. For charters, reserve ahead at P.O. Box 1209, Seward, AK 99664 (☏800/257-7760 or 907/224-3674; www.thefishhouse.net). If you want a small boat, ask to be put on a "six pack," as vessels licensed for six or fewer passengers are known.

HIKING

There are several excellent hiking trails near Seward. You can get a complete list and directions at the Kenai Fjords National Park Information Center (p. 391).

The **Mount Marathon Trail** is a tough hike right to the top of a 3,022-foot mountain in less than 4 miles. The route of the famous Mount Marathon footrace is the most strenuous choice, basically going straight up from the end of Jefferson Street; the hikers' route starts at the corner of 1st Avenue and Monroe Street. Either trail rises steeply to the top of the rocky pinnacle and the incredible views there. Allow all day, unless you're a racer; in that case, expect to do it in under 45 minutes.

The **Caines Head State Recreation Area** (www.alaskastateparks.org, click on "Individual Parks") has a 7-mile coastal trail south of town. Parts of the trail are accessible only at low tide, so it's best done either as an overnight or with someone picking you up or dropping you off in a boat beyond the beach portion—the Miller's Landing water taxi offers this service (see below). The trail has some gorgeous views, rocky shores, and a fascinating destination at the end: a towering promontory with the concrete remains of Fort McGilvray, a World War II defensive emplacement. Take flashlights and you can poke around in the spooky, pitch-dark underground corridors and rooms and imagine what each was used for (going in without lights would be foolhardy). We've rarely enjoyed a hike more. Three campsites are at Tonsina Point, about 2 miles in, and a state park public-use cabin is 2 miles farther (see "Where to Stay," below; and "State Parks Cabin Reservations," p. 360). At North Beach, 4½ miles from the trail head, are two camping shelters, a ranger station, and the trails to the fort and South Beach. For an easy 2-mile hike to Fort McGilvray, start with a boat ride to North Beach. The main trail head is south of town on Lowell Point Road; pull off in the lot right after the sewage plant, then cross the road through the gate and follow the dirt road a bit until it becomes the actual trail. Stop at the Kenai Fjords National Park Information Center for tide conditions and advice.

SEA KAYAKING & WATER TAXI

Sunny Cove Sea Kayaking (☎800/770-9119 for reservations, or 907/224-4426; www.sunnycove.com) has earned a good reputation for guided kayaking in Resurrection Bay and beyond. Their day trips suitable for beginners are offered as part of the Kenai Fjords Tours trips to its Fox Island lodge. For a more ambitious day trip, and for multiday trips, they venture into the fjords themselves (see the Kenai Fjords National Park section, later in this chapter). On a budget, you can take one of Sunny Cove's tours right from Seward. They launch from Lowell Point, following the shore toward Caines Head State Recreation Area, where you can see sea otters, seabirds, intertidal creatures, and the salmon in Tonsina Creek. Three-hour paddles are $65; 8-hour trips are $130. A trip to Fox Island is more expensive but comes with a fjords boat tour and salmon bake, so the cost of the kayaking comes out roughly the same.

Another highly regarded sea kayaking firm in Seward, **Kayak Adventures Worldwide** (☎907/224-3960; www.kayakak.com) offers a wide selection of day trips and expeditions, and offers packages involving other activities, such as glacier hiking, and arranges water-taxi drop-off for clients. Owners Wendy and Dave Doughty have a strong educational and environmental ethic, and they make a point of serving families—they even have a couple of three-seat kayaks so kids can ride in the middle. Their guide training program is impressive. The couple's B&B, Bear Paw Lodge, is listed below.

Miller's Landing, at Lowell Point, 3 miles south of town (☎866/541-5739 or 907/224-5739; www.millerslandingak.com), is the primary water-taxi operator in Seward, charging flat rates to take travelers to remote beaches and public cabins around the bay or to the national park—great for sea kayakers or those who just want to get off on their own or for a one-way day hike to Caines Head (see above). Per person rates are $30 one-way, $43 round-trip to Caines Head; $275 round-trip to the park service cabin in Aialik Bay. The company also rents kayaks ($50 double, $45 single, per day) and skiffs, too ($80 for 4 hr.), and offers many other services (fishing charters, camping, cabins, and even Sat night potluck dinners).

Exploring the Town

Besides the Alaska SeaLife Center (see below), most of Seward's in-town attractions are of the modest, small-town variety. The **Iditarod Trailhead,** on the water just east of the SeaLife Center, is where pioneers entered Alaska. The broken concrete and twisted metal you see on the beach walking north are the last ruins of the Seward waterfront, which was destroyed by a tsunami wave in the 1964 earthquake. Sometimes you can see sea otters swimming just offshore. During silver salmon season, in August and September, it's possible to catch them by casting from shore here, although your chances are far better from a boat (see "Fishing," above).

The **Seward Museum,** at 3rd and Jefferson (℡907/224-3902), is a charming grandma's attic of a place, with clippings, memorabilia, and curiosities recalling the history of the town and of the Iditarod Trail, painter Rockwell Kent, and the ways of the past. Admission is $3 for adults, 50¢ ages 17 and under. It's open during the summer daily from 10am to 5pm, in winter usually weekends noon to 4pm (call ahead). Evening slide programs take place during the summer months.

The steep-roofed **St. Peter's Episcopal Church** (℡907/224-3975; www. stpeters-seward.org) is a sweet little chapel under the mountains at 2nd Avenue and Adams Street finished in 1906, within a few years of the town's founding. Behind the altar is a mural painted in 1925 by Dutch artist Jan Van Emple showing

St. Peter's Episcopal Church.

the Resurrection as if it had happened at Resurrection Bay. The apostles are depicted as real Alaska Natives and pioneers who were living in town at the time, in their contemporary dress. To get into the church, attend a Sunday morning service at 8 or 11am, or ask for the key at the Seward Museum or VanGilder Hotel.

Alaska SeaLife Center ★★★ The center's role as an important research institution makes it an especially vibrant and fascinating aquarium to see creatures from nearby Alaska waters. There's always something happening. You may have seen puffins diving into the water from a tour boat; here you can see what they look like flying *under* the water. Seabirds, harbor seals, octopus, and sea lions reside in three spectacular exhibits viewed from above or below—you can get within a few feet of the birds without glass. There are smaller tanks with fish, crab, and other creatures, a touch tank where you can handle starfish and other tidepool animals, and exhibits on current ocean changes and hot research issues. A remarkable exhibit traces the life cycle of salmon; the staff hatches salmon eggs on a schedule so fish at each stage of development will always be present in their realistic habitats. I don't want to oversell the place, however: The center is not as large as a big-city aquarium, and you'll likely spend no more than a couple of hours unless you sign up for one of the lectures or special behind-the-scenes programs for adults and children that happen all day. To make the most of the admission price, call ahead so you can catch a program that interests you.

301 Railway Ave. (P.O. Box 1329), Seward, AK 99664. **☎888/378-2525** or 907/224-6300. www. alaskasealife.org. $20 adults, $15 students (12–17 or with ID), $10 children 4–11, free for children 3 and under. May 1–Sept 14 Mon–Thurs 9am–6:30pm, Fri–Sun 8am–6:30pm; Sept 15–Apr 30 daily 10am–5pm.

Where to Stay

Alaska's Point of View Reservation Service (**☎907/224-2323;** www.alaskas view.com) is a Seward lodging- and tour-booking agency. The website has a handy search function for B&Bs, cabins, hotel rooms, and all other lodgings. You can get a list of B&Bs from the chamber of commerce visitor center (p. 443).

Seward has several hotels beyond those I can list here; in fact, I'm not aware of a bad hotel in Seward. The **Holiday Inn Express Seward Harbor** (**☎800/ HOLIDAY** [465-4329] or 907/224-2550; www.hiexpress.com/sewardak) stands right on the small boat harbor wall, with its ramp down to the floats, and is only steps from the railroad depot. The hotel has a charter booking office and a tiny pool. The well-equipped rooms have red carpets, but otherwise are typical of a national chain. Summer rates are $189 to $299 double, with the lower-priced units facing the parking lot instead of the harbor. Breakfast is included in the price.

Equally attractive to the Holiday Inn is the downtown **Best Western Hotel Edgewater,** 200 5th Ave. (**☎888/793-6800;** www.hoteledgewater.com). The unique building looks across streets to the ocean on two sides near the SeaLife Center. Rooms vary in shape and size and are decorated in bold colors. All were renovated in 2008 with pillow-top mattresses, flatscreen TVs, and other amenities. Lower-priced units have lesser views or only a frosted window facing the lobby atrium. Summer rates are $199 to $289 double.

Save over either of those choices at Murphy's Motel (**☎800/686-8191** or 907/224-8090; www.murphysmotel.com), near the boat harbor, which has attractive, well-equipped rooms with views and Wi-Fi in a new building and good budget rooms in an older building.

Ballaine House Bed and Breakfast ✒ This 1905 house near downtown is a classic B&B, with wooden floors, a large living room, and tall, double-hung windows. It's on the National Register of Historic Places and the town walking tour, decorated with antiques and handmade quilts. It's a social place with service that is accommodating and fun, and the hostess offers raincoats, binoculars, and other gear for outings, cooks breakfast to order, and even does laundry. The B&B can also book your activities and boats in Seward and some other towns, giving you the booking commission, which can save as much as 20%. The rooms are not large, suitable for only one or two people, and all bathrooms are shared. The B&B does not take children under 8.

437 3rd Ave. (P.O. Box 2051), Seward, AK 99664. ☎**907/224-2362.** www.superpage.com/ballaine. 5 units, none with private bathroom. $99 double. Rates include full breakfast cooked to order. No credit cards. No children under 8. *In room:* TV/DVD, Wi-Fi.

Bear Paw Lodge ★ 📠 An environmentally oriented couple running a Seward kayaking business opened their remarkable log house in a forest outside of town to visitors with the same warmth and energy that has made their paddling business a success. The lodge has four rooms, a big master bedroom under the eaves, and three simpler but very comfortable rooms with shared bath that rent for a bargain $125 a night. Guests use all common rooms, including cooking any meals in the large kitchen and using the broadband-connected computer, and there's a big hot tub on the deck. Check in at the kayak shop downtown; you will need a car and detailed directions to get to the house.

328 3rd Ave. (P.O. Box 2249), Seward, AK 99664. ☎**907/224-3960.** Fax 907/224-2255. www.sewardbearpawlodge.com. 4 units, 1 w/private bathroom. $125 double w/shared bath; $185 double w/private bath. $15 each additional person. Rate includes self-serve continental breakfast. **Amenities:** Grill; hot tub; Internet access; TV/DVD in common room. *In room:* Wi-Fi.

The Breeze Inn ★ Located right at the busy boat harbor, a block back from the water, this three-story hotel completed a large expansion in 2008 that added many spacious rooms in earth tones, all with good amenities and a polished feel. The original wing is a bargain: old-fashioned motel rooms, but clean and well maintained. In whole, the setup lets visitors choose the level of luxury they want and the cost they want to pay, and the property is consistently well run. The location is the most convenient in town for a fishing charter or Kenai Fjords boat trip, which means the building occupies a busy harbor parking lot near the highway and isn't landscaped.

1306 Seward Hwy. (P.O. Box 2147), Seward, AK 99664. ☎**888/224-5237** or 907/224-5237. Fax 907/224-7024. www.breezeinn.com. 100 units. Summer $139–$269 double; winter $49–$119 double. Extra person $10. AE, DC, DISC, MC, V. **Amenities:** Free airport transfers; restaurant; bar. *In room:* A/C, TV, fridge, hair dryer, Wi-Fi.

Harborview Inn ★ ✒ This Inn offers rooms with lots of light and Mission-style furniture for rates that are a bargain by Seward's high standards. The location, midway between the Small Boat Harbor and downtown, puts both within long walking distance. Families and large groups especially should consider a stay, as the inn has a four-bedroom family suite with the features and size of a house—it's 2,500 square feet—renting for $239 double plus $10 for each additional person. Two two-bedroom apartments on the beach along Ballaine Avenue are perfect for families as well and rent for $219 a night for four. There are other suites, too.

804 3rd Ave. (P.O. Box 1584), Seward, AK 99664. ☎888/324-3217 or 907/224-3217. Fax 907/224-3218. www.sewardhotel.com. 35 units, plus 4 apts. High season $149 double, $169–$299 apartment; low season $79 double, $99–$249 apartment. Extra person $10. AE, DISC, MC, V. Closed Oct to mid-May. *In room:* TV, hair dryer, Wi-Fi.

Seward Windsong Lodge ★★ This hotel is the only one near Kenai Fjords National Park with a national park atmosphere. The big lobby, with its high ceiling, huge wood beams, fireplace, and cedar shingles could be at Yellowstone. Moreover, the posh, solidly finished quality of the place puts it in first rank among Seward's hotels. The location is out of town, among spruce trees on the broad valley of the Resurrection River, and the collection of buildings goes on and on. Rooms are in separate lodges with entry from exterior porches. They have a crisp feel, all with two queen beds and rustic-style furniture and good amenities. Family suites are available with TVs and video games in the kids' room.

The hotel restaurant, the **Resurrection Roadhouse,** has lots of natural light, pale wood, and an exhaustive selection of Alaska craft brews on tap. The menu includes fish, venison, and ribs smoked in-house as well as hand-tossed gourmet pizzas. Main courses for dinner range from $9 to $24. The view of the mountains is great and the feeling relaxed, a low-key alternative to a noisy waterfront restaurant. Do call ahead, as they fill at dinner time. The restaurant and lodge close mid-September to mid-May.

Mile ½, Exit Glacier Rd., also known as Herman Leirer Rd. (P.O. Box 1889), Seward AK 99664. ☎888/959-9590 or 907/265-4501 in Anchorage, or 907/224-7116 in Seward. www.sewardwindsong.com. 180 units. High season $249–$299 double; low season $149–$199 double. Extra person age 12 and older $15. AE, DISC, MC, V. Closed Oct–Apr. **Amenities:** Free airport transfers; restaurant; Internet station (in lobby); Wi-Fi (in lobby). *In room:* TV/VCR.

Van Gilder Hotel ★ This 1916 building on the National Register of Historic Places was restored with authentic period details and decorated in a Victorian style that complements the woodwork and stained glass. Old hotels have small bedrooms, and some of the bathrooms that were added are tiny, many with shower stalls, not tubs, but that's all easy to forgive in a place that feels very cozy and very real. The atmosphere is conducive to a fun social visit. A community kitchen on the main floor allows guests to stop for a free hot drink at any time, or even cook their own meals. In Seward's high-priced lodging market, the hotel is a good value, and yet it would be the first choice of many visitors who want to experience an authentic part of this interesting town. All rooms have queen-size beds, and some also have a fold-down Murphy bed for a third person. The location is right downtown.

308 Adams St. (P.O. Box 609), Seward, AK 99664. ☎800/204-6835 or 907/224-3079. Fax 907/224-3689. www.vangilderhotel.com. 23 units. High season $119 double with shared bath, $149–$169 with private bath, $209 suite; low season $59 double with shared bath, $69–$79 with private bath, $139 suite. $10 each additional person. AE, DISC, MC, V. Closed Oct–Mar. *In room:* TV, Wi-Fi.

A HOSTEL, CAMPING & CABINS

A friendly, multi-lingual family that lives in a remote area in the winter comes to Seward in the summer to run the **Moby Dick Hostel,** 432 3rd Ave. (☎907/224-7072; www.mobydickhostel.com). They charge $20 for a bunk, $54 for private hostel rooms, and $65 to $70 for kitchenette rooms. The hostel has Wi-Fi and is centrally located downtown. There is no lock-out or curfew, and the office is open 9 to 11am and 5 to 10pm.

The best campgrounds near Seward are those in Chugach National Forest, described above under "Chugach National Forest: Do-It-Yourself Wilderness," especially Primrose Campground on Kenai Lake (p. 367). The only campground in Kenai Fjords National Park is near Seward, the **Exit Glacier Campground** at mile 8.5 of Herman Leirer Road (aka Exit Glacier Rd.). The campground is on willow-covered, gravel ground that plants haven't yet reclaimed from the retreating ice. Sites are far apart and almost completely private, but lack any amenities—no picnic tables, fire grates, or anything. Use the food lockers and central cooking to keep bears away. Snow lingers into early June; later in the summer, the campground often fills by early evening. There is no fee for the 12 sites, and reservations are not taken. It's open for tents only and has pit toilets and hand-pump water.

In the town of Seward itself, the seaside **Waterfront Park** on Ballaine Boulevard is good for RV camping—units stand side by side like town houses facing the ocean—but the tent sites are too noisy and exposed for my liking. Seward has tried to crack down on drinking and rowdiness in its campgrounds with partial success. The fee is $10 for tents, $15 for dry RV sites, $30 for RV sites with electricity and water; showers are $2. It's operated by the city parks and recreation department (☎ **907/224-4055;** www.cityofseward.net/parksrec). A quieter town campground is **Forest Acres Park,** among the spruce trees at Hemlock and Sealion Boulevard, just off Seward Highway near the Army Recreation Center. Fees are the same. Neither campground accepts reservations. RVs are welcome at Forest Acres, but there are no hookups.

The Alaska Division of Parks maintains two cabins for rent in the **Caines Head State Recreation Area,** south of town, and two in **Thumb Cove State Marine Park,** across the bay from Caines Head (see "State Parks Cabin Reservations," under "Exploring the Kenai Peninsula & Prince William Sound," earlier in this chapter). These cabins are in high demand and difficult to reserve, but there are good areas for camping in both parks. It's possible to hike to the Caines Head cabins (see "Hiking," above), but to get to Thumb Cove you need a boat. Water taxi service is offered by Miller's Landing (p. 382). The Thumb Cove cabins lie in an impossibly steep bowl of mountains, a grand and lovely setting that, along with the excellent salmon fishing nearby, explains their popularity. Camping is permitted along the same beach without a permit, with plenty of space and an outhouse for campers' use.

Cabins in Chugach National Forest and Kenai Fjords National Park are mentioned in those sections.

Where to Dine

There are various places at the harbor to grab a sandwich or other quick meal on the way out to sea; they change too frequently for me to include them here. Downtown, the **Ranting Raven,** 228 4th Ave. (☎ **907/224-2228**), is a great little gift and coffee shop serving pastries and snacks, open April through Christmas. Art shows open on the first Friday of the month through the visitor season, and the shop carries locally crafted jewelry.

Apollo Restaurant ★ ☺ MEDITERRANEAN/SEAFOOD This is a surprisingly good small-town restaurant. Seward families come back for a menu that includes anything they might want: Greek and Southern Italian cuisine, steaks, seafood, pizza, and much more. They'll even cook your own day's catch. But the food is much better than you expect in such a place, especially the seafood dishes, and the service is fast, skilled, and flexible, great for families with children. The dining room, with many booths, takes the Greek theme as far as it will go—I especially enjoyed the miniature Doric columns. They serve beer and wine.

229 4th Ave. ℂ**907/224-3092.** www.apollorestaurantak.com. Main courses $10–$24. AE, MC, V. Daily 11am–11pm.

Christo's Palace ★ SEAFOOD/ITALIAN/MEXICAN I was skeptical of a restaurant with faux 1890s decor and Formica tables serving a family-friendly menu of pizza, pasta, tacos, burgers, subs, fried fish, steaks, and much finer dining, including rack of lamb and stuffed halibut. Who could do so many things well? But I became a believer. First, the service was too friendly and efficient for me to keep up my guard. Next, the children's menu met their needs exactly, and my teen said the pizza was first rate. Finally, the seafood sauté was richly endowed with king crab and other delicacies, and the chicken and artichoke penne pasta was rich and cooked perfectly. Everything was served so quickly the children didn't have time to squirm. Christo's has found the way to please everyone.

133 4th Ave. ℂ**907/224-5255.** Lunch and dinner main courses $8–$38. AE, DC, DISC, MC, V. Daily 11am–11pm.

Ray's Waterfront ★★ STEAK/SEAFOOD The lively, noisy dining room looks out from big windows across the small-boat harbor, with tables on terraces so everyone can see. The atmosphere is fun, and the consistently good food is just right after a day on the water. Unlike many popular waterfront restaurants, Ray's has stayed up with the times, keeping the food interesting while keeping the traditional seafood choices many diners will be looking forward to (such as the famous plank salmon). On my last visit, the seafood chowder was tasty and so thick with goodies the spoon almost stood up in the cup. The jambalaya was beautiful, not too spicy, and loaded with shrimp. Most important, they don't overcook the fresh local fish—and that's really all you can ask. Service is excellent when the restaurant isn't overrun with guests on holiday weekends. They have a full bar.

At the small-boat harbor. ℂ**907/224-5606.** Dinner reservations recommended. Lunch $8–$15; dinner main courses $15–$30. 18% gratuity added for parties of 6 or more. AE, DISC, MC, V. Daily 11am–11pm. Closed Oct to mid-Mar.

KENAI FJORDS NATIONAL PARK

Kenai Fjords is all about remote rocks, mountains, and ice that meet the ocean, and the animals that live there. The park comprises 670,000 acres of the south coast and interior landmass of the Kenai Peninsula. The shore here is exposed to the Gulf of Alaska, whose wild, recurrent storms beat against the mountainous shore unbuffered by any landmass from the vast expanse of the Pacific to the south. Wildlife thrives, but humans have never made a mark.

The geological events that formed this landscape are vast and ongoing. The steep, coastal mountains amount to a dent in the earth's crust where the northward-moving Pacific tectonic plate is colliding and adding land to the southern edge of Alaska. As the Pacific plate pushes under Alaska, it slams islands onto the Alaska coast, then sinks into the molten layer down below. These mountains shrink and rise measurably as the earth convulses. The 1964 earthquake dropped them by 6 to 8 feet. As your boat passes the park's small, sharp, bedrock islands, now populated by seabirds and marine mammals, you are seeing the tips of ancient peaks that once stood far above the shore like today's coastal mountains.

The park's history has barely started. The fjords became a park only in 1980. In 1976, when the National Park Service explored more than 650 miles of coastline, including the park area, they didn't find a single human being. The same was true when geologists came in 1909. British explorer Capt. James Cook made the first maps of the fjords area in 1778, but saw no one and didn't land. We don't know much about Native Americans who lived in the fjords. Scientists have found some areas where people lived, or at least had camps, but no one knows exactly who they were or what they were doing here. The earth, through earthquakes or glacial action, has erased most remains. Anthropologists call these people *Unegkurmiut*, and believe they were Alutiiq, Eskimos who lived on the Pacific Coast, closely related to the people of Prince William Sound and Kodiak Island. Those groups are still around; scientists are studying the Unegkurmiut and what happened to them from the little evidence they can find on the fjord's beaches.

The Natives probably never ventured inland over the impossibly rugged interior of the Kenai Peninsula, leaving its heart to be discovered in 1968, when the first mountain climbers crossed the Harding Ice Field, which covers most of the national park. **Exit Glacier** and all the glaciers of Kenai Fjords flow from this ice-age leftover, which may be a mile thick. The ice field lies in a high bowl of mountains that jut straight out of the ocean to heights of 3,000 to 5,000 feet. When moisture-laden ocean clouds hit those mountains, they drop lots of rain

An endangered bull stellar sea lion claims his territory among a group of females.

Mountain goat and baby near Exit Glacier.

and snow—up on the ice field 40 to 80 feet of snow fall each winter, with a water equivalent of 17 feet. Summer weather isn't warm enough to melt the snow at that elevation, so it packs down ever deeper until it turns into the hard, heavy ice of glaciers and flows downward to the sea.

The area's history finally got an ugly start in 1989, when the tanker *Exxon Valdez* crashed into a rock about 150 miles northeast of the park in Prince William Sound and spilled at least 11 million gallons of oil. Exxon did a poor job of catching the oil before it spread, and by the end of the summer the sticky, brownish-black muck had soiled beaches in the western Sound, across the fjords, and all the way to Kodiak Island and the Alaska Peninsula. More than 1,000 miles of shoreline were oiled to some degree, 30 miles in the park. Thousands of sea otters and hundreds of thousands of seabirds were killed in the Sound and on the islands near the fjords. Nature scrubbed the oil off the rocks again, and you will see no evidence of it in the park today; but government scientists say some of the affected species of birds and animals still haven't come back completely. Nonetheless, there are few places you can see more wildlife than on a boat ride here.

Most of the park is remote and difficult to reach. A large vessel, such as a tour boat operating out of Seward, is the only practical way for most people to see the marine portion of the park. That's not cheap or quick, and there are better destinations for people subject to seasickness. The inland portion is accessible only at Exit Glacier, near Seward.

Essentials

GETTING THERE Seward is the threshold to the park. Exit Glacier is 13 miles from the town by road; the Kenai Fjords National Park Information Center is at the Seward Small-Boat Harbor; and the tour boats that visit the park leave from Seward.

Some visitors try to see the park in a day, coming from Anchorage by train or road, touring the park by boat, then returning that evening. I do not recommend this. To really get to the park, you need to be on an all-day boat trip—most half-day trips barely leave Resurrection Bay and hardly see the park proper. More important, a lot of visitors riding the train back to Anchorage after a 16-hour marathon to Kenai Fjords are so tired they can't keep their eyes open for the extraordinary scenery passing by. A better plan is to spend at least 1 night in Seward and take in the full Kenai Fjords boat trip and Exit Glacier.

VISITOR INFORMATION At the **Kenai Fjords National Park Information Center,** Seward Small Boat Harbor (P.O. Box 1727), Seward, AK 99664 (☎907/224-7500; www.nps.gov/kefj), you will find rangers to answer questions about the park and provide information on the all-important tour boats, and a small but handy bookstore. Call or drop by here for advice on public use cabins for rent in the fjords, guidance on a sea-kayaking expedition there, or information on hikes and trail conditions. They're open late May through early September daily 8:30am to 7pm, the balance of May and September 9am to 5pm. The center is closed October through April.

ACCOMMODATIONS & CAMPING There are no hotels in the park; it's best to base yourself in Seward (see my recommendations earlier in this chapter). The **Exit Glacier Campground,** the only campground in the park, also is listed on p. 387. In the heart of the park you can camp anywhere if you observe correct backcountry precautions. A free park service map shows the location of food lockers and hanging cables to keep your stuff away from bears in the kayaking waters of Aialik Bay and Northwestern Fjord. The Park Service gives voluntary permits to record your itinerary and an emergency contact phone number in case you don't return. The park will send a packet of information, which you can request through the website. They also rent out three **public-use cabins** in the fjords, reachable only by boat or floatplane. Contact the Alaska Public Lands Information Center in Anchorage (p. 292) for a $50-a-day cabin permit, open for reservations starting January 2 each year.

Seeing the Park
SIGHTSEEING & WILDLIFE CRUISES

Kenai Fjords is essentially a marine park. On a boat tour, you'll see its mountains, glaciers, and wildlife. On any of the tours you're sure to see sea otters and sea lions, and you have a good chance, depending on the season, conditions, and luck, of seeing humpback whales, orcas, mountain goats, and black bears. I saw all those on one trip to Aialik Bay. Gray whales come in the early spring and huge fin whales show sometimes, too, but are hard to see. Bird-watchers may see bald eagles; puffins (both tufted and horned); murrelets (marbled, ancient, and Kittlitz's); cormorants (red faced, pelagic, and double-crested); murres (common and thick billed); auklets (rhinoceros and parakeet); and various other sea ducks, alcids, and gulls.

The farther you go into the park, the more you'll see. If you really want to see Kenai Fjords National Park and glaciers that drop ice into the water, the boat has to go at least into Aialik Bay to Holgate Glacier or Aialik Glacier. Northwestern Glacier is even deeper in the park. Half-day Resurrection Bay cruises offer plenty of impressive scenery but pass only one large glacier, and that at a distance. They have less chance of seeing whales, and see fewer species of birds. The longest trips into the heart of the park proper encounter the greatest variety and number of birds and animals. If you're lucky with the weather, you can make it to the exposed Chiswell Islands, which have some of the greatest bird colonies in Alaska, supporting more than 50,000 seabirds of 18 species. I've seen clouds of puffins swarm here. The day-long trips also allow you more time to linger and really see the behavior of the wildlife. Whatever your choice, binoculars are a necessity, but if you didn't bring your own you can often rent them on board.

Prices are around $160 to go to Northwestern Glacier in Northwestern Fjord off Harris Bay, a 10- to 12-hour trip; $130 to $140 to go to Holgate or Aialik Glacier in Aialik Bay, which takes 6 to 8 hours (the most common destinations); and $65 to $85 for a 3- to 5-hour Resurrection Bay tour, which doesn't go to the national park at all. Children's prices are around half off. I have seen vague or misleading publicity material from tour operators, so ask exactly where the boat goes or get a map of the route. Bear Glacier, within Resurrection Bay, is unimpressive, because boats can't get close to it. You have to go at least to Aialik Bay for a noteworthy glacier encounter.

The season begins in April with tours to see the gray whale migration, mostly within Resurrection Bay. That's done by mid-May, when the regular schedule of tours begins, which lasts into September. Fares with each operator differ little, although you can sometimes get early season or Web specials; instead shop for the destination, length of trip, food service, interpretation, and size or intimacy of the boat. Consider the seating arrangement. How many passengers will be on board? Is lunch provided, and what does it consist of? Another important point of comparison is whether you have a ranger doing the commentary, or the captain—some of these captains don't know when to shut up, and they can give inaccurate information.

Try to schedule loosely so that if the weather is bad on the day you choose for your boat trip you can wait and go the next day. If the weather's bad, you'll be uncomfortable and the animals and birds won't be as evident,

Resurrection Bay.

Trying Not to Rock the Boat

A critical factor in choosing your boat tour is your susceptibility to **seasickness**. To reach the heart of the park, vessels must venture into the unprotected waters of the North Pacific. Large, rolling waves are inevitable on the passage from Resurrection Bay to the fjords themselves, although once you're in the fjords the water is calm. On a rough day, most boats will turn back for the comfort of the passengers and change the full-day trip into a Resurrection Bay cruise, refunding the difference in fare. Of course, they'd rather not do that, and the decision often isn't made until the vessel is out there and some people are sick. This has happened to us more than once. On one trip, about 80% of the passengers were already vomiting when the boat turned around. (Even for those who don't lose it, being around that much puke isn't fun.) If you get seasick easily, my advice is to stick to the Resurrection Bay cruise, or take a boat tour in protected Prince William Sound, where the water is always smooth, from Whittier or Valdez (see sections 4 or 11 in this chapter). Detailed advice for seasickness is on p. ###.

or the boat may not go out of Resurrection Bay. If you pay up front to hold a reservation on a boat—probably a good idea in the busy season—find out the company's refund and rescheduling policy.

Most operators offer packages with the Alaska Railroad and the SeaLife Center, or even with a local hotel, which may save money, but make sure you have enough time to do everything you want to do in Seward. All have offices at the Small Boat Harbor in Seward. Here are some of the best.

Kenai Fjords Tours This is the dominant tour operator, with the most daily sailings and choices of destination. The main part of the operation uses 90- to 150-passenger vessels, many of which have forward-facing seats, like an airplane's. They're professionally staffed. The whole operation runs remarkably smoothly, and we found the crew extremely attentive. When the ships are crowded, however, the experience becomes more impersonal. On board, the captain primarily narrates, with other employees sometimes helping. The same company also owns **Mariah Tours,** which operates more intimate 16-passenger vessels. Their trips are more spontaneous and go all the way to Northwestern Fjord every day, weather permitting; the downside is that the smaller boats move more in the waves.

Most of the large Kenai Fjords vessels call on a day lodge the company owns on Fox Island, in Resurrection Bay, for lunch and park service ranger talks. The lodge sits on a long cobble beach near Sunny Cove, where painter Rockwell Kent lived in seclusion with his son in 1918 and 1919 and produced the art that made him famous. It is an inspiring spot. The lodge itself stands on a narrow strip of land between the beach and a pond, which visitors overlook from large wooden decks. Lunch is grilled Alaska salmon and prime rib with an option of adding king crab. Some passengers spend the night at the company's Kenai Fjords Wilderness Lodge on all-inclusive packages, and half-day sea-kayaking paddles from the island are offered for day-trippers or overnight guests: $89 to $99 per person as an add-on for overnighters; or $149 to $169, including a Resurrection Bay tour-boat ride, for day-trippers.

At the Seward Small Boat Harbor. **☎800/478-8068,** 907/224-8068 in Seward, or 907/276-6249 in Anchorage. www.kenaifjords.com.

Major Marine Tours This company pioneered first-class onboard dining and commentary by park rangers, who go on every trip. Their boats are slower than some of the competitors', so they don't make the long trip to Northwest Glacier; they either go to Holgate Glacier or tour Resurrection Bay around Seward. Instead of bringing sandwiches or stopping for a meal, they serve a buffet of salmon and prime rib on board for $19 per person, $9 for children. The food is surprisingly good. I also like their table-seating arrangement with forward-facing seats. Your seat is assigned, so there's no need to rush aboard or try to stake out your spot.

411 W. 4th Ave., Anchorage. **☎800/764-7300** or 907/274-7300, or 907/224-8030 in Seward. www.majormarine.com.

Renown Tours The owner of this company pioneered tours from Seward, left the business, and now is back with this company and also has bought the local operation of Major Marine, mentioned above. Renown's vessels are speedy, steady catamarans, which go to Holgate Glacier in Aialik Bay. All tours to the park carry a park ranger aboard. Lunch consists of smoked salmon, bagels with cream cheese, and such.

411 W. 4th Ave., Anchorage. **☎888/514-8687,** or 907/224-3806 in Seward. www.renowntours.com.

SEA KAYAKING

The fjords are calm yet rugged, intricate, and full of wildlife and soaring vistas. It's hard to imagine a better place for a sea-kayaking expedition. They also are extremely remote and very rainy, however, so a trip there is a poor choice for your very first outing. **Sunny Cove Sea Kayaking** offers a kayaking day trip to Aialik Bay. They take guests out on a small charter boat for a wildlife tour, then you launch and paddle in front of the glacier while the boat stands by. The price for the day trip is $399; expensive, but it is the best of the best. For a visit with time to get more of a feel for the place, spend a couple of days. Sunny Cove's 3-day, 2-night glacier trip costs $1,199; a 5-day, 4-night journey in Northwestern Fjord is $1,399. Experienced cold-water paddlers can rent kayaks and explore Aialik Bay on their own, using the park service cabins for shelter (see above under "Accommodations & Camping"). Miller's Landing rents kayaks and offers water-taxi drop-offs; see the Seward section on p. 382.

EXIT GLACIER

When I visited Italy years ago, I got to the point where I thought I'd scream if I saw another painting of the Madonna. If your trip to Alaska is long, you may start to feel the same way about glaciers. But, although relatively small, Exit Glacier really is unique, and my family still enjoys visits there even as jaded lifelong Alaskans. (And I've probably seen even more glaciers than Madonnas.)

You can walk close to Exit Glacier, see its brittle texture, and feel the cold, dense spires of looming ice. Cold air breathes down on you like air from an open freezer door. Approaching the glacier, you can see the pattern of vegetation reclaiming the land that the melting ice has uncovered, a process well explained by interpretive signs and a nature trail. A National Park Service nature center adds to the comfort and educational content of a visit, and the building is also interesting technically, as it is powered by a hydrogen fuel cell. You can easily spend a couple of hours on a casual, pleasant visit to the glacier (longer if you do a hike). *A safety note:* Big chunks fall off the glacier ever more frequently as Alaska's climate warms. Stay behind the signs or you stand a good chance of being crushed.

The easiest way to get to the glacier is to drive. The clearly marked 9-mile road splits from the Seward Highway 3⅔ miles north of town. In winter, the road is closed to vehicles. If you don't have a car, a shuttle may be available; check with the park information center (p. 391) to see who is currently offering service. Entrance to the park is currently free.

Following the road along the broad bed of the wandering Resurrection River, you'll see in reverse order the succession of vegetation, from mature Sitka spruce and cottonwood trees down to smaller alders and shrubs. It takes time for nature to replace the soil on sterile ground left behind by a receding glacier. As you get closer, watch for signs with dates starting a couple of centuries in the past; they mark the retreat of the glacier through time.

The Exit Glacier Nature Center is open Memorial Day weekend through Labor Day daily 9am to 8pm, sporadically in May, and September daily 9am to 5pm. Ranger-led nature walks start daily at 10am, 2pm, and 4pm on the short trail to the glacier. It's easy to find your way to the glacier and back on a variety of short trails.

One of the glacier's striking features is a high berm of gravel that fits around its leading edge like a necklace. This is a moraine, the glacier's refuse pile. The glacier gouges out the mountains with its immense, moving weight as new ice flows

Exit Glacier.

down from the ice field above and melts here. It carries along the rock and gravel torn from the mountain like a conveyor belt. This moraine is where the conveyor belt ends and the melting ice leaves the debris behind in a big pile. Probably without-out knowing it, you've seen hundreds of moraines all over North America, where the glaciers of the last ice age piled debris into hills, but this is the most obvious moraine I've ever seen, and it helps you understand how they work.

An all-day hike, 8 miles round-trip, climbs along the right side of the glacier to the Harding Ice Field—the glacier gets its name for being an exit from that massive sheet. It's a challenging walk with a 3,000-foot elevation gain, but it's the easiest access I'm aware of to visit an ice field on foot. The upper trail isn't free of snow until late June or early July. The ice field itself is cold and dangerous, and there's an emergency shelter maintained by the park service. Don't trek out on the ice unless you have glacier-climbing experience. The park service leads hikes up the trail Saturdays in July and August, leaving at 9am from the nature center.

The Resurrection River Trail, in Chugach National Forest, begins from the road just short of the last bridge into the Exit Glacier area. It's a pleasant day hike, with lots of wildflowers in the fall, or the start of a long hike deep into the mountains.

COOPER LANDING: ROAD MEETS RIVER

The little roadside community of Cooper Landing, in a wooded mountain valley along Kenai Lake and the Kenai River, begins about 8 miles west of Tern Lake, where the Sterling Highway splits from the Seward Highway, and continues sporadically along the highway for about 7 miles. (The Sterling runs generally west until Soldotna, where it heads south again.) The frothing upper **Kenai River** is the community's lifeline, each summer bringing the salmon that in turn draw visitors, who fill hotels, restaurants, and the date books of fishing guides. The **Russian River** meets the Kenai at the western edge of the community, where a mad fishing frenzy for the July red salmon season occurs. A ferry takes anglers across the river from the highway. For information on how to fish the Kenai, see "Fishing" in "Kenai/Soldotna & Sterling: Giant Salmon," later in this chapter on Kenai/Soldotna; there's additional information in chapter 3.

If you're not an angler, there's not much here—a couple of operators do rafting trips and some trails start here. Cooper Landing is the starting or ending point for backpacking trips in the Chugach National Forest, described under "Chugach National Forest: Do-It-Yourself Wilderness." Look there also for descriptions of several campgrounds for tents or RVs (there are also RV hookups at the Kenai Princess Lodge, reviewed below).

Cooper Landing has a post office, service stations, and small stores selling fishing gear and essentials, but it's not a real center of commerce. For banking or anything else not directly related to catching a salmon, you'll have to drive to Sterling, 30 miles away to the west, or Soldotna, 14 miles beyond that.

Fishing Lodges

The three lodges below can take care of everything, so you can set up your fishing and other activities with a single phone call. If what you need is a simple room or cabin that is clean, comfortable, and inexpensive, try **The Hutch Bed and**

Fishermen clean their bounty at Kenai River.

Breakfast, Mile 48.5, Sterling Highway (☎907/595-1270; wwwarctic.net/~hutch). In nice weather, you can sit at the fire pit and watch the bunny rabbits hop by. The B&B has Wi-Fi and a covered picnic pavilion with a charcoal grill.

Kenai Princess Lodge ★★ This is one of the best in the region. Each room in the red-roofed buildings feels like a remote cabin, with balconies overlooking the wooded valley, woodstoves stocked with firewood, and many unique details; yet they're luxurious hotel rooms at a resort with a fine restaurant. There are three classes of rooms with a $25 to $35 price difference between each. The middle, premium class, is halfway up the hill, with rooms separated by a divider into two parts, like a real cabin. At the top level, the deluxe rooms, highest on the hill, have more of a clean, elegant feel. Bathrooms are surprisingly small in all the rooms. The lodge books guided fishing, horseback riding, tours, and other activities, and there are hiking trails nearby. An attractive 35-space RV park with full hookups is on-site, with access to the facilities.

The Eagle's Crest restaurant has a varied and sophisticated menu, with good use of Alaskan seafood, professional service, and a light dining room that follows the hotel's generally rustic theme. Dinner main courses are $20 to $30; the lunch menu has the expected items, plus choices such as calamari and some unusual salads, generally under $10. Even if you have no reason to stay in Cooper Landing, consider planning your drive to include a meal here that will be several steps up from highway fare and enjoy the relaxing ambience of the lodge.

Up Bean Creek Rd. to Frontier Cir., above Cooper Landing (P.O. Box 676, Cooper Landing, AK 99572). ☎800/426-0500 or 907/595-1425. Fax 907/595-1424. www.princesslodges.com. 86 units. High season $249-$309 double; low season $179-$209 double. RV sites $35. AE, DC, DISC, MC, V. Closed mid-Sept to mid-May. **Amenities:** Restaurant; bar; exercise room; Jacuzzi. In room: TV.

Kenai River Sportfishing Lodge/Kenai Riverside Lodge ★★ The compound lies between the highway and the river, but down among the trees it feels like a remote lodge. I'd call the cabins faux rustic—I've never seen real Bush cabins with smooth walls, wainscoting, bright rag rugs, and private bathrooms, but these trim places still feel like the outdoorsy real thing, with no TVs or phones. The comfortable but not-too-grand central lodge building fits in perfectly, too. In the evening, guests can sit by a fire on a deck at riverside or cook in a woodsy sauna. The young, well-trained staff keeps everything fun and intimate. But the location is the fundamental advantage: Kenai River fishing frontage. White-water rafting rides and fishing floats leave right from the riverfront. The lodge also possesses a scarce resource in its coveted guide permits for the hot fishing river section that runs through the Kenai National Wildlife Refuge.

Everything is covered by one price: transportation from Anchorage, meals in the central lodge building, guided salmon fishing or fly-fishing for rainbow trout in drift or power boats, and, on longer visits, halibut fishing (done from boats in salt water). You pay for your own booze, fishing license, and tips. The company customizes fishing trips of 2 to 7 days, including non-fishing activities such as river rafting, Kenai Fjords sightseeing, or Alaska Railroad tours. Or come as part of a "safari" package that includes outdoor activities and sites, such as the Alaska Wildland Adventures safari that's described in chapter 3 on p. 85.

Alaska Wildland Adventures, Mile 50.1 Sterling Hwy. (P.O. Box 389, Girdwood, AK 99587). **☎800/478-4100** or 907/783-2928. www.alaskasportfish.com. 16 cabins. 3-day, 4-night inclusive package $2,095. MC, V. **Amenities:** Restaurant (family style); sauna; river equipment included.

A Wilderness Lodge

Kenai Backcountry Lodge ★★ On the far side of Skilak Lake from the Sterling Highway, reached by boat, this lodge is not about fishing—it's about being in a beautiful place, hiking to the tree line, lake kayaking, and enjoying quiet in an environmentally sustainable place. The tent cabins and log cabins are hidden in the woods on the lakeshore, connected by gravel paths, and the feeling is authentically wild and remote, but there are flush toilets and hot showers in the shower house, and the food offered in the central lodge is terrific. The owners, Alaska Wildland Adventures, who also have the lodge listed directly above, have established a superb reputation for reliable service and a positive ethic of doing things right. You can stay as part of one of their package trips, or come for the lodge alone. Log cabins are $50 more than tent cabins; a cabin with its own bathroom is $100 more.

Alaska Wildland Adventures, Skilak Lake (P.O. Box 389, Girdwood, AK 99587). **☎800/478-4100** or 907/783-2928. Fax 907/783-2130. www.alaskawildland.com. 10 cabins. $975 adult, $795 child, 2-night stay, double occupancy. All meals and guiding included in price. DISC, MC, V. Closed Sept–May. **Amenities:** Restaurant (family style); boating and other outdoor equipment. *In room:* No phone.

Floating the Kenai River

The Kenai is more famous for fishing than rafting, but the area is beautiful and the Kenai Canyon, below Cooper Landing and above Skilak Lake, has frothy water between vertical canyon walls. **Alaska Wildland Adventures,** at the Kenai Riverside Lodge (**☎800/478-4100** or 907/783-2928), is the most established operator and has a great reputation. They offer a 7-hour float through the canyon for $140 adults, $99 children, and a placid 2-hour float down the upper Kenai for $54 adults, $34 children. Their guided fishing is $275 for a full day, including lunch and gear. **Alaska Rivers Co.,** Mile 50, Cooper Landing (**☎907/595-1226;** www.alaskariverscompany.com), has more than 25 years of experience. They offer scenic rafting three times daily ($49, children half price) and daily canyon floats ($135), as well as guided fishing ($105 half day, $195 all day). They rent cabins, too.

KENAI/SOLDOTNA & STERLING: GIANT SALMON

These quintessential western U.S. towns, dominated by shopping malls and fast-food franchises facing broad highways, have a single claim to fame, but it's a pretty good claim: The largest sport-caught king salmon in the world, almost 100 pounds, came from the Kenai River. The Kenai's kings run so large there's a different trophy class for the river—everywhere else in the state, the Alaska Department of Fish and Game will certify a 50-pounder as a trophy, but on the Kenai it has to be at least 75 pounds. That's because kings in the 60-pound class—with enough wild muscle to fight ferociously for hours—are just too common here. Anglers prepared to pay for a charter will be in their element on the river when the fish are running hot. Catching a big king is not easy or quick, however, and success rates vary greatly year-to-year and week-to-week.

Those not interested in fishing will find, at most, a day's sightseeing in these towns. Instead, use the towns as a base for the outdoors. Kenai has a strangely beautiful ocean beach and the Kenai River mouth, with exceptional bird-watching during migrations. Beyond the towns, you'll find a wealth of outdoor activities, primarily in the lake-dotted **Kenai National Wildlife Refuge,** which has its headquarters in Soldotna. The refuge is covered in the next section.

Kenai came into being with the arrival of the Russians at the mouth of the Kenai River more than 200 years ago, but it came into its own only with the discovery of oil on the peninsula in 1957. Today its economy relies on oil, commercial fishing, and, to a smaller extent, tourism. Soldotna, a smaller, newer, and less attractive town, is the borough seat and the primary destination for anglers. Sterling is just a wide place in the road—incredibly wide, as a matter of fact (no one is quite able to explain why such a small town needs such a big road).

Essentials

GETTING THERE From Anchorage, the drive on the Seward and Sterling highways to Soldotna is 147 miles. Allow 3 hours, without stops: In summer, traffic will slow you down; in winter, speeds are limited by ice and the fear of hitting moose. Kenai is 11 miles from Soldotna on the Kenai Spur Highway, the first major right as you enter Soldotna from the north on the Sterling Highway.

The Stage Line (☎907/235-2252; www.thestageline.net) connects Anchorage, Homer, Seward, and points between with van service. In summer they run to Homer daily from Anchorage and Seward, less frequently in winter. The fare from Anchorage to Soldotna is $66 one-way, $120 round-trip. The pick-up point in Soldotna is the Chamber of Commerce Visitors Center. The Anchorage ticket office is at 412 W. 53rd Ave. (☎907/868-3914).

Kenai receives very frequent flights from Anchorage from **Era Aviation** (☎800/866-8394; www.flyera.com).

GETTING AROUND The area is so spread out that walking most places really isn't practical, and there's no public transportation. Everyone drives. Several major car-rental companies operate at the Kenai airport: **Hertz, Avis, Budget,** and **Payless.** If you plan only to fish, however, you may not need a car, instead getting rides from your guide, your host, or a taxicab. Ask about transportation options when you reserve your rooms. There are several cab companies; try **Alaska Cab** (☎907/283-6000 in Kenai or **907/262-1555** in Soldotna).

VISITOR INFORMATION The **Soldotna Visitor Information Center,** 44790 Sterling Hwy., Soldotna, AK 99669 (☎907/262-9814 or 907/262-1337; www.visitsoldotna.com), is located on the south side of town; drive through the commercial strip and turn right after the Kenai River Bridge. It's open daily in summer from 9am to 7pm; in winter, Monday through Friday from 9am to 5pm. Besides the usual brochures and free maps, they offer help with lodgings, camping, charters, and other services. Anglers should stop in to see the world-record 97-pound King salmon and a 20-pound rainbow trout. Stroll down behind the center to the riverwalk to get close to the water and a handy site for streamside fishing.

In Kenai, the **Kenai Visitors and Cultural Center,** 11471 Kenai Spur Hwy., Kenai, AK 99611 (☎907/283-1991; www.visitkenai.com), is an attraction in itself. The building contains a set of museum galleries. A history and culture exhibit was dismantled for construction in 2009 and will change, but surely will include some old favorites, including first edition journals of Captain James Cook, who explored Cook Inlet in 1778, and the "King of Snags," an immense conglomeration of lost fishing lures, rods, and sticks pulled from the bottom of the river. Large temporary art exhibitions are mounted, too (see below). To get there, follow the Spur Highway past Main Street and look for the large, landscaped building on your left. In summer, admission to the museum portion is $5, free for students through high school; off-season, admission is free. They are open in summer Monday through Friday from 9am to 7pm, Saturday and Sunday from 10am to 6pm; and off-season Monday through Friday from 9am to 5pm and Saturday 11am to 4pm.

SPECIAL EVENTS Kenai Visitors and Cultural Center (see above) hosts invitational art shows each summer. Works usually cross media and include contemporary art and traditional Alaska Native work. Admission is $5 adults, free for minors.

[Fast FACTS] KENAI & SOLDOTNA

Banks You will find them on the Kenai Spur Highway in the middle of town, and in Soldotna, on the Sterling Highway commercial strip. In addition, ATMs are in grocery stores all over the area.

Hospital **Central Peninsula General** is in Soldotna at 250 Hospital Place (☎907/262-4404); from the Sterling Highway, take Binkley Street to Marydale Avenue.

Internet Access Connect to the Web for free at the **Kenai Community Library,** 163 Main St. Loop (☎907/283-4378), or at the **Soldotna Public Library,** 235 Binkley St. (☎907/262-4227).

Police For nonemergencies in Kenai, call the Kenai Police Department (☎907/283-7879); in Soldotna, call the Soldotna Police Department (☎907/262-4455); outside city limits, call the Alaska State Troopers (☎907/262-4453).

Taxes There's a 6% **sales tax** in Kenai and Soldotna, and 2% outside city limits.

In Soldotna, the **Tustumena 200 Sled Dog Race** (☎907/262-3270), an Iditarod qualifier, is held in late January, and helps kick off the mushing season. **Progress Days** (☎907/262-9814), in late July, offers a parade, rodeo, car shows, and other festival events commemorating the completion of a gas pipeline in 1960.

In Ninilchik, the **Kenai Peninsula State Fair** (☎907/567-3670), south at mile 136 on the Sterling Highway, is the third weekend in August (Aug 20–22, 2010), with rodeo, music, crafts, games, agricultural and craft exhibits, and other country attractions, plus a few kids' rides. One-day admission is $8 adults, $6 ages 6 to 12 and seniors.

Fishing

Fishing the Kenai River is the whole point of coming to the area for most visitors. Check at the Soldotna Visitor Information Center (above) for information and regulation booklets, which you must read and understand before fishing. Regulations are also available at sporting goods stores, or contact the **Alaska Department of Fish and Game,** 43961 Kalifornsky Beach Rd., Ste. B, Soldotna, AK 99669 (☎907/262-9368 or 907/262-2737, for a recorded fishing report; www.alaska.gov/adfg). Serious anglers shouldn't miss that website, which includes daily sonar counts of salmon in the river and information on biology and fishing techniques; navigate through "Sport Fish," and click on the Southcentral region on the map. Licenses are for sale on the site and in virtually any sporting goods store. Also, read "A Salmon Primer" and "Fishing" in chapter 3. There are more than two dozen public access points over the 80 miles of the Kenai River. A **guide brochure** with a map is available from the state **Division of Parks,** P.O. Box 1247, Soldotna, AK 99669-1247 (☎907/262-5581; www.alaskastateparks. org); you also can pick up a copy at one of the visitor centers.

KINGS King salmon, the monsters of the river, come in two runs. The early run comes from mid-May to the end of June, peaking in mid-June. On average less plentiful and smaller, in the 20- to 40-pound range, the run also produced the world's record (97 lb., 4 oz.). The second run comes during the month of July and includes more of the massive fish. Most people fish kings from a boat, fishing certain holes. Boats hold stationary or back slowly down the river; or fishermen drift down river. Your chances from the bank are low; on average, with or without a boat, it takes 29 hours of fishing time to land a king (you'll likely get at least a dozen strikes for every fish that makes it into the boat). With a guide, the average time to land a fish is cut in half, but that still means that if you fish for only 1 day, chances are good that you'll get skunked. A boat of three anglers on a half-day guided charter has roughly a 50% chance of landing a king among them.

A guided charter averages $150 to $170 for a 6½-hour day trip, $250 to $265 full day. There are dozens of guides. Contact the visitor center in Kenai or Soldotna (above) to get in touch with a guide; also, many hotels and lodges have their own. It's possible to rent a boat, but this is advisable only if you are experienced in boats and stay out of the hazardous, faster flowing parts of the river. The **Sports Den,** 44176 Sterling Hwy. in Soldotna (☎907/262-7491; www.alaskasportsden.com), is one charter operator, with river and ocean trips for salmon or halibut and fly-in fishing and hunting, and they also offer lodging packages with large units. I've found them friendly and helpful over the years.

REDS The area really goes crazy when the red (or sockeye) salmon join the kings in the river, from mid-July to early August. You can fish reds from the bank or from a boat. Reds are plankton eaters; some say they won't strike a lure, some say they do. In some popular fishing areas regulations allow only the use of flies; check the regulations or contact Fish and Game for details. Most people around here cast the flies with spinning gear, weighting the line 18 inches from the fly so it bounces along the bottom. Cast upstream from shore and allow the fly to drift down, keeping near the bank. While waiting for a strike, debate whether the fish really attack the flies, or if they get caught when they instinctively move their mouths in an eating motion, which they do in quick-moving water.

SILVERS Silvers first arrive in late July, peaking during August, but continue to be in the river through September and even in October. They're easiest to catch anchored in a boat, but you can also do well from shore. Lures work well, as does bait of salmon eggs.

OTHER SPECIES Trophy-size rainbow trout and Dolly Varden char also come out of the river. Anglers using light tackle may also enjoy catching pink salmon, which are plentiful in the Kenai during even-numbered years, arriving in late July and lasting until mid-September. Use spinning gear and lures. Most Alaskans turn up their noses at this easy-to-catch 4-pound fish; just smile and keep hauling them in. Fresh, bright pinks taste great over a campfire.

Exploring the Towns

Kenai's historic sites, beach walking, and bird-watching can occupy you for part of a day. Start at the visitor and cultural center mentioned above and get a copy of the *Old Town Kenai Walking Map;* follow the numbered markers. Not many of the simple, weathered buildings remain from Kenai's life before oil, but those that do are interesting and lie only a few blocks down Main Street from the center, along the Cook Inlet and Kenai River bluff.

The **Holy Assumption of the Virgin Mary Russian Orthodox Church** is the area's most significant building. The parish was founded in 1845, and the present church was built in 1895. It's a quaint, onion-domed church, brightly kept but with old icons. A donation is requested. Several nearby buildings are interesting for their interlocking log construction and weathered exteriors. A charming cafe called Veronica's occupies one of these strange and fascinating little structures (p. 405).

The bluff nearby overlooks the broad, sandy, ocean beach. A dirt path runs down from Alaska Avenue between the apartment building and the houses that contain professional offices (please don't park near here, as an excess of tourists' cars has caused a problem for the apartment building). To drive down, return to the Kenai Spur Highway, turn to the northwest (left), then turn left on South Spruce Street. There's a big parking lot with a $10 fee, which seems strange on the deserted beach unless you arrive during dipnetting season, the last few weeks in July (the only time the fee is actually charged). If you come then, you'll see a fish gold rush. Alaska residents are permitted to fish from this beach by

Holy Assumption of the Virgin Mary Russian Orthodox Church.

scooping up passing red salmon with long-handled dipnets. It's a time for filling freezers and smokers for the winter. That's also when you can see white beluga whales chasing salmon upriver, sometimes in great numbers. If you just want to watch, the viewpoint from the top of the bluff at Erik Hansen Scout Park, at Cook and Mission avenues, is a prime spot. However, the beach also is a lovely place for a walk. It's easy to imagine the Russians' first arrival. On a calm day, the beach sand, the mud flats, and the Inlet's gray, glacial water seem to meld together into one vast, shimmering plain. The water is far too cold and the currents too swift for swimming.

The mouth of the river and the wetlands of its delta make for fine **bird-watching,** especially during spring and fall migrations. One of the best places to get to the tidal Kenai River Flats is along Bridge Access Road, which branches from the Spur Highway, where one sometimes also sees caribou and moose. The state of Alaska has developed viewing areas at each end of the bridge.

Where to Stay

Rates at many hotels are on seasonal schedules with three, four, or even more levels linked to the salmon runs. I've listed the highest and lowest. One unique lodging choice, worth an exploratory visit even if you don't stay there, is the **Historic Kenai Landing** (☏ 907/335-2500; www.kenailanding.com), where a complex of cannery buildings dating from 1912 has been remodeled into simple rooms, a restaurant, and shops. The inexpensive but rather spartan lodgings will appeal most to single-minded fishermen, but the restaurant is well equipped and has live music, and the buildings on a long river dock are interesting and atmospheric. This scenic spot is out of the way, on the opposite side of the river mouth from Kenai: After crossing the bridge, turn right on Kalifornsky Beach Road and right again on Cannery Road.

Aspen Hotel Soldotna ★★ The area's best hotel rooms are here, in a rectangular building just back from the highway strip in Soldotna, near an Arby's but also a stone's throw from fishing on the river bank. The building isn't old, and the management constantly renews it, putting in new carpet, paint, and fabrics in 2009, all in earth tones. The rooms already had high ceilings and a solid feeling of quality, and the improvements gave them a clean but soothing feel. High-end amenities and professional service contribute to an up-to-date corporate style unique in muscular Soldotna. Family suites have bunk beds, privacy between parents and kids, and PlayStation video games. Suites with cooking facilities are available, too, and other handy configurations. The pool was redone in 2009.

326 Binkley Cir., Soldotna, AK 99669. **(888/308-7848** or 907/260-7736. Fax 907/260-7786. www.aspenhotelsak.com. 63 units. High season $169–$179 double, $199 suite; low season $99 double, $119 suite. $10 each additional person age 18 and older. Rates include continental breakfast. AE, DC, DISC, MC, V. **Amenities:** Exercise room, pool, whirlpool. *In room:* TV/DVD, fridge, hair dryer, microwave, Wi-Fi.

Great Alaska Adventure Lodge ★★ For anglers, it's the location that counts, and for that this lodge is hard to top, with a third of a mile of river frontage where the Moose and Kenai rivers converge, a hot fishing spot since time immemorial, as an ancient Native site attests. In the evening, the lodge keeps a guide and campfire on the beach so you can keep casting in the midnight sun. Lodge rooms overlooking the river are spacious and have gas fireplaces and private bathrooms. Unfortunately, the site suffers from vehicle noise from the adjacent Sterling Highway. The lodge offers a wide variety of guided fishing activities, including fly fishing and halibut outings. For guests interested in seeing wildlife, the lodge offers trips to its own backcountry tent camps, including one across Cook Inlet with good brown-bear viewing. Check the lodge's website for information on the many tours and wilderness safaris that they offer as well as rates, which are too extensive to itemize here.

Moose River, 33881 Sterling Hwy., Sterling, AK 99672 (in winter, P.O. Box 2670, Poulsbo, WA 98370). **(800/544-2261** or 907/262-4515. Fax 907/262-8797 in summer, 360/697-7850 in winter. www.greatalaska.com. 25 units. Rates from $295–$550 for a day trip without lodging; packages of 2 to 10 days $1,195–$5,495. Rates include all meals, guide service, pickup in Anchorage. AE, MC, V. Closed Oct to mid-May.

Harborside Cottages Bed and Breakfast ★ On a grassy compound at the top of the bluff over the mouth of the Kenai River in Old Town, these little white cottages make the most of a perfect site. The view and quiet can keep you in a peaceful reverie all day; it's an extraordinarily lovely and calming spot. Inside, the cottages are clean and trim, each with its own light country decoration. They have either king-size beds or pairs of twin beds. There are no tubs, just shower stalls. Outside is a patio with a picnic table and gas barbecue.

13 Riverview Dr. (P.O. Box 942), Kenai, AK 99611. **(888/283-6162** or 907/283-6162. www. harborsidecottages.com. 5 cottages. High season $185 double; low season $150 double. AE, DISC, MC, V. Closed winter. *In room:* TV, fridge, microwave, Wi-Fi.

Log Cabin Inn ★ 🏷 A large family presides at this huge log building on the south side of the Kenai River, across from Kenai, offering comfortable rooms with pleasant views and private bathrooms for bargain rates. The central great room is reminiscent of a big wilderness lodge, with a towering ceiling and lots of rough-hewn wood in every direction. Hosts Teresa and Keith Moyer had to install climbing holds on the central pillar to make it a little safer when one of their five children kept scrambling aloft. The accommodations vary, including large, charming rooms under the eves, cute but smaller units in a half basement, and outdoorsy cabins with refrigerators and microwaves. Teresa serves a full breakfast at the time of individual guests' choosing.

49860 Eider Dr., Kenai, AK 99611. ☎**907/283-3653.** http://alaskalogcabininn.com. 7 units, plus 3 cabins. High season $110–$120 double, $125 cabin for 2; low season $79 double. Rates include full breakfast. AE, MC, V. **Amenities:** Hot tub. *In room:* Wi-Fi.

CAMPING

Soldotna's appealing **Centennial Park Campground** extends along a long section of the Kenai River bluff among thick spruce and birch trees with ramps down to fishing spots on the river, next door to the visitor center and close to stores. Turn right on Kalifornsky Beach Road just after the bridge on the Sterling Highway. Camping fees are $16 a night, and day use is $6.30, payable at a manned entrance booth (plus tax). The park is open May 1 to October 1. There's a dump station, usable for an $11 fee. **Swiftwater Park** is a similar city-operated riverside campground near the Fred Meyer grocery store and Taco Bell as you enter town from the north. For a quieter, oceanfront public campground, see Captain Cook State Recreational Area, p. 409.

RV parks are scattered about. The one with the best location is **Beluga Lookout Lodge and RV Park,** 929 Mission Ave. (☎**907/283-5999;** www.belugalookout.com). It's in Kenai's Old Town, at bluff's edge over Cook Inlet at the mouth of the Kenai River. Full hookups are $35 to $60 a night. They offer bike rentals and charters for salmon and halibut fishing, bear or beluga watching.

Where to Dine

Franchise fast-food and burger-steak-seafood places dominate in Kenai and Soldotna. Among the most popular restaurants without a name brand is **Sal's Klondike Diner,** 44619 Sterling Hwy. (☎**907/262-2220**), a classic Western highway diner, with big portions, fast service, cheap prices, and nothing fancy that doesn't have to be. It's open 24 hours a day all year long under a movie-style false front.

At the other end of the cultural spectrum, **Veronica's Old Town Cafe,** 602 Pederson Way (☎**907/283-2725**), is in a weathered old Russian building of interlocking logs in Kenai's historic area, with a tiny dining room whose low ceiling, bare wood, and cockeyed angles could not be contrived. The coffeehouse cuisine includes sandwiches, wraps, soup, and a specialty, quiche on a polenta crust. It's open in summer Monday through Thursday 8am to 8pm, Friday and Saturday until 9, with live music; in winter the Monday through Thursday hours are 10am to 3pm, while the weekends remain the same.

Charlotte's Bakery, Café, Espresso ★ 🍴 CAFE Some of the best sandwiches I've ever tasted came from this little strip mall restaurant in Kenai. They're anchored by rich-textured bread and enlivened by unique combinations—for example, a sub with olive tapenade, or a turkey sandwich with cranberry cream cheese. The salads, soup, and chili are memorable, too, and the desserts amazing—10 selections, all baked in-house, were on the tray on a typical day when I last visited. Besides the food, the dining experience is a delight, with service by women who seem to know all their customers and work efficiently in a bright, clean room with cheerful, feminine decor.

115 S. Willow, Kenai. ☎**907/283-2777.** All items $5–$12. MC, V. High season Mon–Fri 7am–4pm, Sat 8am–3pm; low season Mon–Fri 7am–3pm, Sat 8am–3pm.

Mykel's ★★★ SEAFOOD This is a traditional fine-dining restaurant for a date or an especially relaxing evening, located in the Soldotna Inn, near the intersection of the Sterling and Kenai Spur highways. The cuisine is exceptional and the service professional and more than friendly. Nothing else in the area even plays in the same league, and Mykel's is only a half step below Alaska's best. The dinner menu contains many familiar beef and chicken dishes done just right. When they "borrowed" the pepper steak created by Jens Hansen at his restaurant in Anchorage, they admitted it on the menu—classy. In addition, the restaurant offers various ways of having local seafood in creative ways. Servings are large, even for the exceptional desserts, so don't order extra courses. The full bar serves 18 wines by the glass and six local microbrews. At lunchtime there are lots of salads to choose from besides the expected sandwiches.

35041 Kenai Spur Hwy., Soldotna. **☎907/262-4305.** www.mykels.com. Reservations recommended. Lunch $8-$18; dinner $15-$35. V. High season daily 11am-10pm; low season Tues-Thurs and Sun 11am-9pm, Fri-Sat 11am-10pm, closed Mon.

Paradisos ★ GREEK The restaurant is a fine example of an old-fashioned type that was once common: a place that's fancy enough to take Grandma for Sunday dinner, but also has a lengthy menu with choices for each member of the family and a relaxed atmosphere where children fit in. I suppose chains have taken over in this category elsewhere—Olive Garden, Applebee's, and such. In business here since 1971, Paradisos has the formula right: big portions of familiar food, reasonable prices, and speedy, friendly service. The owner's specialty is Greek cuisine, but they also turn out Italian and Mexican food, pizza, steaks, crab, and the like.

Main St. and Kenai Spur Hwy. in Kenai. **☎907/283-2222.** Lunch $8-$18; dinner $8-$38. AE, DC, DISC, MC, V. Summer daily 11am-11pm; winter 11am-10pm.

Suzie's Cafe DINER If you are traveling the Sterling Highway and want a pleasant and filling lunch or dinner, you'll do no better than this local favorite on the east side of the road in the town of Sterling itself. Cheerful, efficient servers bring big plates of comfort food and hearty sandwiches. The dining room, heavily decorated in burly country style, has only eight tables and a small lunch counter, and no room for waiting. They offer meals to go, too.

Mile 87.2, Sterling Hwy., Sterling. **☎907/260-5751.** All items $7-$25. MC, V. Summer daily 11:30am-9pm. Closed mid-Sept to May.

KENAI NATIONAL WILDLIFE REFUGE

Floating through the Kenai National Wildlife Refuge in a canoe narrows the world into a circle of green water, spruce, and birch. You can paddle and hike for days without encountering more than a few other people, your only expense the cost of your canoe and the vehicle that carried you to the trail head. Out there with my older son, I once noticed that, other than his voice, the only sounds I had heard in 2 days were the gurgling of the water and the wind shushing in the birch leaves. You rely on yourself, but your greatest tests are not overly taxing. Trail a line behind the canoe, and, when you catch a rainbow trout, land it and make a fire to cook it. Launch your body into the clear, frigid water to rinse off the

Newborn calves in the Kenai National Wildlife Refuge.

sweat on a warm day. Float slowly, eagles circle the treetops and puffy drift like ships past your little world.

Most of the western half of the Kenai Peninsula lies within the 2 million acres of the refuge—it's almost as large as Yellowstone National Park—and much of that land is impossibly remote and truly dedicated to the wildlife. The Kenai River flows through part of the refuge, but the refuge is just a name to the anglers who pursue its salmon. (Information about fishing and rafting the river is above, in the Kenai/Soldotna and Cooper Landing sections.) Canoeists will be more interested in the lowlands on the west side, west of the Sterling Highway and north of Kenai and Soldotna. The lakes there are as numerous as the speckles on a trout's back, or at least that's how they appear from the air. From the ground, the region is a maze of lakes connected by trails—more than 70 lakes you can reach on canoe routes stretching more than 150 miles. It's the easiest way to real Alaska wilderness I know.

Essentials

GETTING THERE The refuge surrounds much of the land from Cooper Landing at the north to Homer at the south and Cook Inlet to the west. The Sterling Highway and roads that branch from it are the main ways to the lakes, trails, and rivers, and there is no practical way there without a vehicle.

VISITOR INFORMATION Stop in at the **Kenai National Wildlife Refuge Visitor Center,** Ski Hill Road (P.O. Box 2139), Soldotna, AK 99669 (☎ 907/ 262-7021; http://kenai.fws.gov), for guidance before plunging into the wilderness. The U.S. Fish and Wildlife Service, which manages the refuge, exhibits natural history displays here, shows a film each hour in the afternoon in the summer, and maintains a 3-mile nature trail. The staff offers advice and sells books and maps that you'll definitely need for a successful backcountry trip. To find the center, turn left just south of the Kenai River Bridge, taking a right turn in front of the building-supply store uphill on the unpaved road. It's open June through August Monday through Friday from 8am to 5pm, Saturday and Sunday from 9am to 5pm; October through May, Monday through Friday from 8am to 4:30pm, Saturday from 10am to 5pm. The website also contains detailed trip-planning information for the canoe routes.

Getting Outside
CANOEING

Once known as the Kenai National Moose Range, the refuge's brushy wetlands are paradise for moose, rich in their favorite foods of willow and birch shoots and pond weeds. Moose like to dine while wading. Waterfowl and other birds,

other aquatic animals are common on the lakes. People
atic to explore the lakes, paddling canoes across their sur-
lily pad passages between lakes, and frequently hiking in
akes while carrying the canoe and camping gear.

in canoe routes, both reached from Swanson River and
of the Sterling Highway from the town of Sterling. The
ute is a 60-mile network of 30 connected lakes. It meets
, allowing a loop of several days, and in between adven-
turers can penetrate many lakes deep into the wilderness, visiting remote lakes
they'll have all to themselves. It's also possible to canoe through to the Moose
River and ride its current 17 miles over a long day back to the Sterling Highway.

Getting anywhere requires frequent portages of a quarter-mile or so, and
more ambitious routes have mile-long portages. You can skip all the portag-
ing, however, by floating 2 days down the **Swanson River** to its mouth, at the
Captain Cook State Recreation Area (see below), joining the river at a landing at
mile 17.5 of Swanson River Road. The water is slow and easy all the way.

The most challenging of the routes is the **Swanson River Canoe Route,**
which connects to the river's headwaters through a series of lakes and longer
portages. The route covers 80 miles, including 40 lakes and the river float. Both
routes have many dozens of remote campsites—just lakeside areas of cleared
ground with fire rings—and most of the portages are well marked and maintained
with wooden planking over the wet areas.

You can rent canoes and everything else you need for a wilderness trip on
the refuge canoe routes near the intersection of Swanson River Road and the
Sterling Highway in Sterling, where the Finch family operates **Alaska Canoe
& Campground** (☎907/262-2331; www.alaskacanoetrips.com). Lightweight
canoes rent for $50 for 24 hours. They offer a shuttle service to carry canoeists
from one entrance to another so you don't have to double back on your trip, and
they can give valuable expert advice. And they rent a lot of other outdoor stuff:
kayaks, mountain bikes, rafts, and so on. Call ahead to check on equipment and
to reserve. Their campground is fully equipped, too, a good base where you can
return for showers and laundry, and they rent a couple of large cabins with full
kitchens and TVs, for $150 a night double, plus $10 for each additional person;
the cabins sleep 8.

The Finches' have offered guided trips, but they stopped because they don't
think guides are really needed for anyone who knows how to paddle a canoe and
use common sense in the wilderness. If you do want a guide, they can give you a
referral. If you go on your own, think about buying a copy of the book *The Kenai
Canoe Trails,* by Daniel L. Quick (Northlite Publishing, $19). The book can be
hard to find, but is available used from online stores such as www.amazon.com.
This extraordinary guide contains superdetailed maps and directions, and advice
on how to plan your trip and fish and camp on your way. I haven't provided detailed driving instructions for the canoe routes because you'll need detailed maps
to go at all. **Trails Illustrated** produces a good detailed map of the whole area,
printed on plastic (p. 367). A serviceable free map is distributed by the refuge
visitor center. There's much more to do in the refuge, too, including several up-
land hiking trails. The refuge visitor center provides guidance and maps.

Camping

For car camping in a wild, oceanfront setting, remote from the region's fishing mayhem, try the **Captain Cook State Recreation Area.** The lovely and underused 3,460-acre area faces Cook Inlet 25 miles north of Kenai on the North Kenai Road at the mouth of the Swanson River. There are lots of attractive sites among large birches, trails, beach walking, a canoe landing at the end of the Swanson River Canoe Route, and lake swimming. The State Parks camping fee is $10.

There are many campgrounds within the refuge, too, some of them lovely, quiet spots on the edge of uninhabited lakes, such as the small **Rainbow Lake** and **Dolly Varden Lake campgrounds,** on Swanson River Road near the start of the canoe routes, and the **Watson Lake** and **Kelly-Peterson Lake campgrounds** on the Sterling Highway between Sterling and Cooper Landing. Get a complete listing from the visitor center. Only two campgrounds have fees: **Hidden Lake** and **Upper Skilak Lake.**

HOMER & KACHEMAK BAY: COSMIC HAMLET BY THE SEA

Homer's leading mystic, the late Brother Asaiah Bates, always maintained that a confluence of metaphysical forces causes a focus of powerful creative energy on this little seaside town. It's hard to argue. Homer is full of creative people: artists, eccentrics, and those who simply contribute to a quirky community in a beautiful place. Indeed, Brother Asaiah may have been the quintessential Homeroid, although perhaps an extreme example, with his gray ponytail, extraordinary openness and generosity, and flowery rhetoric about "the cosmic wheel of life." Homer is full of outspoken, unusual, and even odd individualists —people who make living in the town almost an act of belief. I can say this because I'm a former Homeroid myself.

The geography of Homer—physical as well as metaphysical—has gathered certain people here the way currents gather driftwood on the town's pebble beaches. Homer is at the end of the road; the nation's paved highway system comes to an abrupt conclusion at the tip of the Homer Spit, almost 5 miles out in the middle of Kachemak Bay, and believers of one kind or another have washed up here for decades. There were the "barefooters," a communal group that eschewed shoes, even in the Alaska winter (Brother Asaiah came with them in the early 1950s). There are the Russian Old Believers, who organize their strictly traditional communities around their objection to Russian Orthodox church reforms made by Peter the Great. There are the former hippies who have become successful commercial fishermen after flocking here in the late 1960s to camp as "spit rats" on the Homer Spit beach. And there are even the current migrants— artists and retired people, fundamentalist preachers and New Age healers, wealthy North Slope oil workers and land-poor settlers with no visible means of support—all people who live here simply because they choose to.

The choice is understandable. Homer lies on the north side of Kachemak Bay, a branch of lower Cook Inlet of extraordinary biological productivity. The halibut fishing, especially, is exceptional. The town has a breathtaking setting on Homer Spit and on a wildflower-covered bench high above the bay. The outdoors, especially on the water and across the bay, contains wonderful opportunities. And the arts community has developed into an attraction of its own. There are several exceptional galleries and the Pratt Museum, which has a national reputation. You'll be disappointed, however, if you expect a charming little fishing village. Poor community planning has created a town that doesn't live up to its setting—indeed, highway sprawl is in the process of ruining some of it. Homer Spit in summer is a traffic-choked jumble of cheap tourist development and RVs.

Homer began to take its modern form after two events: In the 1950s the Sterling Highway connected it to the rest of the world, and in 1964 the Good Friday earthquake sank the spit, narrowing a much larger piece of land with a small forest into the tendril that now barely stands above the water. If not for constant reinforcement by the federal government, the spit long since would have become an island, and Homer would hardly exist. As long as it survives, however, the town makes the most of that unique finger into the sea. Whether or not it is a cosmic focal point, it certainly is an exceptional launching point to one of the nation's great marine recreation areas.

Essentials

GETTING THERE **By Car:** At about 235 miles, Homer is roughly 4½ hours from Anchorage by car, if you don't stop at any of the interesting or beautiful places along the way. It's a scenic drive. If you take a rental car, drive it both ways, as the drop-off fees from Anchorage to Homer are high.

By Bus: The Stage Line (☎907/235-2252; www.thestageline.net) runs from Homer to Anchorage and Seward and back daily during the summer, less frequently the rest of the year. The Anchorage-Homer fare is $78 one-way, $144 round-trip. Tickets are for sale at 1213 Ocean Dr. in Homer. In Anchorage, the ticket office is at 412 W. 53rd Ave. (☎907/868-3914).

By Air: Era Aviation (☎800/866-8394; www.flyera.com) serves Homer from Anchorage several times a day. Small air-taxi operators use Homer as a hub for outlying villages and the outdoors.

By Ferry: The **Alaska Marine Highway System** (☎800/642-0066; www.ferryalaska.com) connects Homer to Seldovia, Kodiak, and points west along the Alaska Peninsula and Aleutian Archipelago, with the ferry *Tustumena*. The *Kennicott* also goes to Kodiak, and to the east rounds the Kenai Peninsula to Whittier and thence across the Gulf of Alaska to Southeast Alaska and British Columbia (see "Getting There," under "Whittier: Dock on the Sound"). The run to Kodiak takes 10 hours and costs $74 for an adult walk-on passenger (children 6–11 half off). It's a long trip, but a memorable one.

VISITOR INFORMATION The **Homer Chamber of Commerce Visitor Information Center,** 201 Sterling Hwy. (P.O. Box 541), Homer, AK 99603 (☎907/235-7740; www.homeralaska.org), is on the right as you enter town. In summer, staff is on hand Monday through Friday from 9am to 7pm, Saturday and Sunday 10am to 6pm. Besides answering questions and handing out brochures on local businesses and public lands, they sell tickets for the halibut derby (p. 413). Winter hours are Monday through Friday from 9am to 5pm.

ATTRACTIONS

Art Shop Gallery **8**
Bunnell Street Gallery **3**
Fireweed Gallery **13**
Islands and Oceans
   Visitor Center **11**
Pratt Museum **7**
Ptarmigan Arts **12**
Sea Lion Gallery **17**

ACCOMMODATIONS

Driftwood Inn **2**
Homer Hostel **5**
Land's End Resort **19**
Magic Canyon Ranch B&B **15**
Ocean Shores Motel **1**
Old Town B&B **3**
Pioneer Inn **6**
The Sea Lion Cove **17**

DINING

Boardwalk Fish & Chips **18**
Café Cups **9**
Chart Room **19**
Cosmic Kitchen **14**
Duncan House Diner **10**
Fat Olive's **4**
Fresh Sourdough Express
   Bakery & Cafe **16**

The **Islands and Oceans Visitor Center,** 95 Sterling Hwy., Homer, AK 99603 (☎**907/235-6961;** www.islandsandocean.org), is more than a visitor center. It's one of Homer's best attractions—a sort of museum of the outdoors for the Alaska Maritime National Wildlife Refuge and the Kachemak Bay Research Reserve, the co-sponsoring organizations. Everyone coming to Homer should stop in to see the building, an architectural gem that perfectly reflects the rocky shores that the refuge and reserve take in, and to experience exhibits that use technology and a deft sense of theater to re-create those remote places in thought and feel. A film shows frequently about the research of the brave scientists who work in the fierce wilderness of the refuge's outer reaches, in the Aleutian Islands. The center is also the

Islands and Oceans Visitor Center.

best place to stop for information if you plan to go outdoors anywhere in the area. An easy nature trail descends to the salt marsh below the center. Admission is free. The center is open summer daily 9am to 6pm; check the website or call for winter hours.

The refuge itself consists of islands off Alaska from the Arctic to near British Columbia that include some of the world's most prolific bird and marine mammal habitat. The U.S. Fish and Wildlife Service manages these lands for the benefit of the animals, and people rarely set foot on their shores, but rangers in Homer offer daily programs and walks during peak summer season three times a day, at 11am, 1pm, and 3pm. Call for times and topics. The ranger's birding walks and guided tide-pool treks could be a highlight of your trip. Birders can also call the **Kachemak Bay Bird Alert Information Line** (☎**907/235-7337**) to find out about recent sightings and upcoming birding events, and to leave news of your own observations, in season.

The **Kachemak Bay State Park District Office,** Mile 168.5, Sterling Hwy., 4 miles from town (☎**907/235-7024;** www.alaskastateparks. org), can help answer questions about planning a trip to the trails and beaches across Kachemak Bay from Homer and give advice on renting remote cabins (although you make the reservation through the Anchorage office—see "State Parks Cabin Reservations," p. 360). Depending on staffing, the office should be open Monday through Friday from 9am to 5pm.

GETTING AROUND   The best way to get to and around Homer is by car. If you didn't bring one, you can rent a car at the airport from **Hertz** (☎**800/654-3131** or 907/235-0734; www.hertz.com) or one of three local firms. Taxis are available from **CHUX Cab** (☎**907/235-CHUX** [235-2489]), among others.

For strong riders, a bike is a good way around town. You do have to dodge traffic in places downtown, but a paved trail parallels the road for the 5 miles of the spit and another runs 5 miles east of town. Some excellent mountain-biking routes are mentioned below. **Homer Saw and Cycle,** 1532 Ocean Dr. (☎907/235-8406; www.homersaw.com), rents mountain bikes, street bikes, kids' bikes, and trailers. Bike rentals start at $25 a day and come with helmets and locks. The shop keeps track of trail conditions and is a good source of advice. It is open Monday through Friday from 9am to 5:30pm, Saturday from 11am to 5pm. It's wise to reserve bikes a day or two ahead, especially if an outing depends on getting one.

SPECIAL EVENTS Unless otherwise noted, the **Homer Chamber of Commerce** (☎907/235-7740; www.homeralaska.org) is the best source of information for all these community happenings, and for others listed on the events page of its website. **Homer's Winter Carnival,** in early February, is a big community event, a small-town celebration with a beer-making contest, parade, a Mardi Gras celebration, and auto racing on the ice of Beluga Lake, among other highlights.

The **Winter King Tournament** is a 1-day fishing competition, March 20, 2010, for the largest king salmon caught by a fleet of sportfishing boats trolling for the fish in their winter ocean habitat. The purse exceeds $100,000 in cash and merchandise. The **Jackpot Halibut Derby** (www.homerhalibutderby.com), lasting May 1 to September 30, has a top prize that has reached more than $50,000 for the biggest fish of the season, and smaller monthly prizes and tagged fish prizes. Grand-prize fish are usually 300 pounds or more. Of course, you must buy your $10 ticket before you fish.

The **Kachemak Shorebird Festival,** in early May, includes guided bird-watching hikes and boat excursions, natural history workshops, art shows and performances, and other events. It's organized by Alaska Maritime National Wildlife Refuge and the Homer Chamber of Commerce to mark the return of the annual migration.

The **Kachemak Bay Seafest and Wooden Boat Festival** (www.kbayseafest.org), over Memorial Day weekend, focuses on kayaking,

[FastFACTS] HOMER

Banks Three banks with ATMs, including **Wells Fargo** (which has a lovely mural inside), are on the Sterling Highway near Heath Street.

Hospital **South Peninsula Hospital** is at the top of Bartlett Street, off Pioneer Ave. (☎907/235-8101).

Internet Access Tech Connect Computer Sales

and Services, 432 E. Pioneer Ave. (☎907/235-5248), offers broadband access for $5 an hour on their computers or Wi-Fi on yours. Other Wi-Fi hotspots are not hard to find; the visitor center can give you a list.

Police For nonemergencies within the city limits, call the **Homer Police Department** (☎907/235-3150); outside the city,

phone the **Alaska State Troopers** (☎907/235-8239). The police station is on Heath Street at Pioneer Avenue, right behind the Fire Department.

Post Office Sterling Highway at Heath Street.

Taxes Sales tax in Homer is 7.5%. Outside the city, you pay 3%.

wooden-boat building, and marine safety. You can see handmade boats from around the region and join kayak events, instruction, and paddles.

Concert on the Lawn, over a weekend in late July, by KBBI public radio (✆907/235-7721), is a 2-day outdoor music, craft, and food festival that brings together the whole town.

Exploring the Town

The best activities are on the beaches, in the hilltop meadows, and on Kachemak Bay. The best man-made attractions all somehow relate to that setting. The art inspired by Homer's environment shows in more than a dozen galleries and studios in town, not including those across the bay in Halibut Cove (see below). New shows open all over town on the first Friday of the month, when restaurants hold special evenings and the entire community comes out for an evening of gallery hopping.

FROM TOP: **Fireweed Gallery; Boat at the Kachemak Bay Seafest and Wooden Boat Festival.**

A widely distributed brochure lists most of the galleries in town, with a map. (Find it online at www.fireweedgallery.com/cs4.pdf.) Most are close together on Pioneer Avenue. You'll generally find photography, prints, pottery, fabric, woodwork, and other crafts, since these are small businesses owned by local people trying to make a living. But there is some expensive fine art, too.

Among my favorite galleries are **Ptarmigan Arts,** 471 E. Pioneer Ave. (☎907/235-5345; www.ptarmiganarts.com), an artists' co-op showing a cross-section of what the area offers; the **Fireweed Gallery** (☎907/235-3411; http://fireweedgallery.com), next door to Ptarmigan, with true fine art in an elegant, airy space; and the large, friendly, and well-stocked **Art Shop Gallery** (☎800/478-7076 or 907/235-7076; www.artshopgallery.com), in the two-story, octagonal building at 202 W. Pioneer Ave., which hosts major shows in the summer.

There are galleries on Homer Spit, too, among all the ticky-tacky gift shops, food stands, and fishing charters offices. My favorite there is Gary Lyon's **Sea Lion Gallery,** on the Central Charters Boardwalk at 4241 Homer Spit Rd. (☎907/235-3400; www.sealiongallery.com). Lyon's work captures Alaska wildlife in spectacular detail, but also transforms his subjects with a distinctively dreamy vision. His gallery is a tiny jewel box of valuable works.

Bunnell Street Arts Center ★★ This nonprofit gallery/performance and studio space, located in a perfect space in an old hardware store near Bishop's Beach at the lower end of Main Street, is my favorite in Alaska. Unlike most other Alaska galleries, which double as tourist gift shops, Bunnell was made by and for artists, and the experience is noncommercial and often challenging. You may be tempted to become a member of the nonprofit corporation that runs it, for membership comes with a one-of-a-kind plate made by one of the artists. As with all Homer art, the themes of the work tend to be fishy, and the medium and style can be anything. The arts center also mounts invitational or juried art shows from beyond the community and puts on performance art and art workshops, concerts, poetry readings, and films.

106 W. Bunnell Ave. ☎907/235-2662. www.bunnellstreetgallery.org. Suggested donation $2. Summer daily 10am–6pm; winter Mon–Fri 10am–5pm, Sat noon–4pm.

Norman Lowell Studio & Gallery ★ 📷 Lowell built his own huge gallery on his homestead to show his life's work. The immense oils of Alaska landscapes, which are not for sale, hang in a building that counts as one of Alaska's larger art museums. Although Lowell's work is traditionally representational, many of

Late March Is Perfect

On a spring break trip to Homer, in late March, I enjoyed spectacular cross-country skiing over deep snow on lengthy trails leading to lofty Diamond Ridge, and from there I could see a fleet of hundreds of small boats returning across the bay from a salmon-fishing tournament. We'd spent time viewing the galleries, eating in fantastic restaurants, and staying in a luxurious waterfront room for an amazing bargain price. A smart visitor touring Alaska could combine skiing and fishing in Homer with other March highlights, including the Iditarod Trail Sled Dog Race in Anchorage and the World Ice Art Championships in Fairbanks (see "Alaska Calendar of Events," p. 65). Homer even has a B&B where you can ski the trails from your room, **Alaska Ridgetop Inn** (☎888/357-4343; www.alaskaridgetopinn.com). The owner is one of the volunteer ski-trail groomers.

Pratt Museum.

the paintings carry raw emotions capable of reaching the most cynical viewer. Admission is free, and Lowell and his wife, Libby, usually host guests who walk through. Their old-time Alaskan hospitality is a delight. At the end of the exhibit a large gift shop sells nothing but Lowell's work; paintings range from $750 to $30,000, and prints start at $100. They don't take credit cards. Take a moment to wander the grounds, too, as it's an opportunity to see a real wilderness homestead that has survived largely unchanged from the early days. The Lowells are trying to sell, so stop at this unique place while you still can.

Norman Lowell Dr. ☎907/235-7344. Free admission. Mon–Sat 9am–5pm; Sun 1–5pm. Closed mid-Sept to May 1. Turn from Sterling Hwy. at mile 160.9 (4.5 miles from Anchor Point, about 12 miles from Homer).

Pratt Museum ★★ Homer's award-winning museum is as good as any you'll find in a town of this size. The Pratt displays art and explains local history, too, but it is strongest in natural history. It helped pioneer technology that allows viewing of wildlife through live remote-control cameras without disturbing the animals. Visitors at the museum can watch puffins and other birds on Gull Island, and operate the camera's controls. Another remote camera focuses on the brown bears of Katmai National Park. There is a saltwater aquarium housing local marine life, and if you're curious about all the fishing boats down in the harbor, you can find out about the different types of gear as well as the fish they catch. In the small botanical garden outside you can learn to identify all the local wildflowers, and a forest trail teaches about the area's ecology. There's much more to see, too, including a good gift shop.

3779 Bartlett St. (at Pioneer Ave.). ☏**907/235-8635.** www.prattmuseum.org. Admission $8 adults, $6 seniors, $4 children ages 6–18, $25 family rate. High season daily 10am–6pm; low season Tues–Sun noon–5pm. Closed Jan.

Getting Outside

The best **map of the Kachemak Bay area** is produced by Alaska Road and Recreation Maps and is available all over town.

ON THE HOMER SIDE OF KACHEMAK BAY

EXPLORING TIDE POOLS Exploring Kachemak Bay's tide pools is the best way to really get to know the sea and meet the strange and wonderful animals that live in it, and it doesn't cost anything but the price of a pair of rubber boots. First, check a tide book, available for free in virtually any local store, or ask a local to check one for you. You'll do best on a low tide of –1 or lower, meaning that low water will be at least 1 foot below the normal low, some 25 feet below the high. Extra-low tides expose more of the lower intertidal zone that contains the most interesting creatures. At a –5 tide, you could find octopus and other oddities. Also, the lower the tide, the more time you'll have to look. Keep track of the time: The tide will come in faster than you imagine, and you could get stranded and drown in the cold water.

The best place to go tide pooling right in town is reached from Bishop's Beach Park, near the lower end of Main Street. Walk west on the beach toward the opening of the bay to Cook Inlet. It's at least a half-hour brisk walk to the Coal Point area, where the sand and boulders end. This is where you'll find pools of water left behind by the receding tide, many full of life. Explore patiently and gently—look at the animals and touch them, but always put them back as they were and try not to crush them underfoot. Marine invertebrate identification keys and many other field guides are sold at the Islands and Ocean Visitor Center, above under "Visitor Information," where rangers happily give advice. They also offer ranger-guided tide-pool beach walks. If you want to keep going beyond Coal Point, there's usually a raft of sea otters offshore about 3 miles down the beach. Just continue walking, keeping your eyes on the water. As always with watching wildlife, binoculars will improve the experience.

HIKING & NATURE WALKS The **Wynn Nature Center,** operated by the nonprofit **Center for Alaskan Coastal Studies** (☏**907/235-6667;** www.ak coastalstudies.org), offers a chance to learn about the ecology of the area and see its birds and wildflowers on an easy walk or hike while taking in sweeping ocean views. The center encompasses 140 acres of spruce forest and wildflower meadow off Skyline Drive, with an 800-foot boardwalk accessible to people with disabilities. This is a lovely area, and the center has done a fine job of adding an educational component without diminishing it—including a log cabin where you can meet a host and ask questions. The center is open daily from 10am to 6pm mid-June through Labor Day, with guided walks twice a day. You can also hike on your own with a printed guide. Fees for adults are $7, seniors $6, 17 and under $5. Call about interesting daily programs as well.

More ambitious hikes explore more of the bench of land above Homer or the mountains across the bay at Kachemak Bay State Park (see below). The 7-mile **Homestead Trail** is an old wagon road used by Homer's early settlers. The largely informal trail is lovely and peaceful, tunneling through alders, crossing fields of wildflowers, and passing old homestead cabins. From a hilltop meadow you can see all the way to the inlet and the volcanoes beyond. The eastern trail head is at the reservoir on Skyline Drive—drive up West Hill Road from the Sterling Highway, turn right, and follow Skyline to the fourth left. The western trailhead is on Rogers Loop, which branches from the Sterling Highway just before it crests the last big hill before entering Homer. (That's also the place to join Homer's

Tide pools at Kachemak Bay.

outstanding cross-country ski trails.) A map and guide produced by the Kachemak Heritage Land Trust is available at the visitor center.

HORSEBACK RIDING Ranchers have worked around Kachemak Bay for decades. Drive east of town on East End Road to see pastures overlooking spectacular marine and mountain views. Go beyond the road, and you're in some of Alaska's most beautiful untamed country. Mark Marette guides trail rides to the head of Kachemak Bay, leading every group himself, as he has since 1986. Guests used to typical, boring tourist horseback riding come back thrilled at how adventurous their ride has been. Marette's business is **Trails End Horse Adventures** (☎ 907/235-6393), 11¼ miles out East End. He charges $25 per hour, or $85 for a 4-hour trip. He takes all ages and raw beginners.

MOUNTAIN-BIKING OR DRIVING Several gravel roads around Homer make for exquisite drives or bike rides. Mountain bikers can use the Homestead Trail, too (it is described under "Hiking"). A lovely drive leads out **East End Road,** through seaside pastures, a forest, and the village of Fritz Creek, then follows the bluff line through meadows toward the head of the bay. When the road gets too rough, explore onward on a mountain bike. **Skyline Drive** has extraordinary views of high canyons and Kachemak Bay; drive up East Hill Road just east of Homer. **Homer Saw and Cycle,** the bike shop listed above, under "Getting Around," can give you many more ideas. The great mountain-biking across the bay is described below.

ON & ACROSS KACHEMAK BAY

Along the south side of the Kachemak Bay, glaciers, fjords, and little wooded islands are arrayed like a smorgasbord before Homer. A quick boat ride puts you there for sea kayaking, mountain-biking on unconnected dirt roads, hiking in the mountains, or eating sushi in a top-flight restaurant on pilings. Or gallery hopping, resting at a remote lodge, studying at a nature center, or walking the streets of a forgotten fishing village. The far side of the bay has no road link to import the mundane, mass-produced world, but it does have people, and they make the landscape even richer and more enchanting than it would be alone. And underneath the water, there's a wealth of halibut and salmon.

TRANSPORTATION ACROSS THE WATER Many water taxis operate from Homer to wilderness cabins, kayaking waters, hiking trails, and mountain-biking roads accessible from the Jakolof Bay Dock, Seldovia, Halibut Cove, Kachemak Bay State Park, and other remote points. Rates vary little; it's around $75 per person to get to Kachemak Bay State Park, plus a $4 park fee, for example. **Mako's Water Taxi** (☎907/235-9055; www.makoswatertaxi. com) has experience and a good reputation. Mako Haggerty also rents sea kayaks and drops them off; with his advice, you can plan a one-way paddle, with the water taxi providing a lift at each end. Karl Stoltzfus's **Bay Excursions Water Taxi and Tours** (☎907/235-7525; www.bayexcursions. com) offers transportation across the bay, but also specializes in small-group tours—he takes no more than 12 at a time—for serious bird-watching or, on other days, to encounter sea otters as well as see the bird rookeries. Stoltzfus rents kayaks, too. Contact other water-taxi operators, and make other outdoors booking arrangements, through **Inlet Charters Across Alaska Adventures** (☎800/770-6126; www.halibutcharters.com).

KACHEMAK BAY STATE PARK The park comprises much of the land across the water that makes all those views from Homer so spectacular. For around $75 you can be dropped off there after breakfast, walk the beach, hike in the woods, climb the mountains, and meet your boat in time to be back in Homer for dinner. Enough people are doing it now that some water taxis offer scheduled service to the most popular trail head—perhaps with a stop for espresso at a floating coffeehouse in Halibut Cove on the way home. If you want to be on your own, there are plenty of lesser-used trails, as well.

The park's main office is at the ranger station listed on p. 366. Its center is the summer-only **ranger station** in Halibut Cove Lagoon, where there's a dock and mooring buoys for public use, three public rental cabins over the water, a campsite, and excellent king salmon fishing in mid-June.

The park has about 80 miles of trails, many linking at the ranger station; a free trail guide is available there, but you're well advised to get a good map before you leave Homer. The trails generally start at tidewater amid a lush, mossy forest and rise into the craggy mountains—up sharp peaks, or, if you don't want to climb that much, over the hills to the next secluded beach. The most popular is the **Saddle Trail,** which rises through forest from a staircase at the east side of Halibut Cove over a low ridge to the icy lake in front of Grewink Glacier. It's an easy hike of around 3 miles total. If you want to be away from other hikers, however, discuss choices with a ranger or your water-taxi provider, as there are plenty of quieter trails; since some trails are not adequately maintained, local advice is critical.

All hikers should prepare with proper shoes and clothing and bring mosquito repellent. Review bear avoidance skills (see "Outdoors Health & Safety," in chapter 3). Cellphones work many places on the bay, so bring one along if you have it.

Besides the three cabins at Halibut Cove Lagoon, you can hike to two more public rental cabins less than 3 miles from the lagoon's dock.

The park's fifth cabin is on Tutka Bay, off the Halibut Cove trail network. Cabin permits are $65 a night and usually must be reserved 6 months in advance (see "State Parks Cabin Reservations," p. 360). Seven remote yurts with wood stoves and sleeping platforms are for rent from a concessionaire, **Nomad Shelter** (☎907/235-0132; www.alaskanyurtrentals.com), also for $65, and may be easier to reserve. You use can any of these places as a base for self-guided sea kayaking, and most are at trail heads.

SELDOVIA This historic fishing village is like Homer without all the cars and people: just a lot of quiet, the lovely ocean waters, and some nice places to stay. It belongs in this outdoor section only because there's nothing at all to do there other than bike, paddle, or fish (you can do nothing there very well, too). The trip across Kachemak Bay to Seldovia is one of the best parts of going there. For most people, the **Rainbow Tours** (☎907/235-7272; www.rainbowtours.net) daily round-trips are the practical alternative. They offer shuttle service from Homer Harbor that allows a long day there, and a narrated natural history tour with a 3-hour stop in the village. You don't need to stay overnight in Seldovia to get a feel for the town and take a bike ride, a kayak tour, or just walk around the town. Round-trip fares to Seldovia on the shuttle are $45 adults, $40 seniors, $35 children 12 and under; going one-way is $30 for everyone. For the nature tour, fares are $50 adults, $45 seniors, $40 children.

Go sea kayaking in Seldovia with **Kayak'atak** (☎907/234-7425; www.alaska.net/~kayaks). The couple doing the tours, longtime Seldovia residents, take pride in showing off the wildlife and beauty of this little-used area. They charge $120 for a 5-hour tour, including lunch, or $80 for a 3-hour tour, without lunch. They also rent kayaks and offer overnight trips. For a less taxing look at Seldovia Bay, take their evening skiff tour for $35 per person (with two to four passengers).

King salmon are stocked in Seldovia Slough, which passes right through the town. The run peaks in mid-June, and you can fish from shore. Seldovia also has an edge for halibut anglers, because you start out an hour closer to the **halibut** grounds than Homer, potentially giving you more time to actually fish. The best source of town information is its extraordinary Web portal, www.seldovia.com. You can also leave a message for the **Seldovia Chamber of Commerce** at ☎907/234-7612.

JAKOLOF BAY A state-maintained dock opens an area of gentle shorelines and abandoned roads to visitors who seek the wilderness without paying to stay at a wilderness lodge. West of Kachemak Bay State Park and east of Seldovia, the lands have roads, but the roads aren't connected to anything and are used as much by mountain bikers as by anyone else. You can take a water taxi straight to the Jakolof dock. Lodgings are nearby at **Across the Bay Tent and Breakfast,** p. 428. There's plenty to do in the area. The waters of Jakolof, Little Jakolof, Kasitsna, and Little Tutka bays, and the tiny Herring Islands, are appealing and protected for sea kayaking. Supreme mountain-biking trails lead along the shore and right across the peninsula through forest and meadows for berry picking. The Red Mountain and Rocky River roads are prime routes, different each year depending on wash-outs and intermittent maintenance—that's part of the adventure. A maintained 10-mile road west leads to the charming village of Seldovia, described above.

A DAY TRIP TO halibut COVE

The artists' colony of Halibut Cove sits on either side of a narrow, peaceful channel between a small island and the mainland; the water in this channel is the road. Boardwalks connect the buildings, and stairs reach down to the water from houses perched on pilings over the shore. The post office and espresso stand float on docks. Visitors arrive each afternoon to walk the boardwalks, visit the galleries, and eat at the restaurant, the Saltry. That's a place to sit back on the deck and sip microbrews and eat fresh baked bread, mussels, sushi, and locally grown salads, followed by fresh fish grilled over charcoal.

The classic wooden boat *Danny J* (book through **Central Charters** at ☎**800/478-7847** or 907/235-7847; www.central charter.com) leaves Homer daily in the summer at noon, brings back day-trippers, takes guests to the Saltry Restaurant at 5pm, and brings back the diners later in the evening. The noon trip includes bird-watching at Gull Island. Seating is mostly outdoors, and I would choose something else to do in bad weather. You also take the *Danny J* if you're spending the night in Halibut Cove. The noon trip is $53 for adults, $48 seniors, $33 children; the dinner trip is $30 for everyone, regardless of age, but to go you must have a dinner reservation at the Saltry, usually made

at least a few days ahead, also with Central Charters. On the noon trip only, they sometimes take more passengers than the *Danny J* can carry, putting the overflow aboard the steel *Storm Bird*. Reservations and fares are identical to those of the *Danny J*.

On the afternoon trip you can bring lunch or eat at the Saltry, described above, and then explore the **boardwalk** that runs from the restaurant along Ismailof Island past the galleries, boat shops, and houses. There's also a barn-yard, perched on a patch of ground along the boardwalk, where kids, who will already be in heaven, can look at horses. The summer-only **Halibut Cove's Experience Fine Art Gallery** (☎**907/296-2215**) is the first building past the farm on the boardwalk, on pilings above the water. The airy room contains works by Halibut Cove artists only.

Trails branch from the boardwalk across the island to broad views of the bay or to the quiet opposite end of the island. Exceptionally appealing overnight accommodations at Halibut Cove are covered under "Lodgings Across the Bay," p. 427.

GULL ISLAND The island is a rock across the bay from Homer Spit that is a busy bird colony in the summer. It's easy to get to, and boats can edge close, as the water is deep all around. You can often see tufted and horned puffins, black-legged kittiwakes, common murres, red-faced and pelagic cormorants, pigeon guillemots, and glaucous-winged gulls. Tour boats to Halibut Cove or Seldovia may cruise by the island, and if you are taking a water taxi to Halibut Cove Lagoon, ask to take a look on your way.

ACTIVITIES

FISHING Homer is known for **halibut,** those huge, flat, bottom fish, and the harbor is full of charter boats that will take you out for the day for around $275 per person in the high season. Every day, a few people catch fish that are larger than they are, and halibut more than 50 pounds are common. Using gear and lines that look strong enough to pick up the boat, you jig the bait (chunks of herring or cod) up and down on the bottom. Halibut aren't wily or acrobatic, and fighting one can be like pulling up a sunken Buick. Regulations currently allow anglers to keep two halibut per day in this region, as opposed to one in Southeast Alaska, but those rules could change; if keeping fish is important to you, check before you go. You can download the Alaska Department of Fish and Game regulation booklet from www.adfg. state.ak.us (follow the links to "sportfish"). Getting out to where the fish are plentiful requires an early start and a long ride to unprotected waters. People who get seasick easily shouldn't go, as the boat wallows on the waves during fishing. (For advice on avoiding seasickness, see p. 95.) One good, full-day operator is **Silver Fox Charters (☎800/478-8792** or 907/235-8792; www.silverfoxcharters.com).

Half-day charters have less chance of getting way out to the biggest fish but cost a lot less. **Rainbow Tours (☎907/235-7272;** www.rainbow tours.net) operates a big boat for the shorter outings, charging $105 adult, $95 senior, and $85 12 and under. This choice makes good sense if you are not a fishing fanatic or are taking kids along, as a full day of halibut fishing is exhausting and can be tedious. Other halibut charter boats can be booked through **Inlet Charters Across Alaska Adventures (☎800/770-6126;** www.halibutcharters.com), with many years' experience setting up fishing trips and other activities.

Salmon use Cook Inlet year-round, not only when they're returning to the streams to spawn, and Homer anglers pursue them with trolling gear even in the dead of winter. The town has a Winter King Salmon Tournament in March (check with the chamber of commerce, above). Most people, however, fish salmon in summer. Although Homer lacks the road-accessible streamside fishing found farther north, Kachemak Bay does have good salmon fishing in salt water. A small inlet called the Nick Dudiak Fishing Lagoon on the Spit is stocked with king and silver salmon by the Alaska Department of Fish and Game. Kings return to the lagoon from late May to the end of June. Silvers arrive in mid- to late July, peaking in early August and finishing by mid-month. These salmon have nowhere to spawn, so all must be caught. At the end of the runs, Fish and Game may announce that snagging is permitted, which is something like mugging salmon and can be a lot of fun, if not something you'll brag about later at the Rod and Gun Club.

An angler can easily come back from a halibut charter with 60 pounds of fish that, when cleaned, will yield 30 pounds of filets. A serving is around half a pound of halibut. Eat as much fresh as you can, as it will never be better, but be prepared for how you will deal with the rest of your bounty, which, if bought in a grocery store, would cost as much as $500 (it's illegal to sell sport-caught fish). If it is properly and quickly frozen, it will retain much of its quality well into the winter; if not, you waste this superb food. If you're lucky enough to catch that much salmon, the problem is even more immediate, as salmon is more sensitive to proper handling. Most fishing towns have a sport processor who can vacuum-pack and flash-freeze your catch for $1 to $1.25 a pound. You can get it home conveniently as checked baggage; depending on airline baggage fees, that may be the least expensive option, as well. The processor can provide sturdy fish boxes and cold packs. If you aren't leaving right away, processors may be willing to hold the fish, and many hotels have freezer facilities. If you have to ship it, use an overnight service (expensive) and make sure someone is there to put it in the freezer on the other end. Above all, keep the fish *hard frozen;* thawing and refreezing diminishes the quality of any fish and can turn salmon into mush. Consider having some of your salmon smoked, if possible, making it a ready-to-eat delicacy very welcome as a homecoming gift. Halibut can be smoked, too, but because of its low fat content and delicate flavor and texture, it doesn't come out as well as salmon. See p. 82 for more tips on handling and cooking Alaskan fish. In Homer, Coal Point Trading Co., 4306 Homer Spit (**907/235-3877;** www.welovefish. com), will process and pack your catch as ordered. Ask your charter captain, and they will come and get the fish directly from the boat.

For saltwater salmon fishing in a more natural setting, head across the bay to Halibut Cove Lagoon (see Kachemak Bay State Park, above) or Seldovia. Back up the Sterling Highway, the Anchor River is a lovely fishing stream with steelhead and rainbow trout (both catch-and-release only), salmon, and Dolly Varden char. Several popular fishing streams cross the Sterling Highway farther north toward Soldotna. The **Alaska Department of Fish and Game** maintains a fishing hot line at **907/235-6930.** They're located at 3298 Douglas Place (**907/235-8191**).

FLIGHTSEEING & BEAR VIEWING One gets used to thinking of the mountains across Kachemak Bay from Homer as the far side of a magnificent stage set, so it's somewhat mind-blowing to fly beyond that first line of mountains and see how they are just the beginning of much more complex topography of peaks, glaciers, chasms, and ice fields. The best person to show you that wild country is Bill de Creeft. His **Kachemak Air Service Inc.** (**907/235-8924;** www.alaskaseaplanes.com) offers spectacular scenic flights starting at $175 per person. The tours begin with the thrill of a water take-off from Beluga Lake.

Homer has several air taxis providing access to the very remote areas of the southern Kenai Peninsula and lower Cook Inlet that you can't easily reach by boat. You can also use their scheduled service to explore, flying to Seldovia or even one of the two Alaska Native villages across the bay. If your main objective is to see bears, however, the best guides are at **Emerald Air Service** (☎907/235-6993; www.emeraldairservice.com). Ken and Chris Day specialize in all-day bear-viewing flight expeditions. Unlike some air services I've flown with, whose pilots may not know much about bears and land only briefly, the Days make a point of teaching about bears and their habitat in extended visits. They helped the National Wildlife Federation film an IMAX movie called "Bears," and starred in it along with the title characters. Trips include a flight by floatplanes on fresh or salt water and then a naturalist-guided hike to see the wildlife. The couple prides themselves on their care for the environment. The trips cost $625 per person.

NATURE TOURS The nonprofit **Center for Alaskan Coastal Studies** (☎907/235-6667; www.akcoastalstudies.org) is dedicated to educating the public about the shore, interpreting Kachemak Bay for visitors on daily explorations of the Peterson Bay and China Poot Bay area, across the water from Homer. At low tide they lead guests on a fascinating guided tide-pool walk. The center also has access to lovely woodlands where nature walks cover forest ecology and geology and visit an archaeological site. Saltwater tanks at the lodge contain creatures from the intertidal zone and microscopes to inspect your finds. It's a relaxed and truly Alaskan outing. You can add on guided sea kayaking or a reasonably priced overnight stay in a yurt so you're there ready for an early morning low tide. Reserve by calling the center at the number above. The all-day tour is $105 adults, $73 ages 11 and under, and operates daily Memorial Day to Labor Day. Pack your own lunch, and bring footwear suitable for hiking and potentially wet beach walks and warm clothing for the boat ride.

SEA KAYAKING Silence fell as the boat pulled away from the beach, leaving us behind with the kayaks and our guide. For the rest of the day my son and I absorbed the water-reflected sunlight and glided past fancifully shaped rocks and resident sea otters around Yukon Island. We explored beaches, picnicked, raced, and discovered tiny bays too small for any other craft. At the end of the day, we had a new friend in our quietly cheerful guide, Alison O'Hara, and discovered that she'd imperceptibly taught us a lot about sea kayaking. O'Hara runs **True North Kayak Adventures** (☎907/235-0708; www.truenorth kayak.com). Her 8-hour beginner day trips cost $145, including lunch and passage across the bay. The firm also offers an all-day trip combining a hike with sea kayaking, for $199, and more challenging overnight and multiday trips to remote waters in the area. A $245 package includes the day tour, a night in the attractive Hesketh Island Cabins, and a second day of hiking.

Experienced paddlers can explore Kachemak Bay's protected waters, tiny islands, and remote settlements on your own. Take a water taxi across and explore at will, camping or staying in cabins over much of the bay. Check with Kachemak Bay State Park for guidance. **Mako's Water Taxi** (☎907/235-9055; www.makoswatertaxi.com) offers rides and rents and delivers kayaks. True North Kayak (see the previous paragraph) also rents to experienced paddlers, and rents camping gear. For kayaks expect to pay $65 a day for a double, $45 single.

Where to Stay

Homer has many good B&Bs. The Homer Chamber of Commerce (www.homer alaska.org) has links to a prodigious number of them.

In addition to the places I've listed in detail, **The Sea Lion Cove,** above the Sea Lion Gallery on Homer Spit (**☎907/235-3400** in summer or 907/235-8767 in winter; www.sealiongallery.com/cove), has two spacious units with limited cooking facilities, private phones, and a deck right over the beach where you can hear the waves roll in at night. They rent for $135 and $145 a night.

Up the hill on the other side of town, **A Memorable Experience Bed and Breakfast (☎800/720-9275,** ext. 7374 or 907/235-7374; www.amemorable experience.com) offers huge rooms and a large cottage with spectacular views and an expansive garden setting. The owners know how to do things right. They also run the Fresh Sourdough Express restaurant and, besides a great breakfast, offer guests a voucher for goodies there. Prices range from $135 to $200 per night.

If you just want good, simple lodgings downtown, you'll find an excellent value at the clean and friendly **Pioneer Inn,** 244 W. Pioneer Ave. (**☎800/782-9655** or 907/235-5670; www.pioneerinnhomerak.com), which offers big, apartment-style units starting at $119 in summer with up to four people in the room. Rooms with two twins or a queen bed start at $99 in summer. They also have a house that sleeps up to nine for $275 a night.

Driftwood Inn 🍴 The historic building a block from Bishop's Beach and across from the Bunnell Gallery resembles a lodge or B&B with its large fireplace of beach rock, the hot coffeepot and inexpensive self-serve breakfast in the lobby, and a friendly attitude. The old building has a cozy feel that's somehow enhanced by sloping floors and old fixtures. Its rooms are like Pullman compartments in size and configuration, but they are cute and clean and have some real style. And they're inexpensive. Twelve bedrooms have private bathrooms; nine others share two bathrooms. The upstairs walls are thin, so there's a no-noise policy during evening hours. Two separate new buildings nearer the water have five rooms each with king-size and queen-size beds and large common areas. There's also an appealing 22-site RV park. The inn offers a fish-cleaning station and freezing facility and year-round fishing charters. Smoking is not allowed.

135 W. Bunnell Ave., Homer, AK 99603. **☎800/478-8019** or ☎/fax 907/235-8019. www.the driftwoodinn.com. 33 units, 24 w/private bathroom. High season $65–$195 double; low season $49–$90 double. RV sites $29–$49, full hookup. Extra person $10. MC, V. *In room:* TV.

Land's End Resort ★★★ Traditionally *the* place to stay in Homer, Land's End would be popular no matter what it was like inside because of its location at the tip of Homer Spit, the best spot in Homer and possibly the best spot for a hotel in all of Alaska. It's near the boat harbor, and you can fish right from the beach in front. Buildings sprawl along the low beach crest linked by long corridors, a mismatched collection that resulted from the successive additions over many decades expanding a quaint old nautical hang-out into the well appointed and even luxurious hotel that exists now. The local family that owns the hotel has kept much of the charm while maintaining high standards and making constant improvements. Rooms range widely in size and configuration. The best are a series of privately owned town-house condos next door; for groups or for couples on extended visits, these are the best accommodations in the region, with stylish furniture, lots of space and light, and a beachfront location second to none. The condos rent for $325 to $450 a night, with a 2-night minimum stay in the summer.

The **Chart Room Restaurant** makes good use of its wonderful location, looking out over the beach and bay from big windows. There's a casual, relaxing atmosphere in the long, wood-trimmed dining room. The deck outside has glass wind shields, making it a warm, satisfying place to sit over coffee on a sunny day. You can watch otters, eagles, and fishing boats while you eat. The selection of main courses, priced $16 to $38, is fairly typical of a seaside fine-dining restaurant, and the food is good if not memorable. The appetizer menu, however, is much more extensive and interesting, and the appetizer portions are easily large enough to make a full meal.

4786 Homer Spit Rd., Homer, AK 99603. ℂ**800/478-0400** or 907/235-0400. Fax 907/235-0420. www.lands-end-resort.com. 95 units. High season $125–$245 double; low season $85–$145 double. Extra person $10. AE, DC, DISC, MC, V. **Amenities:** Restaurant; bar; exercise room; outdoor Jacuzzi; indoor lap pool; sauna; spa. *In room:* TV, Wi-Fi.

Magic Canyon Ranch Bed and Breakfast ★ At the top of a canyon road off East End Road, the Webb family shares their charming home, 74 unspoiled acres, a tree house, and sweeping views with guests and a herd of retired llamas. The air is mountain clear and quiet between the high canyon walls—you start to relax as soon as you get out of the car. The Webbs serve sherry in the evening and a full breakfast in the morning. The four rooms, some nestled cozily under the eaves, are decorated in country and Victorian style, with lots of nice details and some family antiques. The house isn't historic by any means, but it feels like it is.

40015 Waterman Rd., Homer, AK 99603. ℂ/fax **907/235-6077.** www.magiccanyonranch.com. 4 units, 2 w/private bathroom. High season $105–$120 double; low season $70–$85 double. Extra adult $25; extra child 12 and under $20. Rates include full breakfast and Wi-Fi. MC, V. Closed winter. **Amenities:** Wi-Fi.

Ocean Shores Motel ★ Buildings on a grassy compound have a commanding view of Kachemak Bay, with a path leading down to Bishop's Beach, yet the location is right off the Sterling Highway as you enter town, within walking distance of downtown Homer. Rooms are fresh and bright, most with private balconies, refrigerators, and microwaves; four have full kitchens (just one rents for only $129). The less expensive rooms lack the views and are older, but are still modern and have cute touches. The place is decorated with photographs and art collected over a family's five generations in Alaska. Smoking is not allowed.

451 Sterling Hwy., Homer, AK 99603 ℂ**800/770-7775** or 907/235-7775. Fax 907/235-8639. www. oceanshoresalaska.com. 38 units. High season $129–$204 double; low season $69–$79 double. Extra person $5. AE, DISC, MC, V. *In room:* TV, fridge, microwave, Wi-Fi.

Old Town Bed and Breakfast ★ 🏨 These rooms combine the artiness of the excellent Bunnell Street Arts Center downstairs (see "Exploring the Town," earlier) and the funky, historic feel of the old trading post/hardware store that the building used to house. The wood floors undulate with age and settling, their imperfections picked out by light from tall, double-hung windows that look out at Bishop's Beach. The antiques, handmade quilts, and wonderful original art fit in as if they have always been there, yet the rooms are comfortable, fresh, and clean. The B&B has no TVs or in-room phones. The rates include a hot breakfast at 8am in the parlor and afternoon tea. This place is not a good choice for people who have any trouble with stairs.

106-D W. Bunnell, Homer, AK 99603. ☎907/235-7558. Fax 907/235-9427. www.oldtown bedandbreakfast.com. 3 units, 1 w/private bathroom. High season $95 double with shared bathroom, $115 with private bathroom; low season $56 double with shared bathroom, $75 double with private bathroom. Extra person $15. Rates include full breakfast. MC, V.

CAMPING & HOSTELS

The most popular place to camp in Homer is out on the spit, amid the sand and pebbles. It can be windy and crowded, but waking up on a bright, pebbled beach makes up for much. The city charges $8 for tents, $15 for RVs, payable at the Camp Fee Office (☎907/235-1583, summer only) in a small log cabin on the spit across the road from the fishing hole (RVers should read the next paragraph for another option on the spit). The city also operates the more protected Hornaday Campground near the hospital: From Pioneer Avenue, take Bartlett Street uphill; turn left on Fairview and right on Campground Road. Both camping areas are managed by **Homer Public Works** (☎907/235-3170; http:// publicworks.ci.homer.ak.us and click "Parks and Recreation").

If RV hookups are a priority, you can still stay on the Homer Spit—for a price. **Heritage RV Park** is on the spit right next to the fishing hole (☎800/380-7787 or 907/226-4500; http://alaskaheritagervpark.com) and has all the usual amenities. Sites with full hookups, including Wi-Fi, telephone with voicemail, and satellite TV, rent for $78 a night. There are plenty of places to go off the spit and get RV hookups more affordably, including the Driftwood Inn, above, and **Oceanview RV Park,** 455 Sterling Hwy. (☎907/235-3951; www.oceanview-rv. com), with 100 spaces near the downtown area overlooking the water and a trail to the beach. Rates are $45 a night for full hookups at peak season, including cable TV. Campers also get halibut charter discounts.

Find conveniently located hostel rooms at **Homer Hostel,** 304 W. Pioneer Ave. (☎907/235-1463; www.homerhostel.com), charging $25 a night for beds in gender-separated or co-ed dorms with four to six bunks each, or $65 double for private rooms (tax included). It's a nice old house with a shared full kitchen, but common areas are small. They also rent bikes and fishing rods and have a grill on the porch guests can use.

LODGINGS ACROSS THE BAY

These places to stay all are based across Kachemak Bay from Homer, each in its own remote cove, bay, or village, and each in its own market niche, from family lodgings to luxurious accommodations. It's wise to reserve rooms at any of these places months in advance (the preceding winter isn't too soon). I regret I can't include many more that are also deserving—and there are many—which you can find listed with links at www.homeralaska.org (click "Accommodations," then "Across Kachemak Bay"). Also have a look at "Kachemak Bay State Park" for the cabins and yurts for rent there. Here are some standouts to consider: the **Otter Cove Resort** (☎800/426-6212 or 907/235-7770; www.ottercoveresort. com), overlooking Eldridge Passage from a collection of attractive, affordable cabins and a shower house, and nearby hiking and sea kayaking; A **Stillpoint In Halibut Cove,** home of the Center for Creative Renewal (☎907/296-2283; www.stillpointlodge.com), which offers an all-inclusive individual wilderness lodge experience, with hiking and kayaking guides, massage, and home-grown organic food, and also offers retreats and workshops for groups—all in a building that's an astonishing work of art itself, full of exquisite stone, dramatic spaces, and even an indoor creek and waterfall; and, in Seldovia, **Alaska Dancing Eagles Cabin Rental** (☎**907/234-7627** in summer or 907/360-6363 in winter; www.dancingeagles.com), a picturesque and relaxing house and cabin on the town's historic boardwalk overlooking calm water and, usually, a sea otter.

Across the Bay Tent and Breakfast ★ Tony and Mary Jane Lastufka created this unique place, a spot where you don't have to be rich to stay for a few days in a backwoods paradise, beachcombing by day and feasting on Tony's grilled seafood in the evening. It looks like a summer camp, with large canvas tents on wooden platforms that stand off by themselves on a steep hillside among towering spruce trees. There's a central house for relaxation, evening games, or conversation, an organic garden to produce the food, two outhouses with stained-glass windows, a bathhouse with plumbing, and a forest volleyball court. The beachfront faces placid Kasitsna Bay—that's where water taxis drop off visitors and where guided sea-kayaking excursions depart ($85 half-day, $105 full day per person). Up the stairs to the road, mountain bikes are for rent ($15 half-day, $25 full day) to explore the area's network of abandoned logging roads or to pedal to Seldovia. The tents have beds, but you sleep in your own bag. You can save further by cooking your own meals. Check the website for workshops you may want to join.

On Kasitsna Bay (P.O. Box 81), Seldovia, AK 99663. ☎**907/235-3633.** (Winter P.O. Box 112054, Anchorage, AK 99511; ☎907/345-2571.) www.tentandbreakfastalaska.com. 6 tents. $75 per person with breakfast; $110 per person with all meals. Half price for children 6–11, free for children 5 and under. MC, V. Closed mid-Sept to Memorial Day.

Kachemak Bay Wilderness Lodge ★★★ I can think of no more idyllic way to become acquainted with Alaska's marine wilderness than by staying at this intimate lodge, run for more than 38 years by hospitable and generous Michael and Diane McBride. The site, on China Poot Bay, is uniquely perfect: on an isthmus, arrayed among big trees, beach grass, and interesting topography, a peaceful and lovely setting with excellent tide pooling, kayaking, and good hiking trails nearby. Environmentally conscious guides, who have included noted experts on the science and history of the area, lead just a few guests at a time for sea kayaking, hiking, wildlife watching, and learning about nature; guests set the agenda, and everything is included. The man-made part of the lodge is extraordinary, too. Instead of trying to pack glossy luxuries into their cabins and main lodge, the McBrides have retained the rough texture of a remote Alaskan camp while subtly enhancing it: One cabin has linoleum floors and well-used furniture, but also fine rugs, a hidden Ethernet connection, and a wine list. The McBrides' meals are legendary, and guests can spend the rest of the evening in yoga classes; in the private, 1930s-vintage sauna; in the hot tub; or viewing a natural history slideshow. Add on a visit to the remote Loonsong Mountain Camp, where Mike and Diane personally guide and cook for just two couples or one family of four at a time in a lodge on its own mountain lake reached by floatplane.

China Poot Bay (P.O. Box 956), Homer, AK 99603. ☎**907/235-8910.** www.alaskawildernesslodge.com. 5 cabins. $1,700 per person for a 2-night stay; $2,400 3-night, $3,500 5-night; children half price, children 6 and younger free. Rates all-inclusive, including boat transportation from Homer. Boating, kayaking, and all guiding included. 2-, 3- or 5-night package only. V. Closed Sept 15–May 25. **Amenities:** Hot tub; sauna.

Quiet Place Lodge ★★★ A series of beautifully finished cabins and lodge buildings perch on the edge of the narrow waterway that is the main street of the artists' colony of Halibut Cove (p. 421), putting a few guests in the heart of this fascinating community in complete, relaxed comfort. You can walk down to the floating dock whenever you like and get aboard your own hand-built wooden rowboat or sea kayak to explore the village or paddle across the water for a spot of sushi at the Saltry Restaurant or an espresso from a stand on a floating dock. The lodge itself serves all meals, included in the package prices. The required 3-day minimum packages also include guided fishing and sea kayaking. A wonderful family created this place and for years has treated guests as friends; their openness and authentic hospitality are among the lodge's best assets.

Halibut Cove (mailing address: 64362 Bridger Rd., Homer, AK 99603). **☎907/235-1800.** www. quietplace.com. 3 cabins. $560 per person, per day. All meals and limited guiding included. 3-day minimum package. MC, V. Closed Sept–May. **Amenities:** Guided fishing; sauna; rowboats; sea kayaks.

Where to Dine

Besides those places listed here, consider the **Chart Room** at Land's End, described under "Where to Stay," above.

Our current favorite in Homer for a quick, casual meal is **Cosmic Kitchen** (**☎907/235-6355;** www.cosmickitchenalaska.com), a cheerful place on Pioneer Avenue producing Mexican lunches and breakfasts, especially large burritos stuffed with fresh, high-quality ingredients along with rice and other side items in disposable baskets. An enormous meal comes in at under $9 per person. Limited indoor seating is supplemented by a pleasant deck out front protected from the wind by glass, but during peak hours the place can be jammed, and taking away your meal may be advisable.

For fresh local halibut and cod, salmon, burgers, chicken, and milkshakes in an attractive beachfront dining room, try **Boardwalk Fish and Chips (☎907/235-7749),** on the boardwalk across from the harbormaster's office on the spit. It's relaxed fast food, but the place is clean and grown-up and serves beer on tap.

Duncan House Diner, downtown at 125 E. Pioneer Ave. (**☎907/235-5344**), is a nice, traditional place for a casual meal in a friendly atmosphere. You can eat at a counter or in booths. It is open for breakfast and lunch daily.

Café Cups ★★★ SEAFOOD The facade of the yellow house on Pioneer Avenue is unmistakable with its elaborate bas-relief sculpture. The small dining room is a work of art, too, a masterpiece of wood, light, and space. Jennifer Olsen seats guests, and her husband, David, is the chef. As the owners, they've combined a love for good food with practicality in a small town. The menu comes in two parts. The regular daily menu is mostly mainstream—aimed at local diners looking for something familiar—but they also have an extensive daily menu of verbally described specials, usually including many interesting choices based on local seafood. Do not make a choice before considering these, which are the heart of the experience. David has a terrific sense of the texture of food—the lamb chops were a sensual delight, crisply seared on the outside, tender and juicy inside, on rich mashed potatoes. Portions are large. They serve beer and wine.

162 W. Pioneer Ave. **☎907/235-8330.** Reservations recommended. Main courses $18–$30. MC, V. Tues–Sat 4:30pm–10pm.

Fat Olives ★★ MEDITERRANEAN Built with great style in a former school bus garage on the Sterling Highway near the visitor center, the restaurant is a wonder of warm Mediterranean colors, shiny metal, and primitive art—not the sort of place you expect to find in a small town in Alaska. The cuisine brings further surprises: bold flavors and textures, a little Tuscany, and plenty of Homer, too, including lots of local seafood. The centerpiece is a wood-fired Italian brick oven that produces pizza, grilled sandwiches, steaks, and much more. They serve local beers on tap and 30 wines by the glass. Although the restaurant is not oriented to children, my kids love it because of the big pieces of pizza available by the slice (which means adults can eat here inexpensively, too). Note that at peak hours it can take a long time to get a table, and they don't take reservations.

276 Olson Lane. ☎907/235-8488. Reservations not accepted. Lunch $7–$12; dinner main courses $16–$26. MC, V. Daily 11am–10pm.

Fresh Sourdough Express Bakery and Restaurant ★ ☺ CAFE Ebullient Donna and Kevin Maltz's organic eatery is quintessential Homer, starting with its motto: "Food for people and the planet." But there's no New Age dogma here. The Sourdough Express is fun and tasty, even as it grinds its own grain and recycles everything in sight. An inexpensive lunch menu includes many vegetarian choices as well as hearty sandwiches. The evening menu includes many specials, elaborate dishes, including huge portions of local seafood with rich sauces, and, perhaps more remarkably, simple, solid choices, too, for those who don't want to spend a lot. All-you-can-eat crab is served from 3 to 8pm. Families will enjoy the relaxed atmosphere, the big sandbox, and an old van out front where kids can play while you wait for your meal. Stop by on the way to the harbor for a brown-bag lunch for your charter fishing trip. Don't miss dessert from the made-from-scratch bakery.

1316 Ocean Dr. ☎907/235-7571. www.freshsourdoughexpress.com. Breakfast $6–$12; lunch $6.50–$15; dinner main courses $10–$25. DISC, MC, V. High season daily 8am–9pm; low season daily 8am–3pm.

The Homestead ★★★ SEAFOOD The ambience is that of an old-fashioned Alaska roadhouse, in a large log building decorated with contemporary art and lots of summer light. The food is terrific, often sophisticated in preparation, and relies largely on fresh Alaskan fish. What I like best is when this perfect seafood is prepared in a way that emphasizes its qualities in flavor and texture without drawing attention away from the fish itself, and that's what I anticipate without disappointment every time I dine here. The portions are generous, and if you want a big piece of rare prime rib, go no farther. After a day outdoors, it's a warm, exuberant place for dinner, but with polished edges: white table linens, usually with intimate, professional service (although our server was overwhelmed and inattentive on our last visit). The owners work hard to bring new flavors and wines to the Homer community in the off season, and even offer wine classes. The wine list is well selected and arranged—not intimidating; plenty of bottles are in the $21 to $34 range. They also have a full bar with local wine, mead, and beer on tap.

Mile 8.2, East End Rd. ☎907/235-8723. www.homesteadrestaurant.net. Reservations recommended. Main courses $21–$39. AE, MC, V. June–Aug daily 5–10pm; Mar–May and Sept–Dec Wed–Sat 5–9pm. Closed Jan–Feb.

Homer Nightlife

The **Pier One Theatre** (☎907/235-7333; www.pieronetheatre.org) is a strong community theater group housed in a small red building on the spit, between the fishing hole and the small-boat harbor. Instead of the ubiquitous gold-rush melo-drama and Robert Service readings, Pier One often presents serious drama, mu-sicals, and comedy—not just schlock. They also produce dance, classical music, and youth theater events during the summer. There's generally something playing Thursday through Sunday nights in the visitor season. Check the *Homer News* or the website for current listings. They strongly recommend making reservations by phone; a reservation can be changed or canceled if necessary. Tickets may also be available at the door.

The landmark **Salty Dawg Saloon** is a small log cabin on the spit with a lighthouse on top. It's the place to swap fish stories after a day on the wa-ter. Wherever you go to hoist a beer, order a draft from the **Homer Brewing Company** (Red Knot Ale is my favorite).

VALDEZ

Big events have shaped Valdez (Val-*deez*). The deepwater port, at the head of a long, dramatic fjord, first developed with the 1898 Klondike gold rush and an ill-fated attempt to establish an alternative route to the gold fields from here. Later, the port and the Richardson Highway, which connected Valdez to the rest of the state, served a key role in supplying materials during World War II. On Good Friday, March 27, 1964, all of that was erased when North America's greatest recorded earthquake occurred under Miners Lake, west of town off a northern fjord of Prince William Sound. It set off an underwater landslide that caused a huge wave to sweep over the waterfront and kill 32 people. The U.S. Army Corps of Engineers moved the town, rebuilding a drab replacement in a safer location that slowly filled with nondescript modern buildings.

The construction of the trans-Alaska pipeline, completed in 1977, brought a new economic boom to Valdez and enduring economic prosperity as tankers came to fill with the oil. Then, on March 24, 1989, on Good Friday 25 years after the earthquake, the tanker *Exxon Valdez,* on its way south, hit the clearly marked Bligh Reef, causing the largest and most environmentally costly oil spill ever in North America. The spill cleanup added another economic boom. Twenty years later, most wildlife populations have recovered and visible signs of the spill are difficult to find, but the spill's impact on people remains indelible and the marine ecosystem has changed.

Today, Valdez is a middle American town, driven by industry but turning to the vast resources of Prince William Sound for outdoor recreation. Despite a spectacular setting and pleasant waterfront, it isn't the sort of historic or charm-ing fishing village that justifies a trip all by itself. A day is enough to tour the two small museums and take a hike or a river float. Instead, come for the setting—the wildlife, fishing, and sightseeing in the Sound, and the spectacular drive down the Richardson Highway.

Because Valdez lies at the end of a funnel of steep mountains that catches moisture off the ocean, the weather tends to be overcast and rainy in summer and extremely snowy in winter.

Essentials

GETTING THERE **By Car:** The **Richardson Highway** ("The Richardson Highway & Copper Center," in chapter 10) dramatically crosses Thompson Pass and descends into the narrow valley where Valdez lies. Try to do the trip in daylight, in clear weather, and stop at the Worthington Glacier. This is the only road to Valdez. The drive from Anchorage is 6 hours without stops.

By Ferry: The **Alaska Marine Highway System** (☎800/642-0066 or 907/835-4436; www.ferryalaska.com) connects Valdez, Whittier, and Cordova by ferry. One time-tested way to see the Sound is to put your vehicle on the ferry in Whittier for the run to Valdez, then drive north on the Richardson Highway. The fast ferry *Chenega* cuts travel time from Anchorage to Valdez to around the same as driving: about 90 minutes by car from Anchorage to Whittier and 4 hours by ferry from Whittier to Valdez. The current fare is $89 for an adult, half price ages 6 through 11, free 5 and under. A 15-foot car costs $105 to take along.

By Air: Era Aviation (☎800/866-8394; www.flyera.com) flies twice a day each way between Anchorage and Valdez.

GETTING AROUND The main part of the town and boat harbor are compact enough to walk, but you will need wheels for the airport, the attractions on Dayville Road, most of the hiking trails, and the two B&Bs I mention below. Rental cars are available at the airport from **Valdez-U-Drive** (☎907/835-4402; www.valdezudrive.com). Taxis are available from **Valdez Yellow Cab** (☎907/835-2500).

VISITOR INFORMATION The Valdez Convention and Visitors Bureau maintains a **Visitor Information Center** at 104 Chenega St., at the corner of Egan Drive (P.O. Box 1603), Valdez, AK 99686 (☎907/835-4636; www.valdezalaska.org). Pick up the free town map and useful *Vacation Planner*. They're open in summer daily 8am to 7pm and winter Monday through Friday 8am to 5pm.

SPECIAL EVENTS The town has three **summer fishing derbies:** The **Halibut Derby** runs all summer, the **Silver Salmon Derby** is late July to early September, and the **Women's Silver Salmon Derby** is the second Saturday in August. Derby tickets are available all over town.

The **Fireweed Bicycle Race Across Alaska** (www.fireweed400.com) covers big mileage on the Glenn and Richardson highways between Sheep Mountain and Valdez, with 50-, 100-, 200-, and 400-mile events, usually the second weekend in July. Finish line festivities in Valdez include a kids' bike rodeo.

The **Last Frontier Theater Conference** (☎907/834-1614; www.pwscc.edu) brings playwrights, directors, and actors from all over the U.S. for seminars and performances. Performances are staged every night over the 8-day event, and workshops and readings last all day. Those interested in literature and theater will find it worth arranging a trip around the event. In 2010, it is being held May 16 to May 23.

Valdez Gold Rush Days includes 5 days of community events, including a parade and fish fry, at the end of July or beginning of August. Contact the visitor center for information.

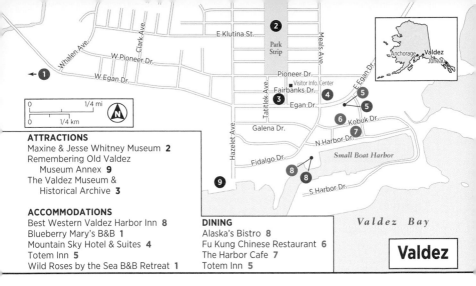

Anchorage • Valdez
Juneau

E Klutina St.

Park Strip

Pioneer Dr.

■ Visitor Info. Center
Fairbanks Dr.

Egan Dr.

Galena Dr.

Kobuk Dr.

N Harbor Dr.

Fidalgo Dr.

Small Boat Harbor

S Harbor Dr.

Whalen Ave. · Clark Ave. · W Pioneer Dr. · W Egan Dr. · Meals Ave. · E Egan Dr. · Tatitlek Ave. · Hazelet Ave.

0   1/4 mi
0   1/4 km

ATTRACTIONS
Maxine & Jesse Whitney Museum **2**
Remembering Old Valdez
   Museum Annex **9**
The Valdez Museum &
   Historical Archive **3**

ACCOMMODATIONS
Best Western Valdez Harbor Inn **8**
Blueberry Mary's B&B **1**
Mountain Sky Hotel & Suites **4**
Totem Inn **5**
Wild Roses by the Sea B&B Retreat **1**

DINING
Alaska's Bistro **8**
Fu Kung Chinese Restaurant **6**
The Harbor Cafe **7**
Totem Inn **5**

Valdez Bay

Valdez

Richardson Highway.

Last Frontier Theater Conference.

[FastFACTS] VALDEZ

Banks Two banks are on Egan Drive, both with ATMs.

Hospital Providence Valdez Medical Center (☎907/835-2249) is at 911 Meals Ave.

Internet Access The comfortable **Valdez Consortium Library**

(☎907/835-4632), at 260 Fairbanks St., has computers and free Wi-Fi, with tables where you can plug in a laptop.

Police For nonemergencies, phone the **Valdez Police Department** (☎907/835-4560) at 212 Chenega Ave.

Post Office Galena Drive and Tatitlek Street, 1 block back from Egan Drive.

Taxes Valdez has no sales tax but does charge a 6% **room tax.**

Getting Outside

The best things to do in Valdez relate to Prince William Sound, so I've put those options first, in order of their interest to most readers.

SIGHTSEEING & WILDLIFE TOURS

For most visitors, a daylong ride on a tour boat into the Sound is likely to be the most memorable part of a visit to Valdez. The main tour-boat company in town is **Stan Stephens Glacier and Wildlife Cruises** (☎866/867-1297 or 907/835-4731; www.stanstephenscruises.com). The office is on the dock at the end of the small boat harbor near the Best Western Valdez Harbor Inn. Stephens has been showing off the Sound and defending it from pollution for decades. After passing through the long fjord of Port Valdez, boats enter an ice-choked bay in front of **Columbia Glacier** on a 6-hour tour that often encounters birds, seals, sea otters, and sea lions, and sometimes whales, for $112 adults. A light lunch is served. Going on to Meares Glacier, farther west, adds 3 hours to the round-trip, but brings you to a glacier you can get a better look at and that may drop ice into the water. That cruise is $147 and includes a hot lunch and a snack. Prices are half for children 2 to 12 on either trip.

SEA KAYAKING & SAILING

Right around Valdez, short sea-kayaking day trips to see wildlife on the Duck Flats may be just what you want for a first try at the sport; but that area is hardly wilderness, as it's also reached by road and is within sight of the oil facilities. Day trips to Shoup or Columbia glaciers get you into more of the beautiful, remote country that makes Prince William Sound so exceptional. **Pangaea Adventures** (☎800/660-9637 or 907/835-8442; www.alaskasummer.com) offers guided sea kayaking from Valdez, or rentals for experienced paddlers, for whom the Sound is a paradise. They also offer multiday guided camping trips deeper into the Sound, or, for those who prefer a bed, lodge, and "mother ship" expeditions, wherein clients paddle by day and stay on board or in a lodge at night. Pangaea offers many other services as well: water-taxi and kayak drop-off, ice climbing and glacier hiking, river rafting and even trips that combine these activities in the Sound and Wrangell–St. Elias National park. Check out the website.

Touring Prince William Sound by boat.

Raven Charters, Slip C-25, Valdez Boat Harbor (☎907/835-5863; www.alaska.net/~ravenchr), is run by a family who shares their home on a substantial 50-foot yawl with clients to sail and explore the Sound. The wind tends to be light and changeable, but a sailboat makes a comfortable base for discovering interesting, isolated places. All-inclusive prices for the whole boat start at $950 per day for up to four passengers, or $800 for a day charter, with discounts for longer trips.

FISHING & BOATING

The ocean waters around Valdez are rich in salmon and halibut. It's possible to fish for salmon from shore. Popular spots include Dayville Road west of the fish hatchery, the city dock near the ferry dock in town, or even the harbor floats. Except at the hatchery, you're hoping a fish swims by your lure or bait at the right moment: There isn't a freshwater destination to concentrate the fish. Chances and the fishing experience are improved if you get out on the water. Many small fishing charter boats are available in the boat harbor, or you can rent your own boat and gear, book either through **Fish Central** (☎888/835-5002 or 907/835-5002; www.fishcentral.net). They can also take care of processing and freezing your catch for shipment.

HIKING & MOUNTAIN-BIKING

Valdez has a broad selection of good day hikes and an overnight. The visitor center can advise you on choices beyond those I list here. In addition, you can join guided hiking and glacier activities, including ice climbing, with Pangaea Adventures (see "Sea Kayaking and Sailing," above).

The easiest hike is a pleasant forest and shore walk to **Dock Point,** starting at the east side of the boat harbor, at the end of North Harbor Drive. It's a peaceful, natural walk close to town, with boardwalks and overlooks and berries along the way in season.

For a longer hike and perhaps an overnight, the **Shoup Glacier Trail** runs 12 miles west from town along the shore of Port Valdez to a lagoon in front of the glacier's face. The going is generally flat, and there are many places to get down to the beach, with wild iris and many other flowers. Cool yourself in a waterfall. Camping is unrestricted, but be sure to bring mosquito repellent and review bear avoidance techniques (see "Outdoors Health & Safety," p. 92). If you plan to go all the way, consider reserving one of the three state parks cabins near the glacier (see "State Parks Cabin Reservations," in "Exploring the Kenai Peninsula & Prince William Sound," earlier in this chapter). Or you can get a lift one-way from a water taxi, such as the service offered by Pangaea Adventures. The trail starts at the end of West Egan Drive.

The **Solomon Gulch Trail** starts across from the fish hatchery on Dayville Road (see below) and goes steeply up to Solomon Lake, where locals swim. Be prepared for bears. Trails off **Mineral Creek Road,** above town off Hanagita Street, are great for walking, mountain-

Bridal Veil Falls.

biking, or berry picking, and in winter there is a fine cross-country skiing trail network. The **Valdez Goat Trail** runs from the spectacular Bridal Veil Falls at mile 13.8 of the Richardson Highway for a distance of 2.5 miles on an abandoned roadbed, past some great views.

RAFTING

Keystone Outfitters and Raft Adventures (☎907/835-2606; www.alaskawhitewater.com) takes five trips a day 4½ miles down the amazing Keystone Canyon, a virtual corridor of rock with a floor of frothing water, past the crashing tumult of the 900-foot Bridal Veil Falls. The whitewater is rated Class III, meaning it is not too wild for most people, but rafting is not without risk—serious mishaps can sometimes occur. They charge $55 per adult, $45 per child. The company also has numerous longer trips, ranging from a day to 10 days, on many of the region's rivers.

HELI-SKIING

Valdez is a magnet for backcountry alpine and extreme skiing and snowboarding thanks to its prodigious snow and limitless steep mountains. A bunch of guide companies offer these trips, operating by helicopter from early March to early May. One established operator is **Valdez Heli-Ski Guides** (☎907/835-4528; www.valdezheliskiguides.com). Expect to pay around $900 for a day of around six runs, or book a package with lodgings and meals.

Exploring the Town

Maxine & Jesse Whitney Museum ★ A couple arriving after World War II spent a lifetime collecting arrowheads, Native crafts, and trophy animal mounts for a roadside museum and rock shop in Fairbanks, then donated everything to the community college in Valdez. As unpromising as that sounds as the basis for a serious museum, the curators here have turned the collection into one of the most evocative exhibits on Alaska anywhere. To do so, they bypassed the usual approach of focusing on the objects—necessitated in part because the Whitneys didn't record the context of the things they collected—instead making a museum about a bygone world, with its old-time roadside rock shop and the tough but warm pioneer culture that surrounded it. Exploring that past is well worth an hour of your visit.

303 Lowe St. **☎907/834-1690.** www.pwscc.edu. $5 adults, $4 seniors and military, $3 ages 5–12, free 4 and under. May to mid-Sept daily 9am–7pm; winter by appointment.

The Solomon Gulch Hatchery When the pink salmon return from late June to early August, they swarm on the hatchery in a blizzard of fish. The hatchery releases more than 200 million pinks and 2 million silvers (or coho) each year. There is no stream for the salmon to return to, so they try to get back into the hatchery, crowding together in a solid sea of fighting muscle. Seals and birds come in to feed, and you can stand on shore and watch (and smell) the spectacle. Surefire fishing is allowed up the shore on Dayville Road. A self-guided tour of the hatchery starts from the parking lot near the Solomon Creek bridge.

On Dayville Rd. on the way to the tanker terminal. **☎907/835-1329.** Free self-guided tour. Summer daily 7am–10pm.

The Valdez Museum and Historical Archive ★★ The museum's primary exhibit is a chronological walk through the area's history from explorers' visits through the oil spill. Objects and photographs bring back some of those moments and places with emotional force, humor, or something like nostalgia—if that's the word to describe longing for a time before one's own birth. Despite its professionalism, the museum has friendly, small-town hospitality and shows items of small-town pride, such as the shiny old fire engines in the lobby, dating back to 1886. An annex, near the ferry dock, is less polished, but shouldn't be missed. It contains the "Remembering Old Valdez" exhibit, a ⅟₂₀-scale model of

Maxine & Jesse Whitney Museum.

"Remembering Old Valdez" exhibit at the Valdez Museum and Historical Archive.

how Valdez looked at its old site, before the 1964 earthquake forced the town to move. Using photographs, records, and old-timers' memories, a dedicated worker brought that lost city back with 400 miniature buildings on tables, such as model train dioramas without the trains. A well-made 37-minute film covers the earthquake's effect on Valdez. The annex is at 436 S. Hazelet Ave. Admission covers both buildings.

217 Egan Dr. ☎**907/835-2764.** www.valdezmuseum.org. $6 adults, $5.50 over age 65, $5 ages 14–17, free for children 13 and under. Memorial Day–Labor Day both buildings daily 9am–5pm. Low season main building Mon–Sat 1–5pm, Sat noon–4pm; annex by appointment.

Where to Stay

The hotels listed here are near the boat harbor and museums, so you may not need a car if you stay there. For the B&Bs you probably will want transportation, as the walk is long.

Best Western Valdez Harbor Inn ★★ This up-to-date hotel commands the best location in town, right on the harbor near the tour boats, although a minority of rooms have good water views. The rooms are decorated in bold colors, with dark blue carpet and wallpaper borders, and with wildlife photography on the walls. They're well equipped, with flatscreen TVs and DVD players and setups to make snacks. Business-class rooms have wired DSL connections and king-size beds. Bathrooms are tiled, and everything is clean and trim. The lobby brings in lots of light from a grassy area by the harbor entrance that's a nice spot to sit and watch boats pass by. There's a welcoming breakfast area, too. Overall, this is the town's most appealing hotel. A good restaurant on-site, Alaska Bistro, is described below.

100 N. Harbor Dr. (P.O. Box 468), Valdez, AK 99686. ☎**888/222-3440** or 907/835-3434. Fax 907/835-2308. www.valdezharborinn.com. 88 units. High season $159–$169 double; low season $99–$109 double. Additional person age 12 or older $15. Rates include continental breakfast. AE, DISC, MC, V. **Amenities:** Restaurant; exercise room. *In room:* TV/DVD, fridge, hairdryer, microwave, Wi-Fi.

Blueberry Mary's Bed and Breakfast ★ 🏷 A lucky few get to sleep under Mary Mehlberg's handmade quilts on her feather beds, gaze at the ocean views, bake in the sauna, and breakfast on her blueberry waffles made from wild berries that grow just outside the house. The two rooms divide off a common room for guests, which is an entrance separate from the family's. The Mehlbergs are friendly, interesting people, and their house on the water's edge, in the woods west of town, feels very Alaskan. The ocean view is mesmerizing. Mary only takes parties of two or fewer and sometimes closes for breaks. Those who do stay here get a good deal on immaculate, handcrafted rooms at a lovely spot.

810 Blueberry Hill Rd., off W. Egan Dr. (P.O. Box 1244), Valdez, AK 99686. ☎907/835-5015. 2 units. $110–$125 double (not including tax). Rates include full breakfast. No credit cards. Closed Sept 15–June 1. **Amenities:** Sauna. *In room:* TV/VCR, fridge, hair dryer, microwave.

Mountain Sky Hotel and Suites ★ Stay here for good standard rooms with few compromises. Service is good and common areas spacious. There's a small pool and the lobby has a handy breakfast area. Rooms are decorated in burgundy, hunter green, and dark wood, with lots of extras, large TVs, and mirrors. Our family of six fit nicely in a family suite, which has a large main bedroom and a separate children's room with bunk beds with its own TV. Ask about many discounts you may qualify for below the rack rates.

100 Meals Ave., Valdez, AK 99686. ☎800/478-4445 or 907/835-4445. Fax 907/835-2437. www. mountainskyhotelsuite.com. 102 units. High season $179 double, $199 suite; low season $99 all units. AE, DISC, DC, MC, V. **Amenities:** Exercise room; Internet station in lobby; indoor pool; spa. *In room:* TV/VCR, fridge, hair dryer, microwave, Wi-Fi.

Totem Inn ★ 🏷 Although the street view of these brown buildings suggests a dated motel, many of the rooms inside have all the qualities of a good modern hotel, including units entered from a breezeway with two queen beds, flatscreen TVs, and many amenities. Reasonably priced suites in a newer two-story building have full kitchens and clothes washers in the unit. The cottages are on the rough side.

The restaurant, where guests check in, is Valdez's primary local hang-out, a traditional small-town diner with a TV always turned on. The food is plentiful, the hours long, and the coffee cups never empty.

114 E. Egan Dr. (P.O. Box 648), Valdez, AK 99686. ☎888/808-4431 or 907/835-4443. Fax 907/834-4426. www.toteminn.com. 69 units. High season $129 double, $169 suite; low season $80 double, $149 suite. AE, DISC, MC, V. **Amenities:** Restaurant; bar. *In room:* TV/DVD, fridge, microwave, Wi-Fi.

Wild Roses by the Sea B&B Retreat ★ Light pours from bay windows that overlook the water and surrounding woods into large, elegantly appointed rooms with high ceilings, decorated with Asian and contemporary art, and finished in light colors, wood floors, and Berber-style carpets. Best of all is the spacious and private "Ocean View Guesthouse," a downstairs suite with a kitchen and living room. The hostess, Rose Fong, prepares elaborate breakfasts in the summer and feeds guests snacks and beverages all day. The location is half a mile from the Shoup Glacier Trail (see above) and less than a mile from a state park beach.

629 Fiddlehead Lane (P.O. Box 3396), Valdez, AK 99686. ☎907/835-2930. www.alaska bytheseabnb.com. 3 units. Summer $134–$177 double, including full breakfast; winter $79 double, including continental breakfast. Extra adult $20, child $15. MC, V. *In room:* TV, hair dryer.

CAMPING

The **Sea Otter RV Park,** P.O. Box 947, Valdez, AK 99686 (☎**907/835-2787**), sits on the outside of the boat harbor breakwater, a mosquito-free spot with views and beachfront where you can fish for salmon or watch the harbor otters. The RV park has a laundry and other facilities, and charges $30 for full hookups.

The best campground in the area is the state's **Blueberry Lake Campground,** 24 miles out of town on the Richardson Highway, just below Thompson Pass. The campground is above the tree line, with mountaintop views and access to limitless alpine hiking. It can be windy and cold. The small lake is stocked with trout. Fifteen well-screened sites are $12 on a self-serve system. There are pit toilets. RVs are welcome, but there are no hookups.

Where to Dine

Alaska's Bistro ★ MEDITERRANEAN A harborside dining room with big windows and an odd, light blue color scheme creates the setting for a small-town restaurant with fine dining aspirations. The menu includes lots of local seafood prepared in Northern Italian and similar styles; the chicken, pork, and beef also get Continental treatment, although you can also get a simple grilled steak. The pizza is European, too, with toppings such as pesto, sun-dried tomatoes, and feta cheese. Overall, the restaurant can be great, but can also be inconsistent. They have a full bar.

102 N. Harbor Dr. ☎**907/835-5688.** Reservations recommended. Lunch $9–$15; dinner $10–$30. AE, MC, V. Daily 6–10:30am, 11:30am–2:30pm, and 5–10pm.

Fu Kung Chinese Restaurant ★ CHINESE This long-established family restaurant near the harbor serves some of the best meals in town; in Valdez, that's not a huge claim to fame, but this place is good. The interior is clean and pleasant, with a fish tank, warm colors, and plenty of room. The food is plentiful and tasty, especially the gingery bean curd with vegetables, the hot and sour soup, and the kung pao chicken. They feature local seafood in Chinese dishes and serve some Thai and sushi selections, too. Service is fast and attentive. In winter, they often close earlier than the hours listed below.

207 Kobuk Dr. (1 block from the boat harbor). ☎**907/835-5255.** Lunch $9–$11; dinner main courses $12–$16. AE, DISC, MC, V. Daily 11am–11pm.

The Harbor Cafe ★ 🍴 The restaurant seems to be trying to pass itself off as a boat-harbor burger joint, with picnic tables outside a boothlike building. The first clue it is something more is the line of relatively mature diners ordering at the window. Choices include burgers, brats, and sandwiches, but also items such as the Caesar salad with blackened shrimp and scallops that I got—a masterpiece of spicy roughness offset by creamy crispness. Friends say the food is always amazing. It's the work of a Peruvian owner, who makes the meals look as well as taste wonderful. (My unique beverage was also fantastic: lemon-ginger juice mixed with a little Sprite.) In the evening and during the colder months, meals are served in a tiny dining room with just a few tables, where a recent menu listed just four entrees, all more than $30—steak, salmon, crab, or halibut, the last of which had a choice of three interesting marinades and sauces.

225 N. Harbor Dr. ☎**907/835-4776.** Lunch $7–$15; dinner $30–$56. MC, V. High season Mon–Sat 11am–8pm, Sun 11am–3pm; low season Tues–Sat 11am–7pm.

CORDOVA: HIDDEN TREASURE

The first time I ever went to Cordova, my companion and I arrived at the Mudhole Smith Airport in a small plane and happened upon an old guy with a pickup truck who offered to let us ride in back with some boards the 10 miles to town. The highway led out onto a broad, wetland plain—among the largest contiguous wetlands in the Western Hemisphere, as it happens. Our guide's voice, studded with profanity, boomed through the back window as he told us proudly about the diversity of the wildlife to be found out there. Then, absolutely bursting with enthusiasm, he leaned on the horn and bellowed, "Look at them f---ing swans!" We looked; trumpeters paddling in the marsh looked back. He would have invited them along to the bar, too, if he'd known how.

Every time I've been to Cordova since, I've been taken under the wings of new friends. Although they usually don't express themselves the same way that first gentleman did, they are just as enthusiastic to show off the amazing natural riches of their little kingdom. Tourists are still something of a novelty here, for Cordova isn't just off the beaten track—it's not on any track at all. There's no road to the rest of the world, and the town is an afterthought on the ferry system. Boosters call their town "Alaska's Hidden Treasure." For once, they're right.

Our family has had some of our happiest times in Cordova, visiting the Childs Glacier and seeing the swans and geese on the delta; hiking into the mountains behind town; boating on the Sound to meet the sea otters, sea lions, eagles, and spawning salmon; hiking and canoeing at a remote lake cabin—and meeting no other people at all. In town, we made new friends whenever we turned around and received hearty greetings from old friends from previous visits. Leaving on the ferry for Valdez, I've watched Cordova shrinking behind us with a wistful hope that it would never change.

So far, I've gotten my wish. You can feel a bit like an anthropologist discovering a tribe lost to time, for Cordova has the qualities small towns are supposed to have had but lost long ago in America. Walking down First Street, you pass an old-fashioned independent grocery store and drug store, the fishermen's union hall, and a gift shop run by the same family since 1909—no chains or franchises. My children thought the street looked like a movie set. The best part of their week was the novel freedom to roam and shop on their own. It was clearly safe. People leave their keys in the car and their doors unlocked at night. When a friend of mine bought one of the quaint, moss-roofed hillside houses years ago, he didn't receive a key—the simple reason was that the front door didn't have a lock.

Cordova owes much of its uniqueness to a rich history and remote location. Its biggest political controversy—simmering for 70 years—concerns whether to build a road to the outside world. The town's heyday was in 1911, when the Copper River and Northwestern Railroad opened, carrying copper ore down from the mine at Kennecott; it hit a low when the mine closed in 1938. Since then, boosters have been trying to get a road built on the old rail line, north along the Copper River to Chitina (that fascinating area is covered in chapter 10, under "Wrangell–St. Elias National Park & Kennecott"). The road builders have made it only about 50 miles out of town so far. From Cordova, the **Copper River Highway** provides access to the best bird-watching and, in my judgment, the most impressive glacier in Alaska, as well as trails and magnificent vistas and areas to see wildlife. In town, the small-boat harbor is a doorway to Prince William Sound.

Essentials

GETTING THERE By Ferry: Cordova is served by ferry from Valdez and Whittier by the **Alaska Marine Highway System** (☎800/642-0066 or 907/424-7333 local dock; www.ferryalaska.com). It's a spectacular ride aboard the fast ferry *Chenega*. The passenger fare from Valdez is $50, from Whittier $89; children 5 to 11 pay half. Taking a vehicle under 15 feet one-way from Valdez to Cordova is $94, Whittier $105. You can also rent a car in Cordova. See "Exploring Southeast Alaska," in chapter 6, for information about the ferry system.

By Air: Alaska Airlines (☎800/426-0333; www.alaskaair.com) flies daily each direction, from Anchorage to the west and Yakutat, Juneau, and Seattle to the southeast, with more flights from Anchorage operated by **Era Aviation** (☎800/866-8394; www.flyera.com).

GETTING AROUND You can easily walk around downtown Cordova, but that's not where the most interesting sights are. To get out on the Copper River Highway, you'll need a car, bus, or, if you're vigorous, a bike. Cars are for rent from **Chinook Auto Rentals** (☎877/424-5279 or 907/424-5279) at Northern Nights Inn (p. 449). Taxis are available from **Cordova Taxi** (☎907/424-5151).

Water taxis and rental of bikes, kayaks, skiffs, canoes, and fishing and camping gear are available at **Cordova Coastal Outfitters,** south of the boat harbor near the Alaska Commercial grocery store (☎800/357-5145 or 907/424-7424; www.cordovacoastal.com). They also offer drop-off and pick-up service on the Copper River Highway, allowing visitors to go for a canoeing or cabin trip without renting a car. They're described in full below.

Copper River Delta Wetlands.

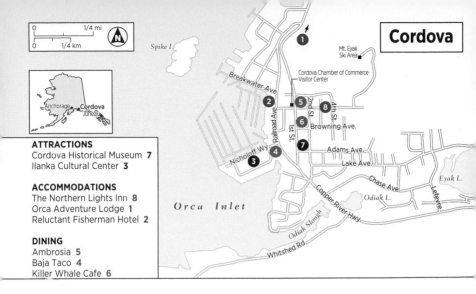

To get to remote cabins and fishing, try **Fishing & Flying (☎907/424-3325)**, operated by Gayle Ranney, a warm and authentic Alaskan bush pilot. She has a choice of planes to get where you want to go and relationships with some other great businesses, including a lighthouse that's for rent in one of the most spectacular, rugged, and out-of-the-way spots in Alaska.

VISITOR INFORMATION The **Cordova Chamber of Commerce Visitor Center** (☎907/424-7260; www.cordovachamber.com) is at 404 First St., north of Council Avenue (P.O. Box 99, Cordova, AK 99574). They're open Monday through Friday 9am to 5pm, with occasional Saturday hours.

The **Cordova Ranger District** of the Chugach National Forest, upstairs in the old white courthouse at 2nd Street and Browning (P.O. Box 280), Cordova, AK 99574 (☎907/424-7661; www.fs.fed.us/r10/chugach), has displays and provides maps and guide information that's indispensable for planning outdoor activities. The staff will sit down and help you figure out what you want to do.

SPECIAL EVENTS The **Cordova Ice Worm Festival,** February 4 to 6, 2010, is a winter carnival culminating in the appearance of the big ice worm—or, to be precise, ice centipede—in a parade. The **Copper River Delta Shorebird Festival,** May 6 to 9, 2010, revolves around the coming of dizzying swarms of millions of shorebirds that use the delta and beaches near the town as a migratory stopover. The whole community gets involved to host bird-watchers and put on a full schedule of educational and outdoor activities that lasts 3 days. **Copper River Wild! Salmon Festival,** July 9 to 11, 2010, includes a marathon and a music festival. For details on any of these happenings, contact the Cordova Chamber of Commerce, or check their website, listed above under "Visitor Information."

[FastFACTS] CORDOVA

Banks There are two banks on 1st Street, with **ATMs.**

Hospital Cordova Community Medical Center and **Ilanka Community Health Center** are located together on Chase Street (**☏907/424-8000**), off the Copper River Highway near the Odiak Slough.

Internet Access Find it at the **Cordova Public Library** (**☏907/424-6667**) and at **Orca Book and Sound** (**☏907/424-5305**), both on 1st Street.

Police For nonemergency business, call **☏907/424-6100.**

Post Office At Railroad Avenue and Council.

Taxes Sales tax is 6%; rooms and car rentals carry an additional 6% tax.

Exploring the Town & Hiking Near Town

ATTRACTIONS Cordova is mostly for outdoor activities (covered below), but save some time to wander around town, make discoveries, and meet people. The **Cordova Historical Museum,** 622 1st St. (**☏907/424-6665;** www. cordovamuseum.org), mostly in one room, does a good job of presenting some valuable artifacts reflecting Cordova's eventful past, a collection of classic Alaskan art, and some odd and fascinating stuff. There's a historic lighthouse lens, a Linotype machine, the interior of a fishing boat, a parka made of bear gut, basketry, and photographs of fishing and historic scenes. Our entire family enjoyed it. The museum is open summer Monday through Saturday from 10am to 6pm, Sunday from 1 to 5pm; winter Tuesday through Friday from 10am to 5pm, Saturday from 1 to 5pm. Recommended donation is $1.

Cordova is a center for the Eyak, a small but linguistically and ethnographically distinct people. Make a point of stopping in at the Native Village of Eyak's **Ilanka Cultural Center,** 110 Nicholoff Way, across from the Fishermen's Memorial at the small boat harbor (**☏907/424-7903;** www. ilankacenter.org). Although small, the center is new and growing, and I always experience a warm link with the Eyak people I meet. The collection includes Eyak, Alutiiq, Tlingit, and Ahtna artifacts, photographs, and oral histories. There is also a fully reconstructed orca whale skeleton. A disturbing and powerful totem pole by Mike Webber, in the Native tradition of the "shame pole," reflects Cordova's still-raw anger and grief over the *Exxon Valdez* oil spill. The gallery sells art, books, and other items made in Alaska, especially by Alaska Natives. Artists sometimes offer classes and demonstrations. Hours are summer Tuesday through Saturday 10am to 5pm. Admission is free, but donations are encouraged.

HIKING Cordova has more good hiking trails per capita than any place I know. The Cordova Ranger Station can provide you with a free trail-guide booklet with lots of ideas and maps. There are three hikes close to town and more on the Copper River Delta, covered below in the section on the Delta, and at Hartney Bay (ask at the ranger station).

The **Tripod Mountain Trail** begins right from town and climbs 1,255 feet over less than a mile up the first mountain back from the shore, a half-day hike with views that present the Sound and Cordova like a map below you. The trail begins at the foot of the town ski lift, on 6th Street—take Browning up the hill.

Partway up Tripod Mountain, near the middle drop-off of the ski lift, a 1-mile trail links to the **Crater Lake Trail,** which eventually joins the **Power Creek Trail** on a loop of 12 miles. An easier start for that route is the Power Creek Road—drive it along the north side of Eyak Lake to the end, 7 miles from town. The creek has spawning red salmon in July and attracts a lot of bears; watch, but don't get out of your car if you come upon one. The trail follows the creek through dramatic scenery 4.3 miles to the Power Creek Forest Service cabin, with a great view (reserve through the system described on p. 360).

The Copper River Delta

The delta and its star attraction, the **Childs Glacier,** make an unforgettable day trip by car or tour bus from Cordova, but if you have a couple of days, you can do much more. The backwaters, sloughs, and ponds beg to be explored by canoe. Bird-watchers will especially enjoy paddling here and visiting the boardwalks and blinds set up by the Forest Service. You can raft the rivers. There are excellent hiking trails and mountain-biking routes branching from the road, and Forest Service cabins to stay in. And the river itself has many miles of deserted sandy beaches for long walks or sand castles on a sunny day.

The delta seems to go on forever, a vast patchwork of marsh, pond, small hills of trees, and the huge, implacable gray river itself. The glacial silt it carries away—some 2 million tons a day—has built this 700,000-acre wetland. A well-maintained gravel road leads across it, all in Chugach National Forest, and the rangers have done a good job of providing ways and places to enjoy and learn about

Million Dollar Bridge.

the area. The road itself is the old bed of the Copper River and Northwestern Railroad. It leads 48 miles to the **Million Dollar Bridge.** Built by Michael Heney, a magician of a 19th-century railroad builder who also constructed the White Pass and Yukon Route in Skagway, the 200-mile Copper River line was an engineering triumph that brought the mind-boggling wealth of the Kennecott Copper Corporation to ships in Cordova (read more about the mine in "Wrangell–St. Elias National Park & Kennecott," in chapter 10). The bridge over the Copper River was built in a race against time between two surging glaciers in 30-foot-deep, fast-flowing glacial water, during winter. It stood for 50 years, until the 1964 earthquake knocked down one end of one of the spans, driving it into the riverbed. In 2004 your highway dollars repaired that span and once again you can drive to the other side, where an unmaintained road soon peters out into a rough trail.

GETTING THERE

BY CAR Driving gives you the most freedom. The Copper River Highway is gravel, but it's wide and level. If you've brought a rental car and your contract does not allow driving on gravel, I recommend parking in Cordova and renting a car there for the drive on the Copper River Highway. The Northern Nights Inn (p. 449) offers rentals. Beyond the Million Dollar Bridge, the road becomes a rough four-wheel-drive track, and if you get stuck you'll be there for a long time. Check at the Forest Service Cordova Ranger Station for the latest news about the road and pick up their road guide.

BY BIKE Mountain-biking the highway is the adventurous way to travel, camping or staying in a Forest Service cabin on the way. The drawbacks are the distances, the delta's strong winds, and a lot of road dust. Of course, you don't have to ride all the way to see lots of birds and wildlife, and there are good mountain biking routes on the delta away from the road. The 3-mile **Saddlebag Glacier Trail,** at mile 25 of the Copper River Highway, leads to a vista of a glacial lake surrounded by rocky peaks. Bikes are for rent from Cordova Coastal Outfitters (see "Out on Prince William Sound," below) for $18 a day.

ALONG THE ROAD

Keep your eyes scanning the wetlands and mountains around you as you drive out the road. The **wildlife** you may see along the way includes black and brown bears, wolves, coyote, moose, and mountain goats. The entire world population of dusky Canada geese nests on the delta, and you're likely to see eagles and trumpeter swans without really looking. The ranger station provides a wildlife-viewing guide, and there are several places to stop along the way designed for bird-watching. The first is a platform with interpretive signs as you leave town, an introduction to the delta; this stretch of the road is fine for bird-watching.

Don't skip the **Alaganik Slough Boardwalk.** Take the 3¼-mile spur road to the right 17 miles out the Copper River Highway; it's marked. The sky here is big and certain, while the land is ambivalent—it doesn't know if it wants to be waving grass of green and gold or shallow, shimmering ponds and tendrils of water. The road leads to the start of the 1,000-foot boardwalk with a blind to a riverside path. Water reflects the sun and the colors of the marsh. We were speechless one evening at sunset, even in the complete absence of birds. Often in the summer you can see breeding trumpeter swans, ducks, and grebes, and in the spring and fall migrating waterfowl and shorebirds make appearances. The path is on the left just before you arrive at the boardwalk and picnic area; the 1-mile Fisherman's Trail is a meandering route among water and brush.

You can stop at any of the bridges crossing the Copper River for a romp in the sand. The river beaches of fine sand extend practically forever.

The highway ends with the area's best attraction, the advancing **Childs Glacier.** This is the most amazing glacier I've ever seen, and no one seems to know about it outside Cordova. The advancing wall of ice, 300 feet tall, comes right down to the quarter-mile-wide river, battling the flowing water for control of the land here. The glacier tries to divert the river while the river tries to cut the glacier like a knife, eroding the base and bringing down huge ice chunks. As you sit on the opposite bank, the glacier on the opposite side is too large to see—it completely fills your field of vision, creating an eerie and hypnotic sense of scale. On a warm summer day, you can feel the glacier's thunder as the ice shifts, and see pieces fall off. A chunk the size of a car barely registers, but when an office building–size hunk falls, there's a roar and gray breakers radiate out across the river. Falling glacier pieces have made waves large enough to uproot trees here, not to mention hurl a few fish around—at the Forest Service viewing and picnic area across the river, salmon have been found high up in the trees and boulders in odd places. Several years ago, such a wave injured some visitors, and now the Forest Service warns that anyone who can't run fast should stay in the observation tower. A path leads less than a mile to the **Million Dollar Bridge,** or drive by on your way out.

The Forest Service maintains a camping and picnic area at the glacier, with RV and tent sites, restrooms, and sheltered tables. RV sites are $25 a night, walk-in tent sites $10, at a self-pay station. Three hand-pump wells produce drinking water.

ACTIVITIES

CANOEING The delta's canoe routes are little used, leading to remote places where birds and aquatic animals rule. You can launch on Alaganik Slough at a picnic area at mile 22 on the Copper River Highway, paddling placid waters into stunningly beautiful marshlands, perhaps headed for the Tiedeman Forest Service Cabin for a few days. Taking the "Wrong Way" route that starts a couple of miles up the road, you can float several miles of challenging water down to McKinley Lake, stay at the Forest Service cabin, then float downstream again to the slough launch, back at the road. It's ideal overnight, or you could do it in a day, or, as we did, spend an extra day and night at the cabin. The couple who runs **Cordova Coastal Outfitters** (see below, under "Out on Prince William Sound") rents canoes for $50 a day (additional days discounted 15%), offers drop-off, and will help you decide what route to take. You can ride out on one of their bicycles and pick up the canoe at the launch site. They rent camping gear, too. Make sure to get their advice on current conditions before setting out on the water.

FISHING Anglers can fish the delta's lakes and streams for all species of Pacific salmon except kings (which you can fish in salt water), as well as Dolly Varden char and rainbow and cutthroat trout. The Cordova Ranger Station can offer guidance, or contact the Cordova office of the **Alaska Department of Fish and Game** (☎907/424-3212; www.alaska.gov/adfg, click "Sport Fish" then the Southcentral region, then "Prince William Sound Area"). See "Fishing" in chapter 3 for general guidance.

Alaganik Slough Boardwalk.

HIKING The Forest Service maintains several trails on the delta. The **Alaganik Slough Boardwalk** and **Saddlebag Glacier Trail** are mentioned on p. 446. The Copper River beaches make for sublime off-trail hikes.

The **Haystack Trail,** starting on the right just past the mile 19 marker on the highway, climbs through mossy rainforest from the delta's floor onto an odd little hill. The glaciers that once covered the delta spared this bedrock outcropping. The trail is steep in places but only three-quarters of a mile in length, and it leads to an overlook.

The **McKinley Lake Trail,** at mile 21.6 on the highway, leads 2.5 miles through rainforest vegetation to a lake bearing trout (although we got no bites), and a little farther to the overgrown ruins of a gold mine. You can also get there by canoe (see above). There are two Forest Service cabins on the trail, the small McKinley Trail Cabin, near the highway, and the McKinley Lake Cabin, beautifully situated among big trees above the lake. Each costs $35 a night and can be reserved through the national system described on p. 360. You can also join a guided glacier hike or ice climb with Alaska River Expeditions (see "Rafting," directly below).

RAFTING The immense quantity of water draining the Wrangell–St. Elias Mountains through the Copper River Delta, and the Copper River Highway that provides river access, make this a perfect venue for rafting. **Alaska River Expeditions** (℄800/776-1864 or 907/424-7238; www.alaskarafters.com) is well regarded by locals. Their diverse territory means they can offer quite a range of trips, from easy floating to white water, or even rafting right in front of the Childs Glacier. Trips range in duration from half- to multiday. A 4½-hour trip is $85 adults, $65 ages 6 to 12; all day, with flightseeing, $350. They guide glacier hikes, ice climbing, and biking, too.

Out on Prince William Sound

The waters of Prince William Sound around Cordova, although lacking the tidewater glaciers found in the western Sound, are protected and rich in marine life. Sea otters don't receive a second glance from locals, congregating in rafts of many dozens or even hundreds. Sea lions can be found predictably, too, and orcas and humpback whales are not out of the ordinary. Bird-watchers can expect harlequin ducks and many other marine birds.

Cordova Coastal Outfitters is a good place to start for any outdoor activities (☎800/357-5145 or 907/424-7424; www.cordovacoastal.com). Andy Craig and Seawan Gehlbach know the equipment, the skills, and the area, and they convey that knowledge with casual enthusiasm. Their office is south of the boat harbor, between the Alaska Commercial grocery store and Baja Taco. They guide sea kayaking, rent kayaks, and offer water-taxi drop-off for kayakers. The **guided sea-kayaking trip** for beginners lasts 4 hours and costs $75, concentrating on wildlife sightings; a 7-hour guided trip is $125, including lunch. An advantage of planning your kayaking here is that there is plenty to see near the harbor and not much boat traffic. If your group isn't up to kayaking, consider renting a motorboat. You won't believe the sense of freedom you feel clearing the harbor breakwater to explore Orca Inlet and the bays of Hawkins Island, on the far side. Boats rent for $150 to $225 a day; fishing gear is extra.

A few vessels are available for fishing charters or day trips to see whales and other wildlife. The chamber of commerce (p. 443) has links to charter operators on its website, or call them for a referral.

Where to Stay

The Northern Nights Inn ★ 🍴 Our family spent a week here, and the visit was supremely relaxing and pleasant, both because of the wonderful hospitality and a big apartment-style room that fit our six perfectly. Cordova is so safe the kids were able to walk out the front door and explore on their own—they couldn't believe it. Each room has been lovingly renovated, with antiques, reproductions, and quilts. They're generally spacious, some have views, and all are loaded with amenities—an almost unreal value. All but one has a full kitchen, and cereal is provided for breakfast. The inn is Becky Chapek and Bill Myers's historic 1906 house, a couple of blocks above the town's main street. Becky loves to talk and share her enthusiasm for Cordova, and you couldn't start with a better person for figuring out what you want to do. She also rents older model vehicles that are okay to drive on the Copper River Highway out to Childs Glacier.

500 3rd St (P.O. Box 1564), Cordova, AK 99574. ☎907/424-5356. Fax 907/424 3291. www. northernnightsinn.com. 5 units. $105–$110 double. Extra adult $20. Children 15 and under stay free in parent's room. AE, DISC, MC, V. **Amenities:** Babysitting; free bike loan. *In room:* TV/VCR, fridge, hair dryer, microwave, Wi-Fi.

Orca Adventure Lodge ★ A picturesque old cannery north of town was renovated into simple guest rooms with private bathrooms (no phones or TVs, however) while retaining the exterior and muscular ambience that made it attractive in the first place. But it's the location and the things you can do here that make the place: on a gravel beach with a dock where sea kayaks, fishing boats, and floatplanes pick up guests, and where thousands of pink salmon spawn in a small creek. In the late winter, helicopters land on the grounds to carry guests to ski in the vast and trackless Chugach Mountains. Guests can use the place as a hotel, paying the regular nightly rates listed below, or come with a package, which includes all meals and outdoor equipment, such as kayaks, bikes, and fishing poles (guiding is extra), for $155 per person per day.

2500 Orca Rd. (P.O. Box 2105), Cordova, AK 99574. ☏866/424-ORCA (424-6722) or 907/424-7249. www.orcaadventurelodge.com. 40 units. Summer $140 double, $175 suite; winter $95 double, $125 suite. **Amenities:** Restaurant.

Reluctant Fisherman Inn ★★ This is where most visitors will stay, the town's main hotel. A commercial fishing family with three generations of history in Cordova bought the failed business and poured money and effort into reviving the place. The sale of Greg Meyer and Sylvia Lange's fishing assets became a new roof, snow white comforters in all the rooms, a sun deck over the harbor, and much else. Their children help staff the desk and make the hotel friendly and homey. The location certainly justifies the effort, with its riveting view at the heart of the town. The rooms have the look and amenities of a good mid-range hotel. The hotel's restaurant serves decent meals, but Sylvia admits it's not the inn's highlight. A continental breakfast is provided to guests in the lobby.

407 Railroad Ave. (P.O. Box 150), Cordova, AK 99574. ☏907/424-3272. Fax 907/424-7465. www.reluctantfisherman.com. 40 units. High season $120–$165 double, $165–$330 suite; low season $85–$120 double, $160 suite. Additional adult in room $10. Children 17 and under free. Rates include continent breakfast. AE, MC, V. **Amenities:** Restaurant; bar; airport shuttle ($10); fish cleaning station; fish freezing; Internet station. *In room:* TV w/HBO, Wi-Fi.

CAMPING

Alaska River Expeditions (☏800/776-1864 or 907/424-7238; www.alaska rafters.com) offers a campground with 20 sites, some with hookups, at mile 12.5 of the Copper River Highway. It has pit toilets and there's an office to check in. A Forest Service campground is located way out of town, at Childs Glacier (p. 447).

Where to Dine

Some of Cordova's best meals—breakfast, lunch, or dinner—come from **Baja Taco** (☏907/424-5599), near the south end of the boat harbor. The kitchen and espresso machine are in an old bus, with a window for ordering, and there are comfortable indoor and outdoor seating areas for diners, with free Wi-Fi. The salmon tacos are exceptional, and all the meals are tasty and generous. The restaurant serves wine and both Alaskan and Mexican beer. It's open April through September.

Ambrosia, 410 1st St. (☏907/424-7175), is a solid standby, a well-run family restaurant in a light storefront with an extensive menu, including pizza. It's the kind of place that stays in business in a small town: The food is reliable, the portions large, and the service friendly and helpful. My children became addicted to the gooey fettuccine alfredo with chicken. The restaurant serves beer and wine. Prices range from $10 to $21. Hours are daily 11:30am to 10pm.

The primary small-town eat-and-meet place is the vegetarian-friendly **Killer Whale Cafe** (☏907/424-7733), on 1st Street. All-day breakfast includes a selection of omelets and other ways of having eggs, and for lunch there are sandwiches in the $8 to $11 range, including salmon and halibut, burgers, and the like. Besides the expected, the cafe serves salmon cakes, biscuits and gravy, smoothies, milkshakes, and espresso. Hours are daily 6:30am to 3pm.

THE DENALI NATIONAL PARK REGION

9

Denali (Den-*al*-ee) stands alone among the national parks: It gives regular people easy access to real wilderness, with sweeping tundra vistas, abundant wildlife, and North America's tallest mountain. Other wilderness areas in Alaska may have equally inspiring scenery and even more animals, but Denali is unique because of its accessibility to visitors—and because that accessibility hasn't spoiled the natural experience, as it has at so many other parks.

It's a sad truth that even the largest national parks in the Lower 48 are too small to comprise complete ecosystems. The dream of leaving nature undisturbed is essentially lost in those places, and only through human intervention do the natural systems within the parks stay as close to their primeval state as they do (this is demonstrated by the efforts of Yellowstone rangers to drive bison back within park boundaries so they won't come to harm outside). Millions of cars driving through the parks further interfere with nature. At Rocky Mountain National Park, there's a crossing guard for bighorn sheep. Yosemite Valley and Grand Canyon Village can be choked with cars in summer, yet attempts to get rid of the cars have so far been thwarted.

On the other end of the spectrum, Alaska has many parks with immense, intact ecosystems that have remained unchanged, still existing as they did before the first white contact. More than two-thirds of America's national park acreage is in Alaska, taking in inconceivably huge swaths of land without roads, buildings, or landing strips. They're natural, all right, but almost no one goes there. Some of these parks receive a few hundred visitors a year—only the indigenous people of the surrounding villages and the hardiest and wealthiest outdoors people. Just chartering a plane to get to some of these places can cost as much as most people spend on their entire vacations. With so many people on the Earth, wilderness survives only when it's rationed somehow. In most of Alaska, the rationing system is simply the expense and difficulty of getting to the wilds.

At Denali, on the other hand, you can see the heart of the park for little more than it would cost for you to visit Yellowstone. And when you get there, it's a pristine natural environment where truly wild animals live in a nearly complete ecosystem without much human interference. A single National Park Service decision makes this possible: The only road through the park is closed to the public. This means that to get into the park, you must ride a bus over a dusty gravel road hour after hour, but it also means that the animals are still there to watch and their behavior remains essentially normal. From the window of the bus, you're likely to see grizzly bears doing what they would be doing even if you weren't there. It may be the only $30 safari in the world.

What's even more unique is that you can get off the bus pretty much whenever you want to, walk across the tundra, out of sight of the road, and be alone in

PREVIOUS PAGE: **Caribou in Denali National Park.**

Dall sheep along the park's bus route.

this wilderness. Unfortunately, many Denali visitors never take the opportunity, which normally would cost a lot of money or require a lot of muscle and outdoor skill. Being alone under the big sky makes many people nervous. But that's the essence of Alaska—learning, deep down, how big creation is and how small you are, one more mammal on the tundra under the broad sky. At Denali, you can experience that wonder, and then, when you're ready to return to civilization, you can just walk to the road and catch the next bus—they come every half-hour.

The Denali experience spreads beyond the park. After all, the park boundary is an artificial line—the wildlife and the scenery of the Alaska Range don't observe its significance. To the east, the **Denali Highway** runs through the same extraordinary terrain, with opportunities for hiking over the tundra and canoeing on the lakes managed by the Bureau of Land Management. To the south, **Denali State Park** and the town of **Talkeetna** provide another vantage on Mount McKinley, with the advantage of salmon fishing in the rivers. The construction of comfortable new lodges and a variety of good outdoor guides have helped make Talkeetna a popular alternative gateway to Denali. Even though it's 150 miles from the park entrance by car, Talkeetna is physically closer to the mountain than is the park headquarters.

Visitors often skip the area's other attractions, however, and focus on **Mount McKinley,** which, at 20,320 feet, is the tallest mountain in North America. It is an impressive peak, but you don't need to go to the park to see it—in fact, most people who do go *don't* see it. Summer weather patterns usually sock in the mountain by midafternoon, at least as seen from the ground in the park.

Unfortunately, Denali has become a thing people feel they *must* do, and seeing Mount McKinley is a thing they must do when they visit Denali. Many package tours rush through the park so quickly it becomes a blur outside a window

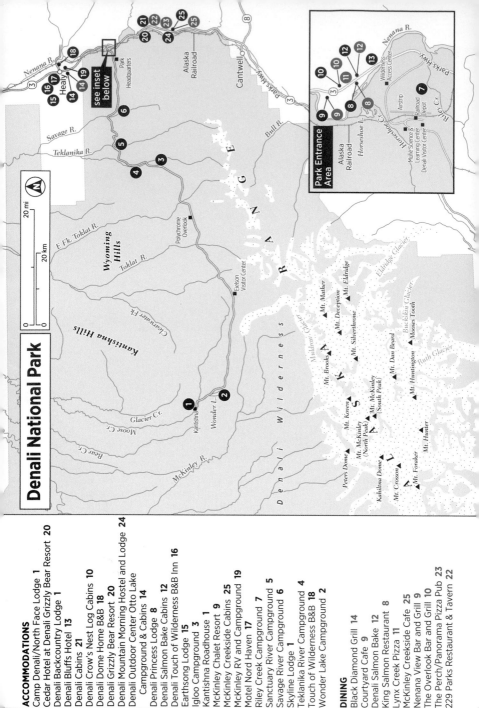

Denali National Park

Park Entrance Area

Alaska Railroad

rather than an experience. If they miss the mountain, passengers may wonder why they traveled so far to stay at a hotel in the developed area near the park's entrance and ride on a bus over a bumpy road. A friend swears she overheard a tourist ask, as she boarded the train leaving Denali, "Why did they put the park way out here in the boondocks?"

The answer is there for you to find, at the bottom of the steps of the shuttle bus door.

PLANNING A VISIT TO THE PARK

Orientation

Denali National Park and Preserve is rock- and ice-robed in tundra and stands of stunted black spruce, a huge slice of the Alaska Range that stands like a pivot in the center of Alaska. It encompasses 6 million acres, a roughly triangular polygon about 20% larger than Massachusetts. The only park entrance is 237 miles north of Anchorage and 120 miles south of Fairbanks on the paved George Parks Highway or the Alaska Railroad. Although **Mount McKinley** is visible from as far away as Anchorage, you can't see it at all from the park entrance (where you will find the railroad depot and all the services accessible by private vehicle) because it's on the far side of the park. A mile north of the park entrance on the Parks Highway, along a cliff-sided canyon of the Nenana River, is **Glitter Gulch,** the local term for the seasonal roadside strip that's home to hotels and restaurants; it's also called **Nenana Canyon,** and local boosters want to stamp out the name "Glitter Gulch," but I keep using it because it is the common name (and descriptive, too). Other services are at **Carlo Creek,** 13 miles south on the Parks Highway; at another roadside development 7 miles south of the park entrance; and in the year-round town of **Healy,** 12 miles north of the park entrance. From the park entrance, a road accessible only by shuttle bus leads west 89 miles through the park, past a series of campgrounds and a visitor center, and ends at the **Kantishna district,** a patch of park-surrounded private land with wilderness lodges.

When to Go & How Far Ahead to Plan

Crowding is relative. Once you're out in the park, Denali is never crowded. The bottleneck created by the shuttle and tour bus system, which prevents vehicles from entering the heart of the park, protects it from overuse. What makes the July to mid-August season difficult is getting through that bottleneck from the crowded park entrance into the wilderness. At that time, travelers who just show up at the visitor center without any reservations might have to spend a day or two outside the park before they can get a desirable shuttle bus seat, a campground site, or a backcountry permit.

The flow of visitors varies greatly from year to year. During past busy years, you needed to make **reservations** by March for a July visit; other years, such as during the recent economic downturn, a few weeks of advance planning has been enough. To be on the safe side, get your shuttle tickets and campsites as soon as you know the dates of your visit. Lodgings also get tight in July but are not as critical to the success of your visit. Reserve a room as far ahead as you can, but don't worry about getting stuck in a dive if you don't get your first choice, as there are few really bad places to stay near the park.

THE DENALI HIGHWAY:
THE drivable DENALI

From Cantwell, 27 miles south of the Denali National Park entrance, the Denali Highway leads 133 miles east to another tiny village, Paxson, on the Richardson Highway. The little-known road is a lesson in how labels influence people. It runs due east from the Denali National Park border, a natural extension of the park over the Alaska Range, with scenery that's equal to and in some ways more impressive than the park's. Yet without the national park name, the terrain along the Denali Highway is comparatively little used.

The Bureau of Land Management (BLM) controls the land along the Denali Highway, and it's pretty much open for any recreational activity. Much of the highway passes through high, alpine terrain, with views that extend infinitely and good chances of seeing caribou, moose, and black and grizzly bears. At **Maclaren Pass,** at 4,086 feet, you stand in high Alaska Range terrain of tundra and rock, with views of Maclaren Glacier. The land invites you to walk at least a little way out across it. The **Tangle Lakes** are perfect canoeing waters, where you can see an extraordinary variety of waterfowl, including trumpeter swans, sandhill cranes, and loons. **Tangle River Inn,** at mile 20 (☎**907/822-3970;** www. tangleriverinn.com), rents canoes for $5 an hour or $35 for 24 hours.

Tangle Lake.

Summer residents come to the park beginning in early May, when snow remains; they migrate south again in mid- to late September, when winter is closing in. In the off season, fewer than 200 residents stay in the area, and sled dog–driving rangers patrol the backcountry. The shuttle bus system doesn't begin operation until the last week of May; going any earlier is inadvisable, and even early June can be iffy. The visitor season gets into high gear in mid-June and starts to wind down in mid-August. There are several weeks of relative quiet, reduced hotel prices, and easy reservations at the end of the season, a wonderful time to go to Denali. The weather gets nippy at night, and there can be surprise snowfalls, but rain is less likely, and the trees and tundra turn wonderful colors. By early September visitors are few. By mid-September the shuttle buses stop

Simply **driving** the road is an experience. If you're traveling to Denali National Park from Anchorage or Fairbanks, consider making a return trip via the Denali Highway and Richardson Highway. But check out road conditions first. The road is gravel and sometimes in poor condition. Consult the Alaska Department of Transportation's **road condition hot line** (☎ 511; http://511.alaska.gov). When the road is good, you can cover its length in less than 4 hours. Agencies that rent cars and RVs for use on these gravel highways are listed under "Equipped for the Backroads," p. 516, and "Car Wheels on Gravel Roads," p. 290. Most companies don't allow their vehicles on the Denali. For the adventurous, **biking** the road is one of the best ways to see it. Trails and remote roads from the highway offer some exceptional mountain-biking and hiking routes, especially in the Tangle Lakes National Register Archaeological District.

Lodgings on the highway are limited to a few small roadhouses. At mile 42, the friendly **Maclaren River Lodge** (☎ 907/822-5444; www.maclarenlodge. com) makes a welcome break with good basic food from the grill and boat tours on the river. Check the cabins before deciding on a night's stay; although inexpensive and clean, they are definitely no-frills. One reportedly has a ghost. The BLM maintains **campgrounds** at Brushkana Creek and Tangle Lakes, and you can camp anywhere you want outside a campground.

For more details, get the BLM's *Denali Highway Points of Interest* road guide and its *Trail Map and Information Guide to the Tangle Lakes Archaeological District.* They're available at the Alaska Public Lands Information Centers in Fairbanks, Anchorage, or Tok, or directly from the BLM's Glennallen Field Office (p. 552), where rangers can give advice on a Denali Highway trip. The agency also has a website devoted to the highway at www.blm.gov/ak/ gdo/denali.html (or just Google it at "BLM Alaska Denali Highway").

operating and private cars can drive on the park road for a few days—the park service holds a lottery in July to determine who will get that treat.

Another way to avoid the crowds is to book a stay in a **wilderness lodge.** Lodges in Kantishna, listed under "Denali Wilderness Lodges," have the right to carry clients to their businesses over the park road in buses and vans, avoiding the bottleneck.

Sample Itineraries

The more you're willing to rough it, the closer you can get to the real Denali. There are no hotels inside the park.

THE HOTEL STAY ITINERARY

Drive to the park or take the train. If arriving by train, choose accommodations near the park—shuttles and courtesy vans can get you around—or rent a car for use while in the area. Visit the exhibits at the Denali Visitor Center, attend a ranger talk, see the *Cabin Nite* dinner-theater show, or go on a short nature walk around the park hotel in the evening. Get to bed early, and the next morning take a shuttle bus by 7am into the park to see the terrain and animals, and possibly to get a view of the mountain. By late morning you'll be at a point with a commanding view of McKinley (in good weather). Now ride partway back toward the entrance before getting off the bus at a place of your choosing for a walk and to eat the bag lunch you've brought along with you (pack out all trash, of course), or take one of the National Park Service guided walks. After enjoying the wilderness for a few hours, head back on the bus, finishing a long day back at the hotel. The next day, try an educational program at the Murie Science and Learning Center or take a rafting ride, a flightseeing trip, or another activity near the park entrance before driving onward or reboarding the train.

THE FAMILY CAMPING ITINERARY

Arrive at the park entrance by car with your camping gear and food for a couple of nights. (You can rent the camping gear and car in Anchorage or Fairbanks.) Camp that evening at the Riley Creek Campground near the visitor center. Enjoy the evening ranger program, see the exhibits at the visitor center, take a nature walk, or go straight to a campsite farther within the park (either way, you'll need to reserve well ahead). The next day, catch a shuttle bus to get deeper into the park for sightseeing and hiking. If you have another day after that within the park, you can do more hikes and have the cushion of a weather day. Add a rafting excursion at the park entrance before driving on, if you like, and possibly a night in a hotel with a soft bed and your very own bathroom.

THE BACKCOUNTRY CAMPING ITINERARY

Arrive by train, bus, or car with your backpack, camping gear, and food for at least several days' hiking. Go immediately to the Backcountry Information Center to orient yourself to the backcountry permit process, buy the information you need for your trek (see "Denali on Foot: Day Hiking & Backpacking," later in this chapter), and choose the unit area that looks most promising. Backcountry permits cannot be reserved in advance; you can apply for them in person only at the center 2 days in advance, and they go fast. If you're lucky, permits will be left for the day after you arrive; more likely, you'll need to camp for a night nearby and arrive at the Backcountry Information Center by the 9am opening (in high season) to get your permit for the following day. Now you've got another day to wait; if you've reserved a shuttle-bus seat, you can get a preview of the park and see some wildlife. The next morning, you can start your backcountry hike, taking the camper bus to your unit and then traveling for up to 2 weeks in a huge area of wilderness reserved almost exclusively for your use.

THE KANTISHNA WILDERNESS LODGE ITINERARY

For those who can afford it, this may be the best way to see Denali. The lodge will drive you through the park and you'll immediately be away from the crowds in remote territory. The lodges all have activities and guides to get you out into the wilderness.

THE TALKEETNA OPTION

Drive or take the train only as far as Talkeetna, about 110 miles north of Anchorage, and board a flightseeing plane from there to the park, perhaps landing on a glacier on Mount McKinley. You'll stand a better chance of seeing the mountain than anyone else, since the weather tends to be better on the south side and you can fly above most clouds. You'll also save yourself hours of driving to the park and the bus ride into the park, and you'll have the pleasure of staying in a town with some character, unlike the park entrance area. If you want the on-the-ground wildlife-viewing opportunities that can be had only in the park, you can fly from Talkeetna for the day, for a price. (See "Talkeetna: Back Door to Denali," later in this chapter, for more information.)

PARK ESSENTIALS
Visitor Information

Getting the information you need to plan your visit is especially important at Denali because of the need for advance reservations.

The most important resource for setting up a trip is the concessionaire: **Doyon/ARAMARK Joint Venture,** 2445 W. Dunlap Ave., Phoenix, AZ 85021 (☎**800/622-7275** or 907/272-7275; fax 907/258-3668; www.reservedenali.com). The concession is operated by a joint venture of ARAMARK, which manages visitor services at many parks around the country, and the Doyon Native Corporation of Interior Alaska. They handle the reservations system for the campgrounds and shuttle buses, as well as several hotels, bus tours, a rafting operation, and a dinner theater. The best place to make in-person contact with the concessionaire is at the reservation and ticketing desks in the **Wilderness Access Center,** on the Denali Park Road, half a mile from the park entrance. The access center is open from mid-May to mid-September daily from 5am to 7pm (reservation desks don't open until 7am); it's closed October through April. You can even buy an espresso inside to drink while you stand in line. Since there's no park entrance station, this center is also a good stop for the park map, a copy of the *Alpenglow* park newspaper, and other handouts. A small store offers a limited selection of conveniences and camping supplies.

The **National Park Service** can be reached at P.O. Box 9, Denali National Park, AK 99755 (☎**907/683-2294;** www.nps.gov/dena). Make contact in person at the spectacular **Denali Visitor Center,** near the railroad depot at mile 1.5 of the park road on the right side. It's open summer daily 8am to 6pm. Find more on park service educational facilities under "Learning About the Park," p. 477.

Besides the centers at the park and the website, you can get park information on the way there at the interagency **Alaska Public Lands Information Centers** in Anchorage (chapter 7) and Fairbanks and Tok (chapter 10). The park's nonprofit publishing arm is the **Alaska Geographic,** Denali Branch, P.O. Box 230, Denali National Park, AK 99755 (☎**907/683-1272** summer, 907/683-1258 off-season; www.alaskageographic.org). They operate the shops in the park visitor centers, and you can use their website to order books, maps, and the *Alpenglow* before coming.

The Reservations System

Here's the system for reserving shuttle-bus tickets and sites at the developed campgrounds. This section may look long, but paying attention to the details of the reservations system greatly improves your chances of a good visit to the park. (The backcountry permit system is covered under "Denali on Foot: Day Hiking & Backpacking.")

FOR ADVANCE RESERVATIONS

Sixty-five percent of shuttle-bus seats and all campground sites (except Sanctuary and Igloo) are offered for booking by Internet, telephone, fax, or mail; the balance is held back for walk-ins up to 2 days before the trip. Use the Doyon/ARAMARK Joint Venture contact information above under "Visitor Information."

Reservations online, or by phone, fax, or mail, open for the whole summer on December 1 of the preceding year. Phone lines are answered daily from 7am to 5pm Mountain Standard Time (that's 2 hr. later than Alaska Standard Time, where the hours would be 5am–3pm, and 2 hr. earlier than Eastern Standard Time, where they would be 9am–7pm). Using the Internet (www.reservedenali.com) allows you to reserve any time. You will need a Visa, MasterCard, American Express, or Discover Card. You can pay by check if you're reserving by phone, mail, or fax; payment is due within 10 days. But this option is not available within 30 days of the date you are arriving. If using mail or fax, you will need to go online or call anyway to get a form.

A **confirmation** will be sent out within 2 days of making the reservation. Take it to the "will call" desk at the Wilderness Access Center; or, if camping, to the check-in at the Riley Creek Mercantile, near the Riley Creek Campground. Exchange the confirmation for a camping permit and bus ticket. The center closes at 8pm, and the Riley Creek Mercantile closes at 11pm. If you'll be later, call ℂ907/683-9274 to avoid losing your site or shuttle seat.

FOR WALK-INS

Internet, mail, and fax orders are not accepted the day before the visit starts (in busy years, the best choices are sold out weeks earlier), but walk-in reservations begin 2 days out, offering 35% of the shuttle-bus seats that are held back and any leftover car-camping sites (usually none), and all sites at Sanctuary and Igloo campgrounds. Desirable shuttle reservations may be snapped up early in the day. That means you may not get a good reservation for the day of your arrival or even the day after, only the next day after that. That's why it's so critical to reserve in advance.

On the other hand, don't despair if you arrive without reservations, as the flow of visitors rises and falls unpredictably. It's perfectly possible that you'll walk into the visitor center and get a good shuttle seat on the same day.

Fees

Park entrance fees are $20 per vehicle (up to eight passengers) or $10 per person, good for 7 days. There is no entrance station to collect the fee, but it is automatically added to your bill when you make shuttle or campground reservations. If you have one of the national passes for senior citizens, those with disabilities, or frequent park users (they're called the "America the Beautiful—National Park and Federal Recreational Lands Pass"), you can get a refund when you get to the park. Entrance fees are in place year-round and are collected at the Murie Science and Learning Center during winter months.

Campground fees are $16 to $28 per night for car or RV camping, $14 for the backpacker's campground at Riley Creek Campground, and $9 at Sanctuary Campground and Igloo Campground (if open). A reservation fee of $4 to $5 is charged for the first night of stays in campgrounds other than Riley Creek and Savage River. (See "Where to Stay," later in the chapter, for more particulars.) **Bus fees** are listed in the chart "Denali Park Road Bus Facts," under "Denali by Shuttle Bus." A $5 fee is charged for canceling or changing a campsite or bus ticket, except for free children's tickets. You can cancel until 11pm the day before arrival for campground reservations or 24 hours before departure for shuttle tickets. Tundra Wilderness Tour reservations can be canceled only 7 days or more in advance.

Getting There

BY TRAIN

The **Alaska Railroad** (☎800/544-0552 or 907/265-2494; www.alaskarailroad. com) pioneered tourism to the park before the George Parks Highway was built in 1972. In summer, trains leave both Anchorage and Fairbanks daily at 8:15am, arriving at the park from Anchorage at 3:45pm and from Fairbanks at 12:15pm, crossing and going on to the opposite city for arrival at 8pm in each. The basic fare from Anchorage to Denali is $146 one-way for adults, from Fairbanks $64, half price for children ages 2 to 11, free 1 and under. First-class "Gold Star" seats are $85 more per leg. Descriptions of the different classes of service are below under "Train Choices." The train also stops in Wasilla and Talkeetna; see the website for details. The full train runs only from mid-May to mid-September, with somewhat lower fares in the first and last few weeks of the season. During the winter, the Alaska Railroad runs a single passenger car from Anchorage to Fairbanks and back once a week—a truly spectacular, truly Alaskan experience.

BY CAR

Renting a car and driving from Anchorage or Fairbanks is far cheaper and far faster than taking the train. It's easy to average 65 mph on a good two lane highway, making the drive about 4½ hours from Anchorage and 2½ hours from Fairbanks. (The train averages 40 mph and takes 7½ hr to get from Anchorage to Denali.) Many of the views along the **Parks Highway** are equal to the views on the train, but large stretches, especially in the Matanuska and Susitna valleys, near Anchorage, have been spoiled by ugly roadside development (which you don't see from the train). A long but spectacular detour around the mess leads through **Hatcher Pass** on a mountainous gravel road open only in the summer (see "Through Hatcher Pass," under "Out from Anchorage: The Matanuska & Susitna Valleys," in chapter 7). Farther north from Anchorage, the Parks Highway passes through **Denali State Park.** If the weather's clear, you can see Mount McKinley from the pullouts there. The state park also contains several campgrounds, public-use cabins, hiking trails, and a veterans' memorial. Byers Lake is a nice stop with a good campground and with canoe and kayak rental from **Denali Southside River Guides** (☎877/425-7238; www.denaliriverguides.com)—the company also offers guided river rafting, kayaking, and fly-fishing. The park has

TRAIN CHOICES

Alaska Railroad executives know that their fares are high for a simple ride to Denali. As one told me, "We're selling entertainment," and that's how you should judge your choices. So, to review the entertainment: All the cars are luxurious, and some are grand and highly memorable; the rail line follows a historic, unspoiled route through beautiful countryside; there's a good chance of seeing moose and caribou; the commentary by well-trained Alaska high-school students is fresh and engaging; and the food is good.

There are disadvantages, too. The train is very expensive. You can rent a small car for a week for the same price as one round-trip on the train. It's slow, adding 3 hours to a trip from Anchorage to the park, and when it's late, it can be very late. And, once you arrive, you have to rely on shuttles and courtesy vans to get around outside the park.

After you decide to ride the train, you have to choose which part of the train. One set of Alaska Railroad locomotives pulls the Alaska Railroad cars and other sets of cars with full glass domes owned by cruise lines, two of which have seats for independent travelers (although 90% or more are filled with their older cruise-ship customers). The two cruise lines are both owned by the same company, and could consolidate their offerings after this goes to press. **Princess Cruises and Tours (☎800/426-0500;** www.princesslodges.com) has tall, all-dome cars with table seating upstairs and dining rooms downstairs; there's plenty of head room and large balconies at the ends of the cars on the lower deck, where you can ride outdoors. **Gray Line of Alaska,** a part of Holland America (☎888/452-1737; www.graylinealaska.com), has newer cars that are even better than Princess's. They're huge and comfortable, with all seats facing forward upstairs—an advantage over table seating—and dining rooms below that are large enough so only two seatings are needed for each meal. (All meals are served at assigned seatings in the cruise-line cars.)

The **Alaska Railroad** offers two classes of service. The basic service is in traditional railroad cars. They're clean and have big windows and forward-facing seats. Passengers stroll around and dine when and how they please rather than at assigned seatings. Old-fashioned Vista Dome cars provide a limited but adequate number of shared dome seats. By paying another $85, you can upgrade to "Gold Star" service, with your own full-dome seat for the entire trip on custom-built double-decker cars like the cruise lines', with a sumptuous white-tablecloth dining room downstairs (eat when you like). These are my favorite cars on the train. They're decorated with original fine art and are very luxurious, but you still know you're on a train, not a cruise ship, and you're not treated as a herd animal. Also, the cars have large outdoor vestibules on the upper deck. The views and open air there are incredible.

All passenger seats are assigned on all the cars. You can't walk from one company's cars to another, but you can walk between cars in your own train section. Fares on all three options are similarly high, but they're more advantageously priced as part of lodging and tour packages, which you can buy from the railroad or the cruise lines.

Alaska Railroad in Denali National Park.

a visitor contact station at the memorial, at mile 147. For information before you go, contact the **Mat-Su Area Park Headquarters** (☎907/746-5000; www. alaskastateparks.org, click on "Individual Parks"). From Fairbanks, the drive is pleasant but rarely spectacular. Allow an hour to stop in the quaint riverside town of Nenana, where you can see an old railroad depot museum (p. 508).

BY BUS

Several van and bus services inexpensively connect Anchorage and Fairbanks to Denali. Most will carry bikes and other gear for an additional fee. **The Park Connection Motorcoach Service** (☎800/266-8625 or 907/245-0200; www. alaskacoach.com) runs big, comfortable coaches to Denali from Anchorage and Seward, with two buses daily in each direction. The Anchorage fare is $90, Seward $145. Children 11 and under ride for half price; those 4 and under need a car seat. **Alaska/Yukon Trails** (☎800/770-7275; www.alaskashuttle.com) also offers daily service from Anchorage and Fairbanks, with stops at any other point on the way. The one way fare is $75 from Anchorage, $55 from Fairbanks.

BY AIR

Talkeetna Aero Services (☎888/733-2899 or 907/683-2899; www.talkeetna-aero.com) offers the only scheduled air service to Denali from their base in Talkeetna, or from Anchorage, in the summer only. The flights are sold as 1-day packages, including flightseeing on the way, a bus tour at the park, a box lunch, and ground transfers. It's the only way to "do" Denali in a day. The package from Anchorage is $525, from Talkeetna $425, and they go only with at least four passengers.

Getting Around

If you take the train or bus, you'll find that most accommodations have arrangements to get you around, although this becomes less convenient as you get farther from the park entrance. Ask how courtesy transportation works when you book your room. There are cabs available, too, but they are an expensive option. If you must rely on cabs, get a firm quote when you call. Try **Denali Transportation** (**877/683-4765** or 907/683-4765). A few cars are for rent at the park from **Keys to Denali,** operated out of Denali Dome Home Bed and Breakfast in Healy (**800/683-1239** or 907/683-1239; www.denalidomehome.com).

[FastFACTS]
DENALI NATIONAL PARK

Bank The region's only bank, **First National Bank of Alaska,** is in Healy, 12 miles north of the park. In addition, a couple of ATMs are in the Glitter Gulch (Nenana Canyon) area, including one at the Lynx Creek Store and Deli.

Emergencies (**911** will work inside the park, but be sure to tell the operator you are within Denali National Park. However, cellphone coverage reaches only along the highway and there are no telephones except at the developed areas. Bus drivers on the park road are equipped with radios.

Gear Rental Denali Mountain Works (**907/683-1542;** www.akrivers.com), a clothing and outfitting shop, rents binoculars, sleeping bags, tents, backpacks, and stoves. It is right across from the McKinley Chalet Resort. Bikes are for rent at **Denali Outdoor Center** (**888/303-1925** or 907/683-1925; www.denalioutdoorcenter.com); see p. 478.

Hospital The seasonal **Canyon Clinic at Denali** (**907/683-4433**) is among the big hotels near the park entrance. It is open daily 9am to 6pm with help on call 24 hours. In Healy, 12 miles north of the park entrance, the year-round **Community Interior Health Center** (**907/683-2211**) is open Monday through Friday 9am to 5pm. Neither clinic has a full-fledged doctor.

Police The **Alaska State Troopers** (**907/683-2232** or 907/768-2202) have a post in Healy, 12 miles north of the park, and in Cantwell, 28 miles south.

Post Office The post office is just within the park entrance, right before the Riley Creek Campground. Check out the bulletin board there for news of local events.

Stores You should do major shopping before leaving Anchorage or Fairbanks, but there are handy stores at Denali. **Riley Creek Mercantile** (**907/683-9246**) is at the Riley Creek Campground, near the park entrance. It's open daily from 7am to 11pm in the summer. Besides convenience groceries, they have firewood, some basic camping supplies, RV supplies, a dump station, made-to-order sandwiches, fax and copy service, binoculars rentals, showers, and laundry. On the highway, near the Denali Salmon Bake, the **Canyon Market and Cafe** is open 24 hours a day during the visitor season.

Taxes The local **room tax** is 7%. There is no sales tax.

If you drive to the park, you'll still need to take the shuttle bus, described below, to get into its heart, except under certain circumstances. You can drive past mile 14 on the park road only if you have a 3-night camping permit at Teklanika Campground, 29 miles in; then your vehicle must remain parked at the campground for the entire 3 days. The rules loosen at the end of the season, when winners of a drawing can drive the road for a few days in late September (check with the park service for lottery details). After the permit driving is over, the road is open to anyone as far as mile 30 until the snow flies; then it's maintained only as far as the headquarters, 3 miles from the entrance.

Bicycles have free access to the park road. For that option, see "Activities Within the Park," later in this chapter.

DENALI BY SHUTTLE BUS

Your visit to Denali will likely revolve around a ride on the shuttle bus into the park to see the wildlife and to stop for a walk in the wilderness. Some planning will make it a more successful trip.

Choosing Your Destination

You can buy shuttle tickets to the Toklat (*Toe*-klat) River, 53 miles into the park, to Eielson Visitor Center, at around 66 miles; Wonder Lake, at 85 miles; or Kantishna, at 89 miles (see "Denali Park Road Bus Facts," below, for fares). On any day trip, you have to go both ways, so you're in for a long ride. If you don't get off the bus along the way, the round-trip takes 5 hours to Toklat, nearly 8 hours to Eielson, 11 hours to Wonder Lake, and 12 hours to Kantishna. You must bring your own water and food.

Pack of gray wolves.

In choosing your destination, you need to balance your stamina, your desire to save time for a day hike, and your desire to see wildlife. There are no firm rules about where wildlife shows up, but my own observations are that, in the early morning, you can often see moose on the first part of the road; in midsummer, brown (grizzly) bears seem to appear most in the higher country, beyond Toklat, which also is the best area for caribou; and in the fall berry season, the grizzlies show up all along the drive.

The best views of Mount McKinley show up beginning around Highway Pass at the east side of the causeway at about mile 58, beyond Toklat (where the mountain cannot be seen at all). The mountain is most likely to be visible in the morning, as clouds often pile up during the day. Going all the way to Wonder Lake provides more amazing views, including the land-covered Muldrow Glacier and many classic images of Mount McKinley. There's really no reason to go as far as Kantishna unless you are headed to a lodge there (see "Denali Wilderness Lodges," later in this chapter). In general, I think Eielson Visitor Center is the best destination for most people, offering them the chance to see the mountain and some wildlife while leaving them time to get out and walk. (I've included ideas on where to hike later.)

You won't be able to time your trip for good weather, as you need to book ahead. But don't despair if it rains—the sun may be out at the other end of the park. The best weather for wildlife sightings is cool, overcast skies without rain. One trick of the system that allows visitors to wait for sun is to stay at Teklanika Campground. If you drive to a campsite there, agreeing to stay for a minimum of 3 nights, you're eligible to buy a special shuttle ticket that's good for rides deeper into the park the entire time you're staying at the campground ($31 for adults, half price for children ages 15–17, free for children 14 and under). Wherever you stay, you can buy a three-trip pass for the price of a two-trip pass.

Denali can be a challenge for families. Young children will go nuts on an 8-hour bus ride and often can't pick out the wildlife—this isn't a zoo, and most animals blend in with their surroundings. Older children also have a hard time

Bus Concerns & Complaints

The Denali concessionaire uses only school bus–type vehicles for shuttles on the park road, which are not as comfortable as highway motorcoaches and do not have bathrooms onboard. Safety concerns permit only these tough, lightweight buses to operate on the narrow, gravel park road. Some of the Tundra Wilderness Tour buses—unlike the shuttles and camper buses—are tricked out with higher-backed cloth seats and video monitors that allow the driver to zoom in on wildlife, but the basic bus is essentially the same. (They sell DVDs of the onboard video after the ride for $40.) The road itself can be an issue, too. I've heard from visitors complaining of white knuckles. The buses act a bit like mountain goats on the heights of Polychrome Pass and near Eielson Visitor Center as the road climbs without guardrails. If you're afraid of heights, it might not be to your liking.

keeping their patience on these trips, as do many adults. The only solution is to get off the bus and turn your trip into a romp in the heather. When you've had a chance to revive, catch the next bus. Besides, just because you buy a ticket to Wonder Lake doesn't mean that you have to go that far. Keep in mind, too, that if your child normally needs a car seat, you must bring the seat along on the bus.

The park has alternatives to the shuttle bus, with commentary, more comfortable seats, and other amenities. Doyon/ARAMARK Joint Venture operates two narrated bus tours, booked mostly as part of package tours. The **Denali Natural History Tour** provides just a taste of the park, going 17 miles down the park road, but also includes a cultural component, with a film, a history talk at a cabin, and a presentation by an Alaska Native, which could include singing, storytelling, or information about living off the land. The **Tundra Wilderness Tour** goes to Toklat when the mountain is hidden by clouds, and 8 miles farther, across Highway Pass to Stony Hill, when it is visible. Programmed commentary provides background on what you are seeing. Food is provided, but you can't get off the bus along the way (that's the fatal flaw, in my opinion). Three narrated tours go all the way to Kantishna, a 13-hour, 190-mile round-trip to the far end of the park road. One is operated by the park's concessionaire and the other two by lodges that have the right to use the road because of where their land is located. The park's own **Kantishna Experience** carries a ranger to provide commentary and to lead a hike and a visit to a historic cabin in Kantishna. The tour costs $155, half price children 14 and under, including lunch and snacks. The private operations, **Kantishna Wilderness Trails** (☎800/230-7275 or 907/683-1475; www.seedenali.com) and **Denali Backcountry Adventure** (☎888/560-2489 or 907/683-2643), run similar tours, but with bus drivers doing the commentary and with different activities at the far end: gold panning (with either) and a sled-dog demonstration (with Kantishna), or a hike (with Denali Backcountry). In any event, it's a marathon and you can't get off the bus along the way. They charge $135 to $169, with no discount for children. But I wouldn't take a child on a 13-hour bus ride and expect to remain sane.

Getting Ready

Reserve your shuttle ticket for as early as you can stand to get up in the morning. This strategy will give you more time for day hikes and enhance your chances of seeing the mountain and wildlife. Many animals are more active in the morning, especially on hot days. During peak season, the first bus leaves the visitor center at 5:30am and then one leaves roughly every 15 to 30 minutes in the morning. A few buses leave in the afternoon, mostly to pick up stragglers on the way back, returning late under the midnight sun.

By taking an early bus, you have more time to get off along the way for a hike, walking back to the road and getting the next bus that comes along with a spare seat. Time it right, and you could have more than 8 hours for hiking plus a tour of most of the park road before returning on a late bus. (To be on the safe side, don't push it to the very last bus.) The sun won't set until after 11pm May through July, and it will be light all night. If you need to get back to the park entrance at a certain time, leave yourself plenty of time, because, after getting off your westbound bus, you can't reserve seats going back the other way, and you may have to wait an hour for a bus with room to take you.

> ## 📎 Shuttle-Bus Etiquette
>
> **It's common courtesy on the shuttle bus to yell out when you see wildlife so others can see it, too. The driver will stop and everyone will rush to your side of the bus. After you've had a look, give someone else a chance to look out your window or get a picture. Be quiet and don't stick yourself, your camera, or anything else out of the bus. You will scare away the animals or, worse, help habituate them to humans.**

Before you leave for the Wilderness Access Center to get on your shuttle bus, you'll need a packed lunch and plenty of water. You should wear sturdy walking shoes and layers of warm and lighter clothing with rain gear packed, you should have binoculars or a spotting scope at the ready, and you should have insect repellent. You may also want a copy of Kris Capps's worthwhile booklet *Denali Road Guide,* sold at the Denali Visitor Center bookstore and published by Alaska Geographic (see "Visitor Information," earlier in this chapter). It provides a milepost commentary you can follow as you ride. Alaska Geographic also publishes guides to Denali birds, mammals, geology, and trails. If you'll be doing any extensive day hiking, you may also want to bring a detailed topographic map printed on waterproof plastic (published by Trails Illustrated and sold for $10 from the visitor center or by ordering from Alaska Geographic), as well as a compass; if you're just going to walk a short distance off the road, you won't need such preparations.

On Your Way

There are no reserved seats on the bus, but if you arrive early, you can find a place on the left side, which has the best views on the way out. Bus riders often see grizzly bears, caribou, Dall sheep, moose, and occasionally wolves, but, as one driver said, the animals aren't union workers, and it's possible that you won't see any at all. Of course, you have to stay on the bus when animals are present.

The shuttle-bus drivers often offer commentary about the sights on the road, but they aren't required to do so. Some do a great job and some don't say much. The tour-bus drivers do a formal presentation, but you can't get off the bus on the way.

A Road Log

Here are some of the highlights along the road (check the visitor center or the park service information handouts to confirm times of the guided walks):

MILE 9 In clear weather, this is the closest spot to the park entrance with a view of Mount McKinley. This section also is a likely place to see moose, especially in the fall rutting season.

MILE 14 At the end of the paved road at the Savage River Bridge, this is generally as far as private vehicles can go. A park service checkpoint stops anyone who doesn't have a proper permit. From the parking lot by the bridge, a simple climb over dry tundra leads to Primrose Ridge, also known as Mount Margaret.

DENALI PARK ROAD BUS FACTS

Note: WAC is Wilderness Access Center. All prices rounded to nearest dollar.

BUS	PURPOSE	ROUTE	FREQUENCY	FARE
Riley Creek Loop	Links facilities within park entrance area	Visitor facilities, learning center, Riley Creek Campground, rail depot	Continuous loop	Free
Savage River Shuttle	Public transport to hiking and picnicking near the Savage River, which can also be reached by car	From visitor center to Savage River day-use area, about 14 miles into the park	Peak season every hour 9am–9pm	Free
Camper Shuttle (Green Bus)	Access to campgrounds and backpacking beyond the park entrance	From the WAC to Wonder Lake Campground, 85 miles into the park	Several times a day	$31 adults, half price ages 15–17, free 14 and younger
Shuttle bus (or just "the shuttle"; Green Bus)	General access to the park and wildlife viewing; limited commentary, depending on the driver; no food or water	From the visitor center as far as Kantishna, 91 miles away through the park	Every 30 minutes to Fish Creek/Eielson, every hour to Wonder Lake, 4 times daily Kantishna	$25 to Toklat, $31 to Eielson, $43 to Wonder Lake, $47 to Kantishna; half price ages 15–17, free 14 and younger
Natural History Tour (Tan Bus)	5-hour guided bus tour at the edge of the park	From the WAC 17 miles into the park	Three times daily	$62 adults, half price ages 14 and younger
Tundra Wilderness Tour (Tan Bus)	7- to 8-hour guided bus tour with lunch provided; passengers may not get off er route	From the WAC to the Toklat River or Stony Hill, 53–61 miles into the park	Twice daily	$104 adults, half price ages 14 and younger
Kantishna Experience	13-hour guided tour and hike to the end of the road	From the WAC to Kantishna	One daily	$155 adults, half price ages 14 and younger

9

THE DENALI NATIONAL PARK REGION | Denali by Shuttle Bus

MILE 17 The vault toilets here are as far as the Natural History Tour bus goes.

MILE 29 An hour and 10 minutes into the drive, a large rest stop overlooks the Teklanika River, with flush toilets, the last plumbing on the road. The Teklanika, like many other rivers on Alaska's glacier-carved terrain, is a braided river—a stream wandering in a massive gravel streambed that's much too big for it. The braided riverbeds, sometimes miles wide, were created by water from fast-melting glaciers at the end of the last ice age. Each is kept free of vegetation by its river, which constantly changes course as it spreads the debris of rock and dust from the glaciers. Flat plains in glacial terrain usually are laid down by this mechanism.

MILE 34 Craggy Igloo Mountain is a likely place to see Dall sheep. Without binoculars, they'll just look like white dots. Manageable climbs on Igloo, Cathedral, and Sable mountains take off along the road in the section from Igloo Creek to Sable Pass.

View from Polychrome Pass.

MILES 38-43 Sable Pass, a critical habitat area for bears, is closed to people. A half-eaten sign helps explain why. Bears show up here mostly in the fall. This is the start of the road's broad alpine vistas.

MILE 46 Here the road tops 5-mile-wide Polychrome Pass, the most scenic point on the ride, and offering a toilet break, 2 hours and 25 minutes into the trip. Caribou look like specks when they pass in the great valley below you, known as the Plains of Murie after Adolph Murie, a biologist who pioneered study here and helped develop the park service's scientific ethic (the name does not always appear on maps, however). Note how the mountains of colored rock on either side of the plain match up—they once were connected before glacial ice carved this valley. Huge rocks on its floor are glacial erratics, plucked from the bedrock by moving ice and left behind when the ice melted.

MILE 53 The Toklat River, another braided river, is a flat plain of gravel with easy walking. The glaciers that feed the river are 10 miles upstream; the river bottom is habitat for bears, caribou, and wolves, and a good place for picnics. There is no food or water, but there are outhouses.

MILE 58 Highway Pass is the highest point on the road. In good weather, dramatic views of Mount McKinley start here. The alpine tundra from here to the Eielson Visitor Center is inviting for walking, but beware: Tundra is soft underfoot and can conceal holes and declivities that can twist an ankle.

MILE 62 Stony Hill Overlook is a mountainous highway point with great views of McKinley, 36 miles away. The Tundra Wildlife Tour turns around here on days with good mountain viewing.

MILE 64 Thorofare Pass, where the road becomes narrow and winding, is a good area to look for bears and caribou. Bus drivers know best where the animals are on any particular day, since they talk to fellow drivers.

MILE 66 This is the site of the newly reconstructed **Eielson Visitor Center,** which reopened in 2008. The center became a model of environmentally sensitive construction and sustainable design, winning an award that marked it as one of the most advanced buildings in the park system. The center has indoor and outdoor viewing areas, exhibits, and spaces for interpretive programs and for visitors to eat. The extravagant geology of the area is evident in the mountains around you. Seismic measurements here show frequent small earthquakes accompanying McKinley's prodigious growth—about an inch every 3 years. This region is a jumble of rocks pushed together by the expanding Pacific tectonic plate; the mountain and the whole Alaska Range are folding upward in that great collision. The facilities and the fine vantage for seeing McKinley make this the best turn-around point for most shuttle-bus riders, balancing the opportunity for wonderful views with saving time for hiking. Shuttle staff operate a dispatch office and can find you a seat on a returning bus if you get off yours.

Eielson Visitor Center.

MILE 68.5 The incredibly rugged terrain to the north is the earth and vegetation covering Muldrow Glacier. The ice extends to McKinley's peak and was an early and arduous route for climbers; these days, they fly to a base camp at a 7,200-foot elevation on the Kahiltna Glacier, on the south side. McKinley's glaciers, falling 15,000 vertical feet and extending up to 45 miles in length, are among the world's greatest. The Ruth Glacier has carved the Great Gorge on the south side, which is almost 6,000 feet deep above the ice and another 4,000 below—almost twice the depth of the Grand Canyon. The park road comes within a mile of the Muldrow's face; then continues through wet, rolling terrain past beaver ponds; and finally descends into a small spruce patch near mile 82.

MILE 86 Wonder Lake campground is the closest road point to Mount McKinley, 27 miles away. Some buses continue another half-hour to Kantishna. The fact that McKinley looks so massive from this considerable distance, dominating the sky, is testament to its stupendous size. You'll likely never see a larger object on this planet. From its base (your elevation here is only 2,000 ft.) to its top is an elevation gain greater than that of any other mountain on Earth. Other mountains are taller overall, but they stand on higher ground.

DENALI ON FOOT: DAY HIKING & BACKPACKING
Day Hiking in the Backcountry

One of the unique aspects of Denali is the lack of developed trails—you really can take off in any direction. I've covered some of the best hiking areas above, in "A Road Log," including Primrose Ridge, Teklanika River, Igloo and Sable mountains, and the Toklat River. The park service long resisted building any trails, but finally gave in and recognized some trails visitors had created, including those at the Eielson Visitor Center and the 2-mile path that leads from the Wonder Lake Campground to the McKinley River Bar, which extends far to the east and west. You can drive or take a free shuttle to the Savage River Day Use Area, at mile 14, which has a 1-mile loop trail and longer, informal routes for great alpine tundra hiking. Kris Capps's *Denali Walks* (Alaska Geographic, $7) is a handy Denali hiking guide covering all the trails in the park. No permit is needed for day hiking.

The broad, hard-gravel flats of the **braided riverbeds,** such as the McKinley, Toklat, Teklanika, and Savage, are among the best routes for hiking in the park. **Stony Creek,** leading up a gorge to the north from the road at mile 60, is an excellent walk into the mountains. You can also hike on the tundra, of which there are two varieties: The **wet tundra** lies on top of permanently frozen ground called permafrost; it's mushy, at best, like hiking on foam rubber laid over bowling balls. At worst, it's a swamp. **Dry tundra** clothes

> ### Ranger Programs in the Park
>
> Check the park newspaper, the *Alpenglow,* for ranger talks and slide shows that happen as often as several times a day in the front-country area (near the entrance) and at the Riley Creek, Savage River, and Teklanika campgrounds.

the mountainsides and generally makes for firmer footing and easier walking. The brush and stunted forest of the region are virtually impenetrable.

The major risks of hiking here relate to the weather and rivers. It can get cold and wet in midsummer, and if you're not prepared with warm, waterproof clothing, you could suffer the spiraling chill of hypothermia. The rivers are dangerous because of their fast flow and icy-cold water. Experienced backcountry trekkers plan their routes to avoid crossing sizable rivers. See the notes on handling river crossings, managing hypothermia, and getting lost in the "Outdoors Health & Safety" section in chapter 3. Bears, which people worry most about, are far less likely to become hazards, but do follow the tips on avoiding them that are found in chapter 3 and are widely distributed at the park.

Hikers at Stony Creek.

For a first foray beyond the trails, consider joining one of the park service guided hikes. One or two daily **Discovery Hikes** take off from the park road. One follows a route well inside the park toward the Eielson Visitor Center, and the other goes nearer to the entrance end of the park. A ranger takes only 11 hikers, leading them into wilderness while teaching them about the nature of the places they visit. Plan a 5- to 11-hour day, including the shuttle ride; actual hiking time is about 4 hours. The hikes generally are not too strenuous for families with school-age children, although it is wise to inquire how steep it will be if you have any doubts. They cost no more than the price of an Eielson shuttle ticket. You need to wear hiking shoes or boots and bring food, water, and rain gear. Reserve a place in advance, as hikes fill up in July, and you'll need to know when and where to catch the special bus. Rangers lead other walks, too, although the lineup can change each year. They added the Alpine Hike in 2009, a strenuous 2-hour climb that goes 900 feet up Thoroughfare Mountain from the Eielson Visitor Center, at mile 66 of the park road. Sign up at the center. Check with any visitor center for the current offerings.

Day Hiking in the Park Entrance Area

There are several trails at the park entrance, weaving through the boreal forest around small lakes. Only one strenuous trail leads from the entrance area, but it is a gem. The steep and spectacular hike to the **Mount Healy overlook** is a 5-mile round-trip. The trail breaks through the tree line to slopes of tundra and rock outcroppings, where you can see just how small the pocket of human infestation at the park entrance area is: The Alaska Range and its foothills extend far into the distance. If you continue on an all-day hike right to the top of Mount

THE alaska-ohio NAME GAME, NEXT GENERATION

Mount McKinley is so large that Athabascan people speaking different languages had different names for it. The Koyukon, on the north and west, called it Deenaalee, while the Dena'ina and Ahtna on the far side called it Dengadh. In 1839 the name was recorded on a Russian map as Tenada. It often has been translated as "the great one," but a closer translation is the more generic "the high one." The Athabascans never named mountains after people, nor did the Denali area get much use, since fish and game are relatively sparse and the weather extreme, but they did regard high places as spiritually important.

The name McKinley became associated with the mountain in the haphazard way common of the Alaska gold-rush period. A businessman and Princeton graduate named William Dickey was prospecting in the area in 1896, constantly arguing with his traveling companions about the big political issue of the day, the gold monetary standard supported by the Republicans and opposed by the Democrats. The Democratic presidential candidate, William Jennings Bryan, declared at his nomination convention that year, "You shall not crucify mankind upon a cross of gold." It was the gold standard that caused a deflationary economic disaster in those years, which was relieved only by the 1898 Klondike gold rush, which also led to Alaska's settlement. Anyway, when Dickey came out of the Bush, he published a piece about his travels in the *New York Sun* in which he reported his "discovery" and his name for North America's highest mountain—in honor of William McKinley, the Republican candidate who won the White House and was later assassinated. Dickey ultimately admitted he chose the name only to spite his former traveling companions.

Alaskans have long believed McKinley is an irrelevant name for the mountain, especially since it already had a name. In 1975, the state of Alaska petitioned the U.S. Geographic Names Board to change the name back to Denali. In 1980, Congress changed the name of the national park to Denali, but a single congressman from Ohio blocked changing the name of the mountain itself. McKinley was an Ohio governor and congressman before running for president. Rep. Ralph Regula, a Republican who represented McKinley's former seat beginning in 1972,

Healy, you can see all the way to McKinley on a clear day. Several new interpretive trails offer the chance to learn, stroll, or even get somewhere. A new bike and pedestrian trail connects the entrance area, near the Riley Creek Mercantile, to Glitter Gulch, allowing pedestrians to get back and forth without walking on the road. The McKinley Station, Morino, and Spruce Forest trails teach about nature and history. Get the book ***Denali Walks,*** mentioned in the previous section, to learn more.

and who even attended William McKinley Law School, found a clever maneuver to keep the name on the mountain. The names board has a policy of taking up no issue that is also being considered by Congress. In each Congress from 1977 onward, Regula introduced a single sentence as a budget amendment or as a standalone bill that states that McKinley is the mountain's permanent name. Although the bill never got so much as a committee hearing, its existence was enough to invoke the board's policy and prevent it from considering the change. In response, Sen. Ted Stevens, R-Alaska, also introduced an annual bill changing the name to Denali, which also went nowhere.

With Regula's retirement and Stevens' defeat in 2008, some Alaskans hoped for an end to the stalemate. But Regula's successor, Rep. Tim Ryan, a Democrat from Niles, Ohio, McKinley's birthplace, took up the cause with the same vigor as the previous generation. Stevens' successor, Democrat Mark Begich, said through staff that he also will keep up the fight. The new blood assures that the issue, entering its fourth decade in Congress, is in no danger of being resolved.

Backpacking

Imagine backpacking over your own area of wilderness, without trails, limits, or the chance of seeing other people. There's no need to retrace your route to get back: Anywhere you meet the 91-mile Denali Park Road you can catch a bus back to the world of people. Any experienced backpacker should consider a backcountry trek at Denali.

Yes, it can be challenging. Hiking on the tundra, broken-rock mountainsides, and braided rivers is tiring, and it's easy to fall or turn an ankle. You must be prepared for river crossings and cold weather, know how to find your way with a map and compass, and know how to avoid attracting bears. But if you've done a backpacking trip in a less challenging area, you surely can manage it here, so long as you prepare and don't underestimate the additional time you'll need in trailless terrain. Nor do you need to trek far—you can camp just a few miles off the road and still be in a place that looks like no one has ever been there before.

You must be flexible about where you're going and be prepared for any kind of terrain because you can't choose the backcountry unit you will explore until you arrive at the Backcountry Information Center, adjacent to

the Wilderness Access Center, and find out what's available. This information, and a map of the units, is posted on a board at the center. Groups of four or more may have a hard time finding a place to hike, but there's almost always *somewhere* to go. You can reserve permits only 2 days in advance, and you're unlikely to get one for the day you arrive, but you can reserve permits for continuation of your trip for up to 14 days at the same time. The first night of a trip is the hard one to get—for one thing, you can reserve only units that are contiguous to the park road for the first night—but after that, each night gets progressively easier. A couple of rangers are

there to help you through the process.

Buy the **Denali National Park and Preserve topographical map,** published by Trails Illustrated, available for $10 from Alaska Geographic, listed earlier in this chapter under "Visitor Information." Printed on plastic, the map includes the boundaries of the 43 backcountry units and much other valuable information. Also, you'll want a copy of the **Backcountry Companion** (Alaska Geographic, $9), which describes conditions and routes in each area. You'll find it at the visitor center, or you can glance at a well-thumbed copy kept at the backcountry desk.

The alpine units from the Toklat River to Eielson Visitor Center are the most popular. That's where you get broad views and can walk across

Backpacking Kesugi Ridge in Denali National Park.

heathery dry tundra in any direction. But to travel far, even there, you may have to climb over rugged, rocky terrain, and the tundra can be deceptively difficult to walk on—it's soft and hides ankle-turning holes. The wooded units are the least popular, since bushwhacking through overgrown country is anything but fun. The best routes for making time here (and anywhere in the Alaska Bush) are along the braided river valleys and streambeds. Be ready to walk in water. You'll have to take the **camper bus** to get to your backcountry unit, at a cost of $31 for each adult.

Before venturing into the backcountry, everyone is required to watch an **orientation film** covering safety and environmental issues, including how not to attract bears. I've spoken to competent backpackers who considered abandoning their trip because of the severity of the warnings they received about bears. That's unfortunate because sensible people taking normal precautions don't need to worry. The park service provides bear-resistant food containers in which you are required to carry all your food. For bear self-defense, you can carry a pepper spray, such as Counter Assault. Bear safety is covered in chapter 3 under "Outdoors Health & Safety."

Before you decide to go backpacking at Denali, however, you may want to broaden your thinking—if you're up to a cross-country hike without a trail, there are tens of millions of acres in Alaska available for backpacking that don't require a permit. Check with the Alaska Public Lands Information Center in Anchorage or Fairbanks for ideas about road-accessible dry tundra and other suitable areas on the Denali Highway (see "The Denali Highway: The Drivable Denali," earlier), and on the Dalton Highway and in Wrangell–St. Elias National Park (see chapter 10). I've listed some great trail hikes in chapter 8, under Chugach National Forest, and in chapter 10, in the sections on Chena Hot Springs Road and the Steese Highway.

ACTIVITIES WITHIN THE PARK
Learning About the Park

Everyone wants to get into the heart of the park to see the wildlife and mountains as soon as possible, but time is well spent as well in the front country, learning about Denali.

The 14,000-square-foot **Denali Visitor Center** introduces the park and its connections to the rest of the world in a building that takes stock of its surroundings. The structure is environmentally advanced, using solar power for electricity and clever design to save solar warmth. Inside, life-size models of cranes overhead lead to an enormous mural, 60×28 feet in size, showing the landscape types found at the park. The carpet simulates a flowing river of gray and brown, making a path to an exhibit area with re-creations of Denali wildlife, including a full-scale moose stepping through deep snow. You will also find exhibits on the Athabascan people, mining, tourism, and scientific research. On the upper floor, a large topographic model of the park demonstrates the arbitrary nature of its boundaries, and another exhibit shows the six-continent routes of migratory birds found at Denali. Drawers open to reveal discoveries: a cross-section of Earth, or of different kinds of trees. An award-winning orientation film, *Heartbeats of Denali*, lasts 18 minutes. The photography is impressive and the narration says much with few words. Summer hours are daily 8am to 6pm; the center is closed in the winter.

The **Murie Science and Learning Center** (☎866/683-1269 or 907/683-1269; www.murieslc.org) supports research and offers programs about the park. It is located about a mile in along the park road on the right side. The lobby houses changing science exhibits. A variety of organizations participate in programming, with evening lectures, morning walk-in science presentations, youth camps, and natural history field seminars for adults and for families with older or younger children. Three-day courses are around $320 per person. Check topics and register well in advance on the website. The center is open summer daily 9:30am to 5:30pm, winter daily 9am to 4pm.

Denali Visitor Center.

Mountain-Biking

A bicycle provides special freedom in the park. Bicyclists can ride past the checkpoint where cars have to turn back, at mile 14 on the park road. Riding is gritty, however, as buses come frequently and kick up a lot of dust. Bikes are not permitted off-road. Park campgrounds have bike stands and, with enough prior planning, you can set up a trip riding from one to the next. The longest stretch on the park road between campgrounds is 52 miles. With a reservation, you can take a bike on the camper bus so you can ride one-way. The shuttle system lacks much capacity for bikes, however, as only two can fit on each camper bus, although the park is considering installing racks on the buses. Given this shortage, it can be hard for cyclists to find room on buses returning to the park entrance; instead, get a reserved spot on an outbound bus and bike back. At least until racks are added, groups larger than two must split up onto different buses. Pick up a copy of the bicycle rules from the Backcountry Information Center before you start. **Denali Outdoor Center** (**☎888/303-1925** or 907/683-1925; www.denalioutdoor center.com) rents front-suspension bikes for $40 for 24 hours, $25 for 6 hours, with discounts for longer rentals. The center has an office in Glitter Gulch and headquarters near Healy, at Otto Lake Road and Parks Highway, mile 247.

Sled-Dog Demonstrations

In the winter, rangers patrol the park by dogsled, as they have for decades. In the summer, to keep the dogs active and amuse the tourists, they run a sled on wheels around the kennel, and a ranger gives a talk, normally at 10am, 2pm, and 4pm. Although it's no substitute for seeing dogs run on snow, you can get a sense of their speed and enthusiasm from the show. It was the highlight of my older son's trip to Denali when he was 3 years old. There's no parking at the kennels, near the headquarters at mile 3.4 on the park road, so take a free bus that leaves the Denali Visitor Center 40 minutes before each show. Times are listed in the *Alpenglow* park newspaper.

Fishing

Fishing is poor at Denali. There are grayling in some rivers, but the water is too cold and silty for most fish. Those who don't care if they catch anything, however, do enjoy fishing in this wonderful scenery. You don't need a fishing license within park boundaries, but you do have to throw back everything you catch. Bring your own gear.

For a better chance of catching something—and an opportunity to learn about fly-fishing, too—go to a private lake outside the park with guide Rick McMahan of **Denali Fly Fishing Guides** (**☎907/768-1127**; www.denalifishing.com). He picks up clients at their hotels and takes them lake or stream fishing, on the bank or wading, mostly for Arctic grayling but also rainbow trout. The per-person cost is $150 for a half-day, $300 for a full day, lunch included. He also provides jet boat trips to wilderness streams for $275.

Climbing Mount McKinley

Because of its altitude and weather, Mount McKinley is among the world's most challenging climbs. Summer temperatures at the high camp average −20° to −40°F

Climber at Summit Ridge.

(–29° to –40°C). If you're looking here for advice, you're certainly not up to an unguided climb. A guided climb is a challenging and expensive endeavor requiring months of conditioning and most of a month on the mountain. Get names of authorized guides from the park service's **Talkeetna Ranger Station,** P.O. Box 588, Talkeetna, AK 99676 (☎**907/733-2231**). The climbing season lasts from late April or early May until the snow gets too soft, in late June or early July. Climbers fly from Talkeetna to a 7,200-foot base camp on Kahiltna Glacier. About 1,200 climbers attempt the mountain annually in about 300 parties; about half typically make it to the top each year, and usually a few die trying.

ATTRACTIONS & ACTIVITIES OUTSIDE THE PARK

Flightseeing

Getting a good, close look at Mount McKinley itself is best accomplished by air. Frequently, you can see McKinley from above the clouds when you can't see it from the ground. Best of all, Talkeetna operators that fly mountaineers also land visitors on the mountain, a unique and unforgettable experience (see "Talkeetna: Back Door to Denali"). Regardless of how close you approach the mountain, a flight shows how incredibly rugged the Alaska Range is.

Small planes and helicopters fly from the park airstrip, from private heliports and airstrips along the Parks Highway, and from the Healy airstrip. **Denali Air** (☎**907/683-2261**; www.denaliair.com) has an office in the Nenana Canyon area and operates flights at mile 229.5 of the Parks Highway. An hour-long flight going within a mile of the mountain costs $350 for adults, $175 for children ages 2 to 12. **McKinley Flight Tours** (☎**888/733-2899** or 907/683-2899; www.flydenali.com), flying out of Healy, is the only operator offering mountain landings from the park area at this writing (others do so from Talkeetna). **Era Helicopters** (☎**800/843-1947** or 907/683-2574; www.erahelicopters.com) has 50-minute flights for $335, including van pickup from hotels in the area. Their heli-hikes land for a 4-hour walk on a mountain ridgeline, the difficulty tailored to the customers' ability, for $465. A 2-hour outing that includes a 70-minute glacier landing costs $435.

Rafting

Rafting on the Nenana River, bordering the park along the Parks Highway, is fun and popular. Several commercial guides float two stretches of the river: an upper portion, where the water is smoother and the guides explain passing scenery; and the lower portion, where the river roars through the rock-walled Nenana Canyon and rafts take on huge splashes of silty, glacial water through Class III and IV rapids. Guides take children as young as 5 on the slow trip (although I wouldn't let my kid go at that age); the youngest accepted for the fast portion is age 12. White-water rafting carries risks you shouldn't discount just because a lot of people do it, as a fatal accident on the supposedly easy tour confirmed in 1999. Each session takes 2 to 2½ hours, including safety briefings, suiting up, and riding to and from the put-in and take-out points. Prices vary from $76 to $112 for adults, with discounted rates for children (from $10 less to half off). **Denali Outdoor Center** (☎888/303-1925 or 907/683-1925; www.denalioutdoorcenter.com) is a professional operation, offering rafting trips and instruction in river techniques. The firm also offers self-paddled inflatable kayaks, popular with those who want to take an active hand in their float. Its riverside office is located at Mile 240, Parks Highway; its main office is at Otto Lake Road, at mile 247; and the company also has an office right in Glitter Gulch. Whoever you go with, plan a shower afterward—the silt in the river water will stick to your skin and hair.

All-Terrain Vehicle Rides

Most Alaskans who venture into the Alaska Range backcountry (outside the park) do so on snow machines or, in the summer and fall, on ATVs. Their purpose is

Rafting on the Nenana River.

usually hunting or trapping, but these balloon-tire buggies are handy just for seeing a lot of country as well. They're easy to drive. **Denali ATV Adventures** (☎907/683-4288; www.denaliatv.com) offers rides on one- or two-person machines north of the park, in the Otto Lake area and on the Stampede Trail, for scenery and wildlife viewing. Commentary is delivered through radio headsets inside riders' helmets. A 2½-hour tour, including instruction, costs $95 as a driver, $45 as a passenger; a 4-hour trip is $175 and $75. The firm has an office in Glitter Gulch and headquarters north of the Denali entrance at Mile 247, Parks Highway.

A Kennel Tour

Like the free dog-sled demonstration at the park, Iditarod champion Jeff King shows off his dogs at his **Husky Homestead Tour** (☎907/683-2904; www.huskyhomestead.com). What makes his tour hugely popular, however, is the program telling about living and raising a family on a homestead in this remote area. Admission is $49 for adults, $29 children 3 to 12; not recommended for children under 3.

WHERE TO STAY
Park Service Campgrounds

I've explained how to make camping reservations under "The Reservations System," p. 460. Camping fees are listed here, but reservation fees and entrance fees may be added when you pay. Only Riley Creek Campground is open after September (water is off in winter). The rest reopen when the snow is gone in May, except Wonder Lake, which opens in June. I have noted where RVs are permitted in the description of each campground. The maximum-size sites are for 40-foot units, and there are not many of those. There are no RV hookups at any campground in the park.

CAR-ACCESSIBLE CAMPGROUNDS

Riley Creek This large campground right across the road from the visitor center is best for those who want to be in the middle of things. It's near the Riley Creek Mercantile, with its showers, laundry, Wi-Fi, and sewage dump station. The free front-country shuttle connects the campground with other facilities. Reservations are relatively easy to get. Sites are wooded with small birch and spruce, and they're adequately separated, but this isn't exactly wilderness camping. Twenty-seven walk-in sites are available only for tent users without vehicles and can be reserved only 2 days ahead, in person.

Near the visitor center. 147 sites; RVs or tents. $22–$28 vehicle sites; $14 walk-in sites. Campfires allowed; flush toilets.

Savage River On the taiga—the thin spruce forest and tundra- this is a wonderful campground with unforgettable views. Campers can wander from their sites on some of the park's best hikes. This is the only campground you can readily drive to that's away from the activity at the park entrance. There is no telephone.

On Denali Park Rd., 13 miles from entrance. 33 sites; RVs and cars or tents. $22 per site. Campfires allowed; flush toilets.

Teklanika River This campground lies beyond the checkpoint on the park road. To hold down traffic, the park service requires campers to keep their vehicles in place for at least 3 nights. Sites are among the small trees of the boreal forest. The big advantage of staying here is that you begin the morning much closer to the heart of the park, cutting the time you have to spend on the bus. You can buy one bus ticket for the regular price and use it for your entire 3-night stay. That makes Teklanika a good base to really explore different areas of the park in varying kinds of weather.

On Denali Park Rd., 29 miles from entrance; access by camper bus, or drive in with a minimum 3-night stay. 53 sites; RVs only, no tents. $20 per site. Campfires allowed; flush toilets.

BUS-ACCESSIBLE CAMPGROUNDS

To use these campgrounds, you'll need a camper ticket on the shuttle bus, which costs $31 for adults, half price for children ages 15 to 17, free for ages 14 and under. There are no businesses and no phones beyond the park entrance area; you must bring in everything you need. Wildlife management concerns sometimes close these campgrounds unexpectedly.

Sanctuary River & Igloo These two small, primitive campgrounds offer a backcountry experience away from cars. You can't reserve sites in advance; permits are available only in person at the visitor center when you arrive.

On Denali Park Rd., Sanctuary River Mile 23, Igloo Mile 34. 7 sites each; tents only. $9 per site. No campfires; stoves permitted; chemical toilets.

Wonder Lake It takes almost 6 hours to get here on the bus, but this campground by placid Wonder Lake, at the foot of Mount McKinley, puts you in the most beautiful and coveted area of the park. Set among a patch of spruce trees on the mountain side of the lake, the sites can be tough to get, especially those with views of McKinley. The secret is to stay more than 1 day. When campers with a coveted site leave in the morning, grab it. A central area with bear-resistant food storage lockers has tables covered by an awning where campers prepare food and meet each other; choose a site away from this area and the noise and foot traffic there. The mosquitoes at Wonder Lake can be horrendous.

On Denali Park Rd., 85 miles from entrance. 28 sites; tents only. $20 per site. No campfires; stoves permitted; flush toilets.

> ### Keeping Clean at Denali
>
> **The only showers within the park are at Riley Creek Mercantile,** the store near the Riley Creek Campground, which also has laundry machines and other services. You pay by the shower, so there's no coin-operated timer to feed. You can also wash your clothes and shower at **Miners Market and Deli/ McKinley RV and Campground** in Healy, covered below under "Commercial Campgrounds." The larger park campgrounds have the typical cold-water bathrooms found in the national parks, while others have vault toilets.
>
> Check the park newspaper, the *Alpenglow,* for ranger talks and slide shows that happen as often as several times a day in the front-country area (near the entrance) and at the Riley Creek, Savage River, and Teklanika campgrounds.

Commercial Campgrounds

There are several commercial campgrounds in the general vicinity of the park entrance, although none in walking distance. **Denali Outdoor Center Otto Lake Campground and Cabins** (☎888/303-1925 or 907/683-1925; www.denalioutdoorcenter.com) will appeal most to those looking for a quiet park setting. Located at .5 Mile, Otto Lake Road (turn west at mile 247 of the Parks Hwy., 10 miles north of the park entrance), the campground has 30 sites, half on the shore of Otto Lake, half on a ridge above the lake with excellent mountain views. On the downside, it can be very windy. Nightly camping rates are $8 per adult, $4 per child. There are no RV hookups. Three basic log cabins sit at lakefront, renting for $92 in the high season, $78 in spring and fall ($10 each additional adult, free children 12 and younger). Showers are extra. The Denali Outdoor Center also guides rafting outings, described above.

Denali Grizzly Bear Cabins and Campground (☎866/583-2696 or 907/683-2696; www.denaligrizzlybear.com) is about 6 miles south of the park entrance at mile 231.1 of the Parks Highway. Some sites sit on an exposed hillside, while others are among small trees. Small cabins and tent cabins dot the property as well; they range from $65 without a bathroom to $260 for a unit with a full bathroom. There are coin-operated showers. Tent sites are $24 for up to four people, with electrical and water hookups $12 more. (The hotel on the property is described on p. 486.)

A campground with birch trees and attractive sites is 10 miles north of the park, next to the highway in Healy. **Miners Market and Deli/McKinley RV and Campground,** at mile 248.5 on the Parks Highway (☎907/683-1418), also has a gas station, a token-operated laundry, and hot showers. Basic tent sites are $11, full hookups $34.

Hotels

Patterns of land ownership and the uncontrolled development around Denali have led to a hodgepodge of roadside hotels, cabins, lodges, campgrounds, and restaurants in pockets arrayed along more than 20 miles of the Parks Highway. There are rooms of good quality in each of the pockets, but the going rates vary widely. The most expensive rooms, and the first booked, are in the immediate vicinity of the park entrance. Better bargains are in pockets south of the park, with prices getting lower the farther you go. Both these areas are entirely seasonal. Good deals are had in **Healy,** too, 12 miles north of the park, where you can find a hotel room for less than a comparable room near the park entrance A few links to B&Bs are on Healy's **Denali Chamber of Commerce** website (www.denalichamber.com, click on "Directory"). If you don't have a car, Healy is not convenient; in that case, stay nearer the park entrance. The other choices are wilderness lodges in the **Kantishna** area (see "Denali Wilderness Lodges"); or **Talkeetna,** the back door to the park (see "Talkeetna: Back Door to Denali"). Despite their high prices, rooms can be hard to find at the peak of the season (although not during the economic recession), and it's wise to book ahead.

NEAR THE PARK

This area, known formally as Nenana Canyon or more commonly as "Glitter Gulch," extends about a mile north of the park entrance on the Parks Highway.

Large, luxurious hotels dominate. Owned by the Princess and Holland American cruise lines, each hotel has superb rooms and public areas that were rebuilt in grand style within the last few years. Objectively the best lodgings in the area, I give them brief mention mainly because they serve escorted-tour passengers nearly to the exclusion of other guests. The giants are **Denali Princess Lodge,** Mile 238.5, Parks Highway (☎800/426-0500 reservations, 907/683-2282 local; www.princesslodges.com), and the **McKinley Chalet Resort,** Mile 239.1, Parks Highway (☎800/276-7234 reservations, 907/683-8200 local; www.denali parkresorts.com). Rack rates are high at each of these places, but you usually don't have to pay them. You can stay for much less if you arrive on one of the days when the flow of cruise-ship passengers is down, or early or late in the season, or if you book one of the owners' packages. Good deals are to be had as well on packages with the Alaska Railroad.

At one time, the canyon contained a variety of smaller, locally owned hotels catering to independent travelers, but the extraordinary value of the property and ever-growing flow of cruise-ship passengers has led to consolidation of lodgings, campgrounds, shops, restaurants, and other businesses into the hands of the two main cruise lines (which are, in reality, only two arms of the same corporation, Carnival), and ARAMARK, the park concessionaire, which operates under the name Denali Park Resorts outside park boundaries.

All the hotels in this area are open only during the tourist season, roughly from May 15 to September 15.

Denali Bluffs Hotel ★ A series of 12 buildings on a steep mountainside looks down on the Nenana Canyon area from above the highway. The light, tastefully decorated rooms have two double beds and good amenities, and those on the upper floor have vaulted ceilings and balconies with great views. There's little to explain the rates, however, other than the overheated Denali market. The courtesy van will take you anywhere in the area. ARAMARK manages the hotel and the 169-room **Grande Denali Lodge,** which perches impossibly high above the Nenana Canyon and charges more for the view. Use caution and observe the mirrors at the switchbacks on the gravel road up from the highway. The information below is for Denali Bluffs, but the toll-free number and website are good for either.

Mile 238.4, Parks Hwy. (Mailing address: 241 North C St., Anchorage, AK 99501). ☎800/276-7234 or 907/276-7234, 907/683-7000 local. www.denaliparkresorts.com. 112 units. High season $256–$291 double. Extra person age 12 and older $20. AE, DISC, MC, V. **Amenities:** Free airport transfers. *In room:* TV.

Denali Crow's Nest Log Cabins ★ Perched in five tiers on the side of Sugarloaf Mountain looking down on Horseshoe Lake and the other, larger hotels, the cabins are roomy and comfortable, especially those on the 100 and 200 level. A log cabin and the warmth of the Crofoot family seem more Alaskan than the modern, standard rooms that have filled the canyon, and the rates are reasonable for the area. You spend a lot of time climbing stairs, however, and the rooms have shower enclosures, not tubs. The restaurant, **The Overlook Bar and Grill,** is recommended separately under "Where to Dine," below.

Mile 238.5, Parks Hwy. (P.O. Box 70), Denali National Park, AK 99755. ☎888/917-8130 or 907/683-2723. Fax 907/683-2323. www.denalicrowsnest.com. 39 cabins. $159 double. Extra person 12 and older $20. All rooms nonsmoking. MC, V. **Amenities:** Free airport transfers; restaurant; bar; outdoor hot tub.

Denali Salmon Bake Cabins 🏷 For those looking to save money while staying near the park entrance, and satisfied with basic shelter, these cabins may be the solution. They're behind the salmon bake that has become the area's hip cultural center, and guests get into the entertainment there without cover charge (see "Dining," below). The highway and busy restaurant are nearby, but the cabins, shielded by trees, are surprisingly well hidden. The least expensive units are tent cabins. Four others with private bathrooms are a bit larger. They're all clean but rustic, one step up from camping.

Mile 238.5, Parks Hwy. (P.O. Box 107), Denali National Park, AK 99755. ☎907/683-2733. Fax 907/683-2259. www.denaliparksalmonbake.com. 12 cabins, 4 with private bath. $69 double with shared bath, $135 double with private bath. Extra person 12 and older $10. AE, DC, DISC, MC, V. **Amenities:** Free airport transfers. *In room:* No phone, Wi-Fi.

IN HEALY

Healy is 10 miles north of the park entrance, but a world away. It's a year-round community with an economy based partly on a coal mine. It sits in a large, windy valley with a few patches of stunted trees and big, open spaces of tundra. There are hotels and B&Bs with rooms well below the cost of those near the park, and most businesses stay open in the winter when the rest of the region shuts down tight. They say the water tastes better, too. On the downside, you need a car to stay in Healy.

Besides the lodgings listed below, **Denali Dome Home** (☎800/683-1239 or 907/683-1239; www.denalidomehome.com) is a neat place, a huge house in a geodesic dome on 5 acres, run year-round by a family for 20 years. The seven rooms are $170 to $190 double in summer and have many amenities, including a cooked-to-order breakfast. Use the same contact information for their **Keys to Denali** car rental.

Denali Touch of Wilderness Bed and Breakfast Inn ★ This special inn has won a place in the hearts of residents of this remote region, who congregate for retreats, quilting, wedding rehearsals, and the like. Visitors will find immaculate rooms, all with private bathrooms and phones, in one large building, decorated in a Victorian-tinged country theme. The common areas create a warm feeling—large sitting rooms with expansive views on the nearby Alaska Range, and a kitchen guests can use. The location is about 3 miles out in the country on the Stampede Road. The hosts serve generous breakfasts from 7 to 9am.

Mile 2.9, Stampede Rd. (P.O. Box 397), Healy, AK 99743 ☎800/683-2459 or 907/683-2459. www.touchofwildernessbb.com. 9 rooms. High season $179–$189 double, 2-night minimum stay suggested; low season $99–$135 double. Extra person $20. AE, DISC, MC, V. Rates include full breakfast. **Amenities:** Guest computer. *In room:* Hair dryer, Wi-Fi.

Earthsong Lodge ★★ 🏷 These solid-log buildings on the windy open tundra, with sweeping views of the Alaska Range, are well off the beaten path, 17 miles north of Denali National Park and 4 miles down the Stampede Trail Road, but it's worth the trip to stay in an authentically Alaskan lodge hosted by year-round residents Jon and Karin Nierenberg. One- and two-bedroom cabins have quilts on the beds and other cozy features. The lodge common rooms include a library and living room, and there's a coffeehouse, Henry's, serving breakfast and dinner and packing sack lunches. In the winter, the lodge operates as the dog-sledding concessionaire for Denali National Park, and in summer you can tour the kennel.

Stampede Trail Rd., off the Parks Hwy. at mile 251 (P.O. Box 89), Healy, AK 99743. **☏907/683-2863.** Fax 907/683-2868. www.earthsonglodge.com. 12 cabins. Summer $155–$195 double. Extra person 18 and over $10, ages 12–17 $5, 11 and under free. DISC, MC, V. **Amenities:** Restaurant (coffeehouse). *In room:* Hair dryer, Wi-Fi.

Motel Nord Haven ★★ This fresh little gray hotel with a red roof has large, immaculate rooms, each with one or two queen-size beds. They're equal to the best standard rooms in the Denali Park area and a lot less expensive. Bill and Patsy Nordmark offer all kinds of extras, even free newspapers and a sitting room with a collection of Alaska books. The rooms, decorated with Alaska art and oak trim, all have interior entrances and have been smoke-free since their construction. Up to four people can stay in the rooms with two beds for the price of a double. There are three kitchenette units. The Nordmarks pack sack lunches for $10.

Mile 249.5, Parks Hwy. (P.O. Box 458), Healy, AK 99743. **☏800/683-4501** or 907/683-4500. Fax 907/683-4503. www.motelnordhaven.com. 28 units. Summer $138–$164; spring/fall $94–$108; winter $80–$85. Summer rate includes continental breakfast. AE, DISC, MC, V. **Amenities:** Free hot drinks; guest computer. *In room:* TV, Wi-Fi.

SOUTH OF THE PARK

Lodgings south of the park are in widely separated pockets of private land concentrated 7 and 14 miles down the highway. (Anything south of that is covered with Talkeetna, under "Talkeetna: Back Door to Denali.") I've listed a few in detail below, but you may also want to try **Denali Cabins,** Mile 229, Parks Hwy. (**☏877/233-6254** or 907/376-1992; www.denali-cabins.com).

Cedar Hotel at Denali Grizzly Bear Resort ★ Four buildings over the Nenana River contain comfortable, modern rooms with the highway mostly out of view. You can hear the water from your bed or emerge on a small deck to enjoy the view (and the company of other guests, who are an arm's length away). Rooms are decorated in the Alaska rustic motif with lots of cedar. The adjoining campground (Denali Grizzly Bear; p. 483) has the same owner.

Mile 231.1, Parks Hwy. (P.O. Box 7), Denali National Park, AK 99755. **☏866/583-2696** or 907/683-2696. www.denaligrizzlybear.com. 105 rooms. High season $179 double; low season $149 double. Extra person $10. DISC, MC, V. **Amenities:** Internet access. *In room:* TV, hair dryer, no phone, Wi-Fi.

Denali Mountain Morning Hostel and Lodge ⚑ The hostel offers cozy accommodations in an octagonal log building. A store mainly carries organic food and a shuttle ($3 one-way, $5 day pass) runs to the park's Wilderness Access Center four times a day. Accommodations include hostel bunks, wall tents, private rooms, or separate private cabins, all reasonably priced with free linens. All guests use the shared bathhouse and have access to a fully equipped kitchen. The hostel is in the Carlo Creek area, where there are a couple of good casual restaurants.

Mile 224.5, Parks Hwy. (P.O. Box 208), Denali National Park, AK 99755. **☏907/683-7503.** www. hostelalaska.com. 14 units (2 female dormitories, 2 male dormitories, 1 co-ed dormitory, 9 private cabins). $32 adult bunk; $19 children 12 and under bunk; $80 double private room; $80–$95 double cabin. Extra adult $10; extra child ages 5–12 $5; extra child under 5 free. 2-night minimum in private rooms and cabins. AE, DISC, MC, V. **Amenities:** Internet access; shared kitchen. *In room:* No phone, Wi-Fi.

McKinley Creekside Cabins ★ These cozy cabins are right by the highway and the pleasant cafe of the same name (covered below), but you would never know it, thanks to how they are situated in the woods on the banks of Carlo Creek. The cabins' rustic decoration, in subdued tones, includes log bedposts made by a local craftsman. They have decks and nice private bathrooms, and some have refrigerators and microwaves. Family units sleep up to six, a real money saver. There are communal spots for visiting around barbecues, horseshoes, and fire pits, some at the creek's edge.

Mile 224, Parks Hwy. (P.O. Box 89), Denali National Park, AK 99755. ☎**888/5DENALI** (533-6254) or 907/683-2277. www.mckinleycabins.com. 30 units (6 rooms, 24 cabins). High season $139–$199 unit for 2–4; low season $99–$149 unit for 2–4. 5th or 6th person in family suite $10 each. DISC, MC, V. Closed Oct–Apr. **Amenities:** Restaurant; barbecue. *In room:* No phone, Wi-Fi.

WHERE TO DINE

Since Denali is entirely seasonal, it lacks the range of inexpensive family restaurants that develop in year-round communities. While you may find reasonably priced food in Healy, to the north, or Carlo Creek, to the south, near the park most meals are overpriced by 25% to 50% due to the short season and captive audience. Unless otherwise stated, all restaurants listed are open only during the visitor season.

Near the Park Entrance

You'll have no trouble finding an espresso at Denali. The large hotels in the canyon each have fine dining and casual restaurants; I've described the best in detail below. There are plenty of spots for a low-key meal or takeout. The **Courtyard Cafe** at the McKinley Chalet Resort serves a buffet and has a children's menu. **Lynx Creek Pizza** is something of a tradition but inconsistent from year to year. **Alaska Fish & Chip Co.** serves the seafood of the name, and more exotic choices, too. Order at the counter and then find a table.

Denali Park Salmon Bake ★ 🎁🍴 GRILL Amid the more corporate places where the casual park atmosphere is relatively contrived, at "The Bake" you'll find a rollicking local hot spot that becomes a center of the community each summer. You can't miss the homemade highway frontage as you enter Glitter Gulch. The extremely casual the staff is friendly, led by owners who in 2008 won the Alaska small business of the year award. The restaurant is also the area's cultural focus, with live music acts coming through regularly during the summer. Check the website for a calendar of who is playing and the amount of the cover charge. The food goes well beyond the $20 grilled salmon entree, also including crab cakes, pulled pork sandwiches, Tex-Mex selections, and even trendier cuisine such as parmesan and asiago-crusted halibut. It's all good, and priced in a broad range appropriate for many budgets. They'll also come to pick you up and drive you back to your hotel. The cabins are described under "hotels," above.

Mile 238.5, Parks Hwy. ☎**907/683-2733.** www.denaliparksalmonbake.com. All items $8–$37. AE, DC, DISC, MC, V. Daily 7am–midnight.

King Salmon Restaurant ★★ SEAFOOD This is a terrific place for a special night of dining out right near the park. The waiting area has a cozy fireplace, and the dining room perches on the edge of the Nenana Canyon, where you can watch rafters float by during your meal. The food and service are up to Princess Tours' excellent standards—steak and salmon, the usual choices for Alaska tourists—expertly prepared. For something a bit more casual, try the Basecamp Bistro next door.

In the Denali Princess Lodge, Mile 238.5, Parks Hwy. ☎907/683-2282. Reservations recommended. Dinner main courses $20–$40. AE, DC, DISC, MC, V. Daily 6–11am, 11:30am–3pm, and 4:30–10pm. Basecamp Bistro daily 3–10pm.

Nenana View Bar & Grill ★ GRILL This is an attractive restaurant in the McKinley Chalet Resort with a fireplace at one end of the dining room and outdoor seating overlooking the river at the other. They serve delicious pizza and great fire-grilled steaks.

Mile 238.9, Parks Hwy., in McKinley Chalet Resort. ☎907/683-8200. All items $12–$28. AE, DISC, MC, V. May–Sept daily 11am–2:30pm and 5–11pm. Bar until 1am.

The Overlook Bar & Grill ★ GRILL This fun, noisy place has the feel of a classic bar and grill, with a vaulted ceiling of rough-cut lumber and a spectacular view of the Nenana Canyon. There are two dining rooms, one with the bar and another, behind a glass partition, which is quieter and has tablecloths. A huge variety of craft beers is available, with several on tap. At times I've gotten excellent fare here. Call ☎907/683-2723 for courtesy transportation from all area hotels.

Mile 238.5, Parks Hwy., up the hill above the Denali Canyon area. ☎907/683-2641. Main courses $9–$15 lunch, $11–$44 dinner. MC, V. Daily 11am–11pm. Bar until 1am.

WITHIN DRIVING DISTANCE

These restaurants are as much as 13 miles from the park entrance, so you will need a car.

Black Diamond Grill ★★ GRILL A unique 9-hole golf course lies amid the mountains and rolling taiga north of the park at a center of activities, including all-terrain vehicle tours, GPS treasure hunts, mini-golf, and covered wagon rides with full-service camp-style meals. The associated restaurant produces excellent food from a menu mostly influenced by Northern Italian cookery, with lots of Alaskan seafood. For lunch, sandwich choices include a pesto chicken hoagie for $7.50, and for dinner there is halibut in parchment with fresh rosemary and garlic for $20. Although not as perfect as at the best restaurants in Anchorage, the cuisine is memorable and satisfying. The dining room is light and cheery, with pine furniture and flowers on the table.

Mile 247, Parks Hwy. (take the hwy. north 10 miles, then turn left at Otto Lake Rd.). ☎907/683-4653. www.blackdiamondgolf.com. Lunch $7.50–$9; dinner $14–$24. AE, DISC, MC, V. Daily 7am–11pm.

McKinley Creekside Cafe ★ ☺ STEAK/SEAFOOD/SANDWICHES This friendly spot in the Carlo Creek area, south of the park, is a favorite of the locals. You can dine on steak or baked salmon with brown sugar, apples, and toasted almonds for around $20, or order a burger for around $9. The food is consistently good, including breakfast, and craft brews and wine are served. There is a

Where to Dine

THE DENALI NATIONAL PARK REGION

playground outside and a kids' menu. They also pack substantial sack lunches for the park shuttle-bus ride.

Mile 224, Parks Hwy. ☎888/533-6254 or 907/683-2277. www.mckinleycabins.com. Lunch $6–$10; dinner $8–$21. DISC, MC, V. Daily 6am–10pm.

The Perch/Panorama Pizza Pub ★ STEAK/PIZZA Two restaurants here. The Perch gets its name from its location, atop an odd, knoblike hill. It's a friendly, family-run place serving a straightforward steak and Alaskan seafood menu—they don't try anything fancy, just good ingredients done right. The home-baked bread is noteworthy. The dining room is light, with well-spaced tables and big picture windows on three sides. Down on the highway level, the Panorama Pizza Pub is a hot spot for pizza and also includes a bakery/deli that packs lunches in cloth tote bags for the park bus. You can often hear local musicians playing here in the evening.

Mile 224, Parks Hwy., 13 miles south of the park. The Perch: ☎888/322-2523 or 907/683-2523. www.denaliperchresort.com. Dinner main courses $14–$40. MC, V. Daily 6–9am and 5–10pm. Panorama Pizza Pub: ☎907/683-2623. Pizza $13–$32. MC, V. Daily 3pm–midnight.

229 Parks Restaurant and Tavern ★★★ INTERNATIONAL The name of the restaurant, which is the best in the area, comes from the milepost, which puts it in a quiet area about 8 miles south of the park entrance in a beautiful post-and-beam building. The owners, Laura and Land Cole, live here year-round. Laura is a professionally trained chef and veteran of Alaska's best dining rooms. Whenever possible, she uses organic ingredients and local produce—eggs are naturally nested by free-range chickens. The menu changes daily and has included main-course items such as tenderloin filet, lemon pasta with asparagus, venison chops, and, of course, salmon. A sweet potato soup with king crab meat was fabulous. The appetizer list is long and interesting, including spring rolls second to none. Breakfast is coffeehouse fare, such as quiche, granola, and fruit. Locals keep the place busy even on winter weekends, but they close at 1pm on winter Sundays so everyone in the community can go play hockey on Deneki Lakes. The restaurant is popular and doesn't take reservations, so you may want to call ahead to check on the wait time.

Mile 229, Parks Hwy. ☎907/683-2567. www.229parks.com. Reservations not accepted. Dinner $18–$33. MC, V. Summer Tues–Sun 7–11am and 5–10pm, winter Fri–Sat 9am–9pm, Sun 9am–1pm (call ahead, because hours can vary in winter).

DENALI NIGHTLIFE

Locals and young people go to the **Denali Park Salmon Bake** in the evening to hear the live music and dance there (see "Where to Eat," above). National touring bands stop in on their way from Anchorage to Fairbanks. A shuttle will come get you. The area also has many other restaurants with bars, many of which I've described.

The main tourist-oriented evening event is the concessionaire's **Cabin Nite Dinner Theater,** at the McKinley Chalet Resort (☎800/276-7234 or 907/683-8200), a professionally produced musical revue about a gold rush–era woman who ran a roadhouse in Kantishna. You can buy the $62 tickets (half price ages 2–12) virtually anywhere in the area. The actors, singing throughout the evening, stay in character to serve big platters of food to diners sitting at long tables, doing a good job of building a rowdy, happy atmosphere for adults and kids. Shows happen nightly at 5:30 and 8:30pm.

Princess Cruises and Tours puts on its own evening show, *The Music of Denali,* at the Denali Princess Lodge. The musical performance lasts an hour, the entire dinner 2 hours. Tickets are for sale at the hotel's tour desk (☎800/426-0500 or 907/683-2282) for $55 (half price ages 6–12).

DENALI WILDERNESS LODGES

Staying in a wilderness lodge makes for a completely different experience of Denali, and that's why I've segregated these choices here. These lodges are self-contained vacations, and if you choose to stay, you don't need to worry about the shuttle bus or the other issues of escaping the "front-country." The lodges also are expensive and require a significant commitment of time. It doesn't make sense to spend fewer than 3 days, and some lodges require longer minimum stays.

All lodges within Denali National Park are in the Kantishna district, on private land where gold miners staked claims before the park was created. The lodge operators who later obtained this land gained something more valuable than gold: the opportunity to bring visitors to the far end of the park from the entrance, as near as a vehicle can get to Mount McKinley, without using the park's shuttle system. Hosts drive visitors to Kantishna in their own buses or vans over the 91-mile park road. These lodges are open only in summer. More wilderness lodges in the wider region are described in chapter 3. Besides the three lodges I have room to describe here in detail, I also recommend **Denali Backcountry Lodge** (☎877/233-6254 or 907/376-1992; www.denalilodge.com).

Camp Denali/North Face Lodge ★★★ In the cabins of Camp Denali, a pioneering eco-tourism establishment, you can wake to the white monolith of Mount McKinley filling your window. Also uniquely, the naturalist guides here have the right to use the park road free of the shuttle system for hiking and field trips to observe wildlife, botany, and birding, all included in the substantial price. During some sessions, nationally respected academics and other experts join the programs. All arrivals and departures are on fixed session dates of 3, 4, or 7 nights. Energy comes from the sun and the lodge's own hydro power: The whole place is about as eco-friendly as you can get. Each of the Camp Denali cabins has its own outhouse, and all share a central bathhouse and lodge common rooms. If your own flush toilet is a priority, North Face Lodge has smallish traditional rooms with private bathrooms, but without the views. Each lodge has its own dining room for family-style meals.

Kantishna area (P.O. Box 67), Denali National Park, AK 99755. ☎907/683-2290. Fax 907/683-1568. www.campdenali.com. 33 units (18 cabins), none with private bathroom at Camp Denali; 15 units with bathroom at North Face Lodge. $505 per adult per night; $379 per child per night. Sessions of 3, 4, or 7 nights only. Rates include all meals, guided activities, and transportation from park entrance. No credit cards. *In room:* No phone.

Kantishna Roadhouse ★★ This property of many buildings along Moose Creek in the old Kantishna Mining District trades on both the mining history and outdoor opportunities of the area. Some rooms are large and luxurious, while others are in smaller single cabins with lofts. The log central lodge has an attractive lobby with people coming and going—it's got more of a hotel feel and might be more attractive to an older, less active set or to families than the other lodges in the Kantishna District. It also has a bar. Rates include guided hikes, fishing, interpretive programs, biking, gold panning, and a daily sled-dog demonstration.

Kantishna District, Denali National Park (Mailing address: 1 Doyon Place, Ste. 300, Fairbanks, AK 99701). **800/942-7420** or 907/683-1475. Fax 907/683-1449. www.seedenali.com. 32 units. $405 per person double; $300 per child ages 3–11. Extra person $320. Rates include all meals, guided activities, and transportation from park entrance. Minimum stay 2 nights. AE, DISC, MC, V. **Amenities:** Bar; mountain bikes; sauna.

Skyline Lodge ★ ✦ Run by pilot Greg LaHaie, owner of Kantishna Air Taxi, the lodge offers a unique alternative in Denali's backcountry: a place you don't have to be a millionaire to afford. With room for only ten guests and a self-serve philosophy, it's far simpler and more casual than the full-service lodges in Kantishna, and costs less than a fourth as much. Also, there's no minimum stay, and you can fly there with Greg. It costs $33 a day to join the family-style lunch and dinner (breakfast is already included in the price). Rooms are in cabins and sleep up to four, each with a double or queen-size bed and a loft. Large windows overlook Moose Creek. The kitchen, TV, and other amenities are in the central lodge building. The most important amenity, however, is that you are in the heart of Denali's backcountry.

Kantishna District (P.O. Box 46), Denali National Park, AK 99755. **907/683-1223.** Fax 907/683-1223. www.katair.com. 4 units, none with private bathroom. $225 double. Extra person age 2 and over $50. Rates include continental breakfast. DISC, MC, V. **Amenities:** Free airport transfers; free mountain bikes; sauna.

TALKEETNA: BACK DOOR TO DENALI

Talkeetna, a historic and funky little town with a sense of humor but not much happening, slept soundly from its decline around World War I until about a decade ago. Now there are paved streets (both of them), a fancy National Park Service building, a larger railroad depot, and two large luxury lodges. It seems that while Talkeetna slumbered in a time capsule, an explosion of visitors was happening at Denali National Park. Now, not entirely voluntarily, Talkeetna has been enveloped in that boom.

As a threshold to the park, Talkeetna has significant pros and cons that you should take into account. On the positive side, it's closer to Anchorage; the development is much more interesting and authentic than that at the park entrance; there's lots to do outdoors; and Mount McKinley is seen more frequently, both because of geography and weather. On the negative side, a big minus: You can't get into the park from here without a long drive or an expensive flight. That may mean you miss the dramatic scenery, easy backcountry access, and unique wildlife viewing on the park road.

The town dates from the gold rush and has many charming log and clapboard buildings. With 16 sites of historic note, the entire downtown area has been listed on the National Register of Historic Places. You can spend several hours looking at two small museums and meeting people in the 2-block main street, then go out on the Talkeetna or Susitna rivers for rafting, a jet-boat ride, or fishing, or take a flightseeing trip to the national park.

Essentials

GETTING THERE Talkeetna lies on a 14-mile spur road that branches from the Parks Highway 99 miles north of Anchorage and 138 miles south of the park entrance. The **Alaska Railroad (℡800/544-0552;** www.alaskarailroad.com) serves Talkeetna daily on its runs to Denali National Park during the summer, and weekly in the winter. (See "Park Essentials," earlier in this chapter, for additional details.) The summer fare from Anchorage to Talkeetna is $89 one-way for adults, half price for children ages 2 to 11, for basic service.

It's possible to stay in Talkeetna but do the Denali National Park shuttle bus ride and other park activities by flying there for the day. **Talkeetna Aero Services (℡888/733-2899** or 907/733-2899; www.talkeetnaaero.com) offers daily round-trips for this purpose during the summer with a flightseeing tour circling Mount McKinley en route. They charge $425 as a package with ground transfers, a bus tour, and a box lunch.

VISITOR INFORMATION Built to serve people aiming to climb Mount McKinley, the **Denali National Park Talkeetna Ranger Station,** at 1st and B streets (P.O. Box 588), Talkeetna, AK 99676 (℡907/733-2231; www.nps. gov/dena), makes a fascinating stop for anyone curious about mountaineering. Inside the handsome structure, a large sitting room contains a river-rock fireplace, climbing books, and pictures of the mountain—it's like an old-fashioned explorers' club. Fascinating records open for inspection cover the history of McKinley climbs. Rangers are on hand to answer questions, too. It's open May through Labor Day daily from 8am to 6pm; winter Monday through Friday from 8am to 4:30pm.

The **Talkeetna/Denali Visitor Center,** located in a tiny cabin at the intersection of the Parks Highway and Talkeetna Spur Road and on Main Street (P.O. Box 688), Talkeetna, AK 99676 (℡800/660-2688 or 907/733-2641; www.talkeetnadenali.com), is a commercial center belonging to a local flight service and providing brochures, information, and advice while earning commissions from bookings. It's the handiest commercial information stop in the region. The center is open daily from 8am to 8pm in summer, and they respond to inquiries year-round with free trip-planning help.

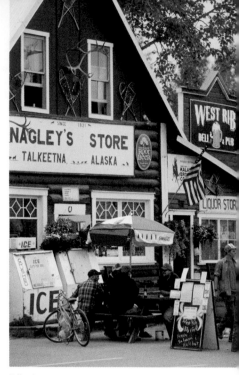

Talkeetna.

SPECIAL EVENTS The **Talkeetna Moose Dropping Festival,** held over the second weekend in July, is the big community event of the year, in its fourth decade as a fundraiser for the Talkeetna Historical Society (☎**907/733-2487;** www.talkeetnahistoricalsociety.org). The named event doesn't involve dropping moose, as an aggrieved animal lover once complained, but tossing moose droppings. Another event, the Mountain Mother Contest, open only to mothers, is a race of Bush skills, including splitting wood and diapering a baby.

Exploring the Town

Talkeetna is famous for its laid-back atmosphere and outdoors, not for "attractions," but there are several places to stop in to get a sense of the place. One is the ranger station mentioned earlier in this section under "Visitor Information." If you come in May or June, you're sure to meet many international mountain climbers; you'll have no difficulty picking them out (see "Climbing Mount McKinley" under "Activities Within the Park"). Along Main Street are shops where artists and craftspeople often can be found at work. For your walk, pick up a copy of the "Talkeetna Historic District Walking Tour" brochure from the museum (in the next paragraph) for a map and informative explanation of the town's story, including details such as the site of its first bathtub, which arrived in 1923.

The **Talkeetna Historical Society Museum,** in five buildings on the Village Airstrip a half-block south of Main Street (☎**907/733-2487;** www.talkeetnahistoricalsociety.org), is well worth a stop. The first building contains artifacts and displays on local mining history, including engaging photographs and biographies of individual characters. The second is an old railroad depot, relocated here and furnished with period decor. The third holds climbing displays and a huge scale model of Mount McKinley and the nearby mountains (don't miss it if you will fly over the mountain). The fourth is a 1916 trapper's cabin and the fifth a 1924 cabin, both with period artifacts. The museum is also a handy information stop. It is open daily in summer from 10am to 6pm; generally closed in winter. Admission is $3, free for children 16 and under.

I've found the most affecting site in town to be the **Mount McKinley Climbers' Memorial** at the town cemetery, near the airstrip on the east side of the railroad tracks. Besides a memorial of granite plaques for lost mountaineers, there is a small garden of monuments to many individual climbers, some in Japanese. The bodies of at least 36 climbers who died on the mountain have never been recovered. The propellers in the cemetery mark the graves of Bush pilots.

Mount McKinley Climbers' Memorial.

[FastFACTS] TALKEETNA

Bank A local credit union is near the Parks Highway on the Talkeetna Spur Road. There is no bank in the town center, but several businesses have ATMs, including Nagley's General Store.

Hospital Talkeetna **Denali Family Medical Clinic,** 125 1st St. (**☎907/733-2708**).

Internet Access Free for up to 30 minutes at the **Talkeetna Public Library** (**☎907/733-2359**), at Mile 13.5 of the Talkeetna Spur Road, just across the tracks.

Police For non-emergencies, call the **Alaska State Troopers** at **☎907/733-2256.** The station is near

the Parks Highway on the Talkeetna Spur Road.

Post Office In the town center, near the intersection of Talkeetna Spur Road and Main Street.

Taxes There is no **sales tax. Room tax** in the area is 5%.

Getting Outside
FLIGHTSEEING

There is no more dramatic or memorable experience available to the typical tourist in Alaska than to fly with one of the glacier pilots who support Mount McKinley climbs. Climbers typically begin with a flight from here to the 7,200-foot level of the Kahiltna Glacier. These immense mountains grow ever larger as you fly toward them until, like a tiny insect, you fly among their miles-tall folds, watching the climbers toiling on the ice below you. I was simply speechless.

Several operators with long experience offer the flights. The least expensive excursions cost around $190 and approach McKinley's south face. If at all possible—and if the weather is good—buy an extended tour that circles the mountain and flies over its glaciers, for $235 to $375 per person. Best of all, arrange

Cessna 180 airplane flying to Mount McKinley.

a landing on the mountain itself, just as the climbers do. The Don Sheldon Amphitheater on the Ruth Glacier is a stunning spot high on McKinley; only after you stand there do you realize the incredible scale of what you have seen from above. In the past this was not possible from mid-July through August, as the snow was too soft for the ski planes to land on the glaciers, but air taxis using different equipment and different landing areas have often been able to land all summer in recent years. These landings are treated as add-ons to the tours mentioned above, for an additional price of $75 to $85 per person, plus the $10 park entrance fee.

Should you reserve ahead or wait to see the weather? It used to be you could reliably walk in and grab a seat, but the popularity of these flights now makes reservations advisable. That's the best way to get a guaranteed price, too; otherwise, prices sometimes depend on the number of passengers aboard the plane. If you do decide on the walk-in approach, make your appearance early in the morning.

A number of air-taxi companies offer these flights, all operating out of the Talkeetna airport, including these three that I can wholeheartedly recommend: **Talkeetna Air Taxi** (☎800/533-2219 or 907/733-2218; www.talkeetnaair.com), **K-2 Aviation** (☎800/764-2291 or 907/733-2291; www.flyk2.com), and **Talkeetna Aero Services** (☎888/733-2899 or 907/733-2899; www.talkeetnaaero.com).

FISHING & JET BOAT TOURS

Talkeetna is at the confluence of the Talkeetna and Big Susitna rivers. **Mahay's Riverboat Service** (☎800/736-2210 or 907/733-2223; www.mahaysriverboat.com) covers these fast moving waters of glacier silt on speedy, comfortable jet boats. Tours that leave several times a day from a dock near the Talkeetna River public boat launch range from 2 to 5 hours, priced at $65 to $155 per person. Owner Steve Mahay is legendary, the only person ever to shoot Devil's Canyon in a jet boat. He offers fishing charters as well.

RAFTING

Talkeetna River Guides, on Main Street (☎800/353-2677 or 907/733-2677; www.talkeetnariverguides.com), offers a 2-hour wildlife river-rafting tour, without white water, over 9 miles of the Talkeetna three times a day for $79 adults, $59 children 10 and under. They also offer longer rafting expeditions.

Where to Stay & Dine

There are good restaurants at each of the lodgings listed here. One other place stands out, **Café Michele,** in a quaint little house at the corner of Talkeetna Spur Road and 2nd Street (☎907/733-5300). It's a classy little bistro, serving sandwiches on homemade focaccia bread for lunch, and with dinner entrees ranging from $23 to $39, including vegetarian dishes. Save room for dessert, as the baking is exceptional—Michele even bakes the area's wedding cakes. It's easy to find a burger, pizza, or sandwich on Main Street.

A public campground for tents only is at the end of Main Street and costs $10. A larger campground with more privacy is at the boat launch (cross the railroad tracks to the airport, then turn left) and charges $13 a night.

Mt. McKinley Princess Lodge ★★ Princess Cruises built the main lodge building to take advantage of a striking view of the mountain, only 42 miles away as the crow flies. The property isn't near any town—100 miles south of the park entrance and about 45 road miles from Talkeetna—but, like a resort, they offer everything you need on-site and a full set of activities, including a short network of trails. If you want a ride to Talkeetna, the lodge provides shuttle service. The design and decoration are an inspired modernization of the classic national park style. There are several dining choices, including a steak and seafood place, a cafe, and a bar and grill.

Mile 133.1, Parks Hwy., Denali State Park, AK 99683. ☏**800/426-0500** or 907/733-2900. Fax 907/733-2922. www.princesslodges.com. 460 units. Summer $189 double, $289 suite; spring and fall $149 double, $249 suite. AE, DC, DISC, MC, V. Closed mid-Sept to mid-May. **Amenities:** 4 restaurants; bar; courtesy shuttle to Talkeetna. *In room:* TV, hair dryer.

Swiss Alaska Inn 🛎 This is the essence of Talkeetna: a family business in the same hands for decades where guests are made to feel like old friends among the real old friends often found sipping coffee with the proprietor in the small restaurant. They serve good, familiar American meals, plus a few German dishes. Most of the rooms are decorated in light colors and, although small, are clean, comfortable, and reasonably priced. The larger rooms in the newer building are quite preferable.

F St., near the boat launch (P.O. Box 565), Talkeetna, AK 99676. ☏**907/733-2424.** Fax 907/733-2425. www.swissalaska.com. 20 units. $141 double. Extra person $10. AE, DISC, MC, V. **Amenities:** Restaurant; bar; courtesy car (to railroad station); Wi-Fi in restaurant. *In room:* TV/DVD (no broadcast reception), hair dryer.

Talkeetna Alaskan Lodge ★★ The Cook Inlet Region Native corporation spared no expense building this magnificent hotel of big timbers and river rock 2 miles from Talkeetna, but it's not a gaudy showplace. Trim of regionally harvested birch finishes rooms and hallways in understated geometric designs, hung with Native art. Because the hotel sits atop a high river bluff, views from common rooms and many guest rooms take in a broad-canvas masterpiece of the Alaska Range, with McKinley towering in the center. Rooms in the main building are somewhat larger and have either one king- or two queen-size beds, and the hallways connect to several sumptuous lobbies with reading areas. As much as I like the hotel, however, the rates are high.

Mile 12.5, Talkeetna Spur Rd. (Mailing address: P.O. Box 727, Talkeetna, AK 99676). ☏**888/959-9590** or 907/265-4501 reservations; 907/733-9500 at lodge. Fax 907/733-9545. www.talkeetnalodge.com. 212 units. Summer $309–$409 double; off-season $189–$259 double. Extra person 11 and over $15. AE, DISC, MC, V. Closed Oct–Apr. **Amenities:** Free airport transfers; 2 restaurants (dining room, bistro); bar; fitness center. *In room:* TV, hair dryer, Wi-Fi.

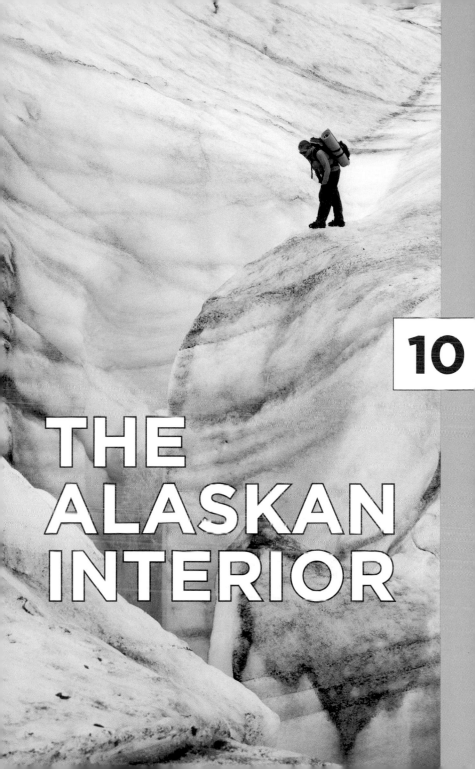

10

THE ALASKAN INTERIOR

A warm summer evening in a campground; a slight breeze rustling the leaves of ghostly paper birches, barely keeping the mosquitoes at bay; the sounds of children playing; a perpetual sunset rolling slowly along the northern horizon—this is Interior Alaska. You know it's time to gather up the kids, separate them according to who belongs to whom, and put them to bed; it's 11 o'clock, for heaven's sake. But it's too difficult to feel that matters, or to alter the pace of a sun-baked day that never ends, meandering on like the broad, silty rivers and empty two-lane highways. Down by the boat landing, some college kids are getting ready to start on a float in the morning. An old, white-bearded prospector wanders out of the bar and, offering his flask to the strangers, tries out a joke while swatting the bugs. "There's not a single mosquito in Alaska," he declares. Waits for the loud, jocular objections. Then adds, "They're all married with big, big families." Easy laughter; then they talk about outboard motors, road work, why so many rabbits live along a certain stretch of highway. Eventually, you have to go to bed and leave the world to its pointless turning as the sun rotates back around to the east. You know it'll all be there tomorrow, just the same—the same slow-flowing rivers, the same long highways, the same vast space that can never be filled.

Interior Alaska is so large—it basically includes everything that's not on the coasts or in the Arctic—you can spend a week of hard driving and not explore it all. Or you can spend all summer floating the rivers and still have years of floating left to do before you see all the riverbanks. It's something like what the great mass of America's Midwest once must have been, perhaps a century and a half ago, when the great flatlands had been explored but not completely civilized and Huckleberry Finn could float downriver into a wilderness of adventures. As it happens, I have a friend who grew up on a homestead in the Interior and ran away from home at age 15 in that exact same fashion, floating hundreds of miles on a handmade raft, past the little river villages, cargo barges, and fishermen. During an Interior summer, nature combines its immensity with a rare sense of gentleness, patiently awaiting the next thunderstorm.

PREVIOUS PAGE: **Root Glacier.**

Winter is another matter. Without the regulating influence of the ocean—the same reason summers are hot—winter temperatures can often drop to –30°F or –40°F (–34°C or –40°C), and during exceptional cold snaps, even lower. Now the earth is wobbling over in the other direction, away from the sun. The long, black nights sometimes make Fairbanks, the region's dominant city, feel more like an outpost on a barren planet, far off in outer space. That's when the northern lights come, spewing swirls of color across the entire dome of the sky and crackling with electricity. Neighbors get on the phone to wake each other and, rising from bed to put on their warmest parkas and insulated boots, stand in the street, gazing straight up. Visitors lucky enough to come at such times may be watching from a steaming hot-spring tub. During the short days, they can bundle up and watch sled-dog racing or race across the wilderness themselves on snowmobiles.

Fairbanks stands second in Alaska in population, with 90,000 in the greater area, but the Interior otherwise is without any settlements large enough to be called cities. Instead, it's defined by roads, both paved and gravel, which are strands of civilization through sparsely settled, often swampy land. Before the roads, development occurred only on the rivers, which still serve as thoroughfares for the Athabascan villages of the region. In the summer, villagers travel by boat. In the winter, the frozen rivers become highways for snowmobiles and sled-dog teams. White homesteaders and gold miners live back in the woods, too. Gold-rush history is written on the land in piles of old gravel tailings and abandoned equipment, as well as in the prettier tourist attractions and historic sites. Gold mining goes on today, in small one-man operations and huge industrial works employing hundreds, but today the economy is based more on military and other government spending, the oil industry, and, of course, tourism. You'll find warm, rural hospitality along with the great vistas on these highways, and, perhaps, a sense of slow-river laziness Huck Finn would have recognized.

EXPLORING THE INTERIOR

More than anywhere else in Alaska, the Interior is the place where having your own car provides you with the freedom to find the out-of-the-way places that give the region its character. Trains and buses run between Fairbanks and Anchorage, but that approach will show you only the larger, tourist-oriented destinations.

If you have the time and money, you may enjoy driving one of the remote gravel highways, or just poking along on the paved highways between the larger towns, ready to stop and investigate the roadhouses and meet the people who live out in the middle of nowhere. You'll find them mostly friendly and often downright odd—*colorful,* to use the polite term. As I drove an abandoned highway a few years ago, I saw a hand-lettered sign advertising coffee. It wasn't your typical espresso stand, just a log cabin dozens of miles from the next nearest building. A squinting high plains drifter stepped out of the cabin, wearing a cowboy hat on his head and a huge revolver on his hip, and asked, "Yeah?" The coffee came from a percolator warming on the woodstove, and the proprietor and I struck up a good conversation in his dark little dwelling. He was living the life of the old-time frontier. Another favorite roadside sign, sighted on the Alaska Highway, in spray paint on plywood: SALE—EEL SKINS—ANVILS—BAIT. I've always wished I'd stopped in

to window-shop and meet the person who came up with that business plan.

Of course, not every mile of back road is scenic; nor are all the stops interesting. Driving a car through Alaska takes a long time, including many hours spent in dull, brushy forest, and calls for a high tolerance for greasy hamburgers and a willingness to occasionally relieve yourself in the bushes. Paved highway sections can develop frost heaves in this often-frozen land—backbreaking dips and humps caused by the freeze and thaw of the road base and ground underneath. The gravel roads generate clouds of dust and quickly fatigue drivers, and windshields and headlights often succumb to their flying rocks. For information on renting a vehicle to drive on gravel roads, see "Equipped for the Backroads," on p. 516.

FROM TOP: **Hick's Creek Roadhouse; Road signs along the Alaska Highway.**

FAIRBANKS: ALASKA HEARTLAND

If the story of the founding of Fairbanks had happened anywhere else, it wouldn't be told so proudly, for the city's father was a swindler and its undignified birth contained an element of chance not usually admitted in polite society. As the popular story goes (and the historians' version is fairly close), in 1901 E. T. Barnette decided to get rich by starting a gold-mining boomtown like the others that had sprouted from Dawson City to Nome as the stampeders of 1898 sloshed back and forth across the territory from one gold find to the next. He booked passage on a riverboat going up the Tanana with his supplies to build the town, having made an understanding with the captain that, should the vessel get stuck, he would lighten the load by getting off with the materials on the nearest bank. Unfortunately, the captain got lost. Thinking he was heading up a slough on the Tanana, he got sidetracked into the relatively small Chena River. That was where the boat got stuck and where Barnette got left, and that was where he founded Fairbanks.

Fortunately for Barnette, an Italian prospector named Felix Pedro was looking for gold in the hills around the new trading post and the next summer made a strike in the Tanana Hills, north of the Chena. On that news, Barnette dispatched his Japanese cook, Jujiro Wada, off to Dawson City to spread the word. Wada's story showed up in a newspaper that winter after Christmas, and a stampede of hundreds of miners ensued, heading toward Fairbanks in weather as cold as –50°F (–46°C). Barnette's town was a success, but the cook nearly got lynched when the stampeders found out how far he'd exaggerated the truth. Much more gold was found later, however, and half the population of Dawson City came downriver to Fairbanks. Barnette had made it big.

The town's future was ensured thanks to a political deal. Barnette did a favor for the territory's judge, James Wickersham, by naming the settlement for Wickersham's hero in Congress, Sen. Charles Fairbanks of Indiana, who later became vice president. Wickersham then moved the federal courthouse to Fairbanks from Eagle—he loaded his records on his dogsled and mushed here, establishing the camp as the region's hub. Wickersham's story is interesting, too. He was a notable explorer, Alaska's first real statesman as a nonvoting delegate to Congress, and father of the Alaska Railroad. Houses he lived in are preserved at Pioneer Park in Fairbanks and in Juneau just up the hill from the capitol building. Barnette didn't do as well in history's eyes: He was run out of the town he founded for bank fraud.

Fairbanks is Alaska's second-largest city now, with a population of about 35,000 in the city limits and 90,000 in the greater metropolitan area, but it has

Rollin' on the River

Floating any of the thousands of miles of the Interior's rivers opens great swaths of wilderness. Beginners will want to take a guided trip before venturing out on their own. (See the lists of operators in chapter 3.) To plan your own trip, start with the **Alaska Public Lands Information Center** in Fairbanks (p. 506), Tok (p. 547), or Anchorage (p. 292). Among the most accessible and historic rivers in the region are the Chena, Chatanika, and Yukon (see the sections on Fairbanks and Chena Hot Springs Rd. and the boxes on the Steese Highway and Dawson City in this chapter).

ALASKA'S highways A LA CARTE

You won't need a detailed highway map of Alaska, because Alaska doesn't have detailed highways. A triangle of paved two-lane highways connects Tok, Fairbanks, and Anchorage. From this triangle, a few routes reach to discrete destinations, and gravel roads penetrate the periphery of the Bush. Beyond a few miles of freeway around Fairbanks and Anchorage, highways all are narrow strips of asphalt or gravel through the wilderness. (See "The Roster of Rural Roads," on p. 532, for a run-down of Alaska's unpaved and minor highways.) Always fill your tank before leaving town, as gas stations are far apart. A centralized report on road conditions and construction is operated by the Alaska Department of Transportation (☎511; http://511.alaska.gov). To help readers figure driving times, I have included my estimate of reasonable average speeds on each road (without stopping). These are based purely on my experience and assume dry, daylight conditions in summer.

Alaska Highway

Route 2 from the border to Delta Junction
Average speed (Alaska section): 55–65 mph

Running nearly 1,400 miles from Dawson Creek, British Columbia, to Delta Junction, Alaska, a couple of hours east of Fairbanks on the Richardson Highway, this World War II road today is paved and generally easy driving. Two tiny towns lie on the Alaska portion of the road, Delta Junction and Tok. The prettiest part is on the Canadian side, in the Kluane Lake area. See section 5, later in this chapter.

Glenn Highway

Route 1 from Anchorage to Tok
Average speed: 55–65 mph, except 45 mph on Matanuska Glacier section

From the Alaska Highway, this is how you get to Southcentral Alaska, including Anchorage, 330 miles southwest of Tok. The northern section, from Tok to Glennallen (sometimes called the "Tok Cut-Off"), borders Wrangell–St. Elias National Park, with broad tundra and taiga broken by high, craggy peaks. Glennallen to Anchorage is even more

spectacular, as the road passes through high alpine terrain and then close by the Matanuska Glacier, where it winds through a deep canyon valley carved by the glacier's river. See section 6, later in this chapter.

Parks Highway

Route 3 from near Anchorage to Fairbanks
Average speed: 60–65 mph

The George Parks Highway goes straight from Anchorage to Fairbanks, 360 miles north, providing access on the way to Denali National Park. The best parts are the vistas of Mount McKinley

Summit Lake.

Glenn Highway.

Canyon and steep Thompson Pass, just out of Valdez (see chapter 8), then passes the huge, distant peaks of southern Wrangell–St. Elias National Park. North of Glennallen, the road climbs into the Alaska Range, snaking along the shores of long alpine lakes. The road descends again to the forested area around Delta Junction and meets the Alaska Highway before arriving in Fairbanks. The highway is covered in section 7 of this chapter.

from south of the park and the alpine terrain on either side of Broad Pass, where the road crosses the Alaska Range and the park entrance. However, the Parks Highway is mostly a transportation route, less scenic than the Richardson or Glenn highway. From the northern (Fairbanks) end, the highway passes Nenana (p. 508), then Denali and Talkeetna (chapter 9), and finally the towns of the Matanuska and Susitna valleys (chapter 7).

Seward Highway
Route 1 from Anchorage to Tern Lake, Route 9 from Tern Lake to Seward
Average speed: 45–60 mph, depending on traffic

The highway leaves Anchorage on the 127-mile drive to Seward following the rocky edge of mountain peaks above a surging ocean fjord. Abundant wildlife and unfolding views often slow cars. Later, the road climbs through high mountain passes above the tree line, tracing sparkling alpine lakes. Alaska's best trail hikes are here. The section from Anchorage 50 miles south to Portage Glacier is covered in chapter 7; the remainder, to Seward, in chapter 8.

Richardson Highway
Route 4 from Valdez to Delta Junction, Route 2 from Delta Junction to Fairbanks
Average speed: 50–60 mph, except 45 mph in Thompson Pass section

The state's first highway, leading 364 miles from tidewater in Valdez to Fairbanks, lost much of its traffic to the Parks Highway, which saves more than 90 miles between Anchorage and Fairbanks, and to the Glenn Highway, which saves about 120 miles from Glennallen to Tok. But it's still the most beautiful paved drive in the Interior. From the south, the road begins with a magnificent climb through Keystone

Sterling Highway
Route 1 from Tern Lake to Homer
Average speed: 50–60 mph, except 45 mph near Cooper Landing

Leading 142 miles from the Seward Highway to the tip of the Kenai Peninsula, the highway has some scenic ocean views on its southern section, but is mostly a way to get to the Kenai River, the Kenai National Wildlife Refuge, Kachemak Bay, and the towns of Cooper Landing, Soldotna, Kenai, and Homer.

Fairbanks

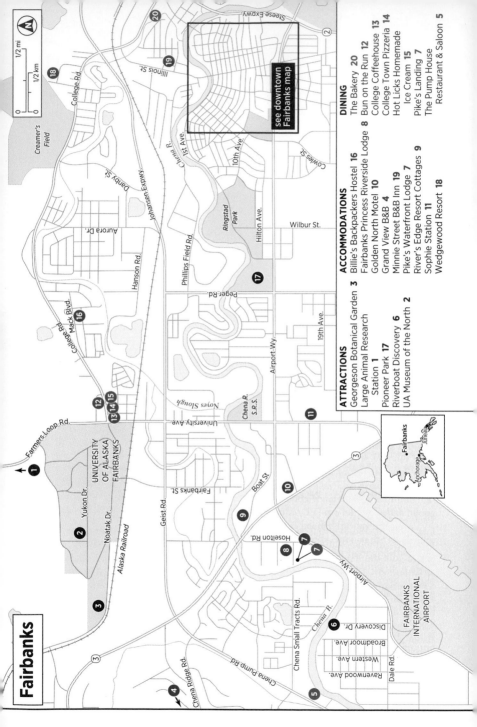

ATTRACTIONS
Georgeson Botanical Garden **3**
Large Animal Research
  Station **1**
Pioneer Park **17**
Riverboat Discovery **6**
UA Museum of the North **2**

ACCOMMODATIONS
Billie's Backpackers Hostel **16**
Fairbanks Princess Riverside Lodge **8**
Golden North Motel **10**
Grand View B&B **4**
Minnie Street B&B Inn **19**
Pike's Waterfront Lodge **7**
River's Edge Resort Cottages **9**
Sophie Station **11**
Wedgewood Resort **18**

DINING
The Bakery **20**
Bun on the Run **12**
College Coffeehouse **13**
College Town Pizzeria **14**
Hot Licks Homemade
  Ice Cream **15**
Pike's Landing **7**
The Pump House
  Restaurant & Saloon **5**

never learned to put on airs. It sprawls, broad and flat, along big highways and the Chena. It's a friendly, easygoing town, but one where people still take gold and their independence seriously. They're still prospecting and mining around here, fighting off environmental regulation and maintaining a traditional Alaskan attitude that "it's us against the world." Fairbanks is the birthplace of strange political movements, including the secessionist Alaskan Independence Party. It's an adamant, loopy, affable place; it doesn't seem to mind being a little bizarre or residing far from the center of things. And that makes it an intensely Alaskan city, for those are the qualities Alaskans most cherish in their myth of themselves.

Fairbanks can strike a visitor a couple of ways, depending on what you expect and what you like. Fairbanks can come across as a provincial outpost, a touristy cross between Kansas and Siberia. Driving one of the franchise-choked commercial strips, you can wonder why you went out of your way to come here. Or you can relax and take Fairbanks on its own terms, as a fun, unpretentious town that never lost its sense of being on the frontier.

My children love it here. There's plenty for families to do in Fairbanks, much of it at least a little corny and requiring drives to widespread sites at the university, on the Chena River, in the gold mining area north of town, and at Pioneer Park. (You *must* have wheels in Fairbanks.) There are good opportunities for hiking and mountain-biking, and great opportunities for canoeing and slow river-float trips.

Essentials

GETTING THERE

BY CAR OR RV Fairbanks is a transportation hub. The Richardson Highway heads east 100 miles to Delta Junction, the end point of the Alaska Highway, then south to Glennallen and Valdez. The Parks Highway heads due south from Fairbanks to Denali National Park, 120 miles away, and Anchorage, 360 miles south.

BY VAN OR BUS Alaska/Yukon Trails (℡800/770-7275; www.alaskashuttle.com) offers daily service in summer (3 days a week in winter) to and from Denali National Park and Anchorage (one-way fares are $55 and $99, respectively). In Fairbanks, the van stops at the visitor center and at Billie's Backpackers and GoNorth hostels (p. 526 and 516), among other places. The shuttle also runs as a tour to Dawson City and Whitehorse, Yukon. On most routes they pick up and drop off along the way, but not in Canada.

BY TRAIN The **Alaska Railroad** (℡800/544-0552; www.alaskarailroad.com) links Fairbanks with Denali National Park and Anchorage, with tour commentary provided along the way. The high-season one-way fare is $64 to Denali and $210 to Anchorage (nearly twice the cost of flying between the cities); first-class, Gold Star service is $149 and $320, respectively.

BY AIR Alaska Airlines (℡800/252-7522; www.alaskaair.com) connects Fairbanks to Anchorage. A bargain round-trip fare is just under $260 at this writing. The airport is a hub for various small carriers to Alaska's Interior and Arctic communities. A cab downtown from the airport is $18 to $20 with **Yellow Cab** (℡907/455-5555). **Airlink Shuttle and Tours** (℡907/452-3337) charges $3.50, with a 3-person minimum and $1 fee per bag, for a ride from the airport to anywhere in town.

VISITOR INFORMATION The new **Morris Thompson Cultural and Visitors Center,** downtown at the corner of Wendell and Dunkel streets, houses the **Fairbanks Convention and Visitors Bureau** (☎800/327-5774 or 907/456-5774; fax 907/459-3787; www.explorefairbanks.com) and the **Alaska Public Lands Information Center** (see below), as well as a non-profit **Alaska Geographic** bookstore (☎907/459-3710; www.alaska geographic.org), and cultural and educational programs. The Fairbanks visitor bureau has information kiosks in the main lobby, as well as a video nook featuring films about the area and Alaska. The staff and volunteers answer questions and provide useful maps, driving tour pamphlets, and walking tour audio players, and can help you find a room with their daily vacancy listing (weekly in winter). Several computers are set up for free e-mail access or to look up travel information. Visitor bureau hours are May to mid-September daily 8am to 9pm, the rest of the year 8am to 5pm. The organization also has information desks at the airport and train depot, staffed summer only, and at Pioneer Park, closed entirely off-season.

The **Alaska Public Lands Information Center** (☎907/459-3730; www.alaskacenters.gov) staffs an information counter at the Morris Thompson center, as well as trip planning tables where you can spread out maps and computers to gather trip planning information. This is an indispensable stop for anyone planning to spend time in the outdoors. The staff is remarkably knowledgeable and can tell you about trips and activities based on firsthand experience. The counter operates in summer daily from 9am to 6pm, in winter Monday through Saturday from 9am to 5pm.

The Morris Thompson center as a whole is also worth visiting, with exhibits and a theater that features daily free films and naturalist programs, and classes, workshops, and demonstrations teaching about Athabascan culture. Parking is plentiful.

GETTING AROUND Fairbanks is designed around the car, and that's the practical way to get around. Without one, sticking only to downtown, you will leave with a low opinion of the place. The city is too spread out to use taxis much. **Avis, Hertz, Dollar, Budget, Payless, Alamo,** and **National** are located at the airport. If you plan on driving any of the region's unpaved highways, see "Equipped for the Backroads," p. 516, as the brand-name agencies do not allow it.

The Fairbanks North Star Borough's **MACS bus system** (☎907/459-1011; www.co.fairbanks.ak.us, click on "Bus Schedules" under "Services") links the university, downtown, the nearby North Pole community, shopping areas, and some hotels. Service is every 30 minutes, at best, worse Saturday, and nonexistent Sunday. Pick up timetables at the visitor center or online. All buses connect at the transit park downtown, at 5th Avenue and Cushman Street. The fare is $1.50 for adults; 75¢ for seniors, children, teens, and people with disabilities; free for children under age 5.

Fairbanks's car-oriented layout does not lend itself to using bikes as the primary means of transportation, but there are great mountain-biking opportunities (see "Getting Outside," later in this chapter).

[FastFACTS] FAIRBANKS

Banks Fairbanks has numerous banks with **ATMs** in the downtown area and along the commercial strips. **Key Bank** is at 100 Cushman.

Business Services & Internet Access FedEx Copy Center is at 418 3rd St. (☎907/456-7348).

You can check e-mail for free at the **Morris Thompson Cultural and Visitors Center** at 101 Dunkel St. (see "Visitor Information," above).

Hospital Fairbanks Memorial is at 1650 Cowles St. (☎907/452-8181).

Police For nonemergency police business, call the **Alaska State Troopers**

(☎907/451-5100), or, within city limits, the **Fairbanks Police Department** (☎907/459-6500).

Post Office At 315 Barnette St.

Taxes Fairbanks has no sales tax. North Pole charges 4%, with a cap of $8 in tax on any one purchase. **Room tax** is 8%.

SPECIAL EVENTS A recording of current local happenings can be reached at ☎907/456-INFO (456-4636), maintained by the Fairbanks Convention and Visitors Bureau, which also posts an event calendar at **www.explore fairbanks.com**.

The **Yukon Quest International Sled Dog Race** (☎907/452-7954; www.yukonquest.com) starts February 6, 2010, in Fairbanks and ends 10 to 14 days later in Whitehorse, Yukon (in odd-numbered years, the direction is reversed). Mushers say this rugged 1,000-mile race is even tougher than the Iditarod.

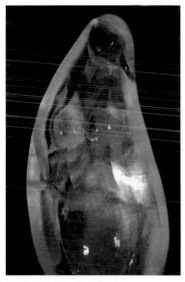

A sculpture at the World Ice Art Championships.

The **Nenana Ice Classic** (☎907/832-5446; www.nenanaiceclassic. com) is a sweepstakes held annually since 1917 based on who can guess closest to the exact minute when the ice will go out on the Tanana River. The classic starts with Tripod Days, the first weekend in March, when they set up the so-called four-legged tripod; when it moves 100 feet it trips a clock, determining the winner. The Tripod Days celebration includes dance performances, dog mushing, and other activities.

Also in March, the **World Ice Art Championships** (☎907/451-8250; www.icealaska.com) brings carvers from all over the world to sculpt immense, clear chunks cut from a Fairbanks pond. It's worth planning a visit around. Ice sculptures stand in the Ice Park near the corner of Peger and Phillips Field roads. In 2010, professional carving will be February 23 to 25 (single block) and

---

Nenana: Tom Sawyer's Alaska

If you are driving south from Fairbanks toward Denali National Park or Anchorage, plan a short stop in the town of Nenana, about 60 miles along your way. It's a town out of a Mark Twain novel, a sleepy, dusty riverside barge stop left over from the past. Here President Warren Harding drove the golden spike on the Alaska Railroad in 1923; a monument with a depiction of the spike is on display outside the memory-stirring old depot museum, although the train hasn't stopped regularly in decades. On the waterfront, riverboats are still loaded with cargo for villages down the Tanana and Yukon rivers. That's also where you can see the Alfred Starr Nenana Cultural Center, with its own little museum and Native craft shop, including some crafts by locals. The oldest building in town is the picturesque 1905 log cabin church on Front Street. Stop in at the visitor center on the Parks Highway to learn more and to see the big book of guesses from the Nenana Ice Classic (www.nenanaakiceclassic.com). The contest is a drawing to guess the exact minute the ice on the Tanana will go out in the spring, with a jackpot around $300,000. Thanks to the game, this is one of the most carefully kept climate measurements in the north; scientists have used it to demonstrate long-term warming of the weather. See "Special Events," above, to learn about ice classic festivities. Learn more about Nenana at the city's website (www.nenanahomepage.com).

February 28 to March 5 (multiblock), with the best viewing of completed sculptures March 5 to 15. Amateur and junior carving events take place during and after the professional events. The park usually stays open until the last Sunday in March, sometimes later if weather allows. Among ice carvers, Fairbanks ice is famous for its clarity and the great size of the chunks. Some spectacular ice sculptures stand as tall as two-story buildings. Check the website for pictures of past winners.

The **North American Sled Dog Championships** (✆907/457-MUSH [457-6874]; www.sleddog.org) are the oldest running, taking place over 2 weekends in mid-March. Sprint mushers from all over the world compete with teams of as many as 24 dogs, streaking away from the starting line on 2nd Avenue or the Chena River.

Lots of events happen around the **summer solstice,** usually June 21. The **Midnight Sun Run** (✆907/452-6046; www.midnightsunrun.us) is a 10K race and walk, with winners chosen for both their times and their funny costumes. The race is run on or near the solstice. It starts at 10pm on the university campus and ends at Pioneer Park.

The **Midnight Sun Baseball Game,** hosted by the semipro Alaska Goldpanners of Fairbanks (✆907/451-0095; www.goldpanners.com), begins at 10:30pm on June 21. The game, which began with a pair of pick-up teams in 1906, is played with no artificial lights. The 'Panners have hosted since 1960.

Also in June, the free **Fairbanks Summer Folk Fest** (www.fairbanks folkfest.org) fills a Pioneer Park lawn with music, food, and art booths; live music starts at 1pm and lasts late into the night.

The Fairbanks Summer Arts Festival, held the last 2 weeks in July on the University of Alaska Fairbanks campus (☎907/474-8869; www.fsaf.org), brings artists of international reputation for performance and teaching. Classes are for all levels in music, dance, Shakespeare, opera, creative writing, visual arts, healing arts, and other subject areas.

The **Tanana Valley State Fair** (☎907/452-3750; www.tananavalleyfair. org), in early August, shows off the area's agricultural production, arts and crafts, businesses and entertainment, and includes rides and competitive exhibits.

In late August, Friends of Creamer's Field (☎907/452-5162) hosts an annual **Sandhill Crane Festival,** with nature walks, lectures, and other activities, mostly at Creamer's Field.

Exploring the Town
STROLLING AROUND DOWNTOWN

Exploring downtown won't take more than an hour or two, but there are a few interesting spots in addition to the ice museum and community museums covered below. Start with the exhibits at the **Morris Thompson Cultural and Visitors Center** at 101 Dunkel St. The visitors bureau there lends audio players with spoken tours for the other sights (you have to leave a credit card imprint as a deposit).

A graceful footbridge spans the river. On the other side peek into the lobby of the **Doyon Native corporation offices** to see Native cultural displays from all over Alaska, the traditional Athabascan tool collection, and the colorful modern

art hanging from the walls and ceiling. Downriver, toward Cushman Street, is the town's most interesting building, the Roman Catholic **Church of the Immaculate Conception.** The white clapboard structure, built in 1904, has ornate gold-rush decoration inside, rare for its authenticity, including a pressed-tin ceiling and stained glass windows—an appealing if incongruous mix of gold-rush and sacred decor.

Crossing back on the Cushman Street Bridge you'll see on the left a large log cabin with a sod roof, the new **headquarters of the Yukon Quest Sled Dog Race,** where you can get race souvenirs and see displays of equipment that teach about the race and dog mushing. Next door, the **Golden Heart Park** is a waterfront plaza with a fountain and a bronze statue of a Native family, where community events often occur. Farther downriver, at 1st Avenue

Church of the Immaculate Conception.

between Kellum and Bonnifield streets, **St. Matthew's Episcopal Church** is a cute old log church with a working rope-pull bell. It was founded by missionary and dog-sled explorer Hudson Stuck in 1904, who organized the first successful climb of Mount McKinley. The original church burned; the present structure dates from 1948.

DOWNTOWN MUSEUMS

At 500 2nd Ave., the **Fairbanks Ice Museum** ★ (☎907/451-8222; www.ice museum.com) aims to show summer visitors a bit of Fairbanks ice carving. A big-screen, high-tech slide show plays hourly, explaining the annual World Ice Art Championships (see "Special Events," above), and four expansive freezers with large picture windows contain ice sculptures with an ice artist usually at work. Admission is $12 for adults, $11 for seniors and military, $6 for children ages 6 to 12, $2 for ages 5 and under. It's open from 10am to 8pm daily from May 1 to September 30. Recently, the Ice Museum's theater began 8pm showings of a unique and striking photographic show called *Auroras: Crown of Light.* Admission for that is $10 for adults, $5 children 12 and younger.

The **Fairbanks Community Museum** ★, in the old city hall at 410 Cushman St. (☎907/457-3669), is well worth a stop for the charming historical exhibits and the sense of local pride it contains. A series of cramped galleries offers up old photographs, maps, newspapers, and other bric-a-brac, as well as skillfully created explanatory exhibits focusing on the 1967 flood and the area's

Seeing the Aurora Borealis

One fall evening I left the house of friends in Fairbanks to the sight of a swirling green glow that filled the dark sky. I knocked on the door and brought them out to see, only to have my friends laugh in my face. They informed me, with mock contempt for my Anchorage home, that in Fairbanks they don't even bother to bend their necks back for northern lights as dim as these. It's true—a bright aurora borealis is routine in Fairbanks. Some of the world's top experts on the phenomenon work here, at the **University of Alaska Geophysical Institute** (their aurora predictions, in season, and extensive background on the aurora are posted at www.gi.alaska.edu). Hours-long displays can be incredibly spectacular and even moving.

Unfortunately, most visitors never see these wild strands of bright colors whipping across the sky, because when most visitors come, the sky is never dark. Alaskans rarely see the stars from late May to early August, and to see the aurora well you need an especially dark night sky. To improve your chances, plan your trip in the fall or winter. An early September trip offers brilliant fall foliage, dark night skies, and the remnants of summer weather. In midwinter, the sky is dark all night and most of the day. Many hotels near Fairbanks cater to travelers coming to see the aurora in winter, as well as visitors who come for such winter sports as dog mushing and snowmobiling; the best for that kind of trip is Chena Hot Springs Resort, covered in the next section of this chapter.

President Harding's railroad car at Pioneer Park.

gold-mining history and development. An exhibit of whimsical photographs shows how modern-day Fairbanksans entertain themselves in the winter. You could lose yourself in this maze of small discoveries. Volunteers run the museum, open Tuesday through Saturday from 10am to 6pm, with reduced hours in the off season. Admission is free, but donations are accepted. It is closed during April.

PIONEER PARK ★★

Built for the Alaska purchase centennial in 1967, **Pioneer Park** (formerly **Alaskaland**) is the boiled-down essence of Fairbanks on grounds at the intersection of Airport Way and Peger Road (☎907/459-1087; www.co.fairbanks. ak.us, click on "Parks and Recreation," then "Parks," then "Pioneer Park"). It's called a theme park, but don't expect Disneyland or anything like it. Instead, Pioneer Park is a city park with a theme. It's relaxing and low-key, entrancing for young children and interesting for adults if you can give in to the charm of the place. Admission to the park is free, and the tours and activities are generally inexpensive. The park is open year-round, but the attractions operate only Memorial Day weekend to Labor Day, daily from noon to 8pm. Pick up a map and schedule when you arrive; here I've listed the highlights, but there is more to see. Depending on the pace you like to keep and the age level of your group, you can spend anything from a couple of hours to most of a day here.

The **SS Nenana ★★** is the park's centerpiece. Commissioned by the federally owned Alaska Railroad in 1933, the large sternwheeler plied the Yukon and Tanana rivers until 1952. In 1967, the *Nenana* came to what was then Alaskaland but was unmaintained and had nearly collapsed from rot when it was saved by a community restoration effort, completed in 1992. Free guided tours explore two decks of sumptuous mahogany, brass, and white-painted promenades, and the wheelhouse, well-preserved engine room, and the like. Self-guided entry is open to the ground-floor cargo deck with its engaging set of dioramas showing all the riverside towns and villages where the boat called, modeled as they looked in its heyday.

Much of Fairbanks's history has been moved to Pioneer Park. A village of log cabins contains shops and restaurants, each marked with its original location and place in town history. **Judge Wickersham's house,** built around 1904, is kept as a museum, decorated appropriately according to the period of the town's founding. The house is less than grand—it may remind you of your grandmother's—but it's worth a stop to strike up a conversation with the historical society volunteers who keep it open. **Pres. Warren Harding's railcar,** from which he stepped to drive the golden spike on the Alaska Railroad, sits near the park entrance. The **Pioneer Air Museum** (☎907/451-0037) is housed in a geodesic dome toward the back of the park. Besides the aircraft there are displays and artifacts of the crashes of Alaska's aviation pioneers. Admission is $2 for adults, free for children 12 and under with a parent, $5 for families.

A different kind of attraction shows off Fairbanks winter in summer. **40 Below Fairbanks,** at Cabin no. 3, just down from the Palace Saloon (☎907/347-5451), puts visitors in 8×10-foot room at a temperature at least –40°F (–40°C), a chill seen at least once most winters here. While in the freezer you can use a rock-solid banana to pound a nail and toss a cup of hot water into the air to watch it explode into steam. Admission is $8.50.

Other park attractions include an illustrated gold-rush show, kayak and bike rentals, a dance hall, an art gallery, and Alaska Native and gold-rush museums. If you have children, you certainly won't escape Pioneer Park without a ride on the **Crooked Creek and Whiskey Island Railroad** that circles the park twice, with a tour guide pointing out the sights; rides cost $2 for adults, $1 for children and seniors. Kids will also enjoy the large **playground,** with equipment for toddlers and older children, where lots of local families come to play, and the two 18-hole miniature golf courses. The only carnival ride is a nice old **merry-go-round,** which costs $1.

Tour groups generally come to Pioneer Park in the evening from mid-May to mid-September for the combined **Alaska Salmon Bake,** at the mining valley area, and the **Golden Heart Revue,** at the Palace Theatre (☎800/354-7274 or 907/452-7274; www.akvisit.com). Cost for all-you-can-eat prime rib and fish (halibut, cod, or salmon) is $31. Beer and wine are available. The seating area is pleasant, with indoor or outdoor dining. The revue, nightly at 8:15pm from mid-May to mid-September, covers the amusing story of the founding of Fairbanks with comedy and song in a nightclub setting; admission is $18 for adults.

UNIVERSITY OF ALASKA FAIRBANKS

The state university's main campus contains several interesting attractions and makes a point of serving tourists. The campus is on the west side of town; major entrances are via Thompson Drive off Geist Road and at the intersection of University Avenue and College Road. A widely distributed brochure lists tours, hours, and fees. A free 2-hour **walking tour,** led by students, meets at Signers Hall Monday through Friday at 10am, June through August. Call ☎907/474-7021, or check www.uaf.edu/visituaf for more information. Several campus attractions are listed below; more are on the website, where you'll also find a campus map. The university's trail system is covered later in this chapter under "Winter Activities."

UA Museum of the North ★★★ The on-campus museum of science and art is one of Alaska's best. The building is a swooping combination of grand, graceful shapes, recalling moving icebergs, or perhaps the northern lights. Alaska's largest natural history collection is here, and its most scholarly, with information presented at advanced as well as elementary levels. Some of the objects have

Iron Eskimo at the UA Museum of the North.

a real wow factor, such as Blue Babe, the mummified steppe bison; a 5,400-pound copper nugget; and the state's largest public display of gold. The art is no less inspiring. A towering gallery contains a thematic presentation of contemporary works alongside Native and archaeological objects, crafts, and much more. A sound and light installation on the second floor, "The Place Where You Go To Listen," received a lengthy review by the *New Yorker* in 2008, which said the piece confirmed Fairbanks composer John Luther Adams as "one of the most original musical thinkers of the new century." Visit the auditorium for presentations on the aurora, winter, and other subjects. Audio players for self-guided tours are available for $4.

907 Yukon Dr. **☎907/474-7505.** www.uaf.edu/museum. Summer admission $15 adults, $14 ages 60 and older, $8 ages 7-17, free ages 6 and under; winter admission $10 adults, $9 ages 60 and older, $5 ages 7-17, free ages 6 and under. Summer daily 9am-9pm; winter Mon-Sat 9am-5pm, closed Sun.

Georgeson Botanical Garden ★ I really enjoy the mix of science and contemplation I find at this relaxed working garden. Plots are laid out to compare seeds and cultivation techniques, usually well posted with explanatory information on the experiment; but at the same time the flowers and vegetables are spectacular and there are peaceful memorials and places to picnic. You don't need a tour to enjoy the garden. Nearby, the barn of the university's experimental farm is open for visitors, and reindeer can be viewed in a neighboring paddock. A children's garden is slowly being created and includes a fun maze in the form of a five-petal flower.

117 W. Tanana Dr. **☎907/474-1944.** www.uaf.edu/salrm/gbg. Admission $2. Summer daily 9am-8pm, store 9am-5pm; free guided tours Fri at 2pm.

Large Animal Research Station ★ The university studies captive musk oxen, reindeer, and caribou here on a property often called the "musk ox farm." Tours are given daily in the high season, with naturalists bringing animals into an amphitheater for close-up viewing. At any time, on a walk along the fence from the parking lot on Yankovich Road, you can see the animals behaving naturally in the large pastures. Best times are the cool morning or evening hours, and binoculars help. A small gift shop specializes in qiviut, the soft underwool of the musk ox.

Yankovich Rd. **☎907/474-7207.** www.uaf.edu/lars. Tours $10 adults, $9 seniors, $6 students, free ages 6 and under. Tours Memorial Day through Labor Day daily each hour 10am-4pm. Call ☎907/474-5724 to check on tour times and changes. Drive north from campus, turn left on Ballaine Rd., left again on Yankovich.

COMMERCIAL TOURIST ATTRACTIONS

Three major for-profit attractions around Fairbanks pack in visitors by the hundreds of thousands, most of them on group tours. These places are educational and fun, as I've described below, but prices for all are high. Whether they're worth your money depends on how much you've got and your level of interest; however, I doubt most budget travelers would feel they got their money's worth.

Riverboat *Discovery.*

The Riverboat *Discovery* ★★ The *Discovery* belongs to the pioneering Binkley family, which has been in the riverboat business since the Klondike gold rush and has run this attraction since 1950. The *Discovery* is a real sternwheeler, a 156-foot steel vessel carrying up to 900 passengers on as many as three trips a day. There's nothing intimate or spontaneous about the 3½-hour ride, which mostly carries package-tour passengers off fleets of buses, but the Binkleys still provide a diverting outing that doesn't feel cheap or phony. After loading at a landing with shops off Dale Road, near the airport, the boat cruises down the Chena and up the Tanana past demonstrations on shore—among others, a bush plane taking off and landing, fish cutting at a Native fish camp, and a musher's dog yard. Finally, the vessel pulls up at the bank for an hour-long tour of a mock Athabascan village.

1975 Discovery Dr. ☎866/479-6673 or 907/479-6673. www.riverboatdiscovery.com. Tours $55 adults, $38 ages 3–12, free ages 2 and under. Sailings mid-May to mid-Sept daily at 8:45am and 2pm.

The El Dorado Gold Mine ★ A train such as you would find at an amusement park carries visitors though an impressively staged educational tour, including a trip through a tunnel in the permafrost. This is like a land version of the riverboat tour that's operated by the same family, the Binkleys. But the gold miners who act as hosts are the real attraction here. Visitors gather around a sluice to hear the amusing and authentic Dexter and Lynette (aka Yukon Yonda) Clark and watch a swoosh of water and gold-bearing gravel rush by. You pan the resulting pay dirt, and everyone goes home with enough gold dust to fill a plastic locket—typically $5 to $35 worth. Drive out to the mine after making reservations, or take a $5 shuttle.

Off the Elliott Hwy., 9 miles north of town. ☎866/479-6673 or 907/479-6673. www.eldorado goldmine.com. Tours $35 adults, $23 ages 3–12, free ages 2 and under. Tours mid-May to mid-Sept daily; call for times.

Gold Dredge Number 8 ★ Authenticity makes this the area's best historic gold-mining site. The centerpiece is a 1927 gold dredge, similar to machines in Dawson City and Nome, standing five stories tall on a barge in a pond it created.

When it operated, huge scoops would dig from one end, the mechanism inside would digest the gold from the gravel, and then it would dump the tailings out the back—in this way, the pond and the dredge it supports crept 4½ miles across the frozen ground north of Fairbanks. Many sterile areas you see in this area were created by these earth-eaters, because little grows on their leavings for decades after. The tour company that bought the historic site added to the dredge with museums housed in relocated gold-camp buildings, showing the harsh, colorless life lived by the miners. A 90-minute tour includes a film, exhibits showing mining techniques, and the dredge, and ends with a chance to pan for gold yourself, with success assured.

1755 Old Steese Hwy. **℡907/457-6058.** www.golddredgeno8.com. Admission $21 tour only, $25 with gold panning, $35 with lunch of stew. Mid-May to mid-Sept tours start hourly 9:30am–3:30pm. To get there, go north on the Steese Expwy. from town, turn left on Goldstream Rd., turn left again on the Old Steese Hwy.

Getting Outside

In this section, I've described the outdoor opportunities local to Fairbanks, but some other choices are barely farther afield: Check out section 3 of this chapter, on Chena Hot Springs Road, and the feature later in this chapter, "The Steese Highway: Drive into the Wild." Get guidance at the **Alaska Public Lands Information Center,** in the Morris Thompson Center at 101 Dunkel St. (**℡907/459-3730;** www.alaskacenters.gov). The staff will advise you on outings, outfitters, and where to find rental equipment. Two publications you can buy at the center could also help greatly. The "Fairbanks Area Wildlife Watching Guide" is a $6 booklet that contains thorough descriptions of the best places to go and tips for success. *Outside in the Interior,* by Kyle Joly (University of Alaska Press, $20), describes more than 50 routes for a variety of activities, and includes

Panning for gold.

detailed maps of each. Published late in 2007, it is the region's only trail guide. Both are for sale in local bookstores as well.

GEARING UP

You can rent most of what you need for outdoor explorations around Fairbanks and along the region's extraordinary rural highways from a set of local businesses that have grown up around the needs of adventurers. Some of the outdoor opportunities I describe require a drive on unpaved roads, including portions of the Steese Highway. Two businesses that rent vehicles you can take on these roads are listed in the feature "Equipped for the Backroads," below. One of those, GoNorth Alaska Adventure Travel Center, also rents canoes, bikes, and camping gear, and offers a shuttle for canoeists and hikers. For ski rentals, see the appropriate sections below.

Alaska Outdoor Rentals & Guides, owned by the knowledgeable Larry Katkin, has its main location on the riverbank at Pioneer Park (☎907/457-2453; www.akbike.com or www.2paddle1.com). The company rents canoes, kayaks, and bikes, and offers pickup or drop off for paddlers in town or farther afield—even for trips on the great Yukon River. For an easy in-town paddle—say from the park to the Pump House Restaurant and Saloon—you would pay $37 for the canoe and $19 for the pickup. If you want to go beyond the road system, Larry also carries foldable canoes that will fit in a bush plane. He also offers lessons. This is a good place to start a mountain-biking outing, too. Bike rental starts at $19 for 3 hours, $27 for a day. You can also rent canoes from the long-established

Equipped for the Backroads

Exploring Alaska's gravel highways—camping and fishing along the way, perhaps launching a canoe in a remote lake—can be tough for visitors to arrange because of the policies of most car-rental agencies, which don't allow clients to drive off pavement. An exception is **Arctic Outfitters** (☎907/474-3530; www.arctic-outfitters.com), which rents the Ford Taurus and Escape. The vehicles are equipped with CB radios, maintenance kits, and two full-sized spare tires. Drivers must be at least 30 years old and have their own insurance. One-day rental rates exceed $200, with discounts for additional days, and mileage charges start after 250 miles.
    GoNorth Alaska Adventure Travel Center, 3500 Davis Rd.

(☎866/236-7272 or 907/479-7272; www.gonorthalaska.com), rents SUVs, vans, and trucks, and also campers on four-wheel-drive pickups and motor homes. All are allowed on gravel roads, but for the motor homes there's an extra fee. The firm also runs a tent-camp hostel; arranges self-guided outdoor trips; rents canoes, bikes, and camping gear; and drives a shuttle for canoeists and hikers. With unlimited mileage, a pickup camper is $137 to $252 a day; insurance of $21 to $27 a day is required unless you present proof of your own coverage, so be sure to ask about what paperwork you will need when you reserve. See "Car Wheels on Gravel Roads," p. 290, for an Anchorage firm.

7 Bridges Boats and Bikes, at 7 Gables Inn, 4312 Birch Lane (**907/479-0751;** www.7gablesinn.com/7bbb), for $35 per day or $100 per week, and they will drop you off at the river and pick you up at your destination for $2.50 per mile out of town, with a $15 minimum. Guests at the inn get free rentals (same phone; www.7gablesinn.com). Street and mountain bikes go for $25 a day.

CREAMER'S FIELD At 1300 College Rd., right in Fairbanks, this 2,000-acre migratory waterfowl refuge is a former dairy farm that was saved from development in 1966 by a community fund drive. In the spring and fall the pastures are a prime stopover point for Canada geese, pintails, and golden plovers, and large flocks of sandhill cranes. We've seen many swans in the spring. Fewer birds are present during mid-summer. The **Friends of Creamers Field** (**907/452-5162;** www.creamersfield.org) operates a small visitor center (**907/459-7307**) in the old farmhouse with displays on birds, wildlife, and history, open mid-May through mid-September daily from 10am to 5pm, off-season Saturdays noon to 4pm. They offer guided nature walks in summer Monday through Friday at 10am and Wednesday at 7pm. But you don't need a guide to explore 3 miles of trails through the forest, field, and wetland. I especially enjoy the Boreal Forest Trail nature walk, interpreted by signs and an excellent booklet you can pick up at the visitor center or from a kiosk at the trail head. The **Alaska Bird Observatory** (**907/451-7159;** www.alaskabird.org) conducts research and educational programs on the Creamer's Field refuge, including bird walks and bird banding that visitors can observe (call for times). It is the farthest north facility of its kind in North America. The organization's building has interpretive displays, a nature store, and a library. Located just west of the refuge on the grounds of the Wedgewood Resort (see below), the observatory can be hard to find—look for the signs.

CHENA LAKE RECREATION AREA This is a wonderful and unique place for a family camping trip. A birch-rimmed lake created for a flood-control project has been developed by the local government to provide lots of recreational possibilities: flat walking and bike trails; a swimming beach; fishing; a place to rent a variety of non-motorized boats; a self-guided 2.5-mile nature trail; a playground; big lawns; volleyball courts; and the terrific campground, with 80 camping sites, from pull-throughs for RVs to tent sites on a little island you can reach only by boat. In the winter, it's a popular area for cross-country skiing, ice fishing, dog mushing, and snowmobiling. Use of the area in summer requires a $4 fee per vehicle. Tent sites are $10 per night, and RV sites are $12. Drive about 15 miles east of Fairbanks on the Richardson Highway and take the exit for Dawson Road. Turn left on Dawson, go under the overpass, then turn right on Mistletoe Drive. When you reach Laurance Road, turn left. Signs are posted along the way. For information, contact Fairbanks North Star Borough Chena Lake Recreation Area (**907/488-1655;** www.chenalakes.com). Follow the same directions to the **Moose Creek Dam Salmon Watch,** driving along the dike past the recreation area. This picnic and viewing site was built by the U.S. Army Corps of Engineers atop the flood-control project so that people could watch spawning salmon in crystal-clear water from late June to the end of July. Use of the salmon watch is free, so tell the recreation-area gatehouse you are going there.

SUMMER ACTIVITIES

CANOEING The rivers in and around Fairbanks are best seen by floating slowly along in a canoe. Paddling is as popular as hiking around here. See "Gearing Up," p. 516, for businesses that rent canoes and provide drop-off and pick-up service along the area's waterways.

The Chena River is slow and meandering as it flows through Fairbanks, and several restaurants on the bank cater to boaters. Farther upriver, the canoeing passes wilder shores, and near the headwaters becomes more challenging (see "Chena Hot Springs Road," later in this chapter). For beginners, try the wilderness section from the Chena Lake Recreation Area downstream (see

Canoeing the Chena River.

"Chena Lake Recreation Area," above). It's 12 to 16 hours from there all the way into town, or you can take out at one of the roads crossing the river along the way. The **U.S. Army Corp of Engineers** (☎907/ **488-2748**) produces the "Chena River Float Guide," with put-in and take-out points and float times, available at the Alaska Public Lands Information Center (see "Visitor Information," earlier).

For something a bit more challenging but still manageable, the clear, Class I water of the Chatanika River is perfect for day trips or relaxed expeditions of a week or more, if you know how to handle river hazards such as sweepers and snags that show up on any Alaska stream. Alaska State Parks produces a brochure covering the float from the Upper Chatanika River Campground, at mile 39 of the Steese Highway, to another campground on the Elliott Highway (get it at the Alaska Public Lands Information Center, above). Low water and logjams requiring portages can slow down the trip so that it takes a long day; in better conditions, expert canoeists can do it in a few hours.

The Steese Highway also meets two National Wild and Scenic Rivers: Beaver Creek, for trips of a week or more over easy Class I water, and Birch Creek, for more expert paddlers. For detailed guidance, check with the Alaska Public Lands Information Center in Fairbanks. Also see "The Steese Highway: Drive into the Wild," p. 536.

BIKING & HIKING Traffic goes fast in Fairbanks, and the separated bike trails are few, but strong cyclists can get by. Mountain-biking is good on many dirt roads and byways within and beyond Fairbanks and on the ski trails at Birch Hill Recreation Area and the University of Alaska Fairbanks (see "Winter Activities," below). The ski trails are also good for easy summer hikes, or go farther afield for more ambitious trail hikes off Chena Hot Springs Road (in the next section of this chapter) or the Steese Highway (p. 536). Inquire about all the options or other ideas at the Alaska Public Lands Information Center.

FISHING Salmon season here is brief and the fish, this far inland, have turned spawning colors and have softer, less palatable flesh compared to coastal salmon. Most fishing is in the streams for Arctic grayling, Northern pike, and burbot, and in stocked lakes for rainbow trout, Arctic char, and silver salmon. You can fish right in the Chena as it flows through town, although getting out of town and hiking away from a road yields better results. Fly-in fishing will further increase your chances and add sheefish and Dolly Varden char to your list, but you can find better salmon fishing to go along with the freshwater fish in Anchorage or another coastal community. The Alaska Public Lands Information Center (p. 506) offers guidance, or contact the **Alaska Department of Fish and Game,** at Creamer's Field, 1300 College Rd., Fairbanks, AK 99701 (☎**907/459-7207;** sportfish information recording ☎907/459-7385; www.alaska.gov/adfg, click on "Sport Fish," then on the Interior region on the map, then "Lower Tanana River Drainage").

WINTER ACTIVITIES

Fairbanks has real Jack London winters. The visitor bureau guarantees it. For the growing number of visitors who want to experience real cold, see the aurora borealis, and ride a dogsled, Fairbanks is the place. Chena Hot Springs Resort (p. 535) and A Taste of Alaska Lodge (p. 523) are the best destinations for winter immersion, but you can also have a good time in town, especially in March, when the days lighten up, the temperatures are moderate, and the town gets busy with dog mushing and the ice-carving contest (see "Special Events," earlier in this chapter).

DOG MUSHING The long winters and vast wild lands make the Fairbanks area a center of dog sledding, both for racers and recreationists, and there are plenty of people willing to take you for a lift, which is really an experience not to be missed. I've heard good things about **Sun Dog Express Dog Sled Tours** (☎**907/479-6983;** www.mosquitonet.com/~sleddog), which

Dog mushing.

charges as little as $15 for a quick spin, up to $250 to learn to drive a team in a half-day. Or try **Paws for Adventure** (**☎907/378-3630;** www.paws foradventure.com), which offers 1-hour rides for about $80 as well as trips up to a week long.

During the summer, learn about mushing by taking a wonderfully intimate tour with Mary Shields, the first woman to finish the Iditarod. Rather than a tour, a visit to Mary's home on the outskirts of Fairbanks feels more like a chat with a fascinating new friend. You'll meet and pet Mary's dogs, talk about dog mushing, and hear tales of her extraordinary experiences as a musher. The tour, called **Alaskan Tails of the Trails** (**☎907/455-6469;** www.maryshields.com), happens every evening in the summer. It costs $28 and lasts 2 hours. Reserve well ahead, as she keeps groups small.

CROSS-COUNTRY SKIING The **Birch Hill Recreation Area,** off the Steese Expressway just north of town, has about 25km of good cross-country ski trails, most groomed for classical or skate skiing, and two warm-up buildings in which to change clothes. Several loops of a few kilometers each offer advanced skiing on the steep southern side of the hill; loops of up to 10km provide more level terrain to the north. Some trails are lighted. The **University of Alaska Fairbanks** offers a trail network of roughly the same length; two-thirds of it groomed for skate technique. Although I prefer Birch Hill, with its mix of ability levels, the University trails pass through lovely lands and have the advantage of a nearby source of rental equipment, the **Outdoor Adventures Program** at the Wood Student Center (**☎907/474-6027;** www.uaf. edu/outdoor). You can rent skis, poles, and boots for a mere $10 a day. One trail head is at the west end of campus, near the satellite dishes at the top of Tanana Loop. Another is off Farmers Loop Road at Ballaine Lake. Find current information, including events, trail conditions, and maps from the website of **Nordic Ski Club of Fairbanks** (www.nscfairbanks.org).

DOWNHILL SKIING Fairbanks has several community-size downhill skiing areas, including the relatively large **Moose Mountain Ski Resort** (**☎907/479-4732;** snow report **☎**907/459-8132; www.shredthemoose.com), with 1,300 vertical feet of skiing. Instead of freezing on a lift, you ride back up the hill and socialize in heated buses.

Shopping

The **Arctic Travelers Gift Shop,** 201 Cushman St. (**☎907/456-7080;** www. arctictravelersgiftshop.com), specializes in Native art and crafts, carrying both valuable art and affordable but authentically Alaskan gifts. The staff is knowledgeable about what they sell. Right next door, at 215 Cushman, **If Only . . . a fine store** (**☎907/457-6659;** www.ifonlyalaska.com), is a charming gift and stationery shop with items to hold locals' as well as visitors' interest—not just tourist stuff.

Near the airport, at 4630 Old Airport Rd., the **Great Alaskan Bowl Company** (**☎800/770-4222** or 907/474-9663; www.woodbowl.com) makes and sells bowls of native birch—salad bowls, of course, but also bowls for many other purposes. Some of these bowls are simply amazing. They can carve up to eight nested bowls from one piece of wood and even laser-engrave a photo inside one. Through a glass wall looking into the shop, you can see workers cutting the

Great Alaskan Bowl Company.

bowls from raw logs. It's hard to depart without buying a bowl. The shop is open daily all year.

Where to Stay

Going the bed-and-breakfast route is a good choice in Fairbanks. At the B&Bs I've listed below, you can save money over a hotel and get a private room just as good while staying in a unique place with interesting people. The **Fairbanks Association of Bed and Breakfasts** lists about 20 more on its website at **www.ptialaska.net/~fabb** The visitor bureau also provides B&B information and up-to-date vacancy data in person at the Morris Thompson center (p. 506), or by calling ☏**907/459-3785.**

EXPENSIVE

There are many more hotels in the expensive category than there is any need to describe here, so I have followed my usual practice of including one for each taste. The enormous **Fairbanks Princess Riverside Lodge** (☏**800/426-0500** or 907/455-4477, fax 907/455-4476; www.princesslodges.com) also merits a mention as a luxurious and well-run hotel in a pleasant setting near the airport (it's quite similar to Pike's Waterfront) However, in summer the Princess usually books fully with the owner's cruise-line clients. Rooms are most often available Friday, Saturday, and Sunday. I can also recommend The **Marriot Fairbanks Springhill Suites** (☏**800/314-0858** or 907/451-6552; fax 907/451-6553; www.marriott.com), which offers spacious rooms in a prime spot in the center of town, and has Lavelle's Bistro (reviewed later in this chapter) and one of the few hotel pools in town.

All Seasons Inn ★ 🎒 This charming and comfortable country inn on a pleasant residential street a couple of blocks from the downtown core is the creation of Mary Richards, a longtime transplant from the southern United States who retains, along with a slight accent, the gentle hospitality and refined style she brought with her. Each cozy room has its own inspired decorative details in bold colors, and the housekeeping has always been perfect on our many visits. For

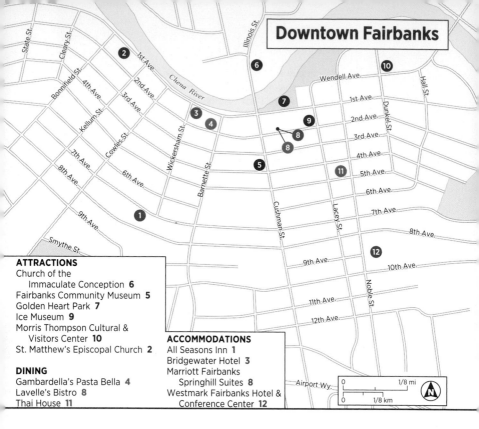

Downtown Fairbanks

ATTRACTIONS
Church of the
  Immaculate Conception **6**
Fairbanks Community Museum **5**
Golden Heart Park **7**
Ice Museum **9**
Morris Thompson Cultural &
  Visitors Center **10**
St. Matthew's Episcopal Church **2**

DINING
Gambardella's Pasta Bella **4**
Lavelle's Bistro **8**
Thai House **11**

ACCOMMODATIONS
All Seasons Inn **1**
Bridgewater Hotel **3**
Marriott Fairbanks
  Springhill Suites **8**
Westmark Fairbanks Hotel &
  Conference Center **12**

visiting with Mary or other guests, a series of elegant common rooms connect downstairs, where you'll find a bar with hot drinks and a sun porch with books and games. Shoes are removed at the front door in winter.

763 7th Ave., Fairbanks, AK 99701. ☏ **888/451-6649** or 907/451-6649. Fax 907/474-8448. www. allseasonsinn.com. 8 units. High season $165–$215 double; low season $89–$109 double. Extra person $35. Rates include full breakfast. DC, DISC, MC, V. **Amenities:** Computer center. *In room:* A/C, TV, hair dryer, Wi-Fi.

Pike's Waterfront Lodge ★★ When Pike's appeared on the Chena River next to the Pike's Landing restaurant (see below), it initially looked like a big rectangle the size and shape of innumerable chain hotels along interstates, but the local owner kept adding features until it became utterly unique, including a greenhouse, an ice cream parlor with an airplane sticking out of it, an extraordinary wildlife art collection, and 28 cabins. Now he's concentrating on going green, with solar panels, low-power TVs, and special cleaning products, paper towels, and carpet. Rooms, while not large, are well equipped, and many look out on the river. The location is a stone's throw from the airport. The place can fill on certain days in the summer with package-tour guests—at this writing, Monday through Wednesday—but usually has room the rest of the week. Summer only, a steak-and-seafood restaurant operates on-site.

1850 Hoselton Dr., Fairbanks, AK 99709. **877/774-2400** or 907/456-4500. Fax 907/456-4515. www.pikeslodge.com. 208 units. High season $149–$225 double, $255–$465 suite; low season $69–$99 double, $89–$235 suite. Extra person age 13 and over $10. Rates include continental breakfast in winter. AE, DC, DISC, MC, V. **Amenities:** Free airport transfers; restaurant (summer); bar; exercise room; sauna; steam room. *In room:* A/C, TV, fridge, hair dryer, microwave, Wi-Fi.

River's Edge Resort Cottages ★★ ☺ An afternoon on a sunny riverbank exemplifies the best of Interior Alaska; this place is built around that knowledge. Trim little cottages stand in a grassy compound along the gentle Chena River, where guests can fish for grayling. Inside, each light, airy cottage is an excellent standard hotel room, with high ceilings and two queen beds. Outside, they're like a little village, where guests can sit on the patio, watch the river go by, and socialize. It's perfect for families, as the outdoor areas are safe for playing and noise inside won't bother the neighbors. A large, summer-only restaurant sits at river's edge, with dining on a deck or inside at round, oak tables. Dinner entrees—steak, seafood, and down-home cooking—range up to $30; a burger is $10.

4200 Boat St., Fairbanks, AK 99709. **800/770-3343** or 907/474-0286. Fax 907/474-3665. www.riversedge.net. 94 units (86 cottages, 8 suites). High season $219 double; low season $149 double. Extra person age 12 and older $10. AE, DISC, MC, V. Closed Oct–Apr. Take Sportsman Way off Airport Way to Boat St. **Amenities:** Free airport transfers; restaurant; bar. *In room:* TV, coffeemaker, hair dryer, Wi-Fi.

Sophie Station Hotel ★ This all-suite hotel, near the university and airport, is well equipped for business travelers or longer stays, with full kitchens, sitting rooms, and separate bedrooms in every suite. The decoration in the rooms is pleasantly muted. Everything is very clean, well maintained, and comfortable. Bathrooms and closets are quite large. I was startled by the quality of the food and service in the hotel restaurant, called **Zach's.** Each dish I selected was perfectly seasoned and done to a turn, servers were attentive without being annoying, and the meals came quickly. The cuisine includes Alaska seafood and familiar American dishes. Dinner main courses top out at $32. They're open year-round.

1717 University Ave., Fairbanks, Alaska 99709. **800/528-4916** reservations, or 907/479-3650 and 907/456-3642. Fax 907/479-7951. www.fountainheadhotels.com. 140 units. High season $169–$205 double; low season $89–$120 double. Extra person $10. AE, DC, DISC, MC, V. **Amenities:** Free airport transfers; restaurant; bar; exercise room; Internet access in lobby. *In room:* A/C, TV, hair dryer, kitchen, Wi-Fi

A Taste of Alaska Lodge ★ Situated atop a grassy slope on 280 acres, facing Mount McKinley, the hand-crafted log main building feels like a wilderness lodge but is less than half an hour from Fairbanks. The family that originally homesteaded this property still lives here and runs the lodge. Each family member I've met is an Alaskan original. A nearby musher offers dog team rides in winter (but make sure that's available when you reserve if it's a priority). During the dark months visitors come for exceptional aurora viewing. Rooms are decorated with handmade quilts, brass beds, and other reproductions, and an incredible array of knickknacks, collectibles, and pictures of Elizabeth Taylor (some will love all this, some may find it a little corny). Each room has a door straight onto the grounds, where moose often wander. The cabins are large and especially luxurious. Breakfast is served at 8am on the dot, and guests have to remove their shoes at the door.

551 Eberhardt Rd. (turn right 5⅓ miles out Chena Hot Springs Rd.), Fairbanks, AK 99712. **☎907/488-7855.** Fax 907/488-3772. www.atasteofalaska.com. 8 units (including 2 cabins). $185 double; $205–235 cabin. Extra person $35. Rates include full breakfast. AE, MC, V. *In room:* TV, Wi-Fi.

Wedgewood Resort ★★ Off College Road near the Creamer's Field Refuge, this well-kept hotel sprawls across a grassy, 23-acre complex in eight large buildings. Seven of them are three-story apartment buildings converted into suites, regularly refitted, without elevators but with large living rooms, separate dining areas, fully equipped kitchens, air conditioners, two TVs, balconies, and phones with voice mail in both the living room and bedroom. The main difference from home is that someone else cleans up after you. Another 157 units are large, standard hotel rooms in the three-story Bear Lodge, which has its own lobby; however, those are closed mid-September to mid-May. A scheduled courtesy van runs to the airport and train depot and various tourist sites in the summer. Several attractions are on-site or nearby: a large new antique auto museum, trails to a pond and Creamer's Field (p. 517), and the Alaska Bird Observatory research and educational center (p. 517). The hotel is nonsmoking.

212 Wedgewood Dr., Fairbanks, AK 99701. **☎800/528-4916** reservations, or 907/452-1442 and 907/456-3642. Fax 907/451-6376. www.fountainheadhotels.com. 462 units (157 rooms, 305 suites). High season $185 double, $154–$225 suite for 2; low season standard double rooms not offered, $75–$120 suite for 2. Extra person in suite $10. AE, DC, DISC, MC, V. **Amenities:** Restaurants (summer only); bar; Internet cafe; courtesy van; computers in each lobby. *In room:* A/C, TV, hair dryer, Wi-Fi.

Westmark Fairbanks Hotel & Conference Center ★★★ This Fairbanks landmark, the town's grand meeting place, owned by Holland America Lines, fills a city block and includes the city's tallest tower (not exactly a skyscraper, but you don't need to be very high for good views in Fairbanks). The decor in newer rooms is the city's most stylish, with a post-mod pastiche that includes fabrics and lamps from the Jetsons along with colonial woodwork; big, manly furniture; and lots of color. I like it. The rooms are packed with amenities, including, in many, little shelves for the coffeemakers so they're not down with your toothpaste. Downstairs, the hotel has a cafe with a dining room that's a work of art (open summer only) and a comfortable steakhouse. A complimentary breakfast is served in the winter months.

Going with the Flow

Many of the large, top quality hotels in Fairbanks—including the Princess, Westmark, Pike's Waterfront Lodge, Sophie Station, River's Edge Resort, and Wedgewood Resort—cater to enormous escorted tours, which flow through town on a rhythm set by the arrival of cruise ships hundreds of miles away. As a result, certain nights are booked up every week many months in advance, while others are wide open. Fortunately, this flow alternates on different nights for different companies, so when one hotel is full another is empty. If you find your first choice is booked, just call one of the others. If they have rooms, ask for a discount, as they may have a lot of empty rooms.

813 Noble St., Fairbanks, AK 99701. **☎800/544-0970** reservations or 907/456-7722. Fax 907/451-7478. www.westmarkhotels.com. 400 units. Summer $225 double, $240–$500 suite; winter $84 double, $94–$500 suite. Extra person 19 and older $15. AE, DC, DISC, MC, V. **Amenities:** Free airport transfers; 2 restaurants; bar; fitness center. *In room:* A/C, TV, hair dryer, Wi-Fi (in most).

MODERATE

Aurora Express Bed and Breakfast ★ ★ 🎁 Susan Wilson's late grandmother
appeared to her in a dream and told her there would be a train on a bank below her house, on the family's 15 acres high in the hills south of Fairbanks. So Wilson went out and got a train—a collection that includes a pair of 1956 Pullman sleepers, a dining car, a locomotive, a caboose, and a World War II hospital car—and her husband, Mike, brought it all up the mountain to install below the house, right in the spot indicated. Some cars are close to their original form, and Susan says older guests sometimes weep over the memories they bring back. Others were elaborately remodeled into rooms, some small, some huge, on themes related to Fairbanks history. A full breakfast is served in the dining car, which also houses the common area, TV, and phone. They're located 6½ miles out of town, so you will need your own car if you stay here. Also consult with the hosts before coming with children, as they discourage visits by the very young.

1540 Chena Ridge Rd. (P.O. Box 80128), Fairbanks, AK 99708. **☎800/221-0073** or 907/474-0949. www.fairbanksalaskabedandbreakfast.com. 7 units. $145–$160 double. Extra person $25–$50. Rates include full breakfast. MC, V. Closed mid-Sept to mid-May. *In room:* No phone.

Bridgewater Hotel ★ 🔑 This older building in a prime downtown location
near the river contains comfortable, immaculate rooms that sacrifice little of substance to places charging as much as $40 a night more. Decoration in pastels creates a feminine, boutique tone in common areas. Rooms are bright and airy, and those on the corners have exceptional views. Most have shower stalls only, not tubs. A cafe serves breakfast, and one of Fairbanks's best restaurants, Gambardella's, is just steps away. A great choice for summertime travelers who like staying in a traditional downtown hotel but don't need luxury hotel trappings. Weekends have the most vacancies and best bargains.

723 1st Ave., Fairbanks, AK 99701. **☎800/528-4916**, or 907/452-6661 and 907/456-3642. Fax 907/452-6126. www.fountainheadhotels.com. 94 units. $129–$169 double. Extra person $10. AE, DC, DISC, MC, V. Closed mid-Sept to mid-May. **Amenities:** Free airport transfers; Internet access. *In room:* A/C, TV, hair dryer, Wi-Fi.

Minnie Street Bed & Breakfast Inn ★ ★ Across the river from the downtown
center, four buildings around a garden courtyard contain large, clean, brightly decorated rooms with stylish furniture and many amenities. The inn reflects the personality of its serene but exacting hosts, managing to feel both homey and polished. A full breakfast is served in a dining room with a high-vaulted ceiling and continental breakfasts in some rooms. Huge one-bedroom suites have kitchens, and extra beds for one or two, and all but one have a Jacuzzi tub. Guests have access to laundry machines, paying on the honor system.

345 Minnie St., Fairbanks, AK 99701. **☎888/456-1849** or 907/456-1802. Fax 907/451-1751. www.minniestreetbandb.com. 16 units, 12 with private bathroom. High season $139–$179 double, $239 suite; low season $75–$89 double, $159 suite. Extra person $35. Rates include full breakfast. AE, DISC, MC, V. **Amenities:** Massage. *In room:* TV, hair dryer, Wi-Fi.

INEXPENSIVE

Golden North Motel 🏷 The Baer family, owners since 1971, works hard to keep up the rooms in this two-story motel, making it the best bargain in town for those seeking a basic budget room. They're always replacing something, and where carpets and furniture are worn they're still quite clean. You have a choice of small rooms and units that combine two of the smaller rooms; although strictly functional, they're very reasonably priced and have extras you might not expect. The building, on a side street near the airport, is a nondescript brown rectangle brightened by flower boxes on the outdoor walkways. Family members greet guests warmly with free pastries and coffee in the small lobby. An adjoining business center has a broadband-connected computer and other business machines, most of the resources free for guest use.

4888 Old Airport Rd., Fairbanks, AK 99709. **☎800/447-1910** or 907/479-6201. Fax 907/479-5766. www.goldennorthmotel.com. 62 units. Summer $89–$106 double; winter $62–$66 double. Extra person 13 or older $10. Rates include continental breakfast. AE, DC, DISC, MC, V. **Amenities:** Free airport transfers. *In room:* TV, VCR/DVD (available from office), fridge and microwave in many, Wi-Fi.

Grand View Bed & Breakfast ★ Perched on 10 acres on Chena Ridge, 15 minutes east of town, a big log house overlooks a panorama of the Tanana Valley and Alaska Range, a view shared by each of the four rooms. The house was crafted of local materials by local craftspeople, even the furniture, and the understated decor makes the most of the logs' rich warmth. Owners Dave and Clodagh Thompson settled here after extensive travels (they speak five languages between them) and are raising three young children, whom they keep from underfoot according to guests' preferences. Rooms have their own full bathrooms, but guests share common areas for TV viewing. Access to the kitchen is open; breakfast is served 8am to 10am.

915 Ridge Pointe Dr., Fairbanks, AK 99709. **☎907/479-3388.** Fax 907/479-3389. www.grandview-bb.com. 4 units. High season $125 double; low season $100 double. Extra person over age 11 $10. Rates include choice of full or continental breakfast. MC, V. **Amenities:** Computer center; hot tub; sauna. *In room:* Wi-Fi.

A HOSTEL & CAMPING

There are several hostels in Fairbanks. Among the best is the homey **Billie's Backpackers Hostel,** near the university, at 2895 Mack Blvd. (**☎907/479-2034;** www.alaskahostel.com). It's a charming place with a charming owner—a real home, but quirky and fun. Billie assigns bunks as people arrive, and you could luck into a private room for the same $27 a night she charges everyone. Rooms are co-ed, and the price includes all linens, coffee and tea, Internet, and much else. The Alaska/Yukon Trails shuttle stops out front (see "Getting There," p. 505). To find the hostel, turn south off College Road on Westwood Way and look for the first house on the left just past Mack Boulevard.

Tent camping is a good way to go in Fairbanks, with its mild summers and ample public lands, but stock up on the mosquito repellent. Right in town, the **Chena River Wayside** (**☎907/452-7275;** www.chenawayside.com) is located where University Avenue crosses the river. (The campground is also known as the Chena River State Recreation Site, and should not be confused with the recreation "area" of the same name described in the next section of this chapter.) Sites are surrounded by birch and spruce, some are near the river, and there are flush toilets. Arrive early to camp close to the river instead of at one of the noisier sites nearer the road. Eleven sites have water and power hookups for RVs and cost $25 a night; another 45 drive-in sites for tent campers or RVs, without hookups, are $17; and 5 tent-only walk-in sites $10. Getting a bit out of town, there are superb public campgrounds at Chena Lake Recreation Area and along Chena Hot Springs Road (covered in section 3 of this chapter).

Fairbanks has plenty of commercial RV parks, some with full service and then some. Pick up a list at the visitor center. Among the best is **River's Edge RV Park and Campground,** at a riverside bend of the Chena at 4140 Boat St., off Airport Way and Sportsman Way (☎800/770-3343 or 907/474-0286; www.riversedge.net), with lots of services, including free shuttles. Full hookups are $35 and tent camping $21. The same people operate the cottage resort and restaurant next door.

Where to Dine
DOWNTOWN

Gambardella's Pasta Bella ★★ ITALIAN This warm, charming restaurant is right in the center of things. The chicken rustico (which sits on polenta) is tasty; they serve seafood in interesting ways; and the lasagna, made with sausage, thin noodles, and a rich, dusky tomato sauce, will improve your opinion of this abused dish. Dining rooms are narrow and segmented, so you always seem to be sitting with just a few other people, with elaborate decoration that adds to a pleasingly busy feeling. The restaurant added more space with a second-story dining room and patio while keeping the cozy ambience. Unlike the synthetic ambience of some of Fairbanks's other fine-dining places, Gambardella's feels real, a place where a family shares its cuisine. Perfect, no—but pleasant and satisfying. They serve beer and wine.

706 2nd Ave. ☎907/456-3417. www.nvo.com/gambardellas. Lunch $7–$13; dinner main courses $14–$28. 15% gratuity added for parties of 5 or more, or for split checks. AE, MC, V. Mon–Fri 7am–10pm, Sat 11am–10pm, Sun 4:30–10pm; closes an hour earlier off season.

Lavelle's Bistro ★★★ BISTRO In a big room of chrome, stone, and glass right downtown (at the base of the Marriott SpringHill Suites), Lavelle's has a grown-up, cosmopolitan feel that is quite welcome when you grow weary of the Alaskan rustic or gold rush themes of many of the area's restaurants. It's also got the advantage of consistently superb food, ambitious in conception and fine in execution, and expert service. The cuisine is difficult to categorize, as Southwest and Italian influences might be brought to a single dish, and Northwest, Asian, and French influences turn up variously. Dinner main courses are mostly more than $20, but you can dine economically on the ample appetizers and salads, or choose a vegetarian lasagna that for only $16 comes with soup or a salad and side dishes. The wine list is impressive, and the 3,000-bottle cellar is behind glass in the middle of the dining room; the owners are on a mission to educate Fairbanks about wine, as they've already done with food by creating one of Alaska's best restaurants.

575 1st Ave. ☎907/450-0555. www.lavellesbistro.com. Reservations recommended. Main courses lunch $11–$16, dinner $16–$40. AE, DC, DISC, MC, V. Summer Mon–Sun 11am–2pm and 4:30–10pm, Sun 4:30–10pm; winter Tues–Sat 4:30–10pm, Sun–Mon 4:30–9pm.

Thai House ★★ THAI In a small, brightly lit dining room in the downtown area, this is a simple, family-run restaurant with authentic Thai cuisine. Every time we've dined here the food came quickly and was deftly seasoned and cooked to a turn. You can rely on the servers, beautifully attired in national costumes, to help you order; just believe that when they say "hot" they really mean it. The first time I ate here, I rechecked the bill because it seemed too small. Thanks to this terrific restaurant and others, Fairbanks has gone a bit Thai crazy, and now, incongruously for such a provincial town, has at least seven Thai restaurants. This one is the most centrally located and among the best, although that debate is part of the fun.

412 5th Ave. **☎907/452-6123.** Lunch items $7–$9; dinner main courses $11–$15. MC, V. Mon–Sat 11am–4pm and 5–9:30pm.

WITHIN DRIVING DISTANCE

Besides the restaurants listed here, consider the salmon bake at Pioneer Park, described earlier, and the restaurant at Sophie Station Hotel (p. 523).

Fairbanks has every flavor of fast food, many of them along the commercial strip of Airport Way, and many a greasy spoon diner, as well. Among the best burgers and shakes can be had at two **Brewsters** restaurants: 3578 Airport Way (**☎907/456-2538**) and 354 Old Steese Hwy. (**☎907/374-9663**).

Some of the best pizza in town comes from **College Town Pizzeria,** near the intersection of College and University roads (**☎907/457-2200**), an East Coast, order-at-the-counter, family place. The crust is wonderful—crisp yet chewy—and they prepare it either in the American style or as Italian gourmet pizza with pesto, spinach, and the like and without tomato sauce. A 16-inch combo is $24. They also serve beer and wine. The pizzeria is closed Sunday.

The Bakery 🍴 DINER There are an infinite number of old-fashioned coffee shops in and around Fairbanks—the kind of place where a truck driver or gold miner can find a hearty, down-home meal, a bottomless cup of coffee, and a motherly waitress. This is one of the better versions. The sourdough pancakes are good, the menu is long and inexpensive, portions are huge (sometimes they require two plates), the service is fast and friendly. Proverbial motherly waitresses call grown men "sweetie." Of course, you can get breakfast all day. They have no liquor license.

Quick Treats Unique to Fairbanks

A shop that makes its own delicious, natural ice cream started near the university and sells its creations in good restaurants all over Alaska. **Hot Licks Homemade Ice Cream,** 3453 College Rd. (**☎907/479-7813;** www.hotlicks.net), has all the standard flavors, plus some of their own, including blueberry and cranberry made in season with local wild berries. If you have children, their joy will be completed by a visit to the playground behind the Radio Shack next door. Right across from Hot Licks on College Road, during summer only, a travel trailer in the parking lot of a sporting goods store contains a bakery called **Bun on the Run,** which turns out fantastic cinnamon rolls and other baked treats, as well as hearty sandwiches.

69 College Rd. **☎907/456-8600.** Lunch items $7–$11; dinner main courses $9–$21. MC, V. Mon-Thurs 6am–4pm; Fri–Sat 6am–7pm; Sun 7am–4pm.

Pike's Landing Riverside Dining ★ STEAK/SEAFOOD The dining room of the fine-dining section overlooks the Chena River near the airport from a series of tiered levels, each with well-separated tables. The menu includes a nice range of simple to more ambitious selections; highlights include the appetizer of spicy crab-stuffed mushrooms with a thick, chowderlike sauce, the salmon Caesar salad, and a lunch of halibut and chips. Portions are quite large. Sunday brunch is big and delicious. Service, in my experience, is not always perfect, however, and the entire restaurant is a bit dated. The deck is open for dining in summers from 11am to 10pm with an inexpensive but limited bar menu offered from 2:30 to 5pm. It's a pleasant choice on a sunny day, less so in cool or rainy weather, when it remains in operation behind plastic.

4438 Airport Way. **☎907/479-6500.** www.pikeslodge.com/pikes-landing.html. Lunch items $9–$16; dinner main courses $10–$40. AE, DC, DISC, MC, V. Mon–Sat 11am–2pm and 5–9pm; Sun 10am–2pm and 5–9pm.

The Pump House Restaurant and Saloon ★★ STEAK/SEAFOOD The historic, rambling, corrugated tin building on the National Register of Historic Places is elaborately decorated and landscaped with authentic gold-rush relics. Sitting on the deck over the Chena, you can watch the riverboat paddle by or a group in canoes stop for appetizers and drinks from the full bar. For dinner, the cuisine is a cut above the area's typical steaks and seafood and includes game you may not have tried, including reindeer and elk. Dishes such as pistachio-encrusted halibut and the seafood chowder—hearty, creamy, and flavorful—make the most of the regional ingredients without trying to get too fancy. Many of the side dishes are a la carte, so although main courses are generous, it's expensive to order a large meal. Besides, you'll want to save room for one of the exceptional desserts. They serve a big Sunday brunch, too.

Mile 1.3, Chena Pump Rd. **☎907/479-8452.** www.pumphouse.com. Main courses $18–$37 AE, DISC, MC, V. Summer Mon–Sat 11:30am–11pm, Sun 10am–11pm; winter Mon–Sat 5–9pm, Sun 10am–2pm and 5–9pm.

The Turtle Club ★ 🏚 AMERICAN Locals pack into this squat, windowless building, with its vinyl tablecloths and stackable metal chairs, for a menu with just a few famous selections: prime rib, lobster, king crab, and prawns. These are simple, burly meals with friendly, roadhouse-style service; the menu is printed on the placemat, and vegetables are an afterthought from an indifferent salad bar. But when the beef comes, you know it—the middle-size prime rib cut is more than an inch thick and covers a large plate, an insanely large portion—and the meat is tender and cooked right. The atmosphere is noisy and super-casual; people laugh loud and don't worry about putting their elbows on the table or spilling a little beer. You won't run into many other tourists here, north of the city in Fox, but you do need reservations, and even with them you often wait half an hour in the smoky bar or a narrow corridor. If this doesn't sound like fun, don't go; but if you get it, the place is energizing.

Mile 10, Old Steese Hwy., Fox. **☎907/457-3883.** Reservations recommended. Main courses $20–$32. AE, DISC, MC, V. Mon–Sat 6–10pm; Sun 5–9pm.

10

THE ALASKAN INTERIOR | Fairbanks

Fairbanks Nightlife

Fairbanks has a lot of tourist-oriented evening activities, as well as entertainment also attended by locals. Call the 24-hour event recording of what's playing currently (☎907/456-INFO [456-4636]), or get a copy of the *Fairbanks Daily News-Miner*. The Regal Goldstream 16-screen **multiplex** (☎907/456-5113) is located on Airport Way. The evening show at the **Palace Theatre** is discussed earlier in this chapter under "Pioneer Park."

There are places to go out in the evening without having to hear about the gold rush (in other words, places locals go). Check out the "Downtown Guide" and "Events" pages of the **Downtown Association of Fairbanks** (☎907/452-8671; www.downtownfairbanks.com) for an updated list of entertainment in that part of town. In the University area, hear local and imported folk music live at the **College Coffeehouse,** 3677 College Rd. (☎907/374-0468; www.college coffeehousefairbanks.com). The website lists upcoming acts. Three miles southwest of town on the Parks Highway, **The Blue Loon** (☎907/457-5666; www.theblueloon.com) has live music, many beers on tap, and good burgers. They even show movies. For something a bit wilder, the **Howling Dog Saloon** out in Fox, 2160 Old Steese Hwy. (☎907/456-4695; www.howlingdogsaloon.com), has long been the place to cut loose in the summer. Besides a bar, "The Dog" offers live music Wednesday to Saturday, a cafe, and volleyball out back. It is open May to September.

CHENA HOT SPRINGS ROAD

The 57-mile paved road east from Fairbanks is an avenue to an enjoyable day trip or a destination for up to a week's outdoor activities and hot-spring swimming. Of all the roads radiating from Fairbanks, this short highway will be most rewarding to outdoors people, and there is a funky and relaxing resort at the end.

The road travels through the Chena River State Recreation Area, with spectacular hikes and float trips and well-maintained riverside campgrounds, and leads to the Chena Hot Springs, where there's a year-round resort perfect for soaking in hot mineral springs and for use as a base for summer or winter wilderness day trips. The resort is open to people who want to rent one of the comfortable rooms or to campers and day-trippers, and it's even more popular in the winter than in the summer (the slow seasons are spring and fall).

The paved road leads through a forest of birch, spruce, and cottonwood, first passing an area of scattered roadside development and then following the Chena River through the state recreation area. On a sunny summer weekend, the people of Fairbanks migrate to the riverside and the hiking trails; on a sunny winter weekend, they take to the hills on snowmobiles, cross-country skis, or dogsleds. It's a pleasant drive at any time, around 1¼ hours each way from Fairbanks, but not particularly scenic.

A pair of prospectors, the Swan brothers, discovered the hot springs in 1905, having heard that a U.S. Geological Survey crew had seen steam in a valley of the upper Chena. Thomas Swan suffered from rheumatism; incredibly, he and his brother poled up the Chena River from Fairbanks, found the hot springs, built a cabin and rock-floored pool, and spent the summer soaking. He was cured! More visitors followed, drawn by stories that whole groups of cripples were able to dance all night after soaking in the pools—by 1915 a resort was in operation, drawing worn-out miners and gold-rush stampeders and many others as well. It has been in constant use ever since.

Essentials

GETTING THERE The Chena Hot Springs Road meets the Steese Expressway about 5 miles north of downtown Fairbanks. (Information on renting a car in Fairbanks can be found in section 2 of this chapter.) The resort offers rides for hotel guests from anywhere in Fairbanks. Rates are $115 round-trip for one person or $75 per person for two or more passengers on the same reservation. Arrange for this at least 72 hours in advance.

VISITOR INFORMATION For outdoors information, check the Fairbanks **Alaska Public Lands Information Center,** in the Morris Thompson center at 101 Dunkel St. (☎907/459-3730; www.alaskacenters.gov).

The **Alaska Division of Parks,** at 3700 Airport Way, Fairbanks, AK 99709 (☎907/451-2695; www.alaskastateparks.org, click on "Individual Parks" and choose the recreation area—not the recreation site), manages the recreation area and produces trail, river, and road guides, which are also available at trail-head kiosks, from the public lands center, on the website, or in the area's *Chena Trailmarker* brochure. You can also contact the parks office with questions about the public cabins in the area (see "State Parks Cabin Reservations," p. 360, for how to reserve).

The Chena River State Recreation Area

The recreation area takes in 254,000 acres along the river valley and over the rolling mountains of heather around it. Some of Interior Alaska's best hiking and floating are found here. As everywhere in the Interior, the mosquitoes are brutal.

Hiking among a giant granite outcropping.

ACTIVITIES

FISHING Several of the ponds in the Chena State Recreation Area are stocked with rainbow trout, which you can keep subject to harvest limits. Signs along the road mark access points to the ponds and river. You can catch and release Arctic grayling in the Chena, but check current regulations and bait restrictions. Contact the **Alaska Department of Fish and Game,** 1300 College Rd., Fairbanks, AK 99701 (☎**907/459-7207;** sportfish information recording 907/459-7385; www.alaska.gov/adfg, click on "Sport Fish," then on the Interior region on the map, then "Lower Tanana River Drainage").

THE ROSTER OF rural ROADS

Like frayed strands extending from the thicker rope of the main highways, these minor roads reach beyond the settled lines through Alaska into places where visitors can have real adventures. Due to the size of the state, I cannot cover everything to be found on these byways, but I have covered some highlights and enough information for you to explore on your own. You will find few other cars or tourists, lots of open land, friendly rural people, and limitless opportunities for solitude and discovery.

Unpaved highways can be hazardous. Plan on driving only 40 to 45 mph on gravel highways, and be aware of the risks of bouncing off the road or damaging your vehicle with rocks. Check road conditions, construction, and weather with the Alaska Department of Transportation (☎511; http://511.alaska. gov). Bring at least one full-sized spare tire and consider carrying extra gasoline in jugs. Most vehicles can make it from one gas station to the next, but what if the station is closed or you have to turn around short of a refill? Insect repellent is an absolute necessity. Drive with your headlights on at all times, and wipe the dust off them and your tail lights periodically. Keep an eye on your rear-view mirror, slowing down or even stopping to allow vehicles to pass; to save your windshield from rocks, it's wise to slow down even for vehicles going the opposite direction. Also, pull off for views or

Dalton Highway.

HIKING & BACKPACKING The best trail hikes in the Fairbanks area are in the Chena Hot Springs State Recreation Area, all of which start on the road. Backcountry camping requires no permit, and many of the trails go above the tree line, so it's a good area for backpackers to get into the wilderness. Trail descriptions are available from the information sources mentioned in the previous section.

The **Angel Rocks Trail** is a sometimes steep hike of around 4 miles, round-trip, to a group of large granite outcroppings, an impressive destination with good views of the valley below. The blackened areas you see are from major fires that burned through the area in 2002 and 2004. Officially

pictures—don't stop on bridges or in the middle of the road, as some people do. (Further safety and packing suggestions for rural highways are in "Driving Safety," p. 96.)

Chena Hot Springs Road A relatively civilized road into the outdoors, this paved 57-mile highway east of Fairbanks meets hiking and river routes on the way to Chena Hot Springs. See "Chena Hot Springs Road," later in this chapter.

Dalton Highway (Rte. 11) Built to haul equipment to the Prudhoe Bay oil fields, about 500 miles north of Fairbanks, the supremely scenic Dalton reaches the heart of the wilderness, crossing the Brooks Range and the North Slope. Services are as much as a day's drive apart. See "The Dalton Highway," later in this chapter.

Denali Highway (Rte. 8) This 133-mile gravel road connects the midpoints of the Parks and Richardson highways, passing stunning alpine vistas high in the Alaska Range that rival those within Denali National Park. Along the way are a rich network of trails and mountain lakes and a good chance to see caribou, bear, moose, and waterfowl (p. 456).

Edgerton Highway & McCarthy Road (Rte. 10) Running east from the Richard-son Highway south of Glennallen, the Edgerton leads to the tiny town of Chitina, where the McCarthy Road, a one-lane track, penetrates Wrangell–St. Elias National Park to the historic sites at McCarthy and Kennecott. The journey of 93 miles takes half a day (p. 558).

Steese Highway (Rte. 6) This road, paved for the first 52 miles, climbs the rounded tundra mountains 162 miles east of Fairbanks to the Native village of Circle, on the Yukon River. It's a rare road deep into Bush Alaska (p. 536).

Taylor Highway (Rte. 5) At times rough, narrow, and a little scary, this dirt road leads 161 miles from a junction on the Alaska Highway east of Tok to the fascinating Yukon River village of Eagle, an island in time (p. 544).

Top of the World Highway (Yukon Rte. 9) Connecting to the Taylor Highway and crossing the Canadian border to Dawson City, a distance of 79 miles, the road rides mountaintop to mountaintop, above the tree line nearly the entire way (p. 544).

a 3.5-mile loop, the trail is better hiked as an out-and-back, because the back part of the loop is in poor shape. A good destination is the top of the main outcroppings, about 2 miles in. The trail head is well marked, at mile 48.9 of the road. A side trail heads from the top of the main outcroppings up to the ridgeline and goes all the way to Chena Hot Springs, a one-way hike of 8.3 miles.

The 15-mile loop of the **Granite Tors Trail,** starting at mile 39.5 of the road, is a challenging day hike, rising through forest to rolling alpine terrain, but the towering tors on top more than reward the effort. (A short-cut loop reduces the hike to 3 miles, but stays in the trees and doesn't make it near the tors.) Like surrealist experiments in perspective, these monolithic granite sentinels stand at random spots on the broad Plain of Monuments, at first confounding the eye's attempts to gauge their distance and size. Like the Angel Rocks, they were created when upwelling rock solidified in cracks in the surrounding earth, which then eroded away. Water is scarce, so bring along plenty. This is an excellent overnight hike, with the driest ground for camping right around the tors. There is a rough public shelter halfway along the trail (first-come, first-served). Massive fires in 2004 burned over much of the trail, but it remains passable, and the Plain of Monuments was practically unscathed.

For a longer backpacking trip, the **Chena Dome Trail** makes a 29-mile loop, beginning at mile 50.5 and ending at mile 49.1. The 3 miles nearest the road at either end pass through forest, but the remaining 23 miles are above the tree line, marked with cairns and with expansive views. The trail summits 4,421-foot Chena Dome after the 10-mile mark. The trail can be quite wet and muddy in parts and steep and rocky elsewhere, and it's wise to bring your water with you. A rough public shelter (first-come, first-served) is near mile 17.

RIVER FLOATING The Chena is a lovely river, growing from a clear, frothy creek near the end of the road to a lazy, brown Class I river as it flows off toward Fairbanks, several days downstream. Where you choose to start depends on your expertise. Easier water is downstream from Rosehip Campground (mile 27), with the slowest of all nearer Fairbanks, but the upper portion is more popular if you are up for something a bit more challenging. The road crosses the river several times, and the state park system has developed other access points, so it's possible to plan a float that matches your time and abilities. Choose your route with the help of the river guide produced by the Alaska Division of Parks (see "Visitor Information," above). Agencies offering canoe rental and shuttle service are covered in the Fairbanks section, above (two are under "Gearing Up," p. 516, and one in the feature "Equipped for the Backroads," p. 516). Chena Hot Springs Resort offers guided raft trips down the Chena (see below).

CAMPING & CABINS

Three beautiful campgrounds with water and pit toilets lie along the road by the Chena River, managed by the Alaska Division of Parks (see "Visitor Information," above). Although they can't be reserved ahead, the campgrounds are unlikely to be full except on a sunny holiday weekend. The **Rosehip Campground,** at mile 27, has 37 sites, well separated by spruce and birch, with 6 suitable for

RVs. Some sites are right on the river, and some are set up for more private tent camping in the woods. The **Granite Tors Campground** is across from the trail head at mile 39.5; it has 24 sites, 7 suitable for RVs. Some sites front a river slough, and, as at Rosehip, float trips can start or end here. The **Red Squirrel Campground,** at mile 42.8, has 12 sites and a pleasant picnic area on the grassy edge of a small, placid pond, where swimming is permitted. Camping is $10 a night at each of these campgrounds.

There are several public-use cabins in the recreation area, three of them easily accessible to summer visitors and not hard to book a month or two ahead. (See "State Parks Cabin Reservations," p. 360, for how to get one.) These are primitive cabins; you must bring your own sleeping bags, lights, fuel, and cooking gear. The **North Fork Cabin** is at mile 47.7 of the road, the **Hunt Memorial Cabin** is at mile 42.3, and the **Chena River Cabin** faces the river at mile 32.2. You can get to all by car or canoe, and each costs $50 a night in the summer, $40 off-season. Most of the other public cabins in the area primarily serve winter users and are difficult to reach when the ground thaws. However, the **Stiles Creek Cabin,** mid-way on a 15-mile multi-use trail, can be reached year-round. The trail meets the road at miles 31.6 and 36.4. As with other off-road cabins, the rent is $25 a night in summer, $20 off-season.

Chena Hot Springs Resort.

The Hot Springs

Chena Hot Springs Resort

★★ Several years ago, Bernie Karl, a Fairbanks recycling entrepreneur, bought the hot springs, the 440-acre valley they lie in, and the old resort there, which had perennially struggled to stay out of the red. As I walked around the grounds with him, he waved his hand here and there while outlining his audacious plans. I admit I nodded patronizingly. Each time I've gone back, however, more of his dream has been realized: an outdoor, boulder-rimmed swimming pond of hot mineral water, without chlorine or treatment; big buildings for large, modern rooms and for recreational activities; geothermal greenhouses growing produce for the restaurant year-round; an innovative geothermal power plant supplying the resort's electricity; and, incredibly, a large arched building made of ice.

Bernie built the ice hotel and filled it with expertly carved ice sculptures and got international publicity—then building inspectors shut it down, citing, of all things, the lack of fire extinguishers. (Their real concern was the complete lack of engineering.) Bernie hired an engineer, got the disagreement worked out (in part by renaming it an ice museum rather than a hotel), and operated it for a winter. That building melted the next summer, but Bernie rebuilt it and has kept it going

THE STEESE HIGHWAY: drive into the wild

Driving the Steese Highway north from Fairbanks is like following a river upstream as it diminishes into its headwaters. First it's a four-lane freeway, then a two-lane highway, then the pavement gives out (at about mile 60), and eventually the gravel gives way to dirt. The road climbs over round tundra mountains, leaves behind the last tiny town, then drifts through uninhabited woods before ending on the banks

of the Yukon River at a tiny Athabascan village, Circle (named for the Arctic Circle, which it isn't on). It's a rough 162-mile drive to nowhere. But if nowhere is where you want to go, the Steese Highway may be the right adventure for you. Just don't forget the mosquito repellent.

Much of the land surrounding the Steese is controlled by the federal **Bureau of Land Management** (BLM), 1150 University Ave., Fairbanks, AK 99709 (☎**800/437-7021** or 907/474-2200). Small- and large-scale gold mining takes place in the area, but most of the land is managed for conservation and recreation, with several campgrounds, some popular river floats, and a couple of beautiful hikes. The BLM website contains a lot of good information, but you'll need to type in this ungainly URL to get started: www.blm.gov/ak/st/en/prog/recreation.html#. In addition, State Parks manages the **Upper Chatanika River Campground,** at mile 39, with 24 sites, pit toilets, a hand pump for water, and a $12 fee. This is the starting point for the most popular

river float on the highway (covered, with others, in the Fairbanks section under "Canoeing," p. 518). Before heading out, call State Parks at ☎**907/451-2705,** as the campground hasn't been consistently open.

Without driving to the bitter end at Circle (where the only attraction is the Yukon River itself), you can make a goal of **Eagle Summit,** at mile 107, the highest place on the highway (3,624 ft.), and a good spot to be on June 21 each year, the summer solstice. Although it's still a degree of latitude below the Arctic Circle, the sun never sets here on the longest day because of the elevation and atmospheric refraction. People come out from Fairbanks and make a celebration of it. The midnight sun is visible for about 3 days before and after the solstice, too, assuming the sky is clear. The BLM has installed a toilet and a viewing deck on a 750-foot loop trail at the trailhead to the 27-mile **Pinnell Mountain National Recreation Trail.** This is a challenging 3-day hike over amazing terrain of rounded, wind-blown, tundra-clothed mountaintops.

year-round with a unique refrigeration system that uses heated water from the hot springs. Whatever he says he will do next, I believe him. Tours of the museum are $15 per person ($7.50 ages 6–12), and you can still rent it for a night (for $600 a night you also get Arctic clothing and an indoor room, too, in case you weary of the cold). You can even take a 2-hour ice-carving class there (call ahead to set it up). The resort also offers free tours of the power plant and greenhouses, which have attracted international attention in this age of energy shortages.

Despite all my affection for the place, however, I have to point out that it still has the rough edges of rural Alaska, and those expecting the standards of service and polish of a corporate resort will likely be disappointed. If you stay, I recommend renting the newest, most expensive rooms. Or camp out. Our family has enjoyed wonderful days here swimming and exploring. Soak in the pools, hike through the woods, and enjoy the sound of the wind in the trees.

The hot springs supply an indoor pool, several indoor and outdoor hot tubs and spas, and the outdoor hot pond (100–110°F/38–43°C). Kids are not allowed in the outdoor pond, allowing adults some respite from the noise of the indoor pool. The locker rooms are tiny, so guests will want to change in their rooms. The swimming facility is open daily from 7am to midnight. Swim passes come with your room if you're staying at the resort; for campers or day-trippers, a day pass is $10 adults, $8 age 60 and older, $7 ages 6 to 17, free children 5 and under. Towel rental is an additional $5, so make sure to bring your own.

Winter is the high season, when the aurora viewing is exceptional, away from city lights, and you can enjoy Nordic skiing groomed for classical or skating techniques, Sno-Cat and snow-machine tours, dog-sled rides, and more. In the summer, you can go horseback riding, rafting, hiking, fishing, mountain-biking, geocaching (a treasure-hunt game using handheld

To hike it in the easier, more downhill direction, start at Eagle Summit and end at Twelvemile Summit, mile 85.5. Two emergency shelters along the trail provide protection from the ferocious weather that can sweep the mountains. Get the free BLM trail brochure before going or check the trail's webpage at the BLM site mentioned above.

The next sensible destination is the tiny town of Central, population 95, which occupies a birch grove 128 miles along the highway. It's a real, old-fashioned gold-mining community and home of the remarkable **Circle District Museum** (☎ 907/520-1893; www.cdhs.us), which displays old mining equipment outdoors and has a large indoor gallery on the area's history. The museum is open during the summer Thursday through Sunday noon to 5pm. The main business in town is the **Steese Roadhouse** (☎ 907/520-5800), which offers rooms, gas, food, and drink. A campground is open in the summer on a spur road to Circle Hot Springs, the site of a historic hotel and swimming pool that have been shut down for years. To learn more about the area, check out these websites maintained by community members: www.steesehighway.org and www.bottomdollar.us.

GPS devices), ATV riding, or flightseeing. Many activities are guided and carry extra fees. Some rental equipment is available.

The accommodations range from simple yurts to the large hotel rooms with televisions, phones, and coffeemakers. The newest rooms, in the Moose building, are solidly built and nicely done up. Noise can be a problem winter nights as guests come and go to look at the aurora. The yurts are basic but adequate if you want inexpensive lodgings and don't mind not having indoor plumbing. The intermediate rooms were cheaply built to start with and will never be great. They have shower stalls, not tubs. The main lodge building contains the restaurant and bar. The menu and staff change fairly frequently, but on our most recent visit the food and service were excellent. Over all, this is a good place to have fun in the real Alaska, but be ready for some rough spots.

Mile 56.5, Chena Hot Springs Rd. (P.O. Box 58740), Fairbanks, AK 99711. ☎907/451-8104. Fax 907/451-8151. www.chenahotsprings.com. 80 units. $189–$249 double; $65 yurts (used mid-May to mid-Sept only). Extra person $20. AE, DC, DISC, MC, V. **Amenities:** Restaurant; bar; guided activities; hot tubs and Jacuzzis; massage; indoor and outdoor pools. *In room:* TV.

THE DALTON HIGHWAY

The original purpose was utilitarian: to haul equipment north from Fairbanks for the trans-Alaska oil pipeline, which runs from Prudhoe Bay, on the Arctic Ocean, to Valdez, on the Pacific. But the experience of the Dalton Highway for a traveler is so far beyond the ordinary as to require a whole new frame of reference to take it all in. The road is so very long, so remote and free of traffic, and the scenery is so mind-boggling in its grandeur and repetition, that after a time it feels like you're living in a dream. At some point you have to swallow and say to yourself, "I guess I didn't know that much about the world after all."

Part of the wonder comes in the difficulty of the drive. There are extreme sports—throwing yourself off the side of a mountain and so forth—and this is an extreme road trip, one that dives into deep wilderness as far from help as most people ever get. In 500 miles there are only three service stations, two of which are within 4 miles of each other. The road averages only 250 vehicles a day over its entire length. Driving the Dalton is not to be taken lightly or done on a whim. You need to prepare and you need to know you want to do it, because you will be rumbling over dirt for many, many hours, breathing dust, and beating the crud out of your car.

The drive starts in Fairbanks (officially, you drive parts of the Steese and Elliott highways before the real Dalton Hwy. begins), crossing the rounded hills and low forest of that region before crossing the Yukon River on a high, wood-decked bridge. Over the miles that follow, trees grow sparser and the road crosses some spectacular alpine plateaus until, entering the Brooks Range, arctic vegetation and the mountains' rocky severity take over. Beyond towering Atigun Pass, the Arctic Slope extends 170 miles, first through sensuous tundra foothills, then over the broad, lake-dotted flatlands that extend to the Arctic Ocean. Arrival at the oil facilities can be a letdown, especially if you haven't made arrangements for the tour that is the only way through to the shore. More on that below.

Wildlife can be accessed all along the road: moose, caribou, and grizzly bears, sport fishing and songbirds. Animals far outnumber people. Two highway businesses are near the Yukon; in Coldfoot there is a truck stop; and Wiseman is 16 miles up the road from Coldfoot, where the 2000 census counted 21 people. And that's it for another 240 miles of dirt road to Prudhoe Bay. There are no ATMs, no grocery stores, no cellphone coverage, no medical facilities—civilization just isn't there. Drive carefully.

Dalton Highway Essentials

PRACTICAL TIPS You can drive the highway yourself, staying in the few motels along the way or in a tent or motor home. From Fairbanks take the Steese Highway north to the Elliot Highway. The total road distance from Fairbanks to the Arctic Ocean is 497 miles. Road conditions are notoriously bad on the gravel-and-dirt Dalton, but now much of it is kept in good condition with pavement working its way steadily north. Speeds of 60 mph are possible on some parts of the road, while doing 35 mph will keep you in one piece on rougher spots; even the good sections can have nasty surprises, however, with unmarked, bone-jarring potholes. The drive takes 12 hours each way, without stops. It's dusty, shoulders are soft, and flat tires are common. In the Fairbanks section I listed two businesses that rent vehicles you can take on the Dalton (see "Equipped for the Backroads," p. 516). Generally, rental companies don't allow their vehicles on the road.

Preparing for the drive is essential. Pick up the road guide produced by the BLM and get firsthand, personal advice (see "Visitor Information," below). Read up on the safety advice under "The Roster of Rural Roads," p. 532. For those who want to let someone else do the driving, a bus package is listed in section 8 of chapter 11, on Prudhoe Bay.

VISITOR INFORMATION Getting up-to-date advice is critical before heading off on the Dalton Highway, and the best place to do that is the Fairbanks **Alaska Public Lands Information Center,** in the Morris Thompson center at 101 Dunkel St., Fairbanks, AK 99701 (℡907/459-3730; www.alaskacenters.gov). Staffers there drive the road annually to stay on top of current conditions.

Much of the road runs through land managed by the **Bureau of Land Management,** 1150 University Ave., Fairbanks, AK 99709 (℡800/437-7021 or 907/474-2200; www.blm.gov/ak/dalton). From the informative website you can download an invaluable *Dalton Highway Visitor Guide,* a 24-page booklet; or get it free at the public lands information center or from any BLM information center, or by mail by calling the number above.

Two information stops are along the highway, both open summer only. A **contact station** at the Yukon River crossing is staffed by BLM volunteers and open daily in summer from 9am to 6pm. It has no phone. The **Arctic Interagency Visitor Center** is at mile 175 on the west side of the highway in Coldfoot (℡907/678-5209 or 678-2014), open late May to early September from 10am to 10pm daily. The free center is far grander than one would expect in the middle of the wilderness. It has award-winning exhibits about the North, a theater for nightly educational programs, a planning room for backcountry trips, a bookstore, and knowledgeable staff. Even if you don't have any questions, you should definitely make this stop.

Trans-Alaska pipeline.

On the Road

The bridge over the Yukon River at mile 56 is the only crossing of the river in Alaska, and many people drive the Dalton just to get to the **Arctic Circle** at mile 115, where you'll find a sign for pictures as well as a crude camping area. Many, many places along the highway have incredible views; among the most famous are Finger Mountain at mile 98, which has a short interpretive nature trail; Gobbler's Knob at mile 132, which offers the first view of the Brooks Range; and 4,739-foot Atigun Pass at mile 245, where the road crosses the Brooks Range, winding through impossibly rugged country. The pass is the highest point on the Alaska road system, and you may find summer snow. All along the highway are opportunities to see birds and animals, including rabbits, foxes, moose, Dall sheep, bears, and caribou. Sit still if you see the skittish caribou, as they are more likely to wander closer to an unmoving vehicle. Beware of wolves, which several times attacked Dalton travelers in 2006, although that's very rare. Keep pets under control, and if a wolf approaches, yell and throw rocks at it.

The road parallels the 4-foot-wide **trans-Alaska pipeline.** The line, completed in 1977, serves America's largest and second-largest oil fields, Prudhoe Bay and Kuparuk, carrying the hot crude 900 miles from the Arctic Ocean to docks in Valdez, where tankers pick it up for shipment primarily to the West Coast. The public road ends before reaching the Prudhoe Bay complex and the Arctic Ocean. The only way through the gate is with a tour operator, and you must make arrangements at least 24 hours ahead to clear security. Call the **Arctic Caribou Inn** (✆907/659-2368; www.arcticcaribouinn.com). See section 8 of chapter 11, on Prudhoe Bay, for more details.

HIGHWAY SERVICES: FOOD, FUEL & LODGINGS

Among the few places offering services along the 414 miles of the Dalton you won't find anything luxurious, or even approaching budget chains. The service is generally quite friendly, but except for two small B&Bs in the tiny town of Wiseman, all lodgings are in former construction camp dormitories.

Near the spectacular suspended bridge over the Yukon River, at mile 56, is a decidedly unspectacular motel, restaurant, and gas station. **Yukon River Camp**

(☎907/474-3557), open daily 9am to 9pm, has a gift shop, fuel (usually), and tire repair as well as food and lodging, and it is open mid-May to mid-September. Just 5 miles up the road from the river, the **Hotspot Café** (☎907/451-7543), open daily 10am to midnight, offers dining, lodging, a gift shop, gas (usually), and tire repair. It also operates only mid-May to mid-September.

The **Coldfoot Camp** truck stop at mile 175 (☎866/474-3400 or 907/474-3500; www.coldfootcamp.com) is the one big stopping place along the road. After the endless wilderness miles on the road, no one could stand to pass it by. The year-round camp includes several buildings on a large gravel pad. Most important are the gas pumps and the 24-hour restaurant where you pay for the fuel—a typical but friendly highway diner. Across the lot, the camp's inn is built of left-over construction camp modular units. The small rooms with low ceilings are perfectly comfortable, with private bathrooms, but far from grand. The camp also provides minor vehicle repairs, RV hookup, laundry, a post office, a gift shop, and a saloon. They offer guided rafting on the Middle Fork Koyukuk River, flight tours to the village of Anaktuvuk Pass, tours of Wiseman, and shuttles for hiking. In the winter the camp offers dog-sled rides and aurora-viewing tours. An air taxi, **Coyote Air** (☎800/252-0603 or 907/678-5995; www.flycoyote.com), offers flightseeing of this amazing country from the air. There are other activities farther afield offered by **Northern Alaska Tour Company** (☎800/474-1986 or 907/474-8600; www.northernalaska.com). Don't miss the remarkable new interagency visitor center, described above. The pleasant BLM Marion Creek Campground is 5 miles north of Coldfoot.

Wiseman, 13 miles north of Coldfoot and 3 miles off the road, is the only real town on the entire drive, and well worth a stop to see a tiny rural community about a century out of time's progress. There's not a thing commercial about it. The general store, Wiseman Trading Company, established 1910, was operating on the honor system when we stopped in. A sign read, "If you need change come to the door and yell for Eight Ball or walk to the cabin across the lawn." Other residents sell furs or crafts from their homes. There's not much to do here but see how our great-grandparents lived, when food came from gardens, streams, and forests. Get advice at the interagency visitor center staff in Coldfoot. To spend the night in a homier place than the Coldfoot truck stop, try Wiseman's **Boreal**

Suspended bridge over the Yukon River.

Lodging (☎907/678-4566; www.boreallodge.com) or **Arctic Getaway Bed and Breakfast** (☎907/678-4456; www.arcticgetaway.com).

After Coldfoot, the next service area is **Deadhorse,** at the end of the road another 240 miles north, with rooms, fuel, restaurants, a post office, vehicle maintenance, a general store, and an airport. See the Prudhoe Bay section in chapter 11.

Getting out of the Car

ACTIVITIES

FISHING The streams and lakes of the Arctic are cold, poor in nutrients, and frozen much of the year; fishing is not a good reason to drive the Dalton. However, if you are taking the adventure anyway, there are fish in streams from July to mid-September and in lakes that don't freeze to the bottom. Many of the streams have Arctic grayling, but you'll want to hike farther than a quarter-mile from the road to increase your chances (off-road vehicles are not allowed). A good bet is the **Jim River area** between miles 140 and 144, where the river follows the road and fishing pressure is spread out. Most North Slope rivers have good Dolly Varden fishing in late August and early September. Many of the lakes along the road have grayling, and the deeper ones north of the Brooks Range have lake trout. Check current regulations. Contact the **Alaska Department of Fish and Game,** 1300 College Rd., Fairbanks, AK 99701 (☎907/459-7207; www.alaska.gov/adfg; click "Sportfish," then the Interior region); they produce a booklet called *Sportfishing Along the Dalton Highway,* which you can download from the website, or get at the office, at some visitor centers, or by mail.

HIKING The road has no established hiking trails, but most of the area is open to self-reliant hikers who know how to pick their own route. Hiking brushy or marshy Interior country isn't fun, but the dry tundra of the ridge tops and mountains creates a wonderful sense of freedom. The country opens up north of the Chandalar Shelf at mile 237. The best hiking area is the zone of dry tundra in the foothills north of the Brooks Range. But even at upper elevations you still run into tussocks, wet ground, and stream crossings. Topographical maps and advice on hiking the Brooks Range are available at the sources listed under "Visitor Information," above. The book *Outside in the Interior* (p. 515) describes a handful of hikes along the road. Remember, this is remote wilderness; do your research, be prepared, and tell someone where you're going and when you'll be back.

Camping

The Bureau of Land Management has a few campgrounds along the road, but there seems little reason to wait to reach them, as there are any number of places to pull off the road on a spot of gravel and spend the night, often in places of stunning beauty. Just take these important precautions for safety and the environment: Get far enough off the road to avoid the fast-moving truck spewing rocks as far as 30 feet; read up on bear avoidance on p. 92; don't leave toilet paper or anything else behind (see "Keeping the Wilderness Clean," p. 79); and stay no longer than 14 days in one spot. The BLM prefers that you don't park on pipeline access, and if you do, be sure not to block the road or security gates. I have listed the BLM's developed areas along the Dalton, which include campgrounds and spots where you can park for awhile and obtain water. Unless the description mentions a formal campground, these are just gravel pads where you can park or sleep in your car. Add 83 miles to the mileposts to get the distance from Fairbanks.

o **Mile 60 (Five Mile):** Undeveloped campground with an outhouse, artesian well with potable water nearby, and free public dump station (this is the last dump station on the hwy.). Don't wash your vehicle here, as it will contaminate the groundwater.

o **Mile 98 (Finger Mountain):** Nice views, outhouse, and wheelchair-accessible trail with interpretive signs.

o **Mile 115 (Arctic Circle):** Outhouses, picnic tables, and an interpretive display; camp only in the undeveloped campground up the hill, which has an outhouse but no water.

o **Mile 150 (Grayling Lake):** Wayside with outhouse.

o **Mile 175 (Coldfoot):** A private campground with hookups is part of the truck stop described above.

o **Mile 180 (Marion Creek):** A developed BLM campground with 27 campsites, 11 of them for large RVs (no hookups). The campground has a potable well and outhouses.

o **Mile 235 (Farthest north spruce tree):** Outhouse; not an attractive camping site due to truck traffic on a steep grade.

o **Mile 275 (Galbraith Lake):** Undeveloped campground with an outhouse and interpretive signs about 4 miles off the highway; follow the access road past the state-operated landing strip, then continue 2½ miles on an unimproved road. Filter or boil water from the nearby creek before use.

o **Mile 301 (Slope Mountain):** Land north of this point is managed by the Alaska Department of Natural Resources, not the BLM; however, you can use the same visitor information sources mentioned above.

o **Mile 355 (Last Chance):** Wayside with an outhouse.

o **Mile 414 (Deadhorse):** The end of the road. Deadhorse has a post office, general store, hotels, and other services. An operator offers tours through to the Arctic Ocean, the only way to get there. Tours must be arranged in advance. See the Prudhoe Bay section in chapter 11.

THE ALASKA HIGHWAY

Detailed coverage of the entire 2,400-mile drive to Alaska is beyond our scope, but chapter 3's "Getting There" section provides the planning basics. Here I've covered the Alaska portion of the road, the 200 miles of the Alaska Highway that run from the border with Canada to the terminus in Delta Junction. This is mostly boring driving, miles of stunted black spruce and brush, either living or burned out. It's a relief when you hit the first major town, **Tok** (rhymes with

DAWSON CITY & EAGLE: detour into history

Instead of taking the Alaska Highway directly from Whitehorse, Yukon, to Tok, consider driving north on the Klondike Highway (Yukon Hwy. 2) to Dawson City, then west and south over the Top of the World Highway and partially unpaved Taylor Highway to rejoin the Alaska Highway just east of Tok. This represents 502 miles of driving, about 127 miles more than if you just stay on the Alaska Highway, and includes 43 miles of sometimes rough dirt road, but it's worth doing at least one way to see historic Dawson City and the fabulous mountain scenery of the Top of the World Highway. Dawson was the destination of the 1898 Klondike Gold Rush; the bed of the Klondike River near here contained thick veins of gold. The town maintains the look of those days, when it was briefly the second largest city on the West Coast, after San Francisco. Many buildings, a gold dredge, and a river boat were restored as part of the Klondike National Historic Sites, managed by **Parks Canada.** Besides the buildings and their setting, there are museums, a working not-for-profit casino, a center of indigenous culture, and other attractions, easily enough for 2 days of sightseeing. The **Klondike Visitor Association,** P.O. Box 389, Dawson City, YT, Canada Y0B 1G0; ☏ **867/993-5575;** fax 867/993-6415; www.dawsoncity.ca), offers information on local businesses, accommodations, and community events. For information on the historic sites, contact **Parks Canada** at P.O. Box 390, Dawson City, YT, Canada Y0B 1G0 (☏ **867/993-7200;** www.parkscanada.gc.ca, click on "National Historic Sites," then "Dawson Historical Complex"). For information on the **Han Nation people** here and their cultural center, call ☏ **867/993-7100** (www.trondek.com).

After passing into the United States on the Top of the World Highway (note that this border crossing is open only during the day, and only during the summer), a further detour leads north on the Taylor Highway to the forgotten town of Eagle on the bank of the Yukon River (going south on the Taylor leads you back to the Alaska Hwy.). The trip to Eagle adds 66 miles each way on a winding, narrow dirt road; allow 2 hours each way. But, if you have the time, the destination more than rewards the effort. Eagle is lost in time, a treasure of a gold-rush river town with many original buildings full of original artifacts from a century ago. It's entirely authentic and non-commercial, with few businesses other than the store, cafe, motel, and a B&B. The **Eagle Historical Society and Museums** (☏ **907/547-2325;**

Coke), 100 miles along. But don't get your hopes up. This is the only place where I've ever walked into a visitor center and asked what there is to do in town, only to have the host hold up her fingers in the shape of a goose egg and say, "Nothing." Another 100 miles (I hope you brought plenty of music, because no radio station reaches out here), and you've made it to **Delta Junction.** There's a little more to do here, but it's still not a destination. Another 100 miles and you're in Fairbanks.

THE ALASKAN INTERIOR | The Alaska Highway

544

www.eagleak.org) shows off the buildings and several museums of materials left behind in this eddy in the stream of history. Their 3-hour walking tour starts once a day at 9am daily, Memorial Day to Labor Day, and costs $5. Sadly, a devastating flood in 2009 severely damaged the town and its historic customs house; I'm hopeful the recovery will be well underway be the time you read this.

To plan a float trip on the Yukon River from Eagle, or for other outdoor information, contact the Eagle Field Office of the **Yukon–Charley Rivers** **National Preserve,** P.O. Box 167, Eagle, AK 99738 (☎ 907/547-2233; www.nps.gov/yuch). The office lies on the far side of the airstrip from the main part of town.

The funny little village of Chicken is the other stop on this drive (the old joke is that they wanted to name the town "Ptarmigan" but didn't know how to spell it). There are a couple of businesses worth a stop for gold panning, a meal, or to shop for gifts. Chicken, too, is mixed up in the area's time warp: The town has never had phone service, but has free Wi-Fi.

The main sources of information for the drive are based in Tok, the first town you hit after you cross the border. It acts as a threshold for the entire state. To plan the journey ahead, contact them, and see "Exploring the Interior" at the beginning of this chapter. If you're headed to Anchorage or other points south, see the sections on the Glenn and Richardson highways later in this chapter; those roads branch from the Alaska Highway at Tok and Delta, respectively.

I've arranged this section in order from the border with Canada heading west.

Crossing the Border

Besides remembering to set your watch back an hour when crossing the border into Alaska—it's an hour earlier than in Yukon Territory—also keep in mind you are spanning an international boundary. An adult U.S. citizen needs a **passport, passport card,** or **enhanced driver's license** to re-enter the country over the road or water; a U.S. child under 18 needs a passport or a birth certificate combined with photo identification. A website explaining the requirements is at www.getyouhome.gov. Canadians need passports but not visas. See chapter 3 to learn more about passports and entry requirements for international visitors. Even with a passport, **children** with their parents should have a birth certificate; children under 18 unaccompanied by parents need a notarized letter from a parent or guardian; and children with a single parent should carry such a letter from the other parent. There are no duties on products made in the United States or Canada. For duties on items that you buy that originated in other countries or on alcohol or smoking supplies, see chapter 3. Products you buy in Alaska made of **wildlife** will probably require special permits to be taken out of the United States, and most marine mammal products cannot be exported (p. 89). If you are a U.S. resident, send the item home by mail without trying to take it through Canada. U.S. authorities no longer let non-citizens into the country with firearms except for permanent resident aliens or foreigners holding both a special permit from the Bureau of Alcohol, Tobacco, Firearms and Explosives and a non-resident hunting license (p. 88). It's complicated for U.S. residents to travel through Canada with **firearms,** as well. Guns other than hunting rifles or shotguns generally are not allowed, and you need to fill out a form and pay a $25 fee for guns that are allowed; contact the Canadian Firearms Center (☎800/731-4000; www.cfc-cafc.gc.ca) before you go to avoid problems. You should also register your firearms with U.S. Customs and Border Patrol (no fee) before entering Canada to ease your return to the United States. **Dogs** more than 3 months old require a rabies certificate with an expiration date before entering the U.S., which should have the signature of a licensed veterinarian that is dated at least 30 days prior to crossing the border. A certificate without an expiration date is honored only 12 months from the date signed. If in doubt about any of these issues, call before you go, as the border is a long way from anywhere: **Canadian Customs** in Whitehorse (☎867/667-3943) or **U.S. Customs and Border Protection** on the highway (☎907/774-2252), in Skagway (☎907/983-2325), or in Anchorage (☎907/271-6855).

FROM THE BORDER TO TOK

The first 65 miles after entering the United States, the road borders the Tetlin National Wildlife Refuge. These broad wetlands and low forests are a migratory stop-over in May and in the fall for thousands of songbirds, birds of prey, and waterfowl, and the summer home of trumpeter swans and lesser sandhill cranes, among 143 other species. The refuge holds a migratory bird festival in May with activities at the refuge and in nearby Tok. Activities change each year. Caribou also show up along the road, especially in the early spring and late fall. Interpretive signs are at six points along the highway. The Fish and Wildlife Service's Tetlin Refuge Visitor Center, 8 miles past the border, at mile 1,229, is open May 15 to September 15 daily from 8am to 4:30pm, longer when staffing allows. There are exhibits, a 1-mile trail, and an observation deck with a great view. The refuge also has two small lakeside campgrounds: Deadman Lake, at mile 1,249, with 14 sites, some okay for RVs; and Lakeview, at mile 1,256, with eight (no RVs more than 30 ft.). Rangers give evening campground programs in the summer at Deadman Lake. The campgrounds do not have drinking water. The refuge headquarters is in Tok (☎907/883-5312; http://tetlin.fws.gov).

Tok

Born as a construction station on the highway, Tok's role in the world has never expanded much beyond being a stop on the road. With its location at the intersection of the Alaska Highway and the Glenn Highway to Anchorage and Prince William Sound (see the next section), the town has built an economy on gas stations, gift stores, cafes, and hotels to serve highway travelers. It brags of being the coldest community in North America, a dubious distinction made possible by both the latitude and the distance from the moderating influence of the ocean.

ESSENTIALS

GETTING THERE You're surely passing through Tok with your own set of wheels. If you get stuck for some reason, one shuttle service or another can get you on your way. **Alaska/Yukon Trails** (☎800/770-7275; www.alaskashuttle.com) runs through Tok between Fairbanks and Dawson City or Whitehorse.

VISITOR INFORMATION Public land agencies jointly operate an informative visitor center to introduce highway travelers to Alaska's outdoors. The **Alaska Public Lands Information Center**, P.O. Box 359, Tok, AK 99780 (☎907/883-5667; www.nps.gov/aplic), is in the same building as the Alaska State Troopers on the right (north) side of the road coming from the direction of Canada on the Alaska Highway. It is open daily from 8am to 7pm in summer and Monday through Friday from 8am to 4:30pm in winter. You can make ferry reservations on the Alaska Marine Highway System here, too.

The next building over, at the intersection of the Alaska Highway and Tok Cut-Off (also known as the Glenn Highway), the town's **Main Street Visitor Center** is operated by the Tok Chamber of Commerce, P.O. Box 389, Tok, AK 99780 (☎907/883-5775, www.tokalaskainfo.com). The center provides information on Tok and anywhere else you may be bound on the highway. They're open from May 1 to September 15 daily from 8am to 7pm.

[FastFACTS] TOK

Bank Denali State Bank has an ATM, as does the Three Bears Food Center, two doors down.

Hospital Tok Clinic is on the Tok Cut-Off across from the fire station (☎907/883-5855).

Police Contact the Alaska State Troopers (☎907/883-5111), next to the visitor center near the intersection of the Alaska and Glenn highways.

Post Office At the highway junction next to the Westmark Hotel.

Taxes There are none in the region.

AN ACTIVITY

A river guide based in Tok offers trips on various Interior rivers. **Canoe Alaska** (**☎907/883-2628;** www.canoealaska.net) specializes in white-water canoe instruction for beginners and intermediate paddlers and leads guided canoe and raft outings and expeditions; a guided trip is around $100 a day. They also rent canoes and offer shuttle service.

WHERE TO STAY

The motels are numerous and competitive in Tok. There are also many B&Bs. Check at the visitor center.

Be sure to get the 50¢ state highway and campground map from the public lands center (see above), which includes all the public campgrounds in Alaska. Three attractive state park campgrounds lie near Tok on the three highway links that radiate from the town. Each has a $15 self-service fee.

There are lots of competitive RV parks in Tok, too. One has wooded sites suitable for tent camping as well as the **Sourdough Campground,** 1½ miles south of town on the Glenn Highway (**☎907/883-5543;** www.sourdough campground.com). They charge $38 for full hookups, $20 dry, showers included. The campground offers some unusual free services, including Wi-Fi and a nightly pancake toss with a chance to win a free breakfast. Besides the pancake breakfasts, they sell evening meals of soup or reindeer chili in sourdough bread bowls.

Snowshoe Motel & Fine Arts and Gifts ⚑ The motel is behind the gift shop. The best units are the newer nonsmoking rooms near the front, and all are reasonably priced. Each is divided into two sections by the bathroom, providing two separate bedrooms—great for families. They have phones. Outside walkways are decorated with flowers. The gift shop carries some authentic Native art as well as highway kitsch. It is open daily in summer, Saturdays in winter.

Across the highway from the information center (P.O. Box 559), Tok, AK 99780. **☎800/478-4511** in Alaska, Yukon, and part of B.C.; or 907/883-4511. Fax 907/883-4517. snowshoe@aptalaska.net. 24 units. High season $90 double; low season $70 double. Extra person $5. MC, V. *In room:* TV, fridge, microwave.

Westmark Tok The central hotel in town is closed in the winter, as its clientele is primarily the package-tour bus trade. It's made up of several buildings connected by boardwalks. Rooms are comfortable, air-conditioned, and regularly updated. The newer section has larger rooms for the same price. The company offers significant discounts for booking on their website. The restaurant serves breakfast and dinner of Mexican and standard American fare, with dinners in the $14 to $23 range.

Intersection of Alaska and Glenn highways (P.O. Box 130), Tok, AK 99780-0130. **☎800/544-0970** (reservations) or 907/883-5174. Fax 907/883-5178. www.westmarkhotels.com. 92 units. $110–$130 double. AE, DC, DISC, MC, V. Closed mid-Sept to mid-May. **Amenities:** Restaurant; bar; computer access and Wi-Fi in lobby. *In room:* A/C, TV, hair dryer.

Young's Motel Good standard motel rooms occupy three one-story structures on the parking lot behind Fast Eddy's restaurant (described below), where you check in. Eighteen newer, smoke-free rooms are the pick of the litter, but all are acceptable.

Delta Junction.

Behind Fast Eddy's Restaurant on the Alaska Hwy. (P.O. Box 482), Tok, AK 99780. ☎ **907/883-4411.** Fax 907/883-5023. 43 units. High season $87 double; low season $64 double. Extra person $5. AE, DISC, MC, V. **Amenities:** Restaurant (described below); bar. *In room:* TV, Wi-Fi.

WHERE TO DINE

A reliable restaurant of many years' tenure, **Fast Eddy's** (☎ **907/883-4411**) is on the right as you enter town from the east. Begun as a typical roadside cafe, it has developed into a place where a wine list and fine-dining entrees don't seem out of place. Yet the proprietor knows that most highway travelers just want a simple, relaxing meal, and the varied menu offers anything they might have in mind. I relish the salad bar and light dishes that offer a break from the usually carnivorous greasy-spoon choices found elsewhere along the highway. The dining room is decorated in maroon, dark wood, and brass. They're open in summer from 6am to 11pm, in winter from 6am to 10pm. Wine and beer are available with meals, but there is no bar.

Delta Junction

This intersection with the Richardson Highway, which runs from Valdez to Fairbanks (see section 7, later), is the official end of the Alaska Highway. It's an earnest little roadside town set in a broad plain between the Delta and Tanana rivers. People make their livings from farming and tourism, by working at a trans-Alaska pipeline pump station south of town and Fort Greely, one of the bases of the national missile defense system. For visitors, there are two historic roadhouse museums, several good campgrounds, and an unpredictable chance to spy a herd of bison—but not enough to hold most for more than a few hours.

[FastFACTS] DELTA JUNCTION

Bank **Wells Fargo,** with an ATM, is next door to the IGA Food Cache on the Richardson Highway at the center of town; another bank with an ATM is just south of the visitor center.

Hospital The **Family Medical Center** is at Mile 267.2. Richardson Highway, 1½ miles north of the visitor center (☎ **907/895-4879** or 907/895-5100).

Police For non-emergency calls, reach the

Alaska State Troopers at ☎ **907/895-4800.**

Post Office On the Richardson, half a mile north of the visitor center.

Taxes None of any kind.

ESSENTIALS

VISITOR INFORMATION A helpful **visitor center** run by the Delta Chamber of Commerce, P.O. Box 987, Delta Junction, AK 99737 (☎877/895-5068 or 907/895-5068, 907/895-5069 summer only; www.deltachamber.org), stands at the intersection of the Alaska and Richardson highways, in the middle of town; it's open from mid-May to mid-September.

EXPLORING THE AREA

Before construction of the first road to Fairbanks in 1917 (today's Richardson Hwy.), travelers to the Interior followed a trail on basically the same route by horse in summer and dogsled in winter, stopping at roadhouses that provided food and shelter a day apart or less on the 2-week trip. Two well-preserved examples of the roadhouse system survive near Delta Junction.

In 1996, the Army saved the 1905 **Sullivan Roadhouse** (☎907/895-4415), which had stood abandoned since 1922 on what became an Army bombing range. Today the log building stands near the town visitor center and is open free of charge in summer Monday through Friday 9am to 5pm. Many of the Sullivans' original belongings have been set back in their original places, giving a strong feel for frontier life, but the heart of the restoration is the authentic hospitality of the local volunteers who show off the place with great pride.

The next stop on the trail beyond Sullivan's Roadhouse was 16 miles toward Fairbanks. **Rika's Roadhouse and Landing,** 8 miles northwest of Delta at mile 275 on the Richardson Highway (☎907/895-4201; www.rikas.com), still makes a pleasant stop on your drive. This roadhouse lasted later than the Sullivans' because drivers had to board a ferry here to cross the Tanana River until the 1940s, and the landing was the end of the line for Tanana sternwheelers. The 1906 log building, on the National Register of Historic Places, has been altered too much by its gift shop to feel authentic, but the grassy 10-acre compound completes a vivid scene of Alaska pioneer life with surviving outbuildings, including telegraph cabins, a museum, a barn, a gorgeous vegetable garden, and livestock pens. The entire site overlooks the riverbank, and an impressive suspension bridge carries the trans-Alaska pipeline over the Tanana just beyond the park. A private operator does a good job of managing the site for the state of Alaska, including operating a restaurant that serves simple meals daily from 9am to 5pm; the grounds and museum are open from 8am to 8pm from May 15 to September 15.

WHERE TO STAY

Check at the visitor center for a referral to one of the many B&Bs. The cute, funny, and hospitable **Kelly's Alaska Country Inn,** at the intersection of Richardson and Alaska highways (☎907/895-4667; www.kellysalaskacountry inn.com), has rooms for $139 double in summer, $109 winter, right in the middle of town. The 20 rooms have TVs, telephones, microwave ovens, refrigerators, and coffee machines; most are small and ordinary, but a funky few are an in old Quonset hut and have arched wood ceilings. This is a family-run business going way, way back.

Alaska 7 Motel, 3548 Richardson Hwy. (☎907/895-4848; www.alaska7 motel.com), is a small, low-slung building containing standard rooms with lots of amenities, including refrigerators, microwave ovens, coffee, Wi-Fi, and satellite TV for $99 double.

CAMPING

Alaska State Parks maintains five campgrounds on the rivers and lakes in and around Delta Junction and a couple of public cabins. Right on the highway near town, the **Delta State Recreation Area campground** lies among large spruce and birch trees, the sites well separated, some with walk-in privacy. It is among the most attractive campgrounds on the highway. The **Quartz Lake State Recreation Area,** 11 miles northwest of town on the Richardson Highway and down a 3-mile turnoff, has more than 100 camping sites on two fishing lakes. The camping fee is $10. For information, contact the **Department of Natural Resources Public Information Center,** 3700 Airport Way, Fairbanks, AK 99709 (☎907/451-2705; www.alaskastateparks.org, click on "Individual Parks").

To park an RV, or if you're tent camping and need a shower, **Smith's Green Acres RV Park and Campground,** 1½ miles north on the Richardson Highway from the visitor center, at mile 267.9 (☎800/895-4369 or 907/895-4369; http:// smithsgreenacres.com), has pull-through RV sites and tent sites among the trees. The place also has cabins, a small playground, laundry facilities, and Wi-Fi. Full hookup sites are $35, tent sites $18.

WHERE TO DINE

For a picnic or quick, simple meal on your drive, try the **IGA Food Cache** (☎907/ 895-4653), on the south side of the highway in Delta. The deli counter sells fried food, subs, and ice cream, and the store also has a bakery counter and coffee stand. You can eat in as well as carry out. They're open Monday through Saturday 6:30am to 9pm, Sunday 8am to 8pm, closing an hour earlier in winter. The **Buffalo Center Drive-In** (☎907/895-4055) is a popular spot on a sunny day, serving burgers, shakes, and other drive-in fare at picnic tables, or brought to your car by a carhop. It is next to the Sullivan Roadhouse on the Richardson Highway just south of the Alaska Highway intersection.

Buffalo Center Diner DINER The locals eat here, for good reason. The dining room is light and clean, decorated with wood and plants, and the menu covers everything you would hope for in a simple family restaurant— plus buffalo burgers and sausage in honor of the Delta herd. Each time I've stopped the food has been good and the atmosphere relaxing. Service has always been friendly and quick, and the waitress called me "hon."

1680 Richardson Hwy. ☎907/895-5089. Lunch $6–$12, dinner $9–$25. MC, V. Summer daily 7am–9pm; winter Mon 11am–8pm, Tues–Sun 7am–8pm.

THE GLENN HIGHWAY

The Glenn Highway, Alaska Route 1, leads from the Alaska Highway at Tok to Anchorage (the section from Tok to Glennallen is also called the Tok Cut-Off). It connects the most populous part of the state to the outside world, a 328-mile strip of blacktop that grows from two lanes in Tok to six or more in urban downtown Anchorage. In this section, I cover the stretch from Glennallen to Palmer. From Tok to Glennallen, the road passes through wilderness. The portion from Palmer to downtown Anchorage is all part of the greater city and encompassed in chapter 7.

Glenn Highway.

Glennallen

The town may look like just a wide place in the road, but this little community near the junction of the Glenn and Richardson highways is the commercial hub for the Copper River Country, a great, thinly settled region. The two highways overlap for a few miles. At their southern split, a handy information stop, the **Copper Valley Chamber of Commerce and Visitor Center,** occupies a gray building next to the Hub gas station and store (P.O. Box 469, Glennallen, AK 99588; **(907/822-5555;** www.traveltoalaska.com). Volunteers open the center May 15 to September 15 daily 9am to 7pm, or longer as manpower allows. Besides the hotel and restaurant listed below, Glennallen has two banks with ATMs, a post office, groceries, a medical center, and government offices, all centered along a strip of the Glenn Highway around mile 187, west of the visitor center.

Apart from Wrangell–St. Elias National Park, much of the outdoor recreation in the Copper River Country occurs on lands managed by the **Bureau of Land Management Glennallen Field Office,** with a log cabin office in town on the north side of the Glenn Highway at mile 186.5 (P.O. Box 147), Glennallen, AK 99588 (**(907/822-3217).** The Internet address is too long to repeat; go to www.blm.gov/ak, and navigate to the "Glennallen Field Office." The office is open Monday through Friday from 8am to 4:30pm. Information is also available from the public land information centers in Anchorage, Fairbanks, and Tok. This huge area, about as large as a midsize eastern U.S. state, is more accessible than most of the national park, but it's still a rough, remote land with few visitor facilities. There are several large alpine lakes, two National Wild Rivers, several hiking trails, and four campgrounds (including the State Park campground just north of Glennallen), all reached on the Richardson, Glenn, and Denali highways. Guides are available for **rafting** and **fishing** in the rivers. Check at the visitor center or BLM office for a list of operators.

Good standard accommodations are at the **New Caribou Hotel,** in town at mile 187 of the Glenn Highway (☎800/478-3302 or 907/822-3302; www. caribouhotel.com). The rooms have the amenities of a roadside chain, but the hotel as a whole has the character of its place. They book up in the summer, so reservations are important. The summer rate is $143 double. Budget rooms are in an annex building, a former pipeline construction camp, for $79 double. Their **Caribou Restaurant** is inexpensive but quite fancy inside, with lots of brass and booths. Choices include burgers, fish, and steak.

The Matanuska Glacier Area

From Glennallen, the highway traverses a broad tundra area where there's a good chance of seeing caribou and other wildlife from a distance. Next, the road climbs between two mountain ranges—the coastal Chugach Mountains that hold the glaciers around Prince William Sound, and the craggy old Talkeetna Mountains to the north. The road winds through steep, rocky terrain with wonderful, scary views, including a good look at the Matanuska Glacier. In the fall, when the tundra and the birches, aspens, and cottonwoods turn yellow and red, this drive is dizzying in its beauty. Plan on driving this section at no more than 45 mph.

The Matanuska Glacier State Recreation Site overlooks the glacier and has a 1-mile interpretive nature trail and a good, 12-site campground ($15 per site or $10 to park overnight in a paved lot). To get closer to the glacier, you have to take a rough side road and pay a fee to the people who own the land in front of it, doing business as **Glacier Park** (☎888/253-4480; www.matanuskaglacier. com). The cost for the self-guided hike is $15 adults; $13 seniors, $10 students and military, $5 children 6 to 12. They also offer camping for $15 a night. Turn at mile 102. The side road is 3 miles, followed by a 15-minute walk to the glacier's face. From October to April it's wise to call to reserve and check conditions.

Two exceptional lodges lie along the highway near the Matanuska Glacier, about 70 miles from Glennallen or 115 miles from Anchorage. In this remote area, phones are in common rooms.

Majestic Valley Wilderness Lodge ★★ ▮▮ This friendly place offers a choice of basic, inexpensive rooms and cabins and more luxurious lodge rooms, and serves excellent family style meals to guests and others who reserve in advance. Dining is in the extraordinary log lodge building with a towering ceiling and wonderful mountain views—a quintessentially Alaskan space that is understandably popular for weddings and the like. It's set in spectacular terrain, a quiet spot off the highway with a 20km network of well-groomed cross-country skiing trails. Anchorage families, such as ours, come here for fun winter or spring weekends, skiing and sledding, playing cards in the evening, and staying in the simple, budget rooms; the four much fancier lodge rooms with satellite TVs, granite counters, and radiant floor heating, still reasonably priced, appeal to another set. In the summer, the hiking here, mostly above tree line, is exceptional, and river rafting, glacier trekking, and flightseeing are offered.

Mile 114.9, Glenn Hwy. (16162 W. Glenn Hwy., Sutton, AK 99674). ☎907/746-2930. Fax 907/746-2931. www.majesticvalleylodge.com. 12 units, 2 cabins. $120–$165 double; $155 cabin double. Extra person age 9 and older $10; extra child ages 3–8 $5. MC, V. **Amenities:** Restaurant.

Sheep Mountain Lodge ★ On a mountainside above the road, a well-loved couple, Zack and Anjanette Steer, preside at this historic log lodge. Zack is a top competitive dog musher, and the lodge attracts many muscle-powered athletes, hosting a December dog-sled race and, in July, the huge Fireweed 400 Bicycle Race that ends in Valdez. Guests can hike and mountain bike over spectacular trails on the tundra-covered mountains in summer and ski-groomed trails in the winter. Cabins are large and stylishly decorated, with high ceilings and walls of rough wood to remind you of the rural location. A few have kitchenettes. The sitting porches have wonderful views down the mountainside. They rent a sleeping-bag bunkhouse, too, and have a guest sauna and indoor hot tub. The little cafe serves simple, healthy food in the summer. Service is very friendly.

Mile 113.5, Glenn Hwy. (17701 W. Glenn Hwy., Sutton, AK 99674). ☎877/645-5121 or 907/745-5121. Fax 907/745-5120. www.sheepmountain.com. 11 cabins. Summer $159 double, $189 with kitchenette, bunkhouse $60 for 4; winter $99–$149 double; bunkhouse $60 for 4. Extra person cabin $10; bunkhouse $5. MC, V. Closed 1 month each in spring and fall (call ahead). **Amenities:** Restaurant; Jacuzzi; sauna.

Chickaloon & Sutton

Road construction projects working along the highway year by year have imposed delays of up to an hour, slow driving, and nighttime closures. Contact ☎511 or check http://511.alaska.gov for the latest. The scenery is attractive, with country-style development cropping up along the road as you approach urban Alaska. Chickaloon is the base of Nova Raft and Adventure Tours, the river riding company listed in the Anchorage chapter; if you're already passing through here, you may want to arrange a float. Sutton is a little town left behind by a coal mine that once operated in these mountains. The charming little historic park there is worthy of a stop to stretch your legs.

THE RICHARDSON HIGHWAY & COPPER CENTER

The 364-mile drive from Fairbanks to Valdez unfolds as a grand cross-section of Alaska. It begins in the broad Interior valleys at the north, rises to the tundra and lakes of the Alaska Range, descends back down to the Copper River Country, and finally climbs over the steep coastal mountains into the Prince William Sound fjord where Valdez resides. This was the first route into Alaska, but today it is little traveled and mostly free of development, an opportunity to see real wilderness by car on paved road.

Delta Junction is covered in section 5, on the Alaska Highway. The intersection with the Denali Highway (see chapter 9) comes 81 miles south of there. This section has the most extraordinary scenery—broad vistas, the Delta River, amazing alpine lakes including long Summit Lake, and many views of the trans-Alaska pipeline. Don't plan on stops or services, although there are a few widely scattered campgrounds and seasonal businesses. The spot on the map known as Paxson, the intersection with the Denali Highway, has a business called the Paxson Inn. You can fill your tanks there, but I wouldn't recommend the restaurant or the rooms.

Copper River Princess Wilderness Lodge.

The next town on the Richardson is Glennallen, which is covered above, in section 6. Fourteen miles south of Glennallen, **Copper Center** is a tiny Athabascan community on the old Richardson Highway near many major rivers, around which people here orient their lives in the summer time. To get out on the water, fishing or just floating, contact **Alaska River Wrangellers** (☎888/822-3967 or 907/822-3967; www.riverwrangellers.com), based at the landing strip, a rafting firm owned by pioneers of the industry in Alaska, Nova Raft and Adventure Tours. They offer half-day floats for as little as $99, with a schedule that allows clients to choose the level of risk, adventure, and remoteness they are comfortable with, or to combine white-water rafting with salmon fishing. Those trips allow access to areas on the Tonsina River most anglers don't brave, for $299 full day.

The town's historic roadhouse, the **Copper Center Lodge** (☎866/330-3245 or 907/822-3245; www.coppercenterlodge. com), has long been worthy of a stop for dinner or even overnight. The history of the lodge dates from the bizarre gold-rush origins of Copper Center and Valdez, when about 4,000 stampeders to the Klondike tried a virtually impossible all-American route from Valdez over the glaciers of the Wrangell–St. Elias region. Few made it, and hundreds who died are buried in Copper Center. The original lodge was built of the stuff they left behind. The existing building dates from 1932. Rooms for up to four are $130 to $165, and they're open year-round.

Copper River Princess Wilderness Lodge ★★ This first-class lodge built by the Princess Cruise Line brings the comforts of the outside world to this rough and isolated corner of the planet. On clear days, the eastward views of mounts Drum, Wrangell, and Blackburn are incredible. Princess has tried to capture the trim, red-and-white look of the historic Kennecott mining district. Inside, common areas are spacious and warm, with a big slate fireplace in the lobby. Rooms are in earth tones, with faux rustic furniture and art reflecting mining history, and have king- and queen-size beds. The restaurant serves three meals a day, including sophisticated cuisine for dinner; those meals are not just in another league, but a completely different game than anything else found on the highway. The smoked salmon eggs Benedict was terrific. Dinner main courses are $16 to $29.

1 Brenwick-Craig Rd. (P.O. Box 422), Copper Center, AK 99573 (turn at mile 102 Richardson Hwy.). ☎800/426-0500 or 907/822-4000. Fax 907/822-4044. www.princesslodges.com. 85 units. High season $179 double; low season $139 double. AE, DISC, MC, V. **Amenities:** Restaurant; courtesy van to Gulkana airport and national park visitor center. *In room:* TV, hair dryer.

Wrangell-St. Elias National Park.

WRANGELL-ST. ELIAS NATIONAL PARK & KENNECOTT

Looking at a relief map of Alaska, you'd think the portion drained by the Copper River was so overweighed with mountains that it might topple the whole state into the Pacific. The Alaska Range, in the center of the state, has the tallest mountain, but this Gulf of Alaska region, straddling the Alaska-Yukon border, has more mass—the second- and fourth-tallest mountains in North America (Logan and St. Elias), plus nine of the tallest 16 peaks in the United States. Four mountain ranges intersect, creating a mad jumble of terrain covering tens of millions of acres, a trackless chaos of unnamed, unconquered peaks. The Copper River and its raging tributaries slice through it all, swallowing the gray melt of innumerable glaciers that flow from the largest ice field in North America. Everything here is the largest, most rugged, most remote; words quickly fall short of the measure. But where words fail, commerce gives a little help: These mountains are so numerous and remote that one guide service makes a business of taking visitors to mountains and valleys that no one has ever explored before.

Ironically for such a wild land, the area's main attraction for visitors is its history. The richest copper deposit in the world was found here in 1900 by a group of prospectors who mistook a green mountaintop for a patch of green grass where they could feed their horses. It was a mountain of almost pure copper, with metallic nuggets the size of desks (one is at the UA Museum of the North in Fairbanks). The deposit produced trainloads of 70% pure copper. The first ore was so rich it required no processing before shipping, then came lots more copper that did need minimal processing. Much more lower-grade ore still lies underground. The Alaska Syndicate, an investment group that included J. P. Morgan and Daniel Guggenheim, built the Kennecott Copper Corporation from this wealth (its name was a misspelling of the Kennicott River and Glacier, where the copper was found). To get the copper out, they paid for an incredible 196-mile rail line up from Cordova (see chapter 8), and created a self-contained company town deep in the wilderness, called **Kennecott.** When the high-grade ore was gone, in 1938, they pulled the plug, leaving a ghost town of extraordinary beauty that still contains machinery and even documents they left behind.

Wrangell–St. Elias National Park and Preserve now owns Kennecott and more than 13 million acres across this region of Alaska. It's the largest national park in the United States by a long shot, six times the size of Yellowstone and about 25% larger than the entire country of Switzerland. The protected land continues across the border in Canada, in **Kluane National Park,** which is similarly massive. Most of that land is impossibly remote, but Wrangell–St. Elias has two rough gravel roads that allow access to see the mountains from a car. The main route is the abandoned roadbed of the Copper River and Northwestern Railroad leading to Kennecott and the historic sites there. It's an arduous but rewarding journey by car, requiring at least 2 days to do it right. Air taxis, river guides, and remote lodges offer other ways into the park's untouched wilderness, mostly starting from **McCarthy,** a historic village near Kennecott. There are a few trails near Kennecott, but only for day hikes. This is a country where experienced outdoors people can get away from any trace of humans for weeks on end.

The Kennecott & McCarthy Area

This historic copper area is the only part of the park most visitors see, as it's the most accessible and has the most services, interesting sites, and paths to explore. It's still not easy to get to, however—that's why it's still so appealing—and there's little point in going without adequate time. You can hit the highlights at Kennecott and McCarthy in a full day, but just getting there takes time. My family and I spent 3 nights and could have stayed longer.

The main event is the ghost town at **Kennecott,** whose red buildings gaze from a mountainside across the Kennecott Glacier in the valley below. Now owned by the Park Service, the buildings made up an isolated company town until 1938, when it abruptly shut down. Tourists coming here as late as the 1960s saw it as if frozen in time, with breakfast dishes still on the tables from the day the last train left. Most of that was looted and destroyed in the 1970s, but when I toured the company store a few years ago, old documents still remained, and the powerhouse and 14-story mill buildings still had their heavy iron and wood equipment. Besides the buildings, there are excellent hiking trails, including one that traverses the glacier. The town now has only a few year-round residents, but in summer is busy with a lodge, a couple of bed-and-breakfasts, guide services, and park rangers.

Kennecott.

Five miles down the road, Kennecott's twin town of **McCarthy** served the miners as a place to drink, gamble, and hire prostitutes on rare days off—the company didn't allow any frivolity in Kennecott or in the bunkhouses high up on the mountain. McCarthy retains the relaxed atmosphere of its past, with businesses and residents living in false-front buildings not much changed from Wild West days. More of a year-round community, McCarthy has a restaurant, lodging, flight services, and other businesses.

Yet even this most populous part of the park is isolated and sparsely inhabited, with few services. Only about 50 people live in the greater area year-round. You will find no banking services, general stores, gas stations, clinics, police, or anything else you're used to relying on. Phones came to McCarthy and Kennecott only in the late 1990s and are still sparse. Bring what you need.

ESSENTIALS
Getting There

BY CAR The paved **Edgerton Highway** starts 17 miles south of Copper Center on the Richardson Highway, then runs east for 33 miles to the tiny, dried-up former railroad town of **Chitina** (*Chit*-na), the last reliable stop for groceries, gas, and other necessities until you return here. Do fill your tank; prudence also demands a full-sized spare tire. Heading east, into the park, the **McCarthy Road** continues along the roadbed of the Copper River and Northwestern Railway. This is 60 miles of narrow dirt road, muddy in wet weather and clouded with dust when it's dry. Each year it has been improved a little, and two-wheel-drive cars can normally make it. The drive is a fun adventure, passing through tunnels of alders and crossing rivers on some of the original wooden railroad trestles; one wood-decked bridge spans a canyon more than 200 feet deep. There are virtually no services, very few buildings, and little traffic on the 3-hour drive. If you are driving a rented car, consider using the van or air options mentioned below, leaving the car in Chitina. I have listed companies that rent cars that can be driven on this unpaved road in Fairbanks (p. 516) and Anchorage (p. 290).

The road ends at a parking lot and collection of temporary businesses on the banks of the Kennicott River. You can drive no farther. Next, you walk across a footbridge or two. Late in the summer the Kennicott Glacier releases a flood from a glacier-dammed lake, but at other times the second channel is a dry wash and the second bridge isn't needed. Handcarts are available to move your luggage across, and on the other side you can catch a van. The place where you are staying will send one, or you can ride the **van** operated by **McCarthy-Kennicott Shuttle** (☎907/554-4411), $2 to McCarthy or $5 per person, one-way, to Kennecott. It runs every half-hour. A public telephone is near the bridge that you can use to call your lodgings.

BY VAN The **Backcountry Connection** (☎866/582-5292 in Alaska only, or 907/822-5292; www.kennicottshuttle.com) runs vans from Glennallen, Copper Center, Kenny Lake, and Chitina to the Kennicott River footbridge daily in summer. The van leaves Glennallen at 7am, Copper Center 7:30am, Kenny Lake 8am, and Chitina at 8:30am, arriving at the footbridge around 11:30am. The return trip departs from the footbridge at 4:30pm, getting back to Chitina around 6:30pm, Kenny Lake 7:30pm Copper Center 8pm, and Glennallen 8:30pm. The same-day round-trip fare is $99, or $139 if you return on a different day; they also offer the option of flying one way.

BY AIR A simple way to Kennecott and McCarthy is to drive to Chitina—as far as you can go on pavement—and fly the rest of the way on one of the air taxis. Once there, get around in the vans that shuttle back and forth over 5 miles of dirt road. **Wrangell Mountain Air** (☎800/478-1160 or 907/554-4411; www.wrangellmountainair.com) offers three flights daily from Chitina to McCarthy for $229 round-trip and includes ground transportation at McCarthy-Kennicott. You can add on lunch and activities, such as a half-day glacier hike or ghost town walking tour. This day trip option gives you enough time at Kennecott without having to spend the night there. A reputable service operating between Chitina and McCarthy on an on-demand basis is **McCarthy Air** (☎907/554-4440; www.mccarthyair.com). Flightseeing over the national park and charters to remote valleys and lakes for backcountry trips are covered below under "Getting Outside: Hiking & Backpacking."

Wednesday or Friday, it's possible to fly in a small prop plane all the way from Anchorage. A couple of flight services team up to do this: You fly on one from Anchorage to Gulkana and then on the mail plane from Gulkana to McCarthy. The fare is about $300 one-way. Contact **Copper Valley Air Service** (☎866/570-4200 or 907/822-4200; www.coppervalleyair.com), which handles all the booking and flies the Gulkana to McCarthy leg.

VISITOR INFORMATION The main park visitor center is on the Richardson Highway near Copper Center (☎907/822-5234; www.nps.gov/wrst). Stop in to buy maps and publications, watch a movie, or get advice from a ranger on outdoor treks. Hours are Memorial Day to Labor Day daily from 9am to 7pm, in winter, Monday through Friday from 8am to 4:30pm. You can write for information to P.O. Box 439, Copper Center, AK 99573. The Park Service is restoring buildings and offers visitor services in Kennecott itself. A former general store has become a visitor center, a good place to stop with questions for rangers, plan a backcountry trip, or join one of the daily guided activities. A ranger station for the less-visited northern area of the park lies on the Nabesna Road near its intersection with the Tok Cutoff Highway, about 80 miles north of Glennallen. That's an area for solitary roadside camping among broad views.

EXPLORING THE TOWNS

CHITINA Chitina lost its reason to exist in 1938, when the last train ran on the Copper River line, but it lives on with 125 residents supporting themselves largely with salmon from the river, produce from their gardens, berries from the forests, and the few tourists who stop. There's a general store and a couple of gas stations (the last gas for many a mile), a wayside interpretive area at the site of the old depot, a pond where you can often see trumpeter swans, and, down by the river, lazily rotating fish wheels plucking salmon from the river. The Copper River is too turbid for angling, but clear water tributaries and stocked lakes in the area have fish. You can also explore south on the old Copper River rail line and even through the tunnels; check with a local or the park headquarters for advice and current conditions before trying it, as landslides sometimes block the way.

Chitina.

MCCARTHY McCarthy feels authentic as soon as you walk down the dirt main street between the false fronts. There are flight-service offices to arrange a trip out, a lodge, and hotel. Then, a street beyond, unbroken wilderness stretches for hundreds and perhaps thousands of miles. On a summer evening, young backpackers and locals stand in the road—there is no traffic, since there are almost no vehicles—meeting and talking, laughing loudly, walking around dogs having their own party. Visitors quickly mix in, as everyone seems eager to talk about the town and its history and their own peculiar wilderness lives. The people here know it's unique, and everyone hopes it doesn't change much.

KENNECOTT This has got to be one of the world's greatest ghost towns, with some 40 buildings, mostly in good enough condition to be reused today—indeed, until the current Park Service restoration project began, the community still played basketball in one structure. Some historic buildings have become lodgings, and the Park Service is using others. Locals still pick rhubarb and chives from the company garden. History has the same kind of immediacy here that you get from holding an old diary in your hand, quite different from the sanitized history-through-glass that you're used to at more accessible sites.

The Park Service bought most of the buildings a few years ago. When we walked through, on the eve of the takeover, items remained out on the ground or on store shelves that would be in museums in many places. If Kennecott were an ordinary industrial site, that would be interesting enough, but this place was something well out of the ordinary: an outpost beyond the edge of the world where men built a self-contained city a century ago. The hardship of the miners' lives and the ease of the managerial families' lives also present a fascinating contrast.

You can take in some of the story by wandering around with a walking tour booklet available from the Park Service and reading signs, but it would be a big mistake to miss going inside the buildings, and to do that you need to join a **guided tour** with **St. Elias Alpine Guides** (☎ **888/933-5427** or 907/345-9048; full listing below under "Hiking & Backpacking"). They have an office in the old Chinese laundry right in the ghost town. Tours, which happen three times daily, last 2½ hours and go into real depth on the geology and history, climbing to the perilous 14th floor of the mill building.

I've never been on another tour like it: fascinating, challenging, and even exciting; I cannot recommend it strongly enough. They operate mid-May to mid-September and charge $25 per person. Consider making a day of it by adding a glacier-hiking trip with the same company. The guides will arrange a custom tour, too.

GETTING OUTSIDE

HIKING & BACKPACKING There are a few trails radiating from Kennecott, for which crude maps are available from the rangers and others around town; or buy the **Trails Illustrated** topographic map, printed on plastic, for sale from some local businesses, or order ahead (see "Fast Facts: Alaska," in chapter 12). An impressive walk continues through the ghost town up the valley, paralleling the Kennicott Glacier and then its tributary, the Root Glacier. You can climb along the Root's edge to a towering ice fall, but a much better outing is to be had by joining a group to walk on the glacier itself. St. Elias Alpine Guides, listed below, accepts walk-ins for daily glacier day hikes and other hikes and tours. A half-day on the glacier goes for $65 a person, while all-day hikes are $100 and ice-climbing lessons $125. We combined the half-day hike with the company's ghost town tour for one of the best days of Alaska tourism we've ever spent. Another fascinating hike you can do on your own leads straight up the mountain behind the Kennecott buildings to the old Bonanza Mine and bunkhouses, 3,000 feet higher on the alpine tundra.

Beyond the trails, the park is endless miles of trackless wilderness—one of Earth's last few places that really deserves that name. Fit hikers without the backcountry experience to mount their own expedition should join one of the guides who work in the area. **St. Elias Alpine Guides (☎888/933-5427** or 907/345-9048; www.steliasguides.com) offers day hikes,

Root Glacier.

rafting, backpacking trips, and alpine ascents, but specializes in guiding extended trips to unexplored territory. Bob Jacobs, the company's founder, stopped guiding on Mount McKinley years ago because of the crowds. At Wrangell–St. Elias it's rare to encounter another party, and peaks remain that have never been climbed by anyone: The firm offers the chance to be one of the first. A 2-week trek and climb, including 4 days of mountaineering instruction, is a big commitment and costs $3,000 and up, but then, first ascents are a finite resource. The St. Elias catalog will make anyone who loves backpacking drool. Trips begin at $650 for a 4-day Donoho Peak trek. They are all-inclusive, but not without hardship and risk—nothing can take away from the severity of this wild country.

Hiking on your own in a wilderness largely without trails is a whole new kind of experience for experienced backpackers and outdoors people who are used to more crowded parts of the planet. You feel like an explorer rather than a follower. At times, there's a fairy-tale sense of the world unfolding around you, as fresh as creation. If you're not prepared to select your own route—a task only for those already experienced in trackless, backcountry traveling—there are various established ways through the park you can follow with a topographic map. You can get a trip synopsis from the visitor center or ranger station, or download from their website (www.nps.gov/wrst). Rangers can help you choose a route to suit your party, although none is easy.

Some routes start from the roads, but a better way to go is to charter a flight into a remote valley from one of the two **air services** in McCarthy, Wrangell Mountain Air or McCarthy Air (p. 559). The planes land on gravel strips, river bars, glaciers, alpine tundra, or any other flat place the pilots know about. These companies make a business of flying out backpackers, and so have established rates for different landing sites and can help you determine a route that's right for you, as well as provide a list of supplies. Wrangell Mountain Air rents bear-proof containers and two-way radios, and McCarthy Air and the Park Service lend the containers. You can charter a flight for $200 to $600 per person, with at least two passengers. Or fly in to a lake for fishing or an alpine area for exploring from a base camp, reducing the worry about how much you pack.

Note: I wouldn't want to scare off anyone who could manage one of these trips, but people do get into trouble in the Alaska wilderness every year, and some of them don't come back. Before you head out into the backcountry, you must know how to take care of yourself where help is unavailable; this includes handling river crossings, bear avoidance, hypothermia prevention, basic first aid, and other issues. Unless you have plenty of backpacking experience in less remote areas, I don't recommend starting here.

MOUNTAIN-BIKING Anywhere else, the 60-mile road that leads to this area would be considered a mountain-biking trail. You also can make good use of bikes between McCarthy, Kennecott, and the footbridge. An old **wagon road** parallels the main road that connects the two towns, 4½ miles each way; the road itself is a one-lane dirt track. Advanced cyclists can also ride the trails around Kennecott described above under "Hiking & Backpacking."

RAFTING Many great, wild rivers drain these huge mountains, which are still being carved by enormous glaciers. The **Kennicott River,** starting at the glacier of the same name, boils with Class III rapids for some 40 minutes starting right from the footbridge at the end of the McCarthy Road. As the area lacks roads, however, most trips must include a plane ride at least one-way, and that makes white-water rafting day trips here more expensive than outings near Copper Center, Valdez, Denali, or Anchorage. At Wrangell–St. Elias, floats punch deep into the backcountry. The Kennicott River meets the Nizina, passing through a deep, dramatic canyon; then the Nizina River flows into the Chitina River, which meets the Copper River near the town of Chitina, 60 miles from the starting point. The Copper River flows to the ocean. A float from the footbridge through the Nizina Canyon takes all day, with lunch and bush plane flightseeing back, which could include a glacier fly-over. St. Elias Alpine Guides (see "Hiking & Backpacking," above) charges $275. Other trips continue for 3 or 4 days to Chitina, for $990 to $1,250 per person; or for 10 to 13 days, 180 miles all the way to the Copper River Delta and the sea (see "Cordova," in chapter 8), for $3,600 per person. This is Alaska on its most grandiose scale, accessible only from the banks of these great rivers. See the previous section for a less expensive option from Copper Center.

WHERE TO STAY & DINE

The closest standard hotel rooms are in Copper Center (in the previous section). In the Kennecott-McCarthy area itself there are several attractive places to stay, all thick with the history the towns represent, but not ordinary American lodgings. Dining is mainly at the lodges. If you're not staying there, it is a good idea to check ahead to make sure they will be ready for you for a meal.

CAMPING & HOSTELLING There is one hike-in campground on the Kennecott-McCarthy side of the Kennicott River footbridge, on the Root Glacier trail. The Park Service allows camping anywhere in the park without a permit, but there are few handy spots on public land (much of the land along the roads is private), except on the Nabesna Road, which is most of a day's drive from the historic zone.

At the end of the McCarthy Road you'll find a couple of private campgrounds and a hostel. **Glacier View Campground** (☎907/554-4490, 907/243-6677 off-season, www.glacierviewcampground.com) charges $20 a night for camping and has a cabin for rent. The owners also rent mountain bikes and offer showers. Their cafe offers barbecue for lunch and dinner and serves beer and wine. Besides the backpacker's hotel mentioned in the review of the **McCarthy Lodge** on p. 564, **Kennicott River Lodge and Hostel** (☎907/554-4441 summer, 941/447-4252 winter; www.kennicottriverlodge.com), located at the end of the road 400 feet from the footbridge, offers bunks for $28 per person. Sheets and pillows are included; other bedding is extra. The lodge also rents rooms for two for $70 to $90 a night and cabins for $100 double, plus $25 for each additional person. They have a common kitchen, lounge, sauna, and showers.

There are three campgrounds on the way to the footbridge. The most attractive is State Parks' **Liberty Falls Campground,** at mile 23 on the Edgerton Highway, which is set among big trees at the foot of a crashing waterfall. Many of the sites are walk-ins, with wooden tent platforms and lots of privacy. The self-service camping fee is $10 per vehicle; the day-use fee is $1. There are pit toilets and no running water.

Kennicott Glacier Lodge ★★ This is the largest and most comfortable accommodation in the Kennecott-McCarthy area, taking the edges off the isolation. The lodge accurately re-creates an old Kennecott building, with the same red-and-white color scheme, and stands among the historic structures of the ghost town. Guests can sip drinks on a long, flower-hung front porch overlooking the glacier, or relax on a lawn with play equipment and the same view. Rooms in the main lodge building are not large and have bathrooms down the hall (six shower rooms and eight bathrooms, all clean but small). The 10 rooms in a newer south wing are larger, with two queen-size beds and private bathrooms. All the bedrooms are remarkably clean and decorated with interesting mine artifacts and papers—telegrams, blueprints, and the like. All but eight overlook the glacier and ghost town, and those on the main floor have second entrances on the veranda.

Filling dinners are served family style at 7pm on long tables, with a fixed menu in the $35 to $45 range, available to non-guests by prior reservation. The food is excellent, and portions are generous. One night we had Copper River salmon with sun-dried tomatoes and pine nuts, the next night prime rib. A large breakfast buffet is $18, continental breakfast $12. Lunch is by menu service, with sandwiches, salads, and specials ranging from $10 to $18. Sack lunches are available, too. There's nowhere else to eat right in Kennecott, so it makes sense to book the inclusive meal package, which is $315 double in the shared-bathroom units, $375 in the newer units; a third person is $85 with the meal package, children aged 4 to 12 half price.

P.O. Box 103940, Anchorage, AK 99510. ✆800/582-5128 or 907/258-2350; in season only, 907/554-4477. Fax 907/248-7975. www.kennicottlodge.com. 35 units, 10 with private bathroom. $199 double with shared bathroom; $259 double with private bathroom. Extra adult $30; extra child age 4–12 $15; free age 3 and under. AE, DISC, MC, V. Closed mid-Sept to mid-May. **Amenities:** Free airport transfers; restaurant.

McCarthy Lodge ★★ The lodge is the center of the relaxed village of McCarthy, 5 miles from the historically more buttoned-up Kennecott. Although you are not among the mining ruins when you stay here, you are in a real community where you can meet year-round residents and the many interesting characters who spend the summer here among historic buildings. The owners of the lodge also own Ma Johnson's Hotel across the street, a saloon, an art shop, and backpacker lodgings. They treasure the history and take great pains with the old buildings and food. Rooms are full of period charm, with antiques, quilts, and memorabilia. The bedrooms—which are small, as always in a historic building—are in a false-front structure that you might see in an old Western movie. Every two rooms share a bathroom. In a separate building, Lancaster's Backpacker's Hotel charges $48 single, plus $20 for each additional person up to four.

The 10-table restaurant is an authentic Bush roadhouse in an unmistakably backwoods structure that was moved here from the abandoned town of Katalla in 1916. The dining room is decorated with artifacts, early photographs, and heavy drapes. Our meals were all perfectly prepared: chicken Alfredo, Cajun halibut, and, best of all, semolina-encrusted Copper River red salmon. The price range for dinner is $15 to $32. Or order from the casual and reasonably priced bar menu of pizza and the like.

P.O. Box MXY, McCarthy, AK 99588. ✆907/554-4402. Fax 877/811-6172. www.mccarthylodge. com. 20 units, none with private bathroom. $159 double. MC, V. Closed mid-Sept to mid-May. **Amenities:** Free airport transfers; restaurant; bar.

11

THE BUSH

The Bush is most of Alaska. On a map of the state, the portion with roads and cities is a smallish corner. Yet most visitors—and, indeed, most Alaskans—never make it beyond that relatively populated corner. Several years ago, a lifelong Anchorage resident was elected to the legislature and appointed chair of its rural issues committee, only to admit he had never been to the Bush. It's common for children to grow to adulthood in Anchorage, Fairbanks, or Southeast Alaska without traveling to the Arctic, the Aleutians, or the vast wetlands of western Alaska. It happens for the same reason most tourists don't go to Bush Alaska—getting there is expensive, and there's not much in the way of human activity once you arrive. Bush Alaska is one of the planet's last barely inhabited areas. But that's a reason to go, not a reason to stay away. You can meet indigenous people who still interact with the environment in their traditional way and see virgin places that remain to be explored by self-reliant outdoors people.

Although there are few people in the Bush, the hospitality of those you do meet is special and warming. In Bush Alaska, where the population is overwhelmingly Alaska Native, it's not uncommon to be befriended by total strangers simply because you've taken the trouble to come to their community and are, therefore, an honored guest. Even in the larger towns, people smile as you pass in the street. If you have a questioning look on your face, they'll stop to help. Living in a small place where people know each other and have to work together against the elements makes for a tight, friendly community.

Alaska Native culture is based more on cooperative than competitive impulses. Respect and consensus carry greater weight than in individualistic white society. Cooperation requires slowing down, listening, not taking the lead. People from our fast-paced culture can leave a village after a visit wondering why no one spoke to them, not realizing that they never shut up long enough to give anyone a chance. The cultural differences here are real, unlike the shadows of past differences we celebrate in most regions of the homogenous United States. Long pauses in conversation are normal, looking down while addressing a person demonstrates respect, punctuality is highly relative, child care is a community function, and when gifts are offered, people really mean it—turning down even a cup of coffee is gauche. (For more on the culture of Alaska's Native peoples, see chapter 2.)

The Native people of the Bush also have terrible problems trying to live in two worlds. There's too much alcohol and too many drugs in the Bush, too

PREVIOUS PAGE: **Iñupiaq Eskimo at sunset.**

much TV, but not enough of an economic base to provide for basic services in many villages. Even in some of the relatively prosperous village hubs described in this chapter, visitors will glimpse a kind of rural poverty they may not have seen before—where prices are extremely high and steady jobs scarce and difficult to hold while pursuing traditional hunting and food gathering. But if you ask why Natives stay, you're missing something. In a world where indigenous cultures struggle to survive, people here are working to retain traditions that give their lives meaning—a sense of place and a depth of belonging that most of us can only envy. It's a work in progress, this combination of tradition and modernity, but there's no question they're slowly succeeding. They control their own land, they're building an economic base, and Native ways are being passed on to younger generations.

The Natives' physical environment is extreme in every respect —the weather, the land, even the geography. There's a special feeling to walking along or upon the Arctic Ocean, the

Native Eskimo girl.

virtual edge of the earth. The quantity and accessibility of wildlife are extreme, too, as are the solitude and the uniqueness of what you can do. Unfortunately, the prices also are extreme. Getting to a Bush hub from Anchorage costs more than getting to Anchorage from Seattle; it's often cheaper to get to Europe from Anchorage than to the Aleutians. And once you're at the rural hub, you're not done. Getting into the outdoors can cost as much again. Many travelers can't afford a Bush sojourn, instead satisfying their curiosity about the state's unpopulated areas on Alaska's rural highways (covered in chapter 10). Most who can afford the trip usually make the most of their time and money with brief prearranged tours or trips directly to wilderness lodges. Only a few explorers head for the Bush unguided, although there are some good places to go that way—Nome, Barrow, Kodiak, and Unalaska among them.

Covering the Bush is a challenge as well for the writer of a book like this one. There are more than 200 Alaska villages; many more lodges, camps, and guides; and a vast, undefined territory to describe. All that information would fill a larger book than this one. I've chosen to provide sections on those few Bush hubs that are most accessible to and popular with visitors, those that have modern facilities and can be used as gateways to more of the state for visitors who want to venture beyond the fringe of civilization.

Crossing a snowfield via snowmobile.

EXPLORING THE BUSH

Alaska's Bush is better defined by what it's like than by where it is. The most common and convenient conception says the Bush is everything beyond the road system. On a map, almost everything north and west of Fairbanks meets that definition, but many Bush villages lie elsewhere in the Interior, in Southcentral, and in Southeast Alaska. In fact, there are some Bush villages you can drive to. No simple definition works. You know a Bush community by how it feels. It's a place where the wilderness is closer than civilization, where people still live off the land and age-old traditions survive, and where you have to make a particular effort to get in or out.

The Regions

THE ARCTIC The Arctic Circle is the official boundary of the Arctic. The line, at 66° 33' north latitude, is the southern limit of true midnight sun—south of it, at sea level, the sun rises and sets, at least a little, every day of the year. But in Alaska, people think of the Arctic as beginning at the **Brooks Range,** which is a bit north of the circle, including **Barrow** and **Prudhoe Bay.** The northwest Alaska region, which includes **Kotzebue** and, south of the Arctic Circle, **Nome,** also is Arctic in climate, culture, and topography. The biggest geographic feature in Alaska's Arctic is the broad **North Slope,** the plain of tundra that stretches from the northern side of the Brooks Range to the Arctic Ocean. It's a swampy desert, with little rain or snowfall, frozen solid all but a few months a year.

Map Pointer

To locate these towns and regions, refer to the "Alaska" map in the front of the book.

WESTERN ALASKA This is the land of the massive, wet **Yukon-Kuskokwim Delta,** or the Y-K Delta, as it's known. Their land never exploited by white explorers, the Yup'ik people here live in some of Alaska's most culturally traditional villages. In places, Yup'ik is still the dominant language. **Bethel** is the main hub city of the delta but holds little attraction for visitors.

SOUTHWEST ALASKA/ALEUTIAN ISLANDS Stretching from the Aleutians—really a region of their own—to the Alaska Peninsula, Kodiak Island, and the southern part of the mountainous west side of Cook Inlet, this is a wild maritime region. The hub of the wet, windy **Aleutians** is **Unalaska** and its port of **Dutch Harbor. Katmai National Park** and the adjoining wild lands are the main attraction of the Alaska Peninsula, although there also are fishing lodges on the salmon-rich rivers and on the lakes to the north, including areas in **Lake Clark National Park** and **Iliamna Lake.** On the peninsula's west side, **Bristol Bay** is known for massive salmon runs, and avid anglers may be interested in its wilderness lodges, using **Dillingham** or **King Salmon** as a hub. The lakes and west side of **Cook Inlet** are accessed primarily by Kenai, Homer, and Anchorage flight services for fishermen and hunters. **Kodiak** is hardly a southwest Bush community, but it fits better in this chapter than anywhere else, and the town is a hub for villages and bear viewing on Kodiak Island.

Getting Around

With a few exceptions for strongly motivated travelers who might take the ferry to Kodiak and Unalaska or drive to Prudhoe Bay, getting to each town in this chapter will require flying. **Alaska Airlines (☎800/252-7522;** www.alaskaair. com) offers the only jet service to Bush hubs. Other, smaller operators serve these towns with prop aircraft. Throughout the chapter, I've listed the plane fare to various communities from Anchorage, based on flying coach and getting a significant discount for advance purchase and some restrictions. Full fares cost more. With the way fuel costs and airfares are fluctuating, I hesitate to mention

A mother and her cubs in Katmai National Park.

firm prices for plane tickets at all. Generally, getting to these towns will cost $400 to $1,000, round-trip, from Anchorage. To get a current fare, use a travel agent or the Internet.

Kodiak, which barely fits in a chapter on the Bush, is the most accessible of the communities in this chapter, but it still requires either a 10-hour ferry ride from Homer or a flight from Anchorage. This charming, historic town is similar to towns in Southeast Alaska or Prince William Sound, but it is also a hub for Native villages on the island and remote wilderness. **Unalaska/Dutch Harbor,** in the Aleutian Islands, is an interesting place to go way off the beaten path while staying in complete comfort. From Anchorage, a visit requires a 3-hour flight on a turbo prop aircraft—fares less than $950 are rarely seen. Otherwise, only a ferry ride that lasts most of a week will get you there. **Prudhoe Bay,** an industrial complex without a real town associated with it, lies on the Arctic Ocean at the end of the 500-mile Dalton Highway and receives Alaska Airlines service. Otherwise, the places in this chapter can be reached only by plane. **Barrow,** the **Pribilof Islands, Kotzebue,** and **Kaktovik** are the most purely Native of the communities in the chapter. **Nome** has the advantages of Arctic surroundings easily accessible on gravel roads, but is more of a gold-rush town than a Native village. Fares from Anchorage range from $450 to $850 for these communities. Buying an **Alaska Airlines package tour** saves money to Nome or Barrow, and gives you something to do when you arrive.

KODIAK: WILD ISLAND

The habitat that makes Kodiak Island a perfect place for bears also makes it perfect for people. Runs of salmon clog unpopulated bays and innumerable, little-fished rivers; the rounded green mountains seem to beg for someone to cross them; the gravel beaches and protected rocky inlets are free of people, but full of promise. But, in this respect, bears are smarter than people. Brown bears own the island, growing to prodigious size and abundant numbers, but Kodiak remains largely undiscovered by human visitors. That's part of the wonder of the place. I'll never forget flying over the luxuriant verdure of Kodiak's mountains and the narrow string of glassy Raspberry Strait on a rare sunny day, seeing no sign of human presence in the most beautiful landscape I had ever beheld.

The narrow streets of the town of Kodiak are a discovery, too. Twisting over the hills in little discernible order, they were the original stomping grounds of **Lord Alexander Baranof,** the first Russian ruler of Alaska, who arrived here in 1790. Kodiak has the oldest Russian building in North America. It was nearly lost in the 1964 Good Friday earthquake, which destroyed most of the town, explaining the general lack of old buildings. The quake brought a 30-foot wave that washed to the building's doorstep. A marker near the police station on Mill Bay Road shows the wave's incredible high-water point. Before the Russians, the **Alutiiq** people lived off the incomparable riches of the island. They're still here, recovering their past in a fascinating little research museum.

The town looks to the sea. Along with the Coast Guard base, fishing makes Kodiak prosperous, creating a friendly, energetic, unpolished community. Kodiak is separate from the rest of Alaska, living its own commercial fishing life without often thinking of what's going on in Anchorage or anywhere else. It's off the beaten path because it doesn't really need anything the path provides.

Kodiak Island.

For the visitor, Kodiak is an undiscovered gem. The town itself is charming and vibrant, and the spectacular wild places around it virtually limitless, yet even in midsummer, you will see few if any other tourists.

There are six **Native villages** on the island. A flight to one of them and back on a clear day is a wonderful, low-cost way to see remote areas of the island and to get a taste of how Alaska Natives live. It's also popular to fly out to see the famous bears on a day trip, or stay at one of several **wilderness lodges** for wildlife watching, fishing, sea kayaking, or hunting.

Essentials

GETTING THERE It's a 1-hour flight from Anchorage to Kodiak on **Alaska Airlines** (☎800/252-7522; www.alaskaair.com). A round-trip ticket from Anchorage costs around $400. **ERA Aviation** (☎800/866-8394; www.flyera. com) also serves the route with prop aircraft, which may save a little money. A **cab,** from **A&B Taxi** (☎907/486-4343), runs about $20 from the airport to downtown.

The ferries *Tustumena* and *Kennicott,* of the **Alaska Marine Highway System** (☎800/642-0066 or 907/486-3800; www.ferryalaska.com), serve Kodiak from Homer, the closest port with a road. The run takes 10 hours, but it is truly memorable. The vessels leave land behind and thread through the strange and exposed Barren Islands. The ocean can be quite rough, and when it is, lots of passengers get seasick; read and follow the advice on p. 95. A cabin is a good idea for an overnight run. Without a cabin, the adult passenger fare from Homer is $74. Fares for children 6 to 12 are half price on all ferries, free if under 6.

The U.S. Fish and Wildlife Service staffs the ferry with a naturalist on runs to Kodiak.

VISITOR INFORMATION The **Kodiak Island Convention and Visitors Bureau,** 100 E. Marine Way, Ste. 200, Kodiak, AK 99615 (☏**800/789-4782** or 907/486-4782; fax 907/486-6545; www.kodiak.org), occupies a small building on the ferry dock. Hours increase in the summer, but the center is open year-round Monday through Friday from 8am to 5pm.

The **Kodiak National Wildlife Refuge Visitor Center** is across from the ferry terminal at Mission Road and Center Street (☏**888/592-6942** or 907/487-2626; www.kodiakwildliferefuge.org). The center provides information on a 1.9-million-acre refuge that covers two-thirds of Kodiak Island and parts of other islands, the home of the famous Kodiak brown bear. It exhibits a complete gray whale skeleton and three full-size replicas of Kodiak brown bears. Hours in summer are daily from 9am to 5pm; the balance of the year Tuesday through Saturday only. There are seven remote public-use cabins around the refuge, reachable by chartered plane. Permits are $45 a night, available though a quarterly drawing of names (Jan. 2 for Apr–June, Apr 1 for Jul–Sept), and after that first-come, first served.

ORIENTATION The Kodiak Archipelago contains Kodiak, Shuyak, and Afognak islands, and many other, smaller islands. Kodiak is the nation's second-largest island (after Hawaii's Big Island). The city of Kodiak is on a narrow point on the northeast side of Kodiak Island, surrounded by tiny islands. There are six Native villages on other parts of the island. The airport and Coast Guard base are several miles southwest of town on **Rezanof Drive,** which runs through town and comes out on the other side. The center of Kodiak is a hopeless tangle of steep, narrow streets—you need the excellent map given away by the visitor center, but it's all walkable. The ferry dock is on **Marine Way,** and most of the in-town sights are right nearby. Several paved and gravel roads, totaling 100 miles, make wonderful exploring from Kodiak to deserted shorelines, gorgeous views, pastures, recreation areas, and salmon streams. The visitor guide contains a mile-by-mile guide to each drive.

GETTING AROUND Several companies rent cars, including **Budget** (☏**800/527-0700** or 907/487-2220; www.budget.com), which has offices at the airport and downtown. **Avis** is at the Kodiak airport (☏**800/331-1212** or 907/487-2264; www.avis.com).

[Fast**FACTS**] KODIAK

Banks Several banks downtown have ATMs, including **Key Bank** and **Wells Fargo** on the mall at the waterfront.

Hospital Providence Kodiak Island Medical Center is at 1915 E. Rezanof Dr. (☏**907/486-3281**).

Internet Access At **A. Holmes Johnson Public Library,** 319 Lower Mill Bay Rd. (☏**907/486-8686**).

Police Contact the **Kodiak Police Department** at ☏**907/486-8000.**

Post Office 419 Lower Mill Bay Rd., at Hemlock Street.

Taxes Sales tax is 6% within city limits and the **room tax** is 5% everywhere on the island; rooms are thus taxed 11% in Kodiak city, 5% elsewhere.

Kodiak Crab Festival.

SPECIAL EVENTS **Russian Orthodox Christmas,** January 7, includes the evening **Starring Ceremony.** A choir follows a parishioner carrying a star to sing at the homes of church members.

The 5-day **Kodiak Crab Festival** (☎907/486-5557), over Memorial Day weekend, is a big event, including a king crab feed, a carnival, many fun community events, the solemn blessing of the fleet, and a memorial service for fishermen and mariners lost at sea.

On Labor Day weekend, the **Kodiak State Fair and Rodeo** has all kinds of small-town contests and family entertainment including bull riding, a horse show, and a wild cow milking contest, in which pairs of amateur cowboys and cowgirls pulled from the audience chase down and milk small cows unleashed in a ring. Call the visitor bureau for information. The bureau also maintains an extensive community calendar online at **www. kodiak.org.**

Exploring the Town

The highlights downtown include the **Fishermen's Memorial,** near the harbormaster's office at the head of the St. Paul Harbor, where a soberingly long list of Kodiak fishermen who have lost their lives at sea is posted on plaques. The warship set in concrete on Mission Way is the *Kodiak Star,* the last World War II Liberty Ship built. It came here as a fish processor after the 1964 earthquake destroyed the canneries and is still in use. Along Shelikof Avenue, overlooking St. Paul Harbor, the **Kodiak Maritime Museum** has mounted 12 attractive and interesting signs explaining the parts of a boat, North Pacific crabbing and geography, and other nautical topics. In the same area, stop in at **Kodiak Island Brewing Co.,** 338 Shelikof St. (www.kodiakbrewery.com), where Ben Millstein brews beer that's mostly organic and offers tours. You can buy a pint to drink on-site or get some for later; local restaurants serve it, too.

At Kashevarof and Mission streets, the **Holy Resurrection Russian Orthodox Church** was founded in 1794, although the present building dates only to 1945, when the original church burned.

Alutiiq Museum ★ This exceptional museum, governed by Natives, seeks to document and revitalize Kodiak's Alutiiq culture, which the Russians virtually wiped out in the 18th century. Besides teaching about Alutiiq culture in a single gallery, the museum manages its own archaeological digs and repatriates Native remains and artifacts, which researchers removed by the thousands until the 1930s. The archaeological repository now includes 100,000 objects.

215 Mission Rd. ☏**907/486-7004.** www.alutiiqmuseum.org. Admission $5 adults, free for kids 15 and under. Summer Mon–Fri 9am–5pm, Sat 10am–5pm; winter Tues–Fri 9am–5pm, Sat 10:30am–4:30pm.

The Baranov Museum ★ The museum occupies the oldest Russian building of only a few left standing in North America, which is Alaska's oldest building of any kind. Alexander Baranof, who ruled Alaska as manager of the Russian American Company, built the log structure in 1808 as a magazine and strong house for valuable sea otter pelts—the treasure that motivated the Russians' interest here. It was his headquarters for the invasion he extended across Alaska and down the Pacific Northwest coast. The museum stands in a grassy park overlooking the water across from the ferry dock. Inside is a little museum rich with Russian and early Native artifacts. The guides know a lot of history and show educational photo albums on various topics. The gift store is exceptional, selling antique Russian items and authentic Native crafts.

101 Marine Way. ☏**907/486-5920.** www.baranovmuseum.org. Admission $3, free for children 12 and under. Summer Mon–Sat 10am–4pm, Sun noon–4pm; winter Tues–Sat 10am–3pm. Closed Feb.

Alutiiq Museum.

Fort Abercrombie State Historical Park.

Getting Outside
TWO RECREATION AREAS

A couple of miles north of town on Rezanof Drive, the **Fort Abercrombie State Historical Park** encompasses World War II ruins set on coastal cliffs amid huge trees. Paths lead to the beaches and good tide-pool walking, a swimming lake, and lots of other discoveries. The gun emplacements, bunkers, and other concrete buildings defended against the Japanese, who had seized islands in the outer Aleutians and were expected to come this way. A group of local World War II buffs have built a museum of war artifacts from the Alaska fighting in the ammunition bunker at Miller Point. Hours change annually, but will be posted at www.kadiak.org (yes, kadiak), or call ☎907/486-7015. The website is extensive. A wonderful 13-site campground sits atop the cliffs among the trees and ruins. Camping is $15. The **Alaska Division of State Parks**, Kodiak District Office, 1400 Abercrombie Dr., Kodiak, AK 99615 (☎907/486-6339; fax 907/486-3320; www.alaskastateparks.org, click on "Individual Parks," then "Kodiak Islands"), maintains an office here where you can ask a question and possibly pick up a walking-tour brochure. Or investigate the tide pools, picking up an identification guide at the park's natural history bookstore.

The **Buskin River State Recreation Site,** 4 miles south of town off Rezanof Drive near the Fish and Wildlife Service visitor center, has 15 campsites, a hiking trail, and access to fishing. Camping is $15.

OUTDOOR ACTIVITIES

BROWN-BEAR VIEWING To count on seeing Kodiak's famous bears you need to get out on a plane or boat and visit at the right time of year. The easiest way is a Kodiak-based floatplane; expect to pay around $475 per person, with a two- or three-person minimum for a guided half-day trip. Landing on the water, you don rubber boots (provided) and walk up to 30 minutes to get to where bears congregate. In early July to early August, depending on salmon runs, flights land on Frazer Lake for viewing at Frazer fish pass. A .8-mile walk on a dirt lane leads to the viewing area. The Kodiak National Wildlife Refuge (☎888/408-3514 or 907/487-2600; http://kodiak.fws. gov; see "Visitor Information," above) controls the viewing area. Flights also sometimes visit Ayakulik and Karluk rivers when fish are present. At any of these sites,

Group of brown bears.

binoculars and telephoto camera lenses are essential. Responsible guides won't crowd Kodiak brown bears so closely that you don't want a lens, although the bears could choose to approach within 50 yards of you. Bears congregate only when salmon are running, so the timing of your visit is critical. From early July to mid-August you have a good chance of seeing bears fishing in streams on Kodiak, sometimes in numbers. Contact the refuge for more information on timing and bear activity.

When fish aren't running on Kodiak, such as in June or after mid-August, air services concentrate on flights to the east coast of the Alaska Peninsula, often in Katmai National Park, to watch bears digging clams from the tidal flats and eating grass and greens on the coastal meadows or catching fish in August. It's interesting and the flight is spectacular, but the viewing may be from a greater distance than on the streams, and the bears will more likely be on their own.

Generally, the flight services charge their standard bear-viewing seat rate regardless of how far they have to fly to find bears; if you charter, it may cost much more, but you will have freedom to determine where the plane goes for added sightseeing. Several small flight services offer bear viewing, including **Sea Hawk Air** (☎800/770-4295 or 907/486-8282; www.sea hawkair.com). If a bear-viewing day trip is the whole reason you're going to Kodiak, compare your options. You can go directly from Homer or Anchorage (see chapters 8 and 7, respectively), or go to Katmai National Park to see bears really close (p. 581).

For additional money, you can see more of Kodiak's bears on a longer outing: a flight service can leave you at a lodge for an extended stay in bear habitat. Check the visitor center for a referral. Harry and Brigid Dodge host small groups at their rustic, solar-powered Aleut Island Lodge in Uyak Bay, taking an environmentally sensitive approach while spending the time to know the bears and their habitat. The business is called **Kodiak Treks** (☎907/487-2122; www.kodiaktreks.com). Rates are $350 per person per night, double, with a 3-night minimum. The rate includes food and activities such as kayaking and fishing, but not the cost of getting there (about $350 per person round-trip from Kodiak).

FISHING The roads leading from Kodiak reach eight good-sized rivers with productive fishing for salmon and Dolly Varden char. At times you can drive to places with fishing pressure as light as at some fly-in locations on the mainland. Going beyond the road network puts you on some of the best and least used fishing opportunities in Alaska. The visitor center provides a list of where to fish and the names and addresses of guides for remote fishing. You can also seek advice and regulations from the **Alaska Department of Fish and Game,** 211 Mission Rd., Kodiak, AK 99615 (℡907/486-1880; www.alaska. gov/adfg; click on "Sport Fish," then on the Southcentral region, then on "Kodiak/Aleutians"). To fish the remote areas, you'll need to charter a plane, going for a day or staying at a remote public-use cabin or wilderness lodge.

About 50 boats are available in the boat harbors for ocean fishing. An advantage of coming to Kodiak is that it puts you near rich halibut grounds—you don't have to take a long boat ride for excellent fishing. Trolling for silvers is good in August, and increasingly anglers troll for king salmon through the summer and fall, although success rates are hard to predict. Check with the visitor center for a referral.

HIKING & BIRD-WATCHING There are good day hikes in Kodiak, some starting from downtown. The local Audubon Society publishes a Kodiak Hiking & Birding Guide that you can pick up at the visitor center. Audubon's guided hikes go to a different place every Saturday and Sunday of the summer, meeting at the visitor center parking lot at 9:30am for car pooling. Again, the center is the best source of information.

SEA KAYAKING The Kodiak Archipelago, with its many folded, rocky shorelines and abundant marine life, is a perfect place for sea kayaking. Kayaks were invented here and on the Aleutian Islands to the west. For beginners it is best to start with a day trip, and the waters around the town of Kodiak are lovely for such a paddle. Several operators can arrange an outing, although most concentrate on more ambitious trips. For a half-day, expect to pay around $140 per person, for a full day $220. One day-trip guide with a strong environmental ethic is Andy Schroeder, whose business is called **Orcas Unlimited Charters** (℡907/539-1979; www.orcasunlimited.com). Schroeder specializes in day trips, but also takes clients on extended outings using a converted fishing boat as a base. Guests paddle by day and sleep and eat aboard.

Shuyak Island State Park, 54 miles north of Kodiak, is famously appealing for sea-kayaking expeditions. The park is a honeycomb of islands and narrow passages in virgin Sitka spruce coastal forest. The Division of State Parks (see addresses under "Two Recreation Areas," above) distributes a free kayaking guide with route descriptions and maintains four public-use cabins, which rent for $75 a night in the summer season. These cabins can be quite hard to get in August. See "State Parks Cabin Reservations," in chapter 8.

Where to Stay

I've listed good places in town and nearby on the roads, but Kodiak has many other B&Bs. Beyond the roads, some of Alaska's best wilderness lodges are on Kodiak Island in remote areas and near Native villages. The visitor center posts links to many B&Bs and lodges on its website at www.kodiak.org.

A Smiling Bear Bed & Breakfast, near Fort Abercrombie (☎907/481-6390; www.asmilingbear.com), has suites with Jacuzzis and serves gourmet breakfasts for $150 to $175 double in the high season. The couple that offers the Galley Gourmet dinner cruise (below) also operates the well-equipped **Cliff House Bed and Breakfast,** with four rooms starting at $125 double. It's on a quiet street with ocean views within walking distance of downtown.

Best Western Kodiak Inn ★ This is the best hotel in downtown Kodiak, with attractive rooms perched on the hill overlooking the boat harbor, right in the center of things. Rooms in the wooden building vary in size and view, but all are acceptable standard units with good amenities, including pillow-top beds and DVD players.

The **Chart Room** restaurant, specializing in seafood and with a great view of the water, is a good choice for a nice dinner out, with entrees in the $18 to $28 range.

236 W. Rezanof Dr., Kodiak, AK 99615. ☎888/563-4254 or 907/486-5712. Fax 907/486-3430. www.kodiakinn.com. 81 units. High season $179 double; low season $109 double. Extra person 18 and older $15. AE, DC, DISC, MC, V. **Amenities:** Free airport transfers; restaurant; bar; outdoor Jacuzzi. *In room:* TV/DVD, fridge, hair dryer, microwave, Wi-Fi.

Comfort Inn Kodiak ★ A 50-room hotel facing the airport parking lot offers some of the area's best standard accommodations. All rooms are equipped with many amenities, and suites are simply larger rooms. The location is 5 miles from Kodiak's downtown or historic sites, but that won't matter much if you rent a car. Those planning remote outdoor activities may prefer it for the close access to air services.

1395 Airport Way, Kodiak, AK 99615. ☎800/544-2202 or 907/487-2700. www.choicehotels.com/hotel/ak025. 50 units. High season $170 double, $240 suite; low season $110 double, $130 suite. Extra person 18 and older $15. AE, DC, DISC, MC, V. Rates include continental breakfast. **Amenities:** Exercise room. *In room:* TV, fridge, hair dryer, microwave, Wi-Fi.

Eider House Bed & Breakfast ★ This attractive B&B 9 miles south of town is a good choice for anglers or anyone who prefers a natural setting. It sits near Sargent Creek, and fishing is within a short walk, with more hot spots not far off. With this in mind, owners Robin and Mike Haight have installed a dedicated fish-cleaning facility for visitor use that includes vacuum-packing equipment and a freezer. The seaside surroundings are inviting for hiking—despite being on the road system, the B&B has aspects of a wilderness lodge. The exceptionally clean bedrooms, all with their own bathrooms, are attractively decorated with reproductions and comforters. A full breakfast is served at convenient hours, and they'll pack a lunch for your charter fishing outing for $10; however, check-in isn't until 5pm except by special arrangement.

782 Sargent Creek Rd., Kodiak, AK 99615. ☎907/487-4315. www.eiderhouse.com. 4 units. High season $145 double; low season $90 double. Extra person $25. AE, MC, V. **Amenities:** Fish processing facility; guest kitchen. *In room:* TV, hair dryer, Wi-Fi.

Where to Dine

Besides the hotel restaurants listed above at the Best Western Kodiak Inn, Kodiak has several restaurants catering to locals.

The best restaurant in town is a coffee shop. **Mill Bay Coffee & Pastries,** about 2 miles out of downtown at 3833 Rezanof Dr. (☎907/486-4411; www.

millbaycoffee.com), is where award-winning, Paris-trained chef Joel Chenet produces wonderful pastries and, for lunch, brilliant combinations of local seafood and international seasonings brought to inexpensive sandwiches—the Kodiak sea burger is made of salmon, crab, shrimp, and cream cheese, among other ingredients, and costs $13. The comfortable, casual dining room, managed by Chenet's wife, Martine, is a local hub, and has Wi-Fi.

Another unique place to eat, this time for dinner, could be a highlight of your trip. Marty and Marion Owen serve dinner for six on their 42-foot yacht the *Sea Breeze*. The meals from **Galley Gourmet** (☎907/486-5079; www.galley gourmet.biz) are usually elaborate seafood creations. The evening starts at 6pm with a 45-minute cruise in the picturesque waters near Kodiak's harbor, where guests may see puffins, sea lions, and whales. Dinner is served at anchor in a quiet lagoon, and you're back at the dock at 9:30pm. The price is $125 per person. The couple offers day-long whale watching and 3-day cruises, too.

Henry's Great Alaskan Restaurant, 512 Marine Way (☎907/486-8844; www.henrysalaska.com), on the waterfront mall, is a bar and grill where you will meet many commercial fishermen and other locals. The menu includes daily specials, local seafood, and good halibut sandwiches, as well as steaks, pasta, and such. The smoked salmon chowder is excellent.

KATMAI NATIONAL PARK

Most of the land of the Alaska Peninsula, pointing out to the Aleutian Archipelago, is in one federally protected status or another, centering on Katmai National Park. The park, pronounced "*Cat*-my," lies just west of Kodiak Island, across the storm-infested Shelikof Strait. Bear and salmon are the main attractions.

Brooks Camp, with a campground and lodge within Katmai, is probably the most comfortable place for foolproof bear viewing in Alaska during its peak

Novarupta.

season. Bears congregate thickly at the falls on the Brooks River when red salmon try to pass up the falls at the beginning of July (more on the seasons below, under "Exploring the Park"). At times, you can sit back on a deck and watch 900-pound brown bears walk by, going about their business of devouring the fish that contribute to their awesome size. (A brown bear is the genetic twin of the grizzly, but generally larger due to its coastal diet of salmon.)

Staying the night will require you to reserve a place in the 16-space campground the previous winter or stay in the pricey lodge, where rooms can book up over a year ahead for the bear season. You can go for a day trip with less planning if you can stand to pay around $650 round-trip airfare from Anchorage for 2 or 3 hours at the camp (this information is covered in "Getting There," below). Bear viewing on the Katmai Coast is covered in the Kodiak section (p. 570), where flight services offers trips. If you're comparing, also look at the flight operators in Homer and Anchorage (p. 359 and 333).

Katmai was set aside in 1918 for reasons unrelated to bears. The area had exploded into world consciousness in 1912 with the most destructive volcanic eruption to shake the earth in 3,400 years. When Katmai's Novarupta blew, it released 10 times more energy than the Mount St. Helens eruption of 1980 and displaced twice as much matter as 1883's Krakatoa. In Kodiak, the sky was black for 3 days, and 2 feet of ash crushed houses and choked rivers. People could clearly hear the blast in Juneau; acid rain melted fabric in Vancouver, British Columbia; and the skies darkened over most of the Northern Hemisphere. At the blast site, all life within a 40-square-mile area was wiped out and buried as deep as 700 feet. But so remote was the area, then still unnamed, that not a single human being was killed. The **Valley of Ten Thousand Smokes,** the vast wasteland created by the blast, belched steam for decades after. Today Novarupta is dormant and the steam is gone, but the area is still a barren moonscape, making a fascinating day tour or hiking trip.

Essentials

GETTING THERE Most people fly to Katmai from Anchorage by way of the village of **King Salmon,** which lies just west of the park. **Alaska Airlines** (☎ **800/252-7522;** www.alaskaair.com) flies to King Salmon daily in the summer, charging around $450 round-trip. For more flight options, you can use their prop partner, **PenAir** (☎ **800/448-4226;** www.penair.com), which can be booked through Alaska Airlines. Air taxis carry visitors the last leg from King Salmon to **Brooks Camp** for a fare of around $180, round-trip. **Katmai Air,** operated by park concessionaire Katmailand (☎ **800/544-0551** or 907/243-5448; www.katmaiair.com), does these flights, and offers round-trip airfare packages from Anchorage that save some money and simplify planning—as a day trip, $619.

As an alternative to Brooks Camp, more and more visitors are exploring the supremely rugged wilderness on the east side of the park from the beaches along **Shelikof Strait.** Air-taxi operators make drop-offs and do bear-viewing day trips from Homer or Kodiak (see the Kodiak section of this chapter, above, or see the Homer section in chapter 8). In a park with more than 2,000 resident brown bears (the world's largest protected population), it's easy for pilots to find them digging clams on the tidal marshes, then land on floats for a good look.

RESERVATIONS & FEES No entry fee or permit applies for day trips to Katmai, but once you're there you have to sign up for an hour on the bear-viewing platforms (see below). Camping costs $8 per person per night. Campground capacity is allocated by person, not by site, and the limit of 60 people per night is far lower than the many visitors who want to stay during the bear season in July. The crowds are smaller in September, but the bears are not quite as numerous. Camping reservations become available for the entire summer as early as January 2, but the exact day changes each year; if you want a spot, check for the date and follow up the moment reservations open. To reserve, call or log on to the **National Recreation Reservation Service** (☎877/444-6777 or 518/885-3639; www.recreation.gov).

VISITOR INFORMATION For advance planning, contact **Katmai National Park Headquarters** at P.O. Box 7, King Salmon, AK 99613 (☎907/246-3305; www.nps.gov/katm). At Brooks Camp the Park Service has a center where all visitors are required to attend a 20-minute orientation called "The Brooks Camp School of Bear Etiquette," designed to train visitors (not bears) and keep them out of trouble. In Anchorage, you can get information at the **Alaska Public Lands Information Center,** 4th Avenue and F Street (☎907/271-2737; see the complete listing in chapter 7). The King Salmon **Visitor Center** is next door to the airport (☎907/246-4250), staffed jointly by the U.S. Fish and Wildlife Service, National Park Service, and Alaska Geographic, a non-profit book publisher. It is open 8am to 5pm daily in the high season, Monday through Saturday in winter.

GETTING AROUND Once you've made it to Brooks Camp, a **bus** carries visitors to the Valley of Ten Thousand Smokes, 23 miles by gravel road from the camp. The park concessionaire, **Katmailand,** charges $88 per person, round-trip, for the all-day guided excursion, plus $8 more for lunch. A ranger leads a walk down into the valley. One-way transfers for hikers are $51.

[FastFACTS] KATMAI & REGION

Bank **Wells Fargo,** with an ATM, is in the King Salmon Mall adjacent to the airport on the Peninsula Highway in King Salmon.

Hospital The **Camai Clinic,** in Naknek (☎907/246-6155), is open during normal business hours; calls to the number go to

emergency dispatchers after hours.

Police In **King Salmon,** call ☎907/246-4222; elsewhere, call **Alaska State Troopers** at ☎907/246-3346 or 907/246-3464. There are no phones or cellular service out in the park.

Shopping The park is remote, and other wild

lands in the region are without businesses other than remote lodges, such as Brooks Camp. King Salmon is the last stop for basic supplies or groceries. This is where you must buy fuel for a camp stove, matches, bear spray, or other needs you can not carry on the jet from Anchorage.

Exploring the Park

Katmai's famous bear viewing occurs at **Brooks Camp** when the bears congregate near the Brooks River to catch salmon. Viewing peaks in early July, but can begin

Bear-viewing at Brooks Camp.

in late June and last through July, with a smaller congregation in September. The summer fish run is when you're assured of seeing bears from the elevated platforms near the Brooks River falls, half a mile from Brooks Camp, even on a day trip. Forty to 60 bears feed here. Indeed, bears are seen all along the trail to the falls and elsewhere—the falls are just the most concentrated spot. Rangers don't guide visitors, but are on hand to manage the foot traffic. The platforms allow a good view of the bears and just enough separation. The Park Service recommends that people with mobility problems avoid this trail when bears are present. Considering the expense and potential difficulty, I'd advise those with trouble getting around to choose another venue for bear viewing. Due to the popularity of the experience, there is a 1-hour limit on the falls platform during the peak season, although the limit is lifted when the platform is below its capacity. After your turn is up, you can sign up on a waiting list to get another chance. The falls platform and trail are closed 10pm to 7am. In September, when the smaller group of bears gathers, they group near the mouth of the river, not the falls, and crowding is less of an issue. Outside of these salmon runs, there are better places to see bears, so if that's your goal, don't spend the money to come here. Bears feed all summer on clams on Katmai's east shore. See "Getting There," above.

The Brooks Camp area has a small Park Service campground, visitor center, and lodge, located where the Brooks River flows into Naknek Lake. When the area was first developed for fishing in the 1950s, the camp was built in the middle of a major bear corridor, where it would never be allowed today, creating a unique opportunity to stay right in some of the most concentrated bear habitat on the globe. The most comfortable way is to stay at the **Brooks Lodge,** operated by Katmailand (**☎800/544-0551** or 907/243-5448; www.brookslodge.com). The lodge has 16 units, with private bathrooms with shower stalls. To save money, book the lodge rooms as packages with air travel from Anchorage. The least expensive, 1-night visit is $931 per person, double occupancy, meals not included;

3 nights is $1,572. A double room without airfare is $714. Peak dates (when the bears are concentrated) book up 12 months out or earlier; for your choice, call as soon as the reservation system opens 18 months ahead, January of the year before the visit. Three buffet-style meals are served daily for guests and visitors who aren't staying in the lodge. Breakfast is $15, lunch $20, and dinner $35. For food, they take MasterCard and Visa at the lodge. Also at Brooks Camp, there's a small store, the park service visitor center, and a campground. See "Reservations & Fees," above, for info on campground reservations, which should be made 6 months in advance. The rangers require special precautions to keep bears away from campers.

The rivers and lakes of Katmai lure human anglers as well as ursine ones. Katmailand operates two lodges within the park other than Brooks Lodge for remote fishing, the **Kulik** and **Grosvenor lodges.** Check their website at www.katmailand.com for fishing details.

The park service also has a list of dozens of fishing, hiking, and air guides. There is no central clearinghouse for remote fishing, but you can find and book a good place through an agency such as **Sport Fishing Alaska,** 9310 Shorecrest Dr., Anchorage, AK 99502 (℡888/552-8674 or 907/344-8674; www.alaskatrip planners.com), listed in full under "Planning an Outdoor Vacation" in chapter 3.

Backcountry hiking in Katmai means crossing a wilderness without trails, including the hazards of river crossings. Only experienced backpackers should plan extended trips. The Park Service asks hikers to obtain a voluntary permit for backcountry travel, thereby clueing them in to your plans in case you need to be rescued. You are required to store food and items with odors in bear-resistant

Valley of Ten Thousand Smokes.

containers, which you can check out from the park. Anyone can walk for the day without such precautions in the desolate **Valley of Ten Thousand Smokes.** This 40-square-mile plain remains a moonscape almost a century after the titanic volcanic blast that buried it, little changed except that the famous plumes of smoke are gone and rivers have sliced through the debris in places to create narrow, white-walled canyons. Although it looks like a desert and is subject to dust storms, rain is common and temperatures rarely go higher than 65°F (18°C). Katmailand operates a tour bus from Brooks Camp, mentioned above under "Getting Around." The visitors on those tours usually stay on a short trail on the valley's rim, where a visitor center is located, but a 3-mile round-trip hike descends 800 feet to the valley floor, where you can get a better look at the ash that creates the bizarre landforms here.

UNALASKA/DUTCH HARBOR: ALEUTIAN BOOMTOWN

After a lifetime of hearing how desolate the Aleutians (Uh-*loo*-shens) were, I felt like I was leaving the edge of the earth the first time I traveled to Unalaska (Un-ah-*las*-ka). Shortly after I arrived, a storm started slinging huge raindrops horizontally through the air so hard that they stung as they splattered on my face. People went on about their business as if nothing special was happening—stormy weather constantly batters these rocks that pop up from the empty North Pacific. My expectations seemed justified.

But the next day, the storm cleared like a curtain opening on a rich operatic scene—simultaneously opening the curtain of my dark expectations. Unalaska may lack trees, but it's not a barren rock. The island is covered with heather and wildflowers. Rounded mountains that invite wandering exploration rise from the ocean like the backs of huge beasts. For sightseeing, it has barely a day's attractions, but for outdoor exploring, bird-watching, and halibut fishing, few places come close.

With the protected port of Dutch Harbor so far out in a ferocious ocean habitat rich in crab and bottom fish, Unalaska has grown from a tiny, forgotten Native village to the nation's largest fishing port. The pattern of growth followed the form of the early gold rushes. There was a wild, lawless time in the 1970s when crab fishermen got rich quick and partied like Old West cowboys. Then the overfished crab stocks crashed, only to be replaced, starting in the mid-1980s, by an even bigger boom, when waters within 200 miles of the U.S. shore were rid of foreign vessels and American bottom fishing took off. Big factory ships began unloading here and huge fish plants were built on flat ground chipped from the rock.

The process of the town's domestication had long ago taken hold when Hollywood discovered it with the hit cable TV program, "Deadliest Catch." As the program shows, crabbing in these waters is dangerous and lucrative—but it's far safer, tamer, and less profitable today than in the days when fishermen died by the dozens every year or came home rich men. The legendary rough bars closed years ago, and in 2008 the last wild nightspot shut down. (How long can that last?) As a visitor, it can be fun to visit the docks and bars, where it's easy enough to strike up a conversation with a fisherman about his adventures and close calls.

Ironically, Unalaska is Alaska's oldest town as well as its newest city. The value of a good port out in the middle of the ocean was recognized from the beginning by the Aleuts. In 1759, the Russians began trading here, and brutally massacred the Aleuts to subjugate them as slaves. The Russians built a permanent settlement here in 1792, their first in Alaska. Unalaska also was a key refueling stop for steamers carrying gold-rush stampeders to Nome a century ago, which brought an epidemic that killed a third of the indigenous population.

In 1940, Dutch Harbor—the seaport on Amaknak Island associated with the town and island of Unalaska—was taken over by the U.S. Navy to defend against Japanese attack. That attack came: In June 1942, Japanese planes bombed Unalaska, killing 43. The Aleut people were removed from the islands for the duration of the war and interned in inadequate housing in Southeast Alaska, where many died of disease. The military pulled out in 1947, but the remains of their defenses are interesting to explore, part of a unique unit of the national park system. Thanks to a 1971 act of Congress settling Native claims, the Aleut-owned Ounalashka Corporation owns much of the land around town. But the National Park Service protects and interprets the World War II historic sites on Native-owned land.

Essentials

GETTING THERE PenAir (**800/448-4226;** www.penair.com) serves Dutch Harbor with large turbo props. You can book directly, or through Alaska Airlines. When a squall is hitting Dutch, planes land on the nearby Alaska Peninsula and wait for it to clear. The flight from Anchorage takes 3 hours and a ticket is $950 or more round-trip.

The **Alaska Marine Highway System** ferry *Tustumena* (**800/642-0066;** www.ferryalaska.com) makes a 4-day trip from Homer to Unalaska just a handful of times a year, from May to August, stopping in Kodiak and the villages along the way. The one-way passenger fare is more than $351, and a two-berth outside (with windows) cabin with shared facilities is $311 more. Travelers who have done this open sea adventure have given me glowing reports of incomparable scenery and wonderful encounters with the people of the villages along the way, best of all if camping on the solarium deck (with duct tape to hold down the tent). Since the ship is in the open ocean, seasickness is a real concern; read the advice on p. 95. Unless you want to spend only 7 hours in Unalaska and then make the long return trip, you'll need to fly back.

VISITOR INFORMATION The **Unalaska/Port of Dutch Harbor Convention and Visitors Bureau,** P.O. Box 545, Unalaska, AK 99685 (**877/581-2612** or 907/581-2612; www.unalaska.info), is at 5th Street and Broadway, in the old part of town.

A visitor center for the **Aleutian WWII National Historic Area** (**907/581-9944;** www.nps.gov/aleu) occupies a war-era building at the airport. The historic area encompasses World War II ruins on the island that stand on Native-owned lands. The National Park Service helped fund the improvements and interprets the history. A $4 entry fee at the visitor center also covers the permit to hike to the ruins (see "Exploring the Town," below). The website is interesting, too (click on "In Depth").

GETTING AROUND The main historic part of the town is a tiny street grid on a narrow peninsula facing Iliuliuk Bay. The **Bridge to the Other Side** (as everyone knows it) leads to Amaknak Island, the site of the airport, the Grand Aleutian Hotel, and the fishing industrial area of Dutch Harbor. Traveling down the road in the other direction leads a little way up into the mountains, a starting point for walks.

Van taxis are the main way of getting around town for the hordes of fishermen. One company is **Blue Checker Taxi** (☎907/581-2186).

[FastFACTS]
UNALASKA/DUTCH HARBOR

Bank **Key Bank** is attached to the Alaska Commercial Store and has an ATM.

Hospital **Iliuliuk Family and Health Services** (☎907/581-1202) is a clinic.

Internet Access Free at the **public library** (☎907/581-5060).

Police Unalaska Department of Public Safety (☎907/581-1233) is just above the bridge on the Unalaska side.

Taxes **Sales tax** is 3%; the total **tax on rooms** is 8%.

Exploring the Town

Unalaska's most significant historic site is the **Holy Ascension Cathedral.** Completed in 1896 on the site of churches that had stood since 1808, the white church with green onion-shaped domes contains 697 icons, artifacts, and artworks, a significant collection that has been continuously in use by the Aleut congregation. The congregation was founded by Father Ivan Veniaminov, who translated the Gospel into Aleut and has been canonized as St. Innocent. Besides his many other accomplishments, he recorded the environmental devastation of Russian fur hunting in this region the 19th century. A $1.3-million restoration saved the church from collapse in 1996. It is a dignified, geometric counterpoint to the soft edge of sparkling Iliuliuk Bay.

The professionally curated **Museum of the Aleutians,** next door to the Ounalashka Corporation on Margaret Bay in Dutch Harbor (☎907/581-5150; www.aleutians.org), contains some of the region's best artifacts, including some from North America's oldest coastal sites on Umnak and Unalaska islands. Exhibits also cover the region's 9,000-year history, including material on World War II in the Aleutians. Of late, more exhibits have focused on relatively contemporary Alaskan art. Admission is $5. It's open summer Tuesday through Saturday from 9am to 5pm, Sunday from noon to 5pm; in winter Tuesday through Saturday from 11am to 5pm.

There are several **World War II military ruins** around town, including some that are still in use, such as the submarine dry dock that today fixes fishing boats. Trails lead over the island to other sites included in the Aleutian World War II National Historic Area, which preserves this evidence of war on American soil and helps tell the story of the Native people who were interned by both the Japanese and Americans during the war (see "The Aleutians: The Quiet After War," below). U.S. Army Fort Schwatka, on Ulakta Head, is about an hour's hike from the airport. The fort once had more than 100 buildings. Many remain, including the best-preserved gun mounts and lookouts of all the nation's coastal defenses from the war. Besides, it's a spectacular site where you can see ships returning. Stop by the historic site visitor center at the airport first; besides learning the context of the park and picking up a tour booklet of Fort Schwatka, your $4 admission fee is your permit for access to the ruins, which belong to the Native-owned Ounalashka Corp. (All use on their land requires a permit; see "Hiking," below.)

Holy Ascension Cathedral.

That's about it for sightseeing in Unalaska, unless you take a walk in the port. The activity there is interesting for the size of the vessels and harvest and the incredible investment in buildings and equipment.

Getting Outside

BIRD-WATCHING Flip through the crisp, unused pages of your bird book to find out what you may see in the Aleutians. Several rare bird species nest in the area, and Asian birds occasionally drop in as accidentals. The whiskered auklet and red-legged kittiwake are among the birds commonly found around Unalaska that you probably haven't seen. You'll have the greatest success taking a boat to a seabird colony. The Grand Aleutian Hotel (below, under "Where to Stay and Dine") offers packages; it's also possible to combine halibut fishing and bird-watching on your own chartered boat (see the next paragraph). You're also likely to encounter sea lions and other marine mammals.

Red-legged kittiwake.

FISHING You can fly out for salmon fishing from black-sand beaches, but Unalaska has become more famous for huge **halibut.** In 1995, a local sport fisherman caught a 395-pound halibut from an 18-foot skiff within a half-mile of town; to kill the behemoth he had to beach it and beat it over the head with a rock. The next year, Fairbanks angler Jack Tragis landed the world's

THE ALEUTIANS: THE quiet AFTER WAR

Once thousands of men died for the rocky islands of the Aleutians. What began as a Japanese military diversion became a ferocious fight for honor, one of the worst of World War II's Pacific Theater. Yet when the fighting was done, most of the islands were abandoned and left uninhabited, littered with military ruins, for half a century. Finally, with the construction of a new National Park Service visitor center in Unalaska, the battle for the Aleutians is just beginning to enter national consciousness.

The Japanese attacked the islands of **Kiska** and **Attu** at the start of the Pacific war to divert the main core of the American navy away from what became the Battle of Midway. But the Americans had intercepted and decoded Japanese transmissions and weren't fooled. Meanwhile, the Japanese had sent 24 ships, including two aircraft carriers, on a fool's errand to bomb the new American naval base at Dutch Harbor and occupy islands in the western Aleutians. Those ships could have tipped the balance at Midway, among the most important battles of the war. Instead, the Japanese met stiff antiaircraft fire in 2 days of bombing at Dutch Harbor; although 43 Americans were killed, the defensive function of the base was not greatly impaired.

The Japanese then took Kiska and Attu, meeting no resistance from 10 Americans staffing a weather station or from an Aleut village whose 43 inhabitants were all—even the children—sent to a prison camp in Japan to mine clay for the duration of the war. About half the prisoners survived to return to Alaska.

The Americans had their own plan to remove the Aleuts, but the idea of depopulating all the islands had been turned down. Now, with the Japanese attack, it was swiftly put into effect. All the Aleuts were rounded up and put on ships. Their villages were burned or trashed by weather and vandalism. With little thought given to their living conditions, the Aleuts were interned in abandoned summer camps and similarly inadequate facilities in Southeast Alaska. Shunned by the local communities and without the basic necessities of life or proper sanitation, 10% died. The U.S. Fish and Wildlife Service took Aleut hunters to hunt furs as virtual slaves, much as the Russians had done 200 years before.

The Japanese and American military fared not much better on their new real estate. Although the Aleutians quickly became irrelevant to the rest of the war, significant resources were committed to a largely futile air and sea battle in the fog and endless storms. Flying at all was difficult and extremely dangerous, and finding the enemy in the fog over vast distances close to impossible. The Americans couldn't spare a land invasion force at first and had to rely on bombing Kiska and Attu to punish the Japanese and try to deter a further advance up the chain. To that end, they built a large base at Adak, among others, so shorter-range fighter escorts could accompany the bombers. Construction in the spongy tundra was difficult in any case, made more so by the length of supply lines.

The Japanese high command never had any intention of advancing up the chain, but also saw no reason to abandon their new Kiska air base when it was causing the Americans to exert such effort. The Japanese concentrated on fortifying Kiska, which became a honeycomb of underground bunkers and heavy antiaircraft guns, and withstood constant bombing raids by the Americans.

Finally, on May 11, 1943, almost a year after the Japanese took the islands, Americans landed on Attu, and a brutal 18-day battle for the rugged island began. The Japanese were massively outnumbered but heavily dug in. Finally, with only 800 soldiers left from an original force of 2,600, the Japanese mounted a banzai attack. Only 28 were taken prisoner—the rest were killed in battle or committed suicide. The Americans lost 549, with 1,148 wounded and 2,132 injured by severe cold, disease, accident, mental breakdown, or other causes. In the end, it was the second most costly island battle in the Pacific, after Iwo Jima.

The battle for Kiska was less dramatic. The Japanese withdrew under cover of fog. After a massive bombardment of the empty island and the rallying of heavy reinforcements, the Americans landed to find that no one was there. Still, 105 American soldiers died in the landing in accidents and fire from their own forces.

After the Aleutian battle was over, American forces in Alaska declined drastically, but a new era had arrived. Military spending was the biggest economic boom the territory had ever seen, connecting it by a new road to the Lower 48 and bringing precious year-round jobs. The advent of the Cold War, and Alaska's prime strategic location in defense against the Soviet Union, brought ever-greater increases in military spending in Alaska. To this day, the military is one of the largest sectors of the Alaska economy.

The end of the war was bitter for the Aleuts. Returning to villages they had departed hastily 3 years before, they found homes and subsistence gear ruined, and even historic Russian Orthodox churches and icons severely damaged. Many who had survived the terrible period of internment never returned. Most of the ancient villages never revived; bureaucrats managing the evacuation wiped them off the map as a cost-saving measure.

Awareness of this injustice began to resurface in the 1980s, and in 1988 Congress and President Reagan formally apologized to the Aleuts and paid compensation of $12,000 to each survivor, then about half the 900 who were evacuated. That act also helped fund restoration of the five historic churches, including the beautiful church in Unalaska, and construction of one replacement. That work has been completed.

Today, the Aleuts own their islands. It's fitting that the National Park Service's Aleutian World War II National Historic Area is their guest, on their land, and the new visitor center belongs to a Native corporation. Stop in to learn about the lives sacrificed here, and to wonder why.

To learn more, see Brian Garfield's readable *The Thousand-Mile War: World War II in Alaska and the Aleutians* (University of Alaska Press, $25).

record halibut here, which weighed 459 pounds. If you're having trouble imagining a fish that big, drop by City Hall, where a replica hangs stuffed in the lobby. The convention and visitor bureau can refer you to a charter boat operator.

HIKING The island's green heather and rounded mountains of wildflowers are inviting for a walk. You can walk pretty much in any direction. Explore the abandoned World War II defenses, or make a goal of a beach or one of the small peaks around the town. There are no bears and not many bugs, but there's great berry picking and beachcombing. The weather can be a threat, however, and fox holes can trip you up. As always in remote outdoor areas, you must be suitably dressed and leave word of where you're going and when you'll be back.

Hikers beyond the World War II historic area have to pay a slightly higher fee to the **Ounalashka Corp. (☎907/581-1276;** www.ounalashka.com), the

Wildflowers along a stream in Unalaska.

Native village corporation that owns much of the land around town. A 1-day hiking permit is $6 per person or $10 per family; permits for longer periods are available, too. Buy permits from the historic area visitor center (p. 585) or the corporation's office at 400 Salmon Way.

Where to Stay & Dine

Grand Aleutian Hotel ★★ It's almost unreal to arrive at this big, luxurious hotel in a hard-driving Alaska Bush community. The Grand Aleutian is the best hotel in the Alaska Bush, with rooms just as good as you find in Anchorage, but minutes away from some of the best halibut fishing and bird-watching anywhere. The accommodations are well designed and comfortable, many with good water views; the lobby is grand, with a huge stone fireplace; and there's a highly civilized lounge—not the rip-roaring Dutch Harbor bar of lore. As you walk outside into a driving gale, it's like teleporting from a big city hotel back to an exposed rock out in the North Pacific.

The **Chart Room** restaurant, on the second floor, allows bird-watchers to see waterfowl in the bay while dining on steak, seafood, or pasta. The menu, although brief, is Unalaska's most sophisticated. Dinner entrees range from $18 to $65. The **Margaret Bay Cafe,** downstairs, also has a good view, with grilled sandwiches and some lighter fare.

The hotel sometimes puts together birding or fishing packages or workshops. Check for current offerings.

498 Salmon Way (P.O. Box 921169), Dutch Harbor, AK 99692. **☎866/581-3844** or 907/581-3844. Fax 907/581-7150. www.grandaleutian.com. 112 units. $184 double; $274 suite. Extra person $20. Packages available. AE, DISC, MC, V. **Amenities:** Free airport transfers; 2 restaurants; 2 bars; limited room service. *In room:* TV, hair dryer, Internet.

THE PRIBILOF ISLANDS: BIRDER'S PARADISE

The Pribilof Islands of St. Paul and St. George sit out in the middle of the Bering Sea, due north of Unalaska, teeming with marine mammals and seabirds. Some 600,000 fur seals meet at the breeding rookeries in the summer, and two million birds of more than 200 species use the rocks. Bird-watchers visit St. Paul for one of the most exotic and productive birding and wildlife-viewing opportunities anywhere. It's best during the spring migration, from mid-May to mid-June, when great numbers of birds show up, including rare Asian accidental species; the fall migration comes in September to mid-October. You can count on making rare sightings any time during the summer. Indeed, the National Audubon Society's *Field Guide to North American Birds* calls this "perhaps the most spectacular sea bird colony in the world."

The islands are extremely remote, however, and the accommodations simple; if you're not interested in birding or in spending a lot of time watching wildlife, it's probably too much money and trouble. The **King Eider Hotel,** at the airport, has basic rooms and shared bathrooms. Guests eat at the Trident seafood-processing plant, where each meal is served buffet style: Breakfast is $10, lunch $14, dinner $18. There are no other dining choices. The island also

Fur seals.

has a grocery store, the AC Value Store, with an ATM and a cappuccino stand. The island's bar is a sometimes hangout of the fishermen from the TV program "Deadliest Catch," and they unload crab at the harbor.

Visitors generally come on tours, which are sold as a package with airfare and guiding by expert birders. With the guides' help and radio communication, your chances of seeing exotic species are much enhanced. The tours are offered by **TDX Corp.,** 4300 B St., Ste. 402, Anchorage, AK 99503 (**☎877/424-5637;** www.alaskabirding.com). Check the website for a wealth of birding news and species details. Packages from Anchorage start at $1,656 for a 2-night visit and operate from mid-May to mid-October. Travelers can choose to ride on a bus as a group or hike on their own. Permanent blinds are in place for watching birds and seals. Count on cool, damp weather.

NOME: ARCTIC FRONTIER TOWN

The accidents of history deposited the streets and buildings of this lusty little town on the shore of Norton Sound, just south of the Arctic Circle in Northwest Alaska, and gave it qualities that make Nome an exceptionally attractive place for a visitor. For once, the local boosters' motto—in this case, "There's no place like Nome"—is entirely accurate, and that's because Nome, although itself nothing special to look at, combines a sense of history, a hospitable and somewhat silly attitude, and an exceptional location on the water in front of a tundra wilderness that's crossed by 250 miles of road. Those roads are the truly unique thing, for Nome is the best place (really, the only place) in Arctic Alaska for a visitor to drive or bike deep into the open country, coming across musk oxen, reindeer, rarely seen birds, Native villages, undeveloped hot springs, and even an abandoned 1881 elevated train from New York City. Elsewhere, you're obliged to fly from rural hubs to get so far into the Bush or drive the endless Dalton Highway, either of which is a more ambitious undertaking for casual explorers.

The accidents of history have been rather frequent in Nome. History has been downright sloppy. Start with the name. It's essentially a clerical error, caused by a British naval officer who, in 1850, was presumably in a creative dry spell when he wrote "? Name" on a diagram rather than name the cape he was sailing past. A mapmaker interpreted that as "Cape Nome." Or so goes one widely

Abandoned elevated train.

Musk oxen.

accepted explanation. The original gold rush of 1898 was caused by prospectors in the usual way, but a much larger 1899 population explosion happened after one of the '98 stampeders, left behind in a camp on the beach because of an injury, panned the sand outside the tent—and found that it was full of gold dust. By 1900, a fourth of Alaska's white population was in Nome sifting the sand. Small-time operators and tourists are still at it. A huge floating gold dredge of the kind that makes for major historic sites in Fairbanks and Dawson City sits idle on the edge of town. In Nome, it stopped operation only in recent years. There are two other, smaller dredges in town, too. Historic structures are few, however, as fires and storms have destroyed the town several times since the gold rush.

Nome has a particular, broad sense of humor. It shows up in the *Nome Nugget* newspaper and in silly traditions such as the Labor Day bathtub race, the sea ice golf tournament, and the polar bear swim. The population is half white and half Native, and the town is run largely by the non-Native group. Some see Nome as a tolerant mixing place of different peoples, while the town strikes others as a bit colonial. Selling booze is outlawed in Kotzebue and Barrow, the Native-dominated cities to the north; but in Nome there is still a sloppy, gold rush–style saloon scene. That sort of thing is prettier as historic kitsch than when it shows up in the form of drunks staggering down Front Street.

But you can ignore that, instead taking advantage of the great bargains to be had on Iñupiaq arts and crafts. And, most important, you can use a pleasant little inn or bed-and-breakfast as a base to get into the countryside that beckons you down one of the gravel roads. Nome is popular with bird-watchers, who find the roads especially useful.

Essentials

GETTING THERE Flying is the only way to get to Nome. **Alaska Airlines** (℡800/252-7522; www.alaskaair.com) flies 90 minutes by jet direct from Anchorage or with a brief hop from Kotzebue. Prices are around $450 round-trip. Many visitors come on escorted tour packages sold by **Alaska Airlines Vacations** (℡866/500-5511; www.alaskaairalaska.com); as a day trip a tour package costs around $575; staying overnight on the package costs around $665 per person, double occupancy.

All taxis operate according to a standard price schedule you can get from the visitor center. A ride to town from the airport is generally $5. There are three companies, including **Louie's Cab** (☎**907/443-6000**).

VISITOR INFORMATION The **Nome Convention and Visitors Bureau,** Front and Division streets (P.O. Box 240), Nome, AK 99762 (☎**907/443-6555;** www.nomealaska.org/vc, new site planned at www.visitnomealaska.com), provides maps and detailed information for diverse interests. The office is open from late May through August daily from 8am to 8pm, the balance of the year Monday through Friday from 9am to 5:30pm.

The **Bering Land Bridge National Preserve Headquarters,** 214 Front St. (P.O. Box 220), Nome, AK 99762 (☎**907/443-2522;** www.nps. gov/bela), is a good source of outdoors information from the rangers who staff a desk and are responsible for a rarely visited 2.7-million-acre national park unit, which covers much of the Seward Peninsula north of the Nome road system. Rangers offer a variety of programs all year, especially during the Iditarod finish in March. Their bird tours and ranger hikes are mentioned below.

Also check the *Nome Nugget* website, at **www.nomenugget.com,** a real window into the community.

GETTING AROUND The town is a street grid along the ocean. **Front Street** follows the sea wall, **1st Avenue** is a block back, and so on. A harbor is at the north end of town, and the gold-bearing beach is to the south. You can mostly walk to see this area. Three roads branch out from Nome. I've described them below, under "Venturing Beyond Town by Road." To get out on the roads, you need to take a tour or rent a car, or bring a bike with you.

Several local car-rental agencies operate in town; the visitor center maintains a list, with rates. **Stampede Rent-A-Car,** 302 E. Front St. (☎**800/354-4606** or 907/443-3838), charges $100 to $150 for SUVs and vans. The same people operate the Aurora Inn (see "Where to Stay," below).

[FastFACTS] NOME

Bank Wells Fargo, with an ATM, is at 250 Front St.

Hospital Norton Sound Regional is at 5th Avenue and Bering Street (☎**907/443-3311**).

Internet Access Nome Public Library is at 200 Front St. (☎**907/443-6626**).

Police At Bering Street and 4th Avenue (☎**907/443-5262**).

Post Office At Front Street and Federal Way.

Taxes The **sales tax** is 5%; the tax on **rooms** totals 6%.

SPECIAL EVENTS The biggest event of the year is the **Iditarod Trail Sled Dog Race** (☎**907/376-5155;** www.iditarod.com), a marathon of more than 1,000 miles that ends in Nome in mid-March. The sled-dog racers, world media, and international visitors descend on the town for a few days of madness, with lots of community events planned. The activities last most of the month; contact the Nome visitor center, or download the calendar from www.nomealaska.org/vc. See p. 48 for an article on the emotional issue of the animal rights opposition to the sport.

One of the March Iditarod events, showcasing Nome's well-developed sense of humor, is the **Bering Sea Ice Golf Classic,** with 6 holes set up on the sea ice. The pressure ridges constitute a bad lie. Various similar silly events take place all year, including the **Polar Bear Swim,** which happens around June 21 as part of the **Midnight Sun Festival.** The festival celebrates the summer solstice, when Nome gets more than 22 hours of direct sunlight. A parade, hand-made raft race, folk festival, bank holdup, and other events headline the festival. Winners of the raft race get possession for a year of the fur-lined honey bucket (known in some places as a chamber pot). For information on any event, contact the Nome Convention and Visitors Bureau (☎907/443-6555; www.nomealaska.org/vc).

Exploring the Town

Most of Nome's original buildings were wiped out by fires or by storms off Norton Sound that tore across the beach and washed away major portions of the business district. A sea wall, completed in 1951, now protects the town. Among the few historic sites that survive are the gold rush–era Board of Trade Saloon, a church, and a bust of Roald Amundsen, who landed near Nome, in Teller, after crossing the North Pole from Norway in a dirigible in 1926. Below the library, at Front Street and Lanes Way, the small **Carrie M. McLain Memorial Museum** (☎907/ 443-6630) contains an exhibit on the town's gold rush. The museum is free and open summer daily from 10am to 5:30pm.

In good weather, a pleasant walk is to be had southeast of town, along the **beach.** Small-time miners may be camped there, but the gold-bearing sand extends for miles more of solitary walking. You can buy a gold pan in town and try your luck, but the sand has been sifted for nearly 100 years, so don't expect to gather any significant amount of gold. The **Swanberg Dredge** you can see from here operated until the 1950s; a large dredge north of town worked into the mid-1990s. The 38 gold dredges that once operated on the Seward Peninsula crept across the tundra, creating their own ponds to float in as they went. The **cemetery,** with white wooden crosses on top of a little hill just out of town, also is worth a look.

If you're in the market for walrus ivory carvings and other **Iñupiaq arts and crafts,** you'll find low prices and an extraordinary selection on Front Street in Nome. Jim West has a legendary collection for sale, assembled in the bar room of the historic **Board of Trade Saloon** that is attached to a shop on Front Street. The **Arctic Trading Post** is more of a traditional gift shop and also has a good ivory collection, as does **Maruskiyas of Nome. Chukotka-Alaska,** 514 Lomen St., is an importer of art and other goods from the Russian Far East. Alaska Native art you find in Nome is likely to be authentic, but still ask; see "Native Art: Finding the Real Thing" (p. 68). International visitors should see chapter 3 to find out about the difficulty of carrying ivory out of the United States.

Venturing Beyond Town by Road

The modest attractions downtown would hardly justify a trip to Nome, but the city's surroundings do. The roads provide unique access to a large stretch of the Seward Peninsula. Unlike other Arctic Bush areas, where someone has to take you into the wilderness, in Nome all you have to do is rent a car and go. There are few cars in Nome (they have to be flown in or shipped by barge), so you won't see many other vehicles on a huge expanse of spectacular territory, with wildlife-viewing opportunities as good as anywhere in the state.

You could see moose, reindeer, foxes, or bears, and nowhere else in the world do you have a better chance of seeing musk oxen from a car. Wildlife sightings are possible anywhere you drive, but check in with the visitor center or the **Alaska Department of Fish and Game,** 103 E. Front St., at the intersection of Steadman Street (☎ 907/443-5796), to find out the best locales to see animals. They can also give you guidance on fishing along the roads and a "Nome Roadside Fishing Guide," or you can download it from www.alaska.gov/adfg (click on "Sport Fisheries," then "Interior," then "Northwest"). Check "Getting Around," above, to find a mode of transportation.

The best option for seeing the nature that Nome's roads open to access may be to join a ranger-guided hike offered by the Bering Land Bridge National Preserve. Call ahead to check on current offerings (see "Visitor Information," above).

ROAD HIGHLIGHTS None of the three roads radiating from Nome has services of any kind—just small Native villages, a few dwellings, and some reindeer herders—so you must be prepared and bring what you need with you, including insect repellent and a good spare tire. The visitor center provides a road guide. Here are some highlights:

A church in Teller.

Bristle-thighed curlew.

The **Nome-Council road** heads 72 miles to the east, about half of that on the shoreline. It turns inland at the ghost town of Solomon, an old mining town with an abandoned railroad train known locally as the Last Train to Nowhere. The engines were originally used on the New York City elevated lines in 1881, then were shipped to Alaska in 1903 to serve the miners along this line to Nome. This is a scenic spot for bird-watching, and fishing is good in the Solomon River, all along the road. Council, near the end of the road, has a couple of dozen families in the summer. A 3-foot-deep river separates the road from the village.

The **Nome-Taylor road,** also known as the Kougarok Road, runs north of town 85 miles from Nome over the tundra and through the Kigluaik Mountains, eventually petering out and becoming impassable. About 40 miles out, you reach lovely Salmon Lake, with a lakeshore campground with picnic tables, grills, and outhouses. A few miles farther, a road to the left leads to the 125°F (52°C) Pilgrim Hot Springs, near a Catholic church. Access is limited to when the caretaker is on hand, so check with the visitor center before going.

The **Nome-Teller road** leads 73 miles to the village of Teller, which has 260 residents and a store. It's an opportunity to see an authentic Arctic Native village.

BIRD-WATCHING Bird-watchers will make many discoveries out on the Nome roads, turning to previously unused pages of their bird books. A bird list is available at the visitor center, and they post recent sightings and can tell you where to look—each of the three roads has a different habitat. The best time to visit for birding is Memorial Day through June and in early August. There's a chance to see Siberian birds, and you are likely to see bluethroats, yellow wagtails, wheatears, Arctic warblers, and Aleutian and Arctic terns.

Nome is the only place to see a bristle-thighed curlew without chartering a plane (but be ready for a strenuous hike). You don't need a guide, although guided field trips do come to Nome (see "Bird-Watching," in chapter 3). National park rangers from the Bering Land Bridge National Preserves offer a Saturday bird outing during the migration in May and June; call ahead to check on current details (see "Visitor Information," above).

THE kotzebue OPTION

The Northwest Arctic's authentic Iñupiaq center of Kotzebue (*Kotz*-eh-biew) isn't my first choice for most visitors. Those interested in Iñupiaq culture should go to Barrow, while those looking for bird-watching or self-guided outdoor sightseeing should go to Nome. Kotzebue lacks activities or attractions geared to the typical tourist, and it doesn't make sense to go there just to walk around.

On the other hand, intrepid travelers seeking real adventure can use Kotzebue as a hub for a vast, spectacular area of Arctic wilderness.

The **National Park Service** (P.O. Box 1029), Kotzebue, AK 99752 (℡**907/442-3760** or 907/442-3890), manages an immense area of protected land in the region, including Kobuk Valley National Park, Cape Krusenstern National Monument, and Noatak and Bering Land Bridge national preserves (find websites to each through www.nps. gov). A new interpretive and educational facility is currently under construction to be called the Northwest Arctic Heritage Center, and planned for opening in the spring of 2010. It will offer classes on traditional Native crafts and medicinal plants, and employees will answer questions about the town as well as the public lands. Year-round hours will be 8am to 5pm. Regardless of the timing of these changes, the park service is the best source of visitor information for Kotzebue and the region, especially since outdoor activities are essentially the only thing to do if you go there.

There are several remote rivers near Kotzebue with easy self-guided floating for experienced outdoors people. This is the best chance to get deep into the Arctic on your own. The great Noatak River originates in the Brooks Range and flows 450 miles through America's largest undisturbed wilderness in the impressive scenery of the Noatak National Preserve. The Selawik, Squirrel, and Kobuk rivers all have long sections of easy water. **Equinox Wilderness Expeditions,** listed in chapter 3 under "Planning an Outdoor Vacation," offers float trips in the area, although not necessarily every year. Expect to pay $4,500 per person. Most river running in the region is self-guided. Get details from *The Alaska River Guide,* by Karen Jettmar, director of Equinox (Menasha Ridge Press, $17). Obviously you should be experienced in the outdoors and in river floating before heading out for a multiday trip in the Arctic. And plan ahead, arranging details well in advance with the park service and your pilot. **Bering Air** (℡**800/478-5422** in Alaska only, or 907/443-5464; www.beringair. com) is one good operator in Kotzebue. A popular way to do a float trip is to use scheduled service into a riverside village.

MOUNTAIN-BIKING The roads of Nome are one of the world's great, undiscovered mountain-biking destinations—where else can you bike past musk oxen and reindeer? There is no bike rental in town, but for bike enthusiasts it may be worth renting a bike in Anchorage or bringing yours from home. There is a bike repair guy in town, Keith Conger, who is a good contact point for information or help with your bike, at **Bering C Bikes,** 500 Spinning Rock Rd. (☎**907/443-4994**).

Kotzebue also offers curious travelers a chance to dig deep into the Iñupiaq way of life with **Arctic Circle Educational Adventures** (☎**907/442-6013** in summer, 907/276-0976 in winter; www.fishcamp.org). The adventure takes place at a fish camp similar to those where Native people spend the summer gathering food for the winter—and to participate in set-net fishing, fish cutting, food gathering, and other traditional subsistence activities as well as hiking, town tours, and bird-watching. You are a participant rather than an observer, and spend real, unmediated time with Native people. The camp, on the beach 5 miles south of town, is as simple as Bush life, but with a modern kitchen, dining room, shower, and sauna. Guests sleep in plywood cabins without plumbing. Elderhostel groups sometimes come for a week. Rates are $150 per person per day for lodging, meals, and transfer from the airport, and an additional $100 per day for tour activities. The season is from late June to mid-August.

Alaska Airlines (☎**800/252-7522;** www.alaskaair.com) offers daily jet service to Kotzebue. Lodging is at the **Nullagvik Hotel** (☎**907/442-3331;** www. nullagvik.com), a comfortable, modern hotel on the beachfront owned by the NANA regional Native corporation. High-season rates are $219 double.

Seeing the Sights in the Air

Nome is a hub for bush plane operators. Flightseeing charters are available, or you can fly on one of the scheduled routes out to the villages and spend a couple of hours touring. The way to do it is to contact a flight service, explain what you have in mind, and follow their advice. Expect to pay $175 to $250. Don't plan to stay overnight in a village without advance arrangements and don't go in bad weather—you'll see little and may get stuck in a tiny village. **Bering Air** (☎**800/478-5422** in Alaska only, or 907/443-5464; www.beringair.com) has a long and illustrious reputation and serves 32 villages from Nome and Kotzebue. They offer flightseeing trips by fixed-wing aircraft or helicopter on hourly charter rates (expensive if there are just one or two of you along). Or they will sell you a seat on a scheduled loop flight that visits various villages, charging the fare only to the closest village on the trip while you enjoy the entire round-trip. They even offer charters across the Bering Strait to the Russian towns of Provideniya and Anadyr.

Where to Stay

There are several good B&Bs and motel rooms besides those listed in full below, including the **Nugget Inn** (☎**877/443-2323** or 907/443-2323). Staying at a B&B makes sense, as your host can introduce you to the community in a less contrived way than a formal tour company. The visitor center and their website can provide information on them.

Aurora Inn Suites ★ Look here for the best traditional hotel rooms in town in a mock country inn on the town's main street. Rooms are nicely furnished and even have some style, a remarkable contrast to the other hotels in Nome. Another plus in this smoky town, there are lots of nonsmoking rooms here. The same company, owned by the Bering Straits Native Corporation, owns a car-rental operation, which is on-site.

302 E. Front St. (P.O. Box 1008), Nome, AK 99762. ☎800/354-4606 or 907/443-3838. Fax 907/443-6380. www.aurorainnnome.com. 56 units. $150–$250 double. Extra person age 16 and older $10. AE, MC, V. **Amenities:** Sauna. *In room:* TV, hair dryer.

Sweet Dreams B&B Convenient to the Iditarod finish line and across from good food at Arctic Pizza, the B&B's best assets are the hosts: Erna and Leo Rasmussen, who are deep wells of Nome history and local knowledge. Leo is a former mayor and a personable and funny man. The two-story house has a rustic, old-fashioned feel, with lots of Alaskan memorabilia and a sun room on top. Two rooms share a bathroom while a third has its own, but not attached. A full breakfast is served when Erna has time to prepare it, and they pick you up from and drop you off at the airport.

406 W. 4th St. (P.O. Box 2), Nome, AK 99762. ☎907/443-2919. 3 units, 2 with shared bathroom. $150 double. Rate includes full breakfast. MC, V.

Where to Dine

You might not go out of your way to dine at any of the restaurants in Nome, but once you're here you can find an adequate meal at various establishments. Several are operated by immigrant families, who offer their national cuisine along with standard American-style fare.

Probably the best place to eat in town is **Airport Pizza,** which no longer is at the airport—it is at 406 Bering St. (☎907/443-7992; www.airportpizza.com). The restaurant serves breakfast, sandwiches, and Tex-Mex as well as pizza, and brews fancy coffee and has 15 microbrews on tap, offers free Wi-Fi, and is open long hours every day. But the delivery service is the biggest claim to fame: They package up pizzas and put them on bush planes out to tiny villages.

Milano's Pizzeria (☎907/443-2924), on 503 Front St. in the Old Federal Building, serves Italian and Japanese meals as well as good pizza. The restaurant accepts Visa and MasterCard. **Twin Dragons,** on Front Street near Steadman Street (☎907/443-5552), serves Chinese food good enough to have kept them in business for many years, and also Vietnamese noodles and pizza. It also takes Visa and MasterCard.

BARROW: WAY NORTH

Half-liquid land comes to an arbitrary point at the northern tip of Alaska, Point Barrow, a long tendril reaching into the Arctic Ocean where bowhead whales pass close to shore during their annual migrations. The Iñupiat settled here more than a thousand years ago because it is such a good whale-hunting spot, and that is still why they live here, dragging their skin boats miles out on the frozen ocean to wait for whales along the cracks in the ice pack. And, according to age-old

Natives prepare to whale hunt.

tradition, here they still share the whales they catch among the entire community. Indeed, even visitors who show up on a Saturday in late June, during the Nalukataq, may be offered a piece of maktak (whale blubber and skin) and a chance to bounce high in the air in the blanket toss.

Barrow is the northernmost settlement on the North American continent, above the 71st parallel, but that's not all that makes it unique. The town of 4,417 is a cultural treasure. It's ancient, but it's also the seat of the North Slope Borough, a county government encompassing an area larger than the state of Nebraska, in which lies North America's largest oil field. The borough has everything money can buy for a local government, yet the people still must contend with crushing ice, snooping polar bears, and utter isolation. From these ingredients, they have concocted an extraordinary mixture of sophisticated modernity and wise tradition. Alaska's largest corporation is based here, its top executives are also subsistence hunters. At the Iñupiat Heritage Center it has been possible to see, on successive nights, traditional dance in the Inupiaq language and avant garde theater in the same language.

Geography and the natural environment also make the place interesting. This is the most heavily instrumented and intensively studied scientific site anywhere in the Arctic. At the labs north of town, cutting-edge work on climate change takes place that could affect the whole world. The tundra around Barrow is dotted with lakes divided by tendrils of swampy tundra no more substantial than the edges of fine lace. On this haven for migratory waterfowl, the flat, wet land and the ocean seem to merge. Indeed, for all but a few months, it's a flat, frozen plain of ocean and land. For 65 days in the winter, the sun never rises. In the summer, it doesn't set. Ice recedes from the shore only for a few brief months. Such extreme geography is a magnet for visitors.

Essentials

GETTING THERE Alaska Airlines (℡800/ 252-7522; www.alaskaair.com) flies a couple of times daily to Barrow from Anchorage, by way of Fairbanks. The fare from Anchorage is $600 and up. You can save by booking their 1-day and overnight tour packages, described in "Exploring the Town & Getting Outside," below. Book them through **Alaska Airlines Vacations** (℡866/500-5511; www.alaska airalaska.com).

VISITOR INFORMATION The City of Barrow's **visitor center,** at Momegana and Ahkovak streets, near the airport and Wiley Post & Will Rogers Monument, operates in the summer only from 10am to 4:30pm, with a guide to talk to, maps (including a numbered walking tour map), and other publications. To obtain advance information, contact the City of Barrow, Office of the Mayor, P.O. Box 629, Barrow, AK 99723 (℡907/852-5211, ext. 231; www.cityofbarrow.org).

Nalukataq blanket toss.

GETTING AROUND Facing the Chukchi Sea, Barrow has two sections, lying on each side of Isatkoak Lagoon. **Browerville,** to the east, has the Iñupiat Heritage Center and the Stuaqpak, or big store, which contains a small food court and many services. The old part of **Barrow,** with the hotels and airport, is to the west. The northern tip of Alaska, **Point Barrow,** is north of the town on a spit. The road leads 6 miles in that direction, but the absolute end is farther out, beyond the road. Other gravel roads lead about 10 miles out of town on the tundra.

The airport is right in town. Depending on where you stay and how much luggage you have, you may be able to walk to your hotel. Taxis are

---

Eskimo Football

The Barrow High School Whalers fielded their first football team in recent years, despite the impossibility of growing a grass field at this latitude. They played home games on bare gravel. The story of Eskimo football players so interested the national media, however, that the team's plight reached the ears of a sympathetic Florida football mom who raised $500,000 for an Astroturf field in Barrow (see her group's website at www.projectalaskaturf. com). The Barrow players got to visit Florida, too, trading in whaling on May sea ice in 10°F (−12°C) temperatures for sand, body surfing, and celebrity.

handy and come quickly, charging $6 or $7 in town, $10 beyond town ($5 for elders), plus $1 for each additional passenger. **Arcticab** (☎907/852-2227) and **Alaska Taxi** (☎907/852-3000) are two of the four cab companies.

SPECIAL EVENTS The return of the sun after 2 months below the horizon is met by traditional celebrations on **January 21.** The **Piuraagiaqta,** a spring festival, takes place in mid-April and includes many fun events. In the tea-making contest couples race to set up a camp stove and melt ice to make tea. If the traditional bowhead whaling season is a success, the **Nalukataq** takes place in late June, usually on a Saturday, but the actual date depends on the preference of the successful captain. It is his responsibility to feed the entire community. The Eskimo blanket toss is also a traditional element of the event (injuries are common, so don't take it lightly). In the fall, generally from early to mid-October, the whale hunt launches from the beaches of town (rather than the ice, as in spring). If you're lucky, you can be on hand as a whale is pulled ashore and butchered by the community. This usually occurs at the NARL runway, north of town; ask around, as everyone will know if a whale has been landed.

[Fast FACTS] BARROW

Alcohol Legality The sale of alcohol is illegal in Barrow and importation for personal use in your luggage is limited and controlled by a permit system. Without going through the permit process, you can bring in 1 gallon of beer, or 1 liter of distilled spirits, or 2 liters of wine. Violating these laws is bootlegging, a serious crime. For more information, call ahead to

Barrow Alcohol Distribution (☎907/852-3788) or the Office of the Mayor (☎907/852-5211, ext. 231). I simply don't drink when I go to Barrow.

Bank Wells Fargo is at 1078 Kiogak St. (☎907/852-6200), with an ATM.

Hospital Samuel Simmonds Memorial Hospital is at 1296 Agvik St. (☎907/852-4611).

Internet Access Free at the **Tuzzy Library,** at the Iñupiat Heritage Center in Browerville.

Police Contact the **North Slope Borough Police Department,** 1068 Kiogak St. (☎907/852-6111).

Taxes Barrow imposes **no sales tax. Room tax** is 5%.

Exploring the Town & Getting Outside

The **Iñupiat Heritage Center** (☎907/852-0422) is the town's main attraction, and one of Alaska's most remarkable cultural institutions. It is part museum, part gathering center, and part venue for living culture. Inside is a workshop for craftspeople where hunters build the traditional boats and tools they use and where drummers build their drums; during the summer, an artist is usually in residence for visitors. There is a performance space for storytellers and dancers, and conference rooms where elders tell old stories or identify a rich store of artifacts. In the museum area, displays of artifacts change regularly, while a permanent exhibit covers Eskimo whaling and the influence of Yankee whaling on it (the quiet pride here carries a real emotional wallop). Iñupiaq dancing and drumming demonstrations, a blanket toss, games, and a craft sale happen every afternoon in the summer from 1:30 to 3:30pm; these are the same programs that are the highlight of the escorted tours. The center is open Monday through Friday from 8:30am to 5pm (to see the program on weekends, call ahead). Regular admission is $10 adults, $5 students, free for seniors and age 6 or younger, with an added fee for the dance program.

The other site that's worthy of a special trip is **NARL,** as the former Navy Arctic Research Laboratory is known. This was once the world's largest Arctic research site, with scores of buildings on the narrow spit of land north of town. Today the navy is long gone, but Barrow's Native corporation took over the buildings and nurtured scientific research here. Once again the facilities are the nation's busiest year-round Arctic research site. It's interesting just to walk around, and the cafeteria in the Ilisagvik College building serves three good meals a day. A few exhibits on the science and culture of the region are housed in the new Barrow Arctic Research Center, behind the NARL complex, where cutting-edge work on climate change is in progress. It is open during normal business hours.

The main tourism business in town is **Tundra Tours** (☎800/882-8478 or 907/852-3900; www.tundratoursinc.com). Arctic Slope Regional Corp., a corporation representing the Iñupiat, owns the company and the Top of the World Hotel. Their tour (the same one sold through Alaska Airlines Vacations) introduces the town to visitors who arrive with little idea of what to expect. The 6-hour summer tour, in a small bus, drives around the town to visit an Eskimo skin boat, the cemetery, and the Arctic Ocean, for a dip of toes. The highlight is a visit to the Heritage Center with a cultural presentation, including Eskimo dance and a chance to buy crafts made by Native artists. The day-trip tour is $499 from Fairbanks, or $599 per person, double occupancy, for the tour and a night in Barrow at the Top of the World Hotel, giving you time on your own without the

Polar bears.

tour group; both prices include airfare and can save over buying a plane ticket alone. Book the tour through Alaska Airlines Vacations or with Tundra Tours at the numbers listed above. If you buy the tour separately when you are already in Barrow, it's $105. They also offer a winter tour for seeing the aurora ($99 separately), which does not include the cultural elements.

In season, Barrow is a good place to see polar bears. The bears are always around when the ice is in; they're dangerous and people take extreme care to avoid them. Barrow and other North Slope communities have minimized the danger of bears in town by setting up sites outside of the villages to dispose of gut piles and other hunting waste. It's a way of bribing the bears to leave the town alone. In Barrow, heavy equipment hauls the leftovers from fall whale butchering—bones and a few inedible organs—out to the very end of the point. Polar bears come for an easy meal whenever the pack ice is close to shore, which is October through June. Commercial tours take visitors out to the point in all-terrain vans or Humvees that can drive on the beach gravel. Arrangements change annually and these are casual home businesses, so if polar-bear viewing is your goal, be sure to make firm arrangements with someone before you go. **Arctic Tours** (**☎907/852-4512** or 907/852-1462 cell) takes visitors out in a Humvee May through September on a 2-hour tour that costs $70 per person, with a two-person minimum. Go only in May, June, or earlier, when the sea ice is in; you stand little chance of seeing a bear during times of open water, in the summer or fall.

Where to Stay

King Eider Inn ★★ The best rooms in town—indeed, some of the best in the Bush—are found in this clapboard building near the airport. They're crisp and airy, with faux rustic furniture, and kept up well. It surely helps that shoes are not allowed in the hotel—you have to take them off at the front door every time you come in. The halls and rooms are decorated with Native art. A room with a kitchenette is $10 more, and the enormous and luxurious Presidential Suite (where Barrow's honeymooners and visiting celebrities stay) is $297 summer, $269 winter. The lobby is comfortable, with a stone fireplace, and free coffee and other hot beverages are offered there around the clock. Bathrooms have large shower stalls, not tubs.

1752 Ahkovak St. (P.O. Box 1283), Barrow, AK 99723. **☎888/303-4337** reservations or 907/852-4700. Fax 907/852-2025. www.kingeider.net. 19 units. Summer $189 double; winter $169 double. Extra person $25. AE, MC, V. No smoking. **Amenities:** Sauna. *In room:* TV, Wi-Fi.

Top of the World Hotel ★ This is a good hotel with familiar standard rooms, worn in places but perfectly comfortable. The staff works to keep the place clean and quiet. Rooms have light furniture and blue carpet, desks, and refrigerators. Those on the water side have remarkable views of the Arctic Ocean, and it's only a few steps to the beach and the heart of Barrow. The lobby is a place where people pass time, somewhat cluttered with a TV and a stuffed polar bear. The hotel is owned by the Native corporation that also operates Tundra Tours, and you stay here if you come on the package tour.

Agvik St. (P.O. Box 189), Barrow, AK 99723. **☎907/852-3900.** www.tundratoursinc.com. 44 units. Summer $150–$220 double; winter $125–$155 double. Extra person $20. AE, DC, DISC, MC, V. *In room:* TV, fridge.

Where to Dine

There are several decent restaurants in Barrow. Generally, they stay open very late, always have a TV on, offer free delivery, and don't brew decaffeinated coffee—people around here run on lots of caffeine and sugar.

Adjoining the Top of the World Hotel, **Pepe's North of the Border,** 1204 Agvik St. (☎907/852-8200), is the most famous place in town thanks to an appearance owner Fran Tate made with Johnny Carson on *The Tonight Show* some 20 years ago. They serve large portions of familiar American-style Mexican food, steak, and seafood. The bus tours come here for lunch, and Tate hands out souvenirs.

Brower's Cafe, 3220 Brower's Hill (☎907/852-3456), occupies the most historic building in town, the 19th-century whaling station and store built by Charles Brower, who introduced Yankee whaling techniques to the Iñupiat and sired one of its most illustrious families. The restaurant serves American and Chinese dishes. Big windows look out on the beach, and a famous whalebone arch is just outside.

Northern Lights Restaurant, in Browerville at 5122 Herman St. (☎907/852-3300), has a very comfortable, clean dining room and is operated by a charming family. Their menu goes on and on, with the owner's own Chinese food, plus deli selections and burgers, and the best pizza in town.

PRUDHOE BAY: ARCTIC INDUSTRY

The Prudhoe (*Prew*-dough) Bay complex is more than a huge oil field, it's an amazing achievement. Massive, complex machinery must operate in winter's deep, dark cold, and in summer must avoid harm to a critical habitat for migrating

Caribou at the Arctic National Wildlife Refuge.

Red fox kittens at the Arctic National Wildlife Refuge.

caribou and waterfowl, on wet, fragile tundra that permanently shows any mark made by vehicles. Workers are forbidden even to set foot on the tundra. Most places, as you look from the edge of one of the gravel pads, the heathery ground looks as undisturbed as a calm sea.

But that doesn't make it a good place to go on your vacation. The grim town of **Deadhorse,** which serves the oil facility, is really more of an industrial yard, barely deserving to be called a town; it certainly isn't anything you'd travel to see. To get beyond it to see Prudhoe Bay, you have to sign up for a tour. The tour has never gone inside the buildings, and under post-9/11 security measures, it doesn't even go close to the most interesting areas. Visitors do get to stop at the Arctic Ocean, the only way to get to the water for those who drive up on the Dalton Highway. That hardly justifies the trip, however, unless you are bent on driving the highway anyway (it is covered in chapter 10, in "The Dalton Highway"). Frankly, I can't recommend spending the time and expense required for a Prudhoe tour. If you're curious about the Arctic, a trip to Barrow or Nome makes more sense.

If you do go to Deadhorse with the objective of touching the Arctic Ocean, you must reserve at least 24 hours ahead and provide information to clear security for the ride. The tours are operated by the **Arctic Caribou Inn,** P.O. Box 340111, Prudhoe Bay, AK 99734 (**☎907/659-2368;** www.arcticcaribouinn. com). They will need your name and identification information such as a driver's license or passport number that British Petroleum can use to run a background check before allowing you on the oil field. The inn also offers the area's visitor services, including a hotel and cafeteria; although tours operate only in the summer, the hotel and restaurant are open year-round. Rooms have two twin beds, and rent for $240 in summer. The restaurant offers breakfast ($15), lunch ($18), and dinner ($20). No alcohol is for sale in the town, and it isn't allowed in the inn. The hotel is near the airport in Deadhorse and serves as the starting point for the tours. The tour itself lasts 2 hours. Visitors are carried by bus past the oil field to the shore, with a 15-minute stop at the Arctic Ocean. It costs $40. There is no other way to get from the end of the road to the water.

Alaska Airlines (☎800/252-7522; www.alaskaair.com) has a couple of flights daily to Prudhoe Bay from Anchorage. A round-trip ticket costs around $800.

Several companies drive bus tours up the Dalton Highway all the way to Prudhoe, flying the other way. **Northern Alaska Tour Company** (☎800/474-1986 or 907/474-8600; www.northernalaska.com) offers these trips, with add-ons to make it more interesting: flightseeing stops, day hikes, village visits, and other choices. The basic 3-day, 2-night tour is $989.

Seeing ANWR for Yourself

The decades-old national controversy about whether to open the Arctic National Wildlife Refuge to oil exploration created strong interest in seeing that extraordinarily remote northeast corner of Alaska, which is best done in summer on a float trip. While interest in these floats may have increased for political reasons, however, their reputation of beauty and adventure has made them an attraction in their own right. The best time to see caribou is in June. **Alaska Discovery** (p. 84) is famous for ANWR expeditions down from the Brooks Range on either the Kongakut or Hulahula river, and also offers float-supported hikes. Expect to pay as much as $5,000 per person, everything included, for a trip of 10 days. Jim Campbell and Carol Kasza's Fairbanks-based **Arctic Treks** has led float trips in ANWR for 3 decades (☎907/455-6502; www.arctictreksadventures.com). As a smaller, locally owned company, they charge somewhat less than Alaska Discovery. They offer shorter base camp trips in ANWR as well as the long river floats and other Arctic journeys.

For those who simply want to see ANWR without a wilderness trip, it's possible to visit the Iñupiaq village of Kaktovik, which lies within the boundaries of the refuge. While I wouldn't recommend the journey for most visitors, those with strong interest in a Bush village sojourn and curiosity about ANWR may enjoy it. Lodging and meals in Kaktovik come from the **Waldo Arms Hotel** (☎907/640-6513), a gathering place known for warm hospitality. Kaktovik is served from Fairbanks by **Frontier Flying Service** (☎800/478-6779 or 907/450-7200; www.frontierflying.com). On the schedule the destination is listed as "Barter Island."

FAST FACTS: ALASKA

Area Codes All of Alaska is in area code **907.** In the Yukon Territory, the area code is **867.** When placing a toll call within the state, you must dial 1, the area code, and the number.

Automobile Organizations Motor clubs will supply maps, suggested routes, guidebooks, accident and bail-bond insurance, and emergency road service. The **American Automobile Association (AAA)** is the major auto club in the United States. If you belong to a motor club in your home country, inquire about AAA reciprocity before you leave. You may be able to join AAA even if you're not a member of a reciprocal club; to inquire, call AAA (☏**800/222-4357;** www.aaa.com). AAA has a nationwide emergency road service telephone number (☏**800/AAA-HELP** [222-4357]).

Business Hours In the larger cities, major grocery stores are open until late at night and carry a wide range of products (even fishing gear) in addition to food. At a minimum, **stores** are open Monday through Friday from 10am to 6pm, on Saturday afternoon, and are closed on Sunday, but many are open much longer hours, especially in summer. **Banks** may close an hour earlier and, if open on Saturday, hours may be short.

Car Rentals Some small towns have only local car-rental agencies; details are listed in each section. For national agencies, see "Airline, Hotel & Car-Rental Websites," p. 614.

Cellular Phone Coverage Pretty much every town that can be reached by road or ferry has cellular voice coverage, as well as some of the paved highways. That means the great majority of the people are covered and the great majority of the land is not. The largest provider is an Alaska company called ACS, which posts maps of its coverage area at www.acsalaska.com (click on "Wireless"). I've found usable coverage is often less than what the companies claim, so don't bet your life on being able to make a call. You may want to check your calling plan to find out if it covers Alaska and, if not, how much you are charged for roaming and long distance.

Drinking Laws The minimum drinking age in Alaska is 21, and ID is frequently checked. Most restaurants sell beer and wine, while some have full bars that serve hard liquor as well. Packaged alcohol, beer, and wine are sold only in licensed stores, not in grocery stores, but these are common and are open long hours every day. Under state law, **bars** don't have to close until 5am, but many communities have an earlier closing, generally around 2am. Open containers of alcohol are not allowed in your car or, with few exceptions, in any public place outside a bar or restaurant. Don't even think about driving while intoxicated, which in Alaska carries mandatory jail time for the first offense. More than 100 rural communities have laws prohibiting the importation and possession of alcohol (this is known as being "dry") or prohibiting the sale but not possession of alcohol (known as being "damp"). With a few exceptions, these are tiny Bush communities off the road network; urban areas are all "wet." Of the communities featured in this book, Kotzebue and Barrow are damp, Kaktovik is dry, and the rest are wet. Before flying into a Native village with alcohol, ask about the law, or check a list online (go to www.dps.state.ak.us/abc and click on "Dry/Damp Communities"). Bootlegging is a serious crime, and serious bad manners, in Alaska Native communities that are trying to address the damage of alcohol abuse.

Electricity As in Canada, the United States uses 110–120 volts AC (60 cycles), compared to 220–240 volts AC (50 cycles) in most of Europe, Australia, and New Zealand. Downward converters that change 220–240 volts to 110–120 volts are difficult to find in the United States, so bring one with you.

Embassies & Consulates All embassies are located in the nation's capital, Washington, D.C. Some consulates are located in major U.S. cities, and most nations have a mission to the United Nations in New York City. If your country isn't listed below, call for directory information in Washington, D.C. (☎202/555-1212), or check **www. embassy.org/embassies**.

The embassy of **Australia** is at 1601 Massachusetts Ave. NW, Washington, DC 20036 (☎202/797-3000; http://usa.embassy.gov/au).

The embassy of **Canada** is at 501 Pennsylvania Ave. NW, Washington, DC 20001 (☎202/682-1740; www.canadianembassy.org). Other Canadian consulates are in Buffalo (New York), Detroit, Los Angeles, New York, and Seattle.

The embassy of **Ireland** is at 2234 Massachusetts Ave. NW, Washington, DC 20008 (☎202/462-3939; www.irelandemb.org). Irish consulates are in Boston, Chicago, New York, San Francisco, and other cities. See website for complete listing.

The embassy of **New Zealand** is at 37 Observatory Circle NW, Washington, DC 20008 (☎202/328-4800; www.nzembassy.com). New Zealand consulates are in Los Angeles, Salt Lake City, San Francisco, and Seattle.

The embassy of the **United Kingdom** is at 3100 Massachusetts Ave. NW, Washington, DC 20008 (☎202/588-7800; www.britainusa.com). Other British consulates are in Atlanta, Boston, Chicago, Cleveland, Houston, Los Angeles, New York, San Francisco, and Seattle.

Emergencies Generally, you can call ☎911 for medical, police, or fire emergencies. On remote highways, there sometimes are gaps in 911 coverage. If you can find a phone, dialing 0 will generally get an operator who can connect you to emergency services. To learn about equipment that can contact help beyond the reach of conventional communications, see "Getting Lost/Wilderness Communications," p. 94.

Gasoline (Petrol) The cost of gasoline changes too quickly to make much sense to list in a book. You can find national and state price averages updated online daily at www.fuelgaugereport.com. Prices in Alaska range from a bit over the national average in Anchorage to much higher in rural areas, where they could be double or more. As elsewhere in the U.S., taxes are already included in the price quoted or on the pump. One U.S. gallon equals 3.8 liters or .85 imperial gallons. Fill-up locations are known as gas or service stations.

Holidays Besides national holidays, banks and state and local government offices close on two state holidays: Seward's Day (the last Mon in Mar) and Alaska Day (Oct 18, or the nearest Fri or Mon if it falls on a weekend). Banks, all government offices, post offices, and many stores, restaurants, and museums are closed on these national holidays: January 1 (New Year's Day), the third Monday in January (Martin Luther King, Jr., Day), the third Monday in February (Presidents' Day), the last Monday in May (Memorial Day), July 4 (Independence Day), the first Monday in September (Labor Day), the second Monday in October (Columbus Day), November 11 (Veterans' Day/Armistice Day), the fourth Thursday in November (Thanksgiving Day), and December 25 (Christmas). The Tuesday after the first Monday in November is Election Day, a federal government holiday in presidential-election years (held every 4 years, and next in 2012).

Insurance See "Travel & Rental-Car Insurance" and "Health & Safety," in chapter 3.

Internet Access See "Using the Internet on the Road" (p. 90), and the "Fast Facts" sections throughout the book for how to get online in each Alaska community.

Legal Aid If you are "pulled over" for a minor infraction (such as speeding), never attempt to pay the fine directly to a police officer; this could be construed as attempted bribery, a much more serious crime. Pay fines by mail or directly into the hands of the clerk of the court. If accused of a more serious offense, say and do nothing before consulting a lawyer. Here the burden is on the state to prove a person's guilt beyond a reasonable doubt, and everyone has the right to remain silent, whether he or she is suspected of a crime or actually arrested. Once arrested, a person can make one telephone call to a party of his or her choice. International visitors should call your embassy or consulate.

Mail At press time, domestic postage rates were 28¢ for a postcard and 44¢ for a letter. For international mail, a first-class letter of up to 1 ounce costs 98¢ (75¢ to Canada and 79¢ to Mexico); a first-class postcard costs the same as a letter. For more information, go to **www.usps.com** and click on "Calculate Postage."

The locations of the post offices in each town in this book are listed in the appropriate "Fast Facts" sections. You can receive mail addressed to you at "General Delivery" at the post office. Always include zip codes when mailing items in the U.S. If you don't know your zip code, visit www.usps.com/zip4.

Maps I've noted the best trail maps in each applicable section throughout this book. For most of the popular areas, I recommend the excellent trail maps published by **Trails Illustrated,** part of National Geographic (☎ **800/962-1643;** www.natgeomaps. com). They're sold in park visitor centers, too. The maps are printed on plastic, so they don't get spoiled by rain; however, they don't cover the whole state. For detailed topographic maps covering all of Alaska, the U.S. Geological Service is still the only place to go. Their map sales office in Anchorage (a fascinating place for anyone interested in cartography) is on the campus of Alaska Pacific University, the **Earth Science Information Center,** at 4230 University Dr. (☎907/786-7011).

Newspapers & Magazines The state's dominant (but rapidly shrinking) newspaper is the *Anchorage Daily News* (www.adn.com); it's widely available in the central part of the state. Seattle newspapers and *USA Today* are often available, and in Anchorage you can get virtually any newspaper. To learn more about Alaska before or after your visit, check out the monthly *Alaska* magazine (www.alaskamagazine.com).

Passports See www.frommers.com/planning for information on how to obtain a passport. See "Embassies & Consulates," above, for whom to contact if you lose yours while traveling in the U.S. For other information, contact the following agencies:

For Residents of Australia Contact the **Australian Passport Information Service** at ☎131-232, or visit the government website at www.passports.gov.au.

For Residents of Canada Contact the central **Passport Office,** Department of Foreign Affairs and International Trade, Ottawa, ON K1A 0G3 (☎800/567-6868; www.ppt.gc.ca).

For Residents of Ireland Contact the **Passport Office,** Setanta Centre, Molesworth Street, Dublin 2 (☎01/671-1633; www.irlgov.ie/iveagh).

For Residents of New Zealand Contact the **Passport Office** at ☎0800/225-050 in New Zealand or 04/474-8100, or log on to www.passports.govt.nz.

For Residents of the United Kingdom Visit your nearest passport office, major post office, or travel agency, or contact the **United Kingdom Passport Service** at ☎0870/521-0410 or search its website at www.ukpa.gov.uk.

For Residents of the United States To find your regional passport office, either check the U.S. State Department website, or call the **National Passport Information Center** toll-free number (☎877/487-2778) for automated information.

Police Dial ☎911 in an emergency. Nonemergency phone numbers for local police departments are listed throughout the book.

Smoking In Alaska's cities, smoking is prohibited in most indoor public places. In Anchorage and Juneau, smoking is prohibited even in bars. Smoking is more common in small towns, where rules are usually less strict. No-smoking rules are so common in hotels and B&Bs, however, that I've stopped listing them; instead, if you must smoke in your room, make that your first question when you book. As a rule, you can never smoke in hotels' common rooms.

Taxes Alaska imposes no state sales tax, but most local governments have a sales tax and a bed tax on accommodations. The tax rates are listed in each town section throughout the book under its "Fast Facts." All prices and rates are listed without tax unless otherwise noted. The United States has no value-added tax (VAT) or other indirect tax at the national level.

Telephones I am assured that all major U.S. calling cards will work in Alaska, but this certainly hasn't been the case in the past. To make sure, contact your long-distance company, or buy a by-the-minute card. They are sold in convenience stores and are often the cheapest way to call home for international visitors. **Local calls** made from public pay phones usually cost 25¢. In smaller Alaska communities, you may have to wait for the person you are calling to answer before quickly putting the money in the phone. Most long-distance and international calls can be dialed directly from any phone. **For calls within the United States and to Canada,** dial 1 followed by the area code and the 7-digit number. **For other international calls,** dial 011 followed by the country code, city code, and the number you are calling. Calls to area codes **800, 888, 877,** and **866** are toll-free but won't work from outside the U.S. or Canada, and occasionally won't work from outside Alaska. For **local directory assistance** ("information"), dial 411; for long-distance information, dial 1, then the appropriate area code and 555-1212.

For **reversed-charge or collect calls,** and for person-to-person calls, dial the number 0 then the area code and number; an operator will come on the line, and you should specify whether you are calling collect, person-to-person, or both. If your operator-assisted call is international, ask for the overseas operator.

The least expensive way to call internationally is by Skype.com and other voice-over-Internet services, which work anywhere you have your computer and a broadband connection. I've found the connection speed spotty in little Alaskan hotels, so don't count on Skype.com working smoothly everywhere you go.

Time Although the state naturally spans five time zones, in the 1980s Alaska's middle time zone was stretched so almost the entire state would lie all in one zone, known as Alaska Standard Time (AST). It's 1 hour earlier than the U.S. West Coast's Pacific Time, 4 hours earlier than Eastern Standard Time. Crossing over the border from Alaska to Canada adds an hour and puts you at the same time as the West Coast. The balance of the continental United States is divided into **four time zones:** Eastern Standard Time (EST), Central Standard Time (CST), Mountain Standard Time (MST), and Pacific Standard Time (PST). When it's 8am in Anchorage it is 9am in Los Angeles (PST), 10am in Denver (MST), 11am in Chicago (CST), noon in New York City (EST), 5pm in London (GMT), and 2am the next day in Sydney.

As with almost everywhere else in the United States, daylight saving time is in effect from 1am on the second Sunday in March (turn your clocks ahead 1 hr.) until 1am on the first Sunday in November (turn clocks back again).

Tipping Tips make up a major part of the compensation for many service workers. To leave no tip in a restaurant is socially unacceptable and leaves your server unpaid. To leave a small tip is a powerful indication of displeasure for bad service; to leave no tip suggests you don't know any better. In restaurants, bars, and nightclubs, tip your server 15% to 20% of the check, depending on the quality of service. Tip **checkroom attendants** $1 per garment, and tip **valet-parking attendants** $1 each time you get your car. Tipping is not expected in cafeterias or fast-food restaurants where you order at a counter. In hotels, tip **bellhops** $1 per bag and tip the **housekeeper** at least $1 to $2 per day. Tip **cab drivers** 15% of the fare and tip **hairdressers** and **barbers** 15% to 20%. Do not tip gas-station attendants and ushers at movies and theaters.

See the box "A Guide to Guide Gratuities" on p. 81 for guidelines on tipping outdoor guides, outfitters, and employees at full-service wilderness lodges.

Toilets You won't find public toilets, or "restrooms," on the streets in most U.S. cities, but they can be found in hotel lobbies, bars, restaurants, museums, department stores, railway and bus stations, and service stations. Large hotels and fast-food restaurants are often the best bet for clean facilities. It can be a long way between any toilets on rural Alaskan highways; see "Keeping the Wilderness Clean" (p. 79).

Visas For information about U.S. Visas, go to **http://travel.state.gov** and click on "Visas." Or go to one of the following websites:

Australian citizens can obtain up-to-date visa information from the **U.S. Embassy Canberra,** Moonah Place, Yarralumla, ACT 2600 (℡02/6214-5600), or by checking the U.S. Diplomatic Mission's website at **http://usembassy-australia.state.gov/consular.**

British subjects can obtain up-to-date visa information by calling the **U.S. Embassy Visa Information Line** (℡0891/200-290), or by visiting the "Visas to the U.S." section of the American Embassy London's website at **www.usembassy.org.uk.**

Irish citizens can obtain up-to-date visa information through the **Embassy of the USA Dublin,** 42 Elgin Rd., Dublin 4, Ireland (℡353/1-668-8777), or by checking the "Visas to the U.S." section of the website at **http://dublin.usembassy.gov.**

Citizens of **New Zealand** can obtain up-to-date visa information by contacting the **U.S. Embassy New Zealand,** 29 Fitzherbert Terrace, Thorndon, Wellington (℡644/472-2068), or get the information directly from the website at **http://wellington. usembassy.gov.**

Water See "Drinking Water," p. 94, to learn about safe water in the outdoors.

AIRLINE, HOTEL & CAR-RENTAL WEBSITES

MAJOR AIRLINES

Air Canada
www.aircanada.com

Alaska Airlines/Horizon Air
www.alaskaair.com

American Airlines
www.aa.com

China Airlines
www.china-airlines.com

Condor Airlines (German)
www.condor.com

Continental Airlines
www.continental.com

Delta Air Lines
www.delta.com

Frontier Airlines
www.frontierairlines.com

Korean Air
www.koreanair.com

Northwest Airlines
www.nwa.com

United Airlines
www.united.com

US·Airways
www.usairways.com

LARGE ALASKAN FLYING SERVICES

Bering Air
www.beringair.com

Era Aviation
www.flyera.com

Frontier Flying Service
www.frontierflying.com

PenAir
www.penair.com

Wings of Alaska
www.ichoosewings.com

MAJOR HOTEL & MOTEL CHAINS

Best Western International
www.bestwestern.com

Clarion Hotels
www.choicehotels.com

Comfort Inns
www.comfortinn.com

Courtyard by Marriott
www.marriott.com/courtyard

Days Inn
www.daysinn.com

Econo Lodges
www.choicehotels.com

Embassy Suites
www.embassysuites.com

Fairfield Inn by Marriott
www.farfieldinn.com

Hampton Inn
www.hamptoninn1.hilton.com

Hilton Hotels
www.hilton.com

Holiday Inn
www.holidayinn.com

Howard Johnson
www.hojo.com

Hyatt
www.hyatt.com

InterContinental Hotels & Resorts
www.ichotelsgroup.com

Marriott
www.marriott.com

Motel 6
www.motel6.com

Omni Hotels
www.omnihotels.com

Quality Inn
www.qualityinn.choicehotels.com

Ramada Worldwide
www.ramada.com

Red Carpet Inns
www.bookroomsnow.com

Red Lion Hotels
www.redlion.rdln.com

Residence Inn by Marriott
www.marriott.com/residenceinn

Rodeway Inn
www.rodewayinn.com

Sheraton Hotels & Resorts
www.starwoodhotels.com/sheraton

Super 8 Motels
www.super8.com

Travelodge
www.travelodge.com

Westin Hotels & Resorts
www.starwoodhotels.com/westin

CAR-RENTAL AGENCIES

Alamo
www.alamo.com

Avis
www.avis.com

Budget
www.budget.com

Dollar
www.dollar.com

Enterprise
www.enterprise.com

Hertz
www.hertz.com

National
www.nationalcar.com

Payless
www.paylesscarrental.com

Rent-A-Wreck
www.rentawreck.com

Thrifty
www.thrifty.com

INDEX

PHOTO CREDITS

p. i: © Alaska Stock/AGE fotostock; p. iii: © Fred Hirschmann/Science Faction/Corbis; p. viii: © Erik Hill; p. 1: © Alaska Stock/AGE fotostock; p. 2: © Alaska Stock/Photolibrary; p. 3: © Chip Porter/Alaska Stock/Photolibrary; p. 6: © Fred Hirschmann/Science Faction/Corbis; p. 7, left: © Courtesy of Celebrity Cruises; p. 7, right: © Alaska Stock/AGE fotostock; p. 8: © John Schwieder/Alamy; p. 9: © Paul Lawrence/Stellar Stock/AGE fotostock; p. 10: © Paul Andrew Lawrence/Alamy; p. 11, top: © Steve Bly/Alamy; p. 11, bottom: © Terry Chick/Photolibrary; p. 12: © Konrad Wothe/Look foto/Photolibrary; p. 13: © Donna Ikenberry/Art Directors/Alamy; p. 14, top: © Ron Sanford/Corbis; p. 14, bottom: © Alaska Stock/AGE fotostock; p. 15: © Matt Hage; p. 16: © Nancy Hoyt Belcher/Alamy; p. 17, top: © Alaska Stock/AGE fotostock; p. 17, bottom: © Alaska Stock/Alamy; p. 19, left: © Greg Vaughn/Alamy; p. 19, right: © Courtesy of Lands End Resort; p. 21: © Alaska Stock/AGE fotostock; p. 23: © Matt Hage; p. 24: © Purcell Team/Alamy; p. 25: © Loukas Hapsis/IML/Aurora Photos; p. 28: © Ken Graham/AGE fotostock; p. 29: © Sam Chrysanthou/All Canada Photos/AGE fotostock; p. 32: © Mark Lyons/epa/Corbis; p. 35: © Peter Barrett/Alaska Stock/Photolibrary; p. 36: © Matt Hage; p. 37: © Alaska Stock/Photolibrary; p. 38, left: © Matt Hage; p. 38, right: © Matt Hage; p. 39: © Scott Dickerson/Alaska Stock/Photolibrary; p. 40: © Alaska Stock/AGE fotostock; p. 41: © Peter Essick/Aurora Photos; p. 43: © Bernd Zoller/Image Broker/AGE fotostock; p. 44: © Minden Pictures/Masterfile; p. 47: © Alaska Stock/AGE fotostock; p. 53: © Bettmann/Corbis; p. 54: © CBS/Photofest; p. 55: © Uwe Bender/Bon Appetit/Alamy; p. 57: © Michael DeYoung/Alaska Stock/Alamy; p. 97: © Rob Howard/Corbis; p. 100: © William Helsel/AGE fotostock; p. 101, top: © Alaska Stock/Photolibrary; p. 101, bottom: © Alaska Stock/AGE fotostock; p. 103: © Ron Buskirk/Alamy; p. 104: © Steven Kazlowski/Alaska Stock/Photolibrary; p. 105, left: © Theo Allofs/Corbis; p. 105, right: © Blaine Harrington III/Alamy; p. 106, left: © Andy Long/Alamy; p. 106, right: © Renaud Visage/AGE fotostock; p. 108, left: © True North Images/AGE fotostock; p. 108, right: © Ian Shive/Aurora Photos; p. 111: © Matt Hage; p. 113, left: © Douglas Peebles/Photolibrary; p. 113, right: © Alaska Stock/AGE fotostock; p. 115: © Alaska Stock/AGE fotostock; p. 116: © Courtesy of Royal Caribbean; p. 141: © Alaska Stock/AGE fotostock; p. 143: © Alaska Stock/AGE fotostock; p. 146: © Alaska Stock/AGE fotostock; p. 151: © Matt Hage; p. 156: © Alaska Stock/AGE fotostock; p. 158: © Don Pitcher/Alaska Stock/Photolibrary; p. 160: © Peter Barrett/Alaska Stock/Photolibrary; p. 161: © Savanah Stewart/Danita Delmont Stock Photography; p. 162: © Clark James Mishler/Alaska Stock/Photolibrary; p. 165: © WorldFoto/Alamy; p. 166: © Matt Hage; p. 172: © Ernest Manewal/Lonely Planet Images; p. 175: © Alaska Stock/AGE fotostock; p. 176: © Alaska Stock/AGE fotostock; p. 179: © Newman Mark/Prisma/AGE fotostock; p. 180: © Greg Vaughn/Alamy; p. 181: © Donna Ikenberry/Art Directors/Alamy; p. 185: © Alaska Stock/AGE fotostock; p. 189: © Douglas Peebles/Photolibrary; p. 191: © Brandon D. Cole/Corbis; p. 192: © Duncan Murrell/Oxford Scientific/Photolibrary; p. 194: © Blaine Harrington/AGE fotostock; p. 202: © Purcell Team/Alamy; p. 203: © Julie Quarry/Alamy; p. 205: © Ken Cedeno; p. 206: © Alaska Stock/AGE fotostock; p. 209: © Alaska Stock/AGE fotostock; p. 217: © Walter Bibikow/Jon Arnold Images/Alamy; p. 218: © Walter Bibikow/Index Stock/Photolibrary; p. 221: © Alaska Stock/AGE fotostock; p. 222: © Marc Dozier/Hemis.fr/Alamy; p. 225: © Altrendo/Getty Images; p. 226: © Lee Foster/Lonely Planet Images; p. 232: © Danny Lehman/Corbis; p. 234: © Alaska Stock/AGE fotostock; p. 239: © Alaska Stock/AGE fotostock; p. 240: © Roy Toft/Oxford Scientific/Photolibrary; p. 248: © Danilo Donadoni/Marka/AGE fotostock; p. 250: © Mira/Alamy; p. 252: © Johnny Johnson/Alaska Stock/Photolibrary; p. 255: © Mark A. Johnson/Alamy; p. 259: © Alaska Stock/AGE fotostock; p. 262: © John Warburton-Lee/Photolibrary; p. 263, top: © Matt Hage; p. 263, bottom: © Photo by Susannah Dowds, courtesy of the Hammer Museum; p. 264: © Alaska Stock/AGE fotostock; p. 269: © Alaska Stock/AGE fotostock; p. 271: © Ron Niebrugge/Alamy; p. 274: © Walter Bibikow/Danita Delmont Stock Photography; p. 276: © Courtesy of Jewell Gardens; p. 278: © Toronto Star/AGE fotostock; p. 283: © Alaska Stock/Alamy; p. 284: © Blaine Harrington/AGE fotostock; p. 285: © Matt Hage; p. 289: © Ken Cedeno; p. 291: © Alaska Stock/AGE fotostock; p. 292: © Matt Hage; p. 294: © WorldFoto/Alamy; p. 307: © Ken Cedeno; p. 309: © Paul Andrew Lawrence/Alamy; p. 312: © Matt Hage; p. 313: © Ken Cedeno; p. 314: © Matt Hage; p. 315: © Ken Cedeno; p. 316: © Matt Hage; p. 317: © Matt Hage; p. 319: © Matt Hage; p. 320: © Ken Cedeno; p. 321: © Matt Hage; p. 323: © Matt Hage; p. 325: © Julie Eggers/Danita Delmont Stock Photography; p. 326: © Photo by Greg Martin, courtesy of Alaska Aces; p. 328: © Matt Hage; p. 329: © Matt

NOTES

NOTES